Lecture Notes in Computer Science

Lecture Notes in Artificial Intelligence   **14339**

Founding Editor

Jörg Siekmann

Series Editors

Randy Goebel, *University of Alberta, Edmonton, Canada*
Wolfgang Wahlster, *DFKI, Berlin, Germany*
Zhi-Hua Zhou, *Nanjing University, Nanjing, China*

The series Lecture Notes in Artificial Intelligence (LNAI) was established in 1988 as a topical subseries of LNCS devoted to artificial intelligence.

The series publishes state-of-the-art research results at a high level. As with the LNCS mother series, the mission of the series is to serve the international R & D community by providing an invaluable service, mainly focused on the publication of conference and workshop proceedings and postproceedings.

Alexey Karpov · K. Samudravijaya ·
K. T. Deepak · Rajesh M. Hegde ·
Shyam S. Agrawal · S. R. Mahadeva Prasanna
Editors

Speech and Computer

25th International Conference, SPECOM 2023
Dharwad, India, November 29 – December 2, 2023
Proceedings, Part II

 Springer

Editors
Alexey Karpov ⓘ
St. Petersburg Federal Research Center
of the Russian Academy of Sciences
St. Petersburg, Russia

K. T. Deepak
Indian Institute of Information Technology
Dharwad
Dharwad, India

Shyam S. Agrawal
KIIT Group of Colleges
Gurugram, India

K. Samudravijaya ⓘ
Koneru Lakshmaiah Education Foundation
Vaddeswaram, India

Rajesh M. Hegde
Indian Institute of Technology Dharwad
Dharwad, India

S. R. Mahadeva Prasanna ⓘ
Indian Institute of Technology Dharwad
Dharwad, India

ISSN 0302-9743   ISSN 1611-3349 (electronic)
Lecture Notes in Artificial Intelligence
ISBN 978-3-031-48311-0   ISBN 978-3-031-48312-7 (eBook)
https://doi.org/10.1007/978-3-031-48312-7

LNCS Sublibrary: SL7 – Artificial Intelligence

This Springer imprint is published by the registered company Springer Nature Switzerland AG
The registered company address is: Gewerbestrasse 11, 6330 Cham, Switzerland

Paper in this product is recyclable.

SPECOM 2023 Preface

The International Conference on Speech and Computer (SPECOM) has become a regular event since the first SPECOM held in St. Petersburg, Russia, in October 1996. The SPECOM conference series was established 27 years ago by the St. Petersburg Institute for Informatics and Automation of the Russian Academy of Sciences (SPIIRAS).

SPECOM is a conference with a long tradition that attracts researchers in the area of speech technology, including automatic speech recognition and understanding, text-to-speech synthesis, and speaker and language recognition, as well as related domains like digital speech processing, natural language processing, text analysis, computational paralinguistics, multi-modal speech, and data processing or human-computer interaction. The SPECOM conference is an ideal platform for know-how exchange – especially for experts working on highly inflectional languages – including both under-resourced and regular well-resourced languages.

In its long history, the SPECOM conference was organized alternately by the St. Petersburg Federal Research Center of the Russian Academy of Sciences (SPC RAS)/SPIIRAS and by the Moscow State Linguistic University (MSLU) in their home towns. Furthermore, in 1997 it was organized by the Cluj-Napoca subsidiary of the Research Institute for Computer Technique (Romania), in 2005 and 2015 by the University of Patras (in Patras and Athens, Greece), in 2011 by the Kazan Federal University (in Kazan, Russia), in 2013 by the University of West Bohemia (in Pilsen, Czech Republic), in 2014 by the University of Novi Sad (in Novi Sad, Serbia), in 2016 by the Budapest University of Technology and Economics (in Budapest, Hungary), in 2017 by the University of Hertfordshire (in Hatfield, UK), in 2018 by the Leipzig University of Telecommunications (in Leipzig, Germany), in 2019 by the Bogaziçi University (in Istanbul, Turkey), in 2020 and 2021 by SPC RAS/SPIIRAS (fully online), in 2022 by the KIIT (in Gurugram, India).

SPECOM 2023 was the twenty-fifth event in the series, this year we celebrated the silver jubilee of the conference. SPECOM 2023 was organized jointly by IIT Dharwad, IIIT Dharwad, NIT Goa, KLE Tech, and KIIT Gurugram. The conference was held during November 29 – December 2, 2023, in a hybrid format, mostly in-person in Hubli-Dharwad, Karnataka, India at Denissons Hotel and online via video conferencing. SPECOM 2023 was sponsored and supported by McAfee, IndSCA, ARM-SOFTECH.AIR, TiHAN, ASM Solutions, the International Speech Communication Association (ISCA) and some other organizations.

This year, beside the regular technical sessions, three special sessions were organized: "Industrial Speech and Language Technology", "Speech Processing and Speech Technology for Under Resourced Languages", and Students Special Session on Speech Analysis. In addition, the one-day Satellite Workshop "Speaker and Language Identification, Verification, and Diarization" was organized by the National Institute of Technology Goa on 2nd December 2023.

During SPECOM 2023, four keynote lectures were given by Bhiksha Raj (Carnegie Mellon University, USA) on "Learning from weak and noisy labels", Visar Berisha (Arizona State University, USA) on "Translating clinical speech analytics from the lab to the clinic: challenges and opportunities", S. Umesh (IIT Madras, India) on "Speech and Language Research For Indian Languages" and Satoshi Nakamura (Nara Institute of Science and Technology, Japan) on "Modeling Simultaneous Speech Translation". In addition, two keynote talks were given at the Satellite Workshop on "Speaker and Language Identification, Verification, and Diarization" by Hema A. Murthy (IIT Madras, India) on "Signal Processing guided Machine Learning" and Oldřich Plchot (Brno University of Technology, Czech Republic) on "Current and emerging trends in extracting speaker embeddings".

This volume contains a collection of submitted papers presented at SPECOM 2023, which were thoroughly reviewed by members of the Program Committee and additional reviewers consisting of more than 120 specialists in the conference topic areas. In total, 94 full papers out of 174 papers submitted for SPECOM 2023 were selected by the Program Committee for presentation at the main conference, the special sessions and the satellite workshop, as well as for inclusion in two volumes of SPECOM 2023 proceedings. Theoretical and more general contributions were presented in common plenary sessions. Problem-oriented sessions as well as panel discussions brought together specialists in niche problem areas with the aim of exchanging knowledge and skills resulting from research projects of all kinds.

We would like to express our gratitude to all authors for providing their papers on time, to the members of the SPECOM 2023 Program Committee for their careful reviews and paper selection, and to the editors and correctors for their hard work in preparing two volumes of the conference proceedings. Special thanks are due to the members of the SPECOM 2023 Organizing Committee for their tireless effort and enthusiasm during the conference organization. We are also grateful to IIT Dharwad, IIIT Dharwad, NIT Goa, KLE Tech, and KIIT Gurugram for organizing and hosting the jubilee 25th International Conference on Speech and Computer SPECOM 2023 in Dharwad, India.

November 2023

Alexey Karpov
K. Samudravijaya
K. T. Deepak
Rajesh M. Hegde
Shyam S. Agrawal
S. R. Mahadeva Prasanna

Organization

The jubilee 25th International Conference on Speech and Computer (SPECOM 2023) was organized by IIT Dharwad, IIIT Dharwad, NIT Goa, KLE Tech, and KIIT Gurugram in Dharwad, Karnataka, India. The conference website is: https://www.iitdh.ac.in/specom-2023/.

General Chairs

B. Yegnanarayana	IIIT Hyderabad, India
Shyam S. Agrawal	KIIT Group of Colleges, Gurugram, India

Program Committee Chairs

Alexey Karpov	St. Petersburg Federal Research Center of the Russian Academy of Sciences, Russia
K. Samudravijaya	Koneru Lakshmaiah Education Foundation, India
K. T. Deepak	IIIT Dharwad, India
Rajesh M. Hegde	IIT Dharwad, India

Program Committee

Chinmayananda A.	IIIT Dharwad, India
Ajish K. Abraham	All India Institute of Speech and Hearing, India
Nagaraj Adiga	Samsung R&D Bangalore, India
Jahangir Alam	Computer Research Institute of Montreal, Canada
Paavo Alku	Aalto University, Finland
Gerasimos Arvanitis	University of Patras, Greece
Elias Azarov	Belarusian State University of Informatics and Radioelectronics, Belarus
Bharathi B.	SSN College of Engineering, India
Nagaratna B. Chittaragi	Siddaganga Institute of Technology, India
Dinesh Babu Jayagopi	IIIT Bangalore, India
Joyanta Basu	CDAC, Kolkata, India
Milana Bojanić	University of Novi Sad, Serbia
Eric Castelli	International Research Center MICA, Vietnam
Vladimir Chuchupal	Federal Research Center "Computer Science and Control" of the Russian Academy of Sciences, Russia

Andrea Corradini   Design School Kolding, Denmark
Govind D.   Koneru Lakshmaiah Education Foundation, India
Dileep A. D.   IIT Mandi, India
Rohan Kumar Das   Fortemedia Singapore, Singapore
Shyamal Kumar Das Mandal   IIT Kharagpur, India
Nauman Dawalatabad   Massachusetts Institute of Technology, USA
Vlado Delić   University of Novi Sad, Serbia
Olivier Deroo   Acapela Group, Belgium
Denis Dresvyanskiy   Ulm University, Germany
Akhilesh Dubey   K L University, India
Anna Esposito   Università degli Studi della Campania
    "L. Vanvitelli", Italy
Vera Evdokimova   St. Petersburg State University, Russia
Mauro Falcone   Fondazione Ugo Bordoni, Italy
Olga Frolova   St. Petersburg State University, Russia
Suryakanth Gangashetty   Koneru Lakshmaiah Education Foundation, India
Philip N. Garner   Idiap Research Institute, Switzerland
Branislav Gerazov   Ss Cyril and Methodius University,
    North Macedonia
Prasanta Kumar Ghosh   Indian Institute of Science, India
Gábor Gosztolya   University of Szeged, Hungary
Ivan Gruber   University of West Bohemia, Czech Republic
Vishwa Gupta   Computer Research Institute of Montreal, Canada
Muralikrishna H.   Manipal Academy of Higher Education, India
Denis Ivanko   St. Petersburg Federal Research Center of the
    Russian Academy of Sciences, Russia
Preethi Jyothi   IIT Bombay, India
Balaji Rao K.   HCLTech, India
Sudarsana Reddy Kadiri   Aalto University, Finland
Ildar Kagirov   St. Petersburg Federal Research Center of the
    Russian Academy of Sciences, Russia
Sishir Kalita   Armsoftech.AIR, India
Shareef Babu Kalluri   National Institute of Technology Karnataka
    Surathkal, India
Narendra Karamangala   NMAMIT, India
Veena Karjigi   Siddaganga Institute of Technology, India
Alexey Kashevnik   St. Petersburg Federal Research Center of the
    Russian Academy of Sciences, Russia
Heysem Kaya   Utrecht University, The Netherlands
Maria Khokhlova   St. Petersburg State University, Russia
Irina Kipyatkova   St. Petersburg Federal Research Center of the
    Russian Academy of Sciences, Russia
Daniil Kocharov   Tampere University, Finland

Liliya Komalova	Moscow State Linguistic University, Russia
Sunil Kumar Kopparapu	Tata Consultancy Services Ltd., India
Evgeny Kostyuchenko	Tomsk State University of Control Systems and Radioelectronics, Russia
Andrew Krizhanovsky	Institute of Applied Mathematical Research of the Karelian Research Centre of the Russian Academy of Sciences, Russia
Mohammad Azharuddin Laskar	Armsoftech Pvt Ltd., India
Benjamin Lecouteux	Université Grenoble Alpes, France
Natalia Loukachevitch	Research Computing Center of Moscow State University, Russia
Elena Lyakso	St. Petersburg State University, Russia
Olesia Makhnytkina	ITMO University, Russia
Maria De Marsico	Sapienza University of Rome, Italy
Yuri Matveev	ITMO University, Russia
Peter Mihajlik	Budapest University of Technology and Economics, Hungary
Nikolay Mikhaylovskiy	Higher IT School of Tomsk State University, Russia
Nobuaki Minematsu	University of Tokyo, Japan
Ganesh S. Mirishkar	IIIT Hyderabad, India
Jagabandhu Mishra	IIT Dharwad, India
Manjunath Mulimani	Tampere University, Finland
Ludek Muller	University of West Bohemia, Czech Republic
Satoshi Nakamura	Nara Institute of Science and Technology, Japan
Géza Németh	Budapest University of Technology and Economics, Hungary
Ruban Nersisson	VIT University, India
Oliver Niebuhr	University of Southern Denmark, Denmark
Dariya Novokhrestova	Tomsk State University of Control Systems and Radioelectronics, Russia
Sergey Novoselov	STC-innovations Ltd., Russia
Stavros Ntalampiras	University of Milan, Italy
Aparna P.	NITK, India
Vasuki P.	SSNCE, India
Win Pa	University of Computer Studies, Yangon, Myanmar
Nick A. Petrovsky	Belarusian State University of Informatics and Radioelectronics, Belarus
Branislav Popović	University of Novi Sad, Serbia
Vsevolod Potapov	Lomonosov Moscow State University, Russia
Rodmonga Potapova	Moscow State Linguistic University, Russia
Saswati Rabha	IIT Guwahati, India

Padmanabhan Rajan	IIT Mandi, India
Kumaraswamy Ramaswamy	Siddaganga Institute of Technology, India
Aleksei Romanenko	STC Ltd., Russia
Sergey Rybin	ITMO University, Russia
Dmitry Ryumin	St. Petersburg Federal Research Center of the Russian Academy of Sciences, Russia
Albert Ali Salah	Utrecht University, The Netherlands
Priyankoo Sarmah	Indian Institute of Technology Guwahati, India
Andrey Savchenko	Sber AI Lab, Russia
Björn Schuller	University of Augsburg, Germany/Imperial College London, UK
Milan Sečujski	University of Novi Sad, Serbia
Guruprasad Seshadri	NXP India Pvt. Ltd., India
Nirmesh Shah	Sony Research India, India
Ajay Kumar Sharma	HCL Technologies Ltd., India
Rajib Sharma	IIIT Dharwad, India
Tatiana Sherstinova	HSE University, St. Petersburg, Russia
Nickolay Shmyrev	Alpha Cephei Inc., Russia
Ingo Siegert	Otto von Guericke University, Germany
Pavel Skrelin	St. Petersburg State University, Russia
Tatiana Sokoreva	Moscow State Linguistic University, Russia
Valery Solovyev	Kazan Federal University, Russia
Victor Sorokin	Institute for Information Transmission Problems of the Russian Academy of Sciences, Russia
Ajay Srinivasamurthy	Amazon Alexa, India
Siniša Suzić	University of Novi Sad, Serbia
Ivan Tashev	Microsoft, USA
Veena Thenkanidiyoor	NIT Goa, India
Laszlo Toth	RGAI, Hungary
Isabel Trancoso	INESC ID Lisboa/IST, Portugal
Jan Trmal	Johns Hopkins University, USA
Moakala Tzudir	IIT Dharwad, India
Vasilisa Verkhodanova	University of Groningen, Campus Fryslan, The Netherlands
Deepu Vijayasenan	NIT-K, India
Anil Kumar Vuppala	IIIT Hyderabad, India
Jainath Yadav	Central University of Bihar, India
Chiranjeevi Yarra	IIITH, India
Zeynep Yucel	Okayama University, Japan
Jerneja Zganec Gros	Alpineon Research and Development Ltd., Slovenia

Organizing Committee

S. R. Mahadeva Prasanna (Chair)	IIT Dharwad, India
Suryakanth V. Gangashetty (Chair)	K L University, India
Ayush Agarwal	McAfee, India
Konjengbam Anand	IIT Dharwad, India
Ananya Angra	IIT Mandi, India
Lalaram Arya	IIT Dharwad, India
Alexander Axyonov	SPC RAS, Russia
Prashanth Bannulmath	IIIT Dharwad, India
Satish Chikkamath	KLE Hubli, India
Amartya R. Chowdhury	IIT Dharwad, India
Dileep A. D.	IIT Mandi, India
Ashwini Dasare	IIIT Dharwad, India
Govind Divakaran	KL University, India
Akilesh Dubay	KL University, India
Amruth Ashok Gadag	IIIT Dharwad, India
Namitha Gokavi	IIIT Dharwad, India
Urvashi Goswami	IIT Mandi, India
Pradyoth Hegde	IIIT Dharwad, India
Denis Ivanko	SPC RAS, Russia
Ildar Kagirov	SPC RAS, Russia
Sishir Kalita	Armsoftech.AIR, India
Alexey Karpov	SPC RAS, Russia
Kanika Kaur	KIIT, Gurugram, India
Kumar Kaustubh	IIT Dharwad, India
Irina Kipyatkova	SPC RAS, Russia
Sujeet Kumar	IIT Mandi, India
Jagabandhu Mishra	IIT Dharwad, India
Sougata Mukherjee	IIT Dharwad, India
Muralikrishna	Manipal Academy of Higher Education, India
Rishith Sadashiv T. N.	IIT Dharwad, India
S. R. Nirmala	KLE Hubli, India
Prakash Pawar	IIIT Dharwad, India
Tonmoy Rajkhowa	IIT Dharwad, India
Dmitry Ryumin	SPC RAS, Russia
Elena Ryumina	SPC RAS, Russia
Sunil Saumya	IIIT Dharwad, India
Kartikay Sharma	KIIT, Gurugram, India
Rajib Sharma	IIIT Dharwad, India
Swapnil Sontakke	IIIT Dharwad, India

Veena Thenkanidiyoor   NIT Goa, India
Akshaya A. V.   IIT Mandi, India

Keynote Speakers

Bhiksha Raj   Carnegie Mellon University, USA
Visar Berisha   Arizona State University, USA
Satoshi Nakamura   Nara Institute of Science and Technology, Japan
S. Umesh   IIT Madras, India
Hema A. Murthy   IIT Madras, India
Oldřich Plchot   Brno University of Technology, Czech Republic

Advisory Board

Rodmonga Potapova   Moscow State Linguistic University, Russia
Andrey Ronzhin   St. Petersburg Federal Research Center of the
                         Russian Academy of Sciences, Russia
Albert Ali Salah   Utrecht University, The Netherlands
Vlado Delić   University of Novi Sad, Serbia
Milos Zelezny   University of West Bohemia, Czech Republic
Nikos Fakotakis   University of Patras, Greece
Géza Németh   Budapest University of Technology and
                         Economics, Hungary
Oliver Jokisch   Meissen University (HSF), Germany
Iosif Mporas   University of Hertfordshire, UK
Samarendra Dandapat   IIT Guwahati, India
Bhiksha Raj   Carnegie Mellon University, USA
Nobuaki Minematsu   University of Tokyo, Japan
Hema A. Murthy   IIT Madras, India
K. Sreenivasa Rao   IIT Kharagpur, India
Hemant A. Patil   DA-IICT, India
Mathew M. Doss   IDIAP, Switzerland
Sriram Ganapathy   IISc Bangalore, India
Hugo L. Rufiner   Universidad Nacional del Litoral, Argentina
Chandra Sekhar S.   IISc Bangalore, India

Additional Reviewers

Abderrahim Fathan
Jovan Galić
Nikša Jakovljević
Prasanna Kumar
Maxim Markitantov
Rohith Mars
Tijana Nosek

Meghna Pandharipande
Elena Ryumina
Nikola Simić
Pratik Singh
Mikhail Uzdiaev
Alena Velichko
Yang Xiao

Contents – Part II

Speech Analysis and Synthesis

Speaker and Language Identification, Verification, and Diarization

Contents – Part I

Digital Signal Processing

Speech Prosody

Speech Processing for Medicine

Industrial Speech and Language Technology

Analysing Breathing Patterns in Reading and Spontaneous Speech

Gauri Deshpande[1,2(✉)] ⬤, Björn W. Schuller[2,3], Pallavi Deshpande[4],
Anuradha Rajiv Joshi[5], S. K. Oza[4], and Sachin Patel[1]

[1] TCS Research, Pune, India
{gauri1.d,sachin.patel}@tcs.com
[2] University of Augsburg, Augsburg, Germany
schuller@ieee.org
[3] Imperial College London, London, UK
[4] Bharti Vidyapeeth (DTU) College of Engineering, Pune, India
{psdeshpande,skoza}@bvucoep.edu.in
[5] Department of Physiology, Bharti Vidyapeeth (DTU) Medical College, Pune, India

Abstract. This paper focuses on the time and phase-domain analysis of speech signals to extract breathing patterns. The speech signals under investigation fall into two categories: reading and spontaneous speaking. We introduce SBreathNet, a deep Long Short-Term Memory (LSTM) based regressive model, to extract breathing patterns from speech signals. SBreathNet is trained with speech collected from 100 individuals reading a phonetically balanced text and extracts the breathing patterns with an average Pearson correlation coefficient (r-value) of 0.61 with the true breathing signal captured using a respiratory belt. The average breaths-per-minute error (BPME) across 100 speakers is 2.50. The analysis is done using leave-one-speaker-out approach. Similarly, when SBreathNet is trained with spontaneous speech signals, it extracts the breathing patterns with an r-value of 0.41 and an average BPME of 3.9. By comparing the performance across speakers, speech categories, and speech-breathing categories, we aim to uncover the factors influencing SBreathNet's effectiveness when applied to these two types of speech signals.

Keywords: Speech analysis · Computational paralinguistics · Speech-breathing patterns · Health informatics

1 Introduction

Speech signals and breathing patterns are inherently interconnected as they both rely on the use of respiratory organs. Moreover, they are both susceptible to being influenced by various psychological and physiological factors. An illustrative instance is the noticeable alteration in an individual's voice when affected by a cough or cold. Similarly, as highlighted in the works of [1,2], breathing patterns serve as an indicator for the presence of respiratory infection, COVID-19.

A. Karpov et al. (Eds.): SPECOM 2023, LNAI 14339, pp. 3–17, 2023.
https://doi.org/10.1007/978-3-031-48312-7_1

In particular, the authors of [1] reveal that breathing signals contain a greater wealth of information regarding COVID-19 infection compared to speech signals.

Among multiple ways of capturing breathing patterns, visual inspection is the simplest of all, but is prone to errors. All other techniques require a measurement instrument connected to the individual under observation. For example, in RIP, a transducer is connected over the chest area to convert the changes in lung volume into digital breathing patterns. The acquisition of such patterns to enable further analysis of the signals requires an instrument called a respiratory belt along with a data acquisition unit. As an individual needs to visit a clinic for an inspection of the breathing pattern, this is usually done only after the difficulty in breathing becomes severe. Consequently, our proposition is to utilise speech signals as a means to extract and analyse breathing patterns, enabling a deeper comprehension of an individual's underlying physiological and psychological states. Speech signals can be conveniently captured using a smartphone microphone, even in non-clinical settings.

1.1 Previous Work

Various approaches have been employed to extract breathing patterns from speech signals. A common metric used to evaluate the performance of predictive models is the Pearson's correlation coefficient, which measures the correlation between the predicted and true breathing patterns. Additionally, breathing parameters like breaths-per-minute (BPM) and tidal volume are also compared between the predicted and true patterns. Several speech features have been utilized to extract breathing patterns from speech. These include Mel Frequency Cepstral Coefficients (MFCCs), Root Mean Square Error, ZCR, and spectral slope, as described in [3]. Cepstrograms, as discussed in [4], and log mel-spectrograms, as explored in [5–8], have also been employed for this purpose. Furthermore, in their work, Nallanthighal et al. [7] have investigated the use of raw speech waveforms fed into deep neural networks.

In [5], simultaneous breathing and conversational speech is collected from 20 healthy subjects. A maximum Pearson correlation (r-value) of 0.47 is achieved with long-short term memory (LSTM) networks for a segment duration of 4 seconds (s). Further breathing parameters such as breathing rate and tidal volume are also calculated with an error rate of 4.3% and 1.8%, respectively. In [6], 40 healthy subjects' data is analysed for the detection of breathing rate using LSTM models. The authors have compared mean squared error (MSE) with BerHu as the regression loss function (similar to Huber loss function – see [6]). They present the hypothesis that the breathing patterns have sudden peaks of inhalation followed by a gradually descending curve of exhalation which can be modelled using a BerHu loss function. They also present the results showing BerHu loss optimises the model better than MSE giving an r-value of 0.42. With the same approach, the authors of [7] have performed cross-corpus analysis and have achieved an r-value of 0.39 when training using Philips-Database and testing on the UCL-SBM database [9] and the r-value of 0.36 with the reversed datasets. The Computational Paralinguistics challengE (ComParE) organised

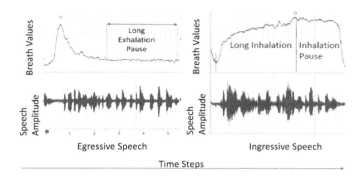

Fig. 1. Two broad categories of the speech-breathing patterns: speech during inhalation called ingressive and speech during exhalation called egressive speech-breathing.

at Interspeech 2020 [9] had in its Breathing Sub-Challenge a baseline Pearson correlation of r = 0.50 on the development (16 speakers), and r = 0.73 on the test data set (17 speakers). The winners of this challenge [10] reported r = 0.76 between the breathing patterns derived from the speech signal and corresponding breathing values of the test set of 17 speakers.

Speech can be primarily categorised into two types: reading speech, which refers to speech produced while reading a paragraph, and spontaneous speech, which pertains to speech generated during natural, unplanned conversations or presentations. The breathing patterns generated during these two speech tasks differ. There have been relatively fewer comparisons made between models that extract breathing patterns from both reading and spontaneous speech. As reported in [11], spontaneous speech task exhibit grammatically inappropriate overlap of speech during exhale duration as compared to reading task. The spontaneous speech task also have longer exhalations overlapping with speech production than the passage reading task. In the study conducted in [7], a performance evaluation of deep learning models is performed on both reading and spontaneous speech tasks. The obtained r-values for the reading and spontaneous speech tasks are reported as 0.56 and 0.51 respectively. It is important to note that the speech data for these tasks is sourced from two separate databases with distinct speakers: the Philips read speech database and the UCL Speech Breath Monitoring (UCL-SBM) database, as mentioned in [9]. Analysing the differences and similarities in the captured breathing patterns of the same set of speakers between reading and spontaneous speech tasks would provide valuable insights.

The main contributions of this paper are as follows:

- We present a deep network: SBreathNet, trained with data from 100 speakers to extract breathing patterns from speech signals.
- We present additional insights with leave-one-speaker-out (LOSO) analysis on r-value and BPME metrics.

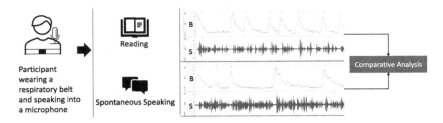

Fig. 2. Simultaneous speech (S) and breathing (B) is collected from the participants while they read and speak spontaneously. The speech signals are analysed for extracting breathing patterns from them. We present a comparison of the performance of the models extracting breathing patterns from reading and spontaneous speech signals.

– We augment the understanding of the speech-breathing patterns. As seen in Fig. 1, the left breathing pattern with a sudden inhalation peak followed by exhalation is called egressive speech-breathing. Here, the speech production happens during exhalation. The right side of Fig. 1 shows the breathing pattern with longer inhalation and a sudden drop during exhalation. This is called ingressive breathing pattern [12]. Here, the speech production happens during inhalation. In this paper, we introduce the impact of ingressive patterns on the model performance.
– We compare SBreathNet performance across 100 speakers, two speech categories (reading and spontaneous speaking), and two speech-breath categories: ingressives and egressives.

2   Methodology

As shown in Fig. 2, speech and breathing patterns are captured simultaneously from the participants while they perform four different tasks: reading a phonetically balanced passage, speaking spontaneously, pronouncing vowels, and laughing out loudly. We present the analysis of speech-derived breathing patterns for the reading and spontaneous speaking tasks and compare their performances. This section explains the study design for capturing the data followed by speech representation techniques explored to build the model for extracting breathing patterns from speech signals.

2.1   Data Acquisition

ADInstruments' respiratory belt transducer is used for recording the breathing patterns and a condenser microphone for recording the speech signals. ADInstruments PowerLab data acquisition system's two channels are connected to these two recording devices to capture the time synchronised signals. The transducer is positioned on the chest (4 centimetres (cm) below the collarbone) and the head mounted microphone is placed at a distance of 4 cm from the mouth. A survey questionnaire is designed to capture the participants' metadata comprising personal and physiological information along with their anxiety level using the state and trait anxiety inventory scale. Personal information includes age group, gender, height, weight and if they have received any formal training of singing. We also ask them if they currently smoke or have smoked in the past. Physiological information includes the momentary pulse rate, and the blood pressure measured using Omron's digital blood pressure monitoring machine.

An approval from the ethical committee of Bharti Vidyapeeth Medical College is taken for execution of the data collection. An informed consent is taken from the participants for collection of data. The participants are seated in a chair and are given approximately 2 min time to relax before starting the experiment. They read the phonetically balanced sentences from the List 2, List 3, List 7, List 8, List 9 and List 10 of Harvard sentences. Harvard sentences are phonetically balanced sentences using specific phonemes at the same frequency as they appear in English [13]. Each participant took around two to three minutes to read these sentences. This activity is called as "Reading Task". After this, the participants are asked to speak spontaneously about any topic they like. They are also given some pointers in the form of questions (such as, what are your hobbies, which is your favourite city and further on) to help them recall any incident they want to narrate. A timer of one minute is set such that they speak at-least for a minute. This is called as "Spontaneous Task". This is followed by the "Vowels Task", in which they pronounce five English vowels and 12 Devnagari vowels. At the end, each participant laughs out loudly (LoL) for around two to three seconds. This is called as "Vowels and LoL Task".

2.2   Speech Representation Analysis

For the extraction of breathing patterns from speech, the significance of the low-level time-domain features is discussed in [14]. Using these features, an r-value of 0.57 is achieved between the speech and the predicted breathing patterns of the ComParE dataset [9]. Among other speech parameters used for understanding the respiratory problems such as COVID-19 from human voice, MFCCs and the phase-domain decomposed filter components (PDDFC) of speech signal are discussed to classify COVID-19 subjects from healthy subjects in [1]. We explore the time-domain features, MFCCs, and PDDFC for training an LSTM-based deep network, to extract the breathing patterns from the speech signals. It is observed that the combination of time-domain features along with PDDFC performs the best. Both the features are calculated for every speech frame of 20 miliseconds (ms). Time domain features form a feature vector of length 16 comprising of: ZCR, kurtosis, RMS, auto-correlation, and 10 time domain difference features [15] and PDDFC forms the feature vector of length 160.

2.3   SBreathNet: LSTM-Based Deep Model

As shown in the Fig. 3, the network architecture is trained using time domain features and PDDFC as input. The network is trained with a batch length of 250 corresponding to a duration of 5 s (A sample for every 20 ms is calculated, hence

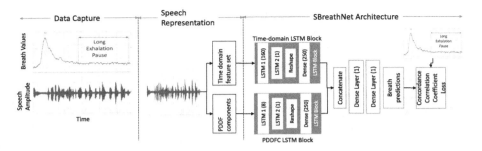

Fig. 3. The speech signals that are captured with breathing patterns are represented using time and phase domain analysis. This representation is then fed to SBreathNet, LSTM-based deep architecture to extract breathing patterns from the speech signals.

250 samples = 250×20 ms = 5000 ms). Both the inputs are passed separately to corresponding LSTM blocks comprising of two LSTMs and a dense layer. The outputs of these two LSTM blocks are concatenated and fed to two consecutive dense layers. This forms the output of the encoder network. The loss function calculates the concordance correlation coefficient (CCC) loss between true and predicted values. The network learns with a learning rate of 0.001 and with an Adam optimiser. The activation function of the last dense layer is the hyperbolic tangent (tanh) function. This causes the prediction values to range between -1 to 1. Figure 3 shows the number of nodes of each network layer in brackets.

3   Results

With the SBreathNet model described in Sect. 2.3, the breathing patterns for both reading and spontaneous speech are extracted when trained with respective speech data. The predicted breathing patterns are then compared with the true breathing patterns captured with the respiratory belt to analyse the respective model performance. We present the separate analysis of reading and spontaneous speech, followed by comparing their performances and the challenges.

3.1   Read Speech

An average r-value of 0.61 is achieved across the 100 speakers' breathing patterns extracted from the speech signals captured while they read the phonetically balanced passage. We experimented with varying batch length values (the time-step value for the LSTM layer) of the network ranging from 1 s to 1 min to understand the impact of the time-series-encoding on the performance. The overall performance is achieved the best for 5 s based analysis. As seen in Fig. 4 (a), the number of speakers having an r-value above 0.50 is 80.

The BPME count for every speaker is calculated on the predictions obtained and compared with that of the true breathing pattern. The peak detection algorithm from scipy [16] is used for the detection of peaks keeping a distance as 100

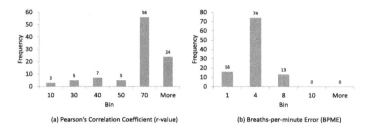

(a) Pearson's Correlation Coefficient (r-value)   (b) Breaths-per-minute Error (BPME)

Fig. 4. (a) Number of speakers belonging to six bins of r-value performance of the SBreathNet model trained with the speech captured during reading task. (b) Number of speakers belonging to five bins of breaths-per-minute error calculated between the true breathing patterns and the breathing patterns predicted using SBreathNet model for the reading task.

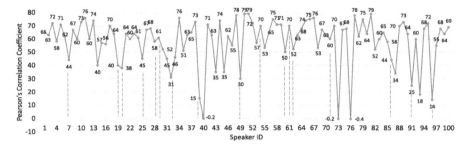

Fig. 5. Pearson's correlation coefficient is calculated between the true breathing patterns and the breathing patterns extracted using SBreathNet for the reading task. The predictions are obtained using Leave-one-speaker-out analysis.

points and a height as 0.2. Using the peak count, further, BPME is calculated for each speaker. An average BPME obtained is 2.50. Figure 4 (b) shows that 90% of the speakers have BMPE less than 4. Hence, SBreathNet can extract breathing patterns with an r-value above 0.50 for 80% speakers and a BPME below 4 for 90% speakers.

Leave One Speaker Out Analysis: Figure 5 visualises the LOSO performance of the SBreathNet architecture. As seen in the Figure, three speaker IDs: 40, 73, and 76 consistently have a negative r-value. As described before, varying batch-lengths from 1 s to 60 s are explored; also regularisation techniques are explored, however, the performance for these three speakers remains unchanged. The speaker-wise BPME for the 100 speakers for the predictions obtained using SBreathNet ranges between 0.3 to 7.5. It is observed that the change in BPME across the speakers is not synchronised with the r-value exhibited by them. This can be seen in the case of speakers with negative r-value of -0.40 and -0.21, who have relatively low BPME of 3 and 2.1, respectively. This shows that SBreathNet captures the breathing event equally well for speakers with low r-value.

Table 1. Number of speakers belonging to each breathing pattern cluster and their corresponding performances. The performance is reported using r-value, BPME, and Centroid-R between the true and the predicted values.

Cluster	Speakers	R	BPME	Centroid-R
0	24	0.60	3.6	0.80
1	20	0.37	1.8	−0.30
2	16	0.68	2.4	0.74
3	26	0.66	2.2	0.68
4	14	0.65	2.6	0.90

Clustering on True Breathing Patterns: To further understand the performance exhibited in LOSO analysis, the true breathing patterns are studied using clustering technique. It is observed that an average breathing cycle duration lasts for around five seconds while a speaker reads loudly. The breathing patterns of the read-task are captured continuously for around 3–4 min from each speaker. Such breathing patterns are segmented into smaller breathlets of 5 s each giving around 35–45 such breathlets per speaker. With each breathlet as a data point, the elbow method indicates that five distinct clusters can be formed using a k-means clustering algorithm. On clustering the breathlets using k-means with random_state defined as zero, the cluster centres show that four of the clusters represent four distinct locations of the inhalation peak in the five seconds duration. These locations are: 1) within first second, 2) between 2–4 s, 3) between 4–5 s, and 4) towards the end of the 5 s. For all these four clusters, the speakers speak during exhalation, hence these four clusters represent the egressive speech-breathing. The fifth cluster represents an inhalation that starts from the first second and the inhalation-pause lasts until five seconds. The speakers belonging to this cluster speak during inhalation, hence, this cluster represents the ingressive speech-breathing. This observation indicates that there are two broad categories of breathing data: ingressive and egressive as shown in Fig. 1. The red dotted lines in Fig. 5 are put against the speaker IDs that belong to cluster 1 and hence are ingressive speakers. It is observed that, the 14 out of 20 (70%) of the speakers exhibiting r-value below 0.50 (low-performers) are ingressives. This contributes to 70% of the total ingressive speakers. These results suggest that, ingressiveness considerably impacts the model performance.

Table 1 explains the average r-value (R) for the five clusters showing the least performance from ingressive cluster; cluster 1. The BPME for the five clusters is as given in Table 1. Once again, we observe a lack of synchronisation between the BPME and the r-values within the cluster. This is particularly evident in cluster 1, which exhibits the lowest average BPME of 1.8. Table 1 also provides an r-value between the mean 5 s breathlet of the five predicted clusters with the corresponding true ones (Centroid-R). For the four egressive clusters, the mean breathlets overlap well with the true ones.

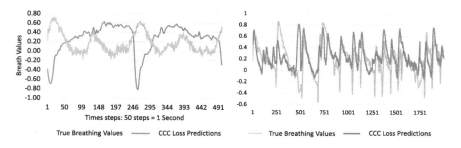

Fig. 6. Breathing predictions for speaker identity 76 (a) and 93 (b). 76 is ingressive and 93 is egressive speaker having an r-value of -0.40 and 0.21 respectively.

Ingressives and Egressives: The average r-value of egressive speaker clusters (1, 3, 4, and 5) is 0.65 and that of ingressive speaker cluster is 0.37 using SBreathNet predictions. From the predicted breathing patterns of SBreathNet, it is observed that the ingressive pattern is apparent in four of the lowest performing ingressive speakers with the speaker IDs 40, 73, 76, and 96. Figure 6 (left) shows the 10 s prediction for speaker 76. As seen in the Figure, the breathing events are correctly identified resulting in predicting the BPME of only 1.2. However, the breathing pattern is inverted such that the inhalation and inhalation pause exhibited by true breathing patterns are not captured by the predictions. Instead, the predictions show an expiration for the corresponding time slot. This explains the absence of synchronisation between the r-value and the BPME across the speakers.

With the proposed model, 6 egressive speakers have a low performance such as speaker ID 93, who has an r-value of 0.21. As seen in Fig. 6 (right), for the 20 s predictions of speaker 93, the peaks are correctly matched as well as the shape. However, the valleys are not matching between the predicted and true values. This is seen when the speakers exhale breath to a large extent resulting in deep valleys. Since the sound of such exhalation activity is not captured in speech or voice, it becomes difficult to trace them. This underscores the second challenge encountered by SBreathNet, which involves identifying the valleys of breathing patterns from speech signals.

3.2   Spontaneous Speech

This section describes the analysis being performed on the speech signals captured while the participants speak spontaneously. The results are obtained using the SBreathNet model trained on the spontaneous speech signal. The calculation of metrics such as the r-value and BPME remains the same as done for read speech. The average r-value, representing the breathing patterns extracted from the speech signals of the same 100 speakers during spontaneous speech, is found to be 0.41. As illustrated in Fig. 7 (a), 42% of the speakers exhibit an r-value above 0.50, while 65% of them have an r-value exceeding 0.40. By experimenting with batch lengths ranging from 1 s to 60 s, we determine that the analysis based

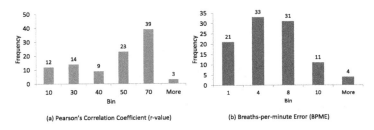

(a) Pearson's Correlation Coefficient (r-value)   (b) Breaths-per-minute Error (BPME)

Fig. 7. (a) Number of speakers belonging to six bins of r-value performance of the SBreathNet model trained with the speech captured during spontaneous speaking task. (b) Number of speakers belonging to five bins of breaths-per-minute error calculated between the true breathing patterns and the breathing patterns predicted using SBreathNet model for the spontaneous task.

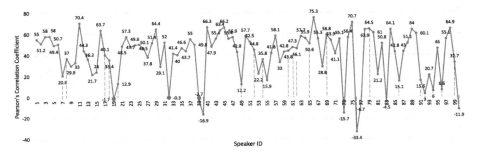

Fig. 8. Pearson's correlation coefficient calculated between the true breathing patterns and the breathing patterns extracted using SBreathNet for the spontaneous task. The predictions are obtained using Leave-one-speaker-out analysis.

on a 5 s batch length produces the most optimal outcome. Figure 7 (b) displays the distribution of BPME across 5 bins. The data reveals that 54% of speakers have a BPME value below 4, whereas 15% of them exhibit a high BPME value surpassing 10.

Leave One Speaker Out Analysis: Based on the LOSO analysis, it is evident that there are eight speakers displaying negative r-values, ranging from -0.3 to -33.4. Speaker ID 66 exhibits the highest correlation of 75.3%. When adjusting the batch length, the performance of the speakers with negative correlation varies, but consistently remains negative. Furthermore, the varying batch length not only impacts individual speaker performance but also affects the overall performance. Figure 8 illustrates the performance obtained using a batch length of 5 s, which yields the best overall results.

Clustering on True Breathing Patterns: To gain deeper insights into the LOSO performance, the true breathing patterns in spontaneous speech are

Table 2. Number of speakers belonging to each breathing pattern cluster and their corresponding performances. The performance is reported using r-value, BPME, and Centroid-R between the true and the predicted values of the spontaneous task.

Cluster	Speakers	R	BPME	Centroid-R
0	32	0.40	5.7	0.41
1	27	0.20	1.9	−0.27
2	17	0.50	4.0	0.71
3	12	0.54	4.2	0.56
4	12	0.56	4.2	0.19

divided into breathlets of 5 s each. This segmentation follows a similar approach to the analysis of breathing in read speech. When considering these actual 5 s breathlets in spontaneous speech as individual data points, the elbow method suggests the presence of five clusters within the data. By utilising the k-means clustering algorithm, these five clusters are successfully identified and formed.

The two main categories of breathing patterns observed in Fig. 1 are also evident within the 5 clusters of spontaneous speech. Among these clusters, one exhibits an ingressive breathing pattern, while the remaining four demonstrate an egressive breathing pattern. Notably, all the eight speakers displaying negative correlation belong to the ingressive cluster. Among the 100 speakers, a total of 27 individuals exhibit ingressive breathing patterns. Within this group, 20 speakers (74%) possess an r-value lower than 0.40, indicating a weaker correlation. To highlight this, red dotted lines are delineated in Fig. 8 to represent the speakers belonging to the ingressive cluster, Cluster 1.

In addition, the performance of the SBreathNet model across the five clusters is illustrated in Table 2. Observing the table, it is evident that cluster 1 exhibits the lowest performance with an average correlation of 0.20. Nevertheless, it is noteworthy that the BPME for this cluster is also the lowest, suggesting accurate identification of breath events within this cluster. Furthermore, the Centroid-R value for the ingressive cluster is negative, indicating a negative correlation. Regarding the egressive clusters, Cluster 3 and Cluster 4 exhibit similar average r-values (R) compared to the other two egressive clusters. However, it is important to highlight that cluster 4 demonstrates notably low correlation in terms of mean breathlet (Centroid-R).

Ingressives and Egressives: According to the findings presented in Table 2, the average correlation of ingressive cluster is 0.20, while that of egressive clusters is 0.48. These results once again highlight the influence of ingressiveness on the model's performance. However, even within egressive speakers, there are other factors that contribute to a decrease in the model's performance. As previously discussed in the context of read speech, the presence of breathing valleys leads to a reduction in correlation since they are not captured in speech. This observation holds true for spontaneous speech as well. Additionally, spontaneous speech presents the additional challenge of random breath events, which can result in a loss of synchronisation between speech signals and breathing patterns across both the speech-breathing categories of egressives and ingressives.

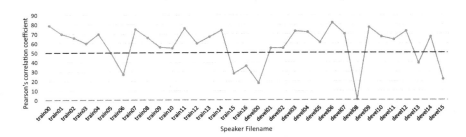

Fig. 9. Leave one speaker out performance of the deep LSTM model SBreathNet on the ComParE dataset.

3.3   Observations on ComPaRe Dataset

As described in [9], the authors have captured the speech and breathing patterns from 49 subjects following a similar protocol as described in Sect. 2.1. The authors mention that spontaneous speech is captured for 4 min per speaker. Training, validation and test partitions of the total data is provided in the challenge organised by the authors. The three partitions have 17, 16, and 17 speakers' data respectively. For the presented discussion, we analyse the training and validation partition data. Figure 9 shows the speaker-wise performance obtained with SBreathNet architecture in the LOSO analysis. We used the same features as defined in Sect. 2.2 along with SBreahNet for this dataset. It is observed from the LOSO analysis of the 33 speakers that 6 speakers have r-value below 0.50. Only one speaker has the r-value as 0.0. On further analysis, it is seen that the breathing patterns of these six speakers follow ingressive pattern. Empirically, they have breathing values above the average value for more than half of the 5 s duration. The average r-value for egressive speakers is 0.67 and for ingressive speakers is 0.24.

The overall performance exhibited by SBreathNet is an r-value of 0.58 on the development partition of ComParE challenge dataset, which is comparable to the winners of this challenge [10] (0.64). Moreover, SBreathNet has 40K parameters as compared to 1.4M and 3.5M parameters of the models discussed in [10].

4   Discussion

In Sect. 3, the results obtained using time and phase domain features with SBreathNet architecture are presented for both read and spontaneous speech. It is observed that the performance for spontaneous speech is 0.2 lower compared to that of read speech. The correlation (r-value) between the predictions of read and spontaneous speech across the 100 speakers is 0.59. This suggests that the predicted breathing patterns for the reading and spontaneous tasks of the same speaker have a similarity index of 59%.

Both categories of speech face similar challenges, including ingressiveness and deep valleys, which have a negative impact on the model's performance. Speakers who exhibit ingressiveness during reading also tend to exhibit the same breathing pattern during spontaneous speech. However, it is not mandatory for the vice-versa to hold true. For instance, speakers with identity 9 and 100 show ingressive patterns while speaking spontaneously but not while reading. Among all the speakers, a total of 14 individuals showcase superior performance in terms of spontaneous speech compared to their performance in read speech. Likewise, 86 speakers demonstrate higher performance in the read speech task.

It is observed from the results that extracting breathing patterns for ingressive speech is difficult. To collect more data belonging to ingressive class, we need to understand such speaker characteristics. We asked further questions on physiological and psychological states to the speakers exhibiting ingressiveness in both reading and spontaneous task. The questions about their involvement in sports, yoga, swimming, if they were infected by COVID-19, about respiratory disorder in their family, the sleep quality, and their metabolic, physical and mental health were asked. We also discussed if they find themselves introvert, if they have stage fear and hence practise talking. None of the conditions are found uniform across all the speakers. For all of them, neither they nor anyone in their family have any respiratory disorders. 9 out of 20 common ingressive speakers reported that they are actively involved in sports activities related to athletics. 3 of them were infected by mild COVID-19 and were asymptomatic. The three ingressive speakers whose r-value is found negative in both reading and spontaneous task reported that they are introverts and had stage fear. They have practised speaking skills. This observation matches with the case study performed in [17]. The authors have found that a subject has used inspiratory speech for 6 years as a means of overcoming the communication problems of long-standing adductor spastic dysphonia. These observations show that not only physiological, but behavioural parameters also impact the breathing patterns of an individual.

5   Conclusion and Future Work

In this paper, we presented the novel SBreathNet architecture consuming time and phase domain features for the extraction of breathing patterns from speech signals during reading and spontaneous tasks. We performed LOSO analysis to understand the r-value between the predicted and the true breathing patterns for each speaker. The speaker-wise analysis helps in understanding the performance variation across speakers. This also reveals the impact of ingressiveness on the model performance. These observations are not evident from the overall performance of the model. We conclude that LOSO analysis is a strong analysis technique to understand the performance better and identify the challenges in extracting breathing patterns from the speech signals. We have presented the impact of the ingressive speech on the model's performance in extracting the breathing patterns accurately. Hence, in future work, we will have a focus on collecting more data and identifying ingressive speech.

During our discussion, we explored the performance of SBreathNet on two speech categories: reading and spontaneous speaking, involving a group of 100 speakers. It was evident that the model achieved superior results in reading speech compared to spontaneous speech. However, both categories encountered common challenges, such as ingressiveness and deep valleys in the breathing patterns. Moreover, the spontaneous speech category presented an additional obstacle: the randomness of breath events, including the start of inhalation and exhalation. We plan to extend our analysis to address these challenges in our future work.

References

1. Deshpande, G., Schuller, B.W.: Covid-19 biomarkers in speech: on source and filter components. In: 43rd Annual International Conference of the IEEE Engineering in Medicine & Biology Society (EMBC), pp. 800–803. IEEE (2021)
2. Brown, C., et al.: Exploring automatic diagnosis of covid-19 from crowdsourced respiratory sound data. arXiv preprint arXiv:2006.05919 (2020)
3. Ruinskiy, D., Lavner, Y.: An effective algorithm for automatic detection and exact demarcation of breath sounds in speech and song signals. IEEE Trans. Audio Speech Lang. Process. **15**(3), 838–850 (2007)
4. Routray, A.: Automatic measurement of speech breathing rate. In: Proceedings of the 27th European Signal Processing Conference (EUSIPCO), pp. 1–5. IEEE, A Coruña, Spain (2019)
5. Nallanthighal, V.S., Strik, H.: Deep sensing of breathing signal during conversational speech. In: Proceedings of the 16th Annual Conference of the International Speech Communication Association, pp. 4110–4114. ISCA, Graz, Austria (2019)
6. Nallanthighal, V.S., Härmä, A., Strik, H.: Speech breathing estimation using deep learning methods. In: Proceedings of the 45th International Conference on Acoustics, Speech and Signal Processing (ICASSP), pp. 1140–1144. IEEE, Barcelona, Spain (2020)
7. Nallanthighal, V.S., Mostaani, Z., Härmä, A., Strik, H., Magimai-Doss, M.: Deep learning architectures for estimating breathing signal and respiratory parameters from speech recordings. Neural Netw. **141**, 211–224 (2021)
8. Mostaani, Z., Nallanthighal, V.S., Härmä, A., Strik, H., Magimai-Doss, M.: On the relationship between speech-based breathing signal prediction evaluation measures and breathing parameters estimation. In: International Conference on Acoustics, Speech and Signal Processing (ICASSP), pp. 1345–1349. IEEE (2021)
9. Schuller, B.W., et al.: The INTERSPEECH computational paralinguistics challenge: elderly emotion, breathing & masks. In: Proceedings of the 21st Annual Conference of the International Speech Communication Association, pp. 2042–2046. ISCA, Shanghai, China (2020)

10. Markitantov, M., Dresvyanskiy, D., Mamontov, D., Kaya, H., Minker, W., Karpov, A.: Ensembling end-to-end deep models for computational paralinguistics tasks: compare 2020 mask and breathing sub-challenges. In: Proceedings of the 21st Annual Conference of the International Speech Communication Association, pp. 2072–2076. ISCA, Shanghai, China (2020)
11. Wang, Y.T., Green, J.R., Nip, I.S., Kent, R.D., Kent, J.F.: Breath group analysis for reading and spontaneous speech in healthy adults. Folia Phoniatr. Logop. **62**(6), 297–302 (2010)
12. Eklund, R.: Pulmonic ingressive phonation: diachronic and synchronic characteristics, distribution and function in animal and human sound production and in human speech. J. Int. Phon. Assoc. **38**(3), 235–324 (2008)
13. Rothauser, E.: IEEE recommended practice for speech quality measurements. IEEE Trans. Audio Electroacoust. **17**, 225–246 (1969)
14. Deshpande, G., Schuller, B.W.: The DiCOVA 2021 challenge-an encoder-decoder approach for covid-19 recognition from coughing audio. In: Proceedings of the 21st Annual Conference of the International Speech Communication Association, pp. 931–935. ISCA (2021)
15. Deshpande, G., Viraraghavan, V.S., Gavas, R.: A successive difference feature for detecting emotional valence from speech. In: Proceedings of SMM19, Workshop on Speech, Music and Mind, vol. 2019, pp. 36–40 (2019)
16. Virtanen, P., et al.: Scipy 1.0: fundamental algorithms for scientific computing in python. Nat. Methods **17**(3), 261–272 (2020)
17. Harrison, G.A., Troughear, R.H., Davis, P.J., Winkworth, A.L.: Inspiratory speech as a management option for spastic dysphonia: case study. Ann. Otol. Rhinol. Laryngol. **101**(5), 375–382 (1992)

Audio-Visual Speaker Verification
via Joint Cross-Attention

Gnana Praveen Rajasekhar$^{(\boxtimes)}$ and Jahangir Alam$^{(\boxtimes)}$

Computer Research Institute of Montreal, Montreal, QC H3N 1M3, Canada
{gnana-praveen.rajasekhar,jahangir.alam}@crim.ca

Abstract. Speaker verification has been widely explored using speech signals, which has shown significant improvement using deep models. Recently, there has been a surge in exploring faces and voices as they can offer more complementary and comprehensive information than relying only on a single modality of speech signals. Though current methods in the literature on the fusion of faces and voices have shown improvement over that of individual face or voice modalities, the potential of audio-visual fusion is not fully explored for speaker verification. Most of the existing methods based on audio-visual fusion either rely on score-level fusion or simple feature concatenation. In this work, we have explored cross-modal joint attention to fully leverage the inter-modal complementary information and the intra-modal information for speaker verification. Specifically, we estimate the cross-attention weights based on the correlation between the joint feature presentation and that of the individual feature representations in order to effectively capture both intra-modal as well inter-modal relationships among the faces and voices. We have shown that efficiently leveraging the intra- and inter-modal relationships significantly improves the performance of audio-visual fusion for speaker verification. The performance of the proposed approach has been evaluated on the Voxceleb1 dataset. Results show that the proposed approach can significantly outperform the state-of-the-art methods of audio-visual fusion for speaker verification.

Keywords: Cross-attention · Audio-visual fusion · Speaker verification · Joint-attention

1 Introduction

Speaker verification is the task of verifying the identity of a person, which is primarily carried out using acoustic samples. It has become a key technology for person authentication in various real-world applications such as customer authentication, security applications, etc [14,19]. In recent years, the performance of speaker verification has been significantly boosted using deep learning models based on acoustic samples such as x-vector [41], xi-vector [20], and ECAPA-TDNN [9]. However, in a noisy acoustic environment, it would be difficult to distinguish different speakers only based on speech signals. Therefore,

A. Karpov et al. (Eds.): SPECOM 2023, LNAI 14339, pp. 18–31, 2023.
https://doi.org/10.1007/978-3-031-48312-7_2

other modalities such as face, iris, and fingerprints are also explored for verifying the person's identity. Out of all the modalities, face and voice share a very close association with each other in identifying a person's identity [16]. Authenticating the identity of a person from videos has been widely explored in the literature by relying either on faces [15,32,44] or voices [2,40,59]. Inspired by the close association between faces and voices, audio-visual (A-V) systems [6,52,55,58] have been proposed for speaker verification. However, effectively leveraging the fusion of voices and faces for speaker verification is not fully explored in the literature [22,46]. Face and voice provide diverse and complementary relationships with each other, which plays a key role in outperforming the performance of individual modalities.

Conventionally, A-V fusion can be achieved by three major fusion strategies: feature-level fusion, model-level fusion, and decision-level fusion [54]. Feature-level fusion (or early fusion) is performed by naively concatenating the features of individual audio and visual modalities, which is further used for predicting the final outputs. Model-level fusion deals with specialized architectures for fusion based on models such as deep networks [56], Hidden Markov Model (HMM) [57], and kernel methods [4]. In decision-level fusion, audio and visual modalities are trained independently end-to-end, and then the scores obtained from the individual modalities are fused to obtain the final scores. It requires little training and is easy to implement, however, it neglects the interactions across the modalities and thereby shows limited improvement over the individual performances of faces and voices. Though feature (or early-level) fusion allows the audio and visual modalities to interact with each other at the feature level, they fail to effectively capture the complementary inter-modal and intra-modal relationships with each other. Most of the existing approaches for speaker verification based on A-V fusion either fall in the category of decision-level fusion, where fusion is performed at score level, or early feature-level fusion, which relies on early feature concatenation of audio and visual modalities. Even though naive feature concatenation or using score level fusion shows improvement in the performance of speaker verification, it does not fully leverage the intra-modal and inter-modal relationships among the audio and visual modalities. In some of the videos, the voices might be corrupted due to background clutter. On the other hand, face images can also be corrupted due to several factors such as occlusion, pose, poor resolution, etc. Intuitively, an ideal strategy of A-V fusion should give more importance to the modality, exhibiting better-discriminating features by fully exploiting the complementary relationships with each other.

Recently, attention mechanisms have been explored to focus on the more relevant modalities of the video clips by assigning higher attention weights to the modality exhibiting higher discrimination among the speakers [38]. In this work, we have investigated the prospect of leveraging the complementary relationships among the faces and voices, while still leveraging the intra-modal temporal dynamics within the same modality to improve the performance of the system than that of individual audio and visual modalities. Specifically, a joint feature representation is introduced to the joint cross-attentional fusion model along with the feature representations of individual modalities to simultaneously capture both the intra-modal relationships and complementary inter-modal relationships. The major contributions of this paper are as follows:

- A joint cross-attentional model is explored for an effective fusion of faces (visual) and voices (audio) by leveraging both the intra-modal and inter-modal relationships for speaker verification.
- Deploying the joint feature representation also helps to reduce the heterogeneity among the audio and visual features, thereby resulting in better A-V feature representations
- A detailed set of experiments are conducted to show that the proposed approach is able to outperform the state-of-the-art A-V fusion models for speaker verification.

2   Related Work

2.1   Audio-Visual Fusion for Speaker Verification

Nagrani et al. [27] is one of the early works to investigate the close association of voices and faces and proposed a cross-modal biometric matching system. They have attempted to match a given static face or dynamics video with the corresponding voice and vice-versa. They have further explored joint embeddings for the task of person verification, where the idea is to detect whether the faces and voices come from the same video or not [26]. Wen et al. [53] also explored shared representation space for voices and faces and presented a disjoint mapping network for cross-modal biometric matching by mapping the modalities individually to their common covariates. Tao et al. [45] proposed a cross-modal discriminative network based on the faces and voices of a given video. They have also investigated the association of faces and voices, whether the faces and voices come from the same person or not, and their application for speaker recognition. Another interesting work on cross-modal speaker verification was done by Nawaz et al. [30], where they analyzed the impact of languages for cross-modal biometric matching tasks in the wild. They have shown that both face and speaker verification systems rely on spoken languages, which is caused due to the domain shift across different languages. Leda et al. [37] attempted to leverage the complementary information of audio and visual modalities for speaker verification using a multi-view model, which uses a shared classifier to map audio and visual into the same space. Wang [50] explored various fusion strategies at the feature level and decision level, and showed that high-level features of audio and visual modalities share more semantic information than low-level features, which helps in improving the performance of the system. Chen et al. [3] proposed a co-meta learning paradigm for learning A-V feature representations in a self-supervised learning framework. In particular, they have leveraged the complementary information among the audio and visual modalities as a means of supervisory signal to obtain robust A-V feature representations. Meng et al. [22] also proposed a co-learning cross-modal framework, where the features of each modality are obtained by exploiting the knowledge from another modality using cross-modal boosters in a pseudo-siamese structure. Tao et al. [46] proposed a two-step A-V deep cleansing framework to deal with the noisy samples. They have used audio modality to discriminate the easy and complex samples as a coarse-grained cleansing, which is further refined as a fine-grained cleansing using the visual modality. Unlike prior approaches, we have investigated the prospect of leveraging attention mechanisms to fully exploit the complementary inter-modal and intra-modal relationships among the audio and visual modalities for speaker verification.

2.2   Attention Models for Audio-Visual Fusion

Attention mechanisms are widely used in the context of multimodal fusion with various modalities such as audio and text [21,25], visual and text [23,51], etc. Stefan et al. [13] proposed a multi-scale feature fusion approach to obtain robust A-V feature representations. They have fused the features at intermediate layers of the audio and visual backbones, which are finally combined with the feature vectors of individual modalities in the shared common space to obtain the final A-V feature representations. Peiwen et al. [43] proposed a novel fusion strategy, that involves weight-enhanced attentive statistics pooling for both modalities, which exhibit a strong correlation with each other. They further obtain keyframes in both modalities using cycle consistency loss along with a gated attention mechanism to obtain robust A-V embeddings for speaker verification. Shon et al. [38] explored an attention mechanism to conditionally select the relevant modality in order to deal with noisy modalities. They have leveraged the complementary information among the audio and visual modalities by assigning higher attention weights to the modality, exhibiting higher discrimination for speaker verification. Chen et al. [5] investigated various fusion strategies and loss functions to obtain robust A-V feature representations for speaker verification. They have further evaluated the impact of the fusion strategies on extremely missing or corrupted modalities by leveraging the data augmentation strategy to discriminate the noisy and clean embeddings. Cross-modal attention among the audio and visual modalities has been successfully explored in several applications such as weakly-supervised action localization [18], A-V event localization [10], and emotion recognition [34,36]. Bogdan et al. [24] explored a cross-attention mechanism for the A-V fusion based on cross-correlation across the audio and visual modalities. The features of each modality are learned under the constraints of other modalities. However, they focus only on inter-modal relationships and fail to exploit the intra-modal relationships. Praveen et al. [33] explored a joint cross-attentional (JCA) framework for dimensional emotion recognition, which is closely related to our work. However, we have further adapted the JCA model for speaker verification by introducing the attentive statistics pooling module.

3   Problem Formulation

For an input video sub-sequence S, L non-overlapping video segments are uniformly sampled, and the corresponding deep feature vectors are obtained from the pre-trained models of audio and visual modalities. Let $\boldsymbol{Z_a}$ and $\boldsymbol{Z_v}$ denote the deep feature vectors of audio and visual modalities respectively for the given input video sub-sequence $\boldsymbol{S}$ of fixed size, which is expressed as:

$$\boldsymbol{Z_a} = \{\boldsymbol{z_a^1}, \boldsymbol{z_a^2}, ..., \boldsymbol{z_a^L}\} \in \mathbb{R}^{d_a \times L} \tag{1}$$

$$\boldsymbol{Z_v} = \{\boldsymbol{z_v^1}, \boldsymbol{z_v^2}, ..., \boldsymbol{z_v^L}\} \in \mathbb{R}^{d_v \times L} \tag{2}$$

where d_a and d_v represent the dimensions of the audio and visual feature vectors, respectively, and $\boldsymbol{z_a^l}$ and $\boldsymbol{z_v^l}$ denotes the audio and visual feature vectors of the video segments, respectively, for $l = 1, 2, ..., L$ segments The objective of the problem is to estimate the speaker verification model $f : \boldsymbol{Z} \to \boldsymbol{Y}$ from the training data $\boldsymbol{Z}$, where $\boldsymbol{Z}$ denotes the set of audio and visual feature vectors of the input video segments and $\boldsymbol{Y}$ represents the speaker identity of the corresponding video sub-sequence S.

4   Proposed Approach

4.1   Visual Network

Faces from videos involve both appearance and temporal dynamics of video sequences, which can provide information pertaining to a wide range of intra-variations of visual modality. Effectively capturing the spatiotemporal dynamics of facial videos plays a key role in obtaining robust feature representations. Long Short-Term Memory Networks (LSTMs) have been found to be promising in modeling the long-term temporal cues in sequence representations for various applications [35,48]. In this work, we have used Resnet18 [12] trained on the Voxceleb1 dataset [28] to obtain the spatial feature representations of the video frames. Conventionally, the size of the visual feature vectors of the last convolutional layer will be $512 \times 7 \times 7$, which is fed to the pooling layer to reduce the spatial dimension from 7 to size 1. However, this spatial reduction may leave out some useful information, which may deteriorate the performance of the system. Therefore, as suggested by [10], we have deployed scaled dot-product of audio and visual feature vectors for each segment in order to leverage the audio feature vectors to smoothly reduce the spatial dimensions of video feature vectors. Then, we encode the temporal dynamics of the segments of the sequence of visual feature vectors using Bi-directional LSTM with residual embedding. Finally, the obtained feature vectors of visual modality are stacked to form a matrix of visual feature vectors as shown by

$$\boldsymbol{X_v} = (\boldsymbol{x_v^1}, \boldsymbol{x_v^2}, ..., \boldsymbol{x_v^L}) \in \mathbb{R}^{d_v \times L} \tag{3}$$

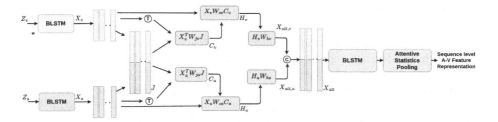

Fig. 1. Block Diagram of the Joint cross-attention model for A-V fusion.

4.2   Audio Network

With the advent of deep neural networks, speaker verification based on deep feature vectors has shown significant improvement over the conventional i-vector [7] based methods. One of the most widely used deep feature vector embeddings is the x-vector paradigm [41], which uses time-delay neural network (TDNN) and statistics pooling. Several variants of TDNN such as Extended TDNN (ETDNN) [42] and Factored TDNN (FTDNN) [47] have been introduced to boost the performance of the system. Recently, ECAPA-TDNN [9] has been introduced for speaker verification, which has shown significant improvement by leveraging the residual and squeeze-and-excitation (SE) components. So we have also explored ECAPA-TDNN to obtain the deep feature vectors of the audio segments. In order to exploit the temporal dynamics in the speech sequence, LSTMs have also been explored for speaker embedding extraction [1,60]. Similar to that of visual modality, we have also used Bi-directional LSTMs with residual embedding to encode the obtained audio feature vectors. Finally, the audio feature vectors of L video clips are stacked to obtain a matrix, shown as

$$X_{\mathbf{a}} = (x_{\mathbf{a}}^1, x_{\mathbf{a}}^2, ..., x_{\mathbf{a}}^L) \in \mathbb{R}^{d_a \times L} \tag{4}$$

4.3   Joint Cross-Attentional AV-Fusion

Though audio-visual fusion can be achieved through unified multimodal training, it was found that multimodal performance often declines over that of individual modalities [49]. This has been attributed to a number of factors, such as differences in learning dynamics for audio and visual modalities [49], different noise topologies, with some modality streams containing more or less information for the task at hand, as well as specialized input representations [29]. Therefore, we have obtained deep feature vectors for the individual audio and visual modalities independently, which are then fed to the joint cross-attentional module for audio-visual fusion.

Since multiple modalities convey more diverse information than a single modality, effectively leveraging the intra-modal and inter-modal complementary relationships among the audio and visual modalities plays a key role in efficient audio-visual fusion. In this work, we have explored joint cross-attentional fusion to encode the intra-modal and inter-modal relationships simultaneously in a joint framework. Specifically, the joint A-V feature representation, obtained by concatenating the audio and visual features is also fed to the fusion module along with the feature representations of individual modalities. By deploying the joint representation, features of each modality attend to themselves, as well as other modalities, thereby simultaneously capturing the semantic inter-modal and intra-modal relationships among audio and visual modalities. Leveraging the joint representation also helps in reducing the heterogeneity among the audio and visual modalities, which further improves the performance of speaker verification. A block diagram of the proposed model is shown in Fig. 1. The joint representation of audio-visual features, J, is obtained by concatenating the audio and visual feature vectors:

$$J = [X_a; X_v] \in \mathbb{R}^{d \times L} \tag{5}$$

where $d = d_a + d_v$ denotes the feature dimension of concatenated features.

The concatenated audio-visual feature representations (J) of the given video sub-sequence (S) are now used to attend to the feature representations of individual modalities X_a and X_v. The joint correlation matrix C_a across the audio features X_a, and the combined audio-visual features J are given by:

$$C_a = \tanh\left(\frac{X_a^T W_{ja} J}{\sqrt{d}}\right) \tag{6}$$

where $W_{ja} \in \mathbb{R}^{L \times L}$ represents learnable weight matrix across the audio and combined audio-visual features, and T denotes transpose operation. Similarly, the joint correlation matrix for visual features is given by:

$$C_v = \tanh\left(\frac{X_v^T W_{jv} J}{\sqrt{d}}\right) \tag{7}$$

The joint correlation matrices C_a and C_v for audio and visual modalities provide a semantic measure of relevance not only across the modalities but also within the same modality. A higher correlation coefficient of the joint correlation matrices C_a and C_v shows that the corresponding samples are strongly correlated within the same modality as well as other modality. Therefore, the proposed approach is able to efficiently leverage the complementary nature of audio and visual modalities (i.e., inter-modal relationship) as well as intra-modal relationships, thereby improving the performance of the system. After computing the joint correlation matrices, the attention weights of audio and visual modalities are estimated.

For the audio modality, the joint correlation matrix C_a and the corresponding audio features X_a are combined using the learnable weight matrices W_{ca} to compute the attention weights of audio modality, which is given by

$$H_a = ReLU(X_a W_{ca} C_a) \tag{8}$$

where $W_{\mathbf{ca}} \in \mathbb{R}^{d_a \times d_a}$ and $H_{\mathbf{a}}$ represents the attention maps of the audio modality. Similarly, the attention maps ($H_{\mathbf{v}}$) of visual modality are obtained as

$$H_{\mathbf{v}} = ReLU(X_{\mathbf{v}}W_{\mathbf{cv}}C_{\mathbf{v}}) \tag{9}$$

where $W_{\mathbf{cv}} \in \mathbb{R}^{d_v \times d_v}$ denote the learnable weight matrices.

Then, the attention maps are used to compute the attended features of audio and visual modalities as:

$$X_{\mathbf{att,a}} = H_{\mathbf{a}}W_{\mathbf{ha}} + X_{\mathbf{a}} \tag{10}$$

$$X_{\mathbf{att,v}} = H_{\mathbf{v}}W_{\mathbf{hv}} + X_{\mathbf{v}} \tag{11}$$

where $W_{\mathbf{ha}} \in \mathbb{R}^{d \times d_a}$ and $W_{\mathbf{hv}} \in \mathbb{R}^{d \times d_v}$ denote the learnable weight matrices for audio and visual modalities respectively.

The attended audio and visual features, $X_{\mathbf{att,a}}$ and $X_{\mathbf{att,v}}$ are further concatenated to obtain the A-V feature representation, which is given by:

$$\widehat{\mathbf{X}} = [X_{\mathbf{att,v}}; X_{\mathbf{att,a}}] \tag{12}$$

The attended audio-visual feature vectors are fed to the Bi-directional LSTM in order to capture the temporal dynamics of the attended joint audio-visual feature representations. The segment-level audio-visual feature representations are in turn fed to the attentive statistics pooling (ASP) [31] in order to obtain the subsequence or utterance-level representation of the audio-visual feature vectors. Finally, the embeddings of the final audio-visual feature representations are used to obtain the scores, where the additive angular margin softmax (AAMSoftmax) [8] loss function is used to optimize the parameters of the fusion model and ASP module.

5   Experimental Methodology

5.1   Datasets

The proposed approach has been evaluated on the VoxCeleb1 dataset [28], obtained from videos of YouTube interviews, captured in a large number of challenging multi-speaker acoustic environments. The dataset contains 1,48,642 video clips from 1,251 speakers, which is gender-balanced with 55% of the speakers being male. The speakers are selected from a wide range of different ethnicities, accents, professions, and ages. The duration of the video clips ranges from 4 s to 145 s. In our experimental framework, we split the voxceleb1 development set (comprised of videos from 1211 speakers) into training and validation sets. We have randomly selected 1150 speakers for training and 61 speakers for validation. We have also reported our results on the Vox1-O (Voxceleb1 Original) test set for performance evaluation. This test set consists of 37720 trials from 40 speakers.

5.2   Evaluation Metric

In order to evaluate the performance of our proposed approach, we used equal error rate (EER) as an evaluation metric, which has been widely used for speaker verification in the literature [7,24]. It depicts the error rate when the False Accept Rate (FAR) is equal to the False Reject Rate (FRR). So the lower the EER, the higher the reliability of the system.

5.3   Implementation Details

For the visual modality, the facial images are taken from the images provided by the organizers of the dataset. For regularizing the network, dropout is used with $p = 0.8$ on the linear layers. The initial learning rate of the network was set to be $1e - 2$ is used for the Adam optimizer. Also, weight decay of $5e - 4$ is used. The batch size of the network is set to 400. Data augmentation is performed on the training data by random cropping, which produces a scale-invariant model. The number of epochs is set to be 50 and early stopping is used to obtain the best weights of the network.

For training the audio network, 80-dimensional Mel-FilterBank (MFB) features are extracted using an analysis window size of 25 ms over a frameshift of 10 ms. The acoustic features are randomly augmented on-the-fly with either MUSAN noise, speed perturbation with a rate between 0.95 and 1.05, or reverberation [39]. In addition, we use SpecAugment [17] for applying frequency and time masking on the MFB features. The initial weights of the audio network are initialized with values from the normal distribution and the network is trained for a maximum of 100 epochs, and early stopping is used. The network is optimized using Adam optimizer with the initial learning rate of 0.001 and the batch size is fixed to be 400. In order to prevent the network from over-fitting, dropout is used with p = 0.5 after the last linear layer. Also, weight decay of $5e - 4$ is used for all the experiments.

For the fusion network, we used hyperbolic tangent functions for the activation of cross-attention modules. The dimension of the extracted features of audio modality is set to 192 and visual modality as 512. In the joint cross-attention module, the initial weights of the joint cross-attention matrix are initialized with the Xavier method [11] and the weights are updated using the Adam optimizer. The initial learning rate is set to be 0.001 and batch size is fixed to be 100. Also, a dropout of 0.5 is applied on the attended A-V features and weight decay of $5e - 4$ is used for all the experiments.

6   Results and Discussion

6.1   Ablation Study

In order to analyze the performance of the proposed fusion model, we compare the proposed fusion model with some of the widely-used fusion strategies for speaker verification. One of the widely used fusion strategies is score-level fusion, where the scores of the individual modalities are obtained and fused together to estimate the identity of a person. Another common approach for A-V fusion is based on early fusion, where the deep features of audio and visual modalities are concatenated immediately after being extracted, and the concatenated version of the individual modalities is used to obtain the final scores. As we can observe in the Table, the proposed fusion model consistently outperforms both the early fusion and the score level (decision level) by leveraging the semantic intra-modal and inter-modal relationships among the audio and visual modalities for speaker verification.

In order to analyze the contribution of the LSTMs in improving the modeling of intra-modal relationships for both individual feature representations and the final attended A-V feature representations, we have carried out a series of experiments with and without Bi-directional LSTMs (BLSTM). The experimental results to analyze the impact of BLSTMs have been shown in Table 1 Initially, we conducted an experiment without using Bi-LSTMs with the proposed fusion model. Then, we introduced Bi-LSTMs only for modeling the temporal dynamics of individual feature representations. We can observe that the performance of the proposed fusion model with the U-BLSTMs for individual feature representations has been improved. Now, we introduce BLSTMs for modeling the temporal dynamics of the final A-V attended feature representations. As observed in Table 1, the performance of the proposed fusion model has been further improved by introducing J-BLSTMs for modeling the temporal dynamics of final A-V feature representations.

Table 1. Performance of various fusion strategies on the validation set.

Fusion Method	EER
Feature Concatenation (Early Fusion)	2.489
Score-level Fusion (Decision-level)	2.521
Proposed Fusion (JCA) without BLSTMs	2.315
Proposed Fusion (JCA) with U-BLSTMs	2.209
Proposed Fusion (JCA) with U-BLSTMs and J-BLSTMs	2.173

6.2   Comparision to State-of-the-Art

In order to compare with state-of-the-art, we have used the recently proposed A-V fusion model based on two-step multimodal deep cleansing [46]. We have used their deep cleansing approach as a baseline and extended their approach by introducing our proposed fusion model to obtain robust A-V feature representations. The experimental results of the proposed approach in comparison to that of [46] are shown in Table 2. We have reported the results for both the validation set and the Vox1-O test partition of the Voxceleb1 dataset. In order to analyze the fusion performance of the proposed model, we have also reported the results for the individual audio and visual modalities. We can observe that the proposed fusion model clearly outperforms the performance of individual modalities. We can also observe that by introducing the proposed fusion model, the performance of the system has been improved better than that of [46].

Table 2. Performance of the proposed approach in comparison to state-of-the-art on the validation set and Vox1-O set.

Fusion Method	Validation Set	Vox1-O Set
Face	3.720	3.779
Speech	2.553	2.529
Tao et al. [46]	2.476	2.4096
Proposed Fusion Model	2.125	2.214

7   Conclusion

In this paper, we present a joint cross-attentional A-V fusion model for speaker verification in videos. Unlike prior approaches, we effectively leverage the intra-modal and complementary inter-modal relationships among the audio and visual modalities. In particular, we obtain the deep features of audio and visual modalities from pre-trained networks, which are fed to the fusion model along with the joint representation. Then semantic relationships among audio and visual modalities are obtained based on the cross-correlation between the individual feature representations and the joint A-V feature representation (concatenated version of audio and visual features). The attention weights obtained from the cross-correlation matrix are used to estimate the attended feature vectors of audio and visual modalities. The modeling of intra-modal relationships in the proposed system has been further improved by leveraging Bi-directional LSTMs to model the temporal dynamics of both the individual feature representations and the final attended A-V feature representations. Experiments have shown that the proposed approach outperforms the state-of-the-art approaches for speaker verification.

Acknowledgments. The authors wish to acknowledge the funding from the Government of Canada's New Frontiers in Research Fund (NFRF) through grant NFRFR-2021-00338.

References

1. Alam, J., Fathan, A., Kang, W.H.: Text-independent speaker verification employing CNN-LSTM-TDNN hybrid networks. In: Speech and Computer, pp. 1–13 (2021)
2. Alam, J., Kang, W.H., Fathan, A.: Hybrid neural network with cross- and self-module attention pooling for text-independent speaker verification. In: IEEE ICASSP, pp. 1–5 (2023)
3. Chen, H., Zhang, H., Wang, L., Lee, K.A., Liu, M., Dang, J.: Self-supervised audio-visual speaker representation with co-meta learning. In: IEEE ICASSP, pp. 1–5 (2023)
4. Chen, J., Chen, Z., Chi, Z., Fu, H.: Emotion recognition in the wild with feature fusion and multiple kernel learning. In: ICMI, pp. 508–513 (2014)
5. Chen, Z., Wang, S., Qian, Y.: Multi-modality matters: a performance leap on VoxCeleb. In: Proceedings of Interspeech, pp. 2252–2256 (2020)
6. Chetty, G., Wagner, M.: Audiovisual speaker identity verification based on cross modal fusion. In: Proceedings of Auditory-Visual Speech Processing, p. paper P37 (2007)
7. Dehak, N., Kenny, P.J., Dehak, R., Dumouchel, P., Ouellet, P.: Front-end factor analysis for speaker verification. IEEE TASLP **19**(4), 788–798 (2011)
8. Deng, J., Guo, J., Xue, N., Zafeiriou, S.: Arcface: additive angular margin loss for deep face recognition. In: IEEE/CVF Conference on CVPR, pp. 4685–4694 (2019)
9. Desplanques, B., Thienpondt, J., Demuynck, K.: ECAPA-TDNN: emphasized channel attention, propagation and aggregation in TDNN based speaker verification. In: Proceedings of Interspeech, pp. 3830–3834 (2020)
10. Duan, B., Tang, H., Wang, W., Zong, Z., Yang, G., Yan, Y.: Audio-visual event localization via recursive fusion by joint co-attention. In: IEEE WACV, pp. 4012–4021 (2021)
11. Glorot, X., Bengio, Y.: Understanding the difficulty of training deep feedforward neural networks. In: ACAIS. vol. 9, pp. 249–256 (2010)
12. He, K., Zhang, X., Ren, S., Sun, J.: Deep residual learning for image recognition. In: CVPR, pp. 770–778 (2016)
13. Hörmann, S., Moiz, A., Knoche, M., Rigoll, G.: Attention fusion for audio-visual person verification using multi-scale features. In: IEEE FG, pp. 281–285 (2020)
14. Jelil, S., Shrivastava, A., Das, R.K., Prasanna, S.R.M., Sinha, R.: Speechmarker: a voice based multi-level attendance application. In: Interspeech, pp. 3665–3666 (2019)
15. Kemelmacher-Shlizerman, I., Seitz, S.M., Miller, D., Brossard, E.: The megaface benchmark: 1 million faces for recognition at scale. In: IEEE Conference on CVPR, pp. 4873–4882 (2016)
16. Kim, C., Shin, H.V., Oh, T.H., Kaspar, A., Elgharib, M., Matusik, W.: On learning associations of faces and voices. In: Proceedings of the ACCV (2018)
17. Ko, T., Peddinti, V., Povey, D., Seltzer, M.L., Khudanpur, S.: A study on data augmentation of reverberant speech for robust speech recognition. In: IEEE ICASSP, pp. 5220–5224 (2017). https://doi.org/10.1109/ICASSP.2017.7953152
18. Lee, J.T., Jain, M., Park, H., Yun, S.: Cross-attentional audio-visual fusion for weakly-supervised action localization. In: Proceedings of the ICLR (2021)
19. Lee, K., Larcher, A., Thai, H., Ma, B., Li, H.: Joint application of speech and speaker recognition for automation and security in smart home. In: INTER-SPEECH, pp. 3317–3318 (2011)

20. Lee, K.A., Wang, Q., Koshinaka, T.: Xi-vector embedding for speaker recognition. IEEE SPL **28**, 1385–1389 (2021)
21. Lee, Y., Yoon, S., Jung, K.: Multimodal speech emotion recognition using cross attention with aligned audio and text. In: INTERSPEECH, pp. 2717–2721 (2020)
22. Liu, M., Lee, K.A., Wang, L., Zhang, H., Zeng, C., Dang, J.: Cross-modal audio-visual co-learning for text-independent speaker verification. In: IEEE ICASSP, pp. 1–5 (2023)
23. Ma, C., Shen, C., Dick, A., Wu, Q., Wang, P., Hengel, A.v.d., Reid, I.: Visual question answering with memory-augmented networks. In: CVPR, pp. 6975–6984 (2018)
24. Mocanu, B., Ruxandra, T.: Active speaker recognition using cross attention audio-video fusion. In: Proceedings of the EUVIP, pp. 1–6 (2022)
25. N., K.D., Patil, A.: Multimodal emotion recognition using cross-modal attention and 1d convolutional neural networks. In: INTERSPEECH, pp. 4243–4247 (2020)
26. Nagrani, A., Albanie, S., Zisserman, A.: Learnable pins: cross-modal embeddings for person identity. In: Proceedings of ECCV (2018)
27. Nagrani, A., Albanie, S., Zisserman, A.: Seeing voices and hearing faces: cross-modal biometric matching. In: IEEE CVPR (2018)
28. Nagrani, A., Chung, J.S., Zisserman, A.: Voxceleb: a large-scale speaker identification dataset. In: INTERSPEECH (2017)
29. Nagrani, A., Yang, S., Arnab, A., Schmid, C., Sun, C.: Attention bottlenecks for multimodal fusion. In: NIPS (2021)
30. Nawaz, S., et al.: Cross-modal speaker verification and recognition: a multilingual perspective. In: Proceedings of the IEEE/CVF Conference on Computer Vision and Pattern Recognition, pp. 1682–1691 (2021)
31. Okabe, K., Koshinaka, T., Shinoda, K.: Attentive statistics pooling for deep speaker embedding. In: Proceedings of Interspeech, pp. 2252–2256 (2018)
32. Parkhi, O.M., Vedaldi, A., Zisserman, A.: Deep face recognition. In: Proceedings of the BMVC, pp. 41.1–41.12 (2015)
33. Praveen, R.G., Cardinal, P., Granger, E.: Audio-visual fusion for emotion recognition in the valence-arousal space using joint cross-attention. IEEE Trans. Biomet., Behav. Identity Sci. **5**(3), 360–373 (2023)
34. Praveen, R.G., Granger, E., Cardinal, P.: Cross attentional audio-visual fusion for dimensional emotion recognition. In: IEEE FG, pp. 1–8 (2021)
35. Praveen, R.G., Granger, E., Cardinal, P.: Recursive joint attention for audio-visual fusion in regression based emotion recognition. In: IEEE ICASSP, pp. 1–5 (2023)
36. Praveen, R.G., et al.: A joint cross-attention model for audio-visual fusion in dimensional emotion recognition. In: 2022 IEEE/CVF Conference on Computer Vision and Pattern Recognition Workshops (CVPRW), pp. 2485–2494 (2022)
37. Sarı, L., Singh, K., Zhou, J., Torresani, L., Singhal, N., Saraf, Y.: A multi-view approach to audio-visual speaker verification. In: IEEE ICASSP, pp. 6194–6198 (2021)
38. Shon, S., Oh, T.H., Glass, J.: Noise-tolerant audio-visual online person verification using an attention-based neural network fusion. In: IEEE ICASSP, pp. 3995–3999 (2019)
39. Snyder, D., Chen, G., Povey, D.: MUSAN: A music, speech, and noise corpus. CoRR abs/1510.08484 (2015). https://arxiv.org/abs/1510.08484
40. Snyder, D., Garcia-Romero, D., Povey, D., Khudanpur, S.: Deep neural network embeddings for text-independent speaker verification. In: Proceedings of Interspeech, pp. 999–1003 (2017)

41. Snyder, D., Garcia-Romero, D., Sell, G., Povey, D., Khudanpur, S.: X-vectors: Robust DNN embeddings for speaker recognition. In: IEEE ICASSP, pp. 5329–5333 (2018)
42. Snyder, D., et al.: The JHU speaker recognition system for the voices 2019 challenge. In: INTERSPEECH, pp. 2468–2472 (2019)
43. Sun, P., Zhang, S., Liu, Z., Yuan, Y., Zhang, T., Zhang, H., Hu, P.: Learning audio-visual embedding for person verification in the wild (2022)
44. Taigman, Y., Yang, M., Ranzato, M., Wolf, L.: Deepface: closing the gap to human-level performance in face verification. In: IEEE Conference on CVPR, pp. 1701–1708 (2014)
45. Tao, R., Das, R.K., Li, H.: Audio-visual speaker recognition with a cross-modal discriminative network. In: Proc. Interspeech, pp. 2242–2246 (2020)
46. Tao, R., Lee, K.A., Shi, Z., Li, H.: Speaker recognition with two-step multi-modal deep cleansing. In: IEEE ICASSP, pp. 1–5 (2023)
47. Villalba, J., et al.: State-of-the-art speaker recognition for telephone and video speech: The JHU-MIT submission for NIST sre18. In: Interspeech, pp. 1488–1492 (2019)
48. Wan, X., Xing, T., Ji, Y., Gong, S., Liu, C.: 3D human action recognition with skeleton orientation vectors and stacked residual BI-LSTM. In: 4th IAPR ACPR, pp. 571–576 (2017)
49. Wang, W., Tran, D., Feiszli, M.: What makes training multi-modal classification networks hard? In: CVPR, pp. 12692–12702 (2020)
50. Wang, Y.: Efficient audio-visual speaker recognition via deep multi-modal feature fusion. In: Proceedings of ICCIS, pp. 99–103 (2021)
51. Wei, X., Zhang, T., Li, Y., Zhang, Y., Wu, F.: Multi-modality cross attention network for image and sentence matching. In: CVPR (2020)
52. Wen, P., Xu, Q., Jiang, Y., Yang, Z., He, Y., Huang, Q.: Seeking the shape of sound: an adaptive framework for learning voice-face association. In: 2021 IEEE/CVF Conference on Computer Vision and Pattern Recognition (CVPR), pp. 16342–16351 (2021)
53. Wen, Y., Ismail, M.A., Liu, W., Raj, B., Singh, R.: Disjoint mapping network for cross-modal matching of voices and faces. In: ICLR (2019)
54. Wu, C.H., Lin, J.C., Wei, W.L.: Survey on audiovisual emotion recognition: databases, features, and data fusion strategies. APSIPA Trans. Signal Inform. Process. 3, e12 (2014)
55. Wu, Z., Cai, L., Meng, H.: Multi-level fusion of audio and visual features for speaker identification. In: Advances in Biometrics, pp. 493–499 (2005)
56. Yang, X., Ramesh, P., Chitta, R., Madhvanath, S., Bernal, E.A., Luo, J.: Deep multimodal representation learning from temporal data. In: CVPR (2017)
57. Zeng, Z., et al.: Audio-visual affect recognition through multi-stream fused hmm for HCI. In: CVPR, pp. 967–972 (2005)
58. Zhao, X., Lv, Y., Huang, Z.: Multimodal fusion-based swin transformer for facial recognition micro-expression recognition. In: IEEE ICMA, pp. 780–785 (2022)
59. Zhao, Z., Li, Z., Wang, W., Zhang, P.: PCF: ECAPA-TDNN with progressive channel fusion for speaker verification. In: IEEE ICASSP, pp. 1–5 (2023)
60. Zhao, Z., et al.: A lighten CNN-LSTN model for speaker verification on embedded devices. Futur. Gener. Comput. Syst. 100, 751–758 (2019)

A Novel Scheme to Classify Read and Spontaneous Speech

Sunil Kumar Kopparapu$^{(\boxtimes)}$

TCS Research, Mumbai, India
sunilkumar.kopparapu@tcs.com
http://www.tcs.com

Abstract. The COVID-19 pandemic has led to an increased use of remote telephonic interviews, making it important to distinguish between scripted and spontaneous speech in audio recordings. In this paper, we propose a novel scheme for identifying read and spontaneous speech. Our approach uses a pre-trained `DeepSpeech` audio-to-alphabet recognition engine to generate a sequence of alphabets from the audio. From these alphabets, we derive features that allow us to discriminate between read and spontaneous speech. Our experimental results show that even a small set of self-explanatory features can effectively classify the two types of speech very effectively.

Keywords: Spoken speech analysis · Read and spontaneous speech · DeepSeech features

1 Introduction

The ability to automatically distinguish read speech[1] from spontaneous speech has several real-world applications. The pandemic introduced constraint on physical travels while there was no such constraint in terms of office work, especially because of the new paradigm of *work from home*. As a result, people saw an opportunity to work for an organization that was hitherto not on their radar because of physical distance. The need to travel to work constraint removed, all work places were an opportunity as a result there was a large movement of people across organizations. The shift to remote work during the pandemic created opportunities for both organizations to hire top talent and for individuals to explore new job prospects. Any movement into an organization is preceded by an *interview* and in the remote work scenario these were in the form of audio or telephone-based interviews. Given the large volume of people who were crisscrossing, several organizations used semi-automated methods to conduct interviews, especially to filter out the initial applicants. One of the critical aspect that required monitoring was to determine *if the candidate was responding to the question spontaneously or was she reading from a prepared or scripted text.*

---

[1] Also called "prepared speech" or "scripted speech".

A. Karpov et al. (Eds.): SPECOM 2023, LNAI 14339, pp. 32–45, 2023.
https://doi.org/10.1007/978-3-031-48312-7_3

The need for an automatic identification of the candidate speech during interview as read speech or spontaneous speech became necessary. In another use case, the ability to distinguish read-speech and spontaneous-speech can have applications in forensics to distinguish *"asked to read"* statement (or confession) from spontaneous statement of a person being investigated. This can possibly be useful to determine if the statement given by the person was given on *their own accord* or was forced to give the statement.

There have been several approaches adopted by researcher in the past which dwell into classification of read and spontaneous speech. Most of these approaches have used deep and intricate analysis of the audio signal or language or both to distinguish read and spontaneous speech. More recently, pivoting on fluency in L2 language, [7] studies the essential statistical differences, based on data collected, in pauses between read and spontaneous speech, for Turkish, Swahili, Hausa and Arabic speakers of English. In [5], the authors describe method to recognize read and spontaneous speech in Zurich German (a specific dialect spoken in Switzerland) language. The authors in [2] discuss the possibility of differentiation between read and spontaneous speech by just looking at the intonation or prosody. Read and spontaneous speech classification based on variance of GMM supervectors has been studied in [1]. From a speaker role characterization perspective, in [6] the authors use acoustic and linguistic features derived from an automatic speech recognition system to characterize and detect spontaneous speech. They demonstrate their approach on three classes of spontaneity labelled French Broadcast News.

Two unrelated works reported in literature three decades apart influence the novel approach proposed in this paper. The first one is an early work on understanding spontaneous speech [15]. It captures the essential differences between read and spontaneous speech while trying to reason out why systems, like automatic speech to text recognition, designed to work for read speech often fail to perform well on spontaneous speech. They equate read speech to written text and spontaneous speech to spoken speech and highlight some of the idiosyncrasies associated with spontaneous speech. Though the authors intent was to outline strategies for speech recognition system trained for read speech to deal with spontaneous spoken speech, it captures some crucial differences in read and spoken speech which can be very helpful in building a classifier to distinguish read and spontaneous speech. Though not directly related to read and spontaneous speech, the second influence is the work reported in [14] where they exploit the pre-trained `DeepSpeech` speech-to-alphabet recognition engine to estimate the intelligibility of dysarthric speech. This paper is influenced by the approach adopted in [14] to identify the differences between read and spontaneous speech as mentioned in [15]. More recently, [11] made use of the differences between spoken language text and written language text, derived from spontaneous and read speech respectively, to build a language model that enhances the performance of a speech to text engine.

The main aim of this paper is to introduce a novel approach to identify features that are not only self-explanatory but are also able to distinguish between read and spontaneous speech. To the best of our knowledge, there is no *known* system to distinguish read and spontaneous speech in literature. Please note that, for this reason, we are unable to compare the performance of the approach proposed in this paper with any prior art. The essential idea is to exploit the available deep pre-trained models to extract features, from speech, that can discriminate between read speech from spontaneous speech. The rest of the paper is organized as follow: In Sect. 2, we describe our approach through an example. In Sect. 3, we present our experimental results and conclude in Sect. 4.

2   Our Approach

The problem of read and spontaneous speech classification can be stated as

Given a recorded audio sample, spoken by a single person, $x(t)$, determine automatically if $x(t)$ was read or spoken spontaneously.

While the approach is simple and straightforward as seen in Fig. 1, the novelty is in the feature extraction block that utilizes *unconventional*, yet explainable set of features, that aid distinguish read and spontaneous speech. Additionally, these features are easily obtained using DeepSpeech a pre-trained speech-to-alphabet recognition engine [10].

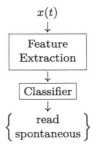

Fig. 1. A high-level read and spontaneous speech classification scheme.

2.1   Speech-to-Alphabet (DeepSpeech)

Mozilla's DeepSpeech [10] is an end-to-end deep learning model that converts speech into alphabets based on the Connectionist Temporal Classification (CTC) loss function. The 6-layer deep model is pre-trained on 1000 hours of speech from the Librispeech corpus [12]. All the 6 layers, except the 4th, have feed-forward dense units; the 4th layer itself has recurrent units.

A speech utterance $x(t)$ is segmented into T frames, as is common in speech processing, namely, $x^\tau(t)$ $\forall \tau \in [0, T-1]$. In DeepSpeech, each frame is of duration 25 msec. Each frame $x^\tau(t)$ is represented by 26 Mel Frequency Cepstral Coefficients (MFCCs), denoted by $\boldsymbol{f}_\tau$. Subsequently, the complete speech utterance $x(t)$ can be represented as $\{\boldsymbol{f}_\tau\}_{\tau=0}^{T-1}$. The input to DeepSpeech is 9 preceding and

9 succeeding frames, namely $\{\boldsymbol{f}_{\tau-9}, \cdots, \boldsymbol{f}_{\tau+9}\}$. The output of the `DeepSpeech` model is a probability distribution over an alphabet set $\mathcal{A} = (a, b, \cdots, z, \diamond, \Box, \prime)$ with $|\mathcal{A}| = 29$. Note that there are three additional outputs, namely, $\diamond$, $\Box$, and $\prime$ corresponding to *unknown*, *space* and an *apostrophe*, respectively in $\mathcal{A}$ in addition to the 26 known English alphabets[2]. The output at each frame, τ is

$$c_\tau^* = \max_{\forall k \in \mathcal{A}} P\left((c_\tau = k) \mid \{\boldsymbol{f}_{\tau-9}, \cdots, \boldsymbol{f}_\tau, \cdots, \boldsymbol{f}_{\tau+9}\}\right) \tag{1}$$

where $c_\tau^* \in \mathcal{A}$. It is important to note that a typical speech recognition engine is assisted by a statistical language model (SLM or LM for short), which helps in *masking* small acoustic mispronunciations. However, as seen in (1), there is no role of LM. This, as we will see later, helps in our task of extracting features that can assist distinguish read and spontaneous speech. As we mentioned earlier, the use of `DeepSpeech` is motivated by its use for speech intelligibility estimation work reported in [14]. Note that (a) `DeepSpeech` outputs an alphabet for every frame of 25 msec, so the longer the duration of the audio utterance, the more the number of output alphabets, (b) the output is always from the finite set $\mathcal{A}$ based on Equation (1). Note that $\Box$ can be treated as the *word separator* and we refer to $\diamond$ token in `DeepSpeech` as an `InActive` alphabet and anything other than that, namely, $\{\mathcal{A}\} - \diamond$ as the `Active` alphabet.

2.2 Feature Extraction

An example of the raw output of `DeepSpeech` to an utterance $x(t) =$

/Declarationofavariableismerelyspecifyingthedata/

is $\mathrm{DS}(x(t)) =$

$\diamond \diamond\, d\, \diamond\, e\, \diamond \diamond \diamond \diamond c\, \diamond \diamond a\, \diamond \diamond r\, \diamond \diamond \diamond \diamond i\, \diamond \diamond \diamond \diamond tiio\, \diamond$
$n\, \diamond \diamond \diamond \diamond \Box\, \diamond \diamond o\, \diamond\, f\, \diamond \diamond \Box\, \diamond \diamond a\, \diamond \diamond \Box r\, \diamond\, e\, \diamond \diamond l\, \diamond \diamond i\, \diamond \diamond \diamond aa\, \diamond \diamond \diamond b\, \diamond\, le\, \diamond \diamond \diamond \diamond \diamond \diamond \diamond \Box\, \diamond$
$\diamond \diamond \diamond i\, \diamond \diamond ss\, \diamond \diamond \diamond \diamond \diamond\, \Box\, \diamond \diamond m\, \diamond \diamond \diamond \diamond e\, \diamond \diamond \diamond r\, \diamond\, e\, \diamond \diamond \diamond \diamond l\, \diamond\, y\, \diamond \diamond s\, \diamond \diamond \diamond \diamond \Box\, \diamond\, p\, \diamond \diamond e\, \diamond\, c\, \diamond$
$\diamond \diamond \diamond i\, \diamond \diamond \diamond \diamond f\, \diamond \diamond \diamond \diamond y\, \diamond \diamond iing\, \diamond \diamond \Box\, \diamond\, thhat\, \diamond\, \Box\, \diamond \diamond \diamond \diamond e\, \diamond \diamond \diamond \diamond \diamond\, t\, \diamond \diamond a\, \diamond \diamond \diamond \diamond \diamond \diamond \diamond \Box$

`DeepSpeech` raw output of an audio signal $x(t)$ is a string of alphabets ($\in \mathcal{A}$). In this paper, we assume $\mathrm{DS}(x(t))$ to represent the audio signal $x(t)$ and hence any signal processing required to extract features from the audio signal translates to simple *string* or text processing. As seen from $\mathrm{DS}(x(t))$, we can easily extract several features using simple string processing scripts. For example, the number of words in the spoken utterance can be identified by the number of occurrences of $\Box$. We can count the total number of alphabets, the total number of `InActive` and `Active` alphabets by processing the alphabet string. Additionally, the knowledge of the duration of the audio $x(t)$ means that we can compute velocity-like features, for example, alphabets per second (APS) or words

---

[2] A collection of letters $\{a, b, \cdots, z\}$.

per second (WPS) etc. or number of InActive or Active alphabets per sec or number of active average word length (AWL) or alphabets per word and so on.

We hypothesize that DS($x(t)$), as a representation of speech $x(t)$, contains sufficient information that can help distinguish between read and spontaneous speech along the lines of [15]. This is motivated by the fact that given the *same information* to be articulated by a speaker, read speech is much faster compared to spontaneous speech, meaning the *duration* of the spontaneous speech is much longer than the read speech. If we consider that spontaneous speech requires thinking time between words, between sentences [15] etc. then the number of InActive alphabets must be more in spontaneous speech compared to read speech. Namely, for the same sentence, the output of DeepSpeech should having more number of InActive alphabets compared to read speech.

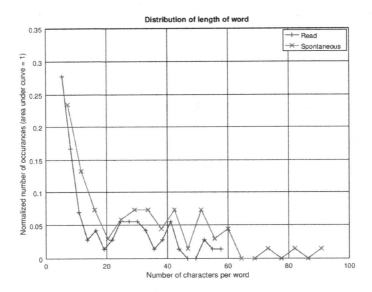

Fig. 2. Word length (# of alphabets per word) for read and spontaneous speech.

2.3   Identifying Features

In the highly data-driven machine learning era, we opted to look for simple, yet effective features that could help in our pursuit. We considered a short technical passage consisting of two sentences and 62 words, which we picked from Wikipedia for our analysis and asked (a) the paragraph to be read as is (read speech) and (b) the paragraph to be held as a reference and spoken in their own words ($\equiv$ spontaneous). We recorded this on a laptop as a 16 kHz, 16 bit, mono in .wav format. This read and spontaneous audio was processed by DS() to produce a string of alphabets ($\in \mathcal{A}$). Figure 2 shows a histogram plot of the number of alphabets in a word and their normalized frequency (area under the curve is 1). It can be clearly observed that, (a) there are more words (with same number of alphabets[3]) in spontaneously spoken passage compared to the read passage (the plot corresponding to spontaneous speech, in red is always above the read speech) and (b) there are more lengthy words in spontaneous speech (the spontaneous speech plot spreads beyond the read speech blue curve), there are words of length 90 alphabets in spontaneous speech compared to < 60 alphabets per word in read speech. This is in line with the observation that there are more InActive alphabets in spontaneous speech.

We extracted a set of 5 meaningful features as mentioned in Table 1 for both the read and spontaneous speech. Note that these measured features are self-explanatory and so we do not describe them in detail. Clearly, there are 3 features (the duration (a), the number of alphabets (c), and the number of Active alphabets (d)) that show promise to discriminate read and the spontaneous speech.

Table 1. Measured features from read and spontaneous speech for the same paragraph. # denotes is the count, an integer.

Measured Values			
SNo	What	Spontaneous	Read
(a)	Duration (sec)	47.62	29.67
(b)	Number of Words (#)	69	72
(c)	Number of Alphabets (#)	2382	1484
(d)	Number of Active alphabets (#)	1915	951
(e)	Number of InActive alphabets (#)	364	413
Derived Features			
Ratio	What	Spontaneous	Read
$(c)/(b)$	Av word len (alphabets/word; AWL)	34.52	20.61
$(c)/(a)$	Speaking Rate (alphabets/sec; APS)	50.02	50.02
$(b)/(a)$	Word Rate (WPS) $[f_3]$	1.45	2.43
$(e)/(a)$	InActive APS $[f_2]$	7.63	13.92
$(d)/(b)$	Active AWL $[f_1]$	27.75	13.21

Based on the differences between read and spontaneous speech mentioned in [15] we derive (see Table 1 Derived Features) features like average word length (AWL), speaking rate, word rate, InActive APS and Active AWL, from the values directly measured from $DS(x(t))$. It can be observed that, while Active average word length (Active AWL) and InActive alphabets per sec (InActive APS) features show promise to be able to discriminate read and spontaneous speech, the speaking rate in terms of alphabets per sec (APS) is a feature that does not allow us to discriminate between read and spontaneous speech, this is

---

[3] We use letter, character and alphabet interchangeably.

to be expected because as we mentioned earlier, the total number of alphabets output by DS() is proportional to the duration of the utterance[4]. Clearly, the `Active` and `InActive` alphabets play an important role in discriminating read and spontaneous speech. As one would expect, there are a large number of ◇ (can be associated with pauses) in spontaneous speech compared to read speech. Figure 3 shows the plot of the ratio of number of `InActive` alphabets to the number of alphabets in a word (arranged in the increasing order). It can be observed that spontaneous speech has more `InActive` alphabets per word compared to the read speech. Note that the curve corresponding to spontaneous speech, in red, is always higher than the read speech (blue curve). This is expected, considering that there is a sizable amount of pause time in spontaneous speech, unlike read speech. We can further observe that the means value of the ratio (number of `InActive` alphabets to the number of alphabets) is higher for spontaneous speech (0.76) compared to read speech (0.64) as seen in Fig. 3.

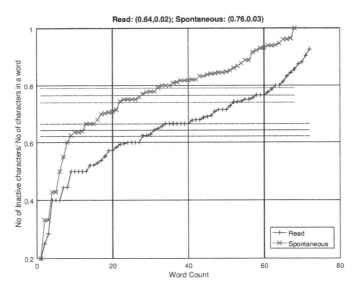

Fig. 3. Ratio of # `InActive` alphabets to the # of alphabets in a word (arranged in the increasing order of ratio).

2.4   Proposed Classifier

As observed in the previous section, there exist features extracted from `DeepSpeech` that are able to discriminate read and spontaneous speech. However, the measured features (Table 1 (a), (c), (d)) though able to discriminate read and spontaneous speech are not useful because it requires *a prior* knowledge of the passage or information spoken by the speaker. On the other hand,

---

[4] One alphabet for every 25 msec.

there are a set of derived features, which are ratios and hence independent of the spoken passage. As seen in Table 1 some of these features are able to strongly discriminate read and spontaneous speech. The three derived features that show promise to discriminate read and spontaneous speech are

1. $[f_1]$ Active AWL
   (Active alphabets per word is higher for spontaneous speech)
2. $[f_2]$ InActive APS
   (InActive alphabets per sec is lower for spontaneous speech)
3. $[f_3]$ WPS
   (Word Rate or Words per sec is lower for spontaneous speech)

Note that these features are independent of the duration of the audio utterance and they do not depend on *what was spoken* and entirely rely on *how the utterance was spoken*. This is important because any feature based on *what was spoken* would have a direct dependency on the performance accuracy of the speech-to-alphabet engine, in our case DeepSpeech. In that sense our approach does not depend explicitly on the performance of the DeepSpeech and does not depend on the linguistic content of the spoken passage. The process of classifying a given utterance $u(t)$ is simple[5]. We extract the features f_1, f_2, f_3 from the DS($x(t)$) for a given spoken passage $x(t)$ and compute a read score $\mathcal{R}$ using (2). We use (3) to determine if $x(t)$ is read speech or spontaneous speech.

$$\mathcal{R} = \frac{1}{1 + exp^{-\lambda_1(f_1 - \tau_1)}} + \frac{1}{1 + exp^{\lambda_2(f_2 - \tau_2)}} + \frac{1}{1 + exp^{-\lambda_3(f_3 - \tau_3)}} \qquad (2)$$

$$x(t) = \text{Read Speech if } \mathcal{R} \geq \tau_{\mathcal{R}}$$
$$= \text{Spontaneous Speech if } \mathcal{R} < \tau_{\mathcal{R}} \qquad (3)$$

We empirically chose $\lambda_{1,2,3} = 1$, $\tau_1 = 6$, $\tau_2 = 10$, and $\tau_3 = 1.75$ based on observations made in Table 1. And $\tau_{\mathcal{R}} = 1.75$, which is in the range $\mathcal{R} \in [0, 3]$.

3   Experimental Validation

The selection of the features to discriminate between spontaneous and read speech is based on an intuitive understanding of the difference between read and spontaneous speech as mentioned in [15] and verified through observation of actual audio data (Table 1).

We collected audio data (150 min; spread over 7 different programs) broadcast by All India Radio [13] called AIR-RS-DB which is available at [9]. This audio data is the recording between a host and a guest and consists of both spontaneous speech (guest) and read speech (host). We used a pre-trained speaker diarization model [4,8] to segment the audio, which resulted in 1028 audio segments. We discarded all audio segments below 2 sec so that there was sizable amount of

---

[5] There is no need to train a conventional classifier.

spoken information in any given audio segment; this resulted in a total of 657 audio segments. All experimental results are reported on this 657 audio segments (see Fig. 4).

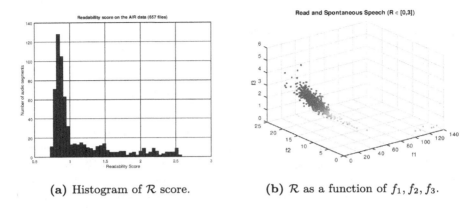

(a) Histogram of $\mathcal{R}$ score.   (b) $\mathcal{R}$ as a function of f_1, f_2, f_3.

Fig. 4. Readability score ($\mathcal{R}$) for 657 audio segments (> 2 sec) from AIR-RS-DB.

For each of these 657 audio segments, f_1, f_2, f_3 were computed and then using (2) $\mathcal{R}$ was computed. Figure 4a shows the distribution of the readability score $\mathcal{R}$ of the audio segments. Clearly a large number of audio segments (535) were classified as spontaneous speech compared to 122, which was classified as read. Figure 4b shows the scatter plot of $\mathcal{R}$ for the 657 audio segments as a function of f_1, f_2, f_3. The colour of the scatter plot represents the value of $\mathcal{R}$. Figure 5 shows the classification of segmented audio into read speech (violet; $\mathcal{R} \geq \tau_{\mathcal{R}}$) and spontaneous speech (yellow; $\mathcal{R} < \tau_{\mathcal{R}}$).

We choose $\delta = 0.05$ and selectively listen to some of the audio segments ($\mathcal{R} > (\tau_{\mathcal{R}} + \delta)$ and $\mathcal{R} < (\tau_{\mathcal{R}} - \delta)$) and found that almost all of the audio segments classified as spontaneous belong to the guest speaker (which is expected), however, several instances of host speech was also classified as spontaneous. We hypothesize, that radio hosts are trained to speak even written text to give a feeling of spontaneity to the listener. We then looked at the 23 audio segments which had $\mathcal{R}$ in the range $[\tau_{\mathcal{R}} - \delta, \tau_{\mathcal{R}} + \delta]$ and hence in the neighbourhood of $\tau_{\mathcal{R}}$ which is more prone to classification errors. We observed that there were 12 and 11 read speech and spontaneous speech segments respectively. Of the 12 audio segments classified as read speech, 4 audio segments were actually spontaneous while of the 11 audio segments classified as spontaneous speech, 3 audio segments were actually read speech (see Table 2). It should be noted that, in the neighbourhood of the $\tau_{\mathcal{R}}$, where the confusion is expected to be very high, the

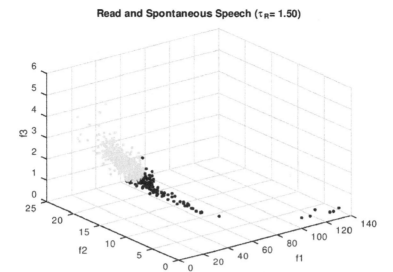

Fig. 5. 657 audio segments from AIR-RS-DB classified as read speech (violet) and spontaneous speech (yellow). (Color figure online)

proposed classifier is able to correctly classify with an accuracy of $\approx 70\%$ (16 of the 23 audio segments correctly classified).

Table 2. Performance on 23 audio segments whose $\mathcal{R} \in [\tau_\mathcal{R} - \delta, \tau_\mathcal{R} + \delta]$. 4 spontaneous speech audio segments were classified as read speech and 3 read speech segments were classified as spontaneous speech.

$\mathcal{R} \in$	Ground Truth	
$[\tau_\mathcal{R} - \delta, \tau_\mathcal{R} + \delta]$	Read Speech	Spontaneous Speech
Read Speech	8	4
Spontaneous Speech	3	8

Very recently, we came across the Archive of L1 and L2 Scripted and Spontaneous Transcripts And Recordings (ALLSSTAR-DB) corpus [3]. We picked up speech data corresponding to 26 English speakers (14 Female and 12 Male). Each speaker spoke a maximum of 8 utterances (4 spontaneous and 4 read) in different settings. The 4 read speech were (a) DHR (20 formal sentences picked from the Universal Declaration of Human Rights; average duration 106.2 s) , (b) HT2 (simple sentences; phonetically balanced which was created for Hearing in Noise Test; average duration 100.5 s), (c) LPP (33 sentences picked from Le Petit Prince, average duration 107.1 s) and (d) NWS (North Wind and the Sun Passage, average duration 32.8 s); while the 4 spontaneous speech utterances were (a) QNA (Spontaneous speech about anything for 5 minutes; average duration 317.5 s), (b) ST2 (wordless pictures from "Bubble Bubble" used to elicit spontaneous speech; average duration 88.8 s), (c) ST3 (wordless pictures from "Just a Pig at Heart"; average duration 78.2 s), and (d) ST4 (wordless pictures from "Bear's New Clothes"; average duration 85.2 s).

Table 3. ALLSSTAR-DB corpus details.

Gen	SpkID	R (DHR, HT2, LPP, NWS)	S (QNA, ST2, ST3, ST4)	(minutes)
F	49	4 (1, 1, 1, 1)	4 (1, 1, 1, 1)	8 (13.47)
	51	4 (1, 1, 1, 1)	4 (1, 1, 1, 1)	8 (16.87)
	56	4 (1, 1, 1, 1)	4 (1, 1, 1, 1)	8 (19.29)
	58	4 (1, 1, 1, 1)	4 (1, 1, 1, 1)	8 (16.73)
	60	4 (1, 1, 1, 1)	4 (1, 1, 1, 1)	8 (12.32)
	62	4 (1, 1, 1, 1)	4 (1, 1, 1, 1)	8 (12.78)
	63	4 (1, 1, 1, 1)	4 (1, 1, 1, 1)	8 (19.42)
	64	4 (1, 1, 1, 1)	4 (1, 1, 1, 1)	8 (16.06)
	65	4 (1, 1, 1, 1)	4 (1, 1, 1, 1)	8 (12.70)
	67	4 (1, 1, 1, 1)	4 (1, 1, 1, 1)	8 (15.04)
	68	4 (1, 1, 1, 1)	4 (1, 1, 1, 1)	8 (12.91)
	69	4 (1, 1, 1, 1)	4 (1, 1, 1, 1)	8 (14.90)
	71	4 (1, 1, 1, 1)	4 (1, 1, 1, 1)	8 (12.87)
	72	4 (1, 1, 1, 1)	4 (1, 1, 1, 1)	8 (15.67)
M	50	4 (1, 1, 1, 1)	4 (1, 1, 1, 1)	8 (14.28)
	52	4 (1, 1, 1, 1)	4 (1, 1, 1, 1)	8 (25.40)
	53	4 (1, 1, 1, 1)	4 (1, 1, 1, 1)	8 (13.27)
	55	4 (1, 1, 1, 1)	4 (1, 1, 1, 1)	8 (13.27)
	57	4 (1, 1, 1, 1)	4 (1, 1, 1, 1)	8 (19.26)
	59	4 (1, 1, 1, 1)	4 (1, 1, 1, 1)	8 (13.60)
	61	4 (1, 1, 1, 1)	4 (1, 1, 1, 1)	8 (14.37)
	66	4 (1, 1, 1, 1)	4 (1, 1, 1, 1)	8 (14.67)
	70	4 (1, 1, 1, 1)	4 (1, 1, 1, 1)	8 (12.97)
	131	4 (1, 1, 1, 1)	2 (1, 1, 0, 0)	6 (11.89)
	132	4 (1, 1, 1, 1)	2 (1, 1, 0, 0)	6 (12.19)
	133	4 (1, 1, 1, 1)	2 (1, 1, 0, 0)	6 (12.64)
Total	26 (Speakers)	104 (26, 26, 26, 26)	98 (26, 26, 23, 23)	202 (388.9)

In all there were 202 audio utterances of which 104 were read utterances and 98 were spontaneous spoken utterances. Note that in all there should have been 104 spontaneous utterances; but 2 spontaneous utterances each were missing from 3 male participants. Table 3 shows the distribution of data from ALLSSTAR-DB. Experiments were carried out on these 202 audio utterances from 26 people. We went through the process of passing through audio utterance through the

`DeepSpeech`, followed by extraction of three features and computing of $\mathcal{R}$ as mentioned in (2). The experimental results are shown as a confusion matrix in Table 4. As can be observed, the performance of our proposed scheme is 88.12%. Figure 6 shows the utterances in the feature space (f_1, f_2, f_3) for ALLSSTAR-DB. The classification based on the approach mentioned earlier in this paper is shown in Fig. 6 (a) the utterances classified as read and spontaneous have been marked in yellow and violet respectively. Figure 6 (b) captures the utterances which have been correctly recognised (represented in green). The read utterances mis-recognized as spontaneous is shown in red (8 utterances) while the utterances corresponding to spontaneous speech which have been recognized as read have been represented in purple (16 utterances).

Table 4. Confusion Matrix. Performance Accuracy on ALLSSTAR-DB 88.12%.

	Ground Truth	
	Read Speech	Spontaneous Speech
Read Speech	88 (84.62%)	8
Spontaneous Speech	16	90 (91.84%)

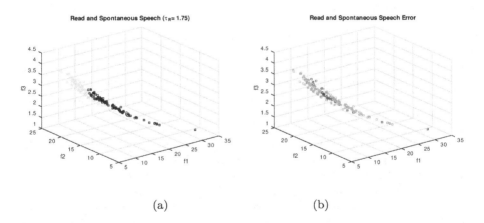

(a)   (b)

Fig. 6. Classification results on ALLSSTAR-DB. (a) Yellow represents read speech while violet corresponds to spontaneous speech and (b) Green shows the correctly recognized utterances (88.12%) while red represents read speech recognized as spontaneous and purple shows the utterances corresponding to spontaneous speech which have been recognized as read. (Color figure online)

We analyzed further to understand the mis-recognized utterances. The spontaneous utterances of speakers with ID $49, 56, 58, 60, 71(2), 57$, and 59 were mis-recognized as read speech while read utterances with speakers ID $56, 58(2), 64(3), 69, 71(2), 50(2), 52, 55, 66(2), 133$ were recognized as being spontaneous. As shown in Table 5 we observe that majority of the speakers were mis-recognized either as reading while they had spoken spontaneously (column 1) or as being spontaneous when they had actually read (column 2). Only speakers with SpkID 56, 58 and 71 (column 3) were mis-recognized both ways, namely their read speech was recognized as spontaneous and vice-versa.

Table 5. Mis-recognition based on Speaker ID. The number in parenthesis shows the number of instances.

	Spontaneous → Read	Read → Spontaneous	Read ↔ Spontaneous
Female	$49(1), 60(1)$	$64(3), 69(1)$	$56(2), 58(3), 71(4)$
Male	$57(1), 59(1)$	$50(2), 52(1), 55(1), 66(2), 133(1)$	-

We observe that the speaker with ID 71 had $\mathcal{R} \in [1.63, 1.82]$; we carefully listened to all the utterances and found very less perceptual difference between read and spontaneous utterances. While the read utterances of the speaker with ID 66 had large silences between sentences (an indication of spontaneous speech) which lead to almost all of the read utterances being recognized as spontaneous.

4   Conclusion

In this paper, we proposed a simple classifier to identify read and spontaneous speech. The novelty of the classifier is in deriving a very small set of features, indirectly from the audio segment. Most of the literature which directly or indirectly address recognition of spontaneous speech have been done by analyzing audio signal for determining speech specific properties like intonation, repetition of words, filler words, etc. We derived a small set of explainable features from a string of alphabets derived from the output of the **DeepSpeech** speech-to-alphabet recognition engine. The features are self-explanatory and capture the essential difference between read and spontaneous speech as mentioned in [15]. The derived features are based on *how* the utterance was spoken and not on *what* was spoken thereby making the features independent of the linguistic content of the utterance. Experiments conducted on our own data-set (AIR-RS-DB) and publicly available ALLSSTAR-DB shows the classifier to perform very well. The main advantage of the proposed scheme is that the features are explainable and are derived by processing the alphabet string output of DS(). It should be noted that while we can categorize our approach as being devoid of deep model training or learning; the dependency on **DeepSpeech** pre-trained deep architecture model (as a black-box) cannot be ignored.

References

1. Asami, T., Masumura, R., Masataki, H., Sakauchi, S.: Read and spontaneous speech classification based on variance of GMM supervectors. In: Fifteenth Annual Conference of the International Speech Communication Association (2014)

2. Batliner, A., Kompe, R., Kießling, A., Nöth, E., Niemann, H.: Can you tell apart spontaneous and read speech if you just look at prosody? In: Speech Recognition and Coding, pp. 321–324. Springer (1995). https://doi.org/10.1007/978-3-642-57745-1_47

3. Bradlow, A.R.: ALLSSTAR: archive of L1 and L2 scripted and spontaneous transcripts and recordings. https://speechbox.linguistics.northwestern.edu/ (2023)

4. Bredin, H., et al.: pyannote.audio: neural building blocks for speaker diarization. In: ICASSP 2020, IEEE International Conference on Acoustics, Speech, and Signal Processing. Barcelona, Spain (2020)

5. Dellwo, V., Leemann, A., Kolly, M.J.: The recognition of read and spontaneous speech in local vernacular: the case of zurich german. J. Phonetics **48**, 13–28 (2015). https://doi.org/10.1016/j.wocn.2014.10.011, https://www.sciencedirect.com/science/article/pii/S009544701400093X, the Impact of Stylistic Diversity on Phonetic and Phonological Evidence and Modeling

6. Dufour, R., Estève, Y., Deléglise, P.: Characterizing and detecting spontaneous speech: application to speaker role recognition. Speech Commun. **56**, 1–18 (2014)

7. Eren, Ö., Kılıç, M., Bada, E.: Fluency in L2: read and spontaneous speech pausing patterns of Turkish, Swahili, Hausa and Arabic Speakers of English. J. Psycholinguist. Res., 1–17 (2021). https://doi.org/10.1007/s10936-021-09822-y

8. Huggingface: speaker-diarization. https://huggingface.co/pyannote/speaker-diarization (pyannote/speaker-diarization@2022072, 2022)

9. Kopparapu, S.K.: AIR-RS-DB: all India radio read and spontaneous speech database. IEEE Dataport (2023). https://doi.org/10.21227/ft5v-xp41

10. Mozilla: Deepspeech. https://github.com/mozilla/DeepSpeech/releases (2019)

11. Mukherji, K., Pandharipande, M., Kopparapu, S.K.: Improved language models for ASR using written language text. In: 2022 National Conference on Communications (NCC), pp. 362–366 (2022). https://doi.org/10.1109/NCC55593.2022.9806803

12. Panayotov, V., Chen, G., Povey, D., Khudanpur, S.: Librispeech: an ASR corpus based on public domain audio books. In: 2015 IEEE International Conference on Acoustics, Speech and Signal Processing (ICASSP), pp. 5206–5210. IEEE (2015)

13. PrasarBharati: All India Radio. https://newsonair.gov.in/ (2022)

14. Tripathi, A., Bhosale, S., Kopparapu, S.K.: Automatic speaker independent dysarthric speech intelligibility assessment system. Comput. Speech & Lang. **69**, 101213 (2021) https://doi.org/10.1016/j.csl.2021.101213, https://www.sciencedirect.com/science/article/pii/S0885230821000206

15. Ward, W.: Understanding spontaneous speech. Speech and Natural Language Workshop, pp. 365–367 (1989)

Analysis of a Hinglish ASR System's Performance for Fraud Detection

Pradeep Rangappa[✉], Aditya Kiran Brahma[✉], Venkatesh Vayyavuru[✉],
Rishi Yadav[✉], Hemant Misra[✉], and Kasturi Karuna[✉]

Applied Research Department, Swiggy, Bengaluru, India
rangan.pradeep@gmail.com, aditya.brahma@swiggy.in,
venkateshvayyavuru@gmail.com, rishi.yadav1907@gmail.com,
hemant.misra@swiggy.in, reachkasturi@gmail.com

Abstract. Speech technology has made significant advancement in the last few decades. Recently it has also made in-roads into the households of the people through products like virtual assistants and voice-controlled devices. At the same time, in the shadows, and away from the eyes of the people, increasingly speech technology has been used gainfully for business tasks such as voice analytic and fraud detection in different industries. If the speech signal needs to be used for down-stream tasks such as developing a conversational voice bot, processing speech signals through an automatic speech recognition (ASR) engine is often an important and first step. Despite significant research in this space, typically the performance of an ASR engine is far from being perfect for all the test conditions it may encounter in the real world. The problem gets more complex when speech data has code-switching. Another equally important aspect while doing deployment of speech technology based products is that it is rather difficult to know if the performance of an ASR engine is adequate for its output to be used for a down-stream task. In this paper, we present our study of how the performance of an ASR engine developed for Hinglish (Hindi code switched with English) for the food domain affects the performance of the final down-stream task of detecting fraud patterns. In addition, we show how the performance of the final task can be improved by using state-of-the-art natural language processing (NLP) techniques like Bidirectional Encoder Representations from Transformers (BERT). The end-to-end system (ASR engine for Hinglish followed by NLP techniques) is successfully deployed in production for fraud detection at Swiggy, one of the largest food delivery platforms in India and the world.

Keywords: Speech recognition · Pattern recognition · Natural language processing · Fraud detection · Food delivery · Hinglish

---

This work was carried out at Swiggy.

1   Introduction

Across the world, in the last decade, speech technology has been actively deployed in consumer electronics such as mobile phones, virtual assistants and voice-activated devices for the English speaking urban/metro population. However, deployment of speech technology based systems has been slow in emerging markets such as India where English is not the language of the masses. For example, in India there is still a large and varied rural and semi-urban population that is currently not getting catered adequately by these systems. Similarly, in India English frequently gets code-mixed with other Indian languages and there is significant opportunity to develop speech technologies that can efficiently manage code-mixed input in different business verticals, for instance, insurance, banking, e-commerce etc. To cater to these segments and verticals effectively, speech technology must address challenges such as code-mixing, robust language support, accurate speech recognition in diverse acoustic environments, and customization for domain-specific terminology and workflows. By developing systems that can manage these challenges, we not only can empower marginalized communities and drive positive socio-economic impact, but also improve customer experience.

Today's state-of-the-art automatic speech recognition (ASR) engines perform exceptionally well for languages and tasks for which there is plenty of annotated speech data available. In fact, some of the ASR engines for English have reached a performance level that is very close to that of a human performance [15,18,21]. Does this mean that there are no more problems to be solved in the area of ASR? Though this may be true that performance of an ASR engine is reasonably good for a selected few languages (such as English) and a few of the use cases (conversational telephone speech in relatively less noisy environment, for example), the performance of an ASR engine for many low resource languages [2,17] and more complex situations like code-switching [8,23] is still far from being close to a human level performance. Although there are many pre-trained ASR models available on hugging face [22], there are several drawbacks of them which include limited language support, domain specificity requiring fine-tuning, resource-intensive hardware requirements, and challenges related to interpretability and explainability.

The second important thing about an ASR system is: though they are typically the first, fundamental and may be the most important step when speech data needs to be processed for insights, they are not the only step in the overall journey of automating and solving a real world problem end-to-end [10,19]. For example, in a voice bot, after the speech gets converted to text by an ASR engine, a natural language understanding (NLU) system is needed to understand the underlying message embedded in the transcribed text, and generate an appropriate response. Having said that, what should be the performance of an ASR system so that the down-stream tasks can be done well is not so well established and understood [9,12,20], and may vary on case-by-case basis.

Developing an ASR engine for food domain data in the Indian context, specifically pertaining to Swiggy, presents unique challenges. Firstly, the food domain involves a wide range of diverse and specialized vocabulary, including dish names, ingredients, restaurant-specific terms and spontaneous speech uttered by the customer. Accurately recognizing and transcribing this domain-specific vocabulary poses a significant hurdle. Additionally, the presence of background noise and varying audio quality in real-world food ordering scenarios adversely affects an ASR engine performance. Moreover, the code-mixing, regional diversity and accents in the Indian context further degrades an ASR engine accuracy. Overcoming these challenges requires domain-specific data collection, robust vocabulary modeling and noise-robust ASR algorithms techniques for reliable and efficient speech recognition.

In this paper first we analyse how the change in performance of an ASR engine effects the performance of a down-stream task of detecting frauds by finding fixed a-priori known patterns (key phrases) that may be present in the speech signal. The second objective of this paper is to understand whether advance NLP techniques which typically are developed (and work very well) for clean text can improve the performance for this down-stream task despite the ASR text output being very noisy.

Rest of the paper is organized as follows: In Sect. 2, we provide a high level description of online food business delivery process at Swiggy and how the DEs circumvent the system and commit fraud. In Sect. 3, we describe the automated end-to-end systems (Rule-based as well as NLP driven) developed for detecting fraud and database that is used for analysing the performance of these systems. The results and our analysis of this work are presented in Sect. 4. In Sect. 5 we conclude and highlight the main contributions of this paper.

2   Problem Statement

2.1   Online Food Delivery at Swiggy

Swiggy is India's second largest and one of the world's largest online food delivery platform. Approximately hundred thousand restaurant partners (RPs) and two hundred thousand delivery executives (DEs) cater to the needs of several million Swiggy customers pan India. In pre-COVID period, every day, on an average, close to a million orders were placed and delivered through our platform. Like many other food delivery platforms, the way Swiggy platform operates is as follows:

- A customer comes to the Swiggy platform using its Android or iOS app or through its website (http://www.swiggy.com) and logins to her/his account.
- The current location of the customer gets detected automatically.
- The customer can search for the restaurants or the dishes in her/his locality (to meet the service level agreement (SLA) of time, Swiggy allows its customer to order from the restaurants that are within 'm' kilometer radius from the current location of the customer).
- The customer can choose the food items she/he wants to order. In an order, the customer can choose the food items she/he wants to order from a single restaurant only (a few exceptions are there where a customer is allowed to

choose food items from more than one restaurant in a single order). Since every order is managed independently, once an order is placed, another order can be placed immediately without waiting for the first order to be delivered.

- The customer confirms the order by making the payment. Certain customers with high ratings are also allowed to choose cash on delivery (CoD) in which case the payment is made to the DE in cash or by various payment apps (like PhonePe, GooglePay and Paytm which use unified payments interface (UPI)) when the DE delivers the order to the customer at her/his premise.
- Apart from other sources of revenue, for every order successfully delivered (not just placed) through its platform, Swiggy gets commission from the restaurant whose order it was.
- If the order faces some problem in delivery because of an issue which is directly or indirectly due to Swiggy's platform and the SLA gets breached (for example, the order getting delayed for reasons such as restaurant not able to prepare food on time, restaurant got closed, food item got over at the restaurant, DE met an accident, DE not able to find the address etc.), a customer can cancel the order without any cancellation charges. When such a cancellation happens, Swiggy doesn't get any commission for that order.

2.2   Use Case: Offline Delivery Abuse

A few DEs of Swiggy try to con the system described above. These DE do the following:

- Pick-up the order from the restaurant.
- Call the customer using the Swiggy DE app and inform that the order hasn't been placed successfully because of a technical problem faced by the platform. Though the DEs can call the customer whose order they are serving using the Swiggy DE app, they don't have access to the customer's phone number.
- Inform the customer that they can get the same food items by placing the order manually with the restaurant, and deliver it to them on payment basis (customer will have to pay the DE at the time of delivery).
- Advise the customer to cancel the order placed through the Swiggy platform. Since the SLA has been breached, the platform allows the customer to cancel the order without paying any cancellation charges.

Typically a customer may agree to this offline delivery arrangement outside the platform since when he/she cancels the order at the platform, his/her money gets reimbursed to him/her, and the same money he/she can give to the DE who delivers the order.

In the above described arrangement, Swiggy looses its commission for that order. Sometimes restaurants may also be involved in this con. If the restaurant is also involved, it may give only a percentage of the originally committed commission to the DE. At Swiggy we call this fraud as **Offline Delivery Abuse**.

3 Systems Description and Database

3.1 Speech Data Recording System

Since the phone number of the customer whose order is being served by a DE is not known to the DE, at least the first time when a DE wants to contact a customer whose order he/she (the DE) is serving, he/she has no other option but to call the customer through the app. All the calls made by a DE to a customer through the app are recorded for quality and monitoring purpose.

Typically a DE may contact a customer whose order is being served for various reasons. The reasons include, but are not limited to, confirming the address, asking for direction, asking for the floor number, informing about unavailability of an item in an order, informing about possibility in delay because of an accident/traffic jam/rain etc.

In cases where a DE wants to do an Offline Delivery Abuse, the first call the DE makes to the customer may typically contain some of the key phrases described in Table 1. It is worth noting that many of these key phrases may occur during a conversation for genuine reasons as well, which makes the problem complex to solve. For example, the DE may ask for the customer's phone number in case where the battery of his/her phone is low and there is need to call the customer using an alternate phone.

Table 1. Examples of some of the key phrases that may be used by the DE for committing fraud.

Key phrase	Brief explanation
Name of any of the UPI payment app	An online payment system in India
Mobile Number	Customer's contact information
Technical issue	DE may state some technical issue at Swiggy because of which the order has not been placed
Cancel	DE may ask the customer to cancel the order

3.2 Hinglish ASR System

India is a federal union comprising 28 states and 8 union territories. Each of its major state may have its own language. It is very common that the mother tongue of a person from a state could be the official language of that state. Moreover, a significant percentage of Indians may be exposed to Hindi, one of the languages spoken in many of the northern states. Apart from this, common words from English such as car, courier, taxi, cancel, refund, technical etc have permeated the day-to-day conversations of people. Considering this, there is an inherent need for the Indian specific ASR engine to deal with code-mixing. Currently we have considered developing only an Hindi-English (Hinglish) ASR engine since Hinglish conversations constitute bulk of our interactions.

The speech data from the Swiggy's customers' and agents' interactions is recorded for quality and monitoring purpose at Swiggy call center. In order to train an Hinglish ASR engine, we took approximately 175 h of Hinglish speech data from Swiggy's call center. This data was divided such that the train set and test set had approximately 155 h and 10 h of speech data, respectively. This speech data was annotated by hiring an external partner and the quality of the annotation was verified by the internal quality analyst team. The words (English as well as Hindi) in the transcripts are transliterated to romanized form before initializing the ASR training process.

ASR Version-1. In ASR, time delay neural network (TDNN) [13] has proven to be an efficient network structure due to its strong ability in context modeling. 40-dimensional Mel-frequency cepstral coefficients (MFCCs) [5] without cepstral truncation are used as input. The input features are spliced by concatenating the "-2,1,0,1,2" frames. Speaker adaptation is utilized by appending 100-dimension iVector with the MFCC input. Finally, the resulting 300-dimensional feature is transformed by a 300-dimension linear discriminant analysis (LDA) and is used as the model input. Truncated back propagation through time (BPTT) with 40 time steps is used in TDNN acoustic model training.

ASR Version-2. The ASR system is retrained using SpecAugment [11], a spectral augmentation technique. It modifies the spectrogram by warping it in the time direction, masking blocks of consecutive frequency channels, and masking blocks of utterances in time. These augmentations have been chosen to help the network to be robust against deformations in the time direction, partial loss of frequency information and partial loss of small segments of speech of the input.

ASR Version-3. By leveraging large-scale unlabelled training data, Wav2Vec2 captures the intricacies of speech, enabling it to excel in real-world applications [1]. This state-of-the-art technology has the potential to revolutionize the performance of ASR engines by making them more accurate and efficient. By leveraging the Wav2vec2-XLSR multilingual pre-trained model [4], Wav2Vec2 becomes a versatile capability of bridging language barriers and supporting speech recognition in different languages and dialects. Especially in low resource settings, fine-tuning of Wav2vec2 architecture has proven to be successful [22]. In our work, we trained Version-3 of the ASR engine by fine-tuning state-of-the-art Wav2Vec2-XLSR with CTC loss.

The performance of all the ASR engines is evaluated in terms of word error rate (WER) (Table 2).

3.3   Fraud Detection Systems

Figure 1 shows the overview of the proposed DE abuse detection framework. In the proposed framework, the DE and customer calls are fetched from the

Table 2. Performance of the three ASR engines on the 10 hour test set.

ASR Version	% WER
ASR Version 1 (without augmentation)	54.42
ASR Version 2 (with augmentation)	50.34
ASR Version 3	35.50

recording database. The recordings are stored in stereo channel, and may include ringtones, IVR prompts and the caller tunes of the customer. Hence, in the pre-processing stage, the irrelevant portions are removed by observing the distribution of the short time energy components across the channels. This pre-processed speech is fed to one of the ASR engines as per the experiment design. The text output from the ASR engine is then fed to: (a) Rule based system and (b) the NLP driven system, to predict a conversation as Fraud or Non-fraud.

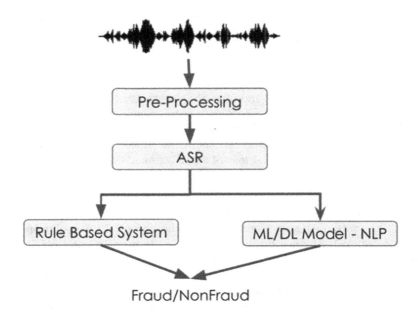

Fig. 1. Overview of the proposed DE fraud detection system.

Rule Based, Aka, Regular Expression Based System. The rule-based system is built to look for specific key phrases (some of them were mentioned in Table 1) in the ASR text outputs, and label a conversation to fraud or non-fraud as per the rules described next.

- Rule-01: If the ASR output has atleast 4 unique fraud related keywords, then the particular utterance is labelled as 'Fraud/Abuse' else it mapped as 'Non-fraud/NoAbuse'. The choice of the threshold is chosen empirically by observing the True positives and the True negatives wrt the ASR outputs for the couple of months of speech data. This data had the Abuse and NoAbuse labels provided by the Business team.
- Rule-02: If the ASR output recognises atleast 5 digits and 3 non-digits from the list of fraud related keywords, then the audio call is mapped as Fraud conversation else it is mapped as Non-fraud.
- Rule-03: In a conversation between the DE and the customer, the DE enquires about the address, flat number, location etc and hence is more likely that digits are spoken in such a scenario. As a result, the ASR output has the presence of the digits. To circumvent this issue, we proposed a method to distinguish a mobile number (Fraud pattern) with a non-mobile number (door number, street number, order price etc.). In the Rule-03, there are three steps to predict the ASR outputs as Fraud or Non-fraud: (a) selection of consecutive digits in the ASR output, (b) fetching lengthy consecutive digit pattern, and (c) applying Rule- 01 on the result of (b).

Two NLP methodologies were also explored for predicting fraud, and are described next.

Machine Learning (ML) Based System. ASR output obtained was processed to create a vocabulary of words using the TF-IDF values. Pre-processing was done such that these words do not contain stop words and unigrams. Total 970 words were selected based on the TF-IDf weightage [7] corresponding to the entire ASR outputs corpus. Selecting these 970 words, each ASR output is transformed into 970 column values where each column represents the TF-IDF weightage of corresponding word based on the ASR output of the Order ID considered. The resultant sparse matrix was passed into an XG-Boost [3] classification algorithm where the hyper parameters were tuned using grid search.

Deep Learning (DL) Based System. Each ASR output was processed to extract phrases which are most relevant to the entire ASR output. BERT [6] based phrase extraction strategy was used here which is done in two steps. First, pre-trained Distilbert [14] model available in hugging face was used to extract the sentence embeddings of overall ASR output of each Order ID. As transformer based models have a token limit, for ASR outputs exceeding the limit we splitted the text into parts and mean pooling strategy was used to get the embedding. The same model was used to get the sentence embeddings of all the top phrases with n-gram range of three to five which are extracted using the TF-IDf strategy mentioned previously. In the second step, top phrases corresponding to each ASR output from the list of phrases are extracted using Maximal Marginal Relevance approach [16]. In this approach input ASR embedding is compared to the embeddings of all the phrases prepared using TF-IDf approach and then top phrases are extracted based on the cosine similarity and Maximal Marginal Relevance. This approach ensures to maximize the diversity of the phrases.

Phrases extracted for each ASR output are concatenated with the actual ASR output and then passed into stacked BiLSTM network. This approach is followed to ensure that the BiLSTM layers can focus more on the relevant keywords of ASR output as they will be present in both phrases and the actual text of ASR. Four BiLSTM layers are stacked on top of each other and then passed into a fully connected dense layer for the binary classification of fraud and non fraud.

3.4 Database

The speech data conversations between the delivery executive and the customer for couple of months is taken for analysis of the DE fraud system. On a daily basis, the Trust and Safety team at Swiggy manually listens to the call and gets confirmation from the customer to label the DE as Fraud or Non-Fraud. We have considered 1756 order ID's and predicted the Fraud/Non-Fraud labels for all the order ID's for rule based system. Later, for developing the NLP driven modelling approach, we considered 3069 order ID's related data for training (the NLP model) and 1219 order ID's as test set.

4   Results and Analysis

4.1 Evaluation of Different Rule Based Systems

Table 3 shows the fraud detection performance by different rule based systems on the output of ASR Version-1. It can be observed that the performance of Rule-03 is much better as compared to that of Rule-02 and Rule-01. This is because the Rule- 03 discriminates between the mobile number and the other category of digits (order value, door number, street number, etc.). Rule-02 outperforms Rule-01 since it considers two conditions to map the ASR output to Fraud/Non-fraud.

Table 3. Evaluation of different rule based fraud detection systems in terms of precision (P), recall (R) and F1 scores (F1) on the output of ASR Version-1.

Logic	Class	Support	P	R	F1	% Acc
Rule-01	Fraud	686	0.57	0.85	0.68	0.69
	Non-Fraud	1070	0.86	0.59	0.70	
Rule-02	Fraud	686	0.58	0.86	0.69	0.70
	Non-Fraud	1070	0.87	0.6	0.71	
Rule-03	Fraud	686	0.6	0.85	0.70	0.72
	Non-Fraud	1070	0.87	0.64	0.74	

Table 4 shows the fraud detection performance on the output of ASR Version-2 for Rule-03. It can be seen that improving the ASR engine accuracy (Version-2) improves the fraud detection rate.

Table 4. Evaluation of Rule-03 based fraud detection system in terms of precision (P), recall (R) and F1 scores (F1) on the output of ASR Version-1 and Version-2.

System	Category	Support	P	R	f1	%Acc
ASR Version-1 + Rule-03	Fraud	686	0.60	0.85	0.70	0.72
	Non-Fraud	1070	0.87	0.64	0.74	
ASR Version-2 + Rule-03	Fraud	686	**0.64**	**0.89**	**0.74**	**0.75**
	Non-Fraud	1070	**0.87**	**0.67**	**0.75**	

4.2 Comparing Rule Based System with ML and DL Based Systems

Table 5 compares the performance of the best rule based system (Rule-03) vis-a-vis that of XGBoost, DL modelling and ensemble techniques. All the results in Table 5 are on the output of ASR Version-2. It can be observed that the ML and DL based systems outperform the Rule-03 based system. XGBoost model being a boosted trees approach is able to capture the combinatorial patterns of keywords that are part of the vocabulary prepared. DL based model trained on the concatenated data of phrase extracted and the ASR output has slightly poor performance as compared to that of the XGBoost model. When trained with ensemble of XGBoost and DL model to understand if there are any additional samples captured correctly, we observe that accuracy further improved to 0.86.

We created another blind test data with increased support values and observed the impact of different ASR versions on XGBOOST based DE fraud

Table 5. Performance of different DE fraud detection systems on the output of ASR Version-2.

System	Category	Support	P	R	f1	%Acc
Rule-03	Fraud	612	0.68	0.61	0.64	0.66
	Non-Fraud	607	0.64	0.71	0.68	
DL	Fraud	612	0.83	0.83	0.83	0.83
	Non-Fraud	607	0.83	0.83	0.83	
XGBoost	Fraud	612	0.82	0.91	0.86	0.85
	Non-Fraud	607	0.9	0.8	0.84	
XGBoost + DL	Fraud	612	0.83	0.9	**0.86**	**0.86**
	Non-Fraud	607	0.89	0.81	**0.85**	

Table 6. Performance of DE fraud detection system on the output of different ASR versions.

System	Category	Support	P	R	f1	%Acc
ASR Version-1	Fraud	1318	0.8	0.77	0.79	0.61
	Non-Fraud	1965	0.7	0.91	0.79	
ASR Version-2	Fraud	1318	0.81	0.78	0.79	0.64
	Non-Fraud	1965	0.7	0.92	0.8	
ASR Version-3	Fraud	1318	0.87	0.64	0.74	0.71
	Non-Fraud	1965	0.66	0.96	0.78	

detector model. The new blind test set is to check model's generalization. Table 6 shows the performance of XGBOOST system trained with different ASR versions. It can be observed from Table 6 that the ASR model trained with Wav2Vec2 representations is able to identify the fraud related keywords more accurately as compared to that of ASR Versions-1 and 2. As a result, the overall precision of DE fraud detection increased from 0.80 to 0.87. On top of it, we observed that the recall on the Non-Fraud cases increased from 0.91 to 0.96 increased the confidence of Non-fraud scenarios. Due to this, the number of manual investigation cases on non-fraud prediction reduced.

4.3   Business Impact

We developed a state-of-the-art ASR engine in the Hinglish language for the food domain from scratch for Swiggy. As a result, the cost of converting speech data to text in Swiggy is as low as INR 2–3 per hour. This cost is mainly incurred due to the infrastructure setup on cloud platform where we save the ASR model and process the offline calls in near real time. The proposed ML based solution was able to catch approximately few hundred DEs per month (with a TAT of a couple of hours) who had abused the system. For confidence scores above 0.90, the system was so robust that approximately one third of the DEs were terminated per month without any human intervention. Potential savings for Swiggy at the current scale in the food vertical because of this system are significant. Though not measured explicitly, this system must have directly helped in improving customer experience as well.

5   Conclusion

This paper is about a practical application of ASR, the task of detecting fraud. The setup used in this paper is that of Swiggy, a food delivery platform, and the fraud use case is that of DEs abusing the platform. Since a DE needs to call a customer for committing this fraud, and the call recordings are getting stored at Swiggy's call center, building an ASR driven system to detect this fraud was the obvious choice. This paper analyzes two things: a) the effect of the performance of Hinglish ASR system on the task of fraud detection, and b) the performance gains that can be achieved by using advanced ML/DL techniques. Improvement in ASR accuracy by approximately 5% leads to an improvement in performance of approximately 4% on the downstream task of fraud detection. The ML/DL techniques lead to an improvement of 20% accuracy (absolute) vis-a-vis a rule based system using regular expressions for matching. The above mentioned end-to-end fraud based system is in production at Swiggy, and helping us detect and stem fraud on day-to-day basis.

References

1. Baevski, A., Zhou, Y., Mohamed, A., Auli, M.: wav2vec 2.0: A framework for self-supervised learning of speech representations. Adv. Neural Inf. Process. Syst. **33**, 12449–12460 (2020)
2. Billa, J.: ISI ASR system for the low resource speech recognition challenge for Indian languages. In: INTERSPEECH, pp. 3207–3211 (2018)
3. Chen, T., Guestrin, C.: Xgboost: a scalable tree boosting system. In: Proceedings of the 22nd ACM SIGKDD International Conference on Knowledge Discovery and Data Mining, pp. 785–794 (2016)
4. Conneau, A., Baevski, A., Collobert, R., Mohamed, A., Auli, M.: Unsupervised cross-lingual representation learning for speech recognition. arXiv preprint arXiv:2006.13979 (2020)
5. Davis, S.B., Mermelstein, P.: Evaluation of acoustic parameters for monosyllabic word identification. J. Acoust. Soc. Am. **64**(S1), S180–S181 (1978)
6. Devlin, J., Chang, M.W., Lee, K., Toutanova, K.: Bert: pre-training of deep bidirectional transformers for language understanding. arXiv preprint arXiv:1810.04805 (2018)
7. Jalilifard, A., Caridá, V.F., Mansano, A.F., Cristo, R.S., da Fonseca, F.P.C.: Semantic sensitive TF-IDF to determine word relevance in documents. In: Thampi, S.M., Gelenbe, E., Atiquzzaman, M., Chaudhary, V., Li, K.-C. (eds.) Advances in Computing and Network Communications. LNEE, vol. 736, pp. 327–337. Springer, Singapore (2021). https://doi.org/10.1007/978-981-33-6987-0_27
8. Li, K., Li, J., Ye, G., Zhao, R., Gong, Y.: Towards code-switching ASR for end-to-end CTC models. In: ICASSP 2019–2019 IEEE International Conference on Acoustics, Speech and Signal Processing (ICASSP), pp. 6076–6080. IEEE (2019)
9. Munteanu, C., Baecker, R., Penn, G., Toms, E., James, D.: The effect of speech recognition accuracy rates on the usefulness and usability of webcast archives. In: Proceedings of the SIGCHI Conference on Human Factors in Computing Systems, pp. 493–502 (2006)
10. Özlan, B., Haznedaroğlu, A., Arslan, L.M.: Automatic fraud detection in call center conversations. In: 2019 27th Signal Processing and Communications Applications Conference (SIU), pp. 1–4. IEEE (2019)
11. Park, D.S., et al.: Specaugment: a simple data augmentation method for automatic speech recognition. arXiv preprint arXiv:1904.08779 (2019)
12. Park, Y., Patwardhan, S., Visweswariah, K., Gates, S.C.: An empirical analysis of word error rate and keyword error rate. In: Interspeech, vol. 2008, pp. 2070–2073 (2008)

13. Peddinti, V., Povey, D., Khudanpur, S.: A time delay neural network architecture for efficient modeling of long temporal contexts. In: Sixteenth Annual Conference of the International Speech Communication Association (2015)
14. Sanh, V., Debut, L., Chaumond, J., Wolf, T.: Distilbert, a distilled version of bert: smaller, faster, cheaper and lighter. arXiv preprint arXiv:1910.01108 (2019)
15. Saon, G., et al.: English conversational telephone speech recognition by humans and machines. arXiv preprint arXiv:1703.02136 (2017)
16. Sharma, P., Li, Y.: Self-supervised contextual keyword and keyphrase retrieval with self-labelling (2019)
17. Srivastava, B.M.L., et al.: Interspeech 2018 low resource automatic speech recognition challenge for Indian languages. In: SLTU, pp. 11–14 (2018)
18. Stolcke, A., Droppo, J.: Comparing human and machine errors in conversational speech transcription. arXiv preprint arXiv:1708.08615 (2017)
19. Sundararaman, M.N., Kumar, A., Vepa, J.: Phoneme-bert: joint language modelling of phoneme sequence and ASR transcript. arXiv preprint arXiv:2102.00804 (2021)
20. Wang, Y.Y., Acero, A., Chelba, C.: Is word error rate a good indicator for spoken language understanding accuracy. In: 2003 IEEE Workshop on Automatic Speech Recognition and Understanding (IEEE Cat. No. 03EX721), pp. 577–582. IEEE (2003)
21. Xiong, W., et al.: Toward human parity in conversational speech recognition. IEEE/ACM Trans. Audio Speech Lang. Process. **25**(12), 2410–2423 (2017)
22. Yi, C., Wang, J., Cheng, N., Zhou, S., Xu, B.: Applying wav2vec2.0 to speech recognition in various low-resource languages. arXiv preprint arXiv:2012.12121 (2020)
23. Yue, X., Lee, G., Yılmaz, E., Deng, F., Li, H.: End-to-end code-switching ASR for low-resourced language pairs. In: 2019 IEEE Automatic Speech Recognition and Understanding Workshop (ASRU), pp. 972–979. IEEE (2019)

CAPTuring Accents: An Approach to Personalize Pronunciation Training for Learners with Different L1 Backgrounds

Veronica Khaustova[1(✉)], Evgeny Pyshkin[1(✉)], Victor Khaustov[2], John Blake[1], and Natalia Bogach[3]

[1] The University of Aizu, Aizuwakamatsu, Japan
{d8231106,pyshe}@u-aizu.ac.jp
[2] Eyes, JAPAN Co. Ltd., Aizuwakamatsu, Japan
[3] Peter the Great St. Petersburg Polytechnic University, St. Petersburg, Russia

Abstract. This paper presents a novel approach to addressing the often-overlooked issue of pronunciation instruction in language learning through a Computer-Assisted Pronunciation Training (CAPT) system. While traditional CAPT systems are based on Automatic Speech Recognition (ASR) models trained on native speakers, we argue that this approach results in low accuracy when applied to non-native speakers. To address this limitation, we propose integrating advancements in ASR and accent recognition technology to create a more tailored and effective system. Specifically, our innovation lies in incorporating an accent recognition model into our mobile applications, allowing us to identify learners' first language (L1) backgrounds and subsequently provide personalized exercises and feedback. By doing so, we enable course content creators to design exercises that are linguistically context-aware, and we employ ASR technology to enhance the accuracy of speech detection and accelerate transcription generation during the content creation phase. Furthermore, we make use of neural style transfer techniques to adapt learners' accents before comparing them to reference pronunciations. The evaluation scores are then generated using the Dynamic Time Warping (DTW) algorithm. The key contribution of this paper lies in demonstrating how the integration of ASR-based and accent-targeted solutions can significantly enhance the effectiveness of CAPT systems. This integrated approach offers learners a more precise and personalized learning experience, thereby optimizing pronunciation training.

Keywords: CAPT · ASR · Accent recognition · Personalized feedback

1 Introduction

The study of pronunciation is an essential part of learning to speak a language. However, it has often been a neglected area of focus, leading to a significant

© The Author(s), under exclusive license to Springer Nature Switzerland AG 2023
A. Karpov et al. (Eds.): SPECOM 2023, LNAI 14339, pp. 59–70, 2023.
https://doi.org/10.1007/978-3-031-48312-7_5

negative impact on the overall effectiveness of language education. From the learner's perspective, pronunciation exercises are often considered as tedious and nonconstructive [8]; thus, contributing little to the measurable progress of the learner in language proficiency. From the teacher's perspective, studies on speech comprehensibility and intelligibility known since the 1990s have been partially contextualized in a discourse on the segmental and suprasegmental aspects of language and on how pronunciation problems impede effective communication [13,17,18].

Prosody teaching systems, by definition, focus on the suprasegmental features, such as intonation and rhythm patterns, and ignore the segmental features, such as the pronunciation of individual phonemes, e.g. consonant and vowel sounds. To address this problem, Computer-Assisted Pronunciation Training (CAPT) environments integrate Automatic Speech Recognition (ASR) systems, which capture both suprasegmental and segmental pronunciation features to "understand" the words and their component phonemes pronounced by the learner. Although the application of ASR in language learning tools has gained popularity in recent years, its primary limitation is that most ASR models are trained predominantly on data from native speakers. Consequently, its accuracy drops substantially when applied to non-native speakers, diminishing the effectiveness of the feedback provided to learners [5]. This paper seeks to address this gap in accuracy by integrating recent advances in accent recognition and applying transfer learning to state-of-the-art ASR models within a CAPT system.

We address an ongoing project on developing a CAPT system, originally oriented toward English pronunciation learning, but which, nevertheless, has demonstrated sufficient robustness and built-in flexibility to accommodate content creation and interface adjustment for instantiating the system for a variety of target second languages (L2).

One of the key innovations presented in this paper is an approach to integrating the accent recognition and modification models into a mobile application, the latter being the end-user component of our CAPT environment. The idea is to "teach" the system to identify the first language (L1) background of a specific learner, thus creating grounds for personalization of pronunciation exercises. The knowledge of the user's L1 background can not only help to apply learner-specific ASR models, leading to a significant improvement in phoneme detection accuracy, but also allow pronunciation course content creators to deliver more personalized teaching material. For that purpose, we introduce the ability to include L1-tailored exercises into the course, powered by an integrated ASR model for content metadata generation. The inclusion of an accent neutralization model (by means of neural style transfer [21]) modifies the learner's accent to facilitate a more accurate comparison with reference pronunciation using the Dynamic Time Warping (DTW) algorithm [23].

2   Background and Related Work

Computer-Assisted Language Learning (CALL) systems have undergone a remarkable transformation, fueled by advances in computational technology and technology-aware pedagogy [20]. Early versions of CALL systems provided basic drill-and-practice exercises, such as typical listen-and-repeat activities in language laboratories; the limited interaction and feedback capabilities often led to less than satisfactory learning outcomes. As CALL was applied to pronunciation, platforms integrating specialized technologies like ASR were developed to analyze and provide feedback on the pronunciation of learners. These CAPT systems provide more effective and personalized learning experiences.

ASR technology has evolved significantly over the years [12]. Initial attempts at ASR were based on simpler models and relied heavily on handcrafted features. The emergence of deep learning has opened up a new period for ASR, resulting in models that can learn more intricate and abstract representations from data. Advances in applying transfer learning to ASR models for non-native speakers further improved the applicability of ASR to a variety of tasks [25]. These models, trained on carefully curated datasets, provided a marked improvement in performance for language learners with different native languages [27]. Datasets, such as L2-ARCTIC [29], have played a pivotal role in this progression.

Accent recognition and classification is an expanding field in speech technology. The ability to identify and classify a speaker's accent may have multiple applications, ranging from personalized language learning to sociolinguistic research [26]. Recognizing that each learner has a unique speech profile influenced by their native language, researchers have developed methods to adapt ASR models to individual accents, providing more accurate feedback on pronunciation.

In the literature on language education, the mother tongue L1 has a dominant influence on the accent of the target language L2. But in a broader sense, the personal accent when learning and speaking some language could be significantly influenced by environmental and other factors such as teacher and learning materials, friends and colleagues, country of living, and previously learned languages, all contributing to varying degrees to the formation of an individual accent.

Accent modification [1] and voice conversion [16] have become another challenging area of study, focusing on the modification of a speaker's accent to facilitate better comprehension and evaluation of speech. One pioneering technique in this field is the use of neural style transfer to modify learners' accents [22]. When such modifications are applied to CAPT learner speech, they improve comparison results with reference pronunciation [6]. This, in turn, leads to significant improvements in pronunciation training, allowing learners to receive more accurate feedback and better understand their pronunciation errors.

This study builds on the available technological and pedagogical advancements to enhance the CAPT system in focus by utilizing ASR, accent recognition, and accent neutralization techniques to provide personalized pronunciation feedback to CAPT system users [24].

3   StudyIntonation—CAPT Environment in Focus

This research aims at improving the current components of the existing multimodal multilingual CAPT environment *StudyIntonation* described in detail in

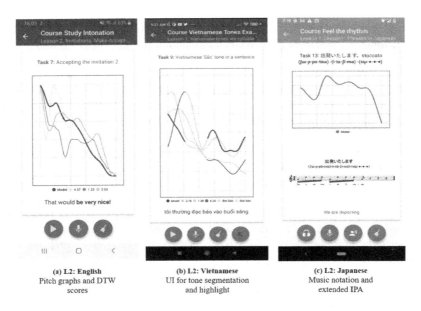

(a) L2: English
Pitch graphs and DTW
scores

(b) L2: Vietnamese
UI for tone segmentation
and highlight

(c) L2: Japanese
Music notation and
extended IPA

Fig. 1. Multimodality in feedback production for different L2.

our previous works [4,15]. The system is a computer-assisted instructional environment that aims to improve the pronunciation skills of learners, with a key focus on prosodic elements, including intonation, stress, and rhythm. The system uses a variety of digital signal processing techniques, such as speech activity identification, pitch visualization modeling using pitch graphs, and evaluation of pronunciation quality.

As shown in Fig. 1, the key interface of the end-user mobile application enables learners to compare their pronunciation pitch graph with a reference model pronunciation (recorded by native speakers). This pitch visualization is accompanied by a number of feedback models that address different levels of system multimodality and various learning styles. In the frame of instantiating the system for a number of target L2 languages representing different language groups (currently, English, Vietnamese, and Japanese), we experimented with the following interface components aiming at tailoring the CAPT feedback to language learners:

- Pitch quality score based on using DTW algorithms [21,23] (known as a robust model to measure the distance between the graphs, which is tempo and scale-invariant);
- Demonstrating a short contextualized video of the exercise (helpful for exercises connected to real-life conversational scenarios);
- Stack of exercise variations (assuming that the same phrase can be trained using a variety of context-dependent intonation patterns);
- Repeated exercise pronunciation patterns (specifically important for mora-timed languages such as Japanese);

- Music notation (helpful for learners with a musical background, especially to represent the language rhythm and higher and lower pitches in mora-timed languages);
- Extended IPA-transcription (with respect to rhythmic units and necessary fragments of silence).

Figure 1 illustrates some of the above-mentioned multimodal feedback interfaces as implemented while instantiating the CAPT environment for different target L2 languages in the process of its multilingual setup. Simultaneously, it is underpinned by an interactive interface designed primarily for mobile devices, tapping into the ubiquity and accessibility offered by today's advanced technology. The application provides a flexible and user-friendly interface designed with learners' needs in mind.

4   Enhancing Pitch Processing Pipeline with ASR Algorithms

In our commitment to offering tailored feedback for learners from diverse L1 backgrounds, we are integrating accent recognition and ASR components into our system. These additions are designed to significantly enhance the personalization of our platform, ensuring a more targeted and effective learning experience for each individual.

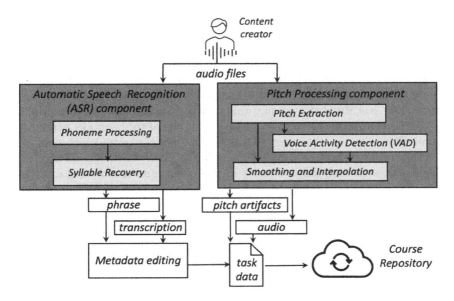

Fig. 2. Workflow of the Course Editor Module.

The key elements of our approach include components such as pitch processing and automatic speech recognition, which are shown in Fig. 2. Pitch processing utilizes the DTW algorithm to provide a tempo-invariant evaluation of the learner's performance. The changes we are implementing concern the neutralization of the accent to produce a more relevant evaluation, as described below. By integrating these different components, our system aims to provide comprehensive and personalized feedback that addresses the specific needs and challenges of each learner.

4.1   Automatic Speech Recognition Component

To achieve efficient processing and robust understanding of diverse accents, we employ transfer learning techniques on an advanced multilingual XLS-R model [2]. This model incorporates the self-supervised learning approach of Wav2Vec2.0 [3] and its capability to learn rich representations from raw audio. Its training on an extensive and varied set of languages enhances its ability to generalize across a wide range of linguistic contexts. It learns contextualized speech representations by randomly masking feature vectors before passing them to a transformer network in the course of self-supervised pre-training. The model is trained to predict the correct speech unit for masked parts of the audio while also learning what the speech units should be. This allows us to capture the nuanced variations of pronunciation across different accents.

To tailor the model to specific accents, we fine-tune the XLS-R model using Connectionist Temporal Classification (CTC) [10] on speech recordings and corresponding transcriptions from the L2-ARCTIC dataset [29], which contains English speech recordings from 24 non-native speakers of six different L1 backgrounds: Arabic, Hindi, Korean, Mandarin, Spanish, and Vietnamese. We resample the audio from 44.1 kHz to the same sampling rate of 16 kHz that was used to pretrain the XLS-R model. We leverage the power of PyTorch [19], an open-source machine learning framework, in tandem with Hugging Face's Transformers library [28], a state-of-the-art natural language processing tool, that provides *Wav2VecFeatureExtractor* to process the speech signal to the model's input format, and *Wav2VecCTCTokenizer* to process the model's output into text.

For the training stage, we implement a data collator that dynamically pads training batches to the longest sample in the batch, and use a word error rate (WER) metric, which is common in ASR, to compute the performance of the model. We load a pretrained checkpoint of XLS-R from Hugging Face Hub, freeze the feature extractor that consists of a stack of CNN layers, and add a linear layer on top of the transformer block to classify each context representation into a token class. For the training configuration and hyperparameter tuning, we follow the recommendations from the XLS-R and Wav2Vec2 papers [2,3] by employing the tri-state learning rate schedule: warm-up, constant stage, and decay stage. This approach helps us to refine and optimize the model, making it more attuned to the idiosyncrasies of different spoken accents, ultimately enhancing its precision and usability for our diverse range of learners. Furthermore, the Transformers library allows us to efficiently execute our language models on mobile devices [9], thus ensuring the wide accessibility and seamless operation of our system for users anywhere and anytime.

4.2   Accent Recognition Component

Building on the foundations laid in our previous research [14], the accent recognition module forms a crucial part of our system. During the initial setup of the application, the learner may read a phrase from the Speech Accent Archive [7], so the application can discern the user's native language.

Subsequent to the recording, the system's analysis yields an accent classification which is then presented to the user for verification. Upon user confirmation of the identified accent, the system may suggest downloading the respective fine-tuned ASR model that has been tailored specifically for that accent. This fine-tuned model will facilitate more precise words and phoneme recognition, enabling the system to provide more accurate and personalized feedback to the learner. If the user decides not to record the phrase or select the L1 background from the list, the generic ASR model is used.

This novel approach to incorporating accent recognition into the initial setup process not only enhances the personalization of our system, but also significantly improves the effectiveness of subsequent pronunciation training exercises. It acknowledges the reality of linguistic diversity and responds by ensuring that the application is adapted to the needs of each individual learner right from the outset.

4.3   Course Editor Module Setup

The Course Editor Module (as shown in Fig. 2) is a purpose-built tool for educators, enabling them to create and structure pronunciation courses tailored to their learners' needs. These custom-designed courses are stored in the Course Repository, where they become readily accessible for students to engage in personalized practice. Each course consists of lessons, and each lesson, in turn, comprises a series of tasks (see Fig. 3).

In our quest to continually enhance the Course Editor and expand its capabilities, we are introducing several key features to empower content creators in developing more personalized and effective language learning courses.

Understanding the profound impact that a learner's L1 can have on their English pronunciation and intonation, we are equipping content creators with the means to design specific exercises that cater to learners from a wide variety of L1 backgrounds. This personalized teaching approach aims to tackle the unique pronunciation hurdles each learner might face due to their L1 influence, paving the way for more effective learning outcomes.

In addition, we are harnessing the power of ASR technology to streamline the content creation process. This innovation automates the generation of transcriptions for recorded tasks, significantly reducing the manual workload of content creators. In case of inaccuracies in the automatically generated transcriptions,

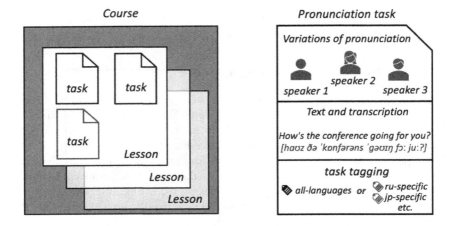

Fig. 3. Course structure.

creators have the flexibility to manually review, edit, and save the corrected version, ensuring the quality and accuracy of the learning materials.

5   Mobile Application

Based on practical possibilities to incorporate the ASR and accent recognition modules into the CAPT environment, we anticipate further extensions of the mobile app interfaces to fit the workflow presented in Fig. 4.

We employ accent recognition and customized ASR models for non-native speakers to help optimize the learning experience tailored to the specific needs of non-native English speakers. This technology helps us to determine the most suitable ASR model to use for each user. Typically, generic ASR models are developed based on the pronunciation patterns of native speakers. However, non-native speakers often exhibit unique pronunciation traits influenced by their L1. The mobile application can use ASR-recognized transcription to highlight the difference between the reference transcription and a recognized one from the learner's recording.

To address this, we refine open-source ASR models for improved accuracy in handling non-native speakers, specifically focusing on those from the most commonly represented L1 backgrounds among the users of the application. By tuning these models to better recognize and understand the pronunciation quirks of different L1 backgrounds, we ensure more accurate and personalized feedback for our users.

One of the challenges in teaching suprasegmental pronunciation is to make sure that the learner not only repeats the intonation correctly but also pronounces the phonemes appropriately. For intonation, the user compares a visualized pitch of their attempt with the reference pitch graph. ASR technology can be deployed directly on the user's mobile device, generating transcriptions of the

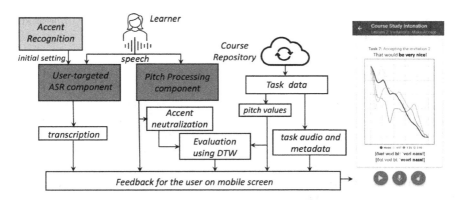

Fig. 4. Workflow of the learning process in the mobile app.

user's spoken utterances. Then, these transcriptions are compared to the reference pronunciation. Any phonemes that differ from the reference are highlighted in red, offering a clear visual indication to the learner of areas where improvement is needed. Figure 4 illustrates the visual feedback of the pitch graphs and the evaluation score extended with the reference and the actual phonetic transcription of the user speech.

Furthermore, accent recognition is employed not only in fine-tuning the ASR but also in categorizing a user's L1 accent. This allows for an even more personalized learning experience, as the system can suggest targeted exercises and provide custom-tailored feedback based on common pronunciation challenges associated with specific L1 accents. By leveraging this technology, we are improving the efficacy of our application, making it an even more powerful tool in the hands of language learners. The courses that provide support for different L1 backgrounds show additional content to practice the corresponding tasks.

We are currently developing a dynamic adaptation module for our system that provides learners with personalized tasks based on their individual performance. This performance is quantified through the use of the DTW evaluation metric—a lower DTW score signifies a higher alignment between the learner's pronunciation and the reference pronunciation, thus indicating better performance.

In cases where a significant discrepancy is detected between the student's pronunciation and the reference standard (indicated by a high DTW score), the system could "intelligently" suggest some additional practice tasks. Such tasks, provisionally added by content creators, are designed to help the learner improve their pronunciation skills in a targeted manner, addressing the areas of difficulty identified through the DTW evaluation. In this way, we aim to foster an adaptive learning environment that tailors instruction to each individual learner's needs, optimizing their language learning journey.

In addition to the possibility of replaying their attempts, users may find helpful an option to adjust the speed of playback. This feature gives learners the opportunity to slow down the audio, making it easier to dissect and understand the intricate phonetic components of the language.

6   Discussion

Enhancing interactive features of a CAPT system, we adapt the learning environment in a way to make it more friendly to users, since the learning process is better tailored to match the individual pace and proficiency level of learners. At the same time, we create more opportunities for teachers (course creators), enabling the promotion of more efficient and learner-centric language acquisition.

Although this contribution is focused on accent-targeted models and L1-specific ASR, it is important to note that these two are not the only feasible ways to produce better personalized CAPT feedback for language learners.

Automatic recognition of the influence of the mother tongue on the target language not only enables CAPT systems to tailor feedback and practice activities to the users but also does so in a discrete yet targeted manner. Accents are often linked to stereotypes, prejudices, and cultural identity, so bypassing the declaration of the influence of an accent helps avoid issues related to, inter alia, privacy, identity, and self-esteem.

The training of ASR models on non-native speaker rather than traditional native speaker datasets enables CAPT systems to move away from the one-size-fits-all model in which all language learners, regardless of mother tongue or language family, are treated the same, viz. as non-native speakers. However, the transition toward targeting specific sets of learners by language family or mother tongue signals a shift to personalized pronunciation training for learners with different L1 backgrounds. We should note that applying transfer learning to the XLS-R model using the L2-Arctic dataset, which contains phrases from out-of-copyright texts from Project Gutenberg books, may decrease the performance of the ASR model for everyday conversations. For that reason, we are working on employing spoken language datasets, such as ICNALE [11].

Although accent recognition plays a valuable role, it is necessary to take into account the complex linguistic landscape in which learners may be exposed to multiple linguistic factors affecting their linguistic repertoire, including the influence of L1 on the target language of the learner.

7   Conclusion

In this paper, we introduce an approach that integrates accent recognition and customized ASR into a CAPT pipeline with the use of ASR-based accent recognition and accent neutralization techniques, along with an approach to design L1-specific exercises and utilizing ASR for transcription generation. A system that incorporates such accent-reflected language-family-specific feedback adjustments could be particularly beneficial for learners whose accents are more heavily influenced by their mother tongue by providing them with implicit but targeted hints on pronunciation improvement.

In conclusion, it is important to note that our CAPT environment is mainly aimed at creating better conditions for the evolution of learners' conversational skills by replicating modeled pronunciation rather than by focusing on the mistakes of the learners. From this point of view, adopting accent recognition techniques to a CAPT system is considered a promising component to be used in conjunction with other approaches towards better CAPT feedback customization, including contextual feedback, enhanced visualization techniques, and multimedia integration.

More experimental and analytical studies are required to evaluate and assess the suggested models in pedagogical practices, including using independent techniques to evaluate learners' progress.

Acknowledgements. This research was funded by the Japan Society for the Promotion of Science (JSPS), grant number 23K00679.

References

1. Aryal, S., Gutierrez-Osuna, R.: Can voice conversion be used to reduce non-native accents? In: 2014 IEEE International Conference on Acoustics, Speech and Signal Processing (ICASSP), pp. 7879–7883. IEEE (2014)
2. Babu, A., et al.: Xls-r: self-supervised cross-lingual speech representation learning at scale. arXiv preprint arXiv:2111.09296 (2021)
3. Baevski, A., Zhou, Y., Mohamed, A., Auli, M.: wav2vec 2.0: a framework for self-supervised learning of speech representations. Adv. Neural Inf. Process. Syst. **33**, 12449–12460 (2020)
4. Bogach, N., et al.: Speech processing for language learning: a practical approach to computer-assisted pronunciation teaching. Electronics **10**(3), 235 (2021)
5. Chakraborty, J., Sinha, R., Sarmah, P.: Influence of accented speech in automatic speech recognition: a case study on Assamese L1 speakers speaking code switched Hindi-English. In: Prasanna, S.R.M., Karpov, A., Samudravijaya, K., Agrawal, S.S. (eds.) Speech and Computer: 24th International Conference, SPECOM 2022, Gurugram, India, 14–16 November 2022, Proceedings, pp. 87–98. Springer, Cham (2022). https://doi.org/10.1007/978-3-031-20980-2_9
6. Felps, D., Bortfeld, H., Gutierrez-Osuna, R.: Foreign accent conversion in computer assisted pronunciation training. Speech Commun. **51**(10), 920–932 (2009)
7. George Mason University. Speech accent archive (2021). https://accent.gmu.edu/
8. Gilbert, J.B.: Teaching Pronunciation: Using the Prosody Pyramid. Cambridge University Press (2008)
9. Gondi, S.: Wav2vec2. 0 on the edge: Performance evaluation. arXiv preprint arXiv:2202.05993 (2022)
10. Graves, A., Fernández, S., Gomez, F., Schmidhuber, J.: Connectionist temporal classification: labelling unsegmented sequence data with recurrent neural networks. In: Proceedings of the 23rd International Conference on Machine Learning, pp. 369–376 (2006)
11. Ishikawa, S.: The ICNALE Guide: An Introduction to a Learner Corpus Study on Asian Learners' L2 English. Taylor & Francis (2023)
12. Karpagavalli, S., Chandra, E.: A review on automatic speech recognition architecture and approaches. Int. J. Signal Process. Image Process. Pattern Recogn. **9**(4), 393–404 (2016)

13. Liu, D., Reed, M.: Exploring the complexity of the l2 intonation system: an acoustic and eye-tracking study. Front. Commun. **6**, 51 (2021)
14. Mikhailava, V., Lesnichaia, M., Bogach, N., Lezhenin, I., Blake, J., Pyshkin, E.: Language accent detection with CNN using sparse data from a crowd-sourced speech archive. Mathematics **10**(16), 2913 (2022)
15. Mikhailava, V., et al.: Tailoring computer-assisted pronunciation teaching: mixing and matching the mode and manner of feedback to learners. In: INTED2022 Proceedings, pp. 767–773. IATED (2022)
16. Mohammadi, S.H., Kain, A.: An overview of voice conversion systems. Speech Commun. **88**, 65–82 (2017)
17. Munro, M.J., Derwing, T.M.: Foreign accent, comprehensibility, and intelligibility in the speech of second language learners. Lang. Learn. **45**(1), 73–97 (1995)
18. Murphy, V.A.: Second language learning in the early school years: trends and contexts. Oxford University Press (2014)
19. Paszke, A.E.A.: Pytorch: an imperative style, high-performance deep learning library. In: Advances in Neural Information Processing Systems, vol. 32, pp. 8024–8035. Curran Associates, Inc. (2019)
20. Pennington, M.C., Rogerson-Revell, P.: English Pronunciation Teaching and Research, vol. 10, pp. 978–988. Palgrave Macmillan, Londres (2019)
21. Permanasari, Y., Harahap, E.H., Ali, E.P.: Speech recognition using dynamic time warping (DTW). J. Phys. Conf. Ser. **1366**, 012091 (2019). https://doi.org/10.1088/1742-6596/1366/1/012091. IOP Publishing
22. Radzikowski, K., Wang, L., Yoshie, O., Nowak, R.: Accent modification for speech recognition of non-native speakers using neural style transfer. EURASIP J. Audio Speech Music Process. **2021**(1), 1–10 (2021)
23. Rilliard, A., Allauzen, A., Boula_de_Mareüil, P.: Using dynamic time warping to compute prosodic similarity measures. In: Twelfth Annual Conference of the International Speech Communication Association (2011)
24. Rogerson-Revell, P.M.: Computer-assisted pronunciation training (CAPT): current issues and future directions. RELC J. **52**(1), 189–205 (2021)
25. Sullivan, P., Shibano, T., Abdul-Mageed, M.: Improving automatic speech recognition for non-native English with transfer learning and language model decoding. In: Analysis and Application of Natural Language and Speech Processing, pp. 21–44. Springer, Cham (2022). https://doi.org/10.1007/978-3-031-11035-1_2
26. Thandil, R.K., Basheer, K.M.: Accent based speech recognition: a critical overview. Malaya J. Matemat. **8**(4), 1743–1750 (2020)
27. Viglino, T., Motlicek, P., Cernak, M.: End-to-end accented speech recognition. In: Interspeech, pp. 2140–2144 (2019)
28. Wolf, T., et al.: Huggingface's transformers: state-of-the-art natural language processing. arXiv preprint arXiv:1910.03771 (2019)
29. Zhao, G., et al.: L2-arctic: a non-native English speech corpus. In: Interspeech, pp. 2783–2787 (2018)

Speech Technology for Under-Resourced Languages

Improvements in Language Modeling, Voice Activity Detection, and Lexicon in OpenASR21 Low Resource Languages

Vishwa Gupta$^{(\boxtimes)}$ and Gilles Boulianne

Centre de Recherche Informatique de Montréal (CRIM), Quebec, Canada
{vishwa.gupta,gilles.boulianne}@crim.ca

Abstract. OpenASR21 evaluation was on 15 low resource languages and 3 case sensitive languages. During the evaluation, participants got significant reduction in word error rates (WER) with text downloaded from the internet for only the case sensitive languages, since the development and evaluation audio contained broadcast news. For the 15 low resource languages, participants showed only small gains for some of the languages. The reason is that the development and test set contain dialog between two people, which is very different from the primarily news texts and web pages available over the internet. Here, we show that training text translated from other OpenASR21 languages reduces the WER for many languages. During the evaluation, one team added words to the lexicon using a 3-gram phone language model, but they do not show what WER reduction they achieve. We show that adding new words in the lexicon from public text is beneficial for languages where the out-of-vocabulary rate is high, and outline conditions for reducing the WER. Adding an attention layer to the TDNN (time delay neural net) based voice activity detector reduced the WER for 17 out of the 18 languages. With all the improvements combined, we are getting lower word error rate for the development set for three languages (Farsi, Kazakh and Tamil) than the site that achieved the best error rate for all the languages during the evaluation period.

Keywords: OpenASR21 · Low-resource · Speech recognition · Language modeling

1 Introduction

The OpenASR21 (Open Automatic Speech Recognition 2021) Challenge set out to assess the state of the art of ASR technologies under low-resource language constraints [11]. The task consisted of performing ASR on audio datasets in up to 15 different low-resource languages and 3 languages with case sensitive scoring, to produce the recognized text. Ten languages were carried over from the OpenASR20 challenge [10], and five new languages were added. A case sensitive scoring was also added for three of these languages: Kazakh, Swahili and Tagalog. In case-sensitive scoring, words capitalized differently from the reference

A. Karpov et al. (Eds.): SPECOM 2023, LNAI 14339, pp. 73–86, 2023.
https://doi.org/10.1007/978-3-031-48312-7_6

transcript will not count as a match. Case-sensitive scoring is used as a proxy for evaluating ASR performance on proper nouns.

We took part in the constrained condition for all the 15 languages and the 3 languages with case sensitive scoring. In the constrained condition, only a 10-hour audio Build dataset for that language can be used for training acoustic models. Additional text data, either from the Build dataset or publicly available resources, can be used for training the language model in the constrained condition. Any such additional training text must be specified in detail in the system description. In the constrained condition, no pre-trained large models were allowed.

A good overview of OpenASR20 is given in [10]. In OpenASR20, two teams achieved very good results [1,17]. They used larger training text and lexicon from Linguistic Data Consortium (LDC) corpora for training language models (LM) and using a larger lexicon. These LMs and larger lexicon reduced the word error rate (WER) significantly for each language.

For OpenASR21 see [11] for a good overview. The team from USTC/iFlytek Research [19] achieved the lowest word error rate (WER) for all the 15 languages. Their WER was significantly lower than any other participant for all the languages. For acoustic modeling, they used TTS to generate additional audio for training either from public text or the Babel training text. This gave them an additional 1.3% average WER reduction for the 15 languages. They also interpolated language model (LM) from LDC text with LM from public text (publicly available text downloaded from internet). This interpolated LM gave them better results for 3 of the 7 languages. They also rescored the decoded lattices with bidirectional LSTMP (LSTM with a recurrent projection layer) [14] language model from public text. This LM was fine tuned with the LDC training text before rescoring. Note that, the leading teams in the OpenASR21 evaluation used hybrid DNN-HMM systems rather than end-to-end systems, since the end-to-end systems perform poorly with only 10 h of audio.

In [18], they do not use any publicly available text for either decoding or for rescoring with LSTM LM. They use a larger lexicon for the 15 languages and 3 case sensitive languages. They generate a 3-gram phone language model from the lexicon, and then generate 12 million sequences from this LM, and keep 1 million most likely sequences not in the lexicon. Words corresponding to these phone sequences are generated using G2P (grapheme to phoneme) methods to augment the lexicon. But they do not show the benefit of using such a large lexicon.

In [4], the authors use three different features (MFCCs, MFCCs+Conformer embeddings, MFCCs + voice activity detector embeddings) to generate 3 different acoustic models for later fusion. They also used publicly available text for language modeling. Instead of generating separate LM from LDC and public text and then interpolating the two [19], they first filter the public text with sentence selection to match the sentences in the LDC training text, and then generate an LM from the combined LDC + filtered public text. The filtered public text is about the same size as the LDC text. This resulted in reduced WER (word error rate) for many languages.

However, the reduction in WER with the added public text was small. The primary reason for this small reduction is that the public text comes mostly from news and web pages, while OpenASR21 contains conversations between two people. So the question is how can we add text corresponding to conversations. Here we introduce a method to generate synthetic conversational text and augment data for a language of interest, using a back-translation approach, and obtain small reduction in WER for that language. Although back-translation has been used to improve machine translation models [15], here it is used for the first time to improve a monolingual model for ASR (to the best of our knowledge).

During the evaluation period, we had used a voice activity detector (VAD) [4] to remove noise segments. This VAD, as outlined in Chime6 track2 speech activity detection[1] had 5 TDNN layers and 2 layers of statistics pooling [2] with an added specAugment layer [8]. We propose to add an attention layer, similar to the one outlined for ASR in [13]. The speech/non-speech segmentation with this attention layer results in small reductions in WER for most languages. The reason is that an attention layer provides longer term context and it improves discrimination between segments with long duration. Silent and speech segments fall in that category.

We also show that increasing the lexicon with new words from public text is effective for languages where OOV (out of vocabulary) rate is high.

As the NIST scoring server for the evaluation set is closed, we only show comparative results for the development set. Through all the improvements in [4], we showed that we got lower WER for the eval set for Tamil than any participant during the evaluation period. In this paper, we show that with all the improvements combined, we get lower single decode WER for development set for Farsi, Kazakh and Tamil than the best team during evaluation [19].

2   Dataset

In the constrained condition, for acoustic model training, we only used the 10-hour Build data set provided by NIST for the language being processed, with corresponding transcripts in UTF-8 encoding. Training and development lexicons were also provided by NIST.

For the 13 languages with LDC packs (all the languages except for Farsi and Somali), we used the expanded lexicon and text provided in those packs. For example, the training text in the OpenASR21 build dataset varies from 66k words for Kazakh to 126k words for Vietnamese, while the training text in the LDC packs varies from 270k words for Kazakh to 989k words for Vietnamese. Overall, the LDC training text is between 4 times and 8 times larger than the text in the OpenASR21 build. The lexicon in the LDC packs is also much larger than the lexicon in the OpenASR21 build. For example, the number of words for Vietnamese in the OpenASR21 lexicon is 3.2k, while in the LDC lexicon there are 6.4k words. For these reasons, training a language model from the training

---

[1] https://chimechallenge.github.io/chime6/track2software.html.

text and lexicon in the LDC packs reduces the word error rate significantly for all the 13 languages with the LDC packs.

3   ASR Approach

Our system is a hybrid HMM-DNN based on WFSTs (Weighted Finite-State Transducers) and trained with the Kaldi toolkit [12]. During the evaluation period, we trained three different acoustic models for decoding the dev and eval sets so that we could combine the multiple results after decoding [4]. In this paper, we just use one set of acoustic models with 40-dim MFCC's and 2-stream TDNN-F architecture (for multi-stream architecture see [5]) for decoding the development (dev) set (we cannot use the eval set since the scoring server at NIST is closed). These models are the same as those used during evaluation. The idea here is to test new algorithms to reduce WER using improved language modeling, better voice activity detector models, and larger vocabulary.

3.1   Enhanced Voice Activity Detector

During the OpenASR21 evaluation [4], we used two voice activity detectors to segment development and evaluation audio into speech/nonspeech segments: one based on DNN-HMM architecture, and another based on TDNN architecture [9] as outlined in Chime6 track2 speech activity detection[2]. This VAD TDNN has 40-dim MFCC features as input, followed by 3 TDNN layers, followed by 2 layers of statistics pooling [2], followed by 2 TDNN layers. During the OpenASR21 evaluation, we showed that adding a specAugment layer after the input layer to this VAD-TDNN results in lower WER for most of the languages [4]. Here we show that by adding an attention layer [13], we can reduce the WER even more for most of the languages. The attention layer is added after the 5th TDNN layer (see Fig. 1). The attention layer has 12 heads, a value dimension of 60, key dimension of 40, and the number of left and right inputs are 5 and 2 respectively. The attention layer has a wider context (108 frames of left context and 69 frames of right context) and it is able to improve speech/non-speech discrimination as speech and non-speech segments are longer in duration. All the TDNN layers have an output dimension of 256. Table 1 compares WER with/without the attention layer in one back-to-back comparison. Except for Swahili, the WER goes down for the other languages. So the attention layer consistently gives lower WER. Overall, the WER is reduced on average by 0.3% absolute. The largest WER reduction is for Cantonese and Georgian (0.7% absolute).

3.2   Enhanced Lexicon

We carried out many experiments to see if adding new words from publicly downloaded text will reduce word error rates. Public text was heavily filtered

---

[2] https://chimechallenge.github.io/chime6/track2software.html.

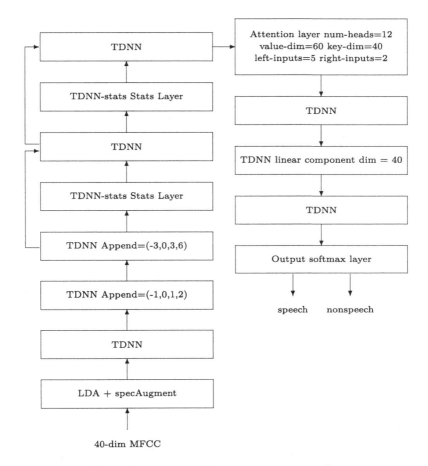

Fig. 1. *VAD TDNN with attention. All the TDNN layers have a dimension of 256.*

by sentence selection to be similar to the LDC training text [4], and the filtered text was about the same size as the LDC text (see Language Model Sec. 3.3). We added new words in this filtered public text to the lexicon. We tried adding frequency one and frequency two words (words not in LDC lexicon occurring at least 2 times in the public text) to the lexicon. To be consistent, we ran all the decoding experiments in this paper with the same acoustic models: LF-MMI (lattice free MMI) training followed by discriminative training of 2-stream acoustic models with 40-dim MFCC [4].

One question is how do we add pronunciations for the new words? We know that the training and test audio are very well transcribed, including the lexicon in the LDC build. The LSP (language specific peculiarities) file in the LDC build contains details about dialects of speakers, any special handling of spelling, character set used for orthographic transcription, romanization scheme, word boundary detection, where the transcribers are from, etc. So the text is

Table 1. WER for the dev set segmented with / without attention layer in VAD-TDNN. CSS stands for case sensitive scoring. (No LSTM LM rescoring is done.)

Lang	no att	att	Lang	no att	att
Amharic	38.0	**37.7**	Mongolian	48.0	**47.9**
Cantonese	47.3	**46.6**	Pashto	48.1	**47.9**
Farsi	52.6	**52.4**	Somali	59.2	**58.9**
Georgian	41.4	**40.7**	Swahili	**36.4**	36.5
Guarani	42.4	**42.3**	Tagalog	44.6	**44.2**
Javanese	53.3	**53.0**	Tamil	61.0	**60.9**
Kazakh	47.3	**46.9**	Kazakh css	53.2	**52.8**
Kurmanji	65.5	**65.3**	Swahili css	48.5	**48.4**
Vietnamese	48.6	**48.0**	tagalog css	47.8	**47.4**

probably quite consistent in transcription, and the words in the LDC lexicon are probably transcribed in a consistent manner. So we did not want to change the transcriptions in this lexicon. This lexicon is transcribed using X-SAMPA[3] phoneme set. To this LDC lexicon, we added pronunciations for the new words in X-SAMPA using two possible scenarios. In one scenario, we train a G2P [7] (grapheme-to-phoneme) from the LDC lexicon (or OpenASR21 lexicon for Farsi and Somali), and then transcribe the new words with this G2P. The second scenario is to use existing G2P from LanguageNet [6] to transcribe the new words. The advantage with LanguageNet is that there are finite state transducers (FSTs) trained for over 120 languages with a large amount of training data for each language. The problem is that some OpenASR21 languages maybe missing (Farsi is missing from LanguageNet). Another problem with LanguageNet is that words are transcribed in IPA symbols, while the OpenASR21 lexicon is transcribed in X-SAMPA. To overcome this, we transcribed the LDC lexicon with the LanguageNet G2P to get a training lexicon with IPA symbols, and then trained another G2P from it to convert IPA phone sequences into X-SAMPA phone sequences. With this conversion capability, we transcribed new words in IPA using languageNet G2P and then converted phoneme sequences in IPA to phoneme sequences in X-SAMPA. So now we had two enhanced lexicons: one from new words transcribed using G2P trained from LDC lexicon[4], and one from new words transcribed with LanguageNet G2P in IPA symbols and then converted to X-SAMPA phone sequences.

We compared the two lexicon with new words added to the LDC lexicon on Amharic and on Somali. The two lexicons gave very similar WER with a small preference for G2P trained from LDC lexicon. So we used the G2P trained from LDC lexicon for the rest of the languages.

---

[3] https://en.wikipedia.org/wiki/X-SAMPA.

[4] Note that in many languages, some new words had graphemes that do not occur in the LDC lexicon, so we removed these new words before transcribing with G2P.

Table 2 shows for each language the OOV (out-of-vocabulary) rate for the development (dev) set, and the WER (word error rate) with/without the enhanced vocabulary. The last column in Table 2 shows the vocabulary size with/without enhancement. For Amharic, Cantonese and Guarani, we used words occurring 2 times or more in the public text for adding to the existing LDC or OpenASR21 lexicon. For the rest of the languages, we added all the new words occurring 1 time or more in the public text to the LDC or OpenASR21 lexicon. From the table we see that the major benefit from adding the new words in the lexicon is for languages where the OOV rate is high: Farsi, Somalese, Kazakh css (case sensitive scoring), Swahili css, and Tagalog css. The reason for high OOV rate for Farsi and Somali is that there is no LDC pack for them, so the lexicon derived from the small training text is small. For the case sensitive scoring languages also there is no LDC pack, so the training text is from only 10 h of audio. But the OOV rate is higher also because words in training text are capitalized where necessary, so many words are OOV if the correct case does not occur in the lexicon.

The decoding scenario for Table 2 is that a 4-gram LM is computed with SRILM toolkit from the LDC training text (where available) with/without the enhanced lexicon. The WER shows decoding results with this LM (without rescoring with LSTM LM).

As we can see from Table 2, decoding with larger lexicon results in WER reduction for languages where OOV rate is high: Farsi, Somali, Kazakh CSS, Swahili CSS, and Tagalog CSS. Why should the error rate go down for languages with larger OOV rate and not for languages with small OOV rate, even though the likelihood for OOVs in the language model is small (since they are assigned a low unigram probability as they do not occur in the LDC text)? For large OOV rate, the words in the enhanced lexicon may come up as top choice despite small LM likelihoods and reduce WER. While for languages with low OOV rate, there are many more new words not in the development set, and if these words show up as top choice, then they will increase the WER. That is why the biggest gain is for the case sensitive scoring (CSS) languages as their OOV rate is the highest (between 17.8% and 23.7%), and the OOV rate reduction with enhanced lexicon is the largest (between 7.6% and 9.7%), as shown in Table 2. Also, the audio for case sensitive languages is from broadcast audio, and so there is a better match between publicly available text and the training text.

3.3 Language Model

We will first outline what we have done in language modeling in the past [4] for OpenASR21 evaluation, and then describe the new improvements. For language modeling (LM) in the constrained condition, we could use any text publicly available over the internet. For 13 of the 15 languages, we used the LDC IARPA Babel language packs from 2016 to 2020 (there were no language packs for Farsi and Somali). The larger LDC training text together with the larger lexicon reduced the WER for all the languages. The LDC text is from conversational speech, and it reduces WER for the dev set significantly as can be seen in [4, 19].

Table 2. OOV rate before and after enhancement, and WER for dev set for each language without/with enhanced lexicon. The last column shows vocabulary size without/with enhancement.

Lang	OOV%	no enh	with enh	vocab no enh/with enh
Amharic	2.0 / 0.7	**37.7**	38.4	36.9k / 46.5k
Cantonese	1.4 / 0	**46.6**	46.6	19.9k / 21.2k
Farsi	9.5 / 6.0	52.4	**52.3**	3.7k / 14.7k
Georgian	1.1 / 0	**40.7**	42.4	35.2k / 130.7k
Guarani	2.0 / 1.1	**42.3**	42.5	28.0k / 30.9k
Javanese	1.0 / 0.6	**53.0**	53.9	15.5k / 44.0k
Kazakh	0.5 / 0.3	**46.9**	48.4	22.3k / 71.4k
Kurmanji	1.1 / 0.2	**65.3**	65.6	14.4k / 63.5k
Mongolian	0.5 / 0.5	**47.9**	48.9	23.9k / 66.9k
Pashto	0.3 / 0	**47.9**	48.0	18.7k / 77.2k
Somali	9.4 / 7.4	58.9	**58.8**	9.6k / 29.3k
Swahili	3.7 / 0.7	**36.5**	37.7	25.2k / 56.9k
Tagalog	1.0/0.8	**44.2**	45.1	22.6k / 59.1k
Tamil	0.5 / 0.2	**60.9**	62.0	58.4k / 104.0k
Vietnamese	0.3 / 0.2	**48.0**	48.1	6.4k / 26.7k
Kazakh css	23.7/14.0	52.8	**48.0**	15.8k / 69.0k
Swahili css	18.6 / 10.9	48.4	**46.3**	11.3k / 58.1k
Tagalog css	17.8 / 10.2	47.4	**43.9**	11.2k / 59.2k

In [4], we also downloaded a significant amount of publicly available monolingual texts from NewsCrawl[5] and CommonCrawl[6], but this text was primarily from news and web sources, and not from conversational speech. So this text significantly increased the perplexity on the development set for every language. We had to resort to sentence selection [16] to use only sentences close to the training text. Through strong sentence selection, we were able to reduce the overall WER after LSTM LM rescoring for 8 of the 15 languages, and all the case sensitive scoring languages (the audio for CSS languages is from broadcast news) [4].

The team with the lowest WER in the evaluation [19] did not filter the downloaded text, but they interpolated the 4-gram LM from this downloaded text with the 4-gram LM from the LDC training text using the SRILM toolkit[7]. They were able to reduce WER for 3 of 7 languages after decoding with this interpolated 4-gram LM.

So the real question is whether we can get additional conversational text that can reduce the perplexity of most of the languages after 4-gram training? In this

[5] https://www.aclweb.org/anthology/W19-5301.
[6] https://data.statmt.org/cc-100/.
[7] https://www.sri.com/platform/srilm/.

paper, we have experimented with Back-translation in order to get additional independent conversation language model training text for each language. Back-translation is used in machine translation [15] to generate synthetic data in a language with scarce resources. Here, since all languages have conversational speech between two speakers on cell phone, we translated the training text in each language to the text in all the other languages. We then combined all translations to a language of interest for generating a 4-gram language model for that language.

For translation we used the Google translation interface[8] in batch mode. We were able to get translations for 14 of the 15 languages (Google translates Mandarin but not Cantonese), thus augmenting LM training data 13-fold for each of these 14 languages. To prepare transcription texts for translation, we merged utterances from the different channel recordings by concatenating them in chronological order, to recreate the full conversation. The transcribed text does not have punctuation marks. We also removed silence and noise markers from this text. At first we considered each utterance as a sentence, but translation results in English made more sense when we concatenated all utterances of a conversation in a single document. Since punctuation marks are added during translation, we used them to split the translated document back into short utterances, then removed the punctuation marks, to make the text similar to the training transcripts.

We have some examples in English (below) that we generated as spot checks for languages. For example, from Vietnamese to English (before punctuation removal):

> hello, hello sister Kieu, oh baby, I haven't eaten yet, have you scratched there, how do you study and only study is normal? what is that dish? my husband just let it go so slowly wear the pink shirt and wear it while it's okay oh my god what is it oh my god what is it my god what is it that makes me laugh everyone studied at this time but didn't go to school at night, did you go to school tonight,

Similarly, translation from Guarani to English is shown below:

> we'll hear we can talk hello hello hello dear brother what's up what's up brother what are you doing right my friend what's the door i aka dehkansándo yeah and here I'll correct and you what are you doing yeah correct what' e here here I'm looking at the movies

Although we cannot actually confirm it, anecdotal evidence suggests that Google translation uses English as the pivot language[9]. We can see that the translation from one language to English is poor, and when English is translated back to another language, it may still be poorer. But we found that in terms of language modeling, this text reduced perplexity more than using the

---

[8] https://cloud.google.com/translation-hub.
[9] https://www.teachyoubackwards.com/extras/pivot/.

downloaded news related text from the internet even after strong filtering. We generated three 4-gram's from three sources: LDC alone (LDC), translated text from 13 languages combined (Trans), and the downloaded and filtered text from the internet (Sel). We then generated two interpolated language models: LDC interpolated with Trans (LDC·Trans), and LDC interpolated with Trans and Sel (LDC·Trans·Sel). The "·" symbol is used here for interpolation. The optimal interpolation weights are found by the iterative E-M (expectation-maximization algorithm) estimation of SRILM. The perplexity and word error rate (WER) for the three 4-grams is shown in Table 3. So for example, in Table 3, perplexity for Amharic dev set with language model trained from LDC is 404, and the WER is 37.7%, perplexity with interpolated LDC·Trans is 394, and the WER is 37.6%, while perplexity with the interpolated LDC·Trans·Sel is 393, and the WER is 37.6%. As can be seen from the Table, we were able to reduce WER for 10 of the 14 languages.

Even though differences reported in Table 3 seem small, the test sets are large samples, between 60K and 112K words for each language, so that confidence intervals[10] for these results range from ±0.20% to ±0.28%. The differences are significant at a 95% level for Farsi, Pashto, Swahili and Vietnamese while for the other languages the differences are not so significant.

Table 3. Perplexity (PPL) and word error rate (WER) for the dev set for each language for 4-gram LMs from LDC, LDC·Trans, LDC·Trans·Sel. No LSTM LM rescoring is done.

Lang	LDC PPL / WER	LDC·Trans PPL / WER	LDC·Trans·Sel PPL / WER	Interp. weights LDC Trans Sel
Amharic	404 / 37.7%	394 / 37.6%	**393 / 37.5%**	0.885, 0.073, 0.042
Farsi	231 / 52.3%	221 / 52.0%	**221 / 52.0%**	0.823, 0.153, 0.024
Georgian	477 / 40.7%	466 / 40.6%	**464 / 40.6%**	0.884, 0.070, 0.046
Guarani	251 /42.3%	**249** / 42.3%	249 / **42.2%**	0.945, 0.036, 0.019
Javanese	271 / **53.0%**	269 / 53.1%	**269** / 53.2%	0.946, 0.039, 0.015
Kazakh	267 / 46.9%	257 /46.8%	**257 / 46.7%**	0.874, 0.097, 0.029
Kurmanji	174 / 65.3%	**170 / 65.3%**	170 / 65.3%	0.904, 0.096, n/a
Mongol	169 / 47.9%	166 / 47.8%	**164 / 47.7%**	0.897, 0.058, 0.045
Pashto	163 / 47.9%	162 / 47.5%	**161 / 47.4%**	0.931, 0.034, 0.035
Somali	279 / **58.8%**	**261** / 59.0%	261 / 59.0%	0.800, 0.179, 0.021
Swahili	319 / 36.5%	306 / 36.3%	**305 / 36.2%**	0.852, 0.094, 0.054
Tagalog	155 / **44.2%**	152 / 44.5%	**152** / 44.4%	0.899, 0.067, 0.034
Tamil	769 / 60.9%	765 / 60.8%	**763 / 60.8%**	0.951, 0.016, 0.033
Vietnam	144 / 48.0%	143 / 48.0%	**140 / 47.8%**	0.885, 0.013, 0.102

[10] We use an 83% confidence interval computed with the Wilson score binomial interval, so that non-overlapping intervals represent a 95% significant difference between the two results [3].

Due to the poor quality of the translation (language → English → another language), the improvement with the translated text is small. However, if we can somehow find two way conversations in English, then we should do much better. It just happens that the switch board[11] data, the call home[12] data, and the Fisher corpus[13] is just that data. These corpus contain millions of words of text. Maybe translating them may lead to appropriate conversational text that can lead to significant reduction in WER. We can even filter this text to be close to the conversations in the training text, and still have a significant amount of additional training text left over. However, we have not exploited this avenue yet.

The final issue is whether all the above improvements (voice activity detector, enhanced lexicon, and translated text) result in significant reduction in WER after LSTM LM rescoring compared to the previous results with LSTM LM rescoring where LSTM LM was trained from LDC + public text or LDC text alone [4]. What we found was that decoding with LDC·Trans·Sel LM followed by rescoring with LSTM LM trained from LDC + translated + filtered public text resulted in lowest WER for Amharic and Farsi. For Guarani and Kazakh, decoding with LDC·Trans LM and rescoring with LSTM LM trained from LDC + filtered public text gave the lowest WER. For other languages, decoding with LDC LM and rescoring with LDC + public text lead to the lowest WER for the dev set. For the case sensitive languages, decoding with 4-gram LM from LDC + public text with enhanced vocabulary, and rescoring with LSTM LM from LDC + public text resulted in the lowest WER. The best WER on dev set in [4] and with all the improvements in this paper is shown in Table 4. For Kurmanji and Swahili, there is no improvement because enhanced VAD, increased vocabulary, translated text and filtered public text did not contribute to WER reduction. So the conversational LDC text for these languages is probably quite different from the text for other languages, and the translation maybe of poor quality. In Table 4, we also compare our results on the dev set for single decode with those of [19] (Table 1, column 1). We can see that we got lower WER for the dev set for three languages: Farsi, Kazakh, and Tamil. For many other languages, our WER for the dev set single decode is close to that in [19].

We also computed confidence intervals for our improvements in WER in Table 4 in a similar manner as for Table 3. The results after the improvements are 95% significant for 13 out of 18 languages[14] (Amharic, Cantonese, Farsi, Georgian, Kazakh, Pashto, Somali, Tagalog, Tamil, Vietnamese, Kazakh css, Swahili css and Tagalog css). When we make a similar comparison of our best WER with the WER in [19], our WER is better than or same as in [19] for 6 out of 15 languages (Farsi, Javanese, Kazakh, Pashto, Tagalog and Tamil) and worse for 9 out of the 15 languages.

---

[11] https://catalog.ldc.upenn.edu/LDC97S62.

[12] https://catalog.ldc.upenn.edu/LDC97T14.

[13] https://catalog.ldc.upenn.edu/LDC2004T19.

[14] We assumed confidence intervals in the same range for Cantonese and the three case-sensitive languages as the other languages since they have similar test sizes.

We also tried to fine tune the LSTM LM language model with LDC training text using a small learning rate. But in each case, we only achieved a 0.1% reduction in WER. The major effect was whether LSTM LM was trained with LDC + translated + filtered public text, or LDC + filtered public text. Another important factor was whether the decoded lattices for rescoring with LSTM LM were generated from LM trained with LDC alone, or from LDC·Trans·Sel, or from LDC + public text with enhanced vocabulary (as described in the previous paragraph).

Table 4. WER for the dev set before and after all the improvements in this paper. CSS stands for case sensitive scoring. Numbers in bold show whether WER before or after was significantly lower. Numbers in underline show that the WER in ref [19] was significantly lower.

Lang	before	After	from ref [19]	Lang	Before	After	from ref [19]
Amharic	37.2	**36.1**	_35.0_	Mongolian	46.4	46.3	_45.4_
Cantonese	45.6	**45.0**	_42.3_	Pashto	45.7	**45.3**	45.2
Farsi	51.7	**50.8**	52.4	Somali	58.6	**57.4**	_55.9_
Georgian	40.3	**39.2**	_37.5_	Swahili	34.6	34.7	_32.3_
Guarani	40.9	40.8	_39.0_	Tagalog	42.8	**42.3**	42.1
Javanese	52.0	51.9	51.9	Tamil	60.3	**59.4**	61.0
Kazakh	45.9	**45.2**	46.1	Kazakh css	51.9	**46.0**	
Kurmanji	64.1	64.1	_63.7_	Swahili css	47.6	**44.2**	
Vietnamese	47.0	**46.3**	_43.9_	Tagalog css	46.3	**41.4**	

4   Conclusion

We participated in all the 15 low resource languages and the three languages with case sensitive scoring in the OpenASR21 Challenge for the constrained condition. In the past, use of downloaded public text has shown small reductions in word error rate (WER) primarily due to mismatched domains (conversational speech versus news sources). We show that we can achieve small reductions in WER by translating training text from other languages in OpenASR21 to the target language. The small improvement is possibly due to the quality of the translation. Translation is the way to possibly improve the language models in low resource languages for conversational speech, since a significant amount of conversational text is available in English (for example, switchboard, call home, Fisher corpus etc.).

We show that we can reduce the WER for a DNN-based voice activity detector by adding an attention layer to the DNN architecture. We also show that increasing the vocabulary for languages in OpenASR21 with high out-of-vocabulary rate reduces the WER significantly.

Overall, for 13 of 18 languages, we reduced the WER for the single decode of the dev set when we combine the three enhancements. For Kazakh css by 5.9% (absolute), for Tagalog css by 4.9%, for Swahili css by 3.4%, for Somali by 1.2%, for Amharic and Georgian by 1.1%, for Farsi and Tamil by 0.9%, for Kazakh and Vietnamese by 0.7%, for Cantonese by 0.6%. These WER reductions are significant in the evaluation scenario.

Acknowledgments. The authors would like to thank Ministry of Economy and Innovation (MEI) of the Government of Quebec for the continued support.

References

1. Alumäe, T., Kong, J.: Combining hybrid and end-to-end approaches for the OpenASR20 challenge. In: Proceedings of the Interspeech, pp. 4349–4353 (2021)
2. Ghahremani, P., Manohar, V., Povey, D., Khudanpur, S.: Acoustic modelling from the signal domain using CNNs. In: Proceedings of the Interspeech, pp. 3434–3438 (2016)
3. Goldstein, H., Healy, M.J.R.: The graphical presentation of a collection of means. J. Roy. Stat. Soc.: Ser. A: Appl. Stat. **158**, 175–177 (1995)
4. Gupta, V., Boulianne, G.: CRIM's speech recognition system for OpenASR21 evaluation with conformer and voice activity detector embeddings. In: Prasanna, S.R.M., Karpov, A., Samudravijaya, K., Agrawal, S.S. (eds.) Speech and Computer, pp. 238–251. Springer International Publishing, Cham (2022). https://doi.org/10.1007/978-3-031-20980-2_21
5. Han, K.J., Pan, J., Tadala, V.K.N., Ma, T., Povey, D.: Multistream CNN for robust acoustic modeling. In: Proceedings of the ICASSP, pp. 6873–6877 (2021)
6. Hasegawa-Johnson, M., Rolston, L., Goudeseune, C., Levow, G.-A., Kirchhoff, K.: Grapheme-to-phoneme transduction for cross-language ASR. In: Espinosa-Anke, L., Martín-Vide, C., Spasić, I. (eds.) SLSP 2020. LNCS (LNAI), vol. 12379, pp. 3–19. Springer, Cham (2020). https://doi.org/10.1007/978-3-030-59430-5_1
7. Novak, J.R., Minematsu, N., Hirose, K.: Phonetisaurus: exploring grapheme-to-phoneme conversion with joint n-gram models in the WFST framework. Nat. Lang. Eng. **22**(6), 907–938 (2016). https://doi.org/10.1017/S1351324915000315
8. Park, D.S., et al.: SpecAugment: a simple data augmentation method for automatic speech recognition. In: Proceedings of the Interspeech, pp. 2613–2617 (2019)
9. Peddinti, V., Povey, D., Khudanpur, S.: A time delay neural network architecture for efficient modeling of long temporal contexts. In: Proceedings of the Interspeech, pp. 3214–3218 (2015)
10. Peterson, K., Tong, A., Yu, Y.: OpenASR20: an open challenge for automatic speech recognition of conversational telephone speech in low-resource languages. In: Proceedings of the Interspeech, pp. 4324–4328 (2021)
11. Peterson, K., Tong, A.N., Yu, J.: OpenASR21: The second open challenge for automatic speech recognition of low-resource languages. In: Proceedings of the Interspeech (2022)
12. Povey, D., et al.: The Kaldi speech recognition toolkit. In: Proceedings of the ASRU (2011)
13. Povey, D., Hadian, H., Ghahremani, P., Li, K., Khudanpur, S.: A time-restricted self-attention layer for ASR. In: 2018 IEEE International Conference on Acoustics, Speech and Signal Processing (ICASSP), pp. 5874–5878 (2018). https://doi.org/10.1109/ICASSP.2018.8462497

14. Sak, H., Senior, A.W., Beaufays, F.: Long short-term memory recurrent neural network architectures for large scale acoustic modeling (2014)
15. Sennrich, R., Haddow, B., Birch, A.: Improving Neural Machine Translation Models with Monolingual Data. In: Proceedings of ACL, pp. 86–96 (2016)
16. Sethy, A., Georgiou, P.G., Ramabhadran, B., Narayanan, S.: An iterative relative entropy minimization-based data selection approach for n-Gram model adaptation. IEEE Trans. Audio Speech Lang. Process. **17**(1), 13–23 (2009)
17. Zhao, J., et al.: The TNT team system descriptions of cantonese and mongolian for IARPA OpenASR20. In: Proceedings of the Interspeech, pp. 4344–4348 (2021)
18. Zhao, J., et al.: The THUEE system description for the IARPA OpenASR21 challenge. In: Proceedings of Interspeech, pp. 4855–4859 (2022). https://doi.org/10.21437/Interspeech.2022-649
19. Zhong, G., et al.: external text based data augmentation for low-resource speech recognition in the constrained condition of OpenASR21 challenge. In: Proceedings of Interspeech, pp. 4860–4864 (2022). https://doi.org/10.21437/Interspeech.2022-649

Phone Durations Modeling for Livvi-Karelian ASR

Irina Kipyatkova(✉) ⓘ and Ildar Kagirov ⓘ

St. Petersburg Federal Research Center of the Russian Academy of Sciences (SPC RAS),
14th Line, 39, 199178 St. Petersburg, Russia
{kipyatkova,kagirov}@iias.spb.su

Abstract. This paper presents the results of experiments conducted during development of an automatic speech recognition system for the low-resource Karelian language (Livvi-Karelian dialect). The main issues addressed within this work are related to acoustic modeling, viz. the treatment of long and short phonemes. There are two approaches to modeling phonological duration in the so-called quantity languages: representation of long and short phonemes as distinct units, and interpretation of long phonemes as reduplicated. There is currently no consensus on which strategy is the most promising. The Livvi-Karelian case is further complicated by the fact that the phonology of Karelian was heavily influenced by Russian, so that a direct transfer of the methods applied to other Balto-Finnic languages is questionable. In the course of the study, experiments were conducted with both approaches, showing that treating long phonemes as reduplicated outperforms the approaches implying introduction of long and short counterparts in the phoneme set. The usage of alternative transcriptions for words with long consonants further improved the recognition accuracy. In addition, the present study contributes to the application of DNN approaches to the tasks of language and acoustic modeling in low-resource languages. In the future works, it is planned to improve the performance of the developed system with transfer techniques and advanced data augmentation procedures.

Keywords: Low-Resource Languages · Automatic Speech Recognition · Livvi-Karelian · Phoneme Duration Modeling

1 Introduction

Automatic speech recognition (ASR) systems play an important role in various domains, such as the development of voice assistants, speech-to-text applications and language learning tools. For a variety of languages, however, the accurate modeling of phoneme durations is crucial for ensuring high recognition accuracy, as the duration of phonemes can carry important linguistic information. The aim of this paper is to investigate and compare two distinct approaches for acoustic modeling in quantity languages (i.e., languages with phonemic distinction between long and short sounds): modeling long and short phonemes as separate units versus representing long phonemes as a sequence of two (or more) short phonemes. The research is conducted on the data from the low-resource Karelian language (Livvi-Karelian dialect).

© The Author(s), under exclusive license to Springer Nature Switzerland AG 2023
A. Karpov et al. (Eds.): SPECOM 2023, LNAI 14339, pp. 87–99, 2023.
https://doi.org/10.1007/978-3-031-48312-7_7

Among the main tasks of this research are evaluating the accuracy of word recognition (WER metrics) when using separate models for long and short phonemes, and comparing this approach with modeling long phonemes as reduplicated units.

In the following sections of the paper, a detailed description of the current approaches to the problem is provided, the collected database and the experiments conducted are presented. The obtained results, including the analysis of the advantages and limitations of different approaches to modeling long and short phonemes in Livvi-Karelian ASR, is discussed among other things. In the conclusion, the research findings and their practical significance, as well as future work projects are outlined.

2 Related Work

2.1 Speech Recognition for Low-Resource Languages

Nowadays, there are two main approaches to development of ASR systems: "traditional" and end-to-end approaches. In the traditional approaches, ASR system is compound of several components: acoustic model (AM), language model (LM), and Pronunciation model (PM). The AM is responsible for mapping acoustic features of each frame to phonetic units, specifically phonemes. The LM associates the phoneme sequence generated by the AM with the sentence having the highest probability. On the contrary, in end-to-end ASR systems there is a single neural model transforming the speech signal to sequence of words [1–3]. Although end-to-end is a state-of-the-art approach showing better performance in terms of decoding speed, it typically requires large training data, and its performance has not surpassed that of traditional models in low-resource speech recognition tasks [4]. Thus, the end-to-end approach is not applicable to low-resource languages, that is, languages for which little data (regarding natural language processing tasks) exists by definition.

Currently, deep neural networks (DNNs) are extensively employed for training both acoustic and language models in ASR systems. For acoustic modeling DNNs are often combined with Hidden Markov Models (HMMs), thus forming hybrid DNN/HMM model. This approach has gained popularity due to its high performance in various applications. For instance, in [5], hybrid DNN/HMM acoustic models were employed for a Sinhala language ASR system. The results demonstrated that these models outperformed HMMs based on Gaussian Mixture Models (GMMs) by achieving a 7.48% improvement in word error rate (WER) on the test dataset.

In another study [6], experiments were conducted on multilingual speech recognition, focusing on low-resource languages including North American Cree and Inuit languages. The researchers investigated the use of factorized time delay neural networks (TDNN-Fs) in hybrid DNN/HMM acoustic models. The findings indicated that this architecture outperformed LSTM-based networks in terms of WER. Similar conclusions were drawn in [7] for the Somali language dataset.

A number of papers addressing languages of India has shown effectiveness of TDNNs in tasks related with low-resource ASRs. For example, the authors of [8] presented research of the application of TDNNs, comparing them with bi-directional residual memory networks (BRMN) and bi-directional LSTM. They reported WER of 13.92%, 14.71%, and 14.06% for Tamil, Telugu, and Gujarati, respectively, using the TDNN and BRMN systems. The authors employed a Kneser-Ney 3-g LM in their study. The introduction of low-rank TDNN with skip connections resulted in an improvement of 0.6–1.1% over the baseline TDNN.

The paper [9] explored the phonetic characteristics relevant to enhancing ASR performance in low-resource Indian languages. They proposed a multilingual TDNN system based on phonetic information. The researchers used a speech corpus provided by Microsoft to construct a system for Gujarati, which exhibited a gradual reduction in WER from GMM (16.95%) to DNN (14.38%) and further to TDNN (12.7%) systems.

Language modeling for low-resource languages is typically performed by n-gram models and recurrent neural network (RNN) based models, with n-gram being applied at the decoding stage, and RNN-based model being applied at the N-best or lattice rescoring stage. For example, this approach was used in [10] for the Sesotho and Zulu languages. The advantage of RNN-based LMs is that they can store the whole context preceding the given word in contrast to feed-forward NNs and n-grams, which store a context of restricted length. It was shown in a range of works, that these types of models have lower perplexity and allows achieving lower WER [11, 12].

Phonemic vocabulary of an ASR system is usually developed automatically by applying some rules converting a sequence of graphemes (letters) to a sequence of phonemic symbols which represent the sounds of speech. When developing ASR systems for Balto-Finnic languages, such as Estonian and Finnish, it is important to consider such features of these languages, as phoneme quantity distinctions. The next section provides the reader with a notion of different approaches to phoneme quantity modeling in ASR for Balto-Finnic languages, focusing on the Finnish and Estonian languages as illustrative examples.

2.2 Approaches to Phoneme Duration Modeling

In Balto-Finnic languages both vowels and consonants exhibit short, long, and overlong (Estonian) quantity degrees [13]. Often these languages are referred to as "quantity languages" due to a significant role of phoneme quantity degrees (as well as other prosodic features like stress and tone). For instance, the variation in the realization of the vowel /a/ as short, long, or overlong in Estonian can result in different meanings for words such as *kalu* ('fish', partitive plural), *kaalu* ('weight', genitive singular), and *kaa:lu* ('weight', partitive singular).

Duration functions in a tool of encoding linguistic information in quantity languages. While some languages, including English, use duration primarily for prosodic purposes such as stress and boundary signaling, quantity languages utilize duration to distinguish between lexical units (see the example above). Studies on various quantity languages have shown that the durational ratios between short and long phonemes remain relatively stable across different articulation rates, indicating their perceptual significance [14]. Absolute durations alone may not be sufficient to convey the quantity distinction, but rather, durational ratios and other acoustic cues contribute to the perception of quantity [15].

When modeling phoneme quantity, researchers typically do not treat different quantity degree representations of the same phoneme type as separate phonological units. Instead, they are represented as one or a sequence of two instances of the same phoneme [16]. The main reason for this approach is that the determination of long/short and long/overlong quantity degrees goes beyond the characteristics of individual phoneme realizations. It depends on the prosodic variables of neighboring syllables and the over-all syllable/word structure.

Another approach implies treating long/short long/overlong as independent phonemes. For example, in [17] distinctive models for short and long variants of all phones (except /j/) were developed for Estonian. However, the distinction between long and overlong duration is argued to be difficult to model and thus was ignored in acoustic modeling by the authors, being unnecessary in written word forms, as they are not visible in orthography except for a few exceptions.

To model long and short durational ratios, a direct expansion of HMM by including an explicit duration model was used in [18], resulting in what is known as hidden semi-Markov models (HSMMs). Other approaches use forced alignment HMM for the computation of duration features [19, 20]. Consequently, HMM states can be expanded into sub-HMMs that share the same acoustic emission density, allowing for explicit modeling of state durations. This modified model is referred to as the expanded state HMM [21]. Unfortunately, both of these techniques tend to reduce recognition efficiency, as stated in [22, 23].

During the current research the authors investigate the modeling of long sounds by selecting appropriate phoneme set taking into account phoneme duration without modification of HMM framework and topology for Livvi-Karelian ASR.

3 Karelian Text and Speech Corpus

Text and speech corpora are used for training ASR system. The text corpus used within this study is based on the data obtained from publications and journals in Livvi-Karelian. In addition, some texts were imported from the open corpus of Vepsian and Karelian VepKar [24]. Another source for text data were transcripts of audio samples from the training part of speech corpus (see below). The text corpus encompasses diverse styles of speech, such as literary, reportage, and colloquial. A portion of the texts were initially in.pdf format and required semi-automatic text recognition for further processing. All texts were eventually made available in.txt format.

During the preparation of the corpus, the data underwent processing and normalization procedures. This involved segmenting texts into sentences, and converting direct and indirect speech clauses into independent sentences.

Further text modifications were made as well. All texts enclosed in brackets were removed, capital letters were converted to lowercase, and punctuation marks were removed. In earlier Karelian editions the grapheme "ü" can be found, and additional work was made to substitute it with "y". To ensure the integrity of the textual data, a thorough assessment was conducted to identify duplicate sentences, as the texts were obtained from different sources, so that the duplication of content was highly plausible. The corpus encompassed approximately 5M word occurrences.

One way of speech corpus collection in scenarios involving low-resource languages, established methodologies often involve the active participation of speakers (readers) who read prepared utterances or a coherent text. Another effective approach for collecting speech data entails utilizing freely accessible speech resources. In the present study, speech data was acquired from radio broadcasts in Livvi-Karelian. A total of 10 broadcasts were used, each broadcast structured in an interview format, featuring a minimum of two speakers (the interviewer and an interviewee). It should be noted that in some broadcasts more than two speakers were present, and interviewers occasionally participated in more than one broadcast. However, no interviewee took part in recording sessions twice. Thus, the recorded speech corpus encompassed 15 speakers, comprising 6 men and 9 women.

The recorded speech data underwent transcription and segmentation (divided into separate statements) procedures conducted by experts in Livvi-Karelian. One significant problem encountered during annotation of texts was simultaneous speech issues, i.e., simultaneous speech from multiple speakers, with interruptions or overlapping. Managing speech overlaps is a complex task, and therefore, phrases containing simultaneous speech of two speakers were excluded from the corpus.

Background noise constituted another factor that hindered the development of the audio corpus. Despite utilizing studio quality recordings, of background noise (music, sounds of turning pages, street noise) were detected. All recordings containing background noise were ultimately removed from the database.

A notable feature of modern Karelian is code-switching [25]. In linguistics, this term generally refers to the spontaneous transition from one language to another. The processing of code-switching in speech recognition demands specialized approaches that were not initially planned for implementation in the system's development. Therefore, all utterances featuring code-switching were excluded from the speech corpus as well.

Proper names present a distinct problem, as they are predominantly borrowed from the Russian language and pronounced according to the Russian phonetic rules. Specifically, stress patterns in names exhibit variability in line with Russian pronunciation. While this problem has yet to be resolved, the most rational solution appears to be compiling a separate dictionary specifically for proper names and transcribing them in accordance with Russian phonetics.

After excluding spoiled segments, the resulting speech corpus amounted to a total duration of more than 3 h (3,819 sentences). The corpus was randomly divided into training and test sets, with 90% of the phrases assigned to the training set and 10% to the test set.

Data augmentation served as an additional tool for expanding the speech data. In this study, augmentation was exclusively applied to the training portion of the speech corpus, utilizing the Sox toolkit [26]. A tempo perturbation augmentation technique was applied to the speech data, the speech rate was varied using a randomly generated coefficient from a uniform distribution ranging between 0.7 and 1.3 for each recording. The augmented speech data was further combined with the authentic training data. As a result, the overall duration of the training data increased from 3 h and 8 min to 6 h and 24 min.

4   Development of a Phonemic Vocabulary

One of the essential prerequisites for developing an automated speech recognition system is the availability of a phonemic transcription dictionary containing words employed by the system. For this purpose, it is necessary to determine a set of phonemes. The main problem arising when creating phoneme set for Karelian is how to treat long sounds. During the current research several types of phoneme alphabet for Karelian were investigated:

- without distinguishing the long sounds (v1);
- treating the long sounds as independent phonemes (v2);
- long vowels are treated as independent sounds, long consonants are treated as reduplicated of the given sound (v3);
- long vowels, as well as long sonorants and fricative consonants are treated as independent sounds, long plosive consonants are treated as reduplicated phonemes (v4).

It should be noted that in all variants of phoneme set, distinctions were made between stressed and unstressed phonemes, additionally, the back row allophone of the /i/ phoneme was considered as an independent phoneme (/i^/). As for consonants, both palatalized and non-palatalized variants were distinguished. The lists of phonemes used in phoneme sets are presented in Table 1. The transcriptions follow the International Phonetic Alphabet (IPA); additionally, the symbol /!/ indicates word stress, and the symbol /'/ represents consonant palatalization. Symbol /:/ means long sound in these phoneme set variants, which distinguish long phonemes as separate phonemes.

There are two main issues to be noted. Although not all phonemes in the standard Livvi-Karelian have long counterparts, some Livvi-Karelian idioms (mainly, local variants) and borrowings from Russian exhibit long phonemes that are not present in the system of the standard Livvi-Karelian. Due to their infrequent use, it is quite difficult to train acoustic models for such "non-native" long sounds. As a consequence, separate phonemes for these sounds were not introduced (for example, the word *seemejärven* was transcribed as /s' e! m' e j ae r v' e n/). However, when treating long sounds as a sequence of two short phonemes, the "non-native" long phonemes were presented as two separate phonemes (for example, *subbotin* was transcribed to /s u! b b o t'i n/).

The second issue is that in spontaneous speech durational ratios are often reduced, and long sounds may be pronounced as short ones. This is especially true for long Plosive consonants that should be pronounced as two separate sounds, but the second sound is often subject to elision. This is illustrated in Fig. 1 where examples of two realizations of phoneme /k'/ in the word *kaikkie* are shown. In Fig. 1a this sound is realized as a two-sound cluster, one can see repetition of closure and explosion on the waveform. In Fig. 1b, the second sound is omitted and the long phone is realized as a short one. Therefore, when creating phonemic transcriptions for words with long consonants and when treating long sounds as reduplicated ones, two alternative transcriptions were created, namely, a transcription with a reduplicated sound and a transcription with one sound. For example, for word "*kaikkie*" two transcriptions were generated: /k a! i k' k' i e/ and /k a! i k' i e/.

All transcriptions for the vocabulary were created automatically using a software module developed for grapheme-phoneme transformation for Livvi-Karelian. Due to the inherent limitations of automatic recognition techniques for printed Karelian texts, words that occurred only once most often turned out to be incorrectly recognized. Therefore, the dictionary includes all words from the transcripts of the training part of speech corpus and words from other sources that were attested at least twice. The final size of the dictionary was 143.5 thousand words.

Table 1. Types of phoneme sets.

Type of phoneme set	Number of phonemes	Type of phonemes		Phoneme List
v1	53	Vowels	Stressed	/a!/, /o!/, /u!/, /i!/, /i^!/, /e!/, /ae!/, /oe!/, /y!/
			Unstressed	/a/, /o/, /u/, /i/, /i^/, /e/, /ae/, /oe/, /y/
		Consonants	Sonorant	/l/, /l'/, /m/, /m'/, /n/, /n'/, /r/, /r'/, /j/
			Fricative	ch/, /ts/, /h/, /h'/, /f/, /f'/, /s/, /s'/, /sh/, /z/, /z'/, /zh/, /v/, /v'/
			Plosive	/b/, /b'/, /d/, /d'/, /g/, /g'/, /k/, /k'/,/p/, /p'/, /t/, /t'/
v2	90	Vowels	Stressed	v1 + /a:!/, /o:!/, /u:!/, /i:!/, /i^:!/, /ae:!/, /y:!/
			Unstressed	v1 + /a:/, /o:/, /u:/, /i:/, /i^:/, /ae:/, /y:/
		Consonants	Sonorant	v1 + /l:/, /l':/, /m:/, /m':/, /n:/, /n':/, /r:/, /r':/
			Fricative	v1 + /ch:/, /ts:/, /h':/, /s:/, /s':/, /sh:/, /v:/, /v':/
			Plosive	v1 + /d':/, /k:/, /k':/,/p:/, /p':/, /t:/, /t':/
v3	67	Vowels	Stressed	v2
			Unstressed	v2
		Consonants	Sonorant	v1
			Fricative	v1
			Plosive	v1
v4	83	Vowels	Stressed	v2
			Unstressed	v2
		Consonants	Sonorant	v2
			Fricative	v2
			Plosive	v1

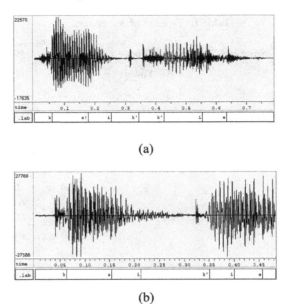

(a)

(b)

Fig. 1. Examples of realization of long phoneme /k'/: a) the long sound is pronounced as two sounds; b) the long sound is pronounced as one sound.

In the case of the Karelian language, generating automatic transcriptions represents a relatively straightforward task. This arises from the fixed stress patterns in Karelian, which consistently fall on the initial syllable, while vowel reduction is infrequent. As a result, the automatic transcription process primarily deals with stress localization, identifying dual graphemes as representations of long phonemes, and finding palatalized consonants preceding front vowels.

5   Karelian ASR System

5.1   Acoustic Modeling

Training and testing of a Karelian ASR system was carried out using the Kaldi toolkit [27]. The architecture of the system is shown in Fig. 2.

Hybrid DNN/HMMs acoustic models based on factorized time-delay neural network (TDNN-F) were used. Mel-frequency cepstral coefficients (MFCCs) with additional 100-dimensional i-vector [28] were used as input features to the network.

The core structure of the DNN consisted of three TDNN-F blocks. The initial block was made up of three TDNN-F layers, responsible for processing input vectors (time context of $\{-1, 0, 1\}$). The next block was a single TDNN-F layer (no splicing). The last block comprised ten TDNN-F layers (time context of $\{-3, 0, 3\}$). Each TDNN-F layer had a dimension of 1024, with a bottleneck of 128.

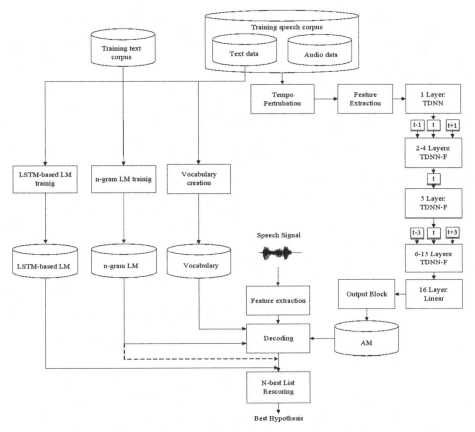

Fig. 2. The Karelian Speech Recognition System.

A Rectified Linear Unit (ReLU) activation function and batch normalization followed each TDNN layers in TDNN blocks. Utilizing skip connections [29], the TDNN layers incorporated the output of each layer (excluding the first layer) by concatenating it with the output of the previous layers. After the TDNN-F layers, a linear layer with a dimension of 256 was employed. The learning rate dynamically adjusted during the training process, starting at 0.0005 and decreasing to 0.00005. The training process was performed in 8 epochs.

5.2 Language Modeling

Both n-gram and LSTM-based LMs were developed, a linear interpolation of these models was made as well. 3-g LM was trained using SRI Language Modeling Toolkit (SRILM) [30]. This model was used at the decoding stage.

LSTM-based LM was trained with the use of TheanoLM toolkit [31]. Experiments were conducted with models with 1, 2 and 3 LSTM layers, the size of LSTM layers was 512. In the models with 2 and 3 LSTM layers dropout at rate 0.5 between LSTM layers was applied. Optimization criteria was Nesterov Momentum. The initial learning rate was equal to 1. The stopping criteria was "no-improvement", which means that learning rate is halved when validation set perplexity stops improving, and training is stopped when the perplexity does not improve at all with the current learning rate [31]. The maximum number of training epoch was 15.

6 Experiments on Karelian Speech Recognition

The results of experiments on Karelian speech recognition are presented in Table 2. Experiments with different types of phoneme sets, as described above, were conducted. When applying phoneme set v3, two types of phonemic transcriptions were applied: those with alternative pronunciation variants for reduplicated consonants and those with a single pronunciation variant. At the decoding stage 3-g LM was applied, while LSTM-based LM and interpolated models were used at the stage of 500-best list rescoring. In the Table 2 the interpolation coefficient of 0 means that only 3-g LM was used (without 500-best list rescoring). In contrast, interpolation coefficient of 1.0 means that 500-best list rescoring was performed using only LSTM LM.

Table 2. Results of Karelian Speech Recognition in Terms of WER, %

Type of phonemic transcription	Interpolation coefficient for LSTM LM						
	0	0.5	0.6	0.7	0.8	0.9	1.0
v1	27.40	24.78	24.70	24.54	24.78	24.86	25.02
v2	26.29	23.63	23.51	23.55	23.43	23.31	23.51
v3 (without alternative transcriptions for words with long sounds)	25.93	23.43	23.39	23.24	23.24	23.31	23.28
v3 (with alternative transcriptions for words with long sounds)	25.57	23.04	**22.80**	22.88	23.08	23.39	23.67
v4 (with alternative transcriptions for words with long plosive consonants)	25.69	23.67	23.47	23.67	23.87	24.03	24.31

As can be seen from the Table 2, phoneme set with reduplicated consonants (v3) demonstrated better results than this treating long consonants as distinct phonemes (v2). Additionally, the results obtained with this type of phoneme set were better than when using only reduplicated phonemes for plosives. The usage of alternative transcriptions for words with long consonants resulted in additional performance improvement. The best speech recognition results were achieved after rescoring of 500-best list with LSTM LM interpolated with 3-g LM. Application of LSTM-based LM interpolated with n-gram LM with interpolation coefficient of 0.6 for N-best list rescoring resulted in 11% WER relative reduction.

7   Conclusions and Future Work

This paper presents an investigation of different approaches to acoustic modeling for a Livvi-Karelian ASR, focusing on phoneme durations representation issues. Two main approaches were compared within the study: modeling long and short phonemes as separate units vs. representing long phonemes as a sequence of two (or more) short phonemes. The experiments were conducted on a dataset collected by the authors of this paper, and the main metric for evaluation of the results obtained was WER.

The results of experiments have shown, that treating long phonemes as reduplicated units, specifically for plosive consonants, demonstrated superior performance over the approach implying differentiation of long and short phonemes. The usage of alternative transcriptions for words with long consonants further improved the recognition accuracy.

Additionally, different language modeling techniques, including n-gram and LSTM-based models, were investigated. The experiments showed that incorporating LSTM-based language models, especially when interpolated with n-gram models, significantly reduced the WER and improved the overall performance of the developed ASR.

Overall, the idea of using hybrid DNN/HMMs AM with TDNN-Fs combined with LSTM-based LM, demonstrated its effectiveness for processing low-resource languages. The system achieved promising results in WER despite the relatively small amount of training data.

Although the present research has provided positive results in the acoustic and language modeling approaches for low-resource speech recognition, there are several issues to be addressed in future work that can potentially enhance the system's performance:

- Data augmentation: in the experiments, tempo perturbation technique was applied to data augmentation. However, exploring other augmentation techniques, such as spectrogram modification or data generation, could improve the robustness of the developed ASR.
- Incorporating prosodic features: Livvi-Karelian, being a quantity language, relies not only on phoneme durations but also on other prosodic features like stress and tone, to convey different semantical nuances. Future work can explore the embedding of different prosodic models into the current system to process Livvi-Karelian speech more accurately. Additionally, using more advanced techniques, such as hidden semi-Markov models, may result in better representation of phoneme durations and improvement of recognition accuracy.
- Knowledge transfer from other (Balto-Finnic) languages: the techniques and approaches used in this study can be enhanced through models developed for other languages sharing similar phonetic and prosodic characteristics. Investigating the applicability of the data from other (Balto-Finnic) languages, viz. Languages with quantity distinctions as well as the usage of pre-trained multilingual model can contribute to the developed system.

By addressing these issues in future works, the authors of this paper are going to contribute to the development of robust and accurate ASRs for low-resource languages.

Acknowledgements. This research was funded by the Russian Science Foundation, grant number № 22-21-00843.

References

1. Wang, D., Wang, X., Lv, S.: An overview of end-to-end automatic speech recognition. Symmetry **11**(8), 1018 (2019)
2. Bahdanau, D., Chorowski, J., Serdyuk, D., Brakel, P., Bengio, Y.: End-to-end attention-based large vocabulary speech recognition. In: Proceedings of 2016 IEEE International Conference on Acoustics, Speech and Signal Processing (ICASSP), pp. 4945–4949. The Institute of Electrical and Electronics Engineers (2016)
3. Hori, T., Watanabe, S., Zhang, Y., Chan, W.: Advances in joint CTC-attention based end-to-end speech recognition with a deep CNN encoder and RNN-LM. In: Proceedings of the 18th Annual Conference of the International Speech Communication Association (Interspeech), pp. 949–953. International Speech Communication Association (2017)
4. Sun, X., Yang, Q., Liu, S., Yuan, X.: Improving low-resource speech recognition based on improved NN-HMM structures. IEEE Access **8**, 73005–73014 (2020)
5. Karunathilaka, H., Welgama, V., Nadungodage, T., Weerasinghe, R.: Low-resource Sinhala speech recognition using deep learning. In: Proceedings of 20th International Conference on Advances in ICT for Emerging Regions (ICTer), pp. 196–201. The Institute of Electrical and Electronics Engineers (2020)
6. Gupta, V., Boulianne, G.: Progress in multilingual speech recognition for low resource languages Kurmanji Kurdish, Cree and Inuktut. In: Proceedings of the 13th Conference on Language Resources and Evaluation (LREC), pp. 6420–6428. European Language Resources Association (2022)
7. Biswas, A., Menon, R., van der Westhuizen, E., Niesler, Th.: Improved low-resource Somali speech recognition by semi-supervised acoustic and language model training. In: Proceedings of 20th Annual Conference of the International Speech Communication Association (Interspeech), pp. 3008–3012. International Speech Communication Association (2019)
8. Pulugundla, B., et al.: BUT system for low resource Indian language ASR. In: Proceedings of 20th Annual Conference of the International Speech Communication Association (Interspeech), pp. 3182–3186. International Speech Communication Association (2019)
9. Fathima, N., Patel, T., Mahima, C., Iyengar, A.: TDNN-based multilingual speech recognition system for low resource Indian languages. In: Proceedings of 19th Annual Conference of the International Speech Communication Association (Interspeech), pp. 3197–3201. International Speech Communication Association (2018)
10. Wills, S., Uys, P., van Heerden, C.J., Barnard, E.: Language modeling for speech analytics in under-resourced languages. In: Proceedings of 21st Annual Conference of the International Speech Communication Association (Interspeech), pp. 4941–4945. International Speech Communication Association (2020)
11. Sundermeyer, M., Ney, H., Schlüter, R.: From feedforward to recurrent LSTM neural networks for language modeling. IEEE/ACM Trans. Audio Speech Lang. Process. **23**(3), 517–529 (2015)
12. Kipyatkova, I.: LSTM-based language models for very large vocabulary continuous Russian speech recognition system. In: Salah, A.A., Karpov, A., Potapova, R. (eds.) SPECOM 2019. LNCS (LNAI), vol. 11658, pp. 219–226. Springer, Cham (2019). https://doi.org/10.1007/978-3-030-26061-3_23
13. Metslang, H.: North and standard estonian. In: Bakró-Nagy, M., Laakso, J., Skribnik, E. (eds.) The Oxford Guide to the Uralic Languages, pp. 350–366. Oxford Academic, Oxford (2022)
14. Nakai, S., Kunnari, S., Turk, A., Suomi, K., Ylitalo, R.: Utterance-final lengthening and quantity in Northern Finnish. J. Phon. **37**(1), 29–45 (2009)
15. Traunmüller, H., Krull, D.: The effect of local speaking rate on the perception of quantity in Estonian. Phonetica **60**, 187–207 (2003)

16. Alumäe, T., Vohandu, L.: Limited-vocabulary Estonian continuous speech recognition system using Hidden Markov models. Informatica **15**(3), 303–314 (2004)
17. Alumäe, T.: Recent improvements in Estonian LVCSR. In: Proceedings of 4th Workshop on Spoken Language Technologies for Under-Resourced Languages (SLTU 2014), pp. 118–123. European Language Resources association (2014)
18. Kermanshahi, M.A., Homayounpour, M.M.: Improving phoneme sequence recognition using phoneme duration information in DNN-HSMM. J. Artif. Intell. Data Min. **7**(1), 137–147 (2019)
19. Qin, Y., Lee, T., Kong, A.P.H., Law, S.P.: Towards automatic assessment of aphasia speech using automatic speech recognition techniques. In: Proceedings of 2016 10th International Symposium on Chinese Spoken Language Processing (ISCSLP), pp. 1–4. The Institute of Electrical and Electronics Engineers (2016)
20. Rosenfelder, I., et al.: FAVE (Forced Alignment and Vowel Extraction) Suite Version 1.1.3. Software. https://doi.org/10.5281/zenodo.9846. Accessed 13 July 2023
21. Johnson, M.: Capacity and complexity of HMM duration modeling techniques. IEEE Signal Process. Lett. **12**(5), 407–410 (2005)
22. Pylkkönen, J.: Phone duration modeling techniques in continuous speech recognition. Master's thesis, Helsinki University of Technology (2004)
23. Pylkkönen, J., Kurimo, M.: Using phone durations in finnish large vocabulary continuous speech recognition. In: Proceedings of the 6th Nordic Signal Processing Symposium (NORSIG), pp. 324–327. The Institute of Electrical and Electronics Engineers (2005)
24. VEPKAR. http://dictorpus.krc.karelia.ru/en. Accessed 13 July 2023
25. Kovaleva, S.V., Rodionova, A.P.: Traditional and Innovative in the Vocabulary and Grammar of Karelian (Based on a Socio-Linguistic Research). KarNC RAN Publ., Petrozavodsk (2011). (in Russian)
26. Sox Toolkit. http://sox.sourceforge.net/sox.html. Accessed 13 July 2023
27. Povey, D., et al.: The Kaldi speech recognition toolkit. In: Proceedings of 2011 IEEE Workshop on Automatic Speech Recognition and Understanding (ASRU), pp. 1–4. Institute of Electrical and Electronics Engineers (2011)
28. Saon, G., Soltau, H., Nahamoo, D., Picheny, M.: Speaker adaptation of neural network acoustic models using i-vectors. In: Proceedings of 2013 IEEE Workshop on Automatic Speech Recognition and Understanding (ASRU), pp. 55–59. Institute of Electrical and Electronics Engineers (2013)
29. Povey, D., et al.: Semi-orthogonal low-rank matrix factorization for deep neural networks. In: Proceedings of 19th Annual Conference of the International Speech Communication Association (Interspeech), pp. 3743–3747. International Speech Communication Association (2018)
30. Stolcke, A., Zheng, J., Wang, W., Abrash, V.: SRILM at sixteen: update and outlook. In: Proceedings of 2011 IEEE Workshop on Automatic Speech Recognition and Understanding (ASRU), p. 5. Institute of Electrical and Electronics Engineers (2011)
31. Enarvi, S., Kurimo, M.: TheanoLM – an extensible toolkit for neural network language modeling. In: Proceedings of the 17th Annual Conference of the International Speech Communication Association (Interspeech), pp. 3052–3056. International Speech Communication Association (2016)

Significance of Indic Self-supervised Speech Representations for Indic Under-Resourced ASR

Sougata Mukherjee[✉], Jagabandhu Mishra, and S. R. Mahadeva Prasanna

Indian Institute of Technology Dharwad, Dharwad, India
{211022004,183081002,prasanna}@iitdh.ac.in

Abstract. Automatic speech recognition is a mature speech technology, almost able to attend human label recognition performance conditioned on the availability of sufficient labeled training data. However, the performance of the system struggles to achieve deployable performance in the under-resourced scenario. In such a scenario, most of the work suggests traditional frameworks are preferable over state-of-the-art deep learning frameworks. This work creates a dataset for the Lambani language of 6 hours duration, and attempts to develop an ASR system. The system provides a character error rate (CER) of 39.1% and 24.1% using the GMM-HMM framework and TDNN framework, respectively for Lambani dataset. The language doesn't have enough publicly available speech and corresponding text transcription resources of its own. Motivating by the same, this work uses the publicly available wav2vec2.0 (W2V) pre-trained model (trained on 23 Indian languages' unlabeled speech data) and fine-tuned it with the labeled data of the Lambani language. After that using the fine-tuned framework as a non-linear feature extractor, the ASR task is performed with GMM-HMM and TDNN framework. The proposed approach provides a relative improvement of 53.4% and 32.1% for the GMM-HMM and TDNN frameworks, respectively.

Keywords: Lambani · Wav2vec2.0 · GMM-HMM · TDNN · W2V Features · MFCC

1 Introduction

Automatic speech recognition (ASR) system converts the spoken utterances to the corresponding textual form. Generally building the state-of-art ASR systems requires a large amount of transcribed speech data having speaker variability, a pronunciation dictionary, and a large amount of text data for building the language model. However, it is difficult to get such repositories for an under-resourced language. On the other hand, to avoid the digital divide and encourage people to use speech-based applications in their own language, it is essential to develop ASR in such languages. Further, such technological intervention in their own language encourages people to use their own language, instead of

A. Karpov et al. (Eds.): SPECOM 2023, LNAI 14339, pp. 100–113, 2023.
https://doi.org/10.1007/978-3-031-48312-7_8

adopting to a resource-rich language. This may help in minimizing the conversion of the resource scare language to the dead language. With this motivation, this work initially attempts to create a dataset suitable for ASR development for the Lambani language. Lambani is a spoken language, doesn't have a written script, and is spoken by the tribal community of Western and Southern parts of India.

Gaussian Mixture Model (GMM)-Hidden Markov Model(HMM) and Time Delay Neural Network (TDNN) [13] are known to be the state-of-art classical approaches for building a speech recognition system. As these approaches do not require a high amount of data, these approaches may be suitable for under-resourced settings [13]. To further improve the performance, the improvement can be done in either of the three levels of the ASR framework, i.e. feature level, modeling level, and decision/hypothesis level. Out of these, this work focuses on the feature level to improve the ASR performance in under-resourced settings.

In wav2vec2.0 in the pretraining stage, the network is trained to predict the masked sub-word units in order to learn about the contextual information [9–11]. In [5], they have shown that when such a learned wav2vec2.0 pre-trained model is used for fine tuning on low-resourced settings it gives a decent performance. Taking motivation from there, in our work, we are using a fine tuned W2V model that has been trained on 23 Indian languages and 10,000 hours of data as a feature extractor. These extracted features are used for GMM-HMM and TDNN training for low-resourced settings in order to get improved performance

The rest of the paper is organized as follows:- Section 2 gives a description of how the lambani corpora was built. Section 3 shows the proposed framework for this paper. Section 4 gives a brief description about the available resources. Section 5 shows the results obtained using MFCC and speech representation extracted from self-supervised wav2vec2.0 approach. Finally, Sect. 6 concludes the report.

2 Building Lambani Corpora

2.1 Text Data Collection

Lambani is a language which has a spoken form, but written form of Lambani is not available. So, the written form of Lambani had to be prepared with a lot of manual effort and time. We had to make sure that the native Lambani speakers could articulate the words easily. So, initially 1000 English sentences containing a swadesh list [16] of words were prepared taking help from a Linguist. These are 4 to 10 word sentences. Examples of short and long sentences from the swadesh list include "All kids want sweet" and "Before I went to her house I changed my clothes". An ASR system requires several hours of speech data to train. The duration of the recording of the sentences containing Swadesh list of words vary from 2 to 4 words. So, the number of sentences had to be increased following the same procedure as discussed above. During the increment in the number of sentences text had to be extracted from several sources. Major sources of English sentences were NCERT and Wikipedia. Among the books published by NCERT, we focused on English language textbooks meant for the students of the lower, middle, and higher secondary schools. For retrieving text, we used text extractors written by us using the Python language. We used optical character recognition to extract sentences from publicly available scanned versions of the books on Lambani and languages using Adobe Reader's API.

2.2   Text Processing

The text data extracted from various sources like NCERT, wikipedia quite often contain incomplete sentences, semantically incorrect sentences, and long sentences which are difficult to speak. Hence The following preprocessing steps were applied to the raw text to improve the readability of the sentences.

- The passages of extracted text were processed to derive a set of sentences. The sentences containing fewer than 3 words were eliminated. Sentences longer than 10 words were removed as they will be difficult to utter for illiterate or older tribal people.
- Incomplete sentences, syntactically or semantically incorrect sentences, and sentences containing symbols and characters not present in the Roman script were removed.
- Sentences containing words that may be too complex for a tribal person to speak were discarded. Text containing controversial statements including political statements was removed from the set of sentences.

The English sentences that successfully passed through the above-mentioned preprocessing steps qualify to be a part of the sentence corpus. The selected English sentences were converted to the Kannada language (contact language) using the Kannada script as it was the formal language in the area. Then, those Kannada sentences were translated to the Lambadi language using the Kannada script by the Lambani native speakers. The Lambani text data in Kannada script was preserved in digital format by writing them in a spreadsheet.

2.3   Speech Files Recording

These sentences collected as text data were spoken by multiple native Lambani speakers which was recorded using Laptop. Graphical User Interface (GUI) was designed to collect data through Laptop. The Lambani sentence is displayed on the GUI. The recorded voice is replayed to assess its quality. If necessary, the GUI offers a feature to re-record the current sentence. Every speaker will record about one hour of data in seven sessions, which means almost 100 recordings per session. The GUI which is used for ASR recording has been shown in Fig. 1

The entire process of data collection strategy can be summarized in the flowchart 2

3   Related Work and Motivation

Efforts have been made to build speech recognition systems for under-resourced languages. But, due to the lack of resources, it becomes very difficult to

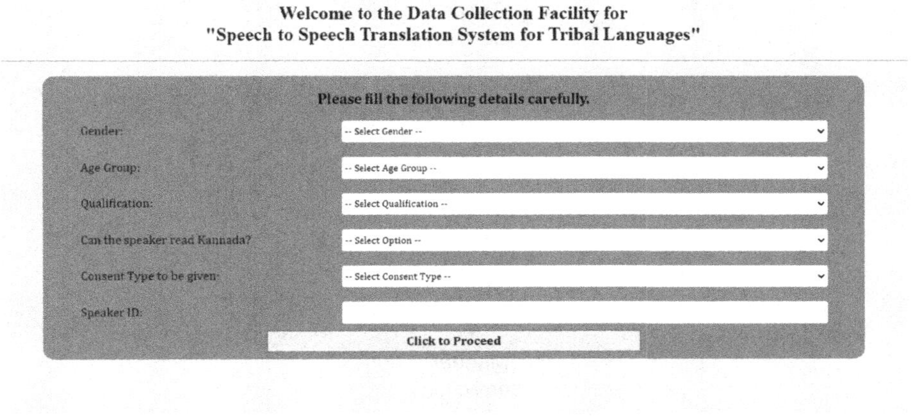

Fig. 1. GUI used for ASR recording

build such systems. Still, people have undergone research in this field applying various methodologies to overcome the challenges. Initially, ASR building for under-resourced language started with cross-lingual adaptation [8] of the Vietnamese language. They also tried to show the potential of cross-lingual context-dependent and independent modeling in this task. The same paper shows grapheme-based acoustic modeling when there is an absence of a pronunciation dictionary. With grapheme based acoustic modeling the performance that they have achieved using data-driven approach is an SLER of 43.9% and a WER of 50.6%.

In [18] they have shown that the performance obtained (36.5% accuracy) from a 30 dimensional posterior features multi-layer perceptron is trained on 15 hrs of German and 16 hrs of Spanish which is adapted to 1 hr of English so that several phonetic attributes of speech get covered from the out-of-language data. Almost in a similar approach, people showed the importance of bottleneck features and tandem features extracted from multi layer perceptron trained 15 hrs of German,16 hrs of Spanish trained on 1 hr of English (low-resource setting) for low-resource large vocabulary continuous speech recognition task [19]. In [6] they have explored multilingual information with KL-HMM when the available data is less than 75 mins and showed how the accuracy of KL-HMM varies with respect to other systems with increase in training data from 5 mins to 808 min. [17] they have explored the performance using both longer acoustic units which are syllables and shorter lexical and language modeling units i.e. morphemes. They have decomposed the rare syllables (if the number is less than 17.9%) into phones and trained the hybrid system. Importance of out-of-domain language data to improve the performance of under-resourced speech recognisers is shown in [7]. Here, they have shown that they are improving the performance using out-of-domain data that using 81 hrs of Dutch data along with 3 hrs of Afrikaans data they are achieving a improved phone accuracy of 68.8% with respect to

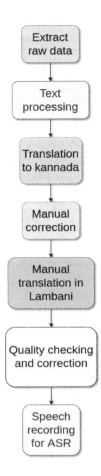

Fig. 2. ASR corpus creation flowchart

the monolingual system which gives a phone accuracy of 60.6%. They have also shown that KL-HMM is giving the best performance after acoustic model adaptation as compared to MLP, MLLR and MAP techniques. In [15] they have discovered a new speech feature named Intrinsic Spectral Analysis (ISA) which is performing better than FBANK,MFCC and PLP features. It gives a phone error rate of 10.42% on a training and testing set of 10.7 hrs and 2.2 hrs of Afrikaans language data. [2] shows that they have achieved best performance of 5.6%for Afrikaans language using multitask learning where they are learning the triphone senones and trigrapheme senones of multiple phonemes and a universal phone set and grapheme set which contains all the phones and graphemes of all the under-resourced languages Afrikaans, Siswati and Sesotho. The entire literature review is summarized in Table 1. [4,20] showed that training pre-trained weights helps to regularize and converge better rather than random initialization. Wav2vec2.0 is known to learn speech representations. So,in our work we

Table 1. Literature review of speech recognition systems for under-resurced languages

Authors	Language	Dataset	Techniques	Performance
Viet-Bac Le et al.	Vietnamese	Training-14 hrs Testing-408 sentences by 3 spkrs	Grapheme based AM	SLER-43.9% WER-50.6%
			Context dependent cross-lingual model adaptation	SLER-36.6% WER-42.7%
Thomas S et al.	English	Training-15 hrs German, 16 hrs Spanish, 1 hr English Testing-1.8 hrs	30D Multi-stream cross-lingual posterior features	Accuracy- 36.5%
Thomas S et al.	English	Training-15 hrs German, 16 hrs Spanish, 1 hr English Testing-1.8 hrs	DNN features	WA-41%
Imseng et al.	Afrikaans	Training-81 hrs Dutch, 3hrs Afrikaans Testing-50 mins	KL-HMM	PA-68.8%
Tachbelie et al.	Amharic	Training-20 hrs Testing-5K set from ATC_120K Corpus	Hybrid acoustic units (phones and syllables)	WER-17.9%
Sahraeian et al.	Afrikaans	Training-10.7 hrs Testing-2.2 hrs	Intrinsic spectral analysis for SGMM	PER-10.2%
Dongpeng et al.	Afrikaans	Train-3.37 hrs	Multitask learning of trigpaheme senones and triphone senones	WER-5.6%

are trying to learn speech representation from multiple Indic languages and then converge the weights accordingly to a particular language of an under-resourced setting.

4   Proposed Framework

As discussed in the previous section, self-supervised learning representations give better results as compared to hand-crafted features . So, MFCC is being replaced by self-supervised speech representations in order to get better performance for under-resource settings. For the build up of these framework we are adopting the following strategies:-

4.1   Character Level Speech Recognition

In this work, kaldi recipes have been used for building frameworks for GMM-HMM and TDNN. Generally, the GMM-HMM and TDNN recipes in kaldi [14] take either word level transcription or phone level transcription as input for training the model and give word level or phone level transcription as decoded output. But in our case due to the absence of a lexicon for under-resourced language Lambani we first built systems which take character level transcription as input for building the trained model and gives character level transcription as decoded output.

For, GMM-HMM framework we have used the TIMIT recipe. There we have replaced the phone level transcription training and testing text files with character level transcription in the data preparation stage. Initially, for speaker independent GMM-HMM training MFCC features, Δ and $\Delta\Delta$ were used. Here, the

MFCCs were subject to cepstral mean variance normalization. But, for speaker dependent case Feature space Maximum Likelihood Linear Regression (FMLLR) features were used [3]. The frame shift and frame width are 10 ms and 25 ms respectively. GMM-HMM acoustic model(AM) was trained using maximum likelihood(ML) condition. Along with these a bi-gram statistical language model (LM) was used while decoding. The training and decoding strategies are shown in the Fig. 3(a)

TDNN is good for modeling long-range temporal dependencies. In the case of TDNN framework, Mini-Libispeech chain recipe in kaldi was followed which uses a factorised TDNN network. In this case, 40 dimensional MFCC and 100 dimensional i-vector was used for every time step. A 13 A Lattice-Free (LF) variant of the Maximum Mutual Information (MMI) criterion is used for chain model training without frame-level cross-entropy pre-training. The training and decoding strategy are shown in the Fig. 3(b)

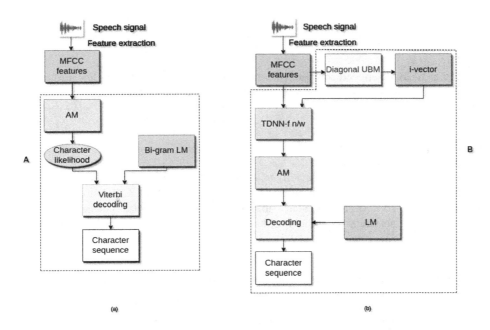

Fig. 3. (a) GMM-HMM framework using MFCC (b) TDNN framework using MFCC

4.2   Wav2vec2.0 Feature Extraction

Before feature extraction wav2vec2.0 involves 2 steps namely pre training and finetuning which are described as follows:-

The pretraining network is shown in the Fig. 4. The latent representations (Z) from raw speech are extracted using convolutional neural networks. The latent representations are quantised to discrete units(Q) which act as targets during the contrastive task. The latent representations are masked randomly and fed to the transformer allowing the network to predict the context representation of the masked regions. Q is compared with C using contrastive and diversity loss. Multilingual pretrained model(CLSRIL-23) [5] which has been trained on 23 indian languages to learn the contextual speech representations has been used here.

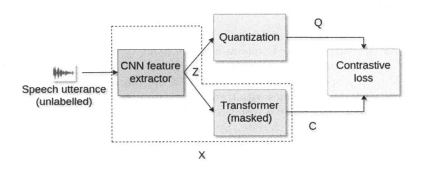

Fig. 4. Wav2vec2.0 pretrainig architechture

The CLSRIL-23 model has been fine tuned on both Mini-Librispeech and Lambani dataset. The fine tuning framework is shown in Fig. 5. During fine tuning as shown in the figure the network X is borrowed from pretraining architecture and a randomly initialized softmax linear layer is added on top of it which is optimized using connectionist temporal classification (CTC). The size of the linear layer is equal to the vocabulary size (V) of the language.

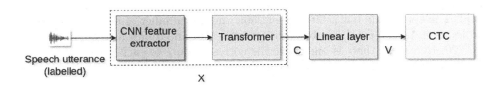

Fig. 5. Wav2vec2.0 finetuning framework

4.3 Modification of Features

CLSRIL-23 pre-trained model is finetuned and has been used as a feature extractor in our proposed framework. In CLSRIL-23 base architecture of the wav2vec2.0 framework is used which contains 12 transformer blocks with a model dimension of 768. Wav2vec2.0(W2V) features which are of 768 dimension is extracted from the last layer of transformer encoder of the fine tuned model with a frame shift of 20 ms and a frame size of 25 ms of the speech signal [10]. These features are used to train the GMM-HMM and TDNN framework in place of MFCC and the rest of the procedure is kept intact. The blocks A and B are the same as shown in Fig. 3(a) and 3(b), only the feature is replaced with W2V features.

5   Database Settings

Two types of language datasets have been used for performing the experiment, those are English and Lambani and the name of the datasets are Mini-Librispeech and Lambani respectively.

The Mini-Librispeech dataset is a subset of the Librispeech data [12]. The Mini-Librispeech dataset comes with transcribed training and testing sets named as train-clean-5 and dev-clean-2 respectively. Train-clean-5 and dev-clean-2 contain 5 hrs and 2 hrs of speech data. Speakers from the dev-clean-2 are chosen randomly so that it sums up to 1hr of testing data. The training set of Mini-Librispeech contains 12 males and 16 females speaker data i.e. 28 speakers data in total, whereas the testing set contains 9 males and 3 females i.e. 12 speakers in total. The speech file has 16 kHz sampling frequency and bit rate of 256 kbits/sec. The number of channels for each speech file is 1. There are 1519 utterances and audio files in the training set and 534 utterances and audio files in the testing set. That means there is one audio file corresponding to each utterance.

The Lambani dataset comes with raw audio files and its corresponding text transcriptions along with the utterance ids. For each utterance there is only one audio file corresponding to that particular utterance. Initially the sampling rate of the speech files were 44.1 kHz which has been changed to 16 kHz which is compatible for all the frameworks. The Lambani training dataset has 7 males and 8 females speaker data which is 15 speakers data in total and the testing data contains 2 females and 1 male speaker data which is 3 speakers data in total. The speech file has a bit rate of 256k and the number of channels of each audio file is 1. The total number of utterances and audio files in the testing set are 770. Here, also there is one audio file corresponding to each utterance.

A summary of the entire dataset is shown in Table 2.

5.1   Experimental Results and Discussion

For GMM-HMM and TDNN based frameworks we have carried out all the experiments using kaldi and for Wav2Vec2.0 we have carried out all the experiments using vakyansh [1] toolkit. We have carried out the experiments with MFCC features and the speech representations from Wav2Vec2.0 which we are calling here as W2V features.The best experimental results are shown in the Table 3.

Table 2. Specification of the dataset after preprocessing and organisation

Parameters	Mini-Librispeech	Lambani
Amount of training data	5 hrs	5 hrs
Amount of testing data	1hrs	1 hrs
No. of spkrs	28(12 males, 16 females) in taining set	12(9 males, 3 females)
	15(7 males, 8 females)	3(2 males, 1 female)
Sampling rate	16 kHz	16 kHz
Bit rate	256k	256k
Channels	1	1
Utterances	1519 in training set	3390 in training set
	534 in testing set	770 in testing set
No. of Audio files	1519 in training set	3390 in training set
	534 in testing set	770 in testing set

Table 3. CER(%) for different frameworks with MFCC and W2V features

FRAMEWORKS	FEATURES	DATASET	
		Mini-Librispeech	Lambani
GMM-HMM	MFCC	38.5	39.1
	W2V	18.2	18.2
TDNN	MFCC	24.1	30.8
	W2V	15.2	20.9

While using MFCC features for building acoustic models for character level ASR systems using GMM-HMM and TDNN frameworks TIMIT recipe and Mini-Librispeech chain recipe from kaldi were used respectively. i-vectors were used in addition to MFCC in the TDNN framework. A bi-gram language model was used while decoding which was built using the text of the entire training data. IRSTLM toolkit was used to build the language model. 5 hours of transcribed Mini-Libispeech and Lambani were used for training and building the acoustic model for the GMM-HMM and TDNN framework.

So, here we can see that W2V features are performing better than the MFCC features for both the frameworks. We have considered speaker adaptation while carrying out the results of Mini-Librispeech but in the case of Lambani it wasn't considered.

Sample for a particular utterance of the decoded transcript for both Lambani and Mini-Librispeech dataset is shown below .

TV stands for truth value

GHM stands predicted sequence for GMM-HMM using MFCC

TM stands predicted sequence for TDNN using MFCC

GHW stands predicted sequence for GMM-HMM using W2V features

TW stands predicted sequence for TDNN using W2V features.

D stand for deletion
I stands for insertion
S stands for sustitution

Mini-Librispeech

```
TV:    *  s h e w a s  i n d e e d a c l e v e r b i r d
GHM:   T  s h e w a s  i n d e e d a c l A v e r P E r d
Eval:  I                            S         S  S
GHW:   W  s h e w a s  i n d e e d a c l e v e r b  i r d
Eval:  I
TM:    *  s h e w a s  E n d e e d a c l I v e r b  U r d
Eval:                  S              S         S
TW:    *  s h e w a s  i n d e e d a c l e v e * b  i r d
Eval:                                           D
```

Lambani

TV:	ವ ಹೊ ಪ ಧಾ ಾಂ ಚ ೯ಸ * ಸಾ ಮ ೯ೕ ಟ ರ ೯ ಪ ೇರ * ಸ ಕ * * ಚ
GHM:	ವ ಋ ಪ ಧಾ * ಕ ೯ ಸ ವ ಋ ಮ ೕ ಟ ರ ೯ * ಬ ರ ೯ ಸ ಕ ತ ೨ ಚ
Eval:	S D S I S S D S I I I
GHW:	ವ ಋ ಪ ಧಾ ಾಂ ಚ * ಸ ವ ಋ ಮ ೨ ಟ ರ * ಪ ೇರ * ಸ ಕ * * ಚ
Eval:	S D I S S D
TM:	ತ ಋ ಪ ಧಾ ನ ಸ ಾಂ ವ * ಋ ಮ ೯ೕ ಟ ರ ೯ ಪ ೇರ * ಸ ಕ ಚ ೨ ಚ
Eval:	S S S S S S S S I I
TW:	ವ ಋ ಪ ಧಾ * ಚ * ಸ ವ ಋ ಮ ೨ ಟ ರ * ಪ ೇರ * ಸ ಕ ರ * ಚ
Eval:	S D D I S S D I

Fig. 6. Lambani predicted text showing its alignment with ground truth

So, we can see that in case of Mini-Librispeech dataset we are getting the least error in the decoded transcription for TDNN framework for W2V features i.e. TW. GHW is also performing better than TM as it has 3 character errors whereas TM has one character error. Among all these GHM is giving the worst result with 4 character error as its performance is the poorest. Here, among the predicted characters the characters which are inserted and substituted are marked in capital letters.Hence the result is justified

As shown in Fig. 6 in the case of the Lambani dataset, GHW is giving the best performance with only 6 character errors. GHM is the worst one with 11 errors. TM has 9 errors and TW has 8 errors so TM has better performance than TW. Hence the result is verified.

6   Conclusion and Future Work

In this work, data collection strategy for an under-resourced language Lambani has been shown. Character level speech recognition for under-resourced settings using GMM-HMM and TDNN has also been explored in this paper. The focus was to show the significance of self-supervised speech representations extracted from wav2vec2.0 for under-resourced settings. So, using the wav2vec2.0 approach as a non-linear feature extractor we are getting a relative improvement of 53.4% and 32.1% for GMM-HMM and TDNN frameworks respectively for under-resourced language Lambani. In the Mini-Librispeech dataset, the relative improvement in the performances are 35.5% and 36.92% for GMM-HMM and TDNN frameworks respectively. Similarly, as a part of future work, this approach can be explored in case of other pretrained models and other deep self-supervised learning methodologies can be explored as a feature extractor in place of wav2vec2.0.

Acknowledgements. The Lambani data collection is a part of the"Speech to Speech translation project". The authors would like to acknowledge the Ministry of Electronics and Information Technology (MeitY), Govt. of India, for funding us in this project. The authors would also like to thank the data associates who have helped in collecting Lambani data. The authors are grateful to Mr.Swapnil Sontakke for building the GUI which played a crucial role in collection of data.

References

1. Chadha, H.S., et al.: Vakyansh: ASR toolkit for low resource Indic languages. arXiv preprint arXiv:2203.16512 (2022)
2. Chen, D., Mak, B.K.W.: Multitask learning of deep neural networks for low-resource speech recognition. IEEE/ACM Trans. Audio Speech Lang. Process. **23**(7), 1172–1183 (2015)
3. Gales, M.J.: Maximum likelihood linear transformations for HMM-based speech recognition. Comput. Speech Lang. **12**(2), 75–98 (1998)
4. Glorot, X., Bengio, Y.: Understanding the difficulty of training deep feedforward neural networks. In: Proceedings of The Thirteenth International Conference on Artificial Intelligence and Statistics, pp. 249–256. JMLR Workshop and Conference Proceedings (2010)
5. Gupta, A., et al.: CLSRIL-23: cross lingual speech representations for Indic languages. arXiv preprint arXiv:2107.07402 (2021)
6. Imseng, D., Bourlard, H., Garner, P.N.: Using kl-divergence and multilingual information to improve ASR for under-resourced languages. In: 2012 IEEE International Conference on Acoustics, Speech and Signal Processing (ICASSP), pp. 4869–4872. IEEE (2012)
7. Imseng, D., Motlicek, P., Bourlard, H., Garner, P.N.: Using out-of-language data to improve an under-resourced speech recognizer. Speech Commun. **56**, 142–151 (2014)
8. Le, V.B., Besacier, L.: Automatic speech recognition for under-resourced languages: application to Vietnamese language. IEEE Trans. Audio Speech Lang. Process. **17**(8), 1471–1482 (2009)
9. Mishra, J., Gandra, J., Patil, V., Prasanna, S.R.M.: Issues in sub-utterance level language identification in a code switched bilingual scenario. In: 2022 IEEE International Conference on Signal Processing and Communications (SPCOM), pp. 1–5. IEEE (2022)

10. Mishra, J., Patil, J.N., Chowdhury, A., Prasanna, S.M.: End to end spoken language diarization with wav2vec embeddings
11. Mishra, J., Prasanna, S.R.M.: Importance of supra-segmental information and self-supervised framework for spoken language Diarization task. In: Prasanna, S.R.M., Karpov, A., Samudravijaya, K., Agrawal, S.S. (eds.) International Conference on Speech and Computer, vol. 13721, pp. 494–507. Springer, Cham (2022). https://doi.org/10.1007/978-3-031-20980-2_42
12. Panayotov, V., Chen, G., Povey, D., Khudanpur, S.: Librispeech: an ASR corpus based on public domain audio books. In: 2015 IEEE International Conference on Acoustics, Speech and Signal Processing (ICASSP), pp. 5206–5210. IEEE (2015)
13. Peddinti, V., Povey, D., Khudanpur, S.: A time delay neural network architecture for efficient modeling of long temporal contexts. In: Sixteenth Annual Conference of The International Speech Communication Association (2015)
14. Povey, D., et al.: The kaldi speech recognition toolkit. In: IEEE 2011 Workshop on Automatic Speech Recognition and Understanding. No. CONF, IEEE Signal Processing Society (2011)
15. Sahraeian, R., Compernolle, D.V., Wet, F.d.: Under-resourced speech recognition based on the speech manifold. In: Sixteenth Annual Conference of the International Speech Communication Association (2015)
16. Swadesh, M.: Lexico-statistic dating of prehistoric ethnic contacts: with special reference to north American Indians and Eskimos. Proc. Am. Philos. Soc. **96**(4), 452–463 (1952)
17. Tachbelie, M.Y., Abate, S.T., Besacier, L.: Using different acoustic, lexical and language modeling units for ASR of an under-resourced language-Amharic. Speech Commun. **56**, 181–194 (2014)
18. Thomas, S., Ganapathy, S., Hermansky, H.: Cross-lingual and multi-stream posterior features for low resource LVCSR systems. In: Eleventh Annual Conference of the International Speech Communication Association (2010)

19. Thomas, S., Ganapathy, S., Hermansky, H.: Multilingual MLP features for low-resource LVCSR systems. In: 2012 IEEE International Conference on Acoustics, Speech and Signal Processing (ICASSP), pp. 4269–4272. IEEE (2012)
20. Yu, D., Deng, L., Dahl, G.: Roles of pre-training and fine-tuning in context-dependent DBN-HMMS for real-world speech recognition. In: Proceedings of NIPS Workshop on Deep Learning and Unsupervised Feature Learning. sn (2010)

Study of Various End-to-End Keyword Spotting Systems on the Bengali Language Under Low-Resource Condition

Achintya Kr. Sarkar[1]([✉])[ID], Tulika Basu[2][ID], Rajib Roy[2][ID], Joyanta Basu[2][ID], Michael Tongbram[3], Yamben Jina Chanu[3][ID], and Priyanka Dwivedi[1]

[1] IIIT Sri City, Chittoor, Andhra Pradesh, India
sarkar.achintya@gmail.com
[2] CDAC, Kolkata, West Bengal, India
[3] NIT Manipur, Imphal, Manipur, India

Abstract. English End-to-end spoken keyword systems (KWS) with limited keywords are commonly available in the literature. This paper aims to study the existing various keyword techniques in the Indian regional Bengali language under low-resource conditions. In this context, we study several KWS techniques which are common in the English language in Bengali namely: Conv1D, Conv2D+attention, Conv2D+multi head attention, VGG, Dense-net, and Vision transformer (ViT). In addition, we also study the effect of voice-activity detection (VAD) on the KWS under real-life scenarios especially when the speech signal could contain the front and tail short pause or silence i.e. without proper segmentation information even under clean conditions. Besides, we also consider cross-lingual transfer learning for tuning the parameters of a pre-trained state-of-the-art transformer model in English to Bengali. Finally, Experimental results demonstrate that VAD significantly improves the accuracy of the KWS detection system using both spectral features and raw audio data. Among the different traditional approaches (without transfer learning), the Densenet technique yields better system accuracy. Overall, cross-lingual transfer learning provides the highest KWS detection than others.

Keywords: VAD · End-to-end DNN · Cross-lingual transfer-learning · KWS · Bengali

1 Introduction

With the immense advent of information and communication technology, accessing and disbursement of information in a more informal and easier way through the medium of computer or mobile devices become very much necessary. Here comes the need for a chatbot through which humans can converse with computers in a natural way. So to converse with a computer, a computer needs to recognize the query of a human, where automatic speech recognition (ASR) takes its place.

A. Karpov et al. (Eds.): SPECOM 2023, LNAI 14339, pp. 114–126, 2023.
https://doi.org/10.1007/978-3-031-48312-7_9

But to run ASR frequently consumes high energy resulting in quick draining of battery in small handheld devices like mobile phones. Hence the rising demand for spoken dialog systems with the emergence of keyword spotting systems takes place. Spoken keyword spotting (KWS) is the task of identifying presumed hits of a text query, target keywords, and phrases in a reference audio file. Basically, the spoken keyword spotting system involves searching for occurrences of certain spoken words amidst a speech utterance. Besides the spoken dialog system, the KWS system has many other applications like audio indexing, command control devices, etc.

In the progress of technology, various DNN-based techniques have been proposed to improve the performance of the KWS such as convolutional neural networks for one-dimensional (Conv1D) data [1] (raw speech signal is fed to train a DNN to discriminate the desire keywords at the output layer), Visual Geometry Group (VGG) [13], Vision transformer (ViT) [4] (feature extracted from speech signal is fed to the DNN for discriminate the keys word at the output layers), Dense Net [7] (speech features are provided to training the DNN), Feed-forward neural network (FF-DNN), Conv2D+attention [12](feature vectors are input to the DNN and a self-supervised attention mechanism is applied), Convolutional neural networks for two-dimensional (Conv2D)+multi head attention [11] (similar to the Conv2D + attention system, the only difference is that multi-head attention is considered). Those techniques commonly explore the Google English command database which consists of well-segmented speech signals (excluding the front and trailing short pause) duration of around 1 seconds for a particular keyword. However, in real scenarios speech collected through a microphone for a particular keyword, is expected to have a short pause/silence at the beginning and end of the recording even under a clean environment. The application of ASR for the segmentation is time-consuming or computationally heavy for handheld devices. On the other hand, the silence/short pause at the beginning and ending is also not useful for the application. Besides Google speech command dataset contains only 35 words whereas the Bengali dataset used in this study contains 100 spoken keywords by 100 farmers. The keywords of Bengali consist of agricultural commodity names spoken by farmers from different districts of West Bengal, India. As the data has been collected from different regions of West Bengal, dialectal variations of the Bengali language and speaker variability have been kept in the dataset. Apart from that different issues related to telephonic recording i.e. channel drop, different types of background noise such as cross-talk, vehicle noise, etc. make the data very challenging to build the system for KWS[3]. Some of the commodity names of the Bengali dataset are given in Table 1.

Recently, various studies are seen in [6,9,15,17] which consider cross-lingual transfer learning for emotion detection to explore the state-of-the-art transformer based model which improves their system performance. The pre-trained model is tuned toward the target downstream.tasks (or language) in this approach.

The previous existing studies motivate us to propose exploring the various KWS techniques of the English database on the low-resource non-English data

Table 1. Sample Keywords of Commodity Names.

Commodity Name in ITRANS	Equivalent IPA	Corresponding English
aalu	/a l u/	Potato
aam	/a m/	Mango
bit'a	/b i ʈ/	Beetroot
caal	/tʃ a l/	Rice
bhind'i	/bʰ i n ɖ i/	Lady's finger

to study its effectiveness. As per our best knowledge, there is no such attempt has been made to develop the KWS system in the Bengali language. Besides, we have also studied the effect of VAD on the KWS especially when every audio file can contain silence or noise at the beginning, middle, and end.

The contributions of the paper are in many folds: first the study of various recent traditional KWS techniques (trained from scratch) namely ViT, Dense Net, Feedforward neural network, Conv2D, Conv2D+attention, and Conv2D+multi head attention for the Bengali with limited data. Secondly, we show the effect of voice activity detection on the KWS, which discards the low energized/unwanted short pause/noninformative part for a given speech signal. Lastly, we consider cross-lingual transfer learning to tune the pre-trained Hubert model in English to Bengali as a downstream task. We show that the incorporation of VAD with the KWS system quite boosts the system performance compared to the counterpart without VAD. Among the different traditional/conventional KWS, *Dense-net* is the best choice with trade-off model parameters and system accuracy. Overall, Hubert pre-trained model with cross-lingual transfer learning significantly boosts the KWS compared to the conventional approaches and is useful for the KWS under limited training data.

The paper is organized as follows: Section 2 deals with methodology. Section 3 describes the experimental setup. Section 4 presents the results and discussion. Finally, the paper is concluded in Sect. 5.

2   Methodology

In this section, we briefly present different KWS techniques in the following subsections:

2.1   KWS-Conv1D with Raw Speech

This is an end-to-end KWS system based on 1D CNN analogous to [1] where the sound classification is performed using raw audio/speech signals. In our case, 1 second of raw audio is fed to the DNN to discriminate the desired commodity (keywords) names as keyword and a non-keyword at the output layer with the cross-entropy-based objective function. Figure 1 illustrates the Conv1D architecture for the KWS in Bengali language.

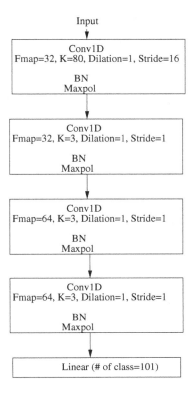

Fig. 1. Bengali spoken KWS with Conv1D based neural network.

2.2   KWS-Conv2D + Attention

In this end-to-end KWS system, the mel-filter bank energy feature of the spoken utterances is fed to the conv2D-based DNN with attention mechanism as per [12] for classification of the spoken desired keywords and a non-keyword (a class consisting of spoken words other than the desired keywords) at the output layer. The system is graphically illustrated in Fig. 2. In the attention mechanism, weightage (a_t) for each time-stamp/frame is calculated by mapping their hidden layer representation $\mathbf{h_t}_{[128 \times 1]}$ into a single score (β_t) as

$$\beta_t = \mathbf{v^T} tanh(\mathbf{Wh_t} + \mathbf{b}) \tag{1}$$

$$a_t = \frac{e^{\beta_t}}{\sum_{i=1}^{n} e^{\beta_i}} \tag{2}$$

where $\mathbf{v}_{[1 \times 128]}, \mathbf{W}_{[128 \times 128]}$ and $\mathbf{b}_{[128 \times 1]}$ are the learn-able parameters. Next output from the attention mechanism is obtained by the weightage combination of each time-stamp/frame as

$$\mathbf{O} = \sum_{i=1}^{n} a_t \mathbf{h_t} \tag{3}$$

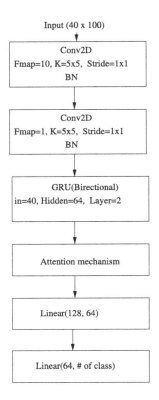

Fig. 2. Bengali spoken KWS using Conv2D based attention mechanism.

2.3   KWS-Conv2D + Multi Head

This system is analogous to the *KWS-Conv2D + attention* except for the attention mechanism, where the multi-head attention mechanism is considered as in [11]. It is shown in [11] that spoken KWS with multi-head attention reduces the classification error over the system without attention by 10% on Google speech commands data sets V2[16]. In this approach, 4 heads have been used and replaced the LSTM with GRU *called MHAtt-RNN*.

2.4   KWS-VGG

In this system, a DNN is trained as per [13], where the feature vector of the speech signals is fed to the DNN to discriminate the desired keyword and non-keyword at-the-output layer with a cross-entropy-based objective function. VGG architecture is a type of convolutional neural network (CNN) that was originally designed for image recognition but can also be applied to audio processing. VGG architecture consists of several layers of convolutional filters, followed by max-pooling layers, and then fully connected layers at the end. The convolutional filters are used to extract features from the input signal, such as frequency, pitch, and energy. The max-pooling layers are used to reduce the dimensionality and complexity of the features while preserving the most important information. The fully connected layers are used to perform the final classification of the input signal into different categories, such as keywords or background noise. One way to use VGG architecture for audio KWS is to first convert the audio signal into a spectrogram, which is a visual representation of the frequency and intensity of the sound over time. Then, the spectrogram can be treated as an image and fed into the VGG network. The network will learn to recognize patterns and features in the spectrogram that correspond to different keywords or phrases. For example, the network might learn that a certain shape or color in the spectrogram indicates the presence of the word "Bing". The network will then output a probability score for each possible keyword or phrase, and the one with the highest score will be selected as the final prediction. Another way to use VGG architecture for audio KWS is to directly feed the raw audio signal into the network, without converting it into a spectrogram. This requires modifying the network to accept one-dimensional inputs instead of two-dimensional inputs. The network will then learn to extract features from the raw audio signal directly, without relying on pre-processing steps. This might result in faster and more accurate predictions, as well as lower computational costs.

2.5   KWS-Dense-Net

In this case, the feature vector of the speech signal is fed to a dense-Net [7] for discriminating the desired keywords and a non-keyword class at the output layer. The Dense-Net architecture comprises a series of cascading convolutional filter layers, succeeded by max-pooling layers, and ultimately culminating in fully connected layers. These convolutional filters serve the vital role of feature extraction from the input signal, encompassing key aspects such as frequency, pitch, and energy. Meanwhile, the max-pooling layers play a pivotal role in diminishing feature dimensionality and intricacy, all the while retaining the salient information of utmost significance. The fully connected layers are used to perform the final classification of the input signal into different categories, such as keywords or background noise.

2.6   KWS-ViT

This KWS system is as per [4], where the feature vector (mel filter bank energy) of the speech signal is split into patches (say, frame) and projected onto the embedded space. The embedded representation is then passed through position embedding. Next, the embedded feature vectors are fed to a transformer encoder. The output of the transformer encoder is average to calculate a single vector and then finally passes to the MLP layer to discriminate the keywords. ViT Transformer consists of several layers of self-attention modules, followed by feed-forward layers, and then fully connected layers at the end. The self-attention modules are used to capture the long-range dependencies and contextual information from the input signal, such as frequency, pitch, and energy. The feed-forward layers are used to perform non-linear transformations on the features while preserving the spatial resolution. The fully connected layers are used to perform the final classification of the input signal into different categories.

2.7   Cross-Lingual Hubert Transfer Learning

In this approach, the pre-trained Hubert [8] trained on the $960h$ data from Librispeech are tuned with the Bengali data. The output layer is modified to the number of classes as per the number of keyword (and non-keyword) classes in our system. However, Hubert is usually pre-trained in a single language, such as English, which limits its applicability to other languages or multilingual scenarios. To address this challenge, cross-lingual Hubert transfer learning is adopted to fine-tune Hubert on a small amount of labeled data from a different language or task, and then the fine-tuned model is used to perform inference on the target language or task. This way, the model can adapt to the new domain and leverage the cross-lingual similarities and transferable knowledge from the pre-trained model.

3   Experiment Setup

All the data used in the experiments have been collected through the Interactive Voice Response (IVR) system. The data collected through the above-mentioned procedure are real environment data covering huge variations of the handset, speaker's age, gender, and last but not least different dialectal variations of Bangla. All the speech data are named properly using the 16 alphanumerical characters, for example, GLNSTDDSXXXXIYYY which comprise of G: Gender, LN: Language, ST: State Name, DD: District, S: Session, XXXX: Speaker Id, I: Sentence type and YYY: Utterance ID [2]. A guided call flow has been designed in order to record speech data. Data has been collected mostly from farmers all over West Bengal. Different types of recording environments such as studios, offices, railway stations, markets, etc. have been kept in mind while collecting data for the system. Altogether 197 agricultural commodities have been recorded by 100 unique speakers of West Bengal. Among them, 100 commodity names were considered as the target, and the rest for the non-keyword class. For the system evaluation, the complete dataset is randomly partitioned into training (80%) and test (20%) for each run of the experiment. Five experiments are conducted to access the overall system performance. Table 2 represents approximately the number of data available for the training and evaluation for each run of experiments (Fig. 3).

Table 2. Number of examples in the training and evaluation set.

	# class	Training	Evaluation
Keyword	100	7988	2012
Non-keyword	1	7772	1928

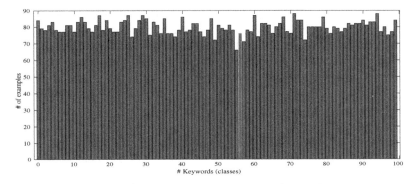

Fig. 3. Illustrates the number of examples (except the non-keyword) available per keyword classes for training the Bengali spoken KWS system in experiment-1.

We include data augmentation during training which consists of random-time shift (randomly shift audio to left/right, the maximum amount of sample shift is kept $0.1 \times samplingrate$), time-stretches (of times series by a fixed rate, the resample offset and resample values are considered respectively, 0.15 and 1) [5] and mix babble noise(15, 10, 5, 0 dBs), reverberation Room impulse response (RIP), MUSAN music and noise (15, 10, 8, 5 dBs). Kaldi toolkits [10] is used for babble noise, RIP, MUSAN music, and noise augmentation. It gives approximately 236400 speech utterances for training DNNs in KWS for each experiment. The training dataset is used for tuning the parameters of the pre-trained Hubert system with transfer learning in KWS.

The DNN in the KWS (except Hubert-based) are trained from scratch with the learning rate 0.001, the weight decaying value 0.0001, and the learning rate decay by 0.1 after 20 epochs. All the DNNs are trained up to 60 epochs.

In the Hubert-based system, the two encoder layers are unfrozen to update their parameters during the transfer learning. Other config parameters are kept as conventional. As Hubert requires 16 kHz speech sampled signal as input, therefore 8 kHz Bengali speech files are first upsampled 16 kHz. The upsampled speech files are then passed through the VAD. The VAD output signals are fixed length of 1 s (similarly to the other KWS) and feed to the Hubert. It is better to note that the parameters in the respective DNN architecture are calculated/optimized using the training data itself. Figure 4 illustrates the spectrogram of two keyword speech signals. It can be observed from Fig. 4 that there is silence/short pause either at the end or at the beginning as well as in between.

Pre-processing: rVAD [14] is applied on the speech signal to discard the low-energized portion of the signal (i.e. silence, noise/short pauses in a speech signal). Afterward, the 1 second duration of the processed signal (zero padding is done in case of a shorter length of signal) is used for the feature extraction. Default parameters are considered as per rVAD[1].

Feature Extraction: For feature extraction, 40 dimensional mel filter bank energy is extracted with $30ms$ hamming window at 10 ms frame rate. It gives around 100 frame per speech file. This feature is then fed to the DNN for the classification of keywords or non-keywords. No zero mean and unit variance normalization is applied to the extracted feature.

4   Results and Discussions

In this section, we analyze the performance of different KWS systems in the Bengali language. Table 3 shows the performance of various end-to-end Bengali KWS systems for different techniques with or without VAD. It can be observed from Table 3 that VAD significantly improves the accuracy of keyword detection.

Table 3. Compares the performance of Keyword identification accuracy (%) for various techniques in the Bengali language with or without VAD.

Exp	w/o VAD	Conv1D -wav	Conv2D +atten	Conv2D + Multihead	Dense -Net	ViT	VGG
1	✓	81.42	85.99	86.65	88.53	82.49	89.49
2	✓	81.17	83.17	85.71	88.50	79.42	88.81
3	✓	81.12	83.20	86.09	88.25	76.73	87.99
4	✓	80.94	83.43	86.17	89.09	79.47	88.65
5	✓	80.58	83.12	85.66	88.71	79.24	88.35
Average		81.04	83.78	86.06	88.62	79.47	88.66
1	×	49.59	53.71	54.31	52.36	50.86	58.38
2	×	49.09	54.80	53.76	53.22	50.03	55.89
3	×	50.18	54.87	53.98	52.74	49.85	57.59
4	×	50.03	54.80	53.78	52.18	50.99	49.42
5	×	50.28	55.76	54.09	53.60	51.27	56.19
Average		49.83	54.79	53.98	52.82	50.60	55.49
# of model Parameters		$\approx 31k$	$\approx 163k$	$\approx 196k$	$\approx 4.25M$	$\approx 5.37M$	$\approx 31.19M$

To understand the reason why VAD significantly improves the performance of KWS, we plot the spectrogram of two speech files shown in Fig. 4. From

---

[1] https://github.com/zhenghuatan/rVAD.

Fig. 4, it can be noticed that low energize/irrelevant information (e.g. short-pause) can exist either at the beginning, ending, middle, or a combination in the spoken speech signal. Therefore, VAD helps the KWS by reducing unwanted or irrelevant information (i.e. unvoiced (0)) from the spoken speech signal. This leads to improved accuracy of the system compared to its counterpart without VAD.

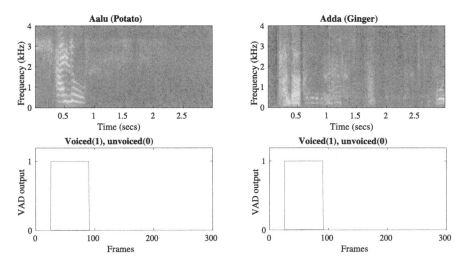

Fig. 4. Illustrates the spectrogram of two keywords - Aalu (Potato) and Aadaa (Ginger).

Among the different KWS with VAD, *Conv2D* with multi-head shows higher accuracy than the simple attention technique as multi-head projects the feature onto different subspaces and so it is able to capture better relation among the feature than the simple case. The KWS system using raw speech modeling i.e. *Conv1D-wav* gives lower accuracy compared to the system using cepstral feature *Conv2D+atten* or *Conv2D+multihead*. It could be due to the fact that the cepstral feature is able to capture more relevant information for the KWS. The *ViT* technique achieves the lowest accuracy compared to the other methods. The fact could be that the limited amount of training data is not sufficient for learning a large number of model parameters in this modeling framework as pointed out in [4]. The KWS performance of *VGG* and *Dense-Net* based system is similar to each other. However, *VGG* consists of a huge number of model parameters than the Dense-Net.

Now if we look at the number of model parameters among the techniques, though *VGG* and *Dense-net* yields similar system accuracy. However, *Dense-net* requires $\approx 7.33\times$ fewer parameters than the *VGG* and so *Dense-net* is computationally and disk space-wise more efficient. With a comparison between *Dense-net* and *Conv2D+multihead* systems, *Conv2D+multihead* system model parameters are $\approx 21\times$ less than the *Dense-net*. However, *Dense-net* gives absolute 2% higher accuracy than the *Conv2D+multihead*. So with trade-off 2% system accuracy, *Conv2D+multihead* can be preferred to the *Dense-net*. Indeed, each system has its own advantages and disadvantages.

Table 4. Comparison the performance of Hubert-based KWS with the traditional *VGG* and *Dense-net* techniques.

(a) Performance (in terms of % Accuracy) of the Bengali KWS system using cross-lingual transfer learning of the Pre-trained Hubert model.

Model	No of experiments					Average
	1	2	3	4	5	
Fine-tunes Hubert (parameters $\approx 14M$)	92.23	90.86	91.26	91.49	91.62	91.49

(b) Comparison perform of *VGG* and *Dense-net* KWS with original (8 kHz) and upsampled 16 kHz version of speech signals.

Model	Speech sampled	No of experiments					Average
		1	2	3	4	5	
Dense-net	8 kHz	88.53	88.50	88.25	89.09	88.71	88.62
	16 kHz	89.24	88.68	87.82	88.50	88.93	88.63
VGG	8 kHz	89.49	88.81	87.99	88.65	88.35	88.66
	16 kHz	89.34	88.10	88.58	87.94	88.71	88.53

Table 4a presents the KWS performance for the system with cross-lingual transfer learning of the pre-trained Hubert model. The system performances are shown only for the VAD as in Table 3 found that VAD quite improves the accuracy of KWS. From Table 4a, it can be seen that Hubert with cross-lingual transfer learning yields more promising accuracy (absolutely around 3% higher than *VGG* and *Dense-net*) than the traditional systems (presented in Table 3). As expected, self-supervised speech presentation to vector and then use with state-of-the-art transformer-based modeling in Hubert is very useful for many downstream tasks, and a similar pattern is observed here for the KWS under limited data conditions. In the context of model parameters, Hubert with transfer learning system consists of $\approx 14M$ parameters which are respectively quite lower and higher than the *VGG* and *Dense-net*. The hubert-based system uses the upsampled 16 kHz speech files whereas the 8 kHz speech files are used by the *VGG* and *Dense-net*. Therefore, we further perform experiments for the *VGG* and *Dense-net* systems presented in Table 4b, where upsampled wav files are considered. It can be noticed that the average performance of the KWS system with VGG and Dense-net with upsampled data does not change. We also believe that the performance of the traditional KWS systems: *VGG, Dense-net, ViT, etc.* could be further improved with the cross-lingual transfer learning concept from the pre-trained model in the respective systems. However, we kept it for the future direction.

5   Conclusion

In this paper, various spoken keyword systems (KWS) are studied for the Bengali language under limited data conditions with or without voice activity detection in a common framework. In addition, the pre-trained Hubert model with cross-lingual transfer learning was considered. We showed that VAD significantly improves the KWS system accuracy and is useful for KWS. Among the different traditional approaches, *Dense-net* is the best choice in trade-off model parameters and system accuracy. Whereas, Hubert's pre-trained model with cross-lingual transfer learning further improves the KWS performance. As future directions for this research, we propose investigating the performance of spoken keyword systems in other languages, such as Assamese and Manipuri, to explore their adaptability across diverse linguistic contexts. Additionally, we suggest exploring advanced VAD techniques and the applications of the KWS system in healthcare. By pursuing these avenues, we aim to extend the impact of our research and contribute to the advancement of natural language processing and speech technology for a wide range of languages and practical applications, including those in the healthcare domain.

Acknowledgments. We gratefully acknowledge the support and funding provided by the Ministry of Electronics and Information Technology (MeitY), Government of India, which made this research possible. We would like to extend our heartfelt thanks to IIT Madras and IIT Guwahati for their invaluable feedback and unwavering support throughout the course of our activities. Additionally, we would like to express our deep gratitude to all the native speakers from West Bengal who generously shared their voice samples for our research endeavors. Without the collective efforts of these individuals and organizations, this work would not have been achievable. A part of this work is supported by NLTM BHASHINI project funding 11(1)/2022-HCC(TDIL) from MeitY, Govt. of India.

References

1. Abdoli, S., Cardinal, P., Koerich, A.L.: End-to-end environmental sound classification using a 1D convolutional neural network. arXiv:1904.08990 (2019)
2. Basu, J., Bepari, M.S., Roy, R., Khan, S.: Design of telephonic speech data collection and transcription methodology for speech recognition systems. In: Proceedings of FRSM, pp. 147–153. India (2012)
3. Basu, J., Bepari, M.S., Roy, R., Khan, S.: Real time challenges to handle the telephonic speech recognition system. In: S, M., Kumar, S. (eds.) Proceedings of the Fourth International Conference on Signal and Image Processing (ICSIP), vol. 222, pp. 395–408. Springer, India (2013). https://doi.org/10.1007/978-81-322-1000-9_38
4. Berg, A., O'Connor, M., Cruz, M.T.: Keyword transformer: a self-attention model for keyword spotting. In: Proceedings of Interspeech, pp. 4249–4253 (2021)

5. Brian, M., et al.: librosa: audio and music signal analysis in python. In: Proceedings of the 14th Python in Science Conference, pp. 18–25 (2015)
6. D. Bruyne, L., Singh, P., D. Clercq, O., Lefever, E., Hoste, V.: How language-dependent is emotion detection? Evidence from multilingual BERT. In: Proceedings of the 2nd Workshop on Multi-lingual Representation Learning (MRL), pp. 76–85. Association for Computational Linguistics (2022)
7. Du, X., Zhu, M., Chai, M., Shi, X.: End to end model for keyword spotting with trainable window function and Densenet. In: Proceedings of IEEE International Conference on Digital Signal Processing, pp. 1–5 (2018)
8. Hsu, W.N., Bolte, B., Tsai, Y.H.H., Lakhotia, K., Salakhutdinov, R., Mohamed, A.: HuBERT: self-supervised speech representation learning by masked prediction of hidden units. arXiv:2106.07447 (2021)
9. Pastor, M., Ribas, D., Ortega, A., Miguel, A., Lleida, E.: Cross-corpus speech emotion recognition with HuBERT self-supervised representation. In: Proceedings of Interspeech, pp. 76–80 (2022)
10. Povey, D., et al.: The kaldi speech recognition toolkit. In: Proceedings of IEEE Workshop on Automatic Speech Recognition and Understanding (2011)
11. Rybakov, O., Kononenko, N., Subrahmanya, N., Visontai, M., Laurenzo, S.: Streaming keyword spotting on mobile devices. In: Proceedings of Interspeech, pp. 2277–2281 (2020)
12. Shan, C., Zhang, J., Wang, Y., Xie, L.: Attention-based end-to-end models for small-footprint keyword spotting. arXiv:1803.10916 (2018)
13. Simonyan, K., Zisserman, A.: Very deep convolutional networks for large-scale image recognition. arXiv:1409.1556 (2015)
14. Tan, Z.H., Sarkar, A.K., Dehak, N.: rVAD: an unsupervised segment-based robust voice activity detection method. Comput. Speech Lang. 59, 1–21 (2020)
15. Uçan, A., Dörterler, M., Akçapınar Sezer, E.: A study of Turkish emotion classification with pretrained language models. J. Inf. Sci. 48(6), 857–865 (2022)
16. Warden, P.: Speech commands: a dataset for limited-vocabulary speech recognition. arXiv:1804.03209 (2018)
17. Yang, J.: Ensemble deep learning with HuBERT for speech emotion recognition. In: Proceedings of IEEE 17th International Conference on Semantic Computing (ICSC), pp. 153–154 (2023)

Bridging the Gap: Towards Linguistic Resource Development for the Low-Resource Lambani Language

Ashwini Dasare[2]([✉]), Amartya Roy Chowdhury[1]([✉]),
Aditya Srinivas Menon[3]([✉]), Konjengbam Anand[1], K. T. Deepak[2]([✉]),
and S. R. M. Prasanna[1]([✉])

[1] Indian Institute of Technology Dharwad, Dharwad, India
{amartya.chowdhury,konjengbam.anand,prasanna}@iitdh.ac.in
[2] Indian Institute of Information Technology Dharwad, Dharwad, India
{ashwini,deepak}@iiitdwd.ac.in
[3] Indian Institute of Information Technology Kottayam, Kottayam, India
adityasrinivas20bcs8@iiitkottayam.ac.in

Abstract. Language technology development is crucial for many downstream applications such as machine translation and language understanding. The lack of linguistic resources makes it challenging for technology development of under-resource languages. This paper aims at developing linguistic tools for Lambamni, an under-resourced tribal language of India through corpora creation, annotation, and transfer learning from contact language. Based on the annotated corpora, we develop the Lambani language tagset and our investigation focused on various methods for developing a Part-of-Speech (POS) tagger and also creating a morphology dictionary for Lambani. A total of eight BIS tagset is found to be present for Lambani language. The experimental results revealed that the statistical approach with GMM-HMM (Gaussian Mixture Model - Hidden Markov Model) achieved POS tagging accuracy of 96% despite the limited dataset containing 6,893 sentences. This success in a low-resource setting highlights the promising potential of GMM-HMM in overcoming challenges posed by the scarcity of annotated data in under-resourced languages. The experiments not only showcase the effectiveness of the proposed methods for low-resource language processing but also shed light on their applications and open new directions for research in language revitalization and the development of digital tools for zero-resource languages.

Keywords: Langauge technology development · Natural language understanding · Lambani · POS tagger · Morphological analysis

1 Introduction

India is a linguistically diverse nation with over 22 officially recognized regional languages [20] and multiple spoken languages. These languages belong to different language families having unique characteristics, including Indo-Aryan,

A. Karpov et al. (Eds.): SPECOM 2023, LNAI 14339, pp. 127–139, 2023.
https://doi.org/10.1007/978-3-031-48312-7_10

Dravidian, Austroa-Asiatic, Sino-Tibetan, and others [8]. While major Indian languages such as Hindi, Kannada and Tamil have abundant linguistic tools and resources [3,19,22,27], there are many widely spoken low-resource languages that do not have written scripts and linguistic tools such as Lambani, Soliga [6] and Mundari.

Technology plays a vital role in language preservation, offering digital tools like audio and video recording devices, online archives, and language documentation software to record and archive endangered languages for future generations. Language apps and online platforms further aid in language learning and revitalization efforts, providing accessible resources for those interested in studying these languages.

Linguistic Resource (LR) for a language typically encompasses various components that facilitate the development, study, and analysis of that particular language. These resources comprise corpora from diverse sources, lexicons, grammar, phonetics and phonology resources, and morphological analysis tools. Well-established Indian languages like Kannada and Hindi have abundant linguistic resources, such as dictionaries, Part of Speech (POS) taggers, morphological tools, and datasets for Natural Language Processing (NLP) tasks while low-resource languages do not have such facilities.

Globalization, urbanization, cultural assimilation, and limited intergenerational transmission threaten many tribal languages. Endangered tribal languages are more than mere communication tools; they are integral to the identity, worldview, and cultural expression of indigenous communities. Protecting endangered tribal languages is crucial to preserve and revitalize indigenous communities' unique linguistic and cultural heritage worldwide. These languages hold valuable knowledge, history, and traditional practices passed down through generations. Hence, efforts to protect and preserve these languages are essential for the well-being of affected communities and for upholding the diverse richness of human languages and cultures.

Preparing the language corpus for low or zero-resource languages is a challenging and time-consuming task. This is particularly true for languages like Lambani, which lack their own script, making manual tagging a significant hurdle in data annotation, and corpus preparation. In this paper, language preservation activity of Lambani language through technological development is discussed.

The Lambani community, also known as the Banjara community, is culturally rich with a nomadic lifestyle and unique traditions [7,21,28]. They have a fascinating history that spans different regions of India, primarily residing in Karnataka, Andhra Pradesh, Telangana, Maharashtra, and Tamil Nadu. There have been few efforts towards technology building for the Lambani language, such as Machine translation [9], and Text to speech synthesis [10]. But to the best of our knowledge, no literature was found regarding basic linguistic tools for Lambani such as morphological analyzer and POS tagger. This works details the effort to build a POS tagger and a Morphological analyser for Lambani language.

The key contributions of this work are as follows:

- We address the problem of developing linguistic technologies for low-resource languages.
- We create lexical corpora for Lambani language by collecting and translating text from various sources.
- Tagset creation and analysis for Lambani language from the created lexical corpora.
- Development of POS tagger for low-resource languages.
- Development of morphology dictionary from a given text corpora.

The rest of the paper is summarized as follows. A brief overview of earlier works in related area is presented in Sect. 2. The proposed approach for Lambani linguistic technology development is presented in Sect. 3. Section 4 details the evaluation of the developed tools and Sect. 5 concludes the work.

2 Related Works

There have been substantial efforts for the development of linguistic tools of Indian languages for various NLP applications. However, limited linguistic resources, such as dictionaries and part-of-speech taggers, make it difficult to develop high-quality NLP applications for under-resourced languages [29]. The current approaches focus on the development of two broad categories of linguistic tools: POS tagger [5,13,15] and morphological analyzer [4,12].

2.1 POS Tagger

POS tagger development works may be classified into (1) rule-based approaches [2,4,12], (2) statistical approaches [13,15,24], and (3) deep learning-based approaches [11,26]. Antony et al. [5] work on different POS taggers for Indo-Aryan languages like Hindi, Bengali, and Panjab, while Merin et al. [14] discuss various tagging methodologies for Dravidian languages such as Kannada, Telugu, Malayalam, and Tamil languages. Srivastava et al. [26] introduced a Deep Learning (DL)-based unsupervised POS tagging method for Sanskrit, employing character-level n-grams. Deshmukh et al. [11] proposed a deep learning-based POS tagger and a Bi-LSTM-based POS tagger, respectively, for Marathi language. This paper works on developing POS tagger for Lambani languages leveraging these extant techniques.

2.2 Morphological Analyzer

There has been considerable work on Morphological Analysers and generators for Indian Languages. Antony et al. [4] proposed rule based morphological analyzer for Kannada. Veen Dixit et al. [12] developed a rule-based spell checker for Marathi Language. However, data scarcity of under-resource language makes it challenging to develop morphological analyzers as they require diverse data to capture language nuances [29].

2.3   Lambani Lingustic Technology

Due to the lack of script, there has not been much written literature found in the Lambani language. As a result, limited work has been carried out for development of Lambani linguistic tools. To overcome the limitations of data scarcity, researchers [29] propose text corpus creation for under-resource language through the use of a contact language. Amartya et al. [9] worked on developing machine translation methods to translate English text to Lambani for Lambani corpora generation. Ashwini et al. [10] proposed the use of Text To Speech synthesis tools for creating Lamabani dataset. This work extend the above works to generate Lambani corpus through the use of Kannada as a contact language.

3   Proposed Approach

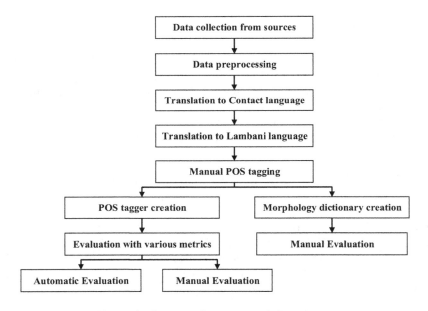

Fig. 1. Architectural overview of the system.

In this section we introduce our proposed system to develop linguistic tools for Lambani. The architectural overview of the system is shown in Fig. 1. The overall process consists of the following steps: (1) Data collection; (2) Data preprocessing; (3) Translation to contact language; (4) Manual POS tagging; (5) POS tagger creation; and (6) Morphology analysis. system undergo the following steps:

3.1   Data Collection

The main objective of this study is to create linguistic resources specifically for Lambani. To overcome the limitation of data scarcity for Lambani language, this step proposes the creation of Lambani language corpora through transfer learning to use in language tool development. The entire data collection process may be summarised in six steps:

- **Gathering text from various sources**: We utilise the Optical Character Recognition (OCR) feature of Adobe Reader to extract sentences from Lambani-based textbooks [7]. Additionally, we extract English texts from the English subject of the National Council of Educational Research and Training (NCERT) textbooks [1]. Our focus lies specifically on English language textbooks intended for lower and middle schools, encompassing classes I to VI. Further, a linguist manually created 1000 sentences using the Swadesh list [17]. This list comprises a set of basic English words that cover fundamental concepts of English grammar, such as pronouns or verbs.
- **Preprocessing**: The extracted text often contains a significant amount of noise, posing challenges for accurate translation by native Lambani speakers. To address this issue, the extracted texts are further subjected to the following preprocessing methods to obtain a clean corpus.
  - It is observed that native Lambani speakers generally communicate using short simple sentences. So, sentences containing fewer than three words and more than eight words are discarded to avoid lengthy sentences.
  - Incomplete sentences provide noisy information and are removed.
  - Manual checking of the text was carried out by a linguist to remove syntactically or semantically incorrect sentences.
  - Sentences containing symbols, URLs and unknown characters are removed.
- **Relevancy pruning**: The sentences are ranked based on relevancy, where 1 is assigned to relevant sentences and 0 otherwise. For example, sentences containing controversial statements including political statements were marked as irrelevant since they are not used in conversations to carry out daily activities. After the sentences have been ranked the relevant sentences are extracted, and the rest of them are discarded. After this step, around 80% of the sentences are retained out of the total 36,000 sentences.
- **Translation to contact language**: For this study, Lambani speakers from northern Karnataka state are considered and they are fluent in both Kannada and Lambani languages. So, Kannada is chosen as a contact language. The English sentences are translated into Kannada by a bilingual English-Kannada speaker. The translated text is validated by another bilingual Kannada-English speaker.
- **Contact language to Lambani Translation**: The Kannada sentences are manually translated to Lambni by a native Lambani speaker who is familiar with Kannada. The translated sentences are written in the Kannada script.
- **Quality checking and correction**: The translated sentences are manually checked and incorrect ones are rectified.

3.2   Developing Lambani Linguistic Resources (LLR)

The linguistic development efforts primarily revolve around creation of essential resources such as a POS tagger and morphological dictionary. These resources would greatly assist in the development of computational tools for the Lambani language.

Lambani POS Tagger. POS tagging is a valuable tool in natural language processing (NLP) as it helps algorithms understand the grammatical structure of sentences and disambiguate words with multiple meanings. It is commonly used to determine the lexical categories and convey the semantics of each word in a sentence. For example, let us take a look at the following sentences.

Sentence 1: *I saw a bear in the forest.*

Sentence 2: *Please bear with me during this difficult time.*

In these two sentences, even though the word "bear" is spelled and pronounced the same, its meaning and POS tag differ based on the context. Sentence 1 refers to the animal "bear", where "bear" is a noun. Sentence 2, however, uses "bear" as a verb, indicating the act of enduring or tolerating. Understanding the POS tag of the word "bear" in both of these sentences helps to disambiguate the meaning. Accurate POS tagging is essential to enhance the performance of these language-processing algorithms and enables the development of various language-based applications.

Manual POS Tagging. As Lambani spoken in northern Karnataka uses Kannada script to write, we propose using Kannada POS tagging rules as a foundation to develop Lambani POS tagger. Utilising the expertise of native Lambani speakers proficient in both English and Kannada, we conducted manual annotations for POS tagging using the standards POS tagset developed by the Bureau of Indian Standards (BIS) [18]. The POS knowledge of the created parallel text corpus comprising English, Kannada, and Lambani is used to annotate the Lambani text corpus. The manual annotation and evaluation by native Lambani speakers ensure the reliability and accuracy of the POS tagging model, providing a strong foundation for further linguistic exploration and application. This meticulous annotated corpus serves as a gold standard for subsequent analysis and testing of the POS tagging model. Table 1 shows examples of Lambani POS along with meaning of words in English.

Developing POS Tagger. We compare various methods for POS tagging for developing Lambani POS tagger, including rule-based, Artificial Intelligence (AI) based, Machine Learning (ML) based, and Deep Learning (DL) based approaches. Rule-based methods for POS tagging involve manually creating linguistic rules, but this is time-consuming, error-prone, and requires language experts. An alternative rule-based approach uses a model to learn rules from a training corpus, leading to AI-based methods. Artificial Intelligence methods employ Hidden Markov Models (HMMs) to automate POS tagging, showing good results. However, the trend is shifting towards Machine Learning (ML) approaches like Naive Bayes, SVMs, and CRFs and Deep Learning (DL) based approaches like Long Short-Term Memory (LSTM) networks, Gated Recurrent Units (GRUs), Convolutional Neural Networks (CNNs) and Transformers. Both these approaches aim to learn the patterns and relationships between words and their corresponding POS tags.

Table 1. Lambani tagset along with examples, English translation and transliteration.

Sl no	Category	Label	Lambani words	English translation
1	Noun	NN	ಭೇಸೆ (bhesi), ಬಳದ (balada)	buffalo, ox
2	Pronoun	PRP	ಏಕ್ (ek), ಮೋರ (vora)	one, his
3	Verb	VB	ಖಾರ್ಚ (khaaricha), ಖುಟಗೋಚ (khutagocha)	eating, finished
4	Adjective	JJ	ಮೋಟೋ (moto), ಆಚೊ (aacho)	big, good
5	Adverb	RB	ಅಚಾನಕ್ (achaanak), ಅತ್ತಜ (attaja)	suddenly, here
6	Conjunction	CCD	ನೆಕಾಣೆ (nikaani), ನೆತರ್ (nitar)	or, but
7	Postposition	PSP	ಮಾಯ್ಇರ (maayira), ಉಪರ (upara)	inside, above
8	Particles	RPD	ಮಾಯ್ (Maayi), ಒರ್ (orr)	in, of

HMM. Hidden Markov Model (HMM) is a stochastic technique used for POS tagging that assigns tags to words based on the most frequent tag in the training data. It follows a step-by-step procedure, extracting unique words, calculating tag occurrence counts, and initializing emission and transmission matrices. These matrices represent probabilities of word-tag observations and tag transitions. The Viterbi algorithm is used to find the most probable sequence of POS tags.

RNN (Recurrent Neural Network). The paper aims leverage different configurations of RNN and LSTM to build a POS tagger for Lambani language. The model implementation involves two LSTM layers, each with 128 neurons, and an output layer with Linear and Softmax components.

BERT. Additionally, the paper explores the use of pre-trained embeddings from a fine-tuned BERT model trained on approximately 29K sentences. Pretrained word or sentence embeddings have become essential in Natural Language Processing. Transformer architectures use Masked Language Modeling (MLM) to train the encoder on text corpora, providing embeddings for downstream tasks like POS tagging. However, these models require large training datasets, which can be challenging for low-resource languages like Lambani. To address this, we will explore two approaches: using multilingual transformers trained on diverse data and reducing the number of parameters to lower data requirements.

Creating Lambani Morphological Dictionary. Identifying root words and affixes are crucial to understanding the fundamental meaning and lexical properties of a word. Table 2 shows examples of English, Hindi, and Lambani words along with their respective root words, prefixes, and suffixes.

Table 2. Examples of root forms and affixes of words in English, Hindi and Lambani.

	Word	Prefix	Root	Suffix
English	unhappiness	un-	happy	-ness
Hindi	किताबें		किताब	ें
Lambani	ಕಾಗದೇನ(kaagadena)	-	ಕಾಗದ(kaagada)	ೀನ

The English word "unhappiness," has the root word is "happy," while the prefix "un-" and the suffix "-ness" modify its meaning and grammatical function. Similarly, in the Hindi word **"किताबें"** (books), the root word is **"किताब"**, represents "book" in English. The suffix **"ें"** indicates plurality, making the word refer to multiple books. Moreover, a Lambani word, **"ಕಾಗದೇನ"** (pronounced as "kaagadena"). The root word in this case is **"ಕಾಗದ"** (pronounced as "kaagada") meaning "paper" in English. Additionally, the suffiix **"ೀನ"** (pronounced as "een") modifies the word's significance.

Building Affix Lexicon. To handle the lexicon specific to the Lambani language, we follow the following steps:

– Vocabulary construction: A vocabulary is constructed that contains all the distinct word forms encountered in the corpus.
– Data cleaning: Non UTF-8 Kannada characters are removed. Additionally, punctuations are also filtered.
– Stemming: As labelled dataset for stemming is not available, the unsupervised Morphessor tool [25] is used for morphological segmentation to get the stem/root words and affixes. The algorithm is based on a set of rules which are applied iteratively until we get the base form of the word. Morphessor uses dynamic programming based Viterbi algorithm to take cleaned vocabulary as input and trains a model that segments words to get stem/root words and affixes.

Table 3 examples of Lambani words along with their POS and morphological affixes obtained after performing morphology analysis.

Table 3. Lambani dictionary after performing morphology analysis.

Lambani word	POS tag	English meaning	English transliteration	Morphology affixes	
ಅಡಗೀರ	NOUN	cooking	adagira	ಅ	ಡಗೀರ
ಅಬೆ	ADVERB	now	abe	ಅ	ಬೆ
ಅತರಾ	DETERMINER	this much	ataraa	ಅತ	ರಾ
ಅಂತೆಮ	ADPOSITION	in the end	antema	ಅಂತ	ೆಮ
ಕಾಳೋ	ADJECTIVE	black	kaalo	ಕಾ	ಳೋ
ಅನಸಾವಚ್	PARTICLE	to feel	anasaavacha	ಅನಸಾವ	ಚ್
ಆರೋಚು	VERB	am coming	aarochu	ಆ	ರೋಚು
ಆದ್ರ	CONJUNCTION	but	aadra	ಆ	ದ್ರ

4   Evaluation

4.1   Dataset Description

The description of the dataset is shown in Table 4. The dataset contains 29,358 sentences collected from various sources of Lambani text. Out of these, 6,893 sentences were manually tagged and divided into training and testing sets using 5-fold cross-validation.

Table 4. Data statistics.

Sl. No.	Total number of sentences
Number of sentences collected	29,358
Number of manually POS tagged sentence	6,893

4.2   Distribution of POS Tags

The distribution of the POS tags is summarised in Table 5. Upon manual labelling of 31640 words, it is inferred that Lambani has 8 part-of-speech tags present, namely Adjective (JJ), Adverb (RB), Conjunction (CCD), Particle (RPD), Noun (NN), Postposition (PSP), Pronoun (PRP) and Verb (VB). It can be observed from Table 5 that we are getting the highest distribution of tags in case of Verb (VB) followed by Noun (NN).

Table 5. Distribution of BIS POS tags in the dataset.

BIS POS Tag	Count (Manual tagging)	Count (GMM-HMM tagging)
Adjective (JJ)	2,743	2,458
Adverb (RB)	1,923	1,727
Conjunction (CCD)	254	296
Particle (RPD)	93	90
Noun (NN)	7,057	7,577
Postposition (PSP)	1,429	1,299
Pronoun (PRP)	6,729	6,496
Verb (VB)	11,412	11,662

4.3   Baseline

For evaluating the performance of POS tagging we use bi-directional RNN based tagger as the baseline. RNN is useful for sequence labelling with variable length inputs. The baseline is compared with BERT based and GMM-HMM based POS tagger. During model training the maximum sequence length is kept at 150 for both the RNN and BERT based models. The training batch size is kept at 32, and a beam size of 5 is adopted. The baseline model contains only 1 RNN layer with an embedding dimension of 768. In case of BERT based models both the encoder and decoder contain 6 layers. For the feed-forward neural network we have used 1024 inner states. Both the encoder and decoder contain 4 heads in each attention layer block. The attention dropout and the dropout applied in the feed forward network is kept constant at 0.1. Both the RNN and BERT are trained using the Adam optimizer. Other than the straightforward RNN and BERT based models we have also conducted experiments using DistilBERT [23] and MicroBERT [16]. DistilBERT uses the concept of knowledge distillation where a large and complex model (BERT) is used to train a smaller and compact model by transferring its knowledge to the smaller model. Whereas MicroBERT uses multitask learning to reduce the model size. MicroBERT has only 1.29 million parameters, thereby making it a better alternative to BERT. The model configurations to both these models are kept unchanged as their default values.

4.4 Evaluation Metrics

To determine the performance of the proposed automatic POS tagger we adopt accuracy, precision, recall and f1 score as the evaluation metrics. The metrics are defined as follows:

- **Precision** is defined as the ratio of total number of correctly predicted POS tags by total number of predicted tags.
- **Recall** is defined as the ratio of total number of correctly predicted POS by the sum of correctly predicted tags and the number of missed tags.
- **F1-score**: Given precision and recall, F-score is defined as follows:

$$F1 - score = 2 * (Precision * Recall)/(Precision + Recall) \qquad (1)$$

- **Accuracy** is defined as the ratio of the total number of correctly predicted POS tags to the total number of tags in the dataset.

4.5 Results

Table 6. Result obtained on various models.

Models	Accuracy	Precision	Recall	F1-score
GMM-HMM	**0.96**	**0.95**	**0.96**	**0.96**
RNN	0.87	0.87	0.87	0.87
BERT+RNN (BRNN)	0.88	0.88	0.88	0.88
Distillbert (D)	0.86	0.86	0.86	0.86
Distillbert + RNN (DRNN)	0.88	0.88	0.88	0.88
Microbert (M)	0.84	0.84	0.84	0.84
Microbert + RNN (MRNN)	0.89	0.89	0.89	0.89

In this section we report the experimental results based on accuracy, precision, Recall and F1-score. Table 6 shows the performance comparison of POS tagging of various methods adopted. The highest metrics compared with the baseline model are highlighted as bold numbers.

POS Taggers Evaluation. We are getting an accuracy of 87% on our baseline model. From Table 6 we can notice that we are getting the highest accuracy of 96% in the case of GMM-HMM which is almost 10% improvement in performance over the baseline model. This may be due to the models ability to handle data sparsity. GMM-HMM tries to learn the joint probability between the words and its corresponding POS tags. Due to its probabilistic approach the model does not assign zero probabilities to unseen word-POS combinations. Moreover, GMM-HMM uses shared parameters across all the states in HMM. This reduces the total number of parameters. In the case of Distillbert (D) we are getting an accuracy of 86% which is an 1% reduction in performance over the baseline model. We are getting the worst performance in the case of Microbert (M). Although M has very few parameters, it is not able to map the POS tags with its corresponding words.

From Table 6 it is quite evident that we are getting a performance improvement when RNN is trained along with BERT models. If we compare between the base BERT models and BERT models that use pre-trained embeddings, we are getting significant improvement while using pre-trained embeddings. As BERT is pre-trained on large amounts of data it was able to capture semantic relationships between various words. Moreover BERT uses contextual embeddings, meaning the embedding of a word depends on the context of the sentence. The BERT+RNN models are almost similar in performance except MRNN which is giving a 1% improvement.

5   Conclusion and Future Work

This paper presents a seminal work to develop a linguistic resource for the under resourced Lambani language. The work involves creating a lexical corpora, a POS tagset, POS tagger, a lexicon dictionary and morphology analyzer for Lambani. We adopt a transfer leaning approach of using parallel corpora in English and Kannada along with Kannada linguistic rules for the work. Upon manual POS tagging of 31640 words, it is observed that the Lambani tagset consists of eight POS tags specified in the BIS tagset. Numerous experiments were conducted to develop an accurate POS tagger that works well with low-resource corpora. For POS tagging, the GMM-HMM approach outperforms the tested methods and gives an accuracy of 96% for POS tagging task. The future efforts will focus on expanding the manually collected parallel corpus in Lambani, both in terms of its size and the amount of annotated POS tags. We will also focus on other variations of BERT like multilingual BERT finetune on the Lambani sentences. The development of a comprehensive Lambani dictionary and further enhancements to the POS tagger will be pursued as well.

Acknowledgement. We would like to thank Prashant Bannulmath, Sunita Rathod, Rajeshwari Naik and Sunil Rathod for helping us in developing the Lambani POS corpus. The authors would also like to thank "Anatganak", high-performance computation (HPC) facility, IIT Dharwad, for enabling us to perform our experiments, and Ministry of Electronics and Information Technology (MeitY), Govt. of India, for supporting us through the "Speech to Speech translation for tribal languages" project.

References

1. National Council of Educational Research and Training. https://ncert.nic.in/textbook.php
2. Aggarwal, N., Randhawa, A.K.: A survey on parts of speech tagging for Indian languages. In: IJCA Proceedings on International Conference on Advancements in Engineering and Technology, ICAET 2015, vol. 3, pp. 29–31 (2015)
3. Anand Kumar, M., Dhanalakshmi, V., Soman, K., Rajendran, S.: A sequence labeling approach to morphological analyzer for Tamil language. Int. J. Comput. Sci. Eng. **2**(06), 1944–1951 (2010)
4. Antony, P., Kumar, M.A., Soman, K.: Paradigm based morphological analyzer for Kannada language using machine learning approach. Int. J. Adv. Comput. Sci. Technol. (2010). ISSN 0973–6107
5. Antony, P., Soman, K.: Parts of speech tagging for Indian languages: a literature survey. Int. J. Comput. Appl. **34**(8), 0975–8887 (2011)
6. Boopathy, S.: Languages of Tamil Nadu: Lambadi, an Indo-Aryan dialect. Census of India 1961, Tamil Nadu ix, part XII (1972)
7. Burman, J.R.: Ethnography of a Denotified Tribe: The Laman Banjara. Mittal Publications (2010)
8. Chandramouli, C., General, R.: Census of India 2011. Provisional Population Totals. Government of India, New Delhi, pp. 409–413 (2011)
9. Chowdhury, A., Deepak, K.T., Prasanna, S. M.: Machine translation for a very low-resource language - layer freezing approach on transfer learning. In: Proceedings of the Fifth Workshop on Technologies for Machine Translation of Low-Resource Languages (LoResMT 2022), pp. 48–55. Association for Computational Linguistics, Gyeongju (2022)
10. Dasare, A., Deepak, K.T., Prasanna, M., Samudra Vijaya, K.: Text to speech system for lambani - a zero resource, tribal language of India. In: 2022 25th Conference of the Oriental COCOSDA International Committee for the Co-ordination and Standardisation of Speech Databases and Assessment Techniques (O-COCOSDA), pp. 1–6 (2022)
11. Dhumal Deshmukh, R., Kiwelekar, A.: Deep learning techniques for part of speech tagging by natural language processing. In: 2020 2nd International Conference on Innovative Mechanisms for Industry Applications (ICIMIA), pp. 76–81 (2020)
12. Dixit, V., Dethe, S., Joshi, R.K.: Design and implementation of a morphology-based spellchecker for Marathi, and Indian language. Arch. Control Sci. **15**(3), 301 (2005)
13. Ekbal, A., Bandyopadhyay, S.: Part of speech tagging in Bengali using support vector machine. In: 2008 International Conference on Information Technology, pp. 106–111 (2008)
14. Francis, M.: A comprehensive survey on parts of speech tagging approaches in Dravidian languages. In: The IIER International Conference, Beijing, China, 26 July 2015 (2015)

15. Gadde, P., Yeleti, M.V.: Improving statistical POS tagging using linguistic feature for Hindi and Telugu. In: ICON, pp. 1–8 (2008)
16. Gessler, L., Zeldes, A.: MicroBERT: effective training of low-resource monolingual BERTs through parameter reduction and multitask learning. In: Proceedings of the The 2nd Workshop on Multi-lingual Representation Learning (MRL), pp. 86–99. Association for Computational Linguistics, Abu Dhabi (Hybrid) (2022)
17. Hymes, D.: Morris swadesh. Word **26**(1), 119–138 (1970)
18. of Indian Standard, B.: Linguistic resources - pos tag set for Indian languages - guidelines for designing tagsets and specification. https://tdil-dc.in/tdildcMain/articles/134692DraftPOSTagstandard.pdf
19. Kumar, D., Singh, M., Shukla, S.: FST based morphological analyzer for Hindi language. Int. J. Comput. Sci. **9** (2012)
20. Metry, K.: tribal languages in 8th schedule. AGPE Royal Gondwana Res. J. Hist. Sci. Econ. Polit. Social Sci. **2**(1), 19–30 (2020)
21. Naik, C., Naik, D.P.: Banjara stastical report Karnatka state, India (2012)
22. Prathibha, R., Padma, M.: Development of morpholoical analyzer for kannada verbs. In: IET, pp. 22–27 (2013)
23. Sanh, V., Debut, L., Chaumond, J., Wolf, T.: Distilbert, a distilled version of bert: smaller, faster, cheaper and lighter. arXiv preprint arXiv:1910.01108 (2019)
24. Sarkar, K., Gayen, V.: A trigram HMM-based POS tagger for Indian languages. In: Satapathy, S.C., Udgata, S.K., Biswal, B.N. (eds.) Proceedings of the International Conference on Frontiers of Intelligent Computing: Theory and Applications (FICTA). AISC, vol. 199, pp. 205–212. Springer, Heidelberg (2013). https://doi.org/10.1007/978-3-642-35314-7_24
25. Smit, P., Virpioja, S., Grönroos, S.A., Kurimo, M.: Morfessor 2.0: toolkit for statistical morphological segmentation. In: Proceedings of the Demonstrations at the 14th Conference of the European Chapter of the Association for Computational Linguistics, pp. 21–24. Association for Computational Linguistics, Gothenburg (2014)
26. Srivastava, P., Chauhan, K., Aggarwal, D., Shukla, A., Dhar, J., Jain, V.P.: Deep learning based unsupervised POS tagging for Sanskrit. In: Proceedings of the 2018 International Conference on Algorithms, Computing and Artificial Intelligence, ACAI 2018. Association for Computing Machinery, New York (2018)
27. Sunitha, K.N., Kalyani, N.: A novel approach to improve rule based Telugu morphological analyzer. In: 2009 World Congress on Nature & Biologically Inspired Computing (NaBIC), pp. 1649–1652 (2009)
28. Trail, R.L.: The grammar of Lamani. SIL of the University of Oklahoma (1970)
29. Yu, X., Vu, N.T., Kuhn, J.: Ensemble self-training for low-resource languages: grapheme-to-phoneme conversion and morphological inflection. In: Proceedings of the 17th SIGMORPHON Workshop on Computational Research in Phonetics, Phonology, and Morphology, pp. 70–78 (2020)

Studying the Effect of Frame-Level Concatenation of GFCC and TS-MFCC Features on Zero-Shot Children's ASR

Ankita$^{(\boxtimes)}$ (iD), Shambhavi, and Syed Shahnawazuddin (iD)

National Institute of Technology Patna, Patna, Bihar, India
{ankita.ph21.ec,s.syed}@nitp.ac.in

Abstract. The work presented in this paper aims at enhancing the recognition performance of zero-shot children's speech recognition task through frame-level concatenation of two complementary front-end acoustic features. The acoustic features chosen are TANDEM-STRAIGHT-based Mel-frequency cepstral coefficients (TS-MFCC) and Gamma-tone frequency cepstral coefficients (GFCC). The GFCC model the cochlear response of the human auditory system. The MFCC features, on the other hand, model the human pitch perception. Therefore, the GFCC and TS-MFCC features capture the acoustic information differently and that too with very low correlation. Consequently, concatenation of TS-MFCC and GFCC feature vectors helps in modeling complementary and a wider range of relevant acoustic information. This, in turn, enhances the recognition performance significantly. The experimental evaluations presented in this paper show that a relative reduction of nearly 12% is achieved by feature concatenation.

Keywords: Zero-shot children's ASR · TS-MFCC · Feature concatenation · GFCC

1 Introduction

Automatic speech recognition (ASR) is the technology that aides in converting human speech into text. Cutting edge computational techniques such as highly efficient deep learning algorithms [5–7,17,20] have boosted the research work in this domain. As a result, ASR systems are employed in several applications such as voice-based digital assistance, voice-to-text conversion for hands-free computing, voice commands to smart home devices, virtual agents, reading tutors, interactive voice response (IVR) systems, live captioning, language learning tools, voice biometrics, automotives, entertainment and clinical note-taking.

To be effective and to generalize well for all kinds of users, ASR systems are supposed to be speaker-independent. For that purpose, a large amount of speech data is used for learning the statistical model parameters. Most of the ASR systems are designed for adult population and hence use data from adult speakers only. Therefore, such ASR systems have high recognition rates with

A. Karpov et al. (Eds.): SPECOM 2023, LNAI 14339, pp. 140–150, 2023.
https://doi.org/10.1007/978-3-031-48312-7_11

respect to adult's speech. However, their performance degrades substantially when they are subjected to the children's speech. Absence of speech data from the child domain in the training set leads to acoustic mismatch between the training and test conditions. This, in turn, results in severe degradation in recognition performance [4,11,19]. This task of recognising children's speech using statistical models trained on adults' speech is referred to as *zero-shot children's* ASR.

The acoustic mismatch between the training and test data can be alleviated by modifying children's speech test set prior to decoding by using techniques like prosody modification [26], formant scaling [9] and vocal-tract length normalization [10,22]. However, those approaches require two-pass decoding in order to optimally modify the test data which, in turn, results in increased computation time. Resorting to out-of-domain data augmentation [8,23,24] as well as developing robust front-end features specifically for children's speech can help overcome the issue of increased computation time. One such acoustic features, suitable for *zero-shot children's* ASR is referred as TS-MFCC, was proposed in [25]. The TS-MFCC feature extraction process employs pitch-synchronous spectrum estimation called TANDEM STRAIGHT (TS). This results in smoothed power spectra that suppresses the ill-effects of pitch harmonics. The Mel-frequency cepstral coefficients (MFCC) computed using the TANDEM-STRAIGHT power spectra are reported to be very effective for *zero-shot children's* ASR task.

In this study, we have revisited the TS-MFCC features and studied its effectiveness in combination with another front-end acoustic feature called Gammatone frequency cepstral coefficient (GFCC) [14]. The GFCC models the human auditory system's cochlear response whereas the MFCC models the human pitch perception. Consequently, the two kinds of features capture and model the acoustic information present in the speech signal differently and that too with a very low correlation. Therefore, it is expected that combining these two front-end acoustic feature vectors will capture a broader range of relevant acoustic information leading to improved recognition performance. Motivated by this fact, in our present work, we have studied the effect of frame-level concatenation of TS-MFCC and GFCC features for *zero-shot children's* ASR task. The ASR system trained on the concatenated feature vectors leads to significantly lower error rates as demonstrated by the experimental evaluations presented later in this paper.

The rest of the sections of this paper is organised as follows: In Sect. 2, the proposed approach is described and the experimental evaluations demonstrating the effectiveness of the proposed approach are presented in Sect. 3. Finally, the paper is concluded in Sect. 4.

2   Proposed Approach

In this work, we have studied the effect of concatenating TS-MFCC and GFCC features in order to enhance the recognition performance of *zero-shot children's* ASR task. The proposed feature concatenation approach is summarized in the block diagram shown in Fig. 1. It involves appending the coefficients of TS-MFCC and GFCC feature vectors at the frame-level. The resultant feature vectors are then used for the training purpose. In this section, we first describe the two kinds of features in detail. Next, we discuss the motivation behind concatenating those two feature vectors.

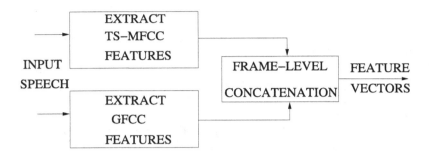

Fig. 1. Block diagram outlining the proposed approach for frame-level concatenation of TS-MFCC and GFCC features.

2.1   Overview of GFCC Features

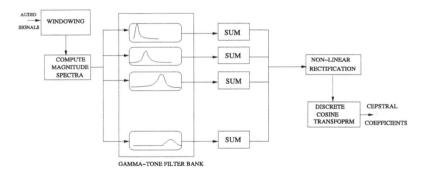

Fig. 2. Block diagram illustrating the process of exctracting GFCC features.

We have borrowed the idea of using Gamma-tone frequency cepstral coefficients [14, 29] from other speech-related research fields where they have been successfully employed for speech recognition [2, 21, 27] and speaker identification [28]. However, it's application in children's speech recognition has not been explored yet. The computation of the GFCC features is similar to that of the MFCC extraction process. The speech signal is first analyzed into short-time frames. The non-stationary speech signal is known to show stationary behaviour in such short frames. This aides in the spectro-temporal signal analysis. Next, each of the frames is processed using a bank of Gamma-tone filters. The Gamma-tone filters are derived by observing the psychophysical and physiological behaviour of the auditory peripheral and hence serve as a standard model for Cochlear filtering. As a consequence, Gamma-tone filtering helps in effectively capturing acoustic information that is left out due to the use of Mel-filterbank.

The cochlea not only amplifies sound waves and converts them into neural signals, but also decomposes complex acoustic waveform into simpler elements. Thus, it acts as mechanical frequency analyzer where each position along the basilar membrane corresponds to a particular frequency. The Gamma-tone filters are designed as such to replicate this process. For this purpose, the magnitude or the power spectrum of the signal is passed through a Gamma-tone filterbank. We have used a bank of 40 filters spaced linearly on the equivalent rectangular bandwidth (ERB) scale whose central frequency varies between 50 Hz and 8000 Hz. The ERB is a psychoacoustic measure of the auditory filter width at each point along cochlea. The frequency conversion from Hz to the ERB scale is given by:

$$ERB = A \times \log_{10}(1 + 0.00437f) \tag{1}$$

where, f is in Hz and A is given by:

$$A = 1000 \frac{\ln(10)}{24.7 \times 4.37} \tag{2}$$

Next, nonlinear cubic-root function is applied on the obtained time-frequency representation to model human loudness perception. To reduce dimensionality and de-correlate the resulting components, discrete cosine transform is applied. The overall GFCC feature extraction process is summarized in Fig. 2.

2.2   Review of TS-MFCC Features

A periodic signal $h(t)$ has a temporally stable power spectrum usually calculated over a sum of two power spectra. To serve this purpose, a pair of time windows are chosen such that they are separated for half of the fundamental period [13]. Let, $h(t)$ has a Fourier transform $H(\omega)$ and assuming that only two harmonic components of the fundamental frequency ($\omega_0 = \frac{2\pi}{T_0}$) occupy the main lobe of $H(\omega)$, then

$$h(t) = e^{jk\omega_0 t} + \alpha e^{j(k+1)\omega_0 t + \beta}. \tag{3}$$

where α and β represent real numbers. Taking Fourier transform of the above equation (assuming $k = 0$ for simplicity):

$$H(\omega) = \delta(\omega) + \alpha e^{j\beta}\delta(\omega - \omega_0). \tag{4}$$

The respective power spectra of the windowed test signal is then

$$P(\omega,t) = |H(\omega)|^2 + \alpha^2|H(\omega - \omega_0)|^2 + 2\alpha H(\omega)H(\omega - \omega_0)\cos(\omega_0 t + \beta). \tag{5}$$

The third term in the above equation is time-dependent and represents the temporal dependency in the spectrum estimation. It can be cancelled by taking an opposite polarity with a window at $t + T_0/2$. The spectrum without any temporal fluctuation i.e., the TANDEM spectrum $T(\omega, t)$ is now given as:

$$T(\omega, t) = \frac{1}{2} \left\{ P(\omega, t) + P(\omega, t + T_0/2) \right\}. \tag{6}$$

The TANDEM spectrum $T(\omega, t)$ results in smoothed vocal-tract response. The suppression of pitch-harmonics through spectral smoothing due to TAN-DEM STRAIGHT analysis was demonstrated in [25]. MFCC features extracted after smoothing out the pitch-harmonics were noted to be effective in the context of *zero-shot children's* ASR task.

2.3 Motivation for Feature Concatenation

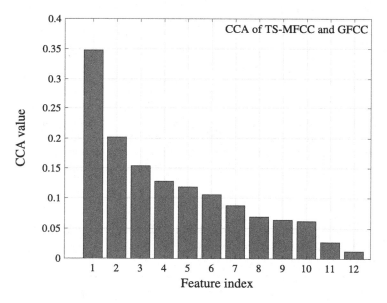

Fig. 3. Canonical correlation between TS-MFCC and GFCC features demonstrating that the two kinds of feature vectors are highly uncorrelated.

As mentioned earlier, the contribution of this work is to explore the effect of frame-level concatenation of two front-end features, i.e., TS-MFCC and GFCC on *zero-shot children's ASR* task. Due to inherent differences in the way the Mel- and Gamma-tone filterbanks are designed and act on a frame of speech, the two kinds of features capture and model complementary acoustic information. To demonstrate that the two kinds of features model the speech data differently and represent a wider range of acoustic attributes, canonical correlation analysis (CCA) was performed on these two features. As evident from Fig. 3, the CCA results in low values (≤ 0.15) for most of the indexes. This, in turn, implies that the TS-MFCC and GFCC features are highly uncorrelated. Hence, their frame-level concatenation is expected to represent a wider range of acoustic attributes as intended. Modeling those will, in turn, help in capturing the missing targeted attributes more robustly and hence improve the recognition performance.

3   Experimental Evaluations

3.1   Database and Experimental Specification

For experimental evaluations, we have used two different British English speech corpora, namely, WSJCAM0 [18] and PF_STAR [1]. The motivation behind using the said corpora is that the mismatches in the recording conditions and the accent of the speakers are minimal. Furthermore, both WSJCAM0 and the PF_STAR databases contain read speech. In our study, the training set was derived from WSJCAM0 and it consisted 15.5 h of speech data from 92 adult speakers (39 females). In order to deal with the unavailability of speech data from child domain, the acoustic attributes of adults' speech training set were modified to make them similar to that of children's speech. For that purpose, we up-scaled the pitch and formant frequencies as well as increased the duration of the adults' speech [8,23]. In addition to that, adults' speech was also subjected to voice-conversion using a generative adversarial network (GAN) to synthetically generate children's like speech [24]. The pitch of the adults' speech training set was increased by a factor of 1.35 while the duration was increased by a factor of 1.4 using the technique reported in [3]. The formant frequencies were up-scaled by a factor of 0.08. For formant modification, the approach proposed in [9] was used which employed scaling of the linear prediction coefficients [12]. These scaling factors were determined by performing experiments on a development set described later. The modified data-sets were then pooled into training. This out-of-domain augmentation approach helps in capturing the missing targeted attributes of children's speech. In addition to that, the overall duration of the training data is increased which, in turn, helps in more robust estimation of model parameters.

Children's speech test set was derived from the PF_STAR corpus and it comprised of 1.1 hours of speech data from 60 speakers (28 females). The age of the child speakers in this test set varied from 4 to 13 years. Furthermore, a development set of children's speech was also derived from the PF_STAR corpus. The development set consisted of 2.1 h of speech data from 63 speakers whose age varied between 6 and 14 years. This set was used for determining the optimal values for the tunable parameters. To gain better insight into the effect of feature concatenation, the test set was split into two, based on the age of the speakers. The first split consisted of nearly 0.6 h of data from children in the age group 4 to 8 years. The second split comprised of nearly 0.5 h of data from speakers belonging to the ages 9 to 13 years. Further to that, another split was done based on the gender of the speakers.

The Kaldi toolkit was used to perform all the experiments [16]. However, front-end speech parameterization was done using MATLAB. The TS-MFCC features reported in [25] were used for front-end speech parameterization in the case of baseline ASR system since those are observed to be more suitable than other existing features in the context of children's speech recognition task. Speech data was analyzed through short-time frames using overlapping Hamming windows of duration 25 ms with a frame-shift of 10 ms. A 40-channel log-Mel-filterbank was used to compute the 13-dimensional base TS-MFCC feature vectors. The base features were time-spliced with context size of ±4 frames and then projected to a 40-dimensional subspace and de-correlated using linear discriminant analysis (LDA) and maximum-likelihood linear transform (MLLT). For feature normalization, cepstral mean and variance normalization (CMVN) as well as feature-space maximum likelihood linear regression (fMLLR) were used. This helps in imparting robustness towards speaker variations. In the case of the GFCC features, frame-size and frame-overlap were chosen as 25 ms and 10 ms. The Gamma-tone-filterbank consisted of 40 channels. Cubic-root function was used for non-linear rectification prior to the application of DCT. The base features extracted in this case were also 13-dimensional. LDA, MLLT, CMVN and fMLLR were then applied in succession to obtain 40-dimensional feature vectors.

Hidden Markov models (HMM) were used for acoustic modeling. The observation probabilities for the HMM states were generated using Gaussian mixture models (GMM) as well as time-delay neural network (TDNN) [15,30]. Cross-word triphone models consisting of eight diagonal covariance components per state were used for the GMM-HMM-based ASR system. Furthermore, decision tree-based state tying was performed with the maximum number of senones being fixed at 2000. Speaker-adaptive training employing fMLLR transforms was used to optimize the final GMM-HMM system. The time-alignments generated using this GMM-HMM-based ASR system were used for initializing the TDNN-HMM. The lattice-free maximum mutual information (LF-MMI) criterion [17] was used for training TDNN-HMM-based ASR system. The TDNN consisted of 13 hidden layers with 1024 nodes per layer. The initial and final learning rates were set to 0.0005 and 0.00005, respectively. Prior to learning the TDNN parameters, 100-dimensional i-vectors were extracted and appended to the base acoustic feature vectors. The universal background model employed for extracting i-vectors consisted of 512 Gaussian components.

A domain-specific 1.5k bi-gram language model (LM) was used while decoding the children's speech test set. This LM was trained on the transcripts of the speech data from PF_STAR corpus after excluding the utterances from the test set. The employed LM had an out-of-vocabulary rate of 1.20% and a perplexity of 95.8 for the children's speech test set. The lexicon consisted of 1969 words including pronunciation variations. The metric used for performance evaluation are word error rate (WER) and character error rate (CER).

3.2   Results and Discussions

The WERs and CERs for the children's speech test set with respect to an ASR system trained on adults' speech and its' modified versions pooled into training

Table 1. WERs and CERs for the children's speech test set with respect to an ASR systems trained on augmented data. The recognition performances are given with respect to the explored front-end features as well as their fame-level concatenation.

Front-end features	Evaluation metrics	
	WER (%)	CER (%)
TS-MFCC	10.01	7.20
GFCC	10.07	7.20
TS-MFCC + GFCC	**8.86**	**6.29**

are given in Table 1. The baseline ASR system is trained using TS-MFCC features as already stated earlier. It is worth mentioning here that, a WER of 19.5% is achieved if only adults' speech is used for training. In other words, the WER gets nearly halved when data augmentation is employed. The WER and CER for GFCC features are almost the same as those obtained using TS-MFCC features. However, on concatenating the two kinds of features, an absolute reduction in WER by 1.15% over the baseline is obtained. Similarly, the absolute reduction in CER is 0.91%. The relative changes in WER and CER over the baseline are shown in Fig. 4. These, results statistically substantiate the efficacy of the proposed approach in the context of *zero-shot children's ASR* task.

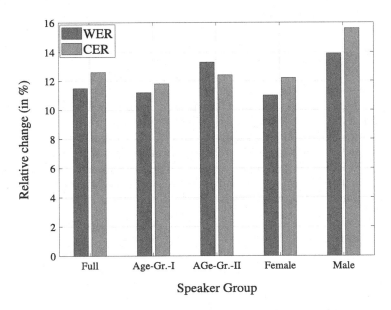

Fig. 4. Age-group and gender-wise relative change in WERs and CERs over the respective baselines obtained by the concatenation of TS-MFCC and GFCC features.

Table 2. Age-group as well as gender-specific WERs and CERs for children's speech with respect to an ASR systems trained on augmented data.

Front-end Features	Speaker Group	Evaluation metrics	
		WER (%)	CER (%)
TS-MFCC	Age-Gr.-I	15.08	11.34
	Age-Gr.-II	6.71	4.36
	Female	11.58	8.59
	Male	8.86	6.16
GFCC	Age-Gr.-I	15.93	12.03
	Age-Gr.-II	6.09	3.91
	Female	11.58	8.59
	Male	8.76	6.16
TS-MFCC + GFCC	Age-Gr.-I	**13.39**	**10.00**
	Age-Gr.-II	**5.82**	**3.82**
	Female	**10.32**	**7.54**
	Male	**7.63**	**5.20**

Next, we performed another study to determine the age-group-specific and gender-specific recognition performances. The age-group as well as gender-specific WERs and CERs are given in Table 2. As evident for the tabulated results, both TS-MFCC and GFCC give similar WER and CER values for each of the speaker groups. However, when the two kinds of feature vectors are concatenated, there are significant reductions in WERs as well as CERs in each of the case. The relative changes in WER and CER obtained over the respective baselines are shown in Fig. 4. In each of the cases, the relative reduction is more than 10%. These results show that the proposed approach is equally powerful not only for Age-Gr.-I kids where the pitch is relatively very high but also for the Age-Gr.-II children having relatively lower pitch values. Similarly, the gains are similar for both male as well as female speakers. Its worth mentioning here that, the pitch values for female speakers are somewhat higher than those for the male children. Thus it can be concluded that the proposed feature concatenation approach imparts pitch-robustness to the ASR system.

4   Conclusion

The work presented in this paper outlines our efforts towards enhancing the recognition performance of *zero-shot children's ASR* system. In this regard, we have implemented frame-level concatenation of two complementary features namely, TS-MFCC and GFCC. The TS-MFCC features employ Mel-filterbank for spectral warping while Gamma-tone filterbank is used in the case of GFCC. Consequently, the two kinds of features model speech data differently and with very low correlation. Hence, on concatenating those at the frame-level helps in capturing a wider range of acoustic attributes. This, in turn, enhances the recognition performance significantly. In our experimental setup, a relative reduction in WER by nearly 12% over the baseline is obtained.

References

1. Batliner, A., et al.: The PF_STAR children's speech corpus. In: Proceedings of Interspeech, pp. 2761–2764 (2005)
2. Cheng, O., Abdulla, W., Salcic, Z.: Performance evaluation of front-end algorithms for robust speech recognition. In: Proceedings of the Eighth International Symposium on Signal Processing and Its Applications, 2005, vol. 2, pp. 711–714 (2005). https://doi.org/10.1109/ISSPA.2005.1581037
3. Damskägg, E.P., Välimäki, V.: Audio time stretching using fuzzy classification of spectral bins. Appl. Sci. **7**(12), 1293 (2017). https://doi.org/10.3390/app7121293
4. Gerosa, M., Giuliani, D., Brugnara, F.: Acoustic variability and automatic recognition of children's speech. Speech Commun. **49**(10–11), 847–860 (2007)
5. Graves, A., Jaitly, N., Mohamed, A.R.: Hybrid speech recognition with deep bidirectional LSTM. In: 2013 IEEE Workshop on Automatic Speech Recognition and Understanding, pp. 273–278. IEEE (2013)
6. Graves, A., Mohamed, A.R., Hinton, G.: Speech recognition with deep recurrent neural networks. In: 2013 IEEE International Conference on Acoustics, Speech and Signal Processing, pp. 6645–6649. IEEE (2013)
7. Hinton, G.E.: Deep neural networks for acoustic modeling in speech recognition. Signal Process. Maga. **29**(6), 82–97 (2012)
8. Kumar, V., Kumar, A., Shahnawazuddin, S.: Creating robust children's ASR system in zero-resource condition through out-of-domain data augmentation. Circuits Syst. Signal Process. **41**(4), 2205–2220 (2022). https://doi.org/10.1007/s00034-021-01885-5
9. Kumar Kathania, H., Reddy Kadiri, S., Alku, P., Kurimo, M.: Study of formant modification for children ASR. In: ICASSP 2020–2020 IEEE International Conference on Acoustics, Speech and Signal Processing (ICASSP), pp. 7429–7433 (2020). https://doi.org/10.1109/ICASSP40776.2020.9053334
10. Lee, L., Rose, R.: A frequency warping approach to speaker normalization. IEEE Trans. Speech Audio Process. **6**(1), 49–60 (1998)
11. Lee, S., Potamianos, A., Narayanan, S.: Acoustics of children's speech: developmental changes of temporal and spectral parameters. J. Acoust. Soc. Am. **105**(3), 1455–1468 (1999)
12. Makhoul, J.: Linear prediction: a tutorial review. Proc. IEEE **63**(4), 561–580 (1975). https://doi.org/10.1109/PROC.1975.9792
13. Morise, M., Takahashi, T., Kawahara, H., Irino, T.: Power spectrum estimation method for periodic signals virtually irrespective to time window position. Trans. IEICE **90**(12), 3265–3267 (2007)
14. Patterson, R.: Auditory filters and excitation patterns as representations of frequency resolution. In: Frequency Selectivity in Hearing (1986)
15. Peddinti, V., Povey, D., Khudanpur, S.: A time delay neural network architecture for efficient modeling of long temporal contexts. In: Proceedings of Interspeech (2015)
16. Povey, D., et al.: The Kaldi Speech recognition toolkit. In: Proceedings of ASRU (2011)

17. Povey, D., et al.: Purely sequence-trained neural networks for ASR based on lattice-free MMI. In: Proceedings of Interspeech, pp. 2751–2755 (2016)
18. Robinson, T., Fransen, J., Pye, D., Foote, J., Renals, S.: WSJCAM0: a British English speech corpus for large vocabulary continuous speech recognition. In: Proceedings of ICASSP, vol. 1, pp. 81–84 (1995). https://doi.org/10.1109/ICASSP.1995.479278
19. Russell, M., D'Arcy, S.: Challenges for computer recognition of children's speech. In: Proceedings of Speech and Language Technologies in Education (SLaTE) (2007)
20. Sainath, T.N., Vinyals, O., Senior, A., Sak, H.: Convolutional, long short-term memory, fully connected deep neural networks. In: 2015 IEEE International Conference on Acoustics, Speech and Signal Processing (ICASSP), pp. 4580–4584 (2015). https://doi.org/10.1109/ICASSP.2015.7178838
21. Schluter, R., Bezrukov, I., Wagner, H., Ney, H.: Gammatone features and feature combination for large vocabulary speech recognition. In: Proceedings of ICASSP, vol. 4, pp. IV-649–IV-652 (2007). https://doi.org/10.1109/ICASSP.2007.366996
22. Serizel, R., Giuliani, D.: Vocal tract length normalisation approaches to DNN-based children's and adults' speech recognition. In: Proceedings of Spoken Language Technology Workshop (SLT), pp. 135–140 (2014)
23. Shahnawazuddin, S., Adiga, N., Kathania, H.K., Sai, B.T.: Creating speaker independent ASR system through prosody modification based data augmentation. Pattern Recogn. Lett. **131**, 213–218 (2020). https://doi.org/10.1016/j.patrec.2019.12.019
24. Shahnawazuddin, S., Adiga, N., Kumar, K., Poddar, A., Ahmad, W.: Voice conversion based data augmentation to improve children's speech recognition in limited data scenario. In: Proceedings of Interspeech, pp. 4382–4386 (2020). https://doi.org/10.21437/Interspeech.2020-1112
25. Shahnawazuddin, S., Adiga, N., Kathania, H.K., Pradhan, G., Sinha, R.: Studying the role of pitch-adaptive spectral estimation and speaking-rate normalization in automatic speech recognition. Digital Signal Process. **79**, 142–151 (2018)
26. Shahnawazuddin, S., Adiga, N., Kathania, H.K.: Effect of prosody modification on children's ASR. IEEE Signal Process. Lett. **24**(11), 1749–1753 (2017)
27. Shao, Y., Jin, Z., Wang, D., Srinivasan, S.: An auditory-based feature for robust speech recognition. In: Proceedings of ICASSP, pp. 4625–4628 (2009). https://doi.org/10.1109/ICASSP.2009.4960661
28. Shao, Y., Wang, D.: Robust speaker identification using auditory features and computational auditory scene analysis. In: 2008 IEEE International Conference on Acoustics, Speech and Signal Processing, pp. 1589–1592 (2008). https://doi.org/10.1109/ICASSP.2008.4517928
29. Valero, X., Alias, F.: Gammatone cepstral coefficients: biologically inspired features for non-speech audio classification. IEEE Trans. Multimedia **14**(6), 1684–1689 (2012). https://doi.org/10.1109/TMM.2012.2199972
30. Waibel, A., Hanazawa, T., Hinton, G., Shikano, K., Lang, K.: Phoneme recognition using time-delay neural networks. IEEE Trans. Acoust. Speech Signal Process. **37**(3), 328–339 (1989). https://doi.org/10.1109/29.21701

Code-Mixed Text-to-Speech Synthesis Under Low-Resource Constraints

Raviraj Joshi[✉][iD] and Nikesh Garera

Flipkart, Bengaluru, India
{raviraj.j,nikesh.garera}@flipkart.com

Abstract. Text-to-speech (TTS) systems are an important component in voice-based e-commerce applications. These applications include end-to-end voice assistant and customer experience (CX) voice bot. Code-mixed TTS is also relevant in these applications since the product names are commonly described in English while the surrounding text is in a regional language. In this work, we describe our approaches for production quality code-mixed Hindi-English TTS systems built for e-commerce applications. We propose a data-oriented approach by utilizing monolingual data sets in individual languages. We leverage a transliteration model to convert the Roman text into a common Devanagari script and then combine both datasets for training. We show that such single script bi-lingual training without any code-mixing works well for pure code-mixed test sets. We further present an exhaustive evaluation of single-speaker adaptation and multi-speaker training with Tacotron2 + Waveglow setup to show that the former approach works better. These approaches are also coupled with transfer learning and decoder-only fine-tuning to improve performance. We compare these approaches with the Google TTS and report a positive CMOS score of 0.02 with the proposed transfer learning approach. We also perform low-resource voice adaptation experiments to show that a new voice can be onboarded with just 3 hrs of data. This highlights the importance of our pre-trained models in resource-constrained settings. This subjective evaluation is performed on a large number of out-of-domain pure code-mixed sentences to demonstrate the high quality of the systems.

Keywords: Code-mixed · Text-to-speech · Encoder-decoder models · Tacotron2 · Waveglow · Transfer learning

1 Introduction

Text to Speech (TTS) systems are widely used in voice-based applications [38]. These systems are used along with automatic speech recognition (ASR) [16] to provide an end-to-end voice interface. It is also prominently used in e-commerce applications like voice assistants, customer experience (CX) voice bots, and user nudges to highlight a feature or product [15,20]. In this work, we describe the approaches used to build the TTS system for e-commerce use cases.

A. Karpov et al. (Eds.): SPECOM 2023, LNAI 14339, pp. 151–163, 2023.
https://doi.org/10.1007/978-3-031-48312-7_12

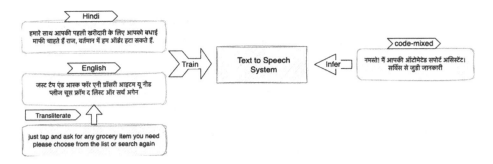

Fig. 1. Code-mixed text to speech synthesis.

In a country like India with high linguistic diversity along with English speaking population 'code-mixing' or 'code-switching' is a common phenomenon. With a large Hindi-speaking diaspora, Hindi-English code-mixing is prevalent in social media and e-commerce platforms [26]. Moreover with product names and service terminologies mostly described in English an e-commerce voice assistant with Hindi as the primary language should support code-mixing as well. For example, a Hindi sentence *"Mafi chahate hai, par aapke product Babolat Super Tape X Five Protection Tape ko wapis nahi kiya jaa sakta hai"* (We're sorry, but your product Babolat Super Tape X Five Protection Tape is non-returnable) contains product name in English. We, therefore, focus on building a code-mixed TTS system for e-commerce use cases.

Building a TTS system requires high-quality studio recordings for training [27]. It is even difficult to build a code-mixed TTS due to a lack of appropriate data sets, complex methods, and coverage issues. A common approach is to create a mixed-script data set by detecting the language of each word and then transliterating it into the corresponding script [31,35]. The mixed script is preferred as the pronunciation of regional tokens is more accurate in the native script. For Hindi-English code-mixed text, the Hindi words are in Devanagari script whereas the English words are in Roman script. Each word is passed to the corresponding language G2P (Grapheme to phoneme) system and the phoneme representations are then passed to the model. An even naive approach is to use a single English G2P model and map Hindi phones to the closest English phones. However, utilizing separate G2P modules for two languages yields good results. These multi-component systems are complex to build and also results in high latency.

In this work, we propose a simple data-oriented approach for our use case. Due to a lack of pure code-mixed data, the proposed solution utilizes individual monolingual (text, audio) pairs in Hindi and English. We use an in-house high-quality transliteration system to convert the English data to a common Devanagari script. The Hindi and English data are mixed to train a TTS model converting Devanagari text to speech. Since the primary language of the end application is Hindi we convert all the data to Devanagari script. We show that independent bi-lingual data sets without pure code-mixing work well for pure code-mixed test sets. This approach is shown in Fig. 1. Although our primary focus is Hindi and Devanagari script with high-quality transliteration systems (English to any Indic Script) the idea can be easily extended to other languages.

For modeling, we implement a two-stage Tacotron2 + Waveglow architecture [30,33]. The Tacotron2 model has been used for text-to-spectrogram conversion and the Waveglow then converts the spectrogram into target audio samples. While there are multiple options available for the spectrogram prediction network and audio synthesis network we choose Tacotron2 + Waveglow as they are competitive with other architectures and still popular in literature [1,10–12]. Moreover, there are single-stage end-to-end deep learning models available but these are not considered in this work due to high data requirements. We also present a comparative analysis of single-speaker and multi-speaker Tacotron2 configurations [14]. The single speaker is a standard setup where single-speaker data is used to train the model. In the muti-speaker setup, we utilize speaker embeddings extracted from an external pre-trained speaker verification model to control the output speaker characteristics. A multi-speaker model allows for zero-shot or few-shot voice adaptation and also has the advantage of cross-speaker learning. These approaches are further augmented using pre-training based transfer learning approach. We initially pre-train the single-speaker model by pooling all the speakers together. This pre-trained model is adapted for target speakers in single-speaker configuration and is also used to initialize the multi-speaker model. We show that the single-speaker adaptation of the pre-trained works the best. We observe that although a single multi-speaker model is capable of generating speech for multiple speakers it leads to a slight degradation in the quality of output. These approaches are evaluated using subjective MOS and CMOS scores on a completely out-of-domain test set from the CX domain while the training data is from the Voice Bot and general domain.

2 Related Work

A host of TTS architectures have been proposed over time with a focus on speed and quality. Recently, single-stage fully end-to-end architectures have been proposed which directly convert text to audio samples. These models include VITS [18], Wave-Tacotron [42], and JETS [24]. However, these models require a large amount of data. The two-stage models (spectrogram generation + speech synthesis) require comparatively less amount of data as the vocoder can be separately trained with audio-only data. The popular spectrogram prediction networks include Tacotron2 [33], Transformer-TTS [23], FastSpeech2 [32], FastPitch [22], and Glow-TTS [17]. There are a wide variety of vocoders to choose from like Clarinet [28], Waveglow [30], MelGAN [21], HiFiGAN [19], StyleMelGAN [25], and ParallelWaveGAN [44]. In terms of voice quality, there is no clear winner among the models and models perform competitively on high-quality datasets.

These architectures have also been extended to multi-speakers by conditioning them on speaker embeddings. The speaker embeddings encode the speaker characteristics of the target audio. The speaker embeddings are either extracted from an external speaker verification model [2, 14] or learned jointly during TTS training [29]. The external embeddings are based on d-vector [40] or x-vector [37] systems. The pre-trained and learnable speaker embeddings were compared in·[6]. The per-trained embeddings were shown to perform superior performance on FastSpeech 2 model. A similar comparison with the Tacotron model has been performed in [8]. They perform zero-shot speaker adaption using different speaker embeddings but still report a gap between similarity scores of seen and unseen speakers. They observed that these models do not generalize well to unseen speakers. A TTS system incorporating different emotions was studied in [43]. They use global style tokens (GSTs) to encode the emotion information add the tokens are jointly trained using emotion labels. Similarly, multi-speaker systems using speaker embeddings are also built in [4, 5, 9].

Relatively less amount of work has been done in code-mixed TTS systems. A preliminary approach for Hindi-English code-mixed TTS using mixed script text was proposed in [34]. A language identification system was employed to distinguish Romanized Hindi and English words followed by the transliteration of Hindi words to the Devanagari script. They however used a common English phone set for both Hindi and English words which might result in accent issues for regional words. Further, different Grapheme to Phoneme (G2P) for English words and regional words were utilized in [31,39]. A single mix-lingual G2P model instead of two separate models were proposed in [3]. In [45], embeddings from an external cross-lingual language model were integrated into the fronted of Tacotron2 model along with the original phone embeddings. The cross-lingual language model encodes words of both languages into the same space thus improving the performance of code-switched TTS. In this work, we make use of a single script and a graphene-based Tacotron frontend thus eliminating the need for such complex high latency modifications. The high quality of the transliteration model also suppresses the pronunciation and accent issues.

3   Methodology

3.1   Code-Mixed TTS

The primary objective of this work is to build a Hindi-English code-mixed or code-switched TTS. Ideally, we would require code-mixed recordings for training such a system. However such recordings are rarely available in practice due to the focus on a single language. To solve for the lack of datasets, we propose a data-oriented approach and utilize monolingual data from the two languages. We use the recordings for Hindi and English text from the same speaker. We propose a single script transliteration-based approach to build a bilingual system. Since the primary language of the end application is Hindi we convert the English text to Devnagari script using an in-house Roman-to-Devanagari transliteration model. The (English text, audio) and (Hindi text, audio) paired data with all the text in the Devanagari script are simply used together to train a single model. We show that this simple mixing works well even for the code-mixed data.

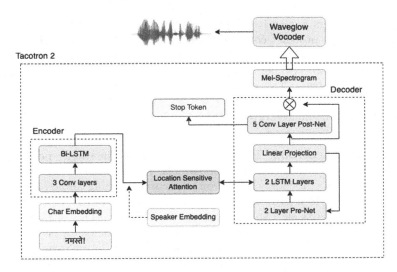

Fig. 2. Model Architecture for single-speaker and multi-speaker configurations. The multi-speaker model has an extra speaker embedding component extracted from a pre-trained speaker verification model.

We compare Hindi-only training and dual-language training to show the effectiveness of using dual languages. The system is evaluated on 500 strong code-mixed examples from the out-of-domain Customer Experience (CX) domain. We also evaluate the system on a 500 English-only product names test set to showcase the English-speaking capabilities of the model.

3.2   Model Architecture

In this work, we use the Tacotron2 spectrogram prediction network and Waveglow vocoder for all our data-oriented experiments. We perform both single-speaker and multi-speaker experiments. For the multi-speaker model, we simply fuse the external x-vector speaker embeddings with the Tacotron model. The model architecture is described in Fig. 2. In the next sub-sections, we describe network architecture and the experimental setup.

Single-speaker Tacotron2. The Tacotron2 [33] is an auto-regressive encoder-decoder model that maps text sequence to spectrogram sequence. We use characters as input to the encoder and the architecture is the same as that described in the original work. The encoder consists of three Conv layers followed by a Bi-LSTM layer. The character embedding size, number of Conv filters, and Bi-LSTM units is 512. The Conv filter size is 5×1. The decoder is an auto-regressive network conditioned on encoder output. It uses location-sensitive attention [7] to compute the context vector. It consists of two uni-LSTM layers with 1024 units. The decoder also consists of a pre-net and post-net added before and after the uni-LSTM layers respectively. The pre-net consists of 2 feedforward layers (256 units) and the post-net consists of 5 Conv layers (512 filters with a size of 5×1). The output of the uni-LSTM is concatenated with the context vector and is passed through two parallel dense layers to compute the stop token and target log-mel spectrogram. The spectrogram is further refined using the post-net and a residual connection connects the output spectrogram to the output of the post-net. The mean squared error (MSE) loss is used for training.

Multi-speaker Tacotron2. This model is the same as the single-speaker model except for the addition of speaker embeddings. An x-vector system is used to extract the speaker embeddings [36] from the corresponding audio sample. The pre-trained model[1] is based on a time-delay neural network (TDNN). It was trained using the VoxCeleb speaker recognition dataset. The 512-dimensional embeddings are subjected to LayerNorm followed by a dense layer of size 512. The output of the dense layer is again passed through a LayerNorm and added to each time step of the encoder output. The decoder is therefore conditioned on the speaker embeddings as well in order to generate audio for the desired speaker. The multi-speaker model again has two configurations as described below.

- **Audio embedding**: This is the regular configuration in which speaker embedding for each audio is computed at run time and passed to the model. The audios from a specific speaker are not explicitly distinguished. We observe that this model shows some generalization to un-seen speakers however at times fails to generate an end token on some audio samples during inference.
- **Avg embedding**: This configuration is similar to speaker selection where each speaker is assigned a single speaker embedding which is the average of speaker embedding from all the audios of the corresponding speaker. With this configuration, we do not see the end token issue however this does not work for unseen speakers.

Pre-training Strategies. We explore transfer learning from public LJSpeech English data and all the available Hindi data from multiple speakers. We observe that pre-training strategies are essential for building a high-quality model. The following strategies are followed for both single-speaker and multi-speaker models.

- **English warmstart**: The Tacotron2 model is initially trained on English LJSpeech corpus with the input in Roman script. During target speaker fine-tuning the character embedding layer has to be discarded since our experiments are based on the Devanagari script.
- **Mix-data warmstart**: In this setup, we initialize the model with weights from English training and then further train the entire model on a mixture of all the speaker's data in the Devanagari script. This model is not directly useful since it is a single-speaker model trained with multi-speakers. This

---

[1] https://huggingface.co/speechbrain/spkrec-xvect-voxceleb.

model will generate different speakers' voices for different sentences and is typically biased toward one specific speaker. However, a rich text encoder obtained from this mixed training hence acts as a very good initialization for target speaker adaptation.

Fine-Tuning Strategies. Based on the pre-training strategies we follow two fine-tuning methods.

- **Full fine-tuning**: The english-warmstart models are subjected to full-finetuning. This is required because of the mismatch in the script for the English text and Devanagari text.
- **Decoder only fine-tuning**: The mix-warmstart models the encoder is already trained on a large amount of Devanagari text. So we freeze the encoder parameters and perform decoder-only fine-tuning. While we can perform full finetuning with mix-warmstart model it gives slightly lower performance than decoder-only finetuning.

We perform an ablation study with pre-training and fine-tuning methods to show that mix-warmstart + decoder-only finetuning works the best.

Low-Resource Voice Adaptation. We perform low-resource voice adaptation experiments in order to understand data requirements for onboarding a new voice/speaker. We use the pre-trained models and perform single-speaker adaptation using different low data configurations like 3 hrs, 5 hrs, and 10 hrs. We observe that 3 hrs of data is sufficient to get a high-quality model with mix-warmstart models. The experiments corresponding to 3 hrs of data are reported in this work. Recently, a TTS system Vall-E [41] has shown extraordinary zero-shot capabilities. However, this system uses a complex architecture and requires 60K hours of pre-training data making it infeasible in low-resource scenarios. Our work uses data of order 15 h and therefore cannot be compared with such system utilizing 60k hours of data.

Waveglow Vocoder. The waveglow [30] model converts mel-spectrogram into audio samples. It is a flow-based generative model which generates audio samples by sampling from a distribution. It performs a series of invertible transforms to convert examples sampled from zero mean and spherical Gaussian distribution into target audio samples. The transformation is also conditioned on mel-spectrogram. The model minimizes the log-likelihood of the data.

The mel-spectrogram is computed using short time fourier transform (STFT). It uses a frame length of 50 ms and a hop size of 12 ms. An 80-channel Mel filter bank is used to transform STFT into Mel scale followed by log compression.

3.3 Dataset Details

The datasets used in this work are described below.

Table 1. Subjective MOS scores for different model configurations on code-mixed CX test set.

TTS Type	eng-warmstart (full train)	mix-warmstart (decoder only train)
single speaker (Hindi only)	4.37 ± 0.78	4.36 ± 0.86
single speaker (Hindi + English)	4.58 ± 0.69	**4.65 ± 0.56**
multi-speaker (audio-embed, Hindi + English)	4.55 ± 0.64	4.65 ± 0.50
multi-speaker (avg-embed, Hindi + English)	4.44 ± 0.95	4.61 ± 0.7

- **English LJSpeech Corpus**: It is a publicly available single-speaker corpus consisting of 13100 (text, audio) pairs [13]. The text is taken from 7 non-fiction English books and the total size of the data is 24 h.
- **Single-Speaker Data**: This is an in-house studio recording from a female speaker. The text for the recordings is taken from the Voice assistant domain and general domain (Wikipedia-like sentences). The total size of the data is 15 hrs consisting of both English and Hindi text. Roughly 65% of the data is Hindi and the rest is English. This speaker is also used for the evaluation of all the models explored in this work. In order to perform low-resource voice adaptation experiments we choose a random subset of 3 h from this data-set.
- **Multi-Speaker Data**: We further create a multi-speaker corpus using additional 4 speakers including 2 male and 2 female speakers. The text from the above single-speaker data is used for recording. The size of data for each speaker is approximately 15 h. These 4 speakers along with the above primary speaker are used for multi-speaker training. The primary female speaker is also chosen for testing the multi-speaker models. Since we use only 5 speakers in multi-speaker training the generated samples are highly similar to the original speaker. Hence similarity tests are not reported in this work. The goal of this work is to create a high-quality primary speaker system and all the evaluations are designed with this objective.
- **Test datasets**: We create two out-of-domain test sets for the evaluation of all the models. These test sets are from customer experience (CX) and product domains. The CX test set consists of customer queries and bot responses with high Hindi-English code-mixing. The product test set consists of English product names from e-Commerce listings. The size of both test sets is 500 text examples. The audios were synthesized for these texts from the corresponding model and used for MOS (Mean Opinion Scores) and CMOS (Comparative MOS) evaluation. For CMOS evaluation, we use the output from out-of-the-box Google speaker 'hi-IN-Standard-A' as the reference audio.

Table 2. Subjective CMOS scores for different model configurations. All the rows except for the last row corresponds to CX test set. The last row indicates numbers for Product test set.

TTS Type	eng-warmstart (full train)	mix-warmstart (decoder only train)
single speaker (Hindi only)	−0.47	−0.35
single speaker (Hindi + English)	−0.45	**0.02**
multi-speaker (audio-embed, Hindi + English)	−0.42	−0.3
multi-speaker (avg-embed, Hindi + English)	−0.8	−0.14
single speaker (Hindi + English, Product test set)	–	**0.12**

Table 3. MOS scores for low-resource voice adaptation experiments on target speaker

Training Strategy	MOS
eng-warmstart + Target (3 h)	4.27 ± 0.95
mix-warmstart + Target (3 h)	4.54 ± 0.58
mix-warmstart + Target (frozen encoder, 3 h)	**4.59 ± 0.68**
mix-warmstart + Target (frozen encoder, 15 h)	4.65 ± 0.58

4   Results

In this work, we evaluate different single-speaker and multi-speaker TTS models for code-mixed speech synthesis tasks. Independent Mean Opinion Scores (MOS) and comparative CMOS scores are used to compare these models. These evaluations are done by 50 trained individuals with each listener evaluating around 30 audios. The audios are presented in random order and specifically, during CMOS the reference audio is randomly chosen. In MOS evaluation the listener is asked to rate the audio on a 1–5 (with a gap of 0.5) scale. A score of 5 indicates a naturally sounding voice with perfect pronunciation. The naturalness and pronunciation are evaluated during MOS, the higher the score better the system.

In the CMOS evaluation user listens to both audios from our TTS and Google TTS. They provide a rating to the second audio in the (−2 to +2) range. Again based on the naturalness and pronunciation of the second audio is given a +ve rating if it is better than the first audio. A score of 0 indicates that both systems are equally better. The speaker for the first and second audios are randomly selected and scores are internally adjusted such that a +ve rating indicates our speaker is better as compared to the Google speaker and a −ve rating indicates vice versa. The reported MOS and CMOS scores are average of all the individual scores. Standard practices are followed to avoid listener fatigue and bias.

All the models are evaluated in two configurations eng-warmstart and mix-warmstart. The eng-warmstart indicates English data pre-training with full fine-

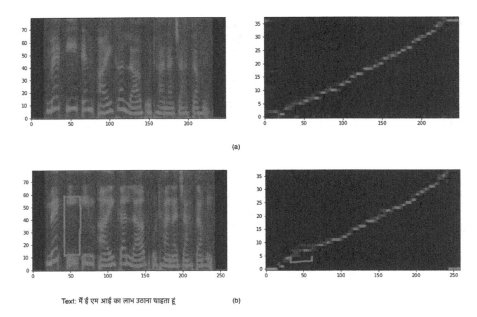

Text: मैं ई एम आई का लाभ उठाना चाहता हूं   (b)

Fig. 3. The Mel-spectrogram and attention alignment plot for a sample sentence using config (a) Mixed [Hindi + English] Training (b) Hindi only training. The difference in the resolution can be clearly seen at the start of the two spectrograms at the word EMI.

tuning whereas mix-warmstart indicates mix data pre-training with decoder-only finetuning. The MOS results are shown in Table 1 and the CMOS scores are shown in Table 2. We show that (Hindi + English) training works better than Hindi-only training via both MOS and CMOS scores. A sample spectrogram for the two configurations is shown in Fig. 3.

The mix-warmstart configuration shows clear improvements over eng-warmstart thus highlighting the importance of Devanagari-based pre-training. While comparing multi-speaker and single-speaker models, the single-speaker based adaptation works better. The difference is more prominent in comparative CMOS score as compared to the MOS score. A positive CMOS score for the single-speaker mix-pretrained model indicates that the system is slightly better than the Google system on code-mixed test sets. Finally, while comparing the two speaker embedding methods for multi-speaker models there is no clear winner. The CMOS scores are in favor of avg-embed whereas MOS scores are in favor of audio-embed. We personally felt that audio-embed systems are slightly better. We also perform a CMOS evaluation of the best single-speaker system on the English product names test set. A high +ve CMOS score indicates that the dual data training is also helping the model beat the Google system.

The results of low-resource speaker adaptation are described in Table 3. We observe that the mix-warmstart models can be adapted to a new speaker using just 3 h of data. We again use decoder-only fine-tuning in this setup. The degradation in MOS scores is very less even after using just 1/5th of the original data.

5 Conclusion

We present different approaches utilized to build a production-quality TTS system for code-mixed e-commerce use cases. We propose a transliteration-based approach to convert the dual language data into a common script and use it for training. We show that this dual language training also works well for code-mixed test sets. We compare different single-speaker and multi-speaker TTS models using two different pre-training methods. We show the advantages of transfer learning from the mix-pretraining setup. The multi-speaker models are further evaluated in reference audio (audio-embed) and speaker selection (avg-embed) configurations. The single-speaker model with mix-data pre-training performs the best and it is also shown to perform better than the Google TTS on code-mixed use cases. We also show that the mix-data pre-trained models with decoder-only fine tuning can be adapted to a new voice with just 3 h of data. This shows the importance of pre-trained models in a low-resource setting.

References

1. Abdelali, A., Durrani, N., Demiroglu, C., Dalvi, F., Mubarak, H., Darwish, K.: Natiq: an end-to-end text-to-speech system for Arabic. arXiv preprint arXiv:2206.07373 (2022)
2. Arik, S., Chen, J., Peng, K., Ping, W., Zhou, Y.: Neural voice cloning with a few samples. Adv. Neural Inf. Process. Syst. **31** (2018)
3. Bansal, S., Mukherjee, A., Satpal, S., Mehta, R.: On improving code mixed speech synthesis with mixlingual grapheme-to-phoneme model. In: INTERSPEECH, pp. 2957–2961 (2020)
4. Casanova, E., Weber, J., Shulby, C.D., Junior, A.C., Gölge, E., Ponti, M.A.: Yourtts: towards zero-shot multi-speaker TTS and zero-shot voice conversion for everyone. In: International Conference on Machine Learning, pp. 2709–2720. PMLR (2022)
5. Chen, M., et al.: Cross-lingual, multi-speaker text-to-speech synthesis using neural speaker embedding. In: Interspeech, pp. 2105–2109 (2019)
6. Chien, C.M., Lin, J.H., Huang, C.Y., Hsu, P.C., Lee, H.Y.: Investigating on incorporating pretrained and learnable speaker representations for multi-speaker multi-style text-to-speech. In: 2021 IEEE International Conference on Acoustics, Speech and Signal Processing (ICASSP 2021), pp. 8588–8592. IEEE (2021)
7. Chorowski, J.K., Bahdanau, D., Serdyuk, D., Cho, K., Bengio, Y.: Attention-based models for speech recognition. Adv. Neural Inf. Process. Syst. **28** (2015)
8. Cooper, E., et al.:: Zero-shot multi-speaker text-to-speech with state-of-the-art neural speaker embeddings. In: 2020 IEEE International Conference on Acoustics, Speech and Signal Processing (ICASSP 2020), pp. 6184–6188. IEEE (2020)
9. Cooper, E., Lai, C.I., Yasuda, Y., Yamagishi, J.: Can speaker augmentation improve multi-speaker end-to-end TTS? arXiv preprint arXiv:2005.01245 (2020)

10. Favaro, A., Sbattella, L., Tedesco, R., Scotti, V.: Itacotron 2: transfering English speech synthesis architectures and speech features to Italian. In: Proceedings of the Fourth International Conference on Natural Language and Speech Processing (ICNLSP 2021), pp. 83–88 (2021)
11. Finkelstein, L., et al.: Training text-to-speech systems from synthetic data: a practical approach for accent transfer tasks. arXiv preprint arXiv:2208.13183 (2022)
12. García, V., Hernáez, I., Navas, E.: Evaluation of tacotron based synthesizers for Spanish and Basque. Appl. Sci. **12**(3), 1686 (2022)
13. Ito, K., Johnson, L.: The LJ speech dataset (2017). https://keithito.com/LJ-Speech-Dataset/
14. Jia, Y., et al.: Transfer learning from speaker verification to multispeaker text-to-speech synthesis. Adv. Neural Inf. Process. Syst. **31** (2018)
15. Joshi, R., Kannan, V.: Attention based end to end speech recognition for voice search in Hindi and English. In: Proceedings of the 13th Annual Meeting of the Forum for Information Retrieval Evaluation, pp. 107–113 (2021)
16. Joshi, R., Kumar, S.: On comparison of encoders for attention based end to end speech recognition in standalone and rescoring mode. In: 2022 IEEE International Conference on Signal Processing and Communications (SPCOM), pp. 1–4. IEEE (2022)
17. Kim, J., Kim, S., Kong, J., Yoon, S.: Glow-TTS: a generative flow for text-to-speech via monotonic alignment search. Adv. Neural. Inf. Process. Syst. **33**, 8067–8077 (2020)
18. Kim, J., Kong, J., Son, J.: Conditional variational autoencoder with adversarial learning for end-to-end text-to-speech. In: International Conference on Machine Learning, pp. 5530–5540. PMLR (2021)
19. Kong, J., Kim, J., Bae, J.: Hifi-gan: generative adversarial networks for efficient and high fidelity speech synthesis. Adv. Neural. Inf. Process. Syst. **33**, 17022–17033 (2020)
20. Kraus, D., Reibenspiess, V., Eckhardt, A.: How voice can change customer satisfaction: a comparative analysis between e-commerce and voice commerce (2019)
21. Kumar, K., et al.: Melgan: generative adversarial networks for conditional waveform synthesis. Adv. Neural Inf. Process. Syst. **32** (2019)
22. Łańcucki, A.: Fastpitch: Parallel text-to-speech with pitch prediction. In: 2021 IEEE International Conference on Acoustics, Speech and Signal Processing (ICASSP 2021), pp. 6588–6592. IEEE (2021)
23. Li, N., Liu, S., Liu, Y., Zhao, S., Liu, M.: Neural speech synthesis with transformer network. In: Proceedings of the AAAI Conference on Artificial Intelligence, vol. 33, pp. 6706–6713 (2019)
24. Lim, D., Jung, S., Kim, E.: Jets: jointly training fastspeech2 and hifi-gan for end to end text to speech. arXiv preprint arXiv:2203.16852 (2022)
25. Mustafa, A., Pia, N., Fuchs, G.: Stylemelgan: an efficient high-fidelity adversarial vocoder with temporal adaptive normalization. In: 2021 IEEE International Conference on Acoustics, Speech and Signal Processing (ICASSP 2021), pp. 6034–6038. IEEE (2021)
26. Nayak, R., Joshi, R.: L3cube-hingcorpus and hingbert: a code mixed Hindi-English dataset and bert language models. In: LREC 2022 Workshop Language Resources and Evaluation Conference, 20–25 June 2022, p. 7 (2022)
27. Ning, Y., He, S., Wu, Z., Xing, C., Zhang, L.J.: A review of deep learning based speech synthesis. Appl. Sci. **9**(19), 4050 (2019)
28. Ping, W., Peng, K., Chen, J.: Clarinet: parallel wave generation in end-to-end text-to-speech. arXiv preprint arXiv:1807.07281 (2018)

29. Ping, W., et al.: Deep voice 3: scaling text-to-speech with convolutional sequence learning. In: International Conference on Learning Representations
30. Prenger, R., Valle, R., Catanzaro, B.: Waveglow: a flow-based generative network for speech synthesis. In: 2019 IEEE International Conference on Acoustics, Speech and Signal Processing (ICASSP 2019), pp. 3617–3621. IEEE (2019)
31. Rallabandi, S.K., Black, A.W.: On building mixed lingual speech synthesis systems. In: Interspeech, pp. 52–56 (2017)
32. Ren, Y., et al.: Fastspeech 2: fast and high-quality end-to-end text to speech. arXiv preprint arXiv:2006.04558 (2020)
33. Shen, J., et al.: Natural TTS synthesis by conditioning wavenet on MEL spectrogram predictions. In: 2018 IEEE International Conference on Acoustics, Speech and Signal Processing (ICASSP), pp. 4779–4783. IEEE (2018)
34. Sitaram, S., Black, A.W.: Speech synthesis of code-mixed text. In: Proceedings of the Tenth International Conference on Language Resources and Evaluation (LREC 2016), pp. 3422–3428 (2016)
35. Sitaram, S., Rallabandi, S.K., Rijhwani, S., Black, A.W.: Experiments with cross-lingual systems for synthesis of code-mixed text. In: SSW, pp. 76–81 (2016)
36. Snyder, D., Garcia-Romero, D., McCree, A., Sell, G., Povey, D., Khudanpur, S.: Spoken language recognition using x-vectors. In: Odyssey, vol. 2018, pp. 105–111 (2018)
37. Snyder, D., Garcia-Romero, D., Sell, G., Povey, D., Khudanpur, S.: X-vectors: robust DNN embeddings for speaker recognition. In: 2018 IEEE International Conference on Acoustics, Speech and Signal Processing (ICASSP), pp. 5329–5333. IEEE (2018)
38. Tan, X., Qin, T., Soong, F., Liu, T.Y.: A survey on neural speech synthesis. arXiv preprint arXiv:2106.15561 (2021)
39. Thomas, A.L., Prakash, A., Baby, A., Murthy, H.A.: Code-switching in INDIC speech synthesisers. In: INTERSPEECH, pp. 1948–1952 (2018)
40. Wan, L., Wang, Q., Papir, A., Moreno, I.L.: Generalized end-to-end loss for speaker verification. In: 2018 IEEE International Conference on Acoustics, Speech and Signal Processing (ICASSP), pp. 4879–4883. IEEE (2018)
41. Wang, C., et al.: Neural codec language models are zero-shot text to speech synthesizers. arXiv preprint arXiv:2301.02111 (2023)
42. Weiss, R.J., Skerry-Ryan, R., Battenberg, E., Mariooryad, S., Kingma, D.P.: Wavetacotron: spectrogram-free end-to-end text-to-speech synthesis. In: 2021 IEEE International Conference on Acoustics, Speech and Signal Processing (ICASSP 2021), pp. 5679–5683. IEEE (2021)
43. Wu, P., Ling, Z., Liu, L., Jiang, Y., Wu, H., Dai, L.: End-to-end emotional speech synthesis using style tokens and semi-supervised training. In: 2019 Asia-Pacific Signal and Information Processing Association Annual Summit and Conference (APSIPA ASC), pp. 623–627. IEEE (2019)
44. Yamamoto, R., Song, E., Kim, J.M.: Parallel wavegan: a fast waveform generation model based on generative adversarial networks with multi-resolution spectrogram. In: 2020 IEEE International Conference on Acoustics, Speech and Signal Processing (ICASSP 2020), pp. 6199–6203. IEEE (2020)
45. Zhou, X., Tian, X., Lee, G., Das, R.K., Li, H.: End-to-end code-switching TTS with cross-lingual language model. In: 2020 IEEE International Conference on Acoustics, Speech and Signal Processing (ICASSP 2020), pp. 7614–7618. IEEE (2020)

An End-to-End TTS Model in Chhattisgarhi, a Low-Resource Indian Language

Abhayjeet Singh, Anjali Jayakumar, G. Deekshitha[✉], Hitesh Kumar,
Jesuraja Bandekar, Sandhya Badiger, Sathvik Udupa, Saurabh Kumar,
and Prasanta Kumar Ghosh

Department of Electrical Engineering, Indian Institute of Science (IISc),
Bangalore 560012, India
{contact.syspin,prasantg}@iisc.ac.in, deekshu50@gmail.com
https://syspin.iisc.ac.in/

Abstract. With the advancement of voice technology, there is a drastic improvement in the realization of Text To Speech (TTS) systems. But the lack of technological support and diversities in the low-resourced Indian languages hinder the development of such systems for the Indian population. SYSPIN is an initiative that aims to develop TTS corpora and AI models in nine Indian languages. The primary motivation behind this work is to set up an initiative to popularize the scope of voice technology for the Chhattisgarhi population. This paper presents 20 h of TTS dataset of 2 speakers in Chhattisgarhi, a low-resourced Indian language with 18 million native speakers. The paper also describes the baseline TTS systems which achieve high subjective scores of 4.38 and 4.46 mean opinion score (MOS) for each speaker.

Keywords: Low-Resourced Indian Dataset · Chhattisgarhi TTS Corpus · End-to-End TTS Model · SYSPIN

1 Introduction

In India, a large number of low-income people, who face barriers of literacy, skills, poverty, gender, and other socioeconomic biases, are unable to utilize digital technologies and corresponding services efficiently. So humanizing speech technology helps these under-skilled populations to access the technologies and services in their own language/ dialect through their own voice. But the advancements in speech technology are yet to meet the requirements in many of the low-resourced Indian languages that suffer from the unavailability of linguistic expertise and resources. This increases the necessity for the development of corpora and various speech technology solutions to provide different voice-based user-friendly applications.

Supported by GIZ-Deutsche Gesellschaft für Internationale Zusammenarbeit, Bonn, Germany.

Chhattisgarh is the ninth largest state in India (around 30 million population) with Chhattisgarhi and Hindi as the official languages. In all 33 districts, Chhattisgarhi is more popular than Hindi. Apart from Chhattisgarh, Chhattisgarhi is used in adjacent areas of Madhya Pradesh, Odisha, and Jharkhand [1]. As per the Linguistic Survey of India, Chhattisgarhi is considered an eastern variant of Hindi and hence is not included as an official language in the Indian constitution. According to the 2011 Linguistic Survey of India, 16.2 million people use Chhattisgarhi as their mother tongue [2]. About 80% of the population of the state is rural and the main livelihood of the villagers is agriculture and agriculture-based small industry [3]. The Average Literacy rate in Chhattisgarh for Urban regions was 84.05% in which female literacy stood at 73.39% [3]. Even though many attempts have been made to introduce voice-based applications to the Chhattisgarhi population, most of them ended up as either pilot studies or specific to some applications due to the lack of data [4–9].

Even though many efforts have been made to develop TTS systems in low-resource languages, no attempts were there on Chhattisgarhi [10–12]. SYSPIN[1] is an initiative that aims at the development of a large TTS corpus for some low-resource Indian languages including Chhattisgarhi. The proposed TTS dataset mainly includes sentences from a few domains that are highly relevant for poor farmers and the women population.

Through this work, we open source a part of the Chhattisgarhi TTS dataset from the SYSPIN initiative for academics, start-ups, researchers, and developers to spur innovation and academic activity in the development of regional voice technologies in India. The proposed dataset includes around 5k sentences and 10 h of recordings from two Chhattisgarhi native voice artists- 1 male and 1 female. An end-to-end Chhattisgarhi TTS model has also been developed as a baseline model.

The paper first presents the details of dataset collection in Sect. 2, from sentence composition to recording. Section 3 deals with the analysis of the collected dataset and Sect. 4 discusses the baseline model development. Finally, the paper summarizes the development of an end-to-end Chhattisgarhi TTS model in Sect. 5 with some future scopes to work.

2 Dataset Preparation

Unlike other high-resource languages like Hindi, online digital or printed texts are not much available for low-resource languages. For those languages, creating the text dataset itself is a challenging task. Figure 1 illustrates the process of Chhattisgarhi TTS dataset preparation, which involves sentence preparation, native voice artist selection, studio recording, and validation.

2.1 Sentence Preparation

Initially, a set of native composers have been selected after pilot validation and were asked to compose sentences on the given topics. People who are able to

---

[1] https://syspin.iisc.ac.in/.

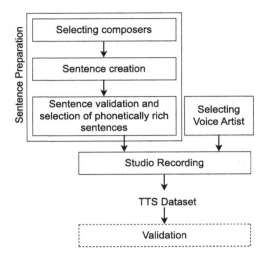

Fig. 1. Flowchart detailing the process of dataset preparation.

compose sentences in Chhattisgarhi (Raipur style) and who followed all the guidelines provided were selected for the particular task. Separate sheets with some topic lists and link to read more about the topics were given to each of the selected composers. The topics for composition were mainly taken from domains like agriculture, finance, education, food, politics, social, Indic, local, healthcare, technology, book continuous, sports, food, books, and websites. Books and website domains include sentences mined from the available printed textbooks as well as online sources. The sentences collected were again validated with another set of validators to check the language style and usage. Programmatic checks on the verified sentences ensure the absence of invalid characters and symbols.

Phonetically Rich Sentence Selection. While training the model, it is good to ensure that the dataset will have all phone combinations in a balanced manner. Before recording, a phonetically rich sub-dataset has been derived from all the validated sentences. The dataset thus created is supposed to cover all major domain vocabulary and phonetic combinations to function well in a practical scenario.

2.2   Voice Artist Selection

We selected the best native Voice Artist (VA) (one male and one female) only after doing a set of pilot checks. For the initial rounds of selection, each voice artist was requested to record some Chhattisgarhi sentences through an app (to keep the recording format uniform across all the speakers). The pilot checks include programmatic checks, reading proficiency checks, voice quality checks, and crowd-sourced perception checks by native speakers. Programmatic checks mainly include speaking rate analysis.

Fig. 2. Picture showing the recording studio setup.

2.3 Recording

After finalising the sentences and voice artists, the next phase of dataset preparation is recording. All the audio files were recorded in a studio setup designed by Bhashini AI Solutions Pvt Ltd[2] with a specification of 48kHz sampling frequency and 24 bits per sample. The studio specification includes a studio microphone: Neumann TLM-103, Audio Interface: UAD Apollo Twin X. Dimensions of the recording room/voice booth is 10'3" x 5'9". Other than the voice artist, there will be 2 other people needed in the studio for recording- one sound engineer and one recording validator.

The Chattisgarhi TTS dataset outsourced in this work is a raw dataset without any audio-text validation. Even though the recorded audio files are expected primarily to match their respective text, but have some mismatches.

3 Chhattisgarhi TTS Dataset Analysis

The proposed Chhattisgarhi TTS Dataset includes 10 h of recording from each male and female voice artist. Table 1 summarizes the major details of the dataset and Table 2 elaborates the distribution files across each domain for the female and male voice artists. Figure 3a illustrates the word counts across different domains for female and male voice artists. Similarly, Fig. 3b shows the distribution of pitch across both speakers. Figure 4 presents the entire vocabulary distribution across the male and female voice artists. It reveals the number of words that are common across male and female voice artists. Similarly, Fig. 5b and Fig. 5a indicate the distribution character length and duration of each file.

Despite the planning and efforts taken to develop an error-free corpus, while inspecting we came across some errors. But the TTS corpus did not go through a complete set of validation steps and, hence, contains different types of errors (as revealed from ongoing validation) a couple of which are illustrated in Fig. 6.

---

[2] https://www.bhashini.ai/.

Table 1. Dataset summary.

Item	Female	Male
Age group of VA	20–25	50–55
Native of VA	Raipur	Raipur
Extra langugaes known	Hindi	Hindi
Number of sentences	5148	4595
Duration	10.00 hr	10.00 hr
Average word length in a sentence	17.27	17.31
Average character length in a sentence	85.25	87.44
Vocabulary size	19872	16416

Table 2. Distribution of dataset across domains for the voice artists.

Female			Male		
Domain	Duration(hr)	# Files	Domain	Duration(hr)	# Files
Healthcare	0.65	341	Healthcare	0.97	470
Books	3.17	1660	Food	1.81	824
Sports	1.68	968	General	0.58	267
Indic	0.75	381	Politics	0.61	295
Local	3.11	1398	Technology	2.26	1085
Others	0.65	968	Website	3.78	1654
Total	10.00	5148	Total	10.00	4595

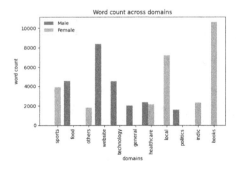

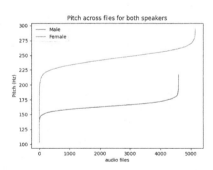

(a) Histogram showing words count across the male and female voice artists in each domain.

(b) Pitch across all the audio files for both speakers.

Fig. 3. Word count and pitch analysis across voice artists.

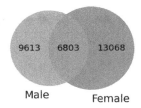

Fig. 4. Vocabulary distribution (all domains together) across the male and female voice artists.

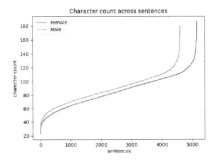
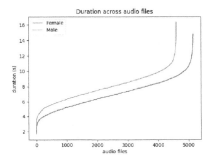

(a) Chart showing the length of each sentence against each voice artist.

(b) Histogram distribution of the duration of each audio against the voice artists.

Fig. 5. Character length and duration distribution in the dataset against each voice artist.

4   The Baseline: End-to-End Chhattisgarhi TTS Model

Separate TTS models are trained for both speakers. We use the VITS [13] model architecture to train the models with the Coqui-ai TTS [14] toolkit. VITS is an end-to-end TTS model capable of directly synthesising the speech waveform without the use of an external vocoder. It is a generative model which uses various formulations such as variational inference, normalising flows, and adversarial training. Along with this, it also learns a stochastic duration prediction, trained using an aligner in an unsupervised way. These specifications lead to various loss functions at the different stages of the model, leading to high-quality speech synthesis.   We perform a subjective evaluation of the trained models with a Mean Opinion Score (MOS). Here the quality of synthesized sentences is rated with respect to reference natural sentences. Evaluators were asked to rate both the synthesized and natural sentences. The evaluators will also listen to unseen natural sentences, randomly mixed with the synthesized audio. A few files will be repeated for each evaluator to identify scoring consistency.

This naturalness evaluation has been conducted on web application built with React and deployed on Firebase. Figure 7 shows the screenshot of the web app created for naturality check. For each speaker model, we synthesise 13 different

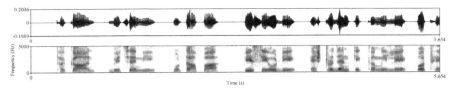

(a) Waveform showing the distortion in the audio file during the speech-end region got chopped off.

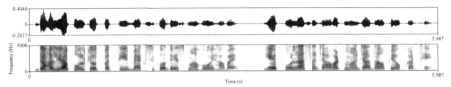

Original Text: डहलिया फूल के उत्पत्ति मेक्सिको देस म होए हवय ए फूल ला सजाबट म जादा उपयोग करथे
Corrected Text: डहलिया फूल के उत्पत्ति मेक्सिको देस म होए हवय ए फूल ला सजाव म जादा उपयोग करथे

(b) Waveform with audio-text mismatch.

Fig. 6. Sample errors found in the dataset.

Fig. 7. Sreenshot of the *React web app* shared with the validators.

unseen sentences. These 26 synthesised audio is then mixed with 4 unseen ground truth audio, and these 30 files are given to manual validators to perform the subjective evaluation. We used 53 native speakers of Chattisgrahi (15 females and 38 males whose ages range from 20-68) to score all the files. The validators rate on a scale of 1-5 as shown in Fig. 7, with 5 representing human-like speech.

Table 3. Mean Opinion Score (MOS) is reported for both TTS models, for real as well as generated samples. The standard deviation is shown in brackets.

TTS model	MOS	
	Real	Generated
Male TTS	4.73(0.62)	4.46(0.61)
Female TTS	4.77(0.52)	4.38(0.67)

The results are shown below in the Table 3. We observe that both models have high MOS scores for generated audio, even with 10 h of data for training.

5   Conclusion

The paper summarizes the efforts taken to realize an end-to-end Chhattisgarhi TTS model. A brief description of the dataset collection, starting from stage 1 of sentence composition to final recording by voice artists is also given in the paper. Further, we have expanded on the details of the corpora, along with training the TTS model. Models on both speakers have shown good performance using the subjective evaluation of Mean Opinion Score with native speakers of the language. In the nearby future, we will look into expanding this database by adding new domains and then do data curation and open-source the biggest Chhattisgarhi TTS dataset to the community.

Acknowledgments. The creation of the dataset has been supported by Deutsche Gesellschaft für Internationale Zusammenarbeit (GIZ) on behalf of the German Ministry for Economic Cooperation and Development. We thank our partners *Bhashini AI Solutions Pvt Ltd* and all others who supported us in this dataset preparation.

References

1. Languages of Chhattisgarh, Chhattisgarh Tourism. https://www.chhattisgarhtourism.co.in/languages-of-chhattisgarh.html. (Accessed 31 July 2023)
2. Census of India 2011. https://censusindia.gov.in/2011Census/C-1625062018NEW.pdf. (Accessed 07 October 2021)
3. Economy of Chhattisgarh. https://www.mapsofindia.com/chhattisgarh/economy/. (Accessed 31 July 2023)
4. Londhe, N.D., Kshirsagar, G.B.: Chhattisgarhi speech corpus for research and development in automatic speech recognition. Int. J. Speech Technol. **21**, 193–210 (2018)
5. Londhe, N.D., Kshirsagar, G.B.: Speaker independent isolated words recognition system for Chhattisgarhi dialect. In: International Conference on Innovations in Information, Embedded and Communication Systems (ICIIECS), Coimbatore, India, pp. 1–6 (2017)

6. Londhe, N.D., Kshirsagar, G.B., Tekchandani, H.: Deep convolution neural network based speech recognition for Chhattisgarhi. In: International Conference on Signal Processing and Integrated Networks (SPIN), Noida, India, pp. 667–671 (2018)

7. Maity, S., Kumar Vuppala, A., Rao, K.S., Nandi, D.: IITKGP-MLILSC speech database for language identification. In: National Conference on Communications (NCC), Kharagpur, India, pp. 1–5 (2012)

8. Gupta, M., Mishra, M., Bagga, J., Mishra, V.: Speech analysis of Chhattisgarhi dialects using wavelet transformation and mel frequency cepstral coefficient. In: International Conference on Advances in Electrical, Computing, Communication and Sustainable Technologies (ICAECT), Bhilai, India, pp. 1–6 (2023)

9. Gaikwad, Y., Yogesh, K.R.: Emotion Recognition from Chhattisgarhi Speech using Neural Network (2014). https://api.semanticscholar.org/CorpusID:212519721

10. Byambadorj, Z., Nishimura, R., Ayush, A., Ohta, K., Kitaoka, N.: Multi-speaker TTS system for low-resource language using cross-lingual transfer learning and data augmentation. In: Asia-Pacific Signal and Information Processing Association Annual Summit and Conference (APSIPA ASC), Tokyo, Japan, pp. 849–853 (2021)

11. Xu, J., et al.: LRSpeech: Extremely Low-Resource Speech Synthesis and Recognition. arXiv: 2008.03687 (2020)

12. Byambadorj, Z., Nishimura, R., Ayush, A., et al.: Text-to-speech system for low-resource language using cross-lingual transfer learning and data augmentation. J. Audio Speech Music Proc. **2021**, 42 (2021)

13. Kim, J., Kong, J., Son, J.: Conditional variational autoencoder with adversarial learning for end-to-end text-to-speech. In: International Conference on Machine Learning, pp. 5530–5540 (2021)

14. Eren, G.: The Coqui TTS Team: Coqui TTS (Version 1.4). Comput. Softw. (2021). https://doi.org/10.5281/zenodo.6334862

An ASR Corpus in Chhattisgarhi, a Low Resource Indian Language

Abhayjeet Singh[1], Arjun Singh Mehta[2], K. S. Ashish Khuraishi[2],
G. Deekshitha[1(✉)], Gauri Date[2], Jai Nanavati[2], Jesuraja Bandekar[1],
Karnalius Basumatary[2], P. Karthika[2], Sandhya Badiger[1], Sathvik Udupa[1],
Saurabh Kumar[1], Prasanta Kumar Ghosh[1], V. Prashanthi[2], Priyanka Pai[2],
Raoul Nanavati[2], Sai Praneeth Reddy Mora[2], and Srinivasa Raghavan[1,2]

[1] Department of Electrical Engineering,
Indian Institute of Science (IISc), Bangalore 560012, India
{contact.respin,prasantg}@iisc.ac.in, deekshu50@gmail.com
[2] Navana Tech (NT), Nanavati Mahalaya 18,
Homi Mody St. Fort, Mumbai 400001, India
https://respin.iisc.ac.in/, https://www.navana.ai/

Abstract. RESPIN is a project that aims at the development of a dialect-rich database and some user-friendly voice-technology applications in 9 Indian languages including Chhattisgarhi. The paper elaborates on the entire process of such a low-resource database preparation in a crowd-sourced manner. Through this work we have open-sourced around 250 h of dialect-rich, domain-rich Chhattisgarhi ASR dataset to popularize the scope of voice technology to the Chhattisgarh population. The paper also describes the development of a base model with a WER score of 11.58% on the test set.

Keywords: Low-Resourced Indian Database · Chhattisgarhi ASR Corpus · Dialect-Rich ASR Corpus · RESPIN

1 Introduction

Interacting with electronic gadgets through one's own voice is the easiest way of communication. Advancements in voice technology help the common man to interact with digital gadgets and gather information by just using their voice and native language. The voice technology advancements will get wide acceptance as they can benefit the population irrespective of their educational or regional or financial or age or gender or health conditions. However, the development of such speech-based technologies is constrained by the availability of data in many Indian languages. Challenges still exist for low-resource languages where the availability of both audio and text is limited [11]. This is further complicated by the presence of multiple dialects of a language, which typically is the case for

---

Supported by Bill & Melinda Gates Foundation (BMGF).

Indian languages. Regional/dialectal variations include variations in vocabulary, pronunciation characteristics, and grammar. The diversities across dialects act as a barrier to standardizing linguistic characteristics.

According to World Bank staff estimates based on the United Nations Population Division's World Urbanization Prospects, 64% of the Indian population is staying in rural regions with nearly 57.8% relying on agricultural households [14]. Advancements in voice technology in Indian languages can potentially help illiterate Indians to use many digital services. Speech recognition for Indian languages is less explored compared to English [13]. Collecting speech databases is the fundamental and most crucial stage for the development of such voice technology systems. Even though there are some initiatives to collect Indian language databases, they are covering only the standard dialect of each language which is intended to serve the educated sector population. Studies [1,5] have found that dialect regions need not have discrete boundaries. Rather, dialectal variations gradually change over distance. To serve the uneducated, financially backward rural population of India, there must be a massive data collection strategy to cover all major dialects in a language.

Chhattisgarh is the ninth largest state in India with around 30 million population. Chhattisgarhi and Hindi are the official languages of this state. In all 33 districts, Chhattisgarhi is more popular than Hindi. Apart from Chhattisgarh, Chhattisgarhi speakers are concentrated in the Indian state of Chhattisgarh and in adjacent areas of Madhya Pradesh, Odisha, and Jharkhand [7]. As per the Linguistic Survey of India, Chhattisgarhi is considered an eastern variant of Hindi and hence is not included as an official language in the Indian constitution. According to the 2011 Linguistic Survey of India, 16.2 million people use Chhattisgarhi as their mother tongue [8]. About 80% of the population of the state is rural and the main livelihood of the villagers is agriculture and agriculture-based small industry [6]. The Average Literacy rate in Chhattisgarh for Urban regions was 84.05% in which female literacy stood at 73.39% [6]. Even though many attempts have been made to introduce voice-based applications to the Chhattisgarhi population, most of them ended up as either pilot studies or specific to some applications due to the lack of data [2–4].

RESPIN[1] is such an initiative that aims to develop a well-performing ASR system in nine Indian languages. Based on the area and population statistics, RESPIN tried to incorporate all major dialects in each of the selected languages. Through this work, we open source a part of the dialect-rich Chhattisgarhi ASR dataset from the RESPIN initiative for academics, start-ups, researchers, and developers to spur innovation and academic activity in the development of regional voice technologies in India. We have identified 5 major dialects in Chhattisgarhi - Kedri (Central), Utti (Eastern), Budati/Khaltahi (Western), Bhandar (Northern), and Rakshahun (Southern) Chhattisgarhi. Given that the Southern dialect has a significantly smaller speaker population than the other dialects, we chose to exclude it from the data collection process as listed in Table 1. The

---

[1] https://respin.iisc.ac.in/.

Table 1. Dialect distribution of Chhattisgarhi.

#	Dialect	District	State
D1	Central	Bilaspur	Chhattisgarh
D2	East	Raigarh	Chhattisgarh
D3	Western	Kabirdham	Chhattisgarh
D4	Northern	Surguja	Chhattisgarh

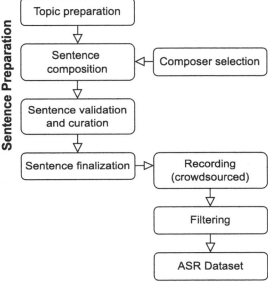

Fig. 1. Flowchart showing the process of database preparation.

paper elaborates on the process of database preparation in detail and describes the development of the baseline model in the following sections.

2   Database Preparation

This section details the efforts taken to collect the so far biggest dialect-rich ASR database in Chhattisgarhi. As Chhattisgarhi is a low-resourced Indian language compared to other Indian languages like Hindi (121 h), Bengali (128 h), Tamil (139 h), and Gujarati (64 h)[2], the collection of dialect-rich, domain-specific sentences from each district can be achieved only through composition/translation tasks with the help of native people (Fig. 1).

---

[2] https://data.ldcil.org/speech.

2.1   Sentence Preparation

In order to collect sentences from each district with maximum vocabulary, we listed different topics (keywords) and subtopics in each domain. Instead of asking people to compose sentences from the agriculture (AGRI)/finance (FIN) domain, topic preparation helps to ensure they reach out to all the related topics in each domain. Topic preparation helped to increase the vocabulary with a variety of sentences by reducing redundancy. Example topics of AGRI domain are *peasant, crop cultivation systems, livestock production systems, production*. Similarly, an example topic of FIN domain is *National rural livelihood mission*.

Native composers from each dialect were shortlisted after having some pilot test rounds. The ones who were good at following the instructions and good enough to compose in the native style were selected and provided with the topics to compose sentences. Manual and programmatic checks were done on the composed sentences to ensure that they are dialect rich as well as it contain only valid characters. Based on these checks the final sentence list was prepared for recording.

Common Sentence Preparation. To study the variance of language styles across dialects, apart from the Generic Sentences-GS, we have collected some common sentences across all dialects. Basically, those common sentences were from agricultural and financial backgrounds and are termed as CA-Common Agri and CB-Common Bank sentences in the database.

2.2   Recording

In order to collect the native recordings from the shortlisted regions with uniform specifications, we have shared a dedicated app with the speakers in the respective regions. As it is a crowd-sourced audio data collection strategy, we added some questions to collect the metadata of the speakers too.

Being crowd-sourced, the audio dataset has some errors too like wrong metadata entries, noisy backgrounds, empty recordings, long silence in between, differences in speaking rates, etc. These errors demanded the need for filtering out the best files to release a part of the dialect-rich Chhattisgarhi ASR database. Table 2 summarises the entire dataset that we have released as a part of this work. As described in Table 2, we have around 458, 395, 375, and 456 speakers from each dialect considered.

To capture the variability in speech, the same sentences were given to different speakers in a region. So each sentence in a dialect will appear multiple times in the corresponding audio database. Figure 2 shows the frequency distribution of sentences in the database. The average frequency of sentences in the database is 9, with 1 and 71 as the lower and upper-frequency boundaries. Domain-rich sentences that are too generic are been recorded multiple times to capture the variability among the maximum speakers. Table 3 shows the distribution of the proposed dataset into train-test and dev.

Table 2. Summary of the proposed dialect-rich Chhattisgarhi ASR corpus.

#	#Sentences	#Audio Files	#Speakers (roughly)	Duration (h)	#Unique words
D1	5084	42, 245	458	64.25	5909
D2	5037	36, 190	395	65.44	5266
D3	5109	25, 886	375	43.16	5757
D4	4769	44, 325	456	74.05	6305
Total	19999	148, 646	1684	246.9	23237

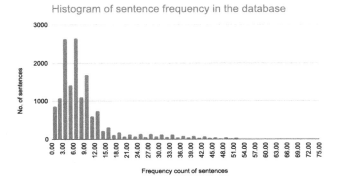

Fig. 2. Histogram of sentences across dialects in the database.

Table 3. Train-Test-Dev split-ups of proposed database for the baseline model.

	Train	Test	Dev
Duration (hours)	239	4	4
# Unique speakers	1583	48	53
# Sentences	15226	2474	2299
# Utterances	143, 096	2828	2722

3   Chhattisgarhi ASR Dataset Analysis

As summarised in Table 3, the proposed Chhattisgarhi ASR Dataset includes
239:4:4 h of recordings for train, test, and dev set. Table 4 explains more characteristics of the training dataset across each dialect. Figure 3 helps to study
the distribution of unique words across each dialect. As represented in those
Venn diagrams, we can claim that each dialect will have some unique words
compared to others. From Fig. 4a and Fig. 4b, it is clear that even though we
have a balanced number of sentences in both AGR and FIN domains across
all dialects, AGR domain sentences are more vocabulary rich compared to FIN
domain. Figure 5a shows the distribution of sentence duration across dialects

Table 4. Split-up of sentences, utterances, and duration across dialects in the training dataset.

	# Sentences				# Utterances				Duration (h)			
	GS	CA	CB	Total	GS	CA	CB	Total	GS	CA	CB	Total
D1	3777	29	27	3833	39646	641	530	40817	60.77	0.85	0.63	62.25
D2	3862	25	24	3911	33941	571	360	34872	62.27	0.69	0.45	63.41
D3	3782	30	29	3841	23475	543	351	24369	40.03	0.69	0.43	41.15
D4	3585	31	25	3641	41717	736	585	43038	70.19	1.04	0.81	72.04
Total				15226				143096				238.85

GS-Generic Sentences, CA-Common Agri and CB-Common Bank

with an average of 5.98 s. Similarly, Fig. 5b shows the distribution of words in a sentence across each dialect, with an average of 15 words in a sentence.

4 Baseline Model

In this paper, as we were focusing much on releasing the dataset collected with a baseline model, we never explored much in different model architectures. Our primary focus was to present all the features of the newly collected low-resource dataset to the research community with a baseline model to show the credibility of the corpus for ASR tasks using TDNN (Table 5).

Table 5. Performance of the baseline ASR.

	D1	D2	D3	D4	Overall
dev	11.80	11.13	11.43	14.63	12.20
test	12.27	9.88	10.42	13.66	11.58

Kaldi ASR toolkit [9] has been used to build an ASR model with time-delay neural network (TDNN) architecture. The lattice-free maximum mutual information (LF-MMI) objective function was used to train the model [10]. Most of the parameters reported in the Kaldi example recipe were used with some adjustments made for adapting it to the Chhattisgarhi corpus. The model architecture of $TDNN$-F^3 consists of 12 TDNN-F layers of dimension 1024 and a linear bottleneck dimension of 128. For decoding purposes, several n-gram language models with different combinations of n-grams were prepared using the

---

[3] https://github.com/kaldi-asr/kaldi/blob/master/egs/wsj/s5/local/chain2/tuning/run_tdnn_1i.sh.

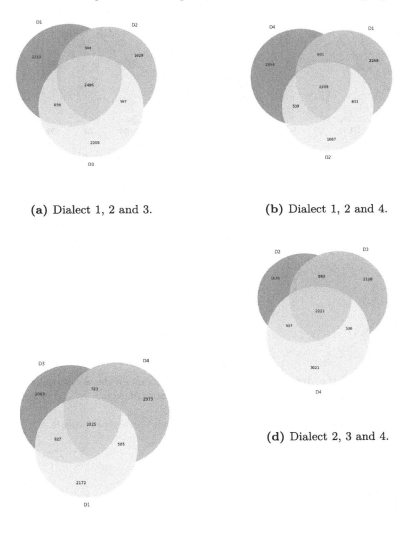

(a) Dialect 1, 2 and 3.

(b) Dialect 1, 2 and 4.

(d) Dialect 2, 3 and 4.

(c) Dialect 1, 3 and 4.

Fig. 3. Unique word distribution across different dialects.

SRILM toolkit [12]. The LM with the best perplexity on the dev set was chosen. All unique sentences in the train set were used for training LM. It is to mention that the phoneme-level lexicon used for these experiments was created manually by the language experts.

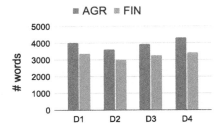

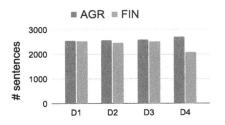

(a) Histogram distribution of the word count across dialects and domains.

(b) Histogram distribution of the sentence count across dialects and domains.

Fig. 4. Histogram analysis across the dialects and domains.

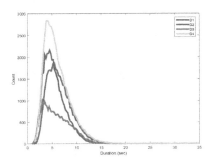

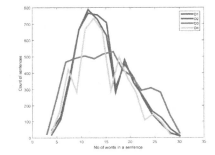

(a) Histogram of the duration of utterances across dialects.

(b) Histogram on the words count in a sentence across dialects.

Fig. 5. Duration and word count analysis across the dialects.

5   Conclusion

In this paper, we described the collection of 250 hours of dialect-rich Chhattisgarhi ASR database. The Chhattisgarhi data described in this paper is Phase 1 of data collected through the RESPIN project which aims to collect speech and text data in nine Indian languages. The entire data has been collected in a crowd-sourced manner, and the data is balanced across dialects and domains. This will encourage the speech research community to explore different speech recognition ideas with this Chhattisgarh dialect-rich ASR database.

As the emphasis was on the release of the dataset collected along with a simple baseline model, we neither explored different model architectures nor compared it with similar state-of-the-art systems. We are planning to explore these in the near future. Further plans include the analysis of subword units in the database and checking whether such units in neighbouring/similar languages can supplement certain categories, for which there are only fewer examples. Apart from these, other future goals include identifying different dialects of the Chhattisgarhi language and developing a language identification system for Indian languages including Chhattisgarhi.

Acknowledgements. We thank everyone who supported us throughout this study. We especially thank the funding agency BMGF, the validators, and other volunteers who contributed to collecting the database.

References

1. Gumperz, J.J.: Speech variation and the study of Indian civilization. Am. Anthropol. **63**(5), 976–988 (1961)
2. Londhe, N.D., Kshirsagar, G.B.: Speaker independent isolated words recognition system for chhattisgarhi dialect. In: 2017 International Conference on Innovations in Information, Embedded and Communication Systems (ICIIECS), pp. 1–6 (2017). https://doi.org/10.1109/ICIIECS.2017.8276169
3. Londhe, N.D., Kshirsagar, G.B., Tekchandani, H.: Deep convolution neural network based speech recognition for chhattisgarhi. In: 2018 5th International Conference on Signal Processing and Integrated Networks (SPIN), pp. 667–671 (2018). https://doi.org/10.1109/SPIN.2018.8474064
4. Londhe, N., Kshirsagar, G.: Chhattisgarhi speech corpus for research and development in automatic speech recognition. Int. J. Speech Technol. **21**, 193–210 (2018)
5. Mandal, R.B.: Patterns of regional geography: an international perspective ·, vol. 2, p. 140 (1990)
6. Maps of India.com: Economy of chhattisgarh. https://www.mapsofindia.com/chhattisgarh/economy/, (Accessed 31 July 2023)
7. MP Tour and Travels.com: Languages of chhattisgarh, chhattisgarh tourism. https://www.chhattisgarhtourism.co.in/languages-of-chhattisgarh.html, (Accessed 31 July 2023)
8. Office of the registrar general: Census of India 2011. https://censusindia.gov.in/2011Census/C-16_25062018_NEW.pdf, (Accessed 07 October 2021)
9. Povey, D., et al.: The Kaldi Speech recognition toolkit. In: Proceedings of ASRU (December 2011)
10. Povey, D., et al.: Purely Sequence-Trained Neural Networks for ASR Based on Lattice-Free MMI. In: Proceedings of Interspeech 2016, pp. 2751–2755 (2016). https://doi.org/10.21437/Interspeech.2016-595
11. Sethi, N., Dev, A.: Survey on automatic speech recognition systems for indic languages. In: Dev, A., Agrawal, S.S., Sharma, A. (eds.) AIST 2021. CCIS, vol. 1546, pp. 85–98. Springer, Cham (2022). https://doi.org/10.1007/978-3-030-95711-7_8
12. Stolcke, A.: SRILM - An extensible language modeling toolkit. In: INTERSPEECH (2002)
13. Vydana, H.K.: Salient Features for Multilingual Speech Recognition in Indian Scenario. Ph.D. thesis (Jan 2019). http://hdl.handle.net/10603/246056
14. World Bank staff estimates based on the United Nations Population Divisions, World Urbanization Prospects: Rural population (% of total population) - india. https://data.worldbank.org/indicator/SP.RUR.TOTL.ZS?locations=IN, (Accessed 31 July 2023)

Cross Lingual Style Transfer Using Multiscale Loss Function for Soliga: A Low Resource Tribal Language

Ashwini Dasare[1]([✉]), B. Lohith Reddy[1], A. Sai Chandra Koushik[1], B. Sai Raj[1], V. Krishna Sai Rohith[1], Satisha Basavaraju[2], and K.T. Deepak[1]

[1] Indian Institute of Information Technology, Dharwad, India
{aswhwini,19bcs014,19bcs006,19bcs061,19bcs016,deepak}@iiitdwd.ac.in
[2] Beltech AI Pvt. Ltd., Bangalore, India
sathisha.iitg@gmail.com

Abstract. Voice conversion is the art of mimicking different speaker voices and styles. In this paper, we present a cross-lingual speaker style adaptation based on a multi-scale loss function, using a deep learning framework for syntactically similar languages Kannada and Soliga, under a low resource setup. The existing speaker adaptation methods usually depend on monolingual data and cannot be directly adopted for cross-lingual data. The proposed method calculates multi-scale reconstruction loss on the generated mel-spectrogram with that of the original mel-spectrogram and adopts its weights based on the loss function for various scales. Extensive experimental results illustrate that the multi-scale reconstruction resulted in a significant reduction of generator noise compared to the baseline model and faithfully transfers Soliga speaker styles to Kannada speakers while retaining the linguistic aspects of Soliga.

Keywords: Low resource cross-lingual speech synthesis · Spoken language generation · Speaker adaptation · Voice conversion · Style transfer

1 Introduction

Tribal languages aid us in understanding our origin, the roots we evolved from, and human race capabilities. India has 22 official spoken languages and 1369 rationalized unofficial languages. About 197 languages of India are listed as endangered by UNESCO [12], and any language spoken by a population less than 10,000 people is considered a potentially endangered language by Govt of India [3]. Many tribal languages of India do not have literary tradition [4]. One such tribal language, Soliga is already on the verge of extinction as it has only a population of fewer than 40,000 people [14], located in Karnataka state. If we do not create digital platforms for languages to be used by respective communities, these languages may vanish in less than a decade [7]

© The Author(s), under exclusive license to Springer Nature Switzerland AG 2023
A. Karpov et al. (Eds.): SPECOM 2023, LNAI 14339, pp. 182–194, 2023.
https://doi.org/10.1007/978-3-031-48312-7_15

Soliga language does not have a script, and to the best of our knowledge, no literature is available in Soliga. Therefore it can be considered as a "zero resource" language. Deep neural networks has been popularly used for TTS, but all of these models need transcripts for each speech file to train the models [10,15,17,19]. For zero-resource languages like Soliga, generating speech data from the written transcript is tedious. But when unlabeled data is used in Speech-to-speech based approaches [2,8], despite the significant improvement in the synthesized audio quality, these approaches tend to miss the prosodic aspects such as speech style, tone, volume, and pitch present in the sample of speech for a given speaker. To train the model for prosodic aspects, we require hundreds of hours of data [22] which is practically not feasible for low-resource languages, especially when the population is as small as Soliga. Finding people to get speech data is a huge time and effort-consuming process. However, cross-lingual style transfer approaches can address the issue of generating speech resources for low-resource languages. The generated speech utterances can be used for applications such as direct speech-to-speech translation, automatic speech recognition, and Speaker recognition and diarization. This can also serve as digital preservation of indigenous tribal languages.

The process of generating a speech sample of a source speaker to a different target speaker while retaining the linguistic content and speaker style characteristics of a source speaker is called Speech style transfer. This paper introduces a cross-lingual, speech-to-speech neural network to transfer the speech style across Soliga and Kannada languages. This work will show the importance of multi-scale reconstruction loss in a speech-style conversion task, thereby preventing the training objective from halting in the local minima.

1.1 Neural Style Transfer

Neural style transfer was introduced for image generation [5]. Since the speech waveform can also be represented in the form of an image in the frequency domain(mel-spectrogram), the same techniques of image style transfer can be applied to Speech data as well. This was shown by [21], in which the model synthesized spoken image descriptions directly without using any text or phonemes. Later using a similar approach of neural style transfer and GAN models, the Speech style transfer technique was proposed [1], which is the baseline model for our implementation. The baseline model uses L_1-loss computed at the input scale to penalize the reconstruction error between the same source and target mel-spectrogram images. However, penalizing the network for the errors at each scale of reconstruction may enable the decoder network to inject speaker-specific style information in the mel-spectrogram image. The overall pipeline is shown in Fig. 1.

The baseline model does not give an intelligible voice for different sources and target languages. Therefore we introduced one more loss function called multi-scale L_1-loss. In computer vision models, it is proven that introducing multi-scale loss significantly improved the accuracy of the image reconstruction [6]. For our mel-spectrogram image, we have adopted this multi-scale reconstruction technique to estimate the loss function along with existing baseline loss functions. In the multi-scale approach, the combination of the individual losses at each scale is the total loss in the decoder, as shown in Fig. 2. Multi-scale reconstruction of the mel-spectrogram improves the performance of the discriminator. We experimented with different scales and discovered that the down-scaling approach works best for our model-detailed explanation in Sect. 3.1.

The overall pipeline is shown in Fig. 1, which is essentially carried out in two steps. In the first step, from a given input language i.e. Soliga, the target speaker's(Kannada) mel-spectrogram is generated, using VAE-GAN network, these spectrograms are fed to, the WaveNet-based vocoder to get the synthesized speech in the time domain. This approach was used in image-to-image style transfer model, and the same is adopted and applied to mel-spectrograms. We retain the base model single encoder structure to generalize and to make it more feasible for multiple target speakers. In this work, we introduce multi-scale loss estimation for mel-spectrograms generation.

The proposed method does not require parallel bilingual data and phoneme representation but only needs bilingual speech data without transcriptions to train a generator model. We claim that this works well for low-resource data for the same language, with different speaking styles. And also works well for languages that share similar syntactic structures. The languages we have chosen for style transfer and voice conversion have syntactically similar utterance patterns and Soliga has kannada word influence [13]. The training is performed in an end-to-end unsupervised manner without any transcript alignments between the input samples.

The paper organization is as follows, Sect. 2 gives data preparation details, Experimental details are given in Sect. 3, Sect. 4 presents Results and Discussion and Sect. 5 discusses concluding remarks and future work.

2   Data Preparation

In order to create a speech database for the Soliga and Kannada languages, we faced the challenge of Soliga being a zero-resource language with no written literature available. To overcome this hurdle, we followed a two-step approach: creating text sentences and recording these sentences with the help of a literate Soliga speaker. The data preparation process involved the following steps:

2.1   Text Sentence Creation

To generate text sentences, we utilized a list of commonly used words in Indian villages known as "swadesh" [20]. Using these words as a foundation, we constructed approximately 10,000 English sentences with lengths ranging from 3 to 15 words. These sentences served as the starting point for our data collection process. As Soliga resides in Karnataka, the contact language is Kannada, and the English sentences were first translated into Kannada, and in the second step, these Kananda sentences were translated into Soliga. Since Soliga does not have its own script, the translated Soliga sentences were written in the Kannada script. This approach ensured that the Soliga speakers, who were more comfortable with Kannada, could understand and read the sentences accurately. Likewise, 5000 parallel translated sentences were prepared for data recording.

2.2 Speech Recording

In the next phase, we sought a female Soliga speaker with a clear voice and good diction to perform studio-quality voice recordings. To facilitate the data collection process, we developed a user interface (UI) that allowed for the recording of speech data while capturing relevant metadata about the speaker, including age, gender, education, and qualifications. Additionally, the speakers were asked to provide their consent for donating their voice for research purposes. The recording sessions took place in a professional studio, with the speech data collected at a sampling rate of 44 kHz to ensure high-quality recordings. The UI displayed the sentences to be read by the speaker, providing an option to listen to each recording and allowing for rerecording in case of any errors or mistakes. Using this methodology, we collected approximately 5,000 utterances from both Kannada and Soliga speakers, resulting in a total duration of about 5 h of recorded speech data for each language.

Furthermore, to expand the number of speakers and incorporate different styles for Soliga to Kannada voice conversion, we augmented our dataset with publicly available Kannada male voice data obtained from sources such as Openslr [16]. By incorporating a diverse range of speakers and styles, we aimed to improve the robustness and flexibility of our model in performing Soliga to Kannada voice conversion.

In summary, the data preparation process involved creating text sentences using a list of common words, translating them into Kannada for Soliga speakers, recording the sentences in a studio environment, and augmenting the dataset with additional Kannada male voice data. These steps ensured the availability of a comprehensive and diverse dataset for training our model.

3   Implementation

The Kannada speaker's voice is converted from the Soliga speaker's input signal while keeping the Soliga speaker's content and style intact. The representation of the mel-spectrogram is created from the input speech signal. Once the spectrogram is generated, it can be treated as a greyscale image, we can employ a neural style transfer model as mentioned in [11], and then the source mel-spectrogram can be converted to the target mel-spectrogram using the style of a target speaker. To convert this mel-spectrogram back into the time domain, we used the WaveNet vocoder [23]

The neural style transfer model used in this research employs a combination of encoder and decoder networks to achieve cross-lingual style transfer between

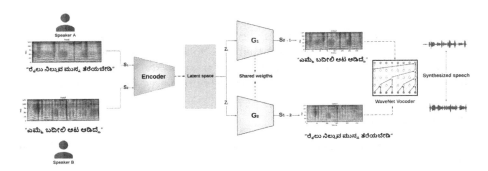

Fig. 1. The style transfer flow between Soliga and Kannada.

Soliga and Kannada languages. The decoder network functions as a generator, responsible for producing the target output speech. On the other hand, the encoder network aims to preserve the linguistic details of the source speech while eliminating speaker identity-related information.

In the proposed model, the encoder architecture remains unchanged from the base paper. Its role is to generate a shared-latent space called "z" that captures only the content of each sample while discarding the identity of the original speaker. By extracting the content information, the encoder helps facilitate the style transfer process. In our approach, we considered two generators, denoted as G_1 and G_2, to accommodate the two speakers for the Kannada and Soliga languages, respectively. Both G_1 and G_2 consist of the same layers as the encoder, but in the opposite order. This arrangement allows the generators to combine the input speech signal's content and style with the target voice, generating the mel-spectrogram of the target speech signal.

To improve the performance of the generator and address the issue of noisy output encountered in the base paper, we introduced additional layers to the generator architecture. Specifically, we incorporated two extra layers for down-scaling and up-scaling experiments. Additionally, we included four more layers for up-down-scaling of the generated mel-spectrogram. This modification enables a more effective transformation of the style while maintaining the integrity of the content. By comparing the generated mel-spectrogram with the original mel-spectrogram, we calculate the multi-scale loss function, which serves as a measure of the style transfer quality. The multi-scale loss function allows us to evaluate the performance of the generator at different levels of abstraction, capturing both local and global style transfer characteristics. In the context of transferring style between Soliga and Kannada languages, the latent space for the two given decoders is switched. This switch allows the generator to effectively capture the style attributes specific to each language and incorporate them into the generated target speech. The swapping of latent spaces facilitates the cross-lingual style transfer process and ensures that the resulting speech aligns with the desired linguistic and stylistic characteristics.

Figure 1 illustrates the architecture and process flow of the proposed model, highlighting the switching of latent spaces between the decoders for Soliga and Kannada languages. By incorporating these modifications to the generator architecture and leveraging the switched latent spaces, our approach improves the style transfer performance and yields more accurate and coherent results compared to the base paper.

3.1 Multi-scale Loss Function Experiments

In this section, we describe the experiments conducted to evaluate the effectiveness of the multi-scale loss functions in improving the performance of the baseline model. In addition to the L_1 loss used in the base paper, we introduced several multi-scale loss functions, including up-scaling, down-scaling, and a combination of up and down-scaling. The purpose of these experiments was to investigate how different scaling operations applied to the generated mel-spectrograms can impact the intelligibility and voice quality of the transferred speech. By analyzing the results, we aimed to identify the most effective approach for enhancing the performance of the baseline model.

In the first experiment, we applied a down-scaling operation to the generated mel-spectrograms. This down-scaling process involved reducing the resolution of the spectrogram while preserving its content and style information. The motivation behind this experiment was to examine whether reducing the resolution could lead to improved speech quality and intelligibility. Next, we conducted an up-scaling experiment, where we increased the resolution of the generated mel-spectrograms. This operation aimed to enhance the fine-grained details in the transferred speech, potentially improving the overall quality and fidelity. Finally, we combined the up-scaling and down-scaling operations in a single experiment. This experiment sought to leverage the benefits of both scaling approaches simultaneously, allowing for a more comprehensive evaluation of their impact on the transferred speech.

After analyzing the results of these experiments, we observed that the down-scaling experiment yielded better intelligibility and voice quality compared to the baseline model. The incorporation of the down-scaling multi-scale loss function appeared to enhance the performance of the baseline model in terms of speech quality. The down-scaling operation likely facilitated a more compact representation of the style and content information in the mel-spectrograms, resulting in clearer and more intelligible speech. By reducing the resolution, the down-scaling operation may have removed some unnecessary noise or artifacts present in the baseline model's output.

While the up-scaling and combined scaling experiments did not demonstrate significant improvements over the baseline model, they provided valuable insights into the effects of scaling operations on the style transfer process. These experiments highlighted the importance of finding the right balance between preserving the content and style information and enhancing the finer details in the transferred speech. Overall, the incorporation of a down-scaling multi-scale loss function proved to be an effective enhancement to the baseline model, leading to improved speech quality and intelligibility. This finding suggests that carefully

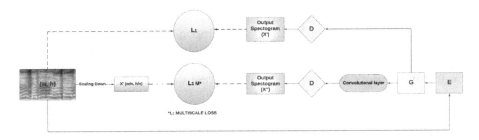

Fig. 2. Loss Function for Down-scaling. Here E is Encoder, G is generator and D is Discriminator

designed scaling operations can contribute to the success of neural style transfer for speech synthesis applications.

In the following sections, we present detailed analyses and discussions of the results obtained from these multi-scale loss function experiments, providing insights into the strengths and limitations of each approach.

Loss of Down-Scale. To improve the efficiency of the discriminator, we added two additional scales to its input by down-scaling the generator output to half and quarter of the original size. We calculated the GAN Loss for each scale and added them to the existing loss calculated from the original mel-spectrogram.

$$L_{GAN} = W_1 \times L_{GAN_1} + W_2 \times L_{GAN_2} + W_4 \times L_{GAN_4} \tag{1}$$

Here the GAN Loss of original input is calculated

$$
\begin{aligned}
L_{GAN_1} = \sum_i & E_{S_i \sim P_{S_i}} [\log D_i (S_i)] \\
& + \sum_{i,j} E (S_{j \to i \mid z_j}) [\log (1 - D_i (S(x))]
\end{aligned}
\tag{2}
$$

The following equation calculates the loss of down-scaling the generator output to half (n = 2) and quarter (n = 4) of the original size.

$$
\begin{aligned}
L_{GAN_n} = \sum_i & E_{S_i \sim P_{S_i}} [\log D_i (S_i)] \\
& + \sum_{i,j} E (S_{j \to i \mid z_j}) [\log (1 - D_i (S(x/n))]
\end{aligned}
\tag{3}
$$

Loss of Up-Scale. In this loss, we add two additional scales to its input by up-scaling the generator output to double and quadrupling the original size. We calculated the GAN Loss for each scale and added them to the existing loss calculated from the original mel-spectrogram (Fig. 3).

$$L_{GAN} = W_1 \times L_{GAN_1} + W_2 \times L_{GAN_2} + W_4 \times L_{GAN_4} \tag{4}$$

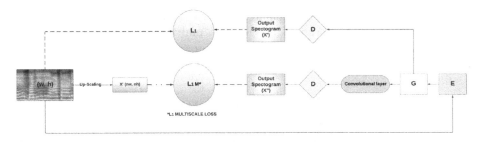

Fig. 3. Loss Function for Down-scaling. Here E is Encoder, G is generator and D is Discriminator

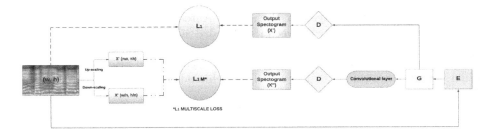

Fig. 4. Loss Function for Up and Down-scaling.

Here the GAN Loss of the original input is calculated,

$$L_{GAN_1} = \sum_i E_{S_i \sim P_{S_i}} [\log D_i (S_i)]$$
$$+ \sum_{i,j} E (S_{j \to i \mid z_j}) [\log (1 - D_i (S(x)))] \tag{5}$$

The following equation calculates the loss of Up-scaling the generator output to double (n = 2) and quadruple (n = 4) of the original size.

$$L_{GAN_n} = \sum_i E_{S_i \sim P_{S_i}} [\log D_i (S_i)]$$
$$+ \sum_{i,j} E (S_{j \to i \mid z_j}) [\log (1 - D_i (S(nx)))] \tag{6}$$

Combined Loss of Up-Scale and Down-Scale. In this case, for calculating loss, the discriminator in a Generative Adversarial Network (GAN), we propose a multi-scale loss approach. This approach involves adding four additional scales to the input of the discriminator. We achieve this by down-sampling and up-sampling the generator output to half and a quarter of the original size and double and four times, respectively (Fig. 3).

For each of these scales, we calculate the GAN Loss and add it to the existing loss calculated from the original image. The multi-scale loss is calculated as the weighted sum of these individual scale losses. The weight of each scale is determined by its size relative to the original image.

$$L_{GAN} = \sum_{i=1}^{5} W_i \times L_{GAN_i} \tag{7}$$

where W_i is the weight for each scale and L_{GAN_1} is the GAN Loss for original input from Eq. (1), L_{GAN_2} , L_{GAN_3} are the GAN Losses for Down-scale input as shown in equation(3) and L_{GAN_4}, L_{GAN_5} are the GAN Losses for Up-scale input as shown in Eq. (6).

The loss function employed by Variational Autoencoder (VAE) models aims to minimize the dissimilarity between the encoded distribution of input data and a prior distribution. This loss function comprises of two terms: the first one is the Kullback-Leibler (KL) divergence between the encoded and prior distributions, while the second term is the negative log-likelihood of the reconstructed input data.

$$L_{VAE} = \lambda_4 \sum_i D_{KL} \left(q\left(z_i \mid S_i\right) \| p\left(z\right)\right)$$
$$- \sum_i E_{z_i \sim q\left(z_i \mid S_i\right)} \left[\log p\, G_i\left(S_i \mid z_i\right)\right] \tag{8}$$

The loss function is used in models that aim to generate new content from existing content. The first term in the equation is the KL divergence between the distribution of the latent codes for the source and target mel-spectrograms. The second term is the negative log-likelihood of the target mel-spectrogram given the source mel-spectrogram and its corresponding latent code.

$$L_{CC} = \lambda_4 \sum_{i,j} D_{KL} \left(q\left(z_i \mid S_{i \rightarrow j}\right) \| p\left(z\right)\right)$$
$$- \sum_{i,j} E_{z_i \sim q\left(z_j \mid S_{i \rightarrow j}\right)} \left[\log p\, G_i\left(S_i \mid z_j\right)\right] \tag{9}$$

Cycle consistency loss we have retained as it is from the baseline model. The regularization parameters in the objective functions, use $\lambda_1 = 100$, $\lambda_2 = 10$, $\lambda_3 = 10$, and $\lambda_4 = e^{-3}$. The regularization parameters are given these values to emphasize the loss from reconstruction in L_{VAE} than the other loss terms.

We have experimented with different values of weights given to the multi-scale loss function. The values $w_1 = 0.5$, $w_2 = 0.25$, and $w_3 = 0.25$ gave better results. We choose these values to give more weight to the original scale compared to other scales. In addition, the WaveNet vocoder is trained independently using the mel-spectrograms generated by both G_1 and G_2 as inputs, while the original waveform of each speaker was used as the reference to compare the utterance and style of the target.

Table 1. Comparison of D and G loss for different models

Soliga-Kannada Style Transfer	D Loss	G Loss
Baseline-model	0.326	32.097
Down-scale model	**0.268**	**24.658**
Up-scale model	0.266	26.616
Up and Down-scale model	0.257	27.236

4   Results and Discussion

The loss reduction of our model compared to the baseline model is represented in
Table 1. The generator loss was calculated using the Kannada-Soliga dataset, in
both cases, our proposed method error is lesser than the baseline model as shown
in the Table 1. Though we have experimented with different loss functions, i.e. by
up-scaling and combining up-scaling and down-scaling, the generator gave less
error for the down-scaling experiment. This could be because error propagation
is high when you upscale the generated mel-spectrograms, the error gets added
to the up-scaled mel-spectrogram as well, and when you downscale the mel-
spectrogram the error will be reduced to down-scaled mel-spectrograms. The
samples of Soliga and Kannada style transfer can be found on Results page [18].

We have visualized the source speaker and target speaker-specific feature
embedding and found that the source features and style transferred features in
the target cluster together in latent space. That gives the overall performance of
our model in terms of the naturalness of the original and synthetic style aspects,
as shown in Fig. 5. "K" stands for Kannada, "S" for Soliga "S-K" stands for Soliga
sentence and style in the Kannada speaker's voice., "K-S" Kannada sentence and
style in Soliga speaker's voice. Essentially the feature embeddings of "S" and "K-
S" cluster together, and "K" and "S-K" should cluster together for good quality
style transfer. Compared to the baseline model all three models proposed have
better clustering of feature embeddings.

We have also conducted subjective evaluations on multi-scale models for intelligibility and style transfer tasks, and Mean Opinion Score(MOS) was taken by
10 Soliga speakers and 10 Kannada speakers to assess the quality of synthesized
speech based on the parameters like intelligibility, style, and accent, on a scale of
1 to 5, where 1 being the poor quality and 5 being the best quality score. It was
found that the Downscale model outperformed the baseline model, as shown in
Table 2. This matches with down-scale Generator loss of Table 1.

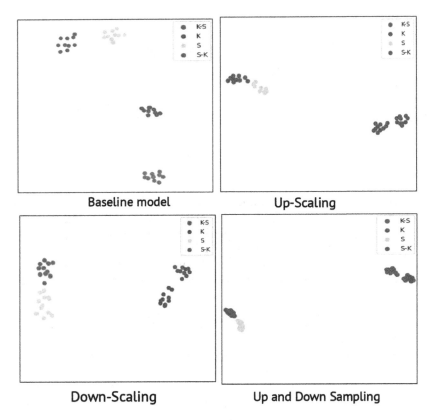

Fig. 5. Features embedding visualization for each speaker on the original and synthesized speech [9]

Table 2. Comparison of Mean Opinion Score (MOS)

Kannada-Soliga	MOS
Baseline-model	3.02
Upscale-model	3.32
Downscale-model	**3.99**
Up and down scale-model	3.50

5   Conclusion and Future Work

In this project, our main objective was to propose a technique for cross-lingual speaker style transfer between Kannada and Soliga, two languages that share similar syntax. We emphasized the significance of utilizing a multi-scale loss in deep neural networks to enable the learning and incorporation of subject-specific style into identity-independent feature embeddings. Through our experiments, we successfully demonstrated that the integration of multi-scale loss in deep neural networks effectively reduced generator noise and facilitated the faithful transfer of Soliga speaker styles to Kannada speakers, while preserving the original speech's content and style. Notably, our model exhibited promising results in voice conversion between different genders. However, further improvements are required to enhance voice conversion within the same gender.

In future research, there is an interesting avenue to explore regarding cross-linguistic speech style transfer between low-resource tribal languages and Indic languages. This area of study presents an opportunity to investigate the adaptation of speech styles across language boundaries, particularly in the context of languages with limited resources and the diverse landscape of Indic languages. By delving into this domain, researchers can uncover novel techniques and approaches for facilitating the transfer of speech styles, which can have a range of practical applications. For instance, it can contribute to the development of speech-to-speech translation systems that seamlessly adapt speech styles, enhance automatic speech recognition systems for low-resource languages, and even improve speaker recognition and diarization technologies for diverse linguistic communities.

Furthermore, exploring cross-linguistic speech style transfer in low-resource contexts can provide insights into the challenges faced by endangered languages and contribute to efforts aimed at their preservation and revitalization. It can help bridge the gap between low-resource tribal languages and the broader ecosystem of Indic languages, fostering better communication and understanding.

Overall, the exploration of cross-linguistic speech style transfer between low-resource tribal languages and Indic languages holds significant promise for future research. It offers an opportunity to better understand the dynamics of speech styles across languages, preserve endangered languages, and develop innovative technologies to bridge linguistic divides.

References

1. AlBadawy, E.A., Lyu, S.: Voice conversion using speech-to-speech neuro-style transfer. In: Interspeech, pp. 4726–4730 (2020)
2. Biadsy, F., Weiss, R.J., Moreno, P.J., Kanevsky, D., Jia, Y.: Parrotron: an end-to-end speech-to-speech conversion model and its applications to hearing-impaired speech and speech separation. arXiv preprint arXiv:1904.04169 (2019)
3. Chandramouli, C., General, R.: Census of india 2011. Provisional Population Totals. New Delhi: Government of India, pp. 409–413 (2011)
4. Dasare, A., Deepak, K., Prasanna, M., Vijaya, K.S.: Text to speech system for lambani-a zero resource, tribal language of india. In: 2022 25th Conference of the Oriental COCOSDA International Committee for the Co-ordination and Standardisation of Speech Databases and Assessment Techniques (O-COCOSDA), pp. 1–6. IEEE (2022)
5. Ghiasi, G., Lee, H., Kudlur, M., Dumoulin, V., Shlens, J.: Exploring the structure of a real-time, arbitrary neural artistic stylization network. arXiv preprint arXiv:1705.06830 (2017)

6. Godard, C., Mac Aodha, O., Firman, M., Brostow, G.J.: Digging into self-supervised monocular depth estimation. In: Proceedings of the IEEE/CVF International Conference on Computer Vision, pp. 3828–3838 (2019)

7. Haokip, T.: Artificial intelligence and endangered languages. Available at SSRN 4212504 (2022)

8. Jia, Y., et al.: Direct speech-to-speech translation with a sequence-to-sequence model. arXiv preprint arXiv:1904.06037 (2019)

9. Joly, C.: Real-time voice cloning (2018). https://doi.org/10.5281/zenodo.1472609

10. Kons, Z., Shechtman, S., Sorin, A., Rabinovitz, C., Hoory, R.: High quality, lightweight and adaptable tts using lpcnet. arXiv preprint arXiv:1905.00590 (2019)

11. Liu, M.Y., Breuel, T., Kautz, J.: Unsupervised image-to-image translation networks. In: Conference on Neural Information Processing Systems (NIPS), pp. 1–9 (2017)

12. Moseley, C.: The UNESCO atlas of the world's languages in danger: Context and process. World Oral Literature Project (2012)

13. Nag, S.: Early reading in kannada: the pace of acquisition of orthographic knowledge and phonemic awareness. J. Res. Reading $30(1)$, 7–22 (2007)

14. Nautiyal, S., Rajasekaran, C., Varsha, N.: Cross-cultural ecological knowledge related to the use of plant biodiversity in the traditional health care systems in biligiriranga-swamy temple tiger reserve, karnataka. Medicinal Plants-Inter. J. Phytomed. Related Indus. $6(4)$, 254–271 (2014)

15. Oord, A.v.d., et al.: Wavenet: a generative model for raw audio. arXiv preprint arXiv:1609.03499 (2016)

16. Openslr. https://www.openslr.org/79/, (Accessed 29 Sept 2023)

17. Ping, W., et al.: Deep voice 3: scaling text-to-speech with convolutional sequence learning. arXiv preprint arXiv:1710.07654 (2017)

18. Results page. https://style-transfer-five.vercel.app/, (Accessed 29th Sept 2023)

19. Shen, J., et al.: Natural tts synthesis by conditioning wavenet on mel spectrogram predictions. In: 2018 IEEE international conference on acoustics, speech and signal processing (ICASSP), pp. 4779–4783. IEEE (2018)

20. Swadesh, M.: Lexico-statistic dating of prehistoric ethnic contacts: with special reference to north American indians and eskimos. Proc. Am. Philos. Soc. $96(4)$, 452–463 (1952)

21. Wang, X., Feng, S., Zhu, J., Hasegawa-Johnson, M., Scharenborg, O.: Show and speak: directly synthesize spoken description of images. In: ICASSP 2021–2021 IEEE International Conference on Acoustics, Speech and Signal Processing (ICASSP), pp. 4190–4194. IEEE (2021)

22. Wang, Y., et al.: Style tokens: unsupervised style modeling, control and transfer in end-to-end speech synthesis. In: International Conference on Machine Learning, pp. 5180–5189. PMLR (2018)

23. Yamamoto, R.: Wavenet vocoder (2018). https://github.com/r9y9/wavenet_vocoder

Preliminary Analysis of Lambani Vowels and Vowel Classification Using Acoustic Features

Leena Dihingia[1]([envelope]) [iD], Prashant Bannulmath[2] [iD], Amartya Roy Chowdhury[3], S.R.M Prasanna[3], K.T Deepak[2], and Tehreem Sheikh[4]

[1] Gauhati University, Guwahati, Assam, India
leena@gauhati.ac.in
[2] Indian Institute of Information Technology, Dharwad, Karnataka, India
{prashantb,deepak}@iiitdwd.ac.in
[3] Indian Institute of Technology, Dharwad, Karnataka, India
amartya.chowdhury@iitdh.ac.in
[4] University of Delhi, New Delhi, India
tehreemsheikh701@gmail.com

Abstract. Lambani is an under-resourced Indo-Aryan language spoken by a nomadic tribe known as the 'Banjara people' across central and southern India. Due to its contact with several major languages of India, Lambani has been influenced both linguistically as well as culturally. One of the major influences has been observed in its phonemic inventory. This paper is a preliminary investigation into the acoustic characteristics of vowels of the language. The paper analyses spectral and temporal features of six Lambani vowels, viz./i,e,a,u,o,ə/ spoken in the Bagalkot district of Karnataka. The results obtained throw light on the distinctiveness of this variety. The paper then uses spectral and temporal features to explore both machine learning and deep learning approaches to classify Lambani vowel perceptual space. Results show that Fully Connected Dense Layer achieves better accuracy in classifying Lambani vowels.

Keywords: Lambani · Formant frequencies · Vowel classification

1 Introduction

Spoken language technologies support the preservation of diverse tribal languages and cultures. However, the limited resources typically available for such tribal languages present numerous challenges. The current study is a preliminary acoustic investigation into the vowel phonemes of the Lambani language spoken in the state of Karnataka in India, by the Banjara people. The paper additionally explores both machine learning and deep learning approaches to classify Lambani vowel perceptual space. Automatic vowel perceptual space classification will help in improving speech intelligibility for machines as well as humans. Exploring vowel sound classification-related issues will help in building spoken language technologies for under-resourced tribal languages.

© The Author(s), under exclusive license to Springer Nature Switzerland AG 2023
A. Karpov et al. (Eds.): SPECOM 2023, LNAI 14339, pp. 195–207, 2023.
https://doi.org/10.1007/978-3-031-48312-7_16

The Banjaras being originally nomadic, are scattered in several states of Central and Southern India. As such, the influence of the other major Indian languages that they have come into contact with has resulted in distinct varieties depending on where it is spoken. There have been a few linguistic studies of the language spoken by the Banjara people [2, 4, 10, 12, 18, 21, 22]. Apart from [12], which is a recent work on the acoustic analysis of vowels of the variety spoken in Telangana state, none have presented a phonetic description of the Lambani phonemes as spoken in Karnataka. Therefore, this paper has stemmed out of a need to provide a phonetic description of the Lambani phonemes as spoken in the state of Karnataka.

It is to be noted that this study is primarily a part of an ongoing larger project on speech-to-speech translation of low-resource tribal languages of two Indian states, Karnataka being one of them. Hence the data extracted and used for the present phonetic analysis consists of speech data that was collected keeping in mind the original intent of the project. Despite the methodological limitations, the authors believe that the current study is a step forward in the understanding of a hitherto understudied tribal language. In the following subsections, we introduce the Banjara community and the Lambani language. Section 2 discusses the methodology adopted for the current study, Sect. 3 discusses the results of the acoustic analysis and the classification tests, and finally, Sect. 4 concludes the findings.

1.1   The Banjara People

Traditionally, the Banjara people were an extremely mobile tribe trading salt, food grain, and other essential commodities on pack bullocks [5]. Even though historically nomadic, most of these people have now settled down to farming and various types of wage labor. In 2020, a PhD thesis on Lambani syntax [22] reported that at present, they are hugely populated in Andhra Pradesh, Telengana, Karnataka, and Maharashtra, as shown in Fig. 1. According to the census report of 2011, the total population of Lambanis in Karnataka is 1,267,036 ecensus:2011. In other central India regions, their strength being comparatively low, the native Banjaras have adopted the socio-cultural and linguistic habits of the dominant people resulting in the erosion of their indigenous speech [10].

On the etymology of the name 'Lambani', [20] reports that the word is derived from Sanskrit 'Lavanah'(salt). Since they were involved in selling lavanah, the people were originally called 'Lavaniga'. Eventually, they come to be named 'Lamani' and later 'Lambani'. However, the speech community has been called by several other names in different parts of the country. These names include Banjara(i), Vanjara, Vanachara, Gormati, Lambada(i), Lambani, Labhani, Lamani, Laman Banjara, Boipara, Sugali, Sukali, and so on [22].

1.2   The Lambani Language

Lambani is described to be an Indo-Aryan language [10, 21]. However, the language is mixed to a greater or lesser extent, with the vernacular of the place

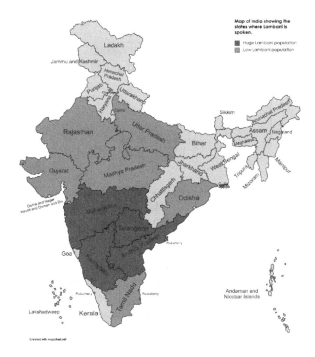

Fig. 1. Banjara population in India, as reported in [22].

wherever the speakers dwell. As a result, Lambani varies in vocabulary and in phonemic inventory from area to area. In Karnataka, Lambani comes in contact with the Dravidian language, Kannada, which is also the official language of the state. Regarding the vowels of Lambani, as spoken in the state of Karnataka, [21]'s report on the language spoken in Gulbarga district, mentions the presence of six distinct phonemes. Whereas [2]'s dissertation on the language spoken in Bijapur district mentions five distinct vowels. Apart from these studies on the Karnataka variety, [4] grammar on the Tamil Nadu variety reports the presence of seven vowels, and [12]'s acoustic description of vowels spoken in Telangana state reports five vowels. Table 1 presents a summary of the Lambani vowels reported so far. Wherever length differences are mentioned, the vowel is reported with the diacritic /:/.

2   Methodology

2.1   Datalist and Vowel Tokens

As mentioned earlier, this study is primarily a part of an ongoing larger project on speech-to-speech translation of low-resource tribal languages. Hence, the vowel data for this study has been extracted from the recordings of Lambani sentences that were majorly collected for the project and not exclusively for

Table 1. Vowels in Lambani as reported in different studies.

	Front			Central			Back	
	High	High-mid	Low-mid	High	Mid	Low	High	High-mid
Gulbarga [21]	i	e			ə	a	u	o
Bijapur [2]	i, iː	e, eː				a, aː	u, uː	o, oː
Tamil Nadu [4]	i, iː	e, eː	ɛ	ɪ		a, aː	u, uː	o, oː
Telangana [12]	i, iː		ɛ, ɛː			a, aː	u, uː	o, oː

a phoneme analysis. The dataset consists of 950 Lambani sentences that were created based on the Swadesh list [9]. The dataset contains a variety of grammatical constructions, in order to obtain as many phonemic combinations as possible in the language. Since Lambani in Karnataka uses the Kannada script, the sentences were written in the said script. They were rechecked and verified by a native Lambani speaker and were then presented to the participants to read out. The sentences were generated in a way such that they can capture the 'colloquial' utterance of the speaker. For linguistic analysis, IPA transcription of the Lambani data list was done by trained linguists after rigorous listening of the recordings. Short and long vowels were marked based on the Kannada script, which distinguishes vowels according to length.

Initially, a total of 7920 vowel tokens, all from a single female speaker were used for the study. These tokens were also used for automatic vowel classification experiments. However, in the later stages of the analysis, data from another female and two male speakers were included. Data from the three speakers contributed to an additional 312 vowel tokens. Since this resulted in a gross imbalance in speaker data, the total number of tokens from the initial participant was reduced to 179. Hence, the acoustic and statistical analysis presented in this paper is based on the final 491 vowel tokens. However, the 7920 tokens for the automatic vowel classification experiments remain unchanged.

2.2   Speaker and Recording Procedure

Two female and two male native Lambani speakers participated in the data collection for this study. The speakers belonged to Bagalkot district of Karnataka and were selected based on the requirements of pronunciation, legibility, and voice modulation for the speech-to-speech project. The recordings were carried out in an enclosed environment inside a sound-proof studio using a MAONO AU-903 cardioid microphone attached to an Acer laptop having a data collection suite with Graphical User Interface (GUI). A database was created for easier retrieval and storage. All recordings were done in .wav format having a sampling frequency of 44100 kHz with a 16bit PCM format.

2.3   Vowel Extraction

The Lambani speech data was segmented at the phoneme, word, and sentence levels using Praat 6.2 [3]. For vowel segmentation, the onset of the vowel formant was considered as the beginning of the vowel and the offset of the formant was considered the vowel ending. The total eleven vowels identified and analyzed for the current study are five short vowels /i,e,a,u,o/, their longer counterparts /iː,eː,aː,uː,oː/ and the vowel /ə/ (In all of the figures used in this study, the vowel /ə/ is represented as 'Q'). The segmented phonemes, along with the time indices, and in-text grid form, were saved separately. Another Praat script using the Burg algorithm was used to estimate the first three formant frequencies (F1, F2, and F3) in Hertz at the mid-20% of the vowel duration. The formant ceiling was kept at 5500 Hz.

2.4   Acoustic and Statistical Analysis

Several studies have considered formant frequency as a reliable measure of vowel quality in speech [7,14,15]. Hence, in order to investigate the vowel quality of Lambani, the first three formants of the vowels were measured as described in Sect. 2.3. Along with formant frequencies, duration, intensity, and F0 of the vowels were also measured. Prior to further analysis, the data were checked for outliers and recording errors. Formant frequencies were normalized using the Lobanov method for speaker-intrinsic effects [16]. The normalized values of the first two formants were then used to plot vowel group means with 1 standard deviation ellipses on F1-F2 space for visual representation. While the positions of the vowels in the vowel space are shown by the formant frequency means, the ellipses show the standard deviation of their distribution within a vowel space. All statistical analyses are conducted using the open-source RStudio platform [19].

2.5   Vowel Classification

To classify Lambani vowel perceptual space, experiments with both machine learning and deep learning approaches were conducted. Intensity (I_0), duration (D_0), fundamental frequency (f_0), and formant frequencies (f_1, f_2, f_3) were used as key features for the classification of vowel space. A general framework for a machine learning-based classifier is shown in Fig. 2.

Assuming we have C classes and our feature vector consists of $f = (f_1, f_2, f_3, f_0, I_0, D_0)$ with 6 features, class representative feature vectors for C^{th} class is given by $f = (f_{1,c}, f_{2,c}, f_{3,c}, f_{0,c}, I_{0,c}, D_{0,c})$. For a given set of class representative feature vector classifier will classify new instants. Popular machine learning algorithm-based classifiers like K-Nearest Neighbor (KNN), Support Vector Machine (SVM), and Random Forest Classifier were used for the classification.

– KNN is a simple efficient machine learning algorithm in classifying non-linear data [11]. It is a non-parametric supervised learning algorithm that uses

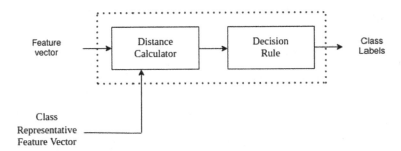

Fig. 2. Block Diagram of Classifier.

attributes from training data for classification. This method has been used for classifying samples based on the nearest training samples in the feature space. The main idea of KNN algorithm is to classify the samples based on the majority class of its nearest neighbors. The current experiment uses the value of K-neighbors = 11 and for measuring the distance from nearest neighbors Euclidean distance is used. SVM is used to classify complex and random data [6]. It works efficiently in cases of limited datasets and can be also used to classify higher dimensional data.

– SVM goes on constructing a discriminative hyperplane to separate different classes until an optimal hyperplane is found. It uses a support vector from the hyperplane to data points to develop maximum width. Depending on the dataset different kernels are used. Linear kernels are used for linearly separable datasets and the radial basis function is used for non-linearly separable datasets. For our experiment, SVM with Radial basis function has been used.
– One of the powerful classifiers that provides a higher level of accuracy in predicting outcomes is the Random Forest Classifier [8]. Training is done on a group of decision classifiers with different random subsets of training data. It gets the prediction from all individual trees to make a decision and one who gets the most votes is predicted. It creates an uncorrelated forest which is more accurate than any individual tree. Bootstrap samples are created by subsampling through the replacement of original data and these predictions are combined by the bootstrap aggregation algorithm.

Deep learning-based methods use Artificial Neural Network (ANN) to build a classifier, and as the name suggests, it is inspired by the biological nervous system [1]. ANN consists of parallel operating simple units trained in such a way that a particular input is converted into a specific target. In our experiment, we have used Single Layer Perceptron and Fully Connected Dense layer network with reLU activation function for the dense layer and softmax activation function for the output layer. The network is trained using rmsprop optimizer until it can approximate a function that maps input vectors to specific output vectors by minimizing categorical cross-entropy.

3   Results

3.1   Acoustic Features

Duration. Table 2 presents the average duration of the Lambani vowels in milliseconds. As observed, the length differences between the short and long vowels are clearly evident in the table. As expected, the vowel /ə/, being a mid-central vowel has the shortest duration. One-way ANOVA with post-hoc Tukey tests was conducted to check the vowels for statistical validation. Results showed significant differences in duration between the Lambani vowels [$F(480) = 30.06$, $p<0.05$]. Post-hoc Tukey tests revealed significant length differences in all short and long vowel counterparts ($p<0.05$), except for the vowel pair /o-oː/ ($p = 0.48$).

Table 2. Lambani vowel duration measured in ms.

Vowel	Av.dur(sd)	Vowel	Av.dur(sd)
/i/	89 (31)	/iː/	109 (35)
/e/	89 (26)	/eː/	101 (33)
/a/	94 (33)	/aː/	112 (35)
/o/	101 (31)	/oː/	110 (35)
/u/	95 (37)	/uː/	127 (33)
/ə/	72 (33)		

Intensity and F0. Table 3 presents the average intensity(in dB) and average F0(in Hz) of the Lambani vowels for female and male speakers. As observed, both intensity and F0 were found to be consistent for the Lambani vowels.

Table 3. Lambani vowel intensity measured in dB and f0 measured in Hz.

Female						Male					
Vowel	Av.in	Av.F0	Vowel	Av.in	Av.F0	Vowel	Av.in	Av.F0	Vowel	Av.in	Av.F0
/i/	71 (4)	270 (50)	/iː/	75 (6)	277 (66)	/i/	74 (5)	181 (24)	/iː/	71 (4)	186 (23)
/e/	74 (3)	253 (41)	/eː/	74 (3)	231 (8)	/e/	74 (2)	169 (16)	/eː/	75 (3)	176 (16)
/a/	75 (4)	257 (39)	/aː/	76 (3)	224 (11)	/a/	76 (4)	183 (20)	/aː/	75 (4)	173 (15)
/o/	71 (5)	240 (40)	/oː/	75 (3)	239 (31)	/o/	77 (5)	192 (24)	/oː/	74 (3)	179 (21)
/u/	71 (5)	267 (45)	/uː/	73 (3)	279 (38)	/u/	73 (7)	172 (15)	/uː/	73 (-)	207 (-)
/ə/	73 (4)	253 (46)				/ə/	75 (4)	177 (18)			

Formant Frequencies. Table 4 presents the mean F1, F2, and F3 values of the Lambani vowels in Hertz. The Lobanov normalized values of F1 and F2 are used to plot these vowels in an F1-F2 space, as visually represented in Figs. 3 and 4 for female and male speakers respectively. It is observed that all the six short vowels

Table 4. Mean F1, F2 and F3 of Lambani vowels measured in Hz.

Female				Male			
Vowel	F1	F2	F3	Vowel	F1	F2	F3
/i/	424 (39)	2691 (247)	3255 (294)	/i/	342 (33)	2257 (139)	2849 (223)
/iː/	352 (53)	3070 (75)	3395 (142)	/iː/	354 (16)	2517 (127)	3184 (231)
/e/	526 (61)	2497 (263)	3155 (276)	/e/	422 (50)	2192 (182)	2750 (229)
/eː/	536 (67)	2535 (156)	3292 (171)	/eː/	439 (66)	2062 (176)	2711 (197)
/a/	853 (155)	1668 (150)	2453 (402)	/a/	845 (112)	1495 (180)	2692 (153)
/aː/	976 (83)	1723 (100)	2836 (237)	/aː/	781 (133)	1331 (176)	2690 (168)
/o/	546 (38)	1296 (217)	3023 (367)	/o/	524 (73)	1057 (51)	2861 (104)
/oː/	587 (72)	1202 (220)	2961 (356)	/oː/	523 (72)	1081 (103)	2851 (141)
/u/	449 (46)	1102 (151)	2653 (798)	/u/	361 (26)	996 (65)	2715 (167)
/uː/	411 (60)	1039 (151)	2563 (872)	/uː/	280 ()	898 (-)	3067 (-)
/ə/	667 (98)	1729 (207)	2836 (539)	/ə/	607 (67)	1442 (190)	2730 (131)

viz. /i,e,a,u,o,ə/ occupy distinct positions in the vowel space for both male and female speakers. The five long vowels /iː,eː,aː,uː,oː/ are also seen to occupy the same positions as their shorter counterparts. In order to ascertain the statistical validity of the vowel positions, one-way ANOVA and post-hoc Tukey tests were conducted on F1 and F2 values. If both the corresponding F1 and F2 values of the short and long counterparts do not show statistically significant differences in the post-hoc tests, it is implied that the two vowels occupy the same position. The post-hoc results of the five short and long vowel pairs are shown in Table 5. Results show that F1 and F2 values of the short and long vowel counterparts do not differ significantly, except for the pairs /i-iː/, /o-oː/ and /a-aː/ which show significant differences ($p < 0.05$) in F2 values in the case of female speakers. However, F1 values for these pairs do not show any significant differences.

Table 5. Results of Tukey post-hoc tests for F1 and F2 conducted on Lambani vowels.

Female			Male		
Vowel pair	p-value for F1	p-value for F2	Vowel pair	p-value for F1	p-value for F2
/i-iː/	0.74 (!)	0.00 (*)	/i-iː/	1.00 (!)	0.08 (!)
/e-eː/	0.99 (!)	0.99 (!)	/e-eː/	0.96 (!)	0.96 (!)
/a-aː/	0.34 (!)	0.03 (*)	/a-aː/	0.47 (!)	0.55 (!)
/o-oː/	0.99 (!)	0.008 (*)	/o-oː/	0.99 (!)	0.99 (!)
/u-uː/	0.99 (!)	0.99 (!)	/u-uː/	0.95 (!)	0.91 (!)

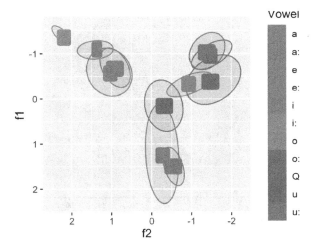

Fig. 3. Normalized formant frequency plots for Lambani vowels with 1 standard deviation ellipses produced by female speakers.

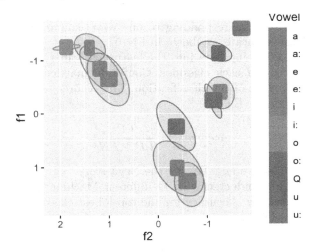

Fig. 4. Normalized formant frequency plots for Lambani vowels with 1 standard deviation ellipses produced by male speakers.

3.2   Classification Accuracy

Feature vectors obtained from available 7920 vowel tokens were split into training data and testing data to fit into the classifier. A total of 80% of extracted feature vectors were used as training data and the remaining 20% of feature vectors were used for testing. Hence, Training data consisted of 6,336 feature vectors each having dimension 6 and one predictor label. Similarly, testing data consisted of 1,584 feature vectors each having dimension 6 and one predictor label. There are

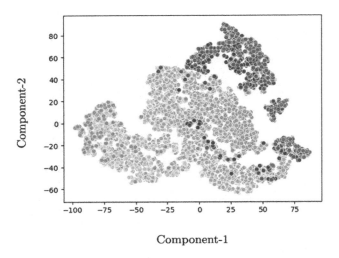

Component-1

Fig. 5. T-SNE Plot.

11 different classes each corresponding to one vowel sound. T-SNE projection
[17] of Lambani vowel data is as shown in Fig. 5.

After fitting the training data into the feature classifier, test data was used
to check the accuracy of each classifier. Confusion matrices were prepared to
indicate the performance of the classification. The accuracy of classification can
be measured through the Eq. 1.

$$Accuracy = \frac{TP}{TP + TN} \tag{1}$$

where TP = True Positive and TN = True Negative.

Experiments were conducted with 12 different Machine Learning and Deep
Learning-based classifiers. Accuracy for the top 5 best classifiers is as shown in
Table 6. The confusion matrix characterizes the performance of classifiers and
helps to understand if members of one class were confused with members of
another class by counting the number of true and false predictions. The confusion
matrices for different classifiers used in the experiments are shown in Fig. 6. For
representation purpose, numerical equivalents of vowels are used, as shown in
Table 7.

Results of the classification experiments show that Random Forest Classifier gives better accuracy compared to KNN and SVM in the case of machine
learning-based approaches. In the case of deep learning-based methods, Fully
Connected Dense Layer outperforms Single Layer Perceptron. Overall, Fully
Connected Dense Layer achieves almost 5% better accuracy than all other classifiers used in the experiment. The accuracy can further be improved with more
amount of training data.

Table 6. Accuracy for different classifiers.

Sl.No	Classifier	Accuracy
1	KNN	70.58
2	SVM	71.46
3	Random Forest	71.96
4	Single Layer Perceptron	71.46
5	Fully Connected Dense Layer	73.46

Table 7. Vowels and numerical equivalent for confusion matrix.

0=/a/	1=/a:/	2=/e/	3=/ə/	4=/e:/	5=/i/	6=/i:/	7=/o/	8=/o:/	9=/u/	10=/u:/

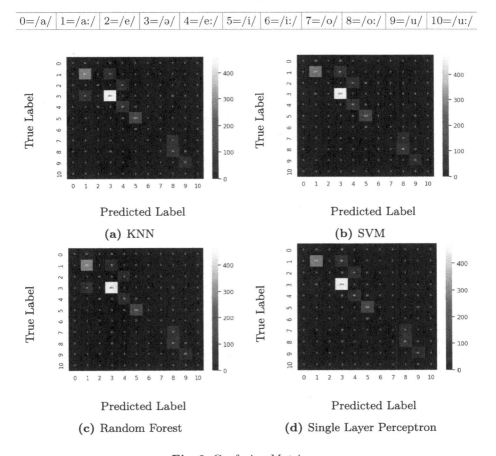

(a) KNN

(b) SVM

(c) Random Forest

(d) Single Layer Perceptron

Fig. 6. Confusion Matrices.

4   Conclusion

This paper presented a preliminary acoustic description of vowels in Karnataka Lambani, providing novel data on an under-resourced language of India. The analyses establish the distinctiveness of the vowels in the case of both formant frequencies and duration. The spectral and temporal features of vowels were then used to classify the Lambani vowels using a number of machine learning and deep learning-based approaches. It was observed that Fully Connected Dense Layer achieved better accuracy compared to other classifiers.

For acoustic analysis, the present study uses data collected from only four Lambani speakers as opposed to the ideal half a dozen speakers of each sex to "satisfy modern standards of phonetic description;; [13]. Another methodological limitation involves vowel context, as vowels can vary depending on their position within the word or phrase. The authors acknowledge these limitations and plan to collect and use data from a more significant number of speakers, as well as in different contexts and syllable structures to provide a descriptive acoustic analysis of the language. Nevertheless, as a preliminary investigation of an under-resourced and under-researched language, the paper contributes to the growing body of studies on vowels and dialect variation as well as is a step forward in developing technology for the language.

Acknowledgment. This paper is part of an ongoing project 'Speech-to-speech translation of low-resource tribal languages' supported by the Ministry of Electronics and Information Technology (MeitY), India. The authors thank Prof. K. Samudravijaya for his suggestions on vowel classification.

References

1. Aguila, M.J., Basilio, H.D.V., Suarez, P.V.C., Dueñas, J.P.E., Prado, S.V.: Comparative study of linear and nonlinear features used in imagined vowels classification using a backpropagation neural network classifier. In: Proceedings of the 7th International Conference on Bioscience, Biochemistry and Bioinformatics, pp. 7–11 (2017)
2. Barikeri, V.: A descriptive analysis of Lambani language spoken in Bijapur district. Ph.D. thesis, Dissertation submitted at the Department of Linguistics, Karnatak University (1982)
3. Boersma, P., Weenink, D.: Praat: doing phonetics by computer (version 6.2.15).[logiciel, en ligne] (2021)
4. Boopathy, S.: Languages of Tamil Nadu: Lambadi, an Indo-Aryan dialect. Census of India 1961, Tamil Nadu ix, part XII (1972)
5. Burman, J.R.: Ethnography of a denotified tribe: the Laman Banjara. Mittal Publications (2010)
6. Clarkson, P., Moreno, P.J.: On the use of support vector machines for phonetic classification. In: 1999 IEEE International Conference on Acoustics, Speech, and Signal Processing. Proceedings, ICASSP 1999 (cat. No. 99CH36258), vol. 2, pp. 585–588. IEEE (1999)
7. Deterding, D.: The formants of monophthong vowels in Standard Southern British English pronunciation. J. Int. Phon. Assoc. **27**(1–2), 47–55 (1997)

8. Devi, T.C., Thaoroijam, K.: Vowel-based meeteilon dialect identification using a random forest classifier. arXiv preprint arXiv:2107.13419 (2021)
9. Dyen, I.: Appendix - The Swadesh 200-Word Basic Vocabulary List, pp. 231–234. De Gruyter Mouton, Berlin, Boston (1975). https://doi.org/10.1515/9783110880830-015
10. Grierson, G.A.: Linguistic Survey of India, vol. 9. Office of the Superintendent of Government printing, India (1928)
11. Kantere, V., Mylopoulos, J., Kiringa, I.: A distributed rule mechanism for multidatabase systems. In: Meersman, R., Tari, Z., Schmidt, D.C. (eds.) OTM 2003. LNCS, vol. 2888, pp. 56–73. Springer, Heidelberg (2003). https://doi.org/10.1007/978-3-540-39964-3_6
12. Kumar, R.R., Duli, B.: An acoustic analysis of the vowels of lambada language. Inter. J. Sci. Res. (IJSR) 3, 1928–1933 (2014)
13. Ladefoged, P.: Phonetic fieldwork. In: Proceedings of 15th ICPhS, Barcelona, pp. 203–206(2003)
14. Ladefoged, P., Maddieson, I.: The sounds of the world's languages. Language 74(2), 374–376 (1998)
15. Lindblom, B.: Phonetic universals in vowel systems. Experim. Phonology, 13–44 (1986)
16. Lobanov, B.M.: Classification of Russian vowels spoken by different speakers. J. Acoust. Soc. Am. 49(2B), 606–608 (1971)
17. Van der Maaten, L., Hinton, G.: Visualizing data using t-sne. J. Mach. Learn. Res. 9(11), 2579–2605 (2008)
18. Maloth, U., Dutta, H.: Language attitudes and lambada youth in a multilingual domain. LINCOM Stud. Socioing. 17 (2018)
19. RStudio Team: RStudio: Integrated Development Environment for R. RStudio, PBC., Boston, MA (2020). https://www.rstudio.com/
20. Thurston, E.: Castes and Tribes of Southern India, vol. IV. Cosmo Publication, New Delhi (1975)
21. Trail, R.L.: The grammar of Lamani. SIL of the Univ. of Oklahoma (1970)
22. Zeenat, T.: Descriptive Analysis of Lambani Syntax. Ph.D. thesis, Dissertation submitted at the Department of Linguistics, Central University of Karnataka (2020)

Curriculum Learning Based Approach for Faster Convergence of TTS Model

Navneet Kaur[✉] and Prasanta Kumar Ghosh

SPIRE Lab, Indian Institute of Science, Bengaluru 560012, India
{knavneet,prasantg}@iisc.ac.in
https://iisc.ac.in/

Abstract. With the advent of deep learning, Text-to-Speech technology
has been revolutionized, and current state-of-the-art models are capable
of synthesizing almost human-like speech. Recent Text-to-Speech models use a sequence-to-sequence architecture that directly converts text
or phoneme sequence into low-level acoustic representation such as spectrogram. These end-to-end models need a large dataset for training, and
with conventional learning methodology, they need days of training to
generate intelligible and natural voice. 'How to use a large dataset to
efficiently train a TTS model?' has not been studied in the past. 'Curriculum learning' has been proven to speed up the convergence of models
in other machine learning areas. For TTS task, the challenge in creating
curriculum is to establish the difficulty criteria for the training samples. In this paper, we have experimented with various scoring functions
based on text and acoustic features and achieved faster convergence of
the end-to-end TTS model. We found 'text-length' or the number of
phonemes/characters in text to be a simple yet most effective measure of
difficulty for designing curriculum for Text-to-Speech task. Using text-
length based curriculum, we validated the faster convergence of TTS
model using three datasets of different languages.

Keywords: Speech synthesis · Text-to-speech · Curriculum learning ·
Tacotron

1 Introduction

Text-to-Speech (TTS) is the technology of automatic conversion of text into
speech waveform. TTS system aims to resemble, as closely as possible, a native
speaker of the language reading that text. A large number of techniques exist in
the literature for TTS [2,9,14,23], but the recent advancements in deep learning
has revolutionized the field. Today, end-to-end speech synthesis models such as
Tacotron [19], TransformerTTS [12], Fastspeech [18] are able to generate human-
like voices. These typically include sequence-to-sequence models that convert
sequence of characters/phonemes into linear or mel-spetrograms. The spectrograms are then used to generate audio waveforms using Griffin-Lim algortithm

A. Karpov et al. (Eds.): SPECOM 2023, LNAI 14339, pp. 208–221, 2023.
https://doi.org/10.1007/978-3-031-48312-7_17

or neural vocoders such as Wavenet [15], WaveGlow [16], MelGAN [10]. These text-to-spectrograms converters and audio generator models are what comprise an end-to-end TTS system.

However, training end-to-end TTS networks requires a sizable set of studio-quality (text, audio) pairs. Training on huge corpus is slow and it takes days of training to get intelligible and natural speech out of these systems. In this paper, we try to answer: 'How to train an end-to-end TTS model using a large dataset such that it converges faster?' To this end, we exploit curriculum learning techniques.

1.1 Curriculum Learning and TTS

Introduced by Yoshua Benjio in [1], curriculum learning (CL) broadly involves presenting the model with easy examples first and then gradually increasing the level of difficulty of examples. This training strategy has been shown both theoretically and empirically to accelerate the learning of deep learning models in [1,7,22]. [21] provides an extensive survey of CL techniques applied in the fields of computer vision, language processing, and speech recognition. Curriculum learning has demonstrated its effectiveness in improving the generalization capability and convergence rate of models from different domains. In the speech domain, curriculum learning has been used for better generalization, but its use for improving the convergence rate has not been explored. Specifically, curriculum learning has been used for robust far-field speech recognition [17], speech emotion recognition from crowd-sourced labels [13], and pre-training for end-to-end speech translation [20].

At the time of this writing, there is only one paper [8] where CL has been used to develop document-level neural TTS. In this paper, the input samples, i.e. (text, audio) pairs are randomly combined to generate progressively longer sentences in successive epochs of training. This curriculum has helped the model to generalize better and generate speech of duration higher than that available in the training set. The aim of the author in [8] has been to generalize the TTS model to the document level, whereas, in our work, we have made an attempt to use curriculum learning to speed up the convergence of the TTS model. To generalize the TTS to larger text, 'text-length' becomes a natural curriculum criterion, and accordingly, the author in [8] has supplemented the dataset with large text lengths by joining (text, audio) samples. However, in order to speed up the convergence of a TTS model, what criteria would be most effective for sorting the given dataset? In this work, we have experimented with different curriculum criteria and compared their effectiveness in speeding up the convergence of the TTS model. The curriculum criteria we have used are inspired by their success in other domains and we made the first attempt to use these criteria for the TTS learning task. Using the best curriculum criterion, we validated faster convergence of TTS model with three datasets of different languages.

2   Model and Datasets

Due to its popularity and simple yet powerful architecture, we have used Tacotron-2 [19] as Text-to-Spectrogram model for our experiments. Tacotron-2 has LSTM based encoder-decoder architecture with location sensitive attention [3]. It is autoregressive in nature and converts the sequence of characters into mel-scale spectrogram, frame by frame. Specifically, we used Nvidia's Pytorch implementation of Tacotron2 as our TTS model and Griffin-Lim algorithm to vocode the resulting spectrograms.

2.1   Three Datasets

We have used the following datasets to carry out experiments and consolidate our findings.

English Dataset. For English, we have used LJ-Speech dataset. It is a publicly available and most widely used dataset for training end-to-end TTS models. The speaker is an American female who reads passages from non-fiction books. We used 12500 utterances having a total duration of about 24 h as the training set for our experiments. The audio ranged from 1 to 10 s in duration.

Hindi Dataset. To consolidate our findings, we did a few experiments with our lab's Hindi dataset of 12 h duration. The dataset consists of 11,156 audio clips of a single female speaker. Audios are recorded at 16 kHz frequency and vary in length from 1 to 7 s. For text, news data from various publications was used along with school textbooks. The recording was done in 2019 with support from *Gnani.ai* team.

Telugu Dataset. This final dataset used for our experiments is created by our lab as a part of SYSPIN: SYnthesizing SPeech in INdian languages project: *syspin.iisc.ac.in*. We took 10,820 utterances as training data for our experiments which resulted in a total of 38 h of data. The text collected spanned across multiple domains: finance, agriculture, politics, education, health and general. The audios were uttered by a male native speaker of Telugu and the recording was done with help of *Bhashini.ai* team in 2021.

2.2   Metrics for Evaluation

Speech synthesis models are generally evaluated using MOS score. For faster turn-around time, we have extensively used objective measures to evaluate the performance of models. We used the following measures: **Mel Cepstral Distortion** (MCD), **Gross Pitch Error** (GPE), **F0 Frame Error rate** (FFE) [6] and **AlignmenT Score** (ATS). The synthesized mel-spectrograms and audios were compared with ground truth or recorded ones using MCD, GPE, and FFE, and the monotonicity of generated alignment map was measured using ATS. MCD computes the difference between the ground truth and generated spectrogram in cepstral domain. We use 13 MFCC coefficients and excluded 0th coefficient for MCD calculation as shown in Eq. 1 where $C_{t,k}/\hat{C}_{t,k}$ is k^{th} MFCC coefficient of reference/synthesized spectrogram at frame index 't', where $1 \leq t \leq T$ with T being the total number of frames.

$$MCD = \frac{10\sqrt{2}}{\ln 10} \frac{1}{T} \sum_{t=0}^{T-1} \sqrt{\sum_{k=1}^{13}(C_{t,k} - \hat{C}_{t,k})^2} \tag{1}$$

GPE and FFE are pitch-based measures as defined in Eq. 2 and 3. $v_t/\hat{v}_t$ are voicing decisions and $p_t/\hat{p}_t$ are pitch values at frame index t in reference/synthesized audio. GPE measures the percentage of voiced frames that deviate by more than 20 percent in the pitch signal of the generated audio compared to the reference audio.

$$GPE = \frac{\sum_t \mathbb{1}[|p_t - \hat{p}_t| > 0.2p_t]\mathbb{1}v_t\mathbb{1}\hat{v}_t}{\sum_t \mathbb{1}v_t\mathbb{1}\hat{v}_t} \tag{2}$$

FFE measures the percentage of frames that either have a 20 percent pitch error or a differing voicing decision between the synthesized and reference audio. F0 contours for audio are obtained using PRAAT software. Since synthesized and ground truth sequences could be different in length, we used dynamic time warping with $l2$ distance as the distance measure to time align both mel-spectrograms and pitch contours before comparing them for MCD, GPE and FFE computation.

$$FFE = \frac{1}{T} \sum_t (\mathbb{1}[|p_t - \hat{p}_t| > 0.2p_t] + \mathbb{1}[v_t \neq \hat{v}_t]) \tag{3}$$

For tracking the convergence of the model, we also use the AlignmenT Score (ATS) of the generated spectrograms. This is defined as the normalized sum of attention weights that lie in the diagonal region of the alignment matrix as shown in Fig. 1. Here, slope Tq/Tv is used to find the diagonal, and the sum of weights in the region 'c' distance away from the diagonal is calculated. We used c=5 frames for our calculations and computed alignment score as shown in Eq. 4 where Tq is sum of all attention weights or equivalently generated spectrogram length. ATS measures the sharpness and monotonicity of the attention maps. A higher ATS score indicates model has learned the alignment well.

$$ATS = \frac{\sum Attention\_weights\_within\_diagonal\_region}{Tq} \tag{4}$$

For final comparison, we also conducted **Mean Opinion Score** (MOS) test, remotely through Google Form. The evaluators were presented with a few sentences and corresponding audios generated by models trained using different

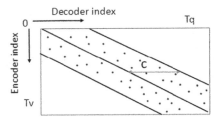

Fig. 1. Computation of Alignment Score: Tq is the number of spectrogram frames, and Tv is character length.

curricula. Different curriculum audios corresponding to the same text were kept together, to bring out relative comparison. To avoid any bias, the order of different curriculum audios was randomly shuffled for each sentence. Also, since some audios may sound very similar, we did not want to burden listeners with hard ranking. Instead, they were asked to rate each audio on a scale of 1 to 5 in terms of naturalness to capture preferences at a finer level.

3   Curriculum Learning Criteria

To apply curriculum learning to any task we need to address two critical questions: how to rank the training examples, and how to modify the sampling procedure based on this ranking. Thus, depending on the application, we need to define two functions: i) Scoring function [1], and ii) Pacing function [1]. To speed up the learning for the TTS task, we experimented with the following scoring functions to rank (text, audio) training examples.

3.1   Text-Length

In neural machine translation tasks, 'text-length' is shown to be an effective measure of the difficulty of training samples. Since, an end-to-end TTS model involves text encoding as that in a neural machine translator, we believed that this intuitive measure of difficulty may be helpful for Text-to-Speech task as well. Specifically, we computed text-length as number of characters in text input of training sample. Being a text-based feature, 'text-length' can be computed for the dataset even before the audio is recorded and thus, can be beneficial in TTS deployment as discussed in Sect. 5.

3.2   Acoustic Feature

We also experimented with an acoustic feature and explored its use for speeding up the convergence of a TTS model. Work done in data selection for TTS in [4,5,11] suggests that utterances with low articulation and low F0 standard deviation generate better-sounding samples when used to train a TTS model.

Here, articulation is defined as shown in Eq. 5 where total energy is computed as the sum of squares of audio samples, and average speaking rate is calculated as the number of vowels divided by utterance length. We experimentally verified the results of the data-selection study using our datasets and found that even an end-to-end TTS model (Tacotron-2) generates more natural voice when trained on a data subset with lower articulation and lower F0 standard deviation. This alludes to the fact that the model learns better and faster if the training samples have low values of articulation and F0 standard deviation. Thus, we constructed an 'acoustic feature' to select audios with low values of these features, as defined in Eq. 6, and used this 'acoustic feature' as a measure of difficulty for implementing CL for TTS.

$$articulation = \frac{total\_energy}{average\_speaking\_rate} \tag{5}$$

$$acoustic\_feature = articulation * F0\_standard\_deviation \tag{6}$$

3.3   Automatic Curriculum Learning

Conventional or pre-defined CL requires us to define the scoring function to rank order the training samples. But, what may be easy for humans may not be easy for the model. Thus, automatic curriculum learning was introduced in which the ranking of samples is model-driven and not human knowledge-driven. As automatic CL is proved to be more advantageous over pre-defined CL in literature, we also experimented with this strategy. Specifically, we trained our TTS model over the entire training corpus for 100 epochs and used this partially trained model to generate mel-spectrograms for all training samples. We then computed DTW-aligned mean squared error distance between synthesized and ground truth mel-spectrograms. Using this distance, we rank-ordered the training examples. The lower the distance, the easier the training sample.

4   Experiments and Results

We primarily used English dataset, LJ-Speech for obtaining the most appropriate difficulty measure for TTS task. We then verified the results on two other data sets: Hindi and Telugu.

4.1   Result on LJ-Speech Dataset

We began the experimentation with LJ-Speech dataset. For each scoring function discussed in section-3, we implemented double step pacing function as follows:
i) We use easiest 8 h of data (as per the scoring function) and trained model for 10k iterations,
ii) Use easiest 15 h of data and trained model for 20k more iterations,
iii) Finally, entire 24 h corpus is used to train the model for further 30k iterations.

As a baseline, we implemented random curriculum in which data subsets are chosen randomly. Table 1 shows the performance of models after each step of curriculum, i.e., after 10k, 30k and 60k iterations. For reference, we have also included results of model trained on 'full data'(entire 24 h corpus) at various stages without any curriculum. We found that for acoustic-feature based curriculum, GPE score which measures the naturalness of speech has reduced the most in 10k iterations, but MCD score remains poor till 30k iterations. On the other hand, we note that after both 10k and 30k iteration points, the MCD score corresponding to 'Text-length' curriculum is the lowest. Also, the GPE score which is poor for 'Text-length' after 10k, is significantly improved or reduced after 30k iterations. 'Text-length' seems to be more effective criterion than the acoustic feature for faster convergence. ATS results favor automatic 'DTW-MSE' based curriculum. The learning curves on validation data are shown in Fig. 2. Considering both the objective scores and learning curves, we find that curriculum learning indeed benefits the convergence and model trains faster as compared to the random curriculum. Especially, 'Text-length' and 'DTW-MSE' based CL prove to be more beneficial. Although DTW-MSE gave the best results, it is an automatic CL and we need to train the model on the complete dataset for implementing this curriculum. On the other hand, 'Text-length' is an easily computed pre-defined feature whose performance is competent with that of a dynamic DTW-MSE feature-based curriculum. We found 'Text-length' to be the most effective and efficient curriculum criteria for accelerated convergence. We thus validate the efficacy of 'Text-length' based curriculum on two other datasets.

Table 1. Performance of models trained using different curricula after 10k/30k/60k iterations. Bold entries correspond to best scoring curriculum.

Feature	MCD	GPE	FFE	ATS
Full-data(No CL)	50.75/32.77 /32.60	0.317/0.175 /0.198	0.211/0.121 /0.137	0.012/0.055 /0.075
Random	54.12/43.12 /32.29	0.343/0.228 /0.194	0.221/0.156 /0.141	0.009/0.010 /0.105
Text-length	**49.57/31.90** /31.75	0.326/0.202 /0.196	0.231/0.145 /0.134	0.016/0.018 /0.037
Acoustic-feature	51.96/36.19 /32.85	**0.269**/0.250 /0.195	0.182/0.163 /0.132	0.014/0.032 /0.030
DTW-MSE	50.75/33.54 /31.67	0.290/**0.186** /0.197	**0.173/0.134** /0.134	**0.017/0.0.056** /0.053

MOS Score Test: To subjectively evaluate the performance of 'text-length' based curriculum versus random curriculum, we conducted MOS score test. For this, we used models after second stage of double step pacing function experiment, i.e. models trained for 30k iterations. For comparison, we also used model trained using entire 23 h data for 30k iterations without curriculum. We synthesized 10 sentences using each of three models, and used 30 synthesized audios for the test. We ensured that the length of test sentences has wide enough range so that 'text-length' curriculum based model trained on shorter sentences gets no undue advantage. Total 46 listeners participated and average scores are shown in Table 2. The results are in agreement with objective evaluation and 'text-length'

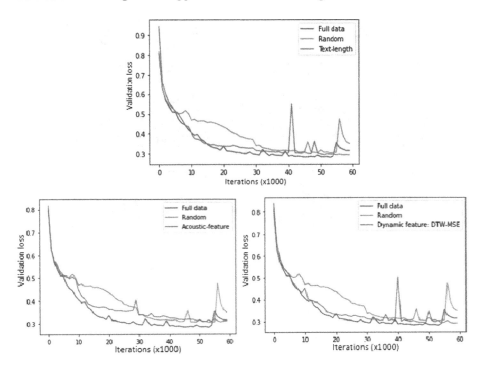

Fig. 2. Validation loss for different curricula: Text-length(top), acoustic feature(bottom-left), DTW-MSE feature(bottom-right) on LJ-Speech.

feature based curriculum has obtained similar MOS score with 15 h data as that of vanilla trained model on 23 h data. The MOS score obtained by random curriculum is, however, very low as the speech synthesized was not very intelligible. The leftmost column in Fig. 3 shows the alignment of a test sentence synthesized by the three models. While 'text-length' based model has achieved sharp monotonic alignment, the alignment obtained from random curriculum trained model still looks blur and hazy.

Table 2. MOS score results for different models trained for 30k iterations. 'Max. duration' is total duration of data the model has seen till this stage of training.

Curriculum	Max. duration	MOS score
Full-data(No CL)	23 h	3.5455
Random	15 h	1.8286
Text-length	15 h	3.5956

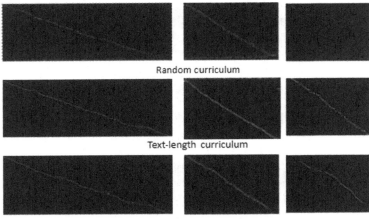

Fig. 3. Attention matrices generated by models trained using different curricula: LJ-Speech (leftmost), Hindi (middle) and Telugu(rightmost).

4.2 Results on Hindi Dataset

We consolidated our results using a Hindi dataset with a total duration of 11.7 h. We implemented 'text-length' based curriculum as follows:

i) We trained Tacotron-2 model for 20k iterations on 5 h easiest data,

ii) Then, followed by 20k iterations on 8 h of easiest data.

Figure 4 shows the validation loss curve and Table 3 shows the objective evaluation results. We observed that the maximum gain of using curriculum learning is observed in the initial phase of training as 'text length' curriculum-based model shows the best performance in terms of all the objective metrics after 15k iterations.

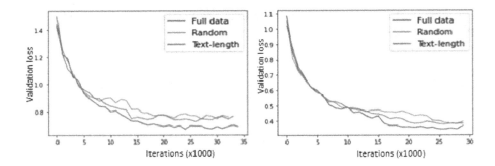

Fig. 4. Validation loss for Hindi(left) and Telugu(right) dataset.

Table 3. Performance of different curriculum models on Hindi dataset. In score format 'x/y//z', 'x/y' represent the score after training model for 15k/20k iterations on 5 h subset, 'z' is the score after further training for 20k iterations with 8 h subsets.

Curriculum	MCD	GPE	FFE	ATS
Full-data	45.37/34.31 //32.27	0.133/0.088 //0.080	0.133/0.060 //0.063	0.036/0.083 //0.109
Random	48.57/35.41 //32.00	0.125/0.088 //0.063	0.117/0.084 //0.059	0.018/0.017 //0.017
Text-length	**41.68**/34.49 //32.46	**0.113**/0.091 //0.063	**0.097**/0.091 //0.060	**0.050**/0.053 //0.085

MOS Score Test: We also conducted MOS score test for Hindi dataset. Ten sentences of varied lengths were synthesized by models trained for 20k iterations on a) 5 h random subset, b) 5 h of shortest text-length subset, and c) full 11.7 h of data. Total 79 responses were recorded and the average scores are reported in Table 4. The middle column in Fig. 3 shows the alignment for a test sentence synthesized by three models. The observations are in agreement with ATS & MOS scores and it is visually clear that the attention of text length curriculum-based model is sharper and better than that obtained by random curriculum model.

Table 4. MOS score results for models trained for 20k iterations on different curricula for Hindi dataset.

Curriculum	Max. duration	MOS score
Full-data(No CL)	11.7 h	3.8202
Random	5 h	1.9759
Text-length	5 h	3.2240

4.3   Results on Telugu Dataset

The total duration of Telugu dataset was 38 h. To experiment with text-length based curriculum learning, we trained Tacotron-2 model for 20k iterations on 10 h easiest data, followed by 10k iterations on 15 h of easier data. Figure 4 shows that the validation loss of text-length based curriculum train remains lower than random curriculum. Also, Table 5 shows that 'Text-length' based curriculum achieves best objective scores, MCD & ATS after 10k/20k iterations, again highlighting that model learns faster using this curriculum.

MOS Score Test: For Telugu dataset, we conducted MOS score test for two stages of learning. MOS-1 and MOS-2 present the scores obtained after 1st and 2nd phase of training. Seven sentences for each stage were synthesized and presented to listeners. A total of 45 responses were collected and results are shown in Table 6. 'Full-data' scores are reported after vanilla training the model for 20k and 30k iterations using the complete 38 h of data. MOS-1 is higher for vanilla learning as compared to curriculum learning as data observed by curriculum learning model is just about 10 h, as compared to 38 h in vanilla training model. MOS-2 however, indicates that using just 39% of training data, i.e. 15 h data, 'text-length' CL based model achieved MOS score competent with that of vanilla training model.

Table 5. Performance of different curriculum models on Telugu dataset; Here, in score format x/y//z, x/y is the score after training for 10k/20k iterations on 10 h subset; z is the score after further training for 10k iterations with 15 h subsets.

Curriculum	MCD	GPE	FFE	ATS
Full-data	40.59/**32.13** //31.25	**0.155/0.143** //0.126	0.104/0.082 //0.087	6.13e-5/0.012 //0.022
Random	37.83/36.71 //30.85	0.158/0.153 //0.133	0.093/0.091 //0.084	7.04e-5/4.04e-5 //9.48e-4
Text-length	**34.40**/33.52 //28.92	0.173/0.151 //0.134	0.104/0.084 //0.079	**1.11e-4/3.93e-4** //1.98e-3

Table 6. Telugu dataset: MOS-1: model trained for 20k iterations on 10 h subset; MOS score-2: model further trained on 15 h data for 10k iterations.

Curriculum	MOS-1 (Max. data)	MOS-2 (Max. data)
Full-data(No CL)	3.3932 (38 h)	3.6015 (38 h)
Random	2.0673 (10 h)	3.2118 (15 h)
Text-length	2.7138 (10 h)	3.5096 (15 h)

5   Discussion

By experimenting with multiple datasets, we found that, we are able to achieve faster convergence using 'text-length' based curriculum as compared to random curriculum. At the same time, 'text-length' based curriculum learning achieves a similar MOS score as that of conventional learning using a significantly lesser amount of data.

We want to highlight that 'text-length' based curriculum learning can provide practical advantages while deploying a TTS system as follows. Conventional TTS system involves text collection, and weeks of audio recording before it is used to train a TTS model. Being a text-based measure, 'text length' can be computed before the audio is recorded. Thus, we can begin the recording with shorter/easier text, and use it to train the model. We can progressively increase the length of the text to be recorded until the model has generalized and the MOS score requirement is achieved. This enables us to achieve faster convergence and record just the sufficient amount of data required to train a TTS model, thus, reducing the cost of data creation.

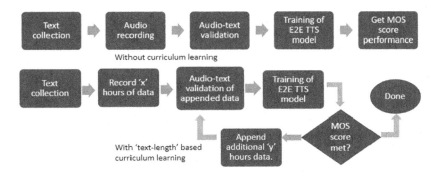

Fig. 5. Conventional TTS system deployment(top) and curriculum enabled TTS deployment(bottom).

As shown in Fig. 5, a conventional TTS system involves text collection, audio recording, and the laborious task of audio-text validation before it is used to train a TTS model. While deploying TTS using a 'text-length' based curriculum, we can begin recording a small chunk of x hours of data, and then keep adding y hours of data until the MOS requirement is achieved. Curriculum learning gives us a criterion to record data in chunks so that we collect just the sufficient amount of data needed to train the model. This also relieves the burden of manual validation of unduly large amounts of data.

6   Conclusion and Future Scope

In this paper, we have established that 'text-length' is an appropriate difficulty measure for curriculum learning in TTS task. We have demonstrated that 'text-length' based curriculum learning helps speed up the convergence of a sequence-to-sequence based Text-to-Speech model on three datasets.

We have worked with Tacotron-2 model which is most widely used text-to-spectrogram model provided by Google, but the results can be extended to other TTS models as well. Work can be done to check the effectiveness of the proposed methods for other auto-regressive and non auto-regressive models for spectrogram generation. Neural vocoder is crucial component of end-to-end TTS system. Even though it does not need paired (text, audio) data for training; it still needs a large amount of audio data and weeks of training to generate high-quality voice. We can explore the use of acoustic feature-based or utterance duration based curriculum learning for vocoders to speed up their training. In this work, we have restricted ourselves to the fixed training schedule. As 'DTW-MSE' loss based curriculum gave positive results on LJSpeech data set, we can work further in the direction of automatic curriculum learning for TTS. We can optimize the training schedule or update it dynamically with the help of model feedback. Finally, we have used simple and clean TTS datasets in our work. In the future, the power of curriculum learning can be explored using other complex datasets.

References

1. Bengio, Y., Louradour, J., Collobert, R., Weston, J.: Curriculum learning. In: Proceedings of the 26th Annual International Conference on Machine Learning, pp. 41–48 (2009)
2. Black, A., Tokuda, K., Zen, H.: An hmm-based speech synthesis system applied to English. In: Proceedings of (2002)
3. Chorowski, J.K., Bahdanau, D., Serdyuk, D., Cho, K., Bengio, Y.: Attention-based models for speech recognition In: Advances in Neural Information Processing Systems 28 (2015)
4. Cooper, E., Levitan, Y., Hirschberg, J.: Data selection for naturalness in hmm-based speech synthesis. In: Speech Prosody (2016)
5. Cooper, E., Wang, X.: Utterance selection for optimizing intelligibility of TTS voices trained on ASR data. Interspeech **2017**, 1 (2017)
6. Fang, W., Chung, Y.A., Glass, J.: Towards transfer learning for end-to-end speech synthesis from deep pre-trained language models. arXiv preprint arXiv:1906.07307 (2019)
7. Hacohen, G., Weinshall, D.: On the power of curriculum learning in training deep networks. In: International Conference on Machine Learning, pp. 2535–2544. PMLR (2019)
8. Hwang, S.W., Chang, J.H.: Document-level neural TTS using curriculum learning and attention masking. IEEE Access **9**, 8954–8960 (2021)
9. Jurafsky, D., Martin, J.H.: Speech and language processing: an introduction to natural language processing, computational linguistics, and speech recognition
10. Kumar, K., et al.: Melgan: generative adversarial networks for conditional waveform synthesis. In: dvances in Neural Information Processing Systems 32 (2019)
11. Kuo, F.Y., Ouyang, I.C., Aryal, S., Lanchantin, P.: Selection and training schemes for improving TTS voice built on found data. In: INTERSPEECH, pp. 1516–1520 (2019)
12. Li, N., Liu, S., Liu, Y., Zhao, S., Liu, M.: Neural speech synthesis with transformer network. In: AAAI Conference on Artificial Intelligence, vol. 33, pp. 6706–6713 (2019)
13. Lotfian, R., Busso, C.: Curriculum learning for speech emotion recognition from crowdsourced labels. IEEE/ACM Trans. Audio, Speech, Lang. Process. **27**(4), 815–826 (2019)
14. Onaolapo, J., Idachaba, F., Badejo, J., Odu, T., Adu, O.: A simplified overview of text-to-speech synthesis. Proc. World Congr. Eng **1**, 5–7 (2014)
15. Oord, A.v.d., et al.: Wavenet: a generative model for raw audio. arXiv preprint arXiv:1609.03499 (2016)
16. Prenger, R., Valle, R., Catanzaro, B.: Waveglow: a flow-based generative network for speech synthesis. In: International Conference on Acoustics, Speech and Signal Processing (ICASSP), pp. 3617–3621. IEEE (2019)
17. Ranjan, S., Hansen, J.H.: Curriculum learning based approaches for robust end-to-end far-field speech recognition. Speech Commun. **132**, 123–131 (2021)
18. Ren, Y., Hu, C., Tan, X., Qin, T., Zhao, S., Zhao, Z., Liu, T.Y.: Fastspeech 2: fast and high-quality end-to-end text to speech. arXiv preprint arXiv:2006.04558 (2020)
19. Shen, J., et al.: Natural TTS synthesis by conditioning wavenet on mel spectrogram predictions. In: International Conference on Acoustics, Speech and Signal Processing (ICASSP), pp. 4779–4783. IEEE (2018)

20. Wang, C., Wu, Y., Liu, S., Zhou, M., Yang, Z.: Curriculum pre-training for end-to-end speech translation. arXiv preprint arXiv:2004.10093 (2020)
21. Wang, X., Chen, Y., Zhu, W.: A survey on curriculum learning. IEEE Trans. Pattern Anal. Mach. Intell. **44**(9), 4555–4576 (2021)
22. Weinshall, D., Cohen, G., Amir, D.: Curriculum learning by transfer learning: Theory and experiments with deep networks. In: International Conference on Machine Learning, pp. 5238–5246. PMLR (2018)
23. Wu, Z., Watts, O., King, S.: Merlin: an open source neural network speech synthesis system. In: SSW, pp. 202–207 (2016)

Rhythm Measures and Language Endangerment: The Case of Deori

Krisangi Saikia$^{(\boxtimes)}$ and Shakuntala Mahanta ⓘ

Department of Humanities and Social Sciences, Indian Institute of Technology Guwahati,
Guwahati 781039, India
{krisangisaikia,smahanta}@iitg.ac.in

Abstract. This paper presents a study on the rhythm in read speech for Deori (L1), a Tibeto-Burman language and Assamese, an Indo-Aryan language (L2) spoken by the Deori speakers in the state of Assam, India. This study aims to explore and analyze the rhythmic patterns exhibited in read speech for Deori, focusing on aspects such as syllable timing, and duration for both L1 and L2 read speech. To analyze the speech rhythm, rhythm measures such as %V, nPVI, rPVI, varco-V, varco-C, ΔV, and ΔC were calculated for the read speech. Regardless of the rhythmic class of Deori (L1), the results on read speech showed that Assamese (L2) are similar to Deori (L1) in terms of nPVI-V, rPVI-C, whereas it exhibits a shift towards the mora-timed class in terms of %V and ΔC. This study provides valuable insights into the complex interplay between L1 and L2 rhythm patterns. These findings highlight the significance of considering factors such as speech rate and prosodic structure when examining rhythmic differences in bilingual speech.

Keywords: Deori · Assamese (L2) · Rhythm · Speech Rate

1 Introduction

Deori is a Tibeto-Burman language spoken in the state of Assam, India. Deori, an endangered language, is currently in a highly vulnerable state, considering it almost moribund. However, a glimmer of hope emerges from a recent study where the research highlights that some young children have been observed learning the Deori language, indicating a potential avenue for extending its existence [1].

Since Deori is spoken in Assam, and almost the entire community is bilingual their speech repertoire comprises their native language as their first language (L1) and Assamese as their second language (L2). In this context, it is important to investigate whether speakers who have an Indo-Aryan language with trochaic prominence as their second language (L2) experience any impact on rhythm. This is particularly relevant when these L2 speakers come from a linguistic background that includes a highly vulnerable language within the Tibeto-Burman language group, which exhibits an iambic prominence pattern characterized by initial vowel lengthening [2]. This paper attempts to study the rhythmic patterns in Deori (L1) and L2 (Assamese). Both of them are compared with the previously analyzed prototypical stress, syllable and mora timed languages.

© The Author(s), under exclusive license to Springer Nature Switzerland AG 2023
A. Karpov et al. (Eds.): SPECOM 2023, LNAI 14339, pp. 222–230, 2023.
https://doi.org/10.1007/978-3-031-48312-7_18

Rhythm is a significant prosodic characteristic that plays a crucial role in the naturalness of speech. Traditionally, spoken languages have been divided into three rhythmic categories, known as "stress-timed," "syllable-timed," and "mora-timed" [3–5]. The categorization is based on the concept of isochrony, which states that speech is divided into relatively equal units of duration: syllables in syllable-timing languages such as French and Italian, inter-stress intervals in stress-timing languages like English and German, and mora intervals in mora-timing languages such as Japanese [6].

However, there is no reliable acoustic evidence that proves the presence of isochronous units [7–9]. Isochrony is thus viewed as a more impressionistic trait that correlates with particular phonological features such as syllable structure, vowel reduction, and stress [7]. Recent research has shifted away from the primary focus on isochrony in favor of a more detailed study of the variability in the durations of consonantal and vocalic intervals for the acoustic perception of rhythmic distinctions. The standard deviation of consonant duration (ΔC), percentage of vocalic duration ($\%V$) [8], and pairwise variability index (PVI) [9] for vocalic and consonant durations are all examples of such measures. Speech rhythm is usually divided into rhythmic classes, with languages being either stress-, syllable-, or mora-timed. So, the basic unit of rhythmic speech is either the foot (e.g., English), syllable (e.g., French), or mora (e.g., Japanese).

Stress-timed languages have complex syllable structure and vowel reduction in contrast to syllable-timed and mora-timed, they have simple syllable structure and avoid vowel reduction [7]. Temporal measurements, such as ΔC (standard deviation of consonantal intervals), ΔV (standard deviation of vocalic intervals), and $\%V$ (percentage of vocalic intervals in an utterance) were measured. Out of these three temporal measures, the combination of $\%V$ and ΔC was considered to best fit for distinguishing rhythm classes. The stressed-timed and syllable-timed languages cluster differently when $\%V$ and ΔC are plotted on an x-y plane [8]. Speaking rate affects measurements like $\%V$, ΔV, and ΔC, making them less efficient in distinguishing rhythm classes. Thus, Pairwise Variability Index (PVI) were proposed to decrease the effect of speaking rate. This approach classifies languages based on durational variability of successive units of speech and can reflect normalized (npvi) or raw (rpvi) values [9]. Whereas Varcos, were developed to minimize the effect of speech tempo [10]. It is important to mention that some claims have been made in the literature suggesting that the existing rhythm metrics are not capable of adequately classifying languages into distinct rhythmic classes [11].

In addition to rhythmic studies on native speech (L1), some studies have investigated rhythmic patterns in non-native speech (L2), such as English as a second language for Mandarin and Cantonese speakers with Mandarin or Cantonese as their first language [12]. Studies also explored the influence of the first language (L1) on the second language (L2) for Dutch, English, and Spanish speakers [13]. It is essential for computer-assisted language learning systems to be able to recognize rhythmic patterns in non-native speech. Some occurrences of rhythmic similarities between the L1 and L2 in non-native speech lend credence to the hypothesis of L1 transfer effects. In other cases, non-native speech shows rhythmic patterns nearly identical to either L1 or L2 [6].

2 Methodology

This work investigates the rhythm of read speech of Deori speakers in Assam. Assamese is the dominant language in Assam so, speakers of Deori are bilingual as they can speak Assamese as L2 and to some extent English L3, especially the younger generation [1]. In this work, we investigated the difference in rhythm of the speakers of Deori (L1) and Assamese (L2) reading the story "The North Wind and the Sun". Conventional rhythm measures, such as %V, nPVI, rPVI, varco-V, varcoC, ΔV and ΔC are calculated for read speech.

2.1 Participants

A total of eight participants, all native speakers of Deori (L1) and also proficient in Assamese (L2), took part in two production experiments. The age range of the participants was between (21 to 36 years), consisting of four male and four female speakers who recorded both languages. Each participant was asked to produce the story four times, ensuring a natural speech rate and intonation pattern. The best three repetitions produced by each speaker were considered for final analysis. The translated story comprises roughly 11 sentences for each language with varied syllable lengths (ranging between 6 to 12 syllables per sentence). The recorded speech data were annotated at the phoneme level in Praat 6.1.06 [14], delineating vocalic and consonantal intervals based on auditory and acoustic cues according to standard segmentation criteria [15].

2.2 Materials

The English version of "The North Wind and the Sun" was translated into Deori and Assamese [16]. Translation has been done by a native speaker of Deori language. Prior to recording, the data sets were given to them to familiarize themselves with the sentences and were allowed to rehearse a couple of times to avoid pauses and hesitations. Speakers were instructed to read the sentences on a sheet at their own pace and as naturally as they would in a conversation.

2.3 Procedure

After the data was recorded, it was annotated at the phoneme level in PRAAT [14]. The *Correlatore* program (version 2.3.4) [17] was used to extract different rhythmic metrics, including Cmean, Vmean, %V, ΔC, ΔV, Varcos (Varco-V, Varco-C), and the PVI (nPVI, rPVI) from the annotated speech data. The *speaking rate* also influences rhythm measures. The speech rate is calculated in terms of the time taken syllables per second and segments per second. The values of these matrices were plotted against each other using the *ggplot* package (Figs. 1 and 2, for example) in the R software (version 4.2.2 (R Core Team, 2022) [18].

3   Results

3.1   Syllable Structure of Deori

Deori typically employs the CV syllable type as the default or unmarked syllable type. This aligns with the moraic theory of syllable weight. Deori follows a canonical syllable structure of (C)V(C), where the onset (initial consonant) and coda (final consonant) are optional [2]. This is also true for Assamese (L2) [19] as can be seen in Fig. 1 for comparison. Deori syllables tend to resemble to French language. Deori (L1) CV- interval shows 75.1% among other syllable types. Whereas Assamese (L2) CV intervals shows 65.5% in the entire passage.

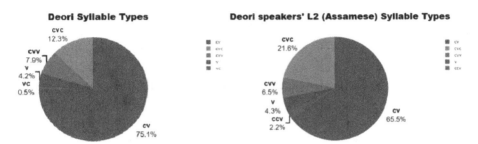

Fig. 1. Syllable types of Deori (L1) on the *left* and Assamese (L2) on the *right* of the read passages in the story *"The North Wind and the Sun"*.

3.2   Correlation of Rhythm Metrics

Several rhythm measures have been demonstrated to be directly or indirectly proportional to the rate of speech in the literature. It has been suggested that utterance length is another aspect to which rhythm metrics are particularly sensitive. It has also been demonstrated that the extent to which these factors influence rhythm measures varies from one language to another. As can be seen in Figs. 2 and 3. Pearson correlation was calculated for each text independently. The figures clearly show that the measurements' correlation varies by language. Rate of articulation, in terms of segments per second (sg/s), has a negative correlation on (L1) and nPVI-V, ΔV. However, there is a robust inverse relationship between Varco-C for both length and syllable per second as can be seen in Fig. 2. In the case of Assamese (L2), the impact of rate of articulation is highly significant across all seven rhythm measures investigated in this study. As seen in Fig. 3, segment/second is negatively correlated with all the rhythm measures.

3.3   Rhythm Measures

Deori (L1) and Deori speaking Assamese (L2) rhythm results are presented in Table 1, along with other languages [8]. This allows us to make direct comparisons to earlier findings. And to compare the results with the previous findings, we plotted the values

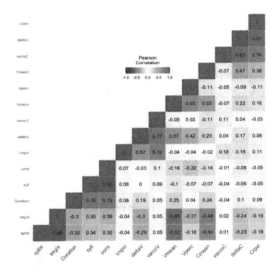

Fig. 2. Pearson correlation matrix of measures for Deori.

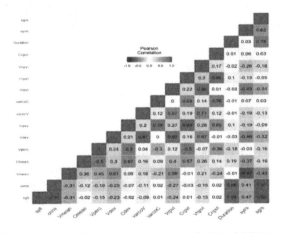

Fig. 3. Pearson correlation matrix of measures for Deori L2 (Assamese).

of %V and ΔC rhythm metrics of Deori (L1) and (L2). As we can see in Fig. 4, the ΔC values for Deori (L1) are close to the other three syllable-timed languages (French, Spanish and Catalan), which makes it clear that Deori should be categorized as syllable-timed while Deori-speaking Assamese (L2), is more a mora-timed language which tends to cluster with Japanese. Whereas in Fig. 5 we plot the values of nPVI-V and rPVI-C with other languages [9]. The results are presented in Table 2. It can be seen that both Deori (L1) and Assamese (L2) the nPVI-V is similar to that of Japanese, but rPVI-C for Deori (L1) showing tendency of shifting towards syllable-timed language and can be seen clustering with French.

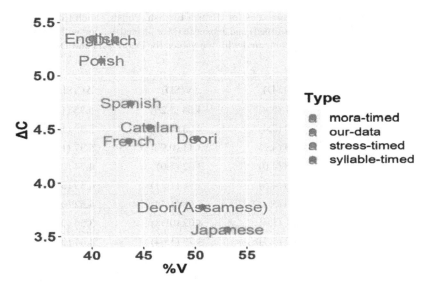

Fig. 4. ΔC and %V for Deori L1 and L2 speech with different languages [8].

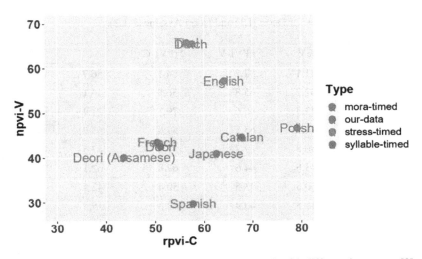

Fig. 5. nPVI-V and rPVI-C for Deori L1 and L2 speech with different languages [9].

Table 1. The values of Rhythm correlates for [British English, Polish, Dutch (Stressed-timed), Spanish, French, Catalan (Syllable-timed) and Japanese (Mora-timed)] along with their standard deviation as proposed by [8] are compared with the values for Deori (L1) and Deori Assamese (L2).

Language	%V(SD)	ΔV(SD)	ΔC(SD)
English	40.1 (5.4)	4.64 (1.25)	5.35 (1.63)
Polish	41.0 (3.4)	4.23 (0.67)	5.33 (1.18)
Dutch	42.3 (4.2)	3.11 (0.93)	5.37 (1.5)
Spanish	43.8 (4.0)	3.32 (1.0)	4.74 (0.85)
French	43.6 (4.5)	3.78 (1.21)	4.39 (0.74)
Catalan	45.6 (5.4)	3.68 (1.44)	4.52 (0.86)
Japanese	53.1 (3.4)	4.02 (0.58)	3.56 (0.74)
Deori	50.2 (5.7)	3.77 (1.64)	4.41 (0.75)
Deori (Assamese)	50.7 (5.8)	3.61 (1.2)	3.77 (0.8)

Table 2. The values of Rhythm correlates for [British English, Thai, Dutch, Polish (Stressed-timed), Spanish, French, Catalan (Syllable-timed) and Japanese (Mora-timed)] as proposed by [9] are compared with the values for Deori (L1) and Deori Assamese (L2).

Language	%V	nPVI-V	rPVI-C	ΔC	ΔV
British English	41.1	57.2	64.1	56.7	46.6
Thai	52.2	65.8	56.5	46.1	74.8
Polish	42.3	46.6	79.1	71.4	44.9
Dutch	44.9	65.5	57.4	53.7	48.4
Spanish	50.8	29.7	57.7	47.5	20.7
Catalan	43.6	44.6	67.8	62.1	33.9
French	50.6	43.5	50.4	42.4	35.5
Japanese	45.5	40.9	62.5	55.5	53.0
Deori	50.2	42.5	51.1	44	37.7
Deori (Assamese)	50.7	40.1	43.6	37.7	36.1

4   Conclusion

We have analyzed the differences in rhythmic patterns of speech of Deori (L1) and Assamese (L2) speakers who were raised speaking Deori as their first language. The rhythmic patterns of read speech were evaluated using nine different rhythm measures. In terms of rate-normalized measures such as nPVI-V and rPVI-C values it was found that L2 speakers gave a rhythmic mode relatively comparable to Deori (L1), and in terms of %V and ΔC values, Assamese (L2) tends to cluster with Mora timed languages, regardless of the rhythmic class of (Deori) L1 which tends to cluster with syllable-timed languages viz., (French, Spanish) as can be seen in Fig. 4. This matches our subjective auditory impression of L2 speech, in which the perceived rhythm may not fit neatly into any of the rhythm class categories. Possible replacement metrics are needed, and the link between rhythmic metrics and other measures of fluency and naturalness must be explored.

Research conducted on Deori phonology reveals that it exhibits an iambic pattern, with a notable lengthening of the second syllable [2]. In contrast, study on Assamese indicates that it displays a trochaic pattern with a preference for heavy syllables [19]. These findings support our observations, considering the vulnerability of Deori and the ongoing language shift observed among Deori speakers. Our research suggests that Deori speakers can attain a high level of proficiency in bilingualism, despite their native language being a Tibeto-Burman language with distinct characteristics such as iambic prominence and remnants of tonal features.

The results of this study contribute to the understanding of rhythm in Tibeto-Burman languages and provide a foundation for further research in the field. The findings show that speakers with extensive language shift to a dominant L1 may be proficient in the subtle feature of the rhythm properties of the L2. This again validates our concern that language endangerment is a gradual process – it starts with gradual bilingualism, extensive proficiency in the L2 and finally acquiring the L2 with great sophistication leading to the complete replacement of the L2 with the L1.

Further, subjective listening tests will be conducted to analyze rhythmic patterns in L1 (native language) and L2 (second language) speech to see if L2 speakers exhibit significant deviations from the rhythmic patterns of their L1. These tests can reveal how speakers, perceive the linguistic features of their native language. If these tests show that individuals have difficulty perceiving or identifying these features, it may indicate that the language is undergoing a shift, and are no longer fully attuned to its linguistic nuances.

References

1. Acharyya, P., Mahanta, S.: Language vitality assessment of Deori: an endangered language. Lang. Doc. Conserv. **13**, 514–544 (2019)
2. Acharyya, P.: Phonology of Deori: an 'endangered' language. Ph.D. dissertation. Indian Institute of Technology, Guwahati, Assam (2019)
3. Abercrombie, D.: Elements of General Phonetics. University Press, Edinburgh (1967)
4. Ladefoged, P.: A course in Phonetics. Harcourt Brace Javanovich, New York (1975)
5. Pike, K.L.: Intonation of American English. University of Michigan Press, Ann Arbor (1945)
6. Gu, W., Hirose, K.: Rhythmic patterns in native and non-native Mandarin speech. In: Social and Linguistic Speech Prosody: Proceedings of the 7th International Conference on Speech Prosody, pp. 587–519 (2014)
7. Dauer, R.M.: Stress-timing and syllable-timing reanalyzed. J. Phon. **11**, 51–69 (1983)
8. Ramus, F., Mehler, J.: Language identification based on supra-segmental cues: a study based on resynthesis. J. Acoust. Soc. Am. **105**(1), 512–521 (1999)
9. Grabe, E., Low.: Durational variability in speech and rhythm class hypothesis. Pap. Lab. Phonol. **7**(515–546) (2002)

10. Dellwo, V.: Rhythm and speech rate: a variation coefficient for deltaC. In: Language and Language-Processing, pp. 231–241. Peter Lang, Frankfurt am Main (2006)
11. Arvaniti, A.: The usefulness of metrics in the quantification of speech rhythm. J. Phon. **40**(3), 351–373 (2012)
12. Mok, P., Dellwo, V.: Comparing native and non-native speech rhythm using acoustic rhythmic measures: Cantonese, Beijing Mandarin and English. In: Proceedings of Speech Prosody, Campinas, Brazil, pp. 423–426 (2008)
13. White, L., Mattys, S.L.: Calibrating rhythm: first language and second language studies. J. Phon. **35**, 50–52 (2007)
14. Boersma, P., Weenink, D.: Praat: doing phonetics by computer (version 5.4). [Computer program]. The Netherlands: University of Amsterdam, Amsterdam (2014). http://www.pra at.org
15. Frota, S., Vigário. M.: On the correlates of rhythmic distinctions: the European Brazilian Portugues case, vol. 13, no. 2, pp.247–275 (2001)
16. Mahanta, S.: Assamese. J. Int. Phon. Assoc. **42**(2), 217–224 (2012)
17. Mairano, P.: Correlatore. 2.1 (2009). https://www.lfsag.unito.it/correlatore/downloadenhtml
18. R Core Team, R: A Language and Environment for Statistical Computing, R Foundation for Statistical Computing, Vienna, Austria (2022). https://www.R-project.org/
19. Mahanta, S.: Some aspects of prominence in Assamese and Assamese-English, MPhil thesis, Central Institute of English and Foreign Languages (2001)

Konkani Phonetic Transcription System 1.0

Swapnil Fadte[1]([✉])[iD], Edna Vaz Fernandes[2,3][iD], Hanumant Redkar[1][iD], and Jyoti D. Pawar[1][iD]

[1] Goa University, Goa, India
{swapnil.fadte,hanumantredkar,jdp}@unigoa.ac.in
[2] Govt College of Arts Science and Commerce Quepem, Goa, India
edna.vaz22@gmail.com
[3] University of Mumbai, Mumbai, India

Abstract. A phonetic transcription system provides pronunciation of words, mostly in International Phonetic Alphabet (IPA) format. Phonetic transcription is the visual representation of phones in the form of characters and symbols represented in the IPA format. This paper describes the development of an automatic phonetic transcription system for an under-resourced Indian language, Konkani. In this paper, we have proposed an automatic phonetic word transcription generation system based on a set of deterministic linguistic rules mainly derived from the available work on Konkani literature. Some general rules, like Schwa deletion, are also considered in the design process. Parallel 101 sentences with 397 unique words have been used to test the accuracy of the system. Our system shows a Word Error Rate (WER) of 60, whereas existing system had a WER of 92.5.

Keywords: Konkani · pronunciation · Phonetic transcription · Transcription system · Konkani phonetic transcription · Phonetic

1 Introduction

Konkani is an Indo-Aryan language that belongs to the Indo-European family of languages[1]. More than 2.5 million people speak Konkani language. It is the official language of the state of Goa in India and is spoken in the western coastal part of India, including Goa, the Konkan region of Maharashtra, Karwar, Mangaluru, other coastal areas of Karnataka, and parts of Kerala, Gujarat, Dadra & Nagar Haveli and Daman & Diu. Konkani is one of the 22 scheduled languages included in the eighth schedule of the Constitution of India[2]. Konkani and Marathi are often referred to as sister languages, as many words have similar formations and semantics with some variations. The first known Konkani inscription dates back to 1187 CE[3].

The work presented here is an attempt to create a resource which can be used for Konkani language development. This paper describes the work of creating a phonetic transcription system for Konkani, which can be considered as one of the important component to develop an Automatic Speech Recognition (ASR) System and Text to Speech (TTS) for any language, in this case, for Konakni language.

---

[1] https://www.britannica.com/topic/Konkani-language.
[2] https://www.mha.gov.in/sites/default/files/EighthSchedule_19052017.pdf.
[3] https://g.co/arts/vyK6hbZbuupN15ru5.

© The Author(s), under exclusive license to Springer Nature Switzerland AG 2023
A. Karpov et al. (Eds.): SPECOM 2023, LNAI 14339, pp. 231–240, 2023.
https://doi.org/10.1007/978-3-031-48312-7_19

The paper is organised as follows:- Sect. 1 provides an introduction of the Konkani language and presents the need for this work. The motivation of this work is briefed in Sect. 2. Section 3 defines the problem statement, Sect. 4 presents the Discussions and Methodology used; Finally, Sect. 6 Concludes the paper with future scope for improvements.

2   Motivation

Konkani is a under-resourced language with very few resources available for R & D. Also, there are hardly any applications for the Konkani language. In the recent decade, efforts have been made to develop resources for Konkani, viz., Konkani Wordnet [3,4,11], ILCI Corpus [2], CIIL Corpus [7], SPTIL Project[4], etc. However, an online Konkani pronunciation dictionary has not been developed as yet. This motivated our research group to create a Konkani phonetic transcription system, which may be beneficial for future research work of TTS and ASR Systems for Konkani Language.

3   Problem Statement

The goal of the work presented in the paper is to design an Automatic phonetic transcription system specific to the Konkani language. This phonetic transcription system takes a Konkani text in written Devanagari form as input and produces phonetic transcription in IPA. The transcriptions are rule-based one-to-one characters to phonemes mapping and currently do not consider the context of the word.

4   Methodology and Datasets Used

4.1   Rules for Phonetic Mapping

The Devanagari character set for Konkani is taken from *A Gold standard Konkani Raw Text Corpus* [8]. Tables 1, 2, and 3 show the mapping of Konkani characters with the IPA symbols. Rules for phonetic transcription are identified using previous work, which is reported by [1,5,9]. Some IPA mapping for the characters not reported through the above work, has also been provided. Some rules are summarized and presented in a tabular form. The Devanagari characters, approximate IPA notation, phonetic transcription for the dictionary and UTF-8 code for the characters are also presented here. Table 4 provides approximate IPA symbols for Devanagari vowels and diphthongs. Konkani has nine vowels out of which six vowels find place in the script whereas three do not. The nine vowels of the language are: [i], [ə], [a], [i], [e], [ɛ], [u], [o], and [ɔ]. The three vowels that are a part of the vowel system of the language but do not have a unique character representing them in the script are: [i], [ɛ], and [ɔ]. There are a few other things that need to be noted with regards to the vowels system of the language:

---

[4] http://sanskrit.jnu.ac.in/projects/sptools.jsp?proj=sptools.

- Vowel length is not phonemic in Konkani. Hence, one of the Devanagari character representing vowel length contrast, namely [i/iː] and [u/uː] is redundant for the language.
- Vowels from Sr. No. 16 in Table 4 are not found in the language.
- The vowel [r̩] occurs in Sanskrit loans only and specifically in proper nouns only. It should be noted that some vowel phonemes in Konkani, like /ə/ and /ɨ/, have the same written representation [5].

Before elaborating on the consonant inventory of the language, it would be worth mentioning that voicing and aspiration is phonemic in the language. Nasalization is phonemic in the language with the vowels displaying oral-nasal contrast in almost all positions. The language also has nasal consonant phonemes /m/, /n/, /ɳ/. Speaking about the labial consonant phonemes, Konkani distinguishes between the voiceless /p/ and the voiced /b/ as well as the aspirated /bʱ/ versus the voiced non-aspirated /b/. With the exception of the voiceless aspirated labial consonant [pʰ], other consonants contrast in voicing and aspiration. Scholars have claimed that [pʰ] did exist in the older stage of the language but was replaced by the labio-dental fricative /f/ due to the large scale Portuguese borrowings in the language. Examples of minimal pairs exhibiting differences between labial sounds are given below:

- There is a contrast between the voiceless plosive /p/ and the voiced plosive /b/., e.g. [paj] 'father-M.SG.' [baj] 'endearment word for a girl child-N.SG.'
- The voiceless plosive /p/ also contrasts with the aspirated voiced plosive /bʱ/), e.g. [puːt] 'son-M.SG.' [bʱuːt] 'ghost-N.SG.'

Four dental phonemes /t̪/, /t̪ʰ/, /d̪/ and /d̪ʱ/ display voicing and aspiration contrast. Examples for these phonemes are given below:

- voiceless dental plosive /t̪/ versus voiced dental plosive /d̪/), e.g., [vaːt̪] 'wick-F.SG.'; 'candle-F.SG.) [vaːd̪] 'dispute', 'argument' (M-SG.)
- voiceless non-aspirated dental plosive /t̪/ versus voiceless aspirated dental plosive /t̪ʰ/, e.g., [t̪aʟi] 'clap-F.SG.' [t̪ʰaʟi] 'small plate for eating-F.SG.'
- voiced non-aspirated dental plosive /d̪/ versus voiced aspirated dental plosive (/d̪ʱ/), e.g., [d̪aːr] 'door-N.SG.' [d̪ʱaːr] 'sharp edge-F.SG.'

With respect to the place of articulation, all the above dental consonants contrast with the retroflex consonant phonemes /ʈ/, /ʈʰ/, /ɖ/, and /ɖʱ/ which also display voicing and aspiration differences. The following pairs of words make this distinction explicit:

- voiceless retroflex plosive /ʈ/ versus voiced retroflex plosive /ɖ/, e.g., [vaːʈ] 'way/path-F.SG.' [vaːɖ] 'growth-F.SG.'
- voiceless unaspirated retroflex plosive /ʈ/ versus voiceless aspirated retroflex plosive /ʈʰ/), e.g., [paːʈ] 'A narrow water course-M.SG.' [paːʈʰ] 'lesson-M.SG.
- voiceless aspirated versus voiced aspirated (/ʈʰ/ versus /ɖʱ/) [ʈʰoː] 'sound of crackers, bullet, etc.' [ɖʱoː] 'loud noise of explosion, fall, etc.'
- Velar consonant phonemes in Konkani namely [k], [kʰ], [g], [gʱ] also display a contrast with respect to voicing and aspiration. Konkani also has the velar nasal [ŋ].

With respect to the place of articulation, all the above dental consonants contrast with the retroflex consonant phonemes /ʈ/, /ʈʰ/, /ɖ/, and /ɖ^ɦ/ which also display voicing and aspiration differences. The following pairs of words make this distinction explicit:

Konkani has dento-palatal affricates /t͡s/, /d͡s/ and /d͡z^ɦ/ which contrast with the palatal affricates /t͡ʃ/, /t͡ʃʰ/, /d͡ʒ/ and /d͡ʒ^ɦ/.

With the exception of the voiceless aspirated counterpart of the dental affricate /t͡s/, all others contrast with respect to place of articulation, voicing and aspiration. However, the written form of the language (the Devanagari script) lacks separate characters for showing the distinction between these sounds.

Minimal pairs exhibiting meaning differences for dento-palatal and palatal phonemes are given below:

– Voiceless unaspirated dento-palatal affricate versus voiced unaspirated versus voiced aspirated affricate (/t͡s/ versus /d͡z/ versus /d͡z^ɦ/)[tsəd] 'climb-IMP.2P.SG.' [dzəd] 'heavy-ADJ.' [d͡z^ɦəd] 'fall-IMP.2P.SG.' [t͡sər] 'graze-IMP.2P.SG.' [d͡zər] 'if' [d͡z^ɦər] 'spring-F.SG.'
– Voiceless unaspirated palatal affricate versus voiced unaspirated palatal affricate (/t͡ʃ/ versus /d͡ʒ/) [t͡ʃar] 'four' [d͡ʒar] 'tired',
– Voiceless unaspirated palatal affricate versus voiced aspirated palatal affricate (/t͡ʃ/ versus /d͡ʒ^ɦ/) [t͡ʃɛlɔ] 'disciple-M.SG. [d͡ʒ^ɦɛlɔ] 'small garland-M.SG.'
– Voiced unaspirated dento-palatal affricate versus voiced unaspirated palatal affricate (/d͡z/ versus /d͡ʒ/ [dzuːn]'mature-ADJ.' [d͡ʒuːn] '(month of) June'

Konkani also has velar consonant phonemes /k/, /kʰ/, /g/, /g^ɦ/ which show contrast in voicing and aspiration. Meaning differences arising from this opposition are shown below:

– voiceless unaspirated velar versus voiceless aspirated velar (/k/ versus /kʰ/) keːl̪ 'banana tree-F.SG. kʰeːl̪ 'sport/game-M.SG.'
– voiced unaspirated velar versus voiced aspirated velar (/g/ versus /g^ɦ/) [gaːj] ;cow-F.SG.' [g^ɦaːj] 'wound-M.SG'

Konkani nasals - Konkani has three nasals - the bilabial nasal [m], the dental nasal [n] and the retroflex nasal [ɳ]. These contrast with each other. The occurrence of the velar nasal [ŋ] and the palatal nasal [ɲ] is predictable in that they occur as homorganic nasals (as in [aŋg] 'body-N.SG', [pəɲt͡ʃ] 'a member of the village council-M/F/N.')

Contrasts between nasal phonemes is given below:

[kaːn] 'ear-M.SG.' [kaːm] 'work-N.SG.'
[b^ɦaːn] 'caution-N.SG.' [b^ɦaɳ] 'a large vessel of copper or iron-N.SG.'

There are four fricatives in the language- the labio-dental fricative [f], voiceless alveolar fricative [s], postalveolar [ʃ] and the voiceless glotal fricative [h]. Some words showing contrast between these sounds are given below:

[faːr] 'explosion-M.SG.' [saːr] 'extract-M.SG.' [ʃaːr] 'city-N.SG.' [haːr] 'python; garland-M.SG.'

The retroflex fricative [ʂ] which is shown in the script, only occurs in the written form as is confined to proper nouns only.

The language has the labio-dental approximant [ʋ] and palatal approximant [j]. Contrast between these is shown below:

[ʋaːd̪] 'argument-M.SG.' [jaːd̪] 'memory-F.SG.'

The language also contrasts between the dental lateral [l] and retroflex lateral [ɭ]. The following pair of words display this contrast.

[paːl] 'lizard-F.SG.' [paːɭ] 'root of a tree-N.SG.'

The language also has the trill [r]. Although so1

me works refer to its place of articulation as dental, it seems to occur in alveolar position in case of some words. Word pair contrasting this sound with the dental approximant [l] is given below:

[raːg] 'anger-M.SG.' [laːg] 'cajolery; wooing-F.SG.'

The Devanagari script used for the language shows two more characters क्ष and ज्ञ which are actually consonant clusters [kʃ] and [dn] respectively. The major limitation of the script is that it does not have characters to show some important contrasts that exist in the language and at times shows characters that are not relevant for the language. A need for revising the script was proposed years back by some scholars

Table 1. Konkani vowels diphthongs and diacritic.

Vowels						Diphthongs		Diacritic
central		front		back				
अ	आ	इ/ई *	ए #	उ/ऊ *	ओ $	ऐ	औ	◌ॅ
[ɨ]	[ə]	[a]	[i / iː]	[e]	[ɛ]	[u / uː]	[o]	[ɔ]	[əi]	[ɔu]	[ə̃]

* Vowel length is not phonemic in Konkani.

\# Orthographic rules provides only one Devanagari character ए to phone e and ɛ

$ Orthographic rules provides only one Devanagari character ओ to phone o and ɔ.

Table 5, presents rules for the vowel diacritics.

In Table 6, transcription rules for Chandrabindu, Anusvara and Visarga are presented. Chandrabindu is used for the tatsama (Sanskrit borrowed) words.

In Table 7, rules for consonant transcription are presented. It should be noted that the place of [pʰ] has been taken by labio-dental fricative [f], which is said to be an effect of Portuguese borrowings into the language. Konkani language also has dental and palatal affricates that are phonemic in the Konkani language but are written alike in the writing system of the Konkani language. Nasalization and aspiration are phonemic in Konkani.

4.2 Dataset Used

For the testing purpose, we created phonetic transcriptions for Konkani text available from [6] which contains 74 sentences. We also created additional 27 transcriptions of sentences to cover all the phones in the language. These data were used for testing the proposed transcription system.

Table 2. Konkani Consonant Set 1.

	Voiceless		Voiced		Nasal
	unaspirated	aspirated	unaspirated	aspirated	(voiced)
Velar	क	ख	ग	घ	ङ
	[k]	[kʰ]	[g]	[gʱ]	[ŋ]
Affricate	च[1]	– –	ज[2]	झ[3]	– –
	[ts]	--	[dz]	[dzʰ]	--
	च[1]	छ	ज[2]	झ[3]	ञ
	[tʃ]	[tʃʰ]	[dʒ]	[dʒʱ]	[ɲ]
Retroflex	ट	ठ	ड	ढ	ण
	[ʈ]	[ʈʰ]	[ɖ]	[ɖʰ]	[ɳ]
Dental	त	थ	द	ध	न
	[t̪]	[t̪ʰ]	[d̪]	[d̪ʰ]	[n]
Labial	प	फ[4]	ब	भ	म
	[p]	[f]	[b]	[bʱ]	[m]

[1] Phone [ts] and [tʃ] has single Devnagari representation च .
[2] Phone [dz] and [dʒ] has single Devnagari representation ज .
[3] Phone [dzʱ] and [dʒʱ] has single Devanagari representation झ .
[4] place of [pʰ] is taken by [f].

Table 3. Konkani Consonant set 2.

य	र	ल	व	श	ष*	स	ह	ळ
[j]	[r]	[l]	[ʋ]	[ʃ]	[ʂ]	[s]	[ɦ]	[ɭ]

* phone [ʂ] occurs only in Sanskrit tatsam words.

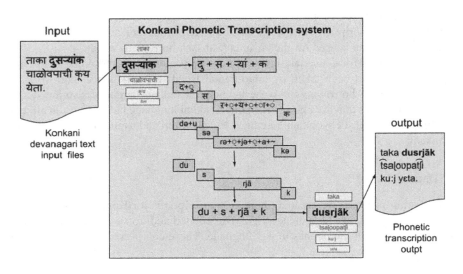

Fig. 1. Konkani Phonetic Transcription System Architecture.

Table 4. Transcription rules for vowels and diphthongs.

Sr. No.	Devanagari	Approximate IPA	Unicode	Example	Gloss
1	अ	[ə]	U+0905	खण [kʰən̪]	'dig-2P.SG.IMP.'
2	अ	[ɨ]	U+0905	खण [kʰɨn̪]	'mine/quarry-F.SG.'
3	आ	[a]	U+0906	आत्मो [at̪mɔ]	'soul-M.SG.'
4	इ	[i]	U+0907	शिकता [ʃikta]	'study-1P.SG.PRS.CONT.'
5	ई	[iː]	U+0908	वीस [viːs]	'twenty-NUM.'
6	उ	[u]	U+0909	उतर [ut̪r]	'word-N.SG.'
7	ऊ	[uː]	U+090A	पूल [puːl]	'bridge-M.SG.'
8	ए	[e]	U+090E	पेर [per]	'guava tree-F.SG.'
9	ॲ	[ɛ]	U+0972	पेर [pɛr]	'guava (fruit)-N.SG.'
10	ऍ	[ɛ]	U+090D	एकारत [ɛkarət̪]	'with only one wick-F.SG.'
11	ओ	[o]	U+0913	दोन [doːn]	'two-NUM'
12	ऑ	[ɔ]	U+0911	बॉल [bɔːl]	'ball-M.SG.'
13	ऐ	[ai]	U+0910	बैल [bəil]	'bull-M.SG.'
14	औ	[əu]	U+0914	औदार्य [ɔudarja]	'grand-heartedness-N.UNC.'
15	ऋ	[r̩]	U+090B	निवृत्त [nivr̩t̪t̪]	retired
16	ॠ	[r̩ː]	U+0960	No example in corpus	
17	ऌ	[l̩]	U+0961	No example in corpus	
18	ॡ	[l̩]	U+096C	No example in corpus	
19	ऎ	[əɛ]	U+096E	No relevant example in corpus	
20	ऒ	[əɔ]	U+0912	No example in corpus	

Table 5. Transcription rules for Vowel Diacritics.

Sr. No.	Devanagari	Approximate IPA	Unicode	Sr. No.	Devanagari	Approximate IPA	Unicode
1	T	[a]	U+093E	10	◌	[ai]	U+0948
2	ि	[i]	U+093F	11	◌	[au]	U+094C
3	ी	[iː]	U+0940	12	◌	[r̩]	U+0943
4	◌	[u]	U+0941	13	◌	[r̩ː]	U+0944
5	◌	[uː]	U+0942	14	◌	[l̩]	U+0962
6	◌	[e]	U+0947	15	◌	[l̩]	U+0963
7	◌	[ɛ]	U+0945	16		[əɛ]	U+0946
8	◌	[o]	U+094B	17	◌	[əɔ]	U+094A
9	◌	[ɔ]	U+0949				

Table 6. Transcription rules for Ayogavaha.

Sr. No.	Devanagari	IPA	Unicode
1	◌	M'	U+0901
2	◌	M	U+0902
3	:	H	U+0903

Table 7. Transcription rules for Consonants.

Sr. No.	Devanagari	Approximate IPA	Unicode	Example	Gloss
1	क	[k]	U+0915	कांसव /ka siv/	tortoise-M.SG.'
2	ख	[kʰ]	U+0916	खारें /kʰarɛ̃/	'dried fish-N.SG.'
3	ग	[g]	U+0917	गोंड /gɔɖ/	'jaggery-N.SG.'
4	घ	[gʰ]	U+0918	घर /gʰər/	'house-N.SG.'
5	ङ	[ŋ]	U+0919	वायङण /vajŋŋ/	'summer (paddy) crop-N.SG.'
6	च	[tʃ]	U+091A	चार /tʃar/	'four-NUM'
7	च	[ts]	U+091A	चार /tsar/	interior esculent of jackfruit-F.SG.'
8	छ	[tʃʰ]	U+091B	छाप /tʃʰaːp/	'impression-M.SG.'
9	ज	[dz]	U+091C	जाळें /dzalɛ̃/	'net-N.SG.'
10	ज	[dʒ]	U+091C	जेवण /dʒevən/	'food-N.SG.'
11	झ	[dzʰ]	U+091D	झाड /dzʰad/	'tree-N.SG.'
12	झ	[dʒʰ]	U+091D	झील /dʒʰiːl/	'bush/undergrowth-F.SG.'
13	ञ	[ɲ]	U+091E	पंच /pɳ/	'member of a village council-M/F/N.SG.'
14	ट	[ʈ]	U+091F	वीट /viːʈ/	'brick-F.SG.'
15	ठ	[ʈʰ/	U+0920	मोठो /mɔʈʰɔ/	'fat-ADJ.M.SG.'
16	ड	[ɖ]	U+0921	घोडो /gʰɔɖɔ/	'horse-M.SG.'
17	ढ	[ɖʰ]	U+0922	गाढव /gaɖʰau/	'donkey-M.SG.'
18	ण	[ɳ]	U+0923	घोण /gʰɔɳ/	'kite(bird)-F.SG.'
19	त	[t̪]	U+0924	तीख /t̪iːkʰ/	'spicy-ADJ.SG.'
20	थ	[t̪ʰ]	U+0925	थुकी /t̪ʰuki/	'spit-F.SG.'
21	द	[d̪]	U+0926	दांत /d̪ãt̪/	'tooth-M.SG.'
22	ध	[d̪ʰ]	U+0927	धुकें /d̪ʰukɛ̃/	'fog-N.SG.'
23	न	[n]	U+0928	नाग /naːg/	'cobra-M.SG.'
24	प	[p]	U+092A	पांख /pãkʰ/	'feather-N.SG.'
25	फ	[f]	U+092B	फेणी /feɳi/	'a kind of a (cashew) alcohol specific to Goa-F.SG.'
26	ब	[b]	U+092C	बडी /bədi/	'stick-F.SG.'
27	भ	[bʰ]	U+092D	भाजी /bʰadʒi/	'vegetable-F.SG.'
28	म	[m]	U+092E	मोर /mor/	'peacock-M.SG.'
29	य	[j]	U+092F	याद /jen/	'memory-F.SG.'
30	र	[r]	U+0930	रात /rat̪/	'night-F.SG.'
31	ल	[l]	U+0932	लागीं /lagĩ/	'near-PSP.'
32	व	[ʋ]	U+0935	वात /ʋat̪/	'wick-F.SG.'
33	श	[ʃ]	U+0936	शेत /ʃet̪/	'field-N.SG.'
34	ष	[ʂ]	U+0937	कृष्ण /kruʂɳ/	'Lord Krishna.M.SG.'
35	स	[s]	U+0938	साक /sak/	'sack; gunny bag-M.SG.'
36	ह	[h]	U+0939	हुंडो /hũɖɔ/	'dowry.M.SG.'
37	ळ	[ɭ]	U+0932	शाळा /ʃaɭa/	'school.F.SG.'
38	ळ	[ɭ]	U+0934	पाळ /paɭ/	'root of a tree-N.SG.'

4.3 Methodology to Create Konkani Phonetic Transcription System and Result

The developed transcription system is a rule-based system and not considering the context of the word. Figure 1 demonstrates the Konkani phonetic transcription system architecture diagram. Various steps were followed in the creation of this phonetic transcription system. Here, the Konkani Devanagari sentence is given as input to the system. This sentence is further broken into tokens or words, and then these words/tokens are broken down into characters for phonetic mapping. Python programming language is used for the design of this system. Mapping from Devanagari to Unicode is done using rules provided in Tables 4, 5, 6 and 7 in this paper. After applying all the transcription rules, we get the final transcription in IPA format.

4.4 Evaluation Metrics

To assess the performance of the phonetic transcription system evaluation metric used is Word Error Rate (WER). WER is the percentage of the words not correctly identified by transcription system from the ground-truth test data set. Word accuracy is calculated by subtracting WER from 100 or it is equal to percentage of the words correctly identified by phonetic transcription system from the from the ground-truth test data set.

5   Results and Discussion

This system exhibits a word accuracy of 40%, with WER of 60. Moreover, when the same dataset is evaluated on the existing Devanagari to Phonetic transcription system [10], it demonstrated a word accuracy of 7.50%. Thus our system performs much better as compared to existing systems. However, there is still scope for improvement in the current system. Errors in the system were mainly with regard to the mapping of some characters to their respective phonemes. In this, the mapping of the character ɘ to phonemes /e/ and /ɛ/ was crucial. The character in the script did not show the closed and open contrast between the phoneme pair. Similar is the case with regard to the back vowels /o/ and ɔ. The phonemes /ə/ and /i/ also contributed to errors significantly. Alike /ə/ and /i/, these phonemes too have the same character अ in the script that represents them. The error was also introduced because the phoneme ə does not get omitted at all places. Identifying schwa deletion rules in depth might help improve the transcription system's performance.

6   Conclusion and Future Work

In this paper, we presented the Konkani pronunciation transcription system. This system is developed by using the rule-based character to phonetic mapping to produce the transcriptions in the International Phonetic Alphabet (IPA) format. This work can be improved by identifying additional transcription rules. In future work, we shall focus on improving the accuracy of the phonetic transcription system by adding more transcription rules. Further, with improved accuracy, this system can lead to the creation of a phonetic dictionary which shall act as an essential component for developing the TTS and ASR system for the Konkani language. Also, building the complete ASR system is possible by creating acoustic and language models.

References

1. Almeida, M.S.: A Description of Konkani. Thomas Stephens Konknni Kendr, Miramar, Panaji (1989)
2. Bansal, A., Banerjee, E., Jha, G.N.: Corpora creation for Indian language technologies-the ILCI project. In: The Sixth Proceedings of Language Technology Conference (LTC'13) (2013)
3. Bhatt, B.S., Bhensdadia, C.K., Bhattacharyya, P., Chauhan, D., Patel, K.: Gujarati wordnet: a profile of the indowordnet. In: Dash, N.S., Bhattacharyya, P., Pawar, J.D. (eds.) The WordNet in Indian Languages, pp. 167–174. Springer Singapore, Singapore (2017). https://doi.org/10.1007/978-981-10-1909-8_9
4. Desai, S.N., Walawalikar, S.W., Karmali, R.N., Pawar, J.D.: Insights on the Konkani wordnet development process. In: Dash, N.S., Bhattacharyya, P., Pawar, J.D. (eds.) The WordNet in Indian Languages, pp. 101–117. Springer Singapore, Singapore (2017). https://doi.org/10.1007/978-981-10-1909-8_6
5. Fadte, S., Fernandes, E.V., Karmali, R., Pawar, J.D.: Acoustic analysis of vowels in Konkani. ACM Trans. Asian Low-Resource Lang. Inform. Process. 21(5), 1–13 (2022). https://doi.org/10.1145/3474358, https://dl.acm.org/doi/10.1145/3474358
6. Fadte, S., Vaz, E., Ojha, A.K., Karmali, R., Pawar, J.D.: Empirical analysis of oral and nasal vowels of Konkani (2023)
7. Kurian, C.: A review on speech corpus development for automatic speech recognition in Indian languages. Int. J. Adv. Netw. Appl. 6(6), 2556 (2015)
8. Ramamoorthy L. and Narayan, C., Saurabh, V., Rajesha, N., Manasa, G.: A gold standard Konkani raw text corpus (2018)
9. Sardesai, M.: Bhasabhas Article on Linguistics. Goa, first edn, Goa Konkani Academy (1993)
10. Ulm, A.: Devanagari to IPA transcription (2022). https://www.ashtangayoga.info/philosophy/sanskrit-and-devanagari/transliteration-tool/
11. Walawalikar, S., et al.: Experiences in building the Konkani wordnet using the expansion approach (2010)

Speech Analysis and Synthesis

E-TTS: Expressive Text-to-Speech Synthesis for Hindi Using Data Augmentation

Ishika Gupta[✉] and Hema A. Murthy

Department of Computer Science and Engineering, IIT Madras, Chennai, India
{ishika,hema}@cse.iitm.ac.in

Abstract. Current state-of-the-art text-to-speech (TTS) systems trained on read-speech have reduced issues with repetition or skipping of words and can produce natural-sounding speech. However, E2E systems have difficulty producing conversational speech, especially in generating out-of-domain terms, and lack appropriate prosody.

This paper proposes a novel data augmentation approach to build intelligible and expressive speech using FastSpeech2 (FS2). Two different studies are performed. Conversational-style phrases/short interrogative sentences are synthesized using a baseline FS2 system and a hidden Markov model-based speech synthesis (HTS) system. Both systems are trained on 8.5 h of read speech in Hindi. This results in DS1 (FS2) and DH1 (HTS) synthetic datasets, respectively. Using DS1 and DH1, we train FS2 models, namely S1 and H1. While S1 sounds natural, H1 is more intelligible on OOD words. An attempt is made to further adapt these systems with as little as 11 min of original prosodically-rich story data from the same speaker to produce systems S2 and H2, respectively. We evaluate three FS2-based models: Baseline FS2 (vanilla FS2), the proposed models, S2, and H2. The subjective evaluation shows that systems S2 and H2 outperform the baseline FS2 system with an average MOS of 4.16 and 4.42, respectively. Further, we observe that H2 is better than S2 in terms of both MOS and intelligibility. We also do the objective evaluation tests and analyze the synthesized speech based on prosodic attributes to support our claim.

Keywords: Text-to-speech · Data-augmentation · Conversational · Expressive speech · HMM models · Prosody transfer · FastSpeech2

1 Introduction

End-to-End (E2E) text-to-speech (TTS) systems have become very popular owing to their naturalness. Nevertheless, they still possess a limitation in requiring a considerable amount of context-rich training data to enhance their intelligibility on out-of-domain (OOD) words. Next, prosodic variation is an essential component in the recognition of spoken communication [9]. These systems lack

A. Karpov et al. (Eds.): SPECOM 2023, LNAI 14339, pp. 243–257, 2023.
https://doi.org/10.1007/978-3-031-48312-7_20

the ability to accurately render the expressiveness in the synthesized voice, which can be critical for some tasks. The motivation for our work is as follows. A scenario where an error-free conversational TTS system is essential is in the task of dubbing educational classroom lectures from English [23] into Indian languages [19]. The word order in Indian languages is distinctly different from that of English; therefore, conversational prosodic transfer from English to an Indian language is non-trivial. The source videos are technical lectures/extempore, which use a conversational style of speech. So, expressiveness is essential in TTS systems when it comes to lip-syncing lectures in other Indian languages, isochronously. Conversational speech is characterized by an unplanned set of words and abrupt sentence endings. The state-of-the-art (SOTA) E2E systems like FastSpeech2 [30] that are trained on clean read speech do not scale for conversational speech synthesis. Moreover, building monolingual conversational speech synthesis systems using conversational corpora is quite challenging, owing to disfluencies, significant syllable rate variation, and diverse prosody patterns. These factors contribute to "buzziness" in the synthesized speech, making the task more complex [22].

We address two issues in this paper: 1) the synthesized speech does not have the prosodic style required for spontaneous speech. This may be because, unlike the traditional parametric synthesis models, the current neural TTS systems do not explicitly model the prosodic attributes.

2) Besides this, it has also been noted that current TTS models do not generalize well to unseen contexts, such as situations where they are trained on read speech and applied to generate conversational speech. This is possibly due to the fact that existing E2E systems are trained on limited domain-specific training data, so they may be unable to pronounce words from an unseen domain correctly. Figure 1 shows examples of Hindi text which is translated from a technical text in English. The highlighted words in the table are mispronounced by the vanilla FastSpeech2 (FS2) trained on the Hindi read-speech corpus.

To overcome these issues, we present a novel methodology based on data augmentation, which results in an intelligible and expressive TTS model. In this work, we have used FastSpeech2 [30] as a baseline model for comparison.

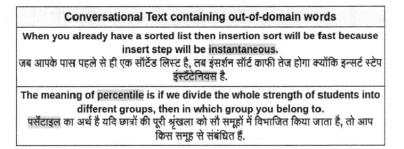

Fig. 1. Different examples of conversational text structure.

The proposed techniques described in this paper can be applied to the JETS (Jointly Training FastSpeech2 and HiFi-GAN for End to End Text to Speech) [17] and VITS (Variational Inference with adversarial learning for end-to-end TTS) [12] frameworks as well. We have also tried training the VITS architecture on our Hindi speech corpus, but we couldn't see much improvement over the FastSpeech2 synthesis output. Also, this model cannot disentangle prosody information from speech [18], so we have not considered VITS in the evaluation. The FastSpeech2 model proves to be a strong baseline system, with its ability to predict pitch and energy information in addition to the mel-spectrogram from the text transcription. This added capability allows the model to capture a wide range of speech variations and nuances. We propose two approaches, each of which involves training on read-speech data and usage of conversational style multi-domain text as new training data, followed by fine-tuning. The training overview is shown in Fig. 2. The use of a multi-domain text gives us the added advantage of not only producing labeled context-rich training data but also broadening the domain of the TTS system. The text comprises short conversational phrases and interrogative sentences. Both FS2 and Hidden Markov model (HMM) based speech synthesis (HTS) systems have the ability to learn prosody from the statistics of the training data by utilizing the pitch and energy information from the ground truth. The findings of this work also indicate that the inclusion of short conversational phrases in the synthetic training data enhances the prosody modeling capability of TTS systems.

The novelty of the work is in the use of classical HMM-based [36] synthesis to direct an E2E system. HTS can handle OOD words to a large extent due to tree-based clustering. These systems explicitly model pitch variations using a multi-space probability density function. Studies have also shown that HTS systems, being statistical models, can be intelligibly trained on smaller amounts of data [29].

Main Contributions: 1) We are able to build expressive TTS with only conversational-style synthetic data and give the model an additive improvement in prosody with a small amount of prosodic-rich data.
2) a scalable language and architecture-agnostic approach for building an expressive TTS system.

The rest of the paper is organized as follows. Section 2 reviews the related literature. Section 3 presents the proposed system overview and approach. Section 4 discusses the analysis done on synthesized speech outputs using qualitative and quantitative measures and presents the results of objective and subjective listening tests performed on the synthesized speech output of the trained systems. Finally, Sect. 5 concludes the paper.

2 Related Work

Several studies have been conducted owing to the growing research interest in expressive speech synthesis. Research in conversational speech synthesis has also led to various approaches towards either recording conversational speech corpora or selectively utilizing existing conversational data.

In TTS applications, [11] generates a large number of synthetic utterances using an auto-regressive (AR) model to improve the quality of non-AR TTS models. [7] uses embedding computed from trained global style tokens (GST) to build multi-style TTS with a good prosodic variation. [24] investigates whether a data mixing strategy can improve conversational prosody for a target voice based on monologue data from audiobooks by adding real conversational data from podcasts. [10] uses synthetic data in the desired speaking style on top of the available recordings generated by applying voice conversion. Further fine-tuning the model on a small amount of expressive samples for the target speaker helps improve naturalness and style inadequacy. [6] focuses on increasing the naturalness of TTS systems on specific domains by adding domain-specific speech to their database. [31] propose an ensemble approach that combines multiple prosody predictors to achieve more accurate and natural-sounding speech. Trained on a diverse dataset of expressive speech samples, the ensemble produces more expressive prosodic patterns by combining predictions from various models.

Parallel efforts to use hybrid paradigms for TTS have also been explored. [20] uses a hybrid approach combining HTS with the neural-network-based Waveglow vocoder [27] using histogram equalization (HEQ) in a low resource setting for improving the quality of speech output. Our work differs in its focus on achieving the challenge of bringing both expressivity and intelligibility in the synthesized speech by combining classical parametric and neural speech synthesis methods.

3 Proposed Approach

We investigate the data augmentation approach using multi-domain text. The overview of our proposed system framework is depicted in Fig. 2. In this study, we propose two TTS systems, namely: FS2 augmented (S1) and HTS augmented TTS system (H1), to build conversational speech synthesis systems. Both the proposed approaches consist of 3 stages: (i) Source model training, (ii) target model training (iii) Fine-tuning the model with as minimal as 11 min of expressive speech data to build proposed systems S2 and H2. The basic modules involved in training the proposed TTS system are described as follows:

3.1 FS2-Based Data Augmentation

Figure 2(a) shows an overview of FS2-based data augmentation. Here, our source model is the FS2 system, which we use to generate synthetic data. Earlier work shows that prosodic phrase breaks can be identified for Indian languages quite accurately if the training data is accurately marked with prosodic phrase marks [26]. During the source model training on read-speech data, the text is manually annotated with phrase breaks to facilitate the learning of the system to predict the pitch for a complete phrase. A fundamental difference between read speech and conversational speech lies in the fact that conversational speech is typically

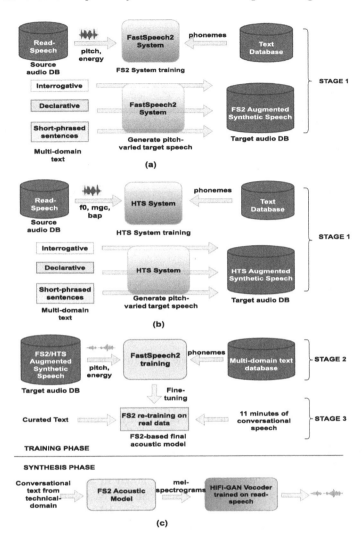

Fig. 2. Overview of the proposed method for building expressive TTS. We have trained the FS2 model using data augmentation: (a) FS2-based data augmentation, (b) HMM-based data augmentation, (c) Shows the training stages 2 and 3 and synthesis phases of both the proposed TTS systems.

composed of short phrases or sentences that are concatenated without punctuation and may have abrupt endings too. A baseline FS2 system attempts to predict the prosody based on the characteristics learned from read speech, which is inadequate for conversational speech owing to its grammatical incorrectness. This is especially evident in conversational speech in Indian languages, where utterances can contain many phrases. Generally, in E2E and HTS systems, prosody at the

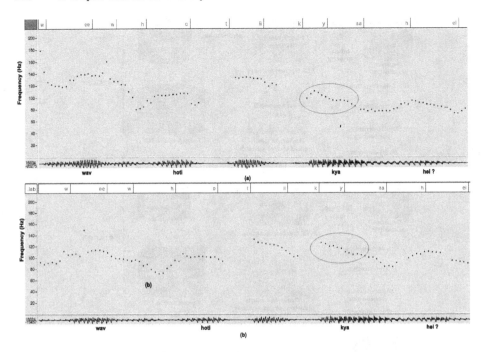

Fig. 3. Pitch contour plotted for a test phrase when (a) it is synthesized as an isolated sentence (b) it occurs in a long sentence.

beginning and end of phrases is learned accurately. Figure 3 and 4 depicts the change in pitch contour and short-term energy when a short phrase is synthesized in isolation and when synthesized as a part of a long sentence. From Fig. 3(a), we can observe that, there is a rise in the pitch at the word '*kya*' and at the end of the question phrase *"wave hoti kya hai?"*, shown in a red oval, whereas the pitch is not modeled so correctly in Fig. 3(b). Similarly, significant fluctuations are visible in the energy plot in Fig. 4(a) than in Fig. 4(b), leading to more stress on words. We can infer that training the FS2 system at a phrase level can help predict pitch better, consequently improving the prosody of synthesized speech. Therefore, while building system S1 (Table 1) on FS2-generated synthetic speech (DS1), we ensure that corresponding multi-domain training data encompasses short conversational phrases and declarative and interrogative sentences.

3.2   HMM-Based Data Augmentation

Figure 2(b) overviews our HTS-based data augmentation. Here, the source model is the HTS system, which we use to generate synthetic data. During training on read-speech data, the same manually annotated text is passed to help the HMM model learn the prosodic cues. Since HMMs explicitly model prosody, we generate HTS synthetic speech dataset (DH1) corresponding to the multi-

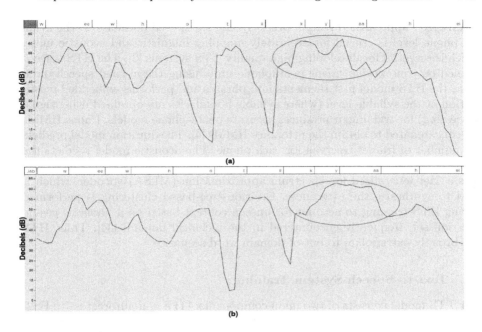

Fig. 4. Short-term energy plotted for a test phrase when (a) it is synthesized as an isolated sentence (b) it occurs in a long sentence.

domain text. While training the FS2 model on this phrasal synthetic speech dataset, the system learns to model the pitch at the start and end of phrases better than what it would have learned with a speech dataset at a sentence level, which is quite depicted in Fig. 3. There have also been some studies that report that prosody modeling is better done at phrase level [26].

3.3 Multi-domain Text Data Collection

We crawled text from Kaggle [2] web source in Hindi for augmenting data. The text data is carefully collected and contains short phrases from various domains ranging from health, lifestyle, science, technology, and ordinary colloquial conversations to interrogative and Yes-No questions. The intent of having such diversity in text data is to train the TTS model with a lot of context information and to enable the TTS model to learn various kinds of phonotactics. Totally we have curated around 14,450 sentences (≈ 15 h) in Hindi. The average number of words per sentence in multi-domain text ranges between 7 to 10.

3.4 HTS Training

To train the HTS model, the text is first transcribed in terms of its constituent phones, which are represented using the common label set (CLS) representation [28]. The speech waveform is aligned at the phone level using a hybrid

HMM-DNN approach. Having a precisely aligned speech database at the syllable/phone level is crucial for accurately mapping linguistic and acoustic units, which is essential for developing high-quality TTS systems [3]. The HTS voice is trained on context-dependent pentaphone units using the aligned speech data. Since the HTS model first segments into phrases and performs embedded reestimation at the syllable level (where syllable boundaries are obtained using signal processing) for training, it produces accurate penta-phone models. Phone HMMs are concatenated to obtain the utterance HMMs [4]. The duration model predicts the number of frames reserved for each phone. The acoustic model predicts the acoustic features for the required number of frames. The HTS engine internally uses a Mel-generalized log spectrum approximation (MLSA) vocoder, which is used to synthesize the utterances. Decision tree-based clustering is performed during HTS training to account for unseen context based on a phonetic yes-no question set, frequently encountered in the technical domain [34]. Thus, HTS can broadly extrapolate to out-of-domain word scenarios.

3.5   Text-to-Speech System Training

Our TTS model consists of two main components: (1) a non-autoregressive FS2-based acoustic model for converting input phoneme sequences into the mel-spectrograms, frame by frame, and (2) a non-autoregressive HiFi-GAN vocoder [13] that is capable of producing high-fidelity speech waveforms from mel-spectro grams. Montreal Forced Aligner (MFA) [21] is used to obtain the alignments between the utterances and the phoneme sequences. Figure 2(c) shows the training process of TTS with the proposed data augmentation. After training the model on the synthetic dataset, we fine-tune the model on 11 min of prosodically-rich expressive speech with the same configurations for 50 more epochs.

4   Analysis of Synthesized Speech

Experiments are conducted in Hindi, which is an Indo-Aryan language, for both male and female data. Studio-recorded Hindi male and female (8.5 h) datasets from the open-source IndicTTS database [5] are considered. We use the HTK [1] [35] and ESPnet toolkits [32] for building voices with default configurations. A HiFi-GAN model is trained separately for Hindi male and female datasets on this 8.5 h of read speech data. Table 1 summarizes various systems trained for each dataset. The text in parentheses indicates the training data used. The synthetic speech produced by baseline FS2, S2, and H2 systems is analyzed on dubbed technical lectures in terms of prosodic parameters.

4.1   Qualitative Analysis

A set of Swayam lectures [25], comprising 347 sentences, is synthesized using the baseline FS2 model (System 2) and our proposed systems S2 and H2. We compare and analyze their pitch and energy distributions.

Table 1. List of systems trained.

Systems	TTS Models
System 1	HTS trained on read-speech (8.5 h)
System 2 (Baseline)	FS2 trained on read speech (8.5 h)
System 3	FS2 trained on FS2 synthesized speech (15 h)**(S1)**
System 4 (Proposed 1)	FS2 trained on FS2 synthesized speech, fine-tuned on conversational speech **(S2)** (8.5 h + 11 min)
System 5	FS2 trained on HTS synthesized speech (15 h) **(H1)**
System 6 (Proposed 2)	FS2 trained on HTS synthesized speech, fine-tuned on conversational speech **(H2)** (8.5 h + 11 min)

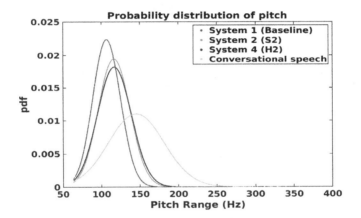

Fig. 5. Pitch plotted for Hindi male synthesized speech on a lecture set and its corresponding English conversational speech.

Pitch. Pitch is a crucial factor in determining the expressiveness of a sentence [31]. From Figure 5, it is observed that there is a wide variation in the pitch trajectory for a conversational speech taken from the lecture. Comparatively, the proposed systems, S2 and H2, are able to capture the finer variations in the pitch better than the FS2 baseline system. This clearly indicates the prosodic richness of S2 and H2 over baseline. A further pitch improvement is noticed in H2 than S2, indicating more closeness toward conversational speech.

Energy. Energy is another critical parameter in speech synthesis quality. The changes in the energy of the speech signal can be used to indicate emphasis on certain words. From Figure 6, we can clearly see a slight increase in the amplitude level for the proposed systems, closer to that of conversational speech in contrast to the baseline. On comparing S2 and H2, further improvement in energy is noticed in system H2.

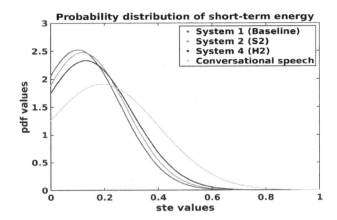

Fig. 6. Energy plotted for Hindi male synthesized speech on a lecture set and its corresponding English conversational speech.

4.2   Subjective Evaluation

Subjective evaluations are performed for the baseline FS2 and the proposed models S2 and H2 for Hindi male and female voices. The comprehension mean opinion score (CMOS) test is performed to assess the system's performance in terms of prosodic variation and intelligibility in the synthetic speech output. Comprehension MOS [33] was proposed to evaluate whether a listener is able to engage with synthetic speech of long durations. Contrast this with sentence-based subjective evaluations. It is a subjective evaluation test that not only assesses the quality of the speech but also checks whether the listener is able to comprehend the content of the audio clearly. It is found in studies that prosodic variations are better realized when long test utterances are presented in context as it helps users to perceive the pitch variations distinctly [8] [15].

We synthesize a coherent paragraph having contextual dependency and then quiz the listener based on the content to check the following: a) expressiveness and b) clarity of the speech. The test includes questions based on the content. 30 native evaluators of Hindi, male, and female, were asked to listen and rate 4 paragraphs presented in random order. MOS is calculated based on the expressiveness of synthetic speech. Listeners were asked to rate the overall quality of synthesized speech on a scale ranging from 1–5, with 1 being poor and 5 being human-like. The intelligibility of the samples is calculated based on the listener's understandability score on a similar scale of 1–5. For the comprehension test, 4 paragraph questions with a mix of translated technical lectures and stories synthesized in Hindi were considered. The comprehension score for each system is obtained by calculating the percentage of correct answers in the evaluation test. CMOS scores are presented in Table 2 and Table 3 for Hindi male and female, respectively. Comparing results of the question: *Rate the audio in terms of expressiveness*, we see that MOS scores are better for H2 than Baseline FS2 and S2, although intelligibility scores are similar for all 3 systems, although H2

Table 2. Comprehensibility MOS scores for Hindi male TTS.

Systems Evaluated	MOS Score	Intelligibility	**Comprehension Score**
Baseline FS2	3.525 ± 0.23	4.425	94.16 %
S2	4.25 ± 0.21	4.575	94.8 %
H2	**4.45 ± 0.18**	**4.65**	**96.4 %**

Table 3. Comprehensibility MOS scores for Hindi female TTS.

Systems Evaluated	MOS Score	Intelligibility	Comprehension Score
Baseline FS2	3.45 ± 0.2	4.325	93.12 %
S2	4.075 ± 0.26	4.495	95.23 %
H2	**4.395 ± 0.19**	**4.557**	**95.71 %**

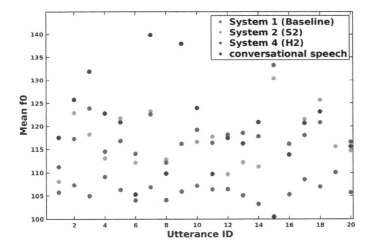

Fig. 7. Mean F0 comparison: baseline system vs. proposed systems.

performs slightly better. A p-test is performed to ensure the results are statistically significant, with both p-values <0.05.

A video lecture demo using the audios synthesized from baseline and the proposed system can be found in this link[1].

4.3 Objective Evaluation

Mean F0: Fundamental frequency (F0) is the most crucial prosody feature [16]. We have used mean F0 as one of the objective evaluation metrics to assess the effectiveness of the proposed systems and how they influence the pitch profile

---

[1] https://www.iitm.ac.in/donlab/preview/web_demo/index.html.

Table 4. Average increment in the mean and std deviation of F0 when the same text is synthesized using System S2 and H2 vs. baseline TTS.

System	System S2	System H2
Mean F0 change	+12.94	+13.41
Std Dev F0 change	+10.25	+14.45

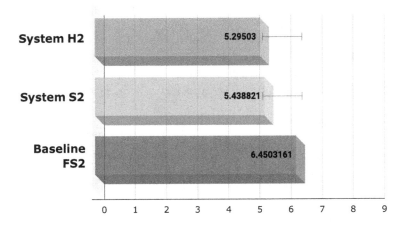

Fig. 8. MCD scores on synthesized utterances across baseline and proposed systems.

of the generated expressive audio with respect to the baseline FS2 system. To calculate the mean F0, 20 synthetic utterances in Hindi male voice were synthesized from the held-out unseen texts using the baseline FS2 and the proposed systems S2 and H2. The mean pitch (F0) is extracted from each system's utterances, including the original conversational speech, and is plotted and compared in Fig. 7.

We observe that mean F0 is higher and varies significantly (like in conversational speech) in both the proposed system's utterances compared to the baseline, even though all utterances were generated in the same speaker's voice. The average difference of mean F0 and standard deviation of F0 between proposed and baseline systems are reported in Table 4.

MCD Score: Mel-cepstral distortion (MCD) [14] serves as a metric to quantify the dissimilarity between two mel cepstral sequences. A smaller MCD score indicates a high degree of similarity between the synthesized and natural speech, indicating that the synthetic speech closely resembles the natural speech. 20 unseen Hindi sentences are synthesized using baseline FS2 and proposed TTS systems S2 and H2 in the male voice. Each system's generated utterances are compared with respect to the corresponding utterances of original conversational speech using dynamic time-warped MCD. The MCD scores for the systems are depicted in Fig. 8. Clearly, systems S2 and H2 scores seem to have less distortion compared to their baseline counterpart, indicating a closer resemblance to conversational speech.

5 Conclusion and Future Work

This work presents a language and architecture-agnostic approach to building expressive TTS systems. Our proposed method explores FS2-based and HTS-based data augmentation methods to build an intonation-based TTS system. We have demonstrated that the model is able to learn expressiveness from synthetic data and result in prosody transfer when coupled with a few minutes of expressive speech data in Hindi. It means there is no requirement to rely on additional conversational corpora for building conversational TTS systems. This makes our proposed approach vastly scalable to other languages. We plan to extend this work to Indo-Dravidian languages too. It's worth noting that there exist other techniques to introduce prosodic cues into the model, such as the pre-training of the FastSpeech2 variance adapters, whereas our work can obtain a similar effect.

Acknowledgement. We want to thank the Ministry of Electronics and Information Technology (MeitY), Government of India (GoI), for funding the project "Speech Technologies in Indian Languages" (SP/21-22/1960/CSMEIT/003119). Our sincere thanks to Anusha Prakash for her help in training the FastSpeech2 TTS model.

References

1. HMM-based toolkit. https://htk.eng.cam.ac.uk/
2. Kaggle Online Community. https://www.kaggle.com/datasets/rushikeshdarge/hindi-text-corpus?select=hi https://www.kaggle.com/datasets/rushikeshdarge/hindi-text-corpus?select=hi
3. Baby, A., Prakash, J.J., Murthy, H.A.: A hybrid approach to neural networks based speech segmentation. Dimension **40**, 3 (2017)
4. Baby, A., Prakash, J.J., Subramanian, A.S., Murthy, H.A.: Significance of spectral cues in automatic speech segmentation for Indian language speech synthesizers. Speech Commun. **123**, 10–25 (2020)
5. Baby, A., Thomas, A.L., Nishanthi, N.L., Consortium, T.: Resources for Indian languages. In: CBBLR - Community-Based Building of Language Resources, pp. 37–43. Tribun EU, Brno, Czech Republic (2016). https://www.iitm.ac.in/donlab/tts/database.php
6. Chu, M., Li, C., Peng, H., Chang, E.: Domain adaptation for TTS systems. In: ICASSP, vol. 1, pp. I-453. IEEE (2002)
7. Chung, R., Mak, B.: On-the-fly data augmentation for text-to-speech style transfer. In: 2021 IEEE Automatic Speech Recognition and Understanding Workshop (ASRU), pp. 634–641. IEEE (2021)
8. Clark, R., Silen, H., Kenter, T., Leith, R.: Evaluating long-form text-to-speech: comparing the ratings of sentences and paragraphs. In: Proceedings of 10th ISCA Speech Synthesis Workshop, 2019, pp. 99–104 (2019)

9. Cutler, A., Dahan, D., Van Donselaar, W.: Prosody in the comprehension of spoken language: a literature review. Lang. Speech **40**(2), 141–201 (1997)
10. Huybrechts, G., Merritt, T., Comini, G., Perz, B., Shah, R., Lorenzo-Trueba, J.: Low-resource expressive text-to-speech using data augmentation. In: ICASSP 2021–2021 IEEE International Conference on Acoustics, Speech and Signal Processing (ICASSP), pp. 6593–6597. IEEE (2021)
11. Hwang, M.J., Yamamoto, R., Song, E., Kim, J.M.: TTS-by-TTS: TTS-driven data augmentation for fast and high-quality speech synthesis. In: ICASSP 2021–2021 IEEE International Conference on Acoustics, Speech and Signal Processing (ICASSP), pp. 6598–6602. IEEE (2021)
12. Kim, J., Kong, J., Son, J.: Conditional variational autoencoder with adversarial learning for end-to-end text-to-speech. In: International Conference on Machine Learning, pp. 5530–5540. PMLR (2021)
13. Kong, J., Kim, J., Bae, J.: HiFi-GAN: generative adversarial networks for efficient and high fidelity speech synthesis. Adv. Neural. Inf. Process. Syst. **33**, 17022–17033 (2020)
14. Kubichek, R.: Mel-cepstral distance measure for objective speech quality assessment. In: Proceedings of IEEE Pacific Rim Conference on Communications Computers and Signal Processing, vol. 1, pp. 125–128. IEEE (1993)
15. Latorre, J., Yanagisawa, K., Wan, V., Kolluru, B., Gales, M.J.: Speech intonation for TTS: Study on evaluation methodology. In: Fifteenth Annual Conference of the International Speech Communication Association (2014)
16. Laures, J.S., Bunton, K.: Perceptual effects of a flattened fundamental frequency at the sentence level under different listening conditions. J. Commun. Disord. **36**(6), 449–464 (2003)
17. Lim, D., Jung, S., Kim, E.: JETS: jointly training fastspeech2 and HiFi-GAN for end to end text to speech. In: Ko, H., Hansen, J.H.L. (eds.) Interspeech 2022, 23rd Annual Conference of the International Speech Communication Association, Incheon, Korea, 18–22 September 2022, pp. 21–25. ISCA (2022)
18. Liu, Z., et al.: Controllable and lossless non-autoregressive end-to-end text-to-speech. arXiv preprint arXiv:2207.06088 (2022)
19. M, M.R.K., Kuriakose, J., S, K.P.D., Murthy, H.A.: Lipsyncing efforts for transcreating lecture videos in Indian languages. In: Proceedings of 11th ISCA Speech Synthesis Workshop (SSW 11), pp. 216–221 (2021)
20. M., M.R.K., Sudhanshu, S., Anusha, P., A, M.H.: A hybrid hmm-waveglow based text-to-speech synthesizer using histogram equalization for low resource Indian languages. In: INTERSPEECH, pp. 2037–2041 (2020)
21. McAuliffe, M., Socolof, M., Mihuc, S., Wagner, M., Sonderegger, M.: Montreal forced aligner: trainable text-speech alignment using kaldi. In: Interspeech, pp. 498–502 (2017)
22. Mukherjeee, B., Prakash, A., Murthy, H.A.: Analysis of conversational speech with application to voice adaptation. In: 2021 IEEE Automatic Speech Recognition and Understanding Workshop (ASRU), pp. 765–772. IEEE (2021)
23. NPTEL: National programme on technology enhanced learning. https://nptel.ac.in/
24. O'Mahony, J., Lai, C., King, S.: Combining conversational speech with read speech to improve prosody in text-to-speech synthesis. In: INTERSPEECH (2022)
25. Paul, P., Bhuimali, A., Kalishankar, T., Aithal, P., Rajesh, R.: Swayam: the platform for modern and enhanced online and flexible education-a knowledge survey. Int. J. Appl. Sci. Eng. **6**(2), 149–155 (2018)

26. Prakash, J.J., Murthy, H.A.: Analysis of inter-pausal units in Indian languages and its application to text-to-speech synthesis. IEEE/ACM Trans. Audio, Speech, Lang. Process. **27**(10), 1616–1628 (2019)
27. Prenger, R., Valle, R., Catanzaro, B.: Waveglow: a flow-based generative network for speech synthesis. In: ICASSP 2019–2019 IEEE International Conference on Acoustics, Speech and Signal Processing (ICASSP), pp. 3617–3621. IEEE (2019)
28. Ramani, B., Christina, S.L., Rachel, G.A., Solomi, V.S., Nandwana, S.K., Samudravijaya, K., et al.: A common attribute based unified hts framework for speech synthesis in Indian languages. In: 8th ISCA Workshop on Speech Synthesis (2013)
29. Rao, K.S., Narendra, N.: Source modeling techniques for quality enhancement in statistical parametric speech synthesis. Springer (2019)
30. Ren, Y., et al.: Fastspeech 2: fast and high-quality end-to-end text to speech. In: International Conference on Learning Representations (2020)
31. Teh, T.H., et al.: Ensemble prosody prediction for expressive speech synthesis. In: ICASSP 2023–2023 IEEE International Conference on Acoustics, Speech and Signal Processing (ICASSP), pp. 1–5. IEEE (2023)
32. Watanabe, S., et al.: Espnet: end-to-end speech processing toolkit. arXiv preprint arXiv:1804.00015 (2018)
33. Wester, M., Watts, O., Henter, G.E.: Evaluating comprehension of natural and synthetic conversational speech. In: Proceedings of speech prosody. vol. 8, pp. 736–740 (2016)
34. Wu, Z., Watts, O., King, S.: Merlin: an open source neural network speech synthesis system. In: SSW, pp. 202–207 (2016)
35. Young, S.J., Young, S.: The HTK hidden Markov model toolkit: Design and philosophy. Design and philosophy (1993)
36. Zen, H., Nose, T., Yamagishi, J., et al., S.: The HMM-based speech synthesis system (HTS) version 2.0. In: SSW, pp. 294–299. Citeseer (2007)

Direct Vs Cascaded Speech-to-Speech Translation Using Transformer

Lalaram Arya[✉], Amartya Roy Chowdhury, and S. R. Mahadeva Prasanna

Indian Institute of Technology Dharwad, Dharwad 580011, India
{202021004,amartya.chowdhury,prasanna}@iitdh.ac.in

Abstract. Direct speech-to-speech translation (DS2ST) is a process of translating speech from one language to another without using a written form of the language. Most of the works attempted for DS2ST utilized the auxiliary network and knowledge from the written form of the language directly or indirectly to improve the performance. This work proposes a transformer-based sequence-to-sequence model to perform the DS2ST task without an auxiliary network. Also, a comparative study is made with a cascaded system. The experiments are performed with the Prabhupadavani dataset in two languages (Hindi and English). The result shows that with our proposed DS2ST model, a BLEU score of 16.46 is achieved without using any auxiliary information. We also augmented the data with speed perturbation and improved the DS2ST performance BLEU score to 18.58.

Keywords: Direct speech-to-speech translation (DS2ST) · Transformer network · Speech-to-speech translation (S2ST) · Data augmentation

1 Introduction

Speech-to-speech translation (S2ST) is the process of translating the speech of one to another spoken language. More than 40% of the languages of the world do not have a written form of the language [1]. Developing translation technology for such languages is a challenging task. The S2ST system for the languages which have resources (E.g., text and audio dataset) is already explored in detail with the help of the cascaded approach [3]. The traditional way to develop the S2ST system is a cascaded approach. A cascaded S2ST system consists of three modules: Automatic speech translation (ASR), Machine translation (MT), and Text to speech synthesis (TTS) [24]. ASR transforms the source language's speech into text. MT translates source language text (generated via ASR) into target-language text. Finally, the target language text is transformed into the speech of the target language using TTS. This approach has a few issues due to cascading error propagation from one module to another. This technique utilizes the text of both source and target languages to develop the S2ST system. Therefore, building the S2ST system for languages without a written form (spoken-only languages) is challenging [1].

A. Karpov et al. (Eds.): SPECOM 2023, LNAI 14339, pp. 258–270, 2023.
https://doi.org/10.1007/978-3-031-48312-7_21

Recently, researchers have started working to develop a direct speech-to-speech translation (DS2ST) system for spoken-only languages [7,27]. Some attempts have been made, such as implementing a sequence-to-sequence model using a Long short-term memory (LSTM) network called Translatotron [4,11]. In the case of a true DS2ST system, the performance of the system was poor, but with the help of an auxiliary network, it was better, where the written form of the language information was utilized to improve the performance. The extension of the same work was done as Translatotron2 to address the over-generation issues by conditioning the spectrogram synthesizer directly on the output from the auxiliary target phoneme decoder [10]. With the auxiliary network, Taranslatotron2 improves the performance but would still require the target language's text. In these two works, a direct mapping is exploited between the source and the target languages. Some more works were attempted by exploiting the mapping function between the discrete representations between the source and the target language [16,18].

To develop speech technology, the availability of suitable datasets in sufficient quantity is essential. Over the period of time, for the cascaded S2ST approaches, sufficient data has been developed [3]. When it comes to the DS2ST system, the nonavailability of data is severe and lagging significantly as it needs a parallel speech dataset. The works attempted in the field of DS2ST, the synthetic data generated using the TTS system is mostly used [12,14]. To overcome this data scarcity, data augmentation could be a valid solution [5,22]. The augmentation techniques can improve the speaker, gender, channel, and session variability in the data artificially. This incorporates more diverse learning for deep learning networks and improves the system's performance by handling the acoustic variation properly encountered during speech translation. Data augmentation offers a practical and effective solution to handle data scarcity and reduces data collection efforts.

We can learn from the literature that most of the DS2ST systems attempted without a written form of the language lag in performance compared to the cascaded approach [11]. So, a comparative study is needed between the cascaded and the DS2ST systems to understand both systems' best use cases and their pros and cons. In this paper, we are exploring the transformer-based DS2ST system. The 80-dimensional Mel filter bank features are extracted from the raw speech and fed to the transformer-based encoder. The features of target spoken speech are fed to the decoder to train the DS2ST system without using the language's written form, as shown in Fig. 1. Apart from the end-to-end DS2ST training, we also experimented and analyzed the performance with one of the data augmentation techniques, speech perturbation, to resolve data scarcity. We augmented the training and the validation dataset with different perturbation factors α. Augmentation increased the dataset by four times compared to the original dataset. We also developed the cascaded S2ST system to compare its performance with the DS2ST system. The comparative analysis helps us to develop a more accurate and efficient DS2ST system. The experiments show that the performance of the DS2ST system improved significantly compared to the previously attempted systems, even without the use of the written form of the language. But compared to the MT and cascaded system, it is still lagging. It gives us proof of concept that with the help of advanced deep learning models and more speech data, the task of the DS2ST may be achievable.

The rest of the paper is organised as follows: Sect. 2 describes the proposed transformer-based DS2ST system, cascaded system and data augmentation using speed perturbation. Section 3 details the experimental setup, results, and analysis while developing the systems. Finally, in Sect. 4 we conclude the work and discuss the future direction.

2   Speech-to-Speech Translation System (S2ST)

Traditionally, the S2ST system can be implemented using the cascaded approach where three modules, ASR, MT and TTS, concatenate together. Another one is DS2ST approach, where the spoken speech of one language is translated directly into another without the use of the written form of the language. In this section, we are discussing these two approaches in detail.

2.1   Proposed Direct Speech-to-Speech Translation (DS2ST) Model

Recently, end-to-end speech translation got the attention to translate speech of one language to another directly without using intermediate text. Attempted works approached this problem in two ways. Firstly, by exploiting the direct mapping function that exists between the speech of the source and the target spoken language. Secondly, by exploiting the mapping function that exists between the discrete representation of the source and the target language speech. In this work, a transformed-based sequence-to-sequence modeling has been utilized instead of the LSTM architecture in [11] to speed up the model training and performance.

Transformer Based Speech-to-Speech Translation. Similar to $Speech - Transformer$ for ASR, we developed a multi-head attention-based transformer architecture [8] for the DS2ST task. The model can be formulated as a sequence-to-sequence model [26]. A sequence-to-sequence model converts an input sequence, $x_i = \{x_1, x_2, ...x_t\}$ into an output sequence, $y_i = \{y_1, y_2, ...y_T\}$ where in most of the cases, the sequences are different in lengths ($t \neq T$). In the speech translation task, the input speech of the source language is translated into the target language speech based on conditional probability. 80-dimensional filter bank features are extracted from both the source as well as target speech to feed into the transformer network. The encoder takes filter bank features of the source language and the decoder takes features of the source language as input. Finally, during inference, the speech in the target language is generated, as shown in Fig. 1. A sequence-to-sequence model mathematically can be formulated as follows:

$$e_t = encoder(x_i, h_{t-1}) \tag{1}$$

$$c_t = attention(h, s_{t-1}) \tag{2}$$

$$d_t = decoder(y_{t-1}, s_{t-1}, c_t) \tag{3}$$

where, e_t and d_t are the output from the encoder and decoder, c_t is the context vector calculated by the attention mechanism.

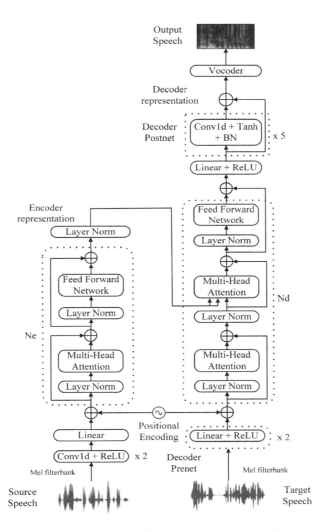

Fig. 1. Transformer based speech-to-speech translation.

Encoder. The encoder takes the input sequence and creates a rich input representation, such as embeddings. In this work, the 80-dimensional filter bank features are extracted as input to the model. The input features are down-sampled to a quarter of its size by two 1D-CNN layers [15]. Down-sampling makes it easier for the encoder layers to process the intact information with features and reduces memory consumption. The encoder consists of 12 transformer layers with 256− dimensional hidden units. Each multi-head attention block contains eight heads in encoder layers. We have used 1024 dimensional inner states for the feed-forward block followed by Layer-Norm.

Decoder. The decoder takes the output of the encoder (contextual information) and generates an output sequence. In this work, the decoder of our model is inspired by transformer TTS [17], which includes a pre-net and a post-net module. The pre-net consists of two fully connected linear layers. The filter bank features of the target speech are passed into the pre-net as input. The dimension of the pre-net module is set to 256, followed by two ReLU activations. We have also experimented by increasing the dimension to 512. However, this increases the training time instead of making any significant improvement. The decoder consists of 6 layers, keeping the same hyper-parameters as the encoder. To reconstruct the target spectrogram from the decoder, we use a 5−layer 1D-CNN, similar to [23], also called the post-net. The decoder representation from the post-net module is then fed to a vocoder, which converts it into target language speech.

2.2   Cascaded Speech-to-Speech Translation

A cascaded S2ST is a system that translates spoken words from one language into another with the help of the written form of the language. The process of S2ST typically involves three modules: ASR, MT and TTS (Fig. 2).

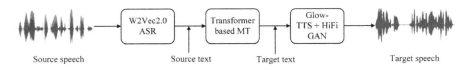

Source speech   Source text   Target text   Target speech

Fig. 2. Cascaded framework of the Speech-to-Speech translation system.

Automatic Speech Recognition (ASR). ASR system recognizes and transcribes the source language speech into the source language text [3]. Wav2Vec 2.0 is a state-of-the-art technique for ASR [6]. By leveraging a self-supervised approach, Wav2Vec 2.0 can effectively learn and extract meaningful speech representations without relying on explicit linguistic supervision. This allows the model to comprehend and identify basic speech elements or phonemes proficiently, even when provided with unlabeled data. We have utilized the pre-trained Wav2Vec 2.0 model and fine-tuned the network weights concerning our dataset. To fine-tune the ASR model, we have used the pertained Vakyansh open source model (CSRIL-23), which is trained on around 10, 000 hours of speech collected in 23 Indict languages. The Prabhupadavani dataset consists of 70.5 hours of labeled speech data and is used for fine-tuning. A fully connected layer is added to the top of the deep network to adapt the pre-trained model for the ASR task. This additional layer was optimized using the connectionist temporal classification (CTC) loss function, a commonly used loss function for sequence labeling tasks in speech recognition. After fine-tuning the model, it achieves a word error rate (WER) of 6.73 in the case of Hindi and 5.91 in the case of the English test dataset.

Machine Translation (MT). MT translates the source language's text into the target language's text [25]. An encoder-decoder transformer-based deep learning network is employed for the MT task in this S2ST system. The transformer network utilizes self-attention and fully connected layers in the encoder and decoder components. The encoder consists of twelve layers, incorporating a multi-head self-attention module and a feed-forward network. Similarly, the decoder consists of six layers, each comprising masked multi-head attention, multi-head attention, and a feed-forward neural network. Transfer learning is employed to enhance the model's performance and adaptability. The training is conducted with the help of Adam Optimizer. Each training batch had a maximum token size of 4096, allowing for efficient computational processing. Byte-pair encoding (BPE) tokenization was applied to all the models, which helps to create smaller dictionaries and enhances vocabulary handling capabilities. By utilizing the transformer network architecture and BPE tokenization, the MT module of the speech-to-speech translation system effectively translates the transcribed text generated by the ASR module into the target language text.

Text-to-Speech Synthesis (TTS). The TTS system synthesizes the speech in the target language from the text translated by the MT in the cascaded S2ST system. To perform this task, the Glow-TTS has been adapted in this work, which was initially proposed for image generation [12]. Using the flow-based generative model, Glow-TTS generates the spectrogram (an intermediate representation of the speech) for the given text. The model uses the invertible convolution and affine coupling layers to learn the conditional distribution of the mel-spectrogram. Also, it leverages the monotonic alignment search (MAS) algorithm to ensure proper and effective alignment during training between the speech and text. After the generation of the spectrogram from the text, a HiFI-GAN vocoder is employed to synthesize it into the target language speech [12]. The vocoder incorporates a generative adversarial network (GAN) that generates high-quality speech. GAN consists of a discriminator and generator, trained using an adversarial learning framework. The model uses a multi-resolution structure, a high-resolution fine-grained feature generator, and a multi-scale discriminator to improve the quality of synthesized speech significantly. This ensures the retention of the acoustic and linguistic characteristics of the desired synthesized speech.

2.3 Data Augmentation

Data augmentation is a technique commonly used to increase the size and diversity of a training dataset artificially. In this work, we have augmented the Prabhupadavani dataset using speed perturbation and investigated the improvement in the performance of DS2ST.

Speed Perturbation. The speed perturbation modified the original speech by resampling the audio signal in the time domain to change its speech rate and duration [9]. If we denote the original audio signal as $x(t)$ and the perturbation factor as α, the resampled audio signal, $y(t)$ can be obtained as follows:

$$y(t) = x(\alpha t) \tag{4}$$

This is equivalent to the following change in the frequency domain:

$$X(f) = \frac{1}{\alpha} x(\frac{1}{\alpha} f) \tag{5}$$

where $X(f)$ and $\frac{1}{\alpha} x(\frac{1}{\alpha} f)$ stand for the respective Fourier transforms of $x(t)$ and $y(t)$. In this way, modifications in speed lead to alterations in the spectral envelope and audio duration.

3 Experiments and Results

In this section, we will discuss our experiments and analyze the results. Firstly, we will discuss the dataset used throughout the experiments and then, with the help of the evaluation matrices, we will analyze the results.

3.1 Data Description

Prabhupadavani dataset is the output of the multi-lingual subtitle generation project of Vanimedia [2]. Under this project, 1080 audio mini-clips were translated, containing conversion, lectures, debates and interviews of swami Prabhupada (founder of an international community called the Society of Krishna Consciousness (ISKCON)). The audio clips contain the conversation about Bhagavad Gita. The primary objective of the project is to translate the audio into 108 languages. Seven hundred dedicated people are working to achieve it. They have to write the translated text according to the given audio clips and the corresponding manually aligned English transcription. The dataset is manually created, so the quality of the corresponding text is excellent. The current release of the dataset consists of 26 languages. In this work, we have taken two languages, Hindi and English, to perform our experiments [21]. For the English language in the dataset, both audio and text are available, but only text is available for Hindi. Table 1 illustrates a few examples of English transcription (source) and the corresponding translations in Hindi from the Prabhupadavani dataset.

Table 1. Some example sentences from Prabhupadavanis dataset

Lang / S.N.	English	Hindi
1	But Caitanya Mahāprabhu said, "No. Anyone can become spiritual master, provided he's conversant with the science.	लेकिन चैतन्य महाप्रभु नें कहा, "नहीं । कोई भी आध्यात्मिक गुरु बन सकता है, अगर वह विज्ञान के साथ परिचित है ।
2	After all, Kṛṣṇa is giving maintenance to everyone.	हिंदी भाषा का उपयोग करके आप अपने दस्तावेज़ में हिंदी पाठ लिख सकते हैं।
3	Prabhupāda: Māyā is nothing. It is a forgetfulness. That's all.	प्रभुपाद: माया कुछ भी नहीं है । यह एक विस्मरण है । बस ।।
4	Punaḥ punaś carvita-carvaṇānām (SB 7.5.30). Adānta-gobhir viśatā tamisra	पुन: पुनश चर्वित-चर्वणानाम (श्रीमद भागवतम ७.५.३०) । अदान्त-गोभिर विशताम तमिश्रम

To perform the S2ST task, we have utilized the fine-tuned TTS described in Sect. 2.2 to generate the Hindi speech from the available transcriptions. We have also observed that the quality of the available source speech with the data in English is noisy as it is recorded in a very open environment during conversation, discussion and lectures. Between the conversion, multiple speaker's voices, long pauses, noise and many filler words are present. The mapping of such speech with the TTS-generated speech is complicated. To overcome such issues during DS2ST, we also generated the source English speech using TTS.

The dataset contains around 53, 398 utterances for each language. The train set consists of 51, 301 utterances, while the test and dev sets contain 1, 048 and 1, 049 utterances, respectively. For further insights, see Table 2.

Table 2. Statistics of Prabhupadavani dataset in terms of number of sentences.

Language	Train	Dev	Test	Total
English	51301	1048	1049	53398
Hindi	51301	1048	1049	53398

3.2   Evaluation Metrics

The evaluation of our system involves assessing both the translation quality and the speech quality of the generated output. We follow the setup outlined in [11] to evaluate the translation quality by applying ASR to the speech output. We compute BLEU scores by comparing the ASR-decoded text to the reference translations. We utilize an open-sourced Hndi ASR model for the ASR component that combines Wav2Vec 2.0 pre-training with self-supervised techniques [6]. This model is pre-trained on 23 Indian languages and fine-tuned on the Prabhupadavani dataset. It achieves a Word Error Rate (WER) of 6.73 on the TTS-generated test set. We normalize the reference text to ensure consistency before computing the BLEU scores using SACREBLEU [20].

3.3 Experimental Set-Up

We have trained the proposed model on the Prabhupadvani corpus [21]. The 80-dimensional Mel-filterbank is computed with $25ms$ of the window and $10ms$ of overlap duration for the input speech. We have also applied spec augment [19]. The down-sampling task consists of two Conv1D layers with a kernel size of 5, stride of 2 and 1024 channels. The encoder and decoder contain eight attention layers with an embedding dimension of 256. We have trained the model for 3000 epochs using Adam optimizer [13] with $\beta_1 = 0.9$ and $\beta_2 = 0.98$. We have also applied a label smoothing of 0.2 and a learning rate of 10^{-5}. We have used an inverse square root learning rate scheduler with $10k$ warm-up steps. The attention dropout and the feed-forward dropout are kept constant at 0.1 throughout the network, while a dropout of 0.5 is applied in the decoder post-net module.

3.4 Results and Discussion

We evaluated the performance of DS2ST and cascaded translation systems developed with Prabhupadavani datasets, which contain speech generated by the TTS system in a male voice. We employed the SACREBLEU metric on ASR transcriptions derived from the translated speech to assess the translation performance. The text obtained from ASR transcriptions was converted to lowercase, excluding punctuation marks and apostrophes. It's important to note that the BLEU score is traditionally used for evaluating machine translation systems based on reference translations. However, in this case, we used ASR as an intermediary step to convert the translation speech to text, which introduces potential errors. Consequently, the BLEU scores obtained from ASR transcriptions represent a distorted estimate, providing a lower bound on the translation quality. To ensure a fair comparison, we utilized an ASR model from Ekstep that was pre-trained on the 23 languages and fine-tuned with the Prabhupada dataset. This ASR model served as a common evaluation framework for all the models, including the baseline models. Furthermore, to generate the audio waveforms from the predicted mel-spectrograms, we employed the HiFi-GAN vocoder consistently across all models. Overall, this evaluation methodology allowed us to objectively compare the translation performance of different speech-to-speech translation models using a standardized ASR model and estimate their translation quality.

Objective Evaluation. In this work, we have performed four experiments. Firstly, we have proposed a DS2ST system, and the system's performance was analyzed on Prabhupadavani's unseen test dataset. We can see from the Table 3 that the system can translate English speech into Hindi without knowing the language's written form. The BLEU score we have achieved is 16.46 without any auxiliary decoder, which was 0.4 in the case of the Translatotron model.

Table 3. Performance analysis of the DS2ST vs cascaded system.

Model	BLEU
MT	37.31
Cascaded model	30.90
DS2ST without Aug	16.46
DS2ST with Aug	18.58

Secondly, we developed a cascaded system to compare the performance of our proposed DS2ST system. From the Table 3, we see that in comparison to the DS2ST system, cascaded leads with a high margin of BLEU score of 14.44. The difference in the BLEU score indicates the difficulty in exploiting the mapping function without the written form of the language. Thirdly, we can see a performance gap when we analyze the result of MT compared to the cascaded system from the Table 3. This again indicates that when we are embedding the ASR, generating the source and the target text degrades the performance by a 6.41 BLEU score. Finally, we have checked the data augmentation technique's capability in the DS2ST system. In this experiment, we have augmented the data by four times with speed perturbation. Table 3 indicates the significant improvement in performance by BLEU score 2.12.

Subjective Evaluation. In the subjective study, we conducted an intelligibility test to assess the performance of different translation models. We randomly selected 20 translated utterances from each translation model under consideration to ensure an unbiased evaluation. During the intelligibility test, the selected utterances from different models were played randomly to the listeners. Each listener was then asked to listen to each utterance once and write down the sentence they heard based on their understanding.

To evaluate the performance, we compared the sentences written by each listener with the ground truth, which consists of the correct original text sentences. The percentage accuracy was calculated by determining the number of words in the sentences that were accurately transcribed out of the total number of words in the sentences played to the listeners. This process helps us to gauge the intelligibility of the translations effectively and provides valuable insights into the effectiveness of the various translation models under study.

Table 4. Performance analysis with intelligibility score (IS) of the DS2ST vs cascaded system.

Model	%IS
Cascaded model	32.79
DS2ST without Aug	17.35
DS2ST with Aug	18.99

The findings from Table 4 indicate that human performance in the intelligibility test aligns with the trends observed in the objective study. Furthermore, it is noticeable that there is a slight discrepancy in the scores between the human evaluation and the BLEU metric. This difference may be attributed to higher human intelligibility and more comprehensive than the assessment provided by automated metrics like BLEU.

4   Conclusion and Future Direction

In this work, we have developed a transformer-based DS2ST system. Experiments are performed with the Prabhupadavani dataset, where we considered English as the source language and Hindi as the target language. We also developed a cascaded S2ST system using the same dataset to compare the performance. A comparative study is made between the DS2ST and the cascaded system. The results show that the system's performance has improved significantly by the BLEU score of 16.60 compared to the earlier DS2ST system (Translatotron 0.4). At the same time, when we compare the performance between the DS2ST and the cascaded system, the DS2ST system still lags significantly. Also, by comparing the cascaded system with MT, we can see that cascading the ASR degrades the system performance by a BLEU score of 6.60. From this, we can conclude that, as of now, the performance of the DS2ST system is lagging compared to the cascaded system, but it is possible to develop the DS2ST system without the use of the written form of language with the advancement in deep learning networks. In the future, we would like to explore other deep learning models and also more data to further improve the performance of the DS2ST system.

Acknowledgment. We extend our gratitude to the "AnantGanak" high-performance computation (HPC) facility at IIT Dharwad for facilitating our research experiments.

References

1. Languages of the world. https://www.ethnologue.com. Accessed 18 Sep 2023
2. Vanimedia. https://vanimedia.org/wiki. Accessed 21 Sep 2023
3. Alhari, S., et al.: Automatic speech recognition: systematic literature review. IEEE Access **9**, 131858–131876 (2021)

4. Arya, L., Agarwal, A., Mishra, J., Prasanna, S.R.M.: Analysis of layer-wise training in direct speech to speech translation using BI-LSTM. In: 2022 25th Conference of the Oriental COCOSDA International Committee for the Co-ordination and Standardisation of Speech Databases and Assessment Techniques (O-COCOSDA), pp. 1–6 (2022)
5. Arya, L., Agarwal, A., Prasanna, S.R.M.: Investigation of data augmentation techniques for BI-LSTM based direct speech to speech translation. In: 2023 National Conference on Communications (NCC), pp. 1–6 (2020)
6. Baevski, A., Zhou, Y., Mohamed, A., Auli, M.: wav2vec 2.0: a framework for self-supervised learning of speech representations. In: Larochelle, H., Ranzato, M., Hadsell, R., Balcan, M., Lin, H. (eds.) Advances in Neural Information Processing Systems. vol. 33, pp. 12449–12460. Curran Associates, Inc. (2020)
7. Chen, P.J., et al.: Speech-to-speech translation for a real-world unwritten language. In: Findings of the Association for Computational Linguistics: ACL 2023, pp. 4969–4983. Association for Computational Linguistics (2023)
8. Dong, L., Xu, S., Xu, B.: Speech-transformer: a no-recurrence sequence-to-sequence model for speech recognition. In: 2018 IEEE International Conference on Acoustics, Speech and Signal Processing (ICASSP), pp. 5884–5888 (2018)
9. Geng, M., et al.: Investigation of data augmentation techniques for disordered speech recognition. In: Interspeech 2020. ISCA (2020)
10. Jia, Y., Ramanovich, M.T., Remez, T., Pomerantz, R.: Translatotron 2: high-quality direct speech-to-speech translation with voice preservation. In: Proceedings of the 39th International Conference on Machine Learning. vol. 162, pp. 10120–10134. PMLR (17–23 Jul 2022)
11. Jia, Y., et al.: Direct speech-to-speech translation with a sequence-to-sequence model. In: INTERSPEECH, pp. 1123–1127 (2019)
12. Kim, J., Kim, S., Kong, J., Yoon, S.: Glow-TTS: a generative flow for text-to-speech via monotonic alignment search. In: Proceedings of the 34th International Conference on Neural Information Processing Systems, NIPS'20 (2020)
13. Kingma, D.P., Ba, J.: Adam: a method for stochastic optimization. In: Bengio, Y., LeCun, Y. (eds.) 3rd International Conference on Learning Representations, ICLR 2015, San Diego, CA, USA, May 7–9, 2015, Conference Track Proceedings (2015)
14. Kong, J., Kim, J., Bae, J.: HiFi-GAN: generative adversarial networks for efficient and high fidelity speech synthesis. In: Proceedings of the 34th International Conference on Neural Information Processing Systems, NIPS'20 (2020)
15. LeCun, Y., Bengio, Y.: Convolutional networks for images, speech, and time series, pp. 255–258, MIT Press (1998)
16. Lee, A., et al.: Direct speech-to-speech translation with discrete units. In: Proceedings of the 60th Annual Meeting of the Association for Computational Linguistics (Volume 1: Long Papers), pp. 3327–3339. Association for Computational Linguistics (2022)
17. Li, N., Liu, S., Liu, Y., Zhao, S., Liu, M.: Neural speech synthesis with transformer network. In: Proceedings of the Thirty-Third AAAI Conference on Artificial Intelligence. AAAI'19, AAAI Press (2019)
18. Li, X., Jia, Y., Chiu, C.C.: Textless direct speech-to-speech translation with discrete speech representation. In: ICASSP 2023–2023 IEEE International Conference on Acoustics, Speech and Signal Processing (ICASSP), pp. 1–5 (2023)
19. Park, D., et al.: Specaugment: a simple data augmentation method for automatic speech recognition. In: Interspeech, pp. 2613–2617. ISCA (09 2019)

20. Post, M.: A call for clarity in reporting BLEU scores. In: Proceedings of the Third Conference on Machine Translation: Research Papers, pp. 186–191. Association for Computational Linguistics, Brussels, Belgium (2018)
21. Sandhan, J., Daksh, A., Paranjay, O.A., Behera, L., Goyal, P.: Prabhupadavani: a code-mixed speech translation data for 25 languages. LaTeCH-CLfL, pp. 24–29 (2022)
22. Shahnawazuddin, S., Adiga, N., Kathania, H.K., Sai, B.T.: Creating speaker independent ASR system through prosody modification based data augmentation. Pattern Recogn. Lett. **131**, 213–218 (2020)
23. Shen, J., et al..: Natural tts synthesis by conditioning wavenet on mel spectrogram predictions. In: 2018 IEEE International Conference on Acoustics, Speech nd Signal Processing (ICASSP), pp. 4779–4783 (2018)
24. Shimizu, T., Ashikari, Y., Sumita, E., Zhang, J., Nakamura, S.: NICT/ATR Chinese-Japanese-English speech-to-speech translation system. Tsinghua Sci. Technol. **13**(4), 540–544 (2008)
25. Tan, Z., et al.: Neural machine translation: a review of methods, resources, and tools. AI Open **1**, 5–21 (2020)
26. Vaswani, A., et al.: Attention is all you need. In: Advances in Neural Information Processing Systems. vol. 30. Curran Associates, Inc. (2017)
27. Zhang, C., Tan, X., Ren, Y., Qin, T., jun Zhang, K., Liu, T.Y.: Uwspeech: speech to speech translation for unwritten languages. In: AAAI Conference on Artificial Intelligence, pp. 14319–14327 (2020)

Deep Learning Based Speech Quality Assessment Focusing on Noise Effects

Rahul Jaiswal[1]([✉])(iD) and Anu Priya[2]([✉])(iD)

[1] Department of Information and Communication Technology,
University of Agder, Grimstad, Norway
`rahul.jaiswal@uia.no`
[2] Scaler Neovarsity, Bangalore, India
`anupreha@gmail.com`

Abstract. This paper investigates the suitability of different speech features in measuring and monitoring speech quality in order to fulfil the expected level of human perceived quality of experience (QoE) while using applications, such as Microsoft Skype, and Apple FaceTime to name a few. To this end, two speech features, namely; line spectral frequencies (LSF), and multi-resolution auditory model (MRAM) are extracted from the speech signal after processing it through a voice activity detector (VAD). A series of deep neural network (DNN)-based objective no-reference speech quality models (SQMs) are then developed employing a single speech feature and combining both speech features. Two noisy speech datasets, namely; Supplement-23 and NOIZEUS-2240 are used for the experiment. Simulation results demonstrate that the SQM developed using combined speech features results in a better speech quality prediction as compared to the SQM developed using a single speech feature, when tested with distinct types of speech degradations.

Keywords: DNN · QoE · Speech Feature · Speech Quality · VAD

1 Introduction

In the past few years, the working mode of people has changed due to the COVID-19 pandemic. Most people prefer to work at a home-based office. Important meetings and communications are carried out online using different applications, for instance, Google Meet, and Microsoft Skype to name a few. To perceive a better quality of experience (QoE) [5] using these applications that are free from any type of noise disruptions, one needs to measure and monitor real-time speech quality. It can assist internet service providers to recognise the possible impairments present in their speech processing systems and install QoE management services to fulfil the desired QoE level of the end-user. In practice, a speech quality model is required to measure speech quality. Moreover, in practice, only noisy or degraded speech signals are available to measure speech quality. Hence, it is named as *no-reference speech quality model*, which is a fast and practical

A. Karpov et al. (Eds.): SPECOM 2023, LNAI 14339, pp. 271–282, 2023.
https://doi.org/10.1007/978-3-031-48312-7_22

method to measure speech quality objectively. On the contrary, traditionally, the quality of speech is measured subjectively, where a group of people provides their speech quality ratings after listening to the speech sample in a noise-free room. This method of speech quality rating is referred to as absolute category rating (ACR) [1]. However, this method is slow, time-consuming, and needs specific people who have no listening impairments. This work primarily focuses on the development of an objective speech quality model that leverages meaningful speech features to measure accurate speech quality.

There have been different objective speech quality models (SQMs) developed in the literature. However, to develop an effective SQM, the extraction of meaningful speech features is important. For instance, the classical P.563 [22], standardized by the International Telecommunication Union (ITU), uses the most dominant speech feature among several speech features for its mapping to speech quality. The ANIQUE+ [19] model employs the temporal envelope of the speech signal. However, it is not open-access. The author in [9] constructs an artificial reference model using the Gaussian mixture model (GMM) to compare noisy speech. The deep and sub-band autoencoder speech features are used in [25] for measuring speech quality. The model in [15] uses mean opinion score (MOS) as a salient feature to develop a deep neural network (DNN) based speech quality model. The LCQA [4] model uses speech variance, spectral flatness, spectral dynamics, and spectral centroid features. However, the performance of LCQA is poor for the competing speaker type degradations.

Our motivation in this work is driven towards first extracting meaningful speech features and then developing DNN-based SQMs which can result in a better prediction of speech quality. Along this line, we extract two distinct features from the voiced components of the speech signal, namely; line spectral frequencies (LSF), and multi-resolution auditory model (MRAM). The voiced components mainly contain speech activities and are obtained using a voice activity detector (VAD). Then, we develop DNN-based SQMs employing a single speech feature and combining both speech features in order to investigate their suitability in measuring accurate speech quality.

The structure of the remaining paper is designed as: Sect. 2 discusses VAD, feature extraction from speech samples, and the development of DNN-based SQMs. Section 3 describes the experimental dataset. The evaluation methodology is explained in Sect. 4. Section 5 discusses simulation results. Conclusion and future work are presented in Sect. 6.

2   Background

This section discusses the VAD, the approach for extracting features from speech samples, and the design of SQMs.

2.1   Voice Activity Detector

The author in [10] has shown that speech quality is measured poorly when silences are present in the speech signal. In other words, silence does not play any significant role in speech quality measurement. As a result, in our experiment, we use a VAD to segregate the silences and consider only voiced components of the speech signal to extract speech features [16]. Notice that only voiced components contain speech activities.

Along this line, we employ our designed *weighted spectral centroid (WS) VAD* [14], which extracts spectral centroid features from each frame (15–30 ms) of the speech signal. Then, it compares with a dynamic threshold to segregate the silence and the voiced components. Under distinct non-stationary noises, WS VAD has been shown to perform outstandingly. The complete mathematical formulation of VAD can be seen in [14].

After obtaining the voiced components, we extract distinct speech features from it, which is discussed further.

2.2   Feature Extraction

For developing DNN-based SQMs, extraction of meaning information from the speech sample is required. To this end, LSF and MRAM features are extracted.

LSF: The spectral information of speech is encoded by LSF. LSF is calculated from the linear predictor coefficients (LPC) [3]. A smaller amount of coefficients is required by LSF to capture the formant structure effectively. Moreover, the interpolation of LSF is better.

After processing the speech sample from WS VAD (see Sect. 2.1), the obtained frame-wise (frame duration of 16 ms) voiced components are used to compute the 10-dimensional (10-D) LSF feature. In general, LSF features are acquired by computing mean, variance, skewness and kurtosis [22]. However, only mean is used to obtain 10-D LSF as it is sufficient to represent spectral information or spectral envelope of the speech sample.

MRAM: Time-frequency resolution of speech samples is constructed by MRAM. After processing the speech sample from WS VAD (see Sect. 2.1), the obtained frame-wise (frame duration of 16 ms) voiced components are used to compute the 68-D MRAM feature using the following steps.

- Decomposition of speech energy into distinct critical band energies (CBE) using wavelet packet decomposition [18].
- Incorporation of absolute hearing threshold using outer and middle ear weights for the CBE.
- Exploitation of spectral spreading to each CBE.
- Exploitation of temporal smearing for temporal masking.
- Exploitation of power law compression [24] for effective subjective loudness.
- Computation of mean, variance, skewness and kurtosis [22] for 17 critical bands.
- Exploitation of principal component analysis [23] to obtain 22-D MRAM as it captures 99.9% speech energy.

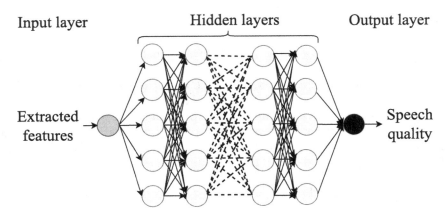

Fig. 1. Illustration of DNN-based SQM.

2.3 Speech Quality Model

We employ fully-connected DNN [21] to map the extracted features into speech quality score (MOS). DNN is a universal function approximator and the complex connection between extracted features and perceptual quality score can be learnt by DNN effectively.

To this end, in this experiment, the measurement of speech quality is stated as a regression task. Each extracted speech feature and combination of both extracted speech features, respectively, are considered as the input of DNN. The subjective MOS is the output of DNN. A simple illustration of DNN-based SQM is depicted in Fig. 1.

3 Experimental Dataset

The noisy speech datasets used in our experiment are discussed in this section.

3.1 Supplement-23 Dataset

Supplement-23 dataset [2] consists of coded speech samples. Out of three experiments performed by these samples for codec characterization test [7], only the samples of experiment 1 and 3 which use ACR [1] test for measuring speech quality, are used in our experiment. Experiment 1 consists of 3 sub-experiments, namely; A, D, and O, each consisting of 176 samples. Experiment 3 consists of 4 sub-experiments, namely; A, C, D, and O, each consisting of 200 samples. This results in 1328 ($3 \times 176 + 4 \times 200$) noisy samples. These samples are present at distinct conditions of random noise, such as vehicle, street, and hoth at 20 dB SNR, for the American English, French, Japanese, and Italian languages. They are down-sampled from 22 kHz to 8 kHz (narrow-band). The average duration of each sample is 8 s. The subjective speech quality rating is present for each sample.

3.2 NOIZEUS-2240 Dataset

This dataset comprises 20 clean IEEE English sentences, pronounced by 3 male and 3 female speakers aged between 18–65 years. These clean samples are added with 4 distinct noises, that is, babble, car, street, and train at two SNRs (5 dB and 10 dB). The noise samples are acquired from the AURORA repository [11]. This results in 160 (20 × 4 × 2) noisy samples. These noisy samples are then processed through 14 state-of-the-art speech enhancement algorithms [12]. It enhances the quality of speech samples [17]. As a result, one can obtain 2240 (160 × 14) processed samples. Down-sampling is performed for samples from 25 kHz to 8 kHz (narrow-band). The average duration of each sample is 3 s. The samples are present in .wav (16 bit PCM, mono). The author in [8] provided the subjective speech quality rating of each sample.

4 Evaluation Methodology

To predict objective speech quality, Fig. 2 shows the experimental setup which mainly comprises three scenarios. Under the first scenario, the degraded or noisy samples are processed through our designed WS VAD (see Sect. 2.1) to obtain voiced components. LSF features are then extracted for these voiced components. These extracted features are the input to the DNN (see Fig. 1). The output of DNN is the corresponding subjective quality rating. With these settings, we train the DNN to predict objective speech quality. We represent this SQM model as "SQM_{LSF}". Similarly, under the second scenario, the same procedure is followed for DNN training by extracting the MRAM feature. We represent this SQM model as "SQM_{MRAM}". However, under the third scenario, we follow the same procedure for DNN training by extracting both LSF and MRAM features from the degraded samples. We represent this SQM model as "SQM_{Hybrid}".

For each scenario of DNN training, we split the total degraded samples (see Sect. 3). The training samples comprise 70% of the total samples, and the test samples comprise 30% of the total samples. Moreover, for the evaluation of each SQM in terms of training and test accuracy, 5-fold cross-validation [6] is used.

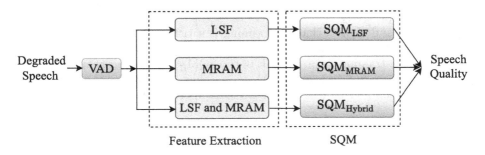

Fig. 2. Experimental setup.

Next, to investigate the association between the subjective quality rating (MOS-LQS) and the predicted objective quality rating (MOS-LQO), we calculate the Pearson's correlation (ρ_p), Spearman's correlation (ρ_s), and root mean square error (RMSE) for all test samples employing each SQM. Suppose, there is n number of samples. $s_1, s_2, ..., s_n$; $\hat{s}_1, \hat{s}_2, ..., \hat{s}_n$; μ_s; $\mu_{\hat{s}}$, and d_i are the subjective and predicted objective quality rating, respectively, their corresponding means μ, and difference between their corresponding quality rating ranks. We compute these measures as [13]:

$$\rho_p = \frac{\sum_{i=1}^{n}(\hat{s}_i - \mu_{\hat{s}})(s_i - \mu_s)}{\sqrt{\sum_{i=1}^{n}(\hat{s}_i - \mu_{\hat{s}})^2(s_i - \mu_s)^2}}. \tag{1}$$

$$\rho_s = 1 - \frac{6\sum_{i=1}^{n}d_i^2}{n(n^2-1)}. \tag{2}$$

$$\text{RMSE} = \sqrt{\frac{1}{n}\sum_{i=1}^{n}(s_i - \hat{s}_i)^2}. \tag{3}$$

5   Results and Discussions

The obtained results are presented and discussed in this section.

5.1   Experiment with Supplement-23 Dataset

Model Analysis of Each SQM: The objective speech quality is predicted by training the DNN-based SQM using each extracted feature and combining both extracted features, respectively. This results in three distinct DNN-based SQMs, represented as SQM_{LSF}, SQM_{MRAM}, and $\text{SQM}_{\text{Hybrid}}$, respectively (see Fig. 2). Tables 1, 2 and 3 show distinct parameters and hyper-parameters for each SQM and the training and test accuracy in terms of mean square error (MSE) [26]. Moreover, depending on the dimension of the speech feature, each DNN-based SQM requires a distinct number of neurons in its input layer. For instance, 10, 22, and 32 neurons are present in the input layer of SQM_{LSF}, SQM_{MRAM}, and $\text{SQM}_{\text{Hybrid}}$, respectively.

Tables 1, 2 and 3 show that the training is satisfactory for each SQM, that is, the training MSE and the test MSE are comparable, showing no overfitting. Specifically, the training and test MSE of the $\text{SQM}_{\text{Hybrid}}$ are less than the corresponding values in SQM_{LSF} and SQM_{MRAM}. This signifies that the training of each SQM is good and we can employ these SQMs to predict the speech quality of test samples.

Performance Analysis of Each SQM: Table 4 presents the ρ_p, ρ_s, and RMSE of each SQM. We can observe that the ρ_p, ρ_s, and RMSE of each SQM are significantly good. In particular, the ρ_p, and ρ_s of the $\text{SQM}_{\text{Hybrid}}$, where both speech features are combined, are better as compared to the SQM_{LSF} and SQM_{MRAM}.

Table 1. Model learning of the SQM_{LSF}.

Input layer neurons	10
Hidden layers	4
Neurons in each hidden layer	256, 128, 64, 32
Activation function in each hidden layer	ReLU
Batch normalization after 1st hidden layer	default setting
Dropout after 2nd hidden layer	0.30
Output layer neurons	1
Output layer activation function	ReLU
Optimizer	Adam [20]
Learning rate	0.0001
Loss function	MSE
Size of each batch	32
Training-Testing split	70:30
Training MSE	0.022484
Test MSE	0.025924

Table 2. Model learning of the SQM_{MRAM}.

Input layer neurons	22
Remaining parameters and hyper-parameters are the same as in Table 1.	
Training MSE	0.012294
Test MSE	0.026344

Table 3. Model learning of the SQM_{Hybrid}.

Input layer neurons	32 (10+22)
Remaining parameters and hyper-parameters are the same as in Table 1.	
Training MSE	0.010224
Test MSE	0.01975

Table 4. Correlations and RMSE of each SQM.

Description of each scenario	ρ_p	ρ_s	RMSE
Scenario 1: Degraded speech → VAD → SQM_{LSF} → MOS-LQO	0.691	0.691	0.161
Scenario 2: Degraded speech → VAD → SQM_{MRAM} → MOS-LQO	0.700	0.708	0.162
Scenario 3: Degraded speech → VAD → SQM_{Hybrid} → MOS-LQO	0.774	0.778	0.140

Moreover, the RMSE is also less for SQM_{Hybrid}. There is an improvement of around 11% in both ρ_p and ρ_s, and a decrement of around 13% in RMSE under Scenario 3 in contrast to Scenario 1. Similarly, there is an improvement of around 10% in both ρ_p and ρ_s, and a decrement of around 13% in RMSE under Scenario 3 in contrast to Scenario 2. This signifies that the SQM_{Hybrid} developed by combining both speech features (Scenario 3) is the most appropriate SQM for capturing meaningful information from speech samples and predicting objective speech quality.

5.2   Experiment with NOIZEUS-2240 Dataset

Model Analysis of Each SQM: The objective speech quality is predicted by training the same DNN-based SQM (see Fig. 2) employing a single extracted feature and combining both extracted features, respectively. Tables 5, 6 and 7 show distinct parameters and hyper-parameters for each SQM and the training and test accuracy in terms of MSE.

Tables 5, 6 and 7 show that the training is satisfactory for each SQM, that is, the training MSE and the test MSE are comparable, showing no overfitting. Specifically, the training and test MSE of the SQM_{Hybrid} are less than the corresponding values in SQM_{LSF} and SQM_{MRAM}. This signifies that the training of each SQM is good and we can employ these SQMs for predicting the speech quality of test samples.

Table 5. Model learning of the SQM_{LSF}.

Input layer neurons	10
Remaining parameters and hyper-parameters are the same as in Table 1.	
Training MSE	0.015178
Test MSE	0.017361

Table 6. Model learning of the SQM_{MRAM}.

Input layer neurons	22
Remaining parameters and hyper-parameters are the same as in Table 1.	
Training MSE	0.009743
Test MSE	0.012279

Table 7. Model learning of the SQM_{Hybrid}.

Input layer neurons	32 (10+22)
Remaining parameters and hyper-parameters are the same as in Table 1.	
Training MSE	0.008384
Test MSE	0.012099

Table 8. Correlations and RMSE of each SQM.

Description of each scenario	ρ_p	ρ_s	RMSE
Scenario 1: Degraded speech → VAD → SQM_{LSF} → MOS-LQO	0.612	0.609	0.131
Scenario 2: Degraded speech → VAD → SQM_{MRAM} → MOS-LQO	0.747	0.748	0.110
Scenario 3: Degraded speech → VAD → SQM_{Hybrid} → MOS-LQO	0.764	0.761	0.109

Performance Analysis of Each SQM: Table 8 presents the ρ_p, ρ_s, and RMSE of each SQM. We can observe that the ρ_p, ρ_s, and RMSE of each SQM are significantly good. In particular, the ρ_p, and ρ_s of the SQM_{Hybrid}, where both speech features are combined, are better as compared to the SQM_{LSF} and SQM_{MRAM}. Moreover, the RMSE is also less for SQM_{Hybrid}. There is an improvement of around 20% in both ρ_p and ρ_s, and a decrement of around 17% in RMSE under Scenario 3 in contrast to Scenario 1. Similarly, there is an improvement of around 20% in both ρ_p and ρ_s, and a decrement of around 1% in RMSE under Scenario 3 in contrast to Scenario 2. This again signifies that the SQM_{Hybrid} developed by combining both speech features (Scenario 3) is the most appropriate SQM for capturing meaningful information from speech samples and predicting objective speech quality.

5.3   Scatter Plots

For visualizing the efficacy of a single speech feature and combined speech features in order to develop a better SQM, the mean opinion score listening quality objective (MOS-LQO) obtained using each SQM is compared with the corresponding mean opinion score listening quality subjective (MOS-LQS). The comparison is made for the test speech samples of each dataset, as illustrated in Fig. 3(a)–(c), and Fig. 4(a)–(c), respectively.

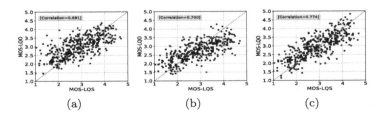

(a)   (b)   (c)

Fig. 3. Subjective and objective speech quality comparison for the test samples of Supplement-23 dataset using: (a) SQM_{LSF}, (b) SQM_{MRAM}, and (c) SQM_{Hybrid}.

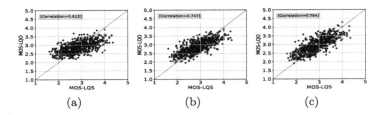

Fig. 4. Subjective and objective speech quality comparison for the test samples of NOIZEUS-2240 dataset using: (a) SQM_{LSF}, (b) SQM_{MRAM}, and (c) SQM_{Hybrid}.

Both scatter plots show that there is no proper distribution or spread of speech samples towards the diagonal line while employing the SQM trained with only the LSF feature, that is, SQM_{LSF}, resulting in a poor correlation (see Fig. 3(a) and Fig. 4(a)). However, there is a slight spread of speech samples towards the diagonal line while employing the SQM trained with only the MRAM feature, that is, SQM_{MRAM}, resulting in an improved correlation (see Fig. 3(b) and Fig. 4(b)). On the other hand, a very good distribution of speech samples can be seen towards the diagonal line while employing the SQM trained with both LSF and MRAM features, that is, SQM_{Hybrid}, resulting in a better correlation (see Fig. 3(c) and Fig. 4(c)), as compared to SQM_{LSF} and SQM_{MRAM}. This again reflects that the combination of both speech features results in a better SQM for predicting speech quality as compared to the SQM which is developed using a single speech feature.

6   Conclusion and Future Work

This paper examines deep learning-based SQMs in measuring accurate speech quality under noisy surroundings as the noise degrades the speech quality. Along this line, two features are extracted from the speech sample after processing it through a VAD. DNN-based SQMs are then developed using a single feature and combining both features. Simulation results show that the Hybrid SQM, which is developed using both features, performs better in contrast to the SQM which is developed using only a single feature. It also suggests that the combination of both features contains meaningful information about the speech sample and is beneficial for real-time speech quality measurement. Internet service providers can easily deploy the Hybrid SQM for measuring and monitoring speech quality in order to fulfil the expected QoE level of the end-user. In future, we aim to examine highly complex speech features for developing SQMs. We also aim to examine developed SQMs with noisy samples containing real-world noise and noisy samples that comprise native speakers.

References

1. ITU-T recommendation P.800: Methods for subjective determination of transmission quality (1996)

2. ITU-T Coded-Speech Database. Series P, Supplement 23 (1998)
3. Alim, S.A., Rashid, N.K.A.: Some commonly used speech feature extraction algorithms. In: IntechOpen (2018)
4. Bruhn, S., Grancharov, V., Kleijn, W.B.: Low-complexity, non-intrusive speech quality assessment. US Patent 8,195,449 (2012)
5. Brunnström, K., Beker, S.A., De Moor, K., Dooms, A., Egger, S.: Qualinet white paper on definitions of quality of experience (2013)
6. De Rooij, M., Weeda, W.: Cross-validation: a method every psychologist should know. Adv. Methods Pract. Psychol. Sci. **3**(2), 248–263 (2020)
7. Dubey, R.K., Kumar, A.: Non-intrusive speech quality assessment using several combinations of auditory features. Int. J. Speech Technol. **16**(1), 89–101 (2013)
8. Dubey, R.K., Kumar, A.: Comparison of subjective and objective speech quality assessment for different degradation/noise conditions. In: IEEE International Conference on Signal Processing and Communication, pp. 261–266 (2015)
9. Falk, T.H., Xu, Q., Chan, W.Y.: Non-intrusive GMM-based speech quality measurement. In: IEEE ICASSP, vol. 1, pp. 125–128 (2005)
10. Hines, A., Gillen, E., Harte, N.: Measuring and monitoring speech quality for voice over IP with POLQA, ViSQOL and P.563. In: Interspeech, pp. 438–442 (2015)
11. Hirsch, H.G., Pearce, D.: The Aurora experimental framework for the performance evaluation of speech recognition systems under noisy conditions. In: ASR2000-Automatic Speech Recognition: Challenges for the New Millenium ISCA Tutorial and Research Workshop (ITRW) (2000)
12. Hu, Y., Loizou, P.C.: Subjective comparison and evaluation of speech enhancement algorithms. Speech Commun. **49**(7–8), 588–601 (2007)
13. Jaiswal, R.: Influence of silence and noise filtering on speech quality monitoring. In: 11th IEEE International Conference on Speech Technology and Human-Computer Dialogue (SpeD), pp. 109–113 (2021)
14. Jaiswal, R.: Performance analysis of voice activity detector in presence of non-stationary noise. In: Proceedings of the 11th International Conference on Robotics, Vision, Signal Processing and Power Applications. LNEE, vol. 829, pp. 59–65. Springer, Singapore (2022). https://doi.org/10.1007/978-981-16-8129-5_10
15. Jaiswal, R., Dubey, R.K.: CAQoE: a novel no-reference context-aware speech quality prediction metric. ACM Trans. Multimedia Comput. Commun. Appl. **19**(1s), 1–23 (2023)
16. Jaiswal, R., Hines, A.: The sound of silence: how traditional and deep learning based VAD influences speech quality monitoring. In: 26th Irish Conference on Artificial Intelligence and Cognitive Science (2018)
17. Jaiswal, R., Romero, D.: Implicit wiener filtering for speech enhancement in non-stationary noise. In: 11th International Conference on Information Science and Technology, pp. 39–47. IEEE (2021)
18. Karmakar, A., Kumar, A., Patney, R.: Design of optimal wavelet packet trees based on auditory perception criterion. IEEE Signal Process. Lett. **14**(4), 240–243 (2007)
19. Kim, D.S., Tarraf, A.: ANIQUE+: a new American National Standard for non-intrusive estimation of narrow-band speech quality. Bell Labs Tech. J. **12**(1), 221–236 (2007)
20. Kingma, D.P., Ba, J.: Adam: a method for stochastic optimization. In: 3rd International Conference on Learning Representations (ICLR) (2015)
21. LeCun, Y., Bengio, Y., Hinton, G.: Deep learning. Nature **521**(7553), 436–444 (2015)
22. Malfait, L., et al.: The ITU-T standard for single-ended speech quality assessment. IEEE Trans. Audio Speech Lang. Process. **14**(6), 1924–1934 (2006)

23. Naik, G.R.: Advances in Principal Component Analysis: Research and Development. Springer, Heidelberg (2017). https://doi.org/10.1007/978-981-10-6704-4
24. Schroeder, M.R.: Computer Speech: Recognition, Compression, Synthesis. Springer, Heidelberg (2004). https://doi.org/10.1007/978-3-662-03861-1
25. Soni, M.H., Patil, H.A.: Non-intrusive quality assessment of noise-suppressed speech using unsupervised deep features. Speech Commun. **130**, 27–44 (2021)
26. Wang, Z., Bovik, A.C.: Mean squared error: love it or leave it? a new look at signal fidelity measures. IEEE Signal Process. Maga. **26**(1), 98–117 (2009)

Quantifying the Emotional Landscape of Music with Three Dimensions

Kirtana Sunil Phatnani[1]([✉])[iD] and Hemant A. Patil[2]

[1] Fractal Analytics, Mumbai, Maharashtra, India
Kirtana.Phatnani@fractal.ai
[2] Speech Research Lab, Dhirubhai Ambani Institute of Information and
Communication Technology, Gandhinagar, India
Hemant_Patil@daiict.ac.in

Abstract. Music is a powerful art form that fosters a deep connection between the listener and the sound. Yet, sentiment analysis alone is limited in capturing the breadth and depth of emotions conveyed in songs, especially as individuals' perceptions and interpretations of music vary widely. Our goal is to offer a more immersive and meaningful experience for listeners by harnessing the emotional contagion elicited by each song and gauging it through a multifaceted lens that considers identity, setting, and sentiment metrics. By analyzing the lyrics of songs that garnered similar Vader sentiment scores, we demonstrate that our innovative approach not only captures the essence of each composition but also uncovers nuanced differences in sentiment that escape traditional sentiment analysis. The divergence between our methodology integrating first-person sentiment shows variation of sentiment scores from –0.32 to 0.65 across the 10 songs having sentiment of approximately 0.99 (based on the traditional sentiment analysis method). Expanding the dataset to 47 positive songs and 48 negative songs from the Moody Lyrics dataset [3], we observe a variance of approximately 0.22 in positive and 0.19 in the negative songs (as compared to 0 in the traditional sentiment analysis), underscoring the remarkable intricacies that our approach can reveal. We also propose optimizing song recommendation using Reinforcement Learning (RL) utilizing these dimensions as states, choice of music as actions and accurate choice as reward. We propose this analysis can help dive deeper into the potential of emotions in music impacting the society as a whole.

Keywords: Music cognition · Temporal sentiment Analysis · Emotional Contagion · Lyrical Analysis

1 Introduction

The notion that music can elicit emotions was not thoroughly explored until the debate between Kivy and Radford in 1993 [13]. Kivy claimed that music had never made him feel sad, while Radford argued that it could. In the ensuing

A. Karpov et al. (Eds.): SPECOM 2023, LNAI 14339, pp. 283–294, 2023.
https://doi.org/10.1007/978-3-031-48312-7_23

three decades, researchers from various disciplines, including psychology, neuroscience, and computer science, have delved into the complex relationship between music and emotion. Initially, psychologists struggled to fully grasp music perception due to its highly subconscious nature, [9] where only conscious perceptions were evident. However, over time, the connection between music and emotions became clearer. Juslin's research was particularly instrumental in developing a comprehensive understanding of musical emotions, which identified seven key phenomena: brain stem reflex, rhythmic entertainment, emotional contagion, evaluative conditioning, episodic memory, and mental visual imagery [15].

Brain stem reflex is an innate response to the intensity and progression of sounds that we have developed through evolution [12]. On the other hand, rhythmic entertainment involves the synchronization of our body's physiological rhythms, such as heart rate, with the rhythm of the music [25]. These two phenomena occur at a physiological level without any intervention from the conscious mind. The predictability and regularity offered by rhythmic entertainment have been found to aid in the therapy of individuals with Autism Spectrum Disorder (ASD), as they struggle with uncertainty [24]. The repetition inherent in music allows individuals with ASD to engage with it without cognitive overload [23].

In addition, music is known to induce emotions in listeners through emotional contagion, which refers to the transfer of emotions from the music to the listener in a manner similar to the spread of a contagious disease [10,14]. This phenomenon is linked to the activation of mirror neurons in the brain, which are most active during face-to-face interactions such as concerts or music videos [22]. However, emotional contagion can also be elicited through the lyrics of a song, which allow the listener to relate to the expressions of the singer and the emotions conveyed in the music [2].

Furthermore, music has the ability to trigger evaluative conditioning, which is the association of certain events or emotions with specific musical stimuli. This can lead to the recreation of those events or emotions in the listener's mind upon listening to the music again [11,28]. Episodic memory, on the other hand, refers to the flashbacks or recollections that listeners experience when listening to music, leading to strong emotional responses [21,26]. Finally, mental visual imagery involves the use of vivid descriptions in music that can stimulate the imagination and activate affect systems in the brain [19].

The different responses of our brain to music, such as emotional contagion, evaluative conditioning, episodic memory, and mental visual imagery, all heavily rely on our emotional reactions to music. To enable machines to select appropriate music for us, it is essential to identify and understand the emotions evoked by a musical piece. In this study, we propose a three-dimensional sentiment analysis to enhance the field of Music Emotion Recognition (MER). Additionally, we argue that music is a vital medium of social mass communication, and understanding its emotional impact is crucial to understanding communication [4].

Every music episode, even if for the same piece of music, is different for the listener [13]. This is because music activates different mental imagery and meaning to the experience depending on the present state of the listener. In instrumental music, the emotional contagion derived from music is much more subjective owing to the memories people associate with the musical piece. Recent studies report a high level understanding of the valence and arousal of soundscapes in music [18]. Studies also offer the viewpoint of how common sounds present in our environment and music share similar frequencies for same sentiments [17]. Juslin also speaks about how the sentiment that may be evoked by listening to music may be very much similar to the same sentiment produced through speech [13]. For lyrical music, the experience is relatively more objective and deeper due to the deterministic nature of language. Hence, for the purpose of this paper we delve deep into the lyrics contained in music.

This study aims to develop a novel approach to Music Emotion Recognition (MER) by designing statistical reasoning of emotions that can have optimal effects on our bodies. In doing so, we address some of the limitations of recent approaches in the field, including:

- Most studies in the field of MER label an entire music piece with one emotional label, without considering the hills and valleys of different emotions in the musical piece [30].
- Many studies in music literature have proposed that the concepts of *consonance* and *dissonance* are the fundamental principles of music and that emotion recognition studies rely on these concepts [29]. However, as stated in [16], recent studies have revealed that some cultures do not conform to this standard when assessing the impact of music.
- Emotions from a lyrical music piece arise from the story between its characters, and hence, the emotional journey of each character and their relationship is important in the musical journey.

Therefore, we propose an approach that takes into account the emotional journey of each character in a lyrical music piece for MER. The rest of the paper is organized as follows: Sect. 2 describes the statistical reasoning of emotions and the dataset used. Section 3 presents results and analysis of the identity-wise sentiment analysis. Section 4 proposes how a reinforcement learning algorithm can be used to recommend songs using this analysis of sentiments. and Sect. 5 summarizes the paper with a conclusion.

2   Materials and Methods

From a human perspective, every sentence in a lyric offers a glimpse into an event's context. Such events can be positive, negative, or neutral. They might occur in the past, present, or future. By considering tense, we gain an added layer to assess the positioning of sentiments in time. After pinpointing these feelings tied to time, we identify the characters or entities in the song. These entities are distinguished by the pronouns they are associated with. To determine each entity, we look at the narrative framework of the song, where characters are differentiated by pronouns like first, second, or third person, or relationship. We also model relationship as a part of identifying identity as we find many songs describe not only how the protagonist feels but also how the state of their relationship with objects, places, people are. According to neuroscience, studies show that during the dream state the brain attempts to model relationships we have in our world [5]. Hence, relationships become a key facet to model. To summarize, this study focuses on the three-dimensional sentiment extraction of musical pieces using the dimensions of identity, emotion, and setting (time) [20]. Figure 1 provides an overview of the three dimensions. After segmenting the musical piece, we extract the final emotion for each identity, the identity's emotional journey.

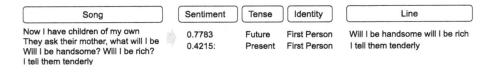

Fig. 1. Each song is composed of multiple lines, each line is composed of identity, time, and emotion.

Post segmenting the musical piece, we extract:

- Final emotion for that identity
- Journey of the identity from the past to the present and into the future and,
- Finally, we propose song recommendation using Reinforcement Learning (RL) algorithm.

To segment into identity dimensions, we analyze sentences in the lyrics based on the pronouns used. We extract the tense of the verb to identify when the sentiment occurred. For sentiment analysis, we utilized Vader's lexicon analysis library in Python [7].

To track the emotional journey of a character in a song, we estimate its weighted average using the recency heuristic [6]. We use the recency heuristic because brain is an anticipating machine. Hence, it anticipates the future using the memories of the present and the past [27]. We use the recency heuristic because the time scale of emotions weighs future > present > past, which can be thought of as synaptic weights re-adjusting from the past to present in order to best predict the future. To that effect, we use the following formula to estimate the final sentiment of each identity i:

$$f_i = \frac{w\_past * \overline{past_i} + w\_present * \overline{present_i} + w\_fut * \overline{fut_i}}{w\_past + w\_present + w\_fut} \tag{1}$$

where $w\_fut = 1000$, $w\_present = 100$, and $w\_past = 10$. We adopt a weight scheme that emphasizes recent events over past ones, with the weights increasing in power from the past to the future. This enables us to assign more importance to the most recent events. To determine the trajectory of the identity, we utilize two deltas: d_1 represents the difference between the present and past sentiment, while d_2 represents the difference between the future and present sentiment. We calculate these differences for each identity i, taking into account the unequal weighting of sentiments. To accomplish this, we assign weights from a geometric progression with a common ratio of 1.5 and a starting value of 1. Thus, the past has a weight of 1, the present a weight of 1.5, and the future a weight of 1.5 multiplied by 1.5. To normalize the values of d_{1_i} and d_{2_i}, we divide them by the maximum possible value. Hence, we have:

$$d_{1_i} = \frac{1.5 * \overline{present_i} - \overline{past_i}}{2.5}, \tag{2}$$

$$d_{2_i} = \frac{1.5 * 1.5 * \overline{future_i} - 1.5 * \overline{present_i}}{3.75}, \tag{3}$$

where d_{1_i} and $d_{2_i} = 0$, when $\overline{present_i} = 0$ and $\overline{future_i} = 0$, respectively. To classify a song as uplifting, from the possible combinations of d_{1_i} and d_{2_i}, when it satisfies the following equation:

$$d1_i + d2_i > 0. \tag{4}$$

Utilizing these measures, we can discern the range of emotions experienced by each character and their emotional progression throughout the song. With this information, we can classify whether the overall mood of the song is uplifting or not. Our analysis in this study centers on the songs listed in Table 1.

Table 1. Details of Songs Used in this Study for Data Collection. After [1].

Song Title	Singer
Memories	Maroon 5
So Will I	Ben Platt
Que Sera Sera	Doris Day
Supermarket Flowers	Edward Sheeran,
Tenerife Sea	Edward Sheeran
Still	Niall Horan
Flicker	Niall Horan
Black and White	Niall Horan
I See Fire	Ed Sheeran
Saving Grace	Kodaline

3   Results and Analysis

Analyzing the Table 2, we can further reinforce that the "Sentiment" column alone does not offer an exhaustive view of the intricate nature of the songs' themes, narrative perspectives, and emotional fluctuations.

Table 2. Identity-wise sentiment, delta 1 and delta 2 analysis.

Song	Sentiment	FP	SP	TP	R	FP		SP		TP		R	
						d1	d2	d1	d2	d1	d2	d1	d2
Que Sera Sera	0.93	0.65	0	0	0.42	0.05	0.5	0	0	0	0	0	0
Memories	0.97	0.03	0.44	0	0.08	0.13	0	0	0	0	0	−0.33	−0.23
Black and White	1	0.27	0.61	0	0.6	−0.04	0.21	0	0	0	0	0.22	0.64
Tenerife Sea	0.99	−0.32	0.7	0	0.59	0	−0.42	0	0	0	0	0	0
Saving Grace	−0.92	0.42	−0.35	0	0.25	0	0	−0.12	0	0	0	0	0.04
So Will I	0.97	0.24	−0.32	0	0.22	−0.13	0.05	0	0	0	0	−0.03	−0.05
Supermarket Flowers	1	0.64	0.31	0.61	0.53	0	0	0.06	0	0	0.61	0.21	0.64
Flicker	0.92	0.47	0.03	0.23	0.39	0	0.5	0	0	0	0	0.03	0
Still	0.92	−0.29	0.69	−0.01	0.4	0	−0.31	0	0	−0.07	−0.18	0	0
I See Fire	−0.99	−0.17	0	−0.44	−0.08	−0.27	−0.34	0	0	0	0	0	−0.34

1. *Diversity in Narrative Perspectives:*
   - *Que Sera Sera* and *Memories* have non-zero values in the First Person (FP) and Second Person (SP) columns but zero in Third Person (TP), indicating a diversity in narrative perspectives, which would be imperceptible with only the "Sentiment" column.
   - *Supermarket Flowers* shows sentiment across all perspectives including Relationship (R), indicating a multi-dimensional narrative not reflected in a singular sentiment value.
2. *Temporal Changes in Sentiments:*
   - *Tenerife Sea* and *Still* show negative delta values in SP and TP respectively, hinting at the temporal development or regression in themes or sentiments, unobservable with the overall sentiment value alone.
   - *I See Fire* has negative delta values in FP, revealing a decline in sentiment within the first-person perspective, providing more nuanced insights into the song's emotional trajectory.
3. *Complex Emotional Structures:*
   - *Black and White* and *Supermarket Flowers* have varying sentiments across FP, SP, TP, and R, indicating the presence of complex emotional structures and differing thematic elements within the songs, unaccounted for in the overall sentiment value.
   - *Saving Grace* presents a negative overall sentiment value but displays positive sentiment in FP, underscoring the contrast and depth in emotional elements within the song.
4. *Varied Relationship Dynamics:*
   - *Supermarket Flowers* displays sentiments in the Relationship (R) column along with changes in delta values, highlighting the varying dynamics in relationships depicted in the song.
   - The presence of non-zero delta values in the Relationship (R) column in songs like *Black and White* illustrates changes in relationship dynamics or themes over time, adding another layer to the interpretation of the songs.

5. *Contrasting Sentiments:*
   - Songs like *So Will I, Saving Grace* and *Still* with overall positive and negative "Sentiment" values respectively, show contrasting sentiments in individual perspectives (FP, SP, TP), showcasing the juxtaposition of emotions and themes within the songs.

In our endeavor to refine and statistically substantiate our preliminary findings, we meticulously broadened our dataset to encompass 100 songs from the distinguished Moody Lyrics database [3]. The database was bisected into two segments, allocating 50 songs to both the positive and negative sentiment classes, respectively. Through meticulous analysis and curation, we successfully procured the lyrics for 47 songs categorized as Positive and 48 dubbed as Negative.

Following this enlargement of our data set, we deployed analogous analytical methodologies on these newly acquired classes and generated the results as depicted in Table 1 and Table 2. Table 3 enumerates the top five songs with positive sentiment along with the respective artist, whereas Table 5 lists the top five songs within the negative class.

Table 3. Positive Songs from Moody Lyrics Dataset(top 5 songs).

Artist	Songs	Sentiment
The Jackson 5	ABC	1
Kenny Lattimore	And I Love Her	1
Megadeth	Angry Again	1
Jordin Sparks	Battlefield	1
J. Holiday	Bed	1

Table 4. Positive Songs identity-wise sentiment (top 5 songs).

Song	FP	SP	TP	R
ABC	0.67	0	0	0.46
And I Love Her	0.74	0	0	0.58
Angry Again	−0.32	0.77	0.36	−0.46
Battlefield	−0.23	0.44	0	0.03
Bed	0.56	0.4	0	0.43

The Tables 3 and 5, give a glimpse into the list of songs used for the analysis. Table 4 and Table 6 reveal intriguing insights into the variations and complexities in emotional structures within the songs, enabling a nuanced appreciation of the intricacies in lyrical content. Table 7 and 8 describe the temporal variations across each identity in the songs. To further scrutinize the disparities in sentiment

Table 5. Negative Songs from Moody Lyrics Dataset (top 5).

Artist	Songs	Sentiment
Cassandra Wilson	A Day In The Life Of A Fool	−1
Testament	Apocalyptic City	−1
High On Fire	Bastard Samurai	−1
All That Remains	Become The Catalyst	−1
Love Is All	Bigger Bolder	−1

Table 6. Negative Songs identity-wise sentiment (top 5 songs).

Song	FP	SP	TP	R
A Day In The Life Of A Fool	−0.25	0	0	−0.18
Apocalyptic City	−0.13	0	0	−0.22
Bastard Samurai	0	0	0	−0.46
Become The Catalyst	0.02	0	0	−0.27
Bigger Bolder	−0.57	0	0	0.57

Table 7. Positive songs temporal-wise sentiment (top 5 songs).

Song	FP		SP		TP		R	
	d1	d2	d1	d2	d1	d2	d1	d2
ABC	0.06	0	0	0	0	0	0.27	0
And I Love Her	0.13	0	0	0	0	0	0.15	0
Angry Again	−0.02	0	0.12	0	0.12	0	0.12	0
Battlefield	0.38	0	0	0	0	0	0.36	0
Bed	0.06	0	0.12	0	0	0	0.12	0

Table 8. Negative songs temporal-wise sentiment (top 5 songs).

Song	FP		SP		TP		R	
	d1	d2	d1	d2	d1	d2	d1	d2
A Day In The Life Of A Fool	0	−0.58	0	0	0	0	0.29	0
Apocalyptic City	0.05	0.03	0	0	0	0	−0.01	−0.12
Bastard Samurai	0	0	0	0	0	0	−0.14	−0.5
Become The Catalyst	−0.2	−0.27	0	0	0	0	0.57	0.69
Bigger Bolder	0	0	0	0	0	0	−0.08	0

elucidation between the Vader sentiment and our bespoke method, we delved deeper into the comparative.

To further scrutinize the disparities in sentiment elucidation between the Vader sentiment and our bespoke method, we delved deeper into the comparative variances within songs described in Table 9.

Table 9. Variance in Vader sentiment analysis and the proposed emotional contagion analysis.

	Vader Sentiment Variance	Emotional Contagion variance
Positive	0	0.22
Negative	0	0.19

the variance in sentiment for positive songs was identified to be *0.22*, and for negative songs, it was *0.19*. This quantified variance underscores a pivotal revelation; it illustrates the nuanced intricacies and the multiplicity of emotional layers interwoven within each song. Such granularity and multifaceted insights are pivotal, reflecting not just the diversity in emotional tones but also unmasking the subtle, often overlooked, thematic elements inherent within the lyrical compositions. In essence, this substantiates our assertion that a singular sentiment value might not adequately represent the myriad emotional textures and thematic intricacies embedded within a song. It becomes imperative to integrate a more refined and multifaceted analytical approach to genuinely comprehend and interpret the multi-dimensional nature of songs, thereby offering a more comprehensive and insightful exploration into the world of music and lyrics.

Conclusion

The detailed perspectives (FP, SP, TP), relationship dynamics (R), and their changes over time (Delta Values) play a crucial role in understanding the multi-faceted nature of the songs. The singular "Sentiment" column may oversimplify the complex interplay of themes, emotions, and perspectives within each song, necessitating a more granular approach for a comprehensive interpretation of the songs' lyrical content.

4   Discussion

Using the quantification of the qualitative aspects of music, we can employ reinforcement learning to optimize song selection for listeners. We propose that these three metrics: identity sentiment, d_1 and d_2 across four identities: first person, second person, third person and relationship, can be used to define states and be mapped to a positive reward when the listener chooses to listen to a particular song. We propose forming the $Q - table$ based on serialization of the sentiment across these 12 columns, and updating the $Q - table$ based on the respective choice of the song with Eq. 5. We can utilize these dimensions as states, choice of music as actions and accurate choice as reward. With the RL algorithm, we can optimize the song selection based on where in the space does a particular song lie and accordingly choose it for the listener.

$$Q[action][state] = Q[action][state] + \qquad (5)$$
$$(1/N[action][state] * (R[action] - Q[action][state]))$$

5   Summary and Conclusions

Emotions are the fabric of our lives, allowing us to understand and navigate our experiences. Music, in particular, is deeply intertwined with our emotions, and we seek to uncover the emotional landscape of each musical piece through our methodology. To identify emotional hills and valleys through each musical piece, we identify three dimensions. The three dimensions consist of identity, setting, and sentiment. Following this, we employ the recency heuristic to ascertain the emotion of each identity, while also tracking the emotional trajectory of the song by evaluating the weighted difference between present and past, and future and present sentiments. Through this, we can determine if a song is uplifting for a given identity. Post splitting, we elicit what is the emotion of each identity using the recency heuristic. Additionally, we track the emotional trajectory of the song by measuring the difference between the present and past, and the present and future sentiment. Furthermore, this study has the potential to revolutionize emotion recognition and regulation by utilizing uplifting music that resonates with individual contexts. This can be utilizing our methodology for music recommendation system based on RL and sentiment analysis Moreover, the insights derived from this study can be applied to promote social good, such as in Assistive Technology for Listening, where music therapy has shown remarkable results in enhancing neural connections and providing relief to individuals suffering from mental illnesses [8].

6   Future Research

In future endeavors, the deltas derived from this study are envisioned to be instrumental in developing models for musical expectancy, shedding light on the intricate dynamics of emotional anticipation within music. This approach will unearth the various ways emotions are conveyed, interpreted, and internalized in the realm of music, offering a richer perspective on the emotional nuances and subtleties embedded within musical compositions.

To further enhance our understanding of music's emotional landscape, we plan to incorporate sophisticated data visualization techniques to delve deeper into the phenomenon of emotional contagion as elicited by music. Utilizing these techniques will render the multifaceted emotional interactions and resonances more discernible, offering detailed insights into the layers of emotions and their transmission through musical expressions.

Moreover, we aspire to expand our analytical scope beyond the initial identities, encompassing all entities-objects, places, people, and other elements-that humans forge relationships with. This broader perspective is crucial for portraying a comprehensive representation of relational dynamics within music, which, in turn, contributes to a more inclusive and elaborate exploration of the diverse relational sentiments depicted in musical narratives.

Additionally, there's a keen interest in exploring the roles and impacts of metaphors and symbolism within musical pieces. By deciphering the metaphorical and symbolic elements inherent in songs, we aim to uncover the deeper and often concealed meanings, revealing the intricate layers of emotional expressions and thematic profundities embedded within. Such an exploration will elucidate how these literary elements augment the overall emotional atmosphere of a piece and how they resonate with listeners, offering a more profound comprehension of the sophisticated interplay between the musical content and the emotional response it evokes.

In essence, our future research is aimed at fostering a holistic and detailed understanding of the thematic and emotional aspects of music by exploring various identities, relationships, emotions, and literary devices within musical narratives. The adoption of advanced visualization and modeling techniques will facilitate a meticulous examination of the emotional nuances and representations, thereby paving the way for enhanced insights into the intricate and diverse world of musical expression.

References

1. AZLyrics: AZLyrics - Song Lyrics from A to Z. https://www.azlyrics.com. Accessed 13 Apr 2020
2. Batcho, K.I.: Nostalgia and the emotional tone and content of song lyrics. Am. J. Psychol. **120**(3), 361–381 (2007)
3. Çano, E., Morisio, M.: Moodylyrics: a sentiment annotated lyrics dataset. In: Proceedings of the 2017 International Conference on Intelligent Systems, Metaheuristics & Swarm Intelligence, pp. 118–124 (2017)
4. Cross, I.: Music and communication in music psychology. Psychol. Music **42**(6), 809–819 (2014)
5. Fischmann, T., Russ, M.O., Leuzinger-Bohleber, M.: Trauma, dream, and psychic change in psychoanalyses: a dialog between psychoanalysis and the neurosciences. Front. Hum. Neurosci. **7**, 877 (2013)
6. Gigerenzer, G.: Introduction: taking heuristics seriously. In: The Behavioral Economics Guide 2016, pp. V–XI. Behavioral Science Solutions (2016)
7. Gilbert, C., Hutto, E.: Vader: A parsimonious rule-based model for sentiment analysis of social media text. In: Eighth International Conference on Weblogs and Social Media (ICWSM-14), vol. 81, p. 82 (2014). http://comp.social.gatech.edu/papers/icwsm14.vader.hutto.pdf. Accessed 13 Apr 2020
8. Gitlow, L.: Assistive technology and everyday technology used by people with serious mental illness. In: Assistive Technology Industry Association, *ATIA* (2015)

9. Hassin, R.R., Uleman, J.S., Bargh, J.A.: The New Unconscious. Oxford University Press, Cambridge (2004)
10. Hatfield, E., Cacioppo, J.T., Rapson, R.L.: Emotional contagion. Curr. Dir. Psychol. Sci. **2**(3), 96–100 (1993)
11. Hofmann, W., De Houwer, J., Perugini, M., Baeyens, F., Crombez, G.: Evaluative conditioning in humans: a meta-analysis. Psychol. Bull. **136**(3), 390 (2010)
12. Juslin, P.N., Barradas, G., Eerola, T.: From sound to significance: exploring the mechanisms underlying emotional reactions to music. Am. J. Psychol. **128**(3), 281–304 (2015)
13. Juslin, P.N.: Musical Emotions Explained: Unlocking the Secrets of Musical Affect. Oxford University Press, New York (2019)
14. Juslin, P.N., Laukka, P.: Communication of emotions in vocal expression and music performance: different channels, same code? Psychol. Bull. **129**(5), 770 (2003)
15. Juslin, P.N., Västfjäll, D.: Emotional responses to music: the need to consider underlying mechanisms. Behav. Brain Sci. **31**(5), 559–575 (2008)
16. McDermott, J., Schultz, A., Undurraga, E., Godoy, R.: Consonance preferences are not universal: indifference to dissonance among native amazonians. J. Acoust. Soc. Am. (JASA) **139**(4), 1994–1994 (2016)
17. Ntalampiras, S.: A transfer learning framework for predicting the emotional content of generalized sound events. J. Acoust. Soc. Am. **141**(3), 1694–1701 (2017)
18. Ntalampiras, S.: Emotional quantification of soundscapes by learning between samples. Multimedia Tools Appl. **79**(41–42), 30387–30395 (2020)
19. Pearson, J.: The human imagination: the cognitive neuroscience of visual mental imagery. Nat. Rev. Neurosci. **20**(10), 624–634 (2019)
20. Phatnani, K.S., Patil, H.A.: Music footprint recognition via sentiment, identity, and setting identification. Multimedia Tools Appl. 1–16 (2022)
21. Platel, H., Baron, J.C., Desgranges, B., Bernard, F., Eustache, F.: Semantic and episodic memory of music are subserved by distinct neural networks. Neuroimage **20**(1), 244–256 (2003)
22. Ramachandran, V., Blakeslee, S., Dolan, R.J.: Phantoms in the brain probing the mysteries of the human mind. Nature **396**(6712), 639–640 (1998)
23. Rudovic, O., Lee, J., Dai, M., Schuller, B., Picard, R.W.: Personalized machine learning for robot perception of affect and engagement in autism therapy. Sci. Rob. **3**(19), eaao6760 (2018)
24. Szalavitz, M.: Unbroken Brain: A Revolutionary New Way of Understanding Addiction. St. Martin's Press, New York (2016)
25. Thaut, M.H., McIntosh, G.C., Hoemberg, V.: Neurobiological foundations of neurologic music therapy: rhythmic entrainment and the motor system. Front. Psychol. **5**, 1185 (2015)
26. Tulving, E.: Episodic memory: from mind to brain. Ann. Rev. Psychol. **53**(1), 1–25 (2002)
27. Vuust, P., Heggli, O.A., Friston, K.J., Kringelbach, M.L.: Music in the brain. Nat. Rev. Neurosci. **23**(5), 287–305 (2022)
28. Walther, E., Nagengast, B., Trasselli, C.: Evaluative conditioning in social psychology: facts and speculations. Cogn. Emot. **19**(2), 175–196 (2005)
29. Wang, Q.J., Spence, C.: 'striking a sour note': assessing the influence of consonant and dissonant music on taste perception. Multisens. Res. **29**(1–3), 195–208 (2016)
30. Yang, X., Dong, Y., Li, J.: Review of data features-based music emotion recognition methods. Multimedia Syst. **24**(4), 365–389 (2018)

Analysis of Mandarin *vs* English Language for Emotional Voice Conversion

S. Uthiraa[(✉)] and Hemant A. Patil

Speech Research Lab, DA -IICT, Gandhinagar, Gujarat, India
{uthiraa_s,hemant_patil}@daiict.ac.in

Abstract. Emotional Voice Conversion (EVC) is a method to convert the emotional state of an utterance to another without changing the linguistic information and speaker's identity. Its application is enormous in human-machine interaction, development of emotional Text-To-Speech (TTS), etc. This study focuses on analyzing the characteristics of Mandarin and English language for EVC between these languages. Prosodic features, such as energy, fundamental or pitch frequency (F_0), duration, pauses/silences, and loudness are compared using several techniques, such as narrowband spectrograms, Root Mean Square Energy (RMSE), and Zero-Crossing Rate (ZCR). Teager Energy Operator (TEO) based features are studied to analyze the energy profile of emotions. The Emotional Speech Dataset (ESD) is used in this work. Experiments were performed on 5 emotions, namely, anger, happiness, neutral, sad, and surprise. Results showed that tonal language (i.e., Mandarin) has steep and multiple fluctuations in F_0 contour as it is pitch-dependent, as compared to the stress-time language (English), which had less F_0 fluctuations, and is stable for the most duration of the sentence. Loudness and silences are also different in the two languages. These findings may serve as important cues for EVC task.

Keywords: Emotional Voice Conversion · Emotional Speech Database (ESD) · Narrowband Spectrogram · Fundamental Frequency · Teager Energy Operator

1 Introduction

Communication, "the mode for transferring, sharing, and receiving information", which is performed by either verbal, non-verbal or visual means. Language, "a structured system of communication", conveyed through speech (spoken), writing or signs. In this paper, we focus on the spoken aspect of language. In this era, where population and technology is increasing rapidly, communication among and between them is essential. Language plays its role well for human interaction as well as for human-machine interaction. Moreover, language is the engine of cultivation and human speech is its most powerful form.

Voice Transformation (VT) aims at changing one or more aspects of a speech signal while preserving its linguistic information. Voice Conversion (VC) aims at

© The Author(s), under exclusive license to Springer Nature Switzerland AG 2023
A. Karpov et al. (Eds.): SPECOM 2023, LNAI 14339, pp. 295–306, 2023.
https://doi.org/10.1007/978-3-031-48312-7_24

changing *source* speaker's voice in such a way that, it sounds as if the *target* speaker has spoken that sentence [7]. In this context, Emotional Voice Conversion (EVC) aims to convert the emotional state of the utterance, while preserving the linguistic and speaker information [14]. This paper focuses on analysis of emotions in Mandarin *vs.* English in the context of EVC as it has significant application in human-machine interaction [9], and aids at developing emotional Text-To-Speech (TTS).

The earlier work on EVC dates back to around 2003 [5], where neutral speech was converted to other emotions, such as joy, anger, happiness, etc. For emotion recognition, one of the prominent features is prosodic feature extraction, which includes tone, rhythm, intonation, energy, duration, fundamental frequency (F_0), and loudness parameters [10]. For this paper, we use prosodic features, such as energy, loudness, F_0 to compare the emotions produced in Mandarin and English languages. This feature is selected as Mandarin is known to be a *tonal* language and English is a stress-timed language and thus, prosodic features will aid in its analysis [12].

In this paper, we analyze five emotions, namely, anger, happy, neutral, sad, and surprise in English and Mandarin language using narrowband spectrograms, F_0, Root Mean Square Energy (RMSE) and Zero-Crossing Rate (ZCR) to investigate prosodic parameters that are essential and more significant for emotional voice conversion between languages. Observations indicate that RMS and ZCR values can be used for EVC between languages.

The rest of the paper is organized as follows: In Sect. 2, we discuss the proposed work. Section 3 gives the details of the experimental setup. Section 4 presents the analysis of the results. Section 5 concludes the paper along with potential future research directions.

2   Proposed Work

Several languages in Southeast Asia and Africa are tonal languages, where pitch or F_0 differences are used to differentiate meanings of words or to convey grammatical distinctions. In contrast, English is a stress-timed language, i.e., in this language, the tone is used to convey an attitude or change a statement to a question, however, it does not affect the meaning of individual words [1].

In the baseline paper [13], EVC was performed in the same language, i.e., English neutral was converted to English sad or happy. The analysis presented in this paper is useful for conversion between languages and between emotions. In this paper, we analyze the loudness parameter using RMSE, voiced and unvoiced components using ZCR, and F_0 and its harmonics using narrowband spectrograms.

2.1   Spectrographic Analysis

Spectrograms are a visual representation of acoustic signals with time (X-axis), frequency (Y-axis), and amplitude measures in parameter representation. Pauses and harmonic components are also seen. In this paper, we study the narrowband spectrograms (as they give good frequency resolution, i.e., show pitch source harmonics as horizontal striations, useful for tonal language analysis), and F_0 of English and Mandarin sentences spoken in 5 emotions, namely, anger, happy, neutral, sad, and surprise. The energy distribution, pitch source harmonics, and silences are compared. Figures 1 and 2 shows the F_0 changes, plot, and spectrograms of female speakers uttering the same sentence in English and Mandarin, respectively.

2.2 Root Mean Square (RMS) Energy

RMS for speech signal is a crucial acoustic cue for target speech perception [11]. It is the squared signal value (amplitude), averaged over time, and its square root is calculated. In particular,

$$RMS_t = \sqrt{1/K \sum_{n=t.K}^{(t+1)(K-1)} |s(n)^2|},$$ (1)

where $s(n)^2$ is the energy of nth sample, then we sum the energies of all the samples at time t. To get the mean, it is then divided by frame size, K.

This feature has significant applications in audio segmentation and music genre classification. In this paper, we plot the RMS values of audio to find the loudness measure. Amplitude envelope (AE) can also be used to measure loudness, however, RMS is preferred as it is less sensitive to outliers than the AE. In addition, it gives us perceived loudness, i.e., the way our ear perceives loudness. In Fig. 3, each plot depicts the RMS values of the same sentences spoken in English (yellow colored) and Mandarin (Red colored) by 2 female (1 for English and 1 for Mandarin) speakers in 5 emotions, namely, anger, happy, neutral, sad, and surprise, respectively.

2.3 Zero-Crossing Rate (ZCR)

ZCR is "the rate at which a signal changes from positive to zero to negative or from negative to zero to positive". Historically, it is known to have a correlation with formants, thus, helpful for speech perception [6]. Its expressed as-

$$ZCR_t = (1/2). \sum_{n=t.K}^{(t+1)(K-1)} |sgn(s(n)) - sgn(s(n+1)),$$ (2)

where s(n) and s(n+1) represent the amplitude at sample n and its consecutive amplitude sample, respectively.

It is an useful measure to recognize percussive (random ZCR) *vs.* pitched sounds (stable ZCR) [4]. For this work, we use ZCR for monotonic pitch estimation and for analyzing the voiced and unvoiced segments of audio signal [3]. Figure 4 shows the ZCR plot for 2 females (1 for English and 1 for Mandarin) speaking the same sentence in both languages with 5 emotions, namely, anger, happy, neutral, sad, and surprise, respectively.

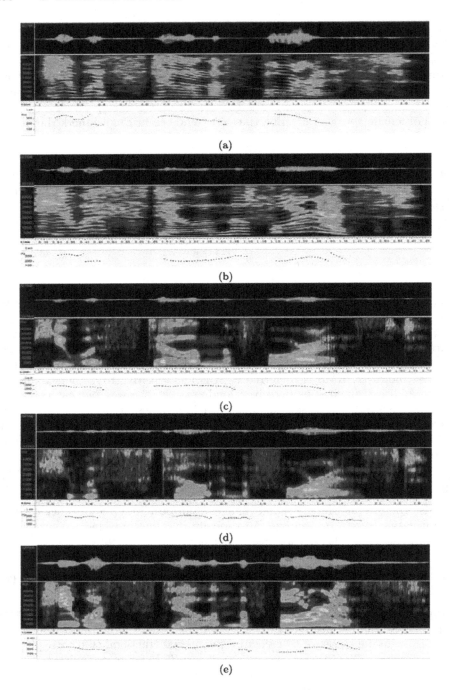

Fig. 1. Time-domain signal, narrowband spectrograms, F_0 contour of English sentences by female speakers in 5 emotions: (a) anger, (b) happy, (c) neutral, (d) sad, and (e) surprise.

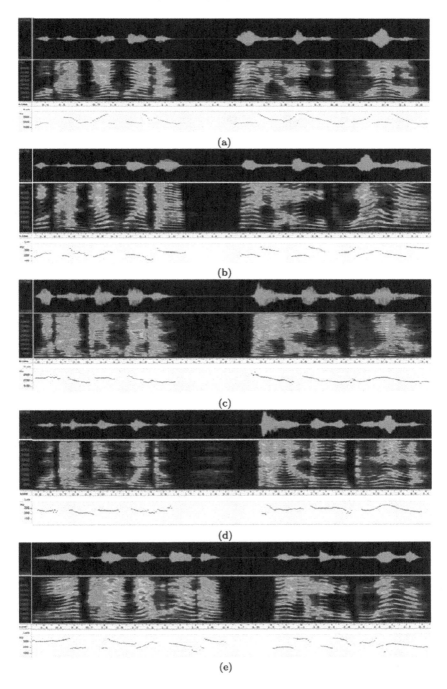

Fig. 2. Time-domain signal, narrowband spectrograms, F_0 contour of Mandarin sentences by female speakers in 5 emotions: (a) anger, (b) happy, (c) neutral, (d) sad, and (e) surprise.

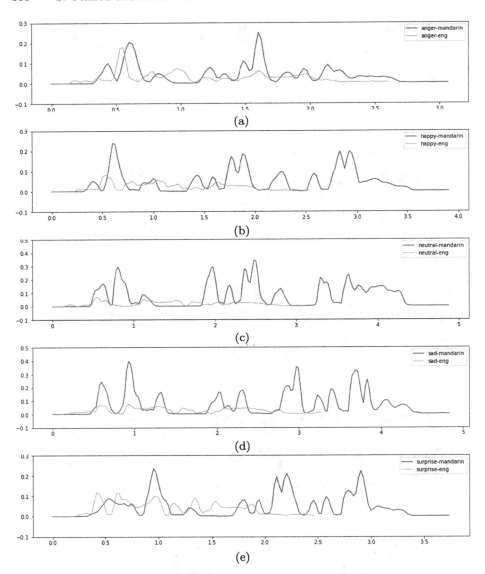

Fig. 3. RMS for Mandarin *vs.* English for a sentences in (a) anger, (b) happy, (c) neutral, (d) sad, and (e) surprise by female speakers.

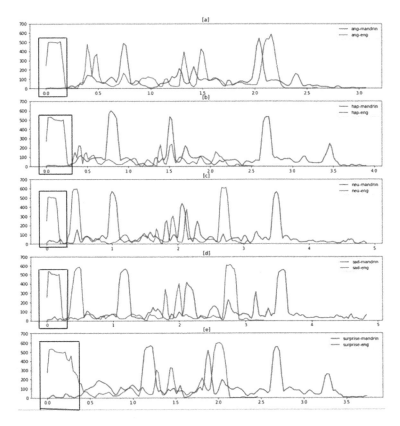

Fig. 4. ZCR for Mandarin *vs.* English for a sentences in [a] anger, [b] happy, [c] neutral, [d] sad, and [e] surprise by female speakers. The box at the beginning of the plot indicates the whisper sound —h— in "he" uttered.

2.4   Teager Energy Operator (TEO)

Speech is produced by non-linear, vortex airflow interaction in the vocal tract. A stressful situation affects the muscle tension of the speaker which results in an alteration of the airflow during the production of the sound [2]. This is captured *via* TEO, in particular, $\Psi\{x(n)\} = x^2(n) - x(n+1)x(n-1)$, where $\Psi\{\}$ is the Teager Energy Operator (TEO), and $x(n)$ is the discrete-time signal. TEO features are extensively used in distinguishing genuine *vs.* replay speech in spoofing. In this paper, we use TEO to analyze the glottal closure impact, i.e., bumps within the glottal cycle are studied [8]. Figures 5 and 6 have the TEO profile of a female speaker uttering the same sentence with 5 emotions in English and Mandarin, respectively, with the X-axis representing frames and the Y-axis, amplitude. Figures 5 and 6 show that the TEO gives a running estimate of the signal's energy w.r.t. time. Further, the TEO profile seems to vary across emotions for a particular language (here, either Mandarin or English).

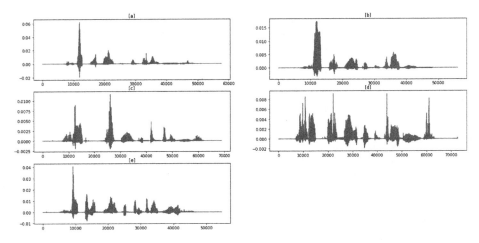

Fig. 5. TEO profile of a female speaker uttering an English sentence in [a] anger, [b] happy, [c] neutral, [d] sad, and [e] surprise.

3 Experimental Results

3.1 Dataset Used

In this paper, we have used a recently developed ESD dataset [13]. It consists of 350 parallel utterances spoken by 10 native English (5 female and 5 male), and 10 native Mandarin speakers (5 female and 5 male) speakers. The emotions captured in it are - anger, happy, neutral, sad, and surprise, whose audio is sampled at 16 kHz. This dataset is chosen as it is a relatively large-scale, multi-speaker and publicly available dataset with good recording conditions [14], thus, making the analysis relatively accurate.

3.2 Experimental Results

All the results mentioned are generalized results which were taken and compared with atleast 5 sentences for each emotion, but for the paper readability, results using only 1 sentence (from female speakers) are given. The analysis for male speakers was similar to that of female speakers, but the distinction between emotions was clearer for females than males. The detailed analysis of spectrograms (shown in Figs. 1 and 2) is presented in Fig. 7. We infer that high energy contents are seen in all 5 emotions of Mandarin speech and thus, indicating that Mandarin speech is usually louder in comparison to English speech. A significant difference seen in spectrograms is that all English sentences with 5 emotions had energy components present only at the higher frequency at the end of a sentence, which wasn't seen in any spectrograms for Mandarin. The width between the two consecutive horizontal striations in the narrowband spectrogram gives pitch

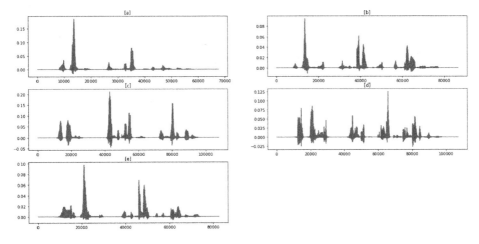

Fig. 6. TEO profile of a female speaker uttering a Mandarin sentence in [a] anger, [b] happy, [c] neutral, [d] sad, and [e] surprise.

(the way the auditory system perceives frequency) information, which is higher in Mandarin than in English. The silences were seen more in Mandarin than in English.

The study of F_0 contour is represented in the form of a boxplot (which gives the spread or variance of F_0) in Fig. 8. It is noted that neutral emotion has the least spread in both languages and the highest spread is seen in emotions; surprise and anger in English and Mandarin speech, respectively. Almost no outliers are seen for Mandarin speech, i.e., there is not much difference between the F_0 values as compared to English. Another distinction seen is that the median values for all emotions in Mandarin are higher than that in English. These conclude that the F_0 contours are at higher frequencies, and with wide fluctuations for Mandarin speech.

In the RMS plots (Fig. 3), it is observed that all the emotional sentences spoken in Mandarin has significant fluctuations in peaks compared to the English statements. Anger and surprise emotions have similar peaks in both the languages. Neutral and sad sentences in English have almost no variations in peaks. Happy in Mandarin has broader peaks. These results state that Mandarin sentences are perceived louder (as have more energy content, as seen from spectrograms) than the corresponding English sentences.

Characteristics	Anger	Happy	Neutral	Sad	Surprise
Energy Content	High energy content is not uniformly distributed in English as compared to Mandarin.	High energy content is more prominent in lower frequencies in Mandarin but also seen at higher frequencies in the beginning of the sentence in English.	Very less high energy content in English but in Mandarin, high energy content is present.	Very less high energy content in English. In Mandarin, high-energy content seen towards the end of sentence.	Almost similar high energy content seen in both English and Mandarin.
Width	Width between harmonics is higher in Mandarin than in English.	Width between harmonics is more in Mandarin than in English.	Width between harmonics is more in Mandarin than in English.	Width between harmonics is more in Mandarin than in English.	Width between harmonics is more in Mandarin than in English.
Pauses	Clear and distinct in Mandarin than in English.	More are distinct pauses seen in Mandarin than in English.	Clear and low duration pauses in English. In Mandarin, clear and higher duration pauses seen.	Similar pauses seen in both English and Mandarin except for 1 long pause in Mandarin.	Distinct pauses seen in Mandarin.

Fig. 7. Analysis of narrowband spectrograms for English *vs.* Mandarin emotions.

The ZCR plots shown in Fig. 4, give the idea on percussive *vs.* pitched sounds. We can consider two extreme cases of spectral energy density, i.e., the low frequency and high frequency regions. It is observed that ZCR peaks are less in lower frequency regions and high in higher frequency regions of spectrograms. ZCR peaks of Mandarin are less than that of English as tonal sounds are pitch-dependent and have voiced speech as compared to English, which has unvoiced and whisper elements (beginning of the sentence, as shown in Fig. 4 for the sentence analyzed, and thus, proving that ZCR peaks are high for unvoiced sounds in comparison to their voiced counterpart).

The TEO plots in Figs. 5 and 6 show that Mandarin sentences have higher energy profiles (peaks reach higher amplitudes) than English sentences. This is because a higher pitch leads to higher loudness and thus, higher amplitude.

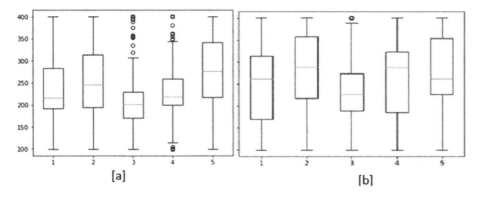

Fig. 8. Boxplot of F_0 contour of female speaker uttering an [a] English and [b] Mandarin sentence in [1] anger, [2] happy, [3] neutral, [4] sad, and [5] surprise.

4   Summary and Conclusion

In this study, we analyze a tonal language (Mandarin), and a stress-timed language (English) using prosodic features, such as energy, F_0, loudness, and TEO-based features. Our analysis indicate, Mandarin language has higher F_0 fluctuations due to variations in pitch, are louder, and have higher energy profiles than English language. Therefore, for EVC, RMS, and ZCR features can be used to maintain the speaker's identity. It would be interesting to analyze how RMS and ZCR features would work if, replaced with F_0 in the baseline paper [13] for EVC. The study presented in this paper may help in analyzing the confusion matrices that are obtained from the SER task. Future work includes using these results in classifiers for performing EVC in the same and in multi-languages and developing more datasets w.r.t. EVC.

Acknowledgements. The authors are thankful to the Ministry of Electronics and Information Technology (MeitY), New Delhi, Government of India, for sponsoring the project, "National Language Translation Mission (NLTM): BHASHINI with the objective of Building Assistive Speech Technologies for the Challenged (Grant ID: 11(1)2022-HCC (TDIL)).

References

1. An introduction to Tonal languages. https://ceas.sas.upenn.edu/sites/default/files/. Accessed 9 Sep 2022
2. Alex, S.B., Mary, L., Babu, B.P.: Attention and feature selection for automatic speech emotion recognition using utterance and syllable-level prosodic features. Circuits Syst. Signal Process. **39**(11), 5681–5709 (2020)
3. Bachu, R., Kopparthi, S., Adapa, B., Barkana, B.: Separation of voiced and unvoiced using zero crossing rate and energy of the speech signal. In: American Society for Engineering Education (ASEE) Zone Conference Proceedings, pp. 1–7. American Society for Engineering Education (2008)

4. Brata, I., Darmawan, I.: Comparative study of pitch detection algorithm to detect traditional balinese music tones with various raw materials. J. Phys.: Conf. Ser. **1722**, 012071 (2021)

5. Kawanami, H., Iwami, Y., Toda, T., Saruwatari, H., Shikano, K.: GMM-based voice conversion applied to emotional speech synthesis. In: 8th European Conference on Speech Communication and Technology, EUROSPEECH 2003 - INTERSPEECH 2003, Geneva, Switzerland (2003)

6. Licklider, J.C.R., Pollack, I.: Effects of differentiation, integration, and infinite peak clipping upon the intelligibility of speech. J. Acoust. Soc. Am. **20**(1), 42–51 (1948)

7. Mohammadi, S.H., Kain, A.: An overview of voice conversion systems. Speech Commun. **88**, 65–82 (2017)

8. Patil, H.A., Parhi, K.K.: Development of TEO phase for speaker recognition. In: 2010 International Conference on Signal Processing and Communications (SPCOM), pp. 1–5. IISc Bangalore, India (2010)

9. Pittermann, J., Pittermann, A., Minker, W.: Handling Emotions in Human-computer Dialogues. Springer (2010). https://doi.org/10.1007/978-90-481-3129-7

10. Swain, M., Routray, A., Kabisatpathy, P.: Databases, features and classifiers for speech emotion recognition: a review. Int. J. Speech Technol. **21**(1), 93–120 (2018). https://doi.org/10.1007/s10772-018-9491-z

11. Wang, L., Wu, E.X., Chen, F.: Contribution of RMS-level-based speech segments to target speech decoding under noisy conditions. In: INTERSPEECH, pp. 121–124, Shangai China (2020)

12. Zhou, K., Sisman, B., Li, H.: Transforming spectrum and prosody for emotional voice conversion with non-parallel training data. arXiv preprint arXiv:2002.00198 (2020)

13. Zhou, K., Sisman, B., Liu, R., Li, H.: Seen and unseen emotional style transfer for voice conversion with a new emotional speech dataset. In: ICASSP 2021–2021 IEEE International Conference on Acoustics, Speech and Signal Processing (ICASSP), Toronto, Canada, pp. 920–924 (2021)

14. Zhou, K., Sisman, B., Liu, R., Li, H.: Emotional voice conversion: theory, databases and ESD. Speech Commun. **137**, 1–18 (2022)

Audio DeepFake Detection Employing Multiple Parametric Exponential Linear Units

Md Shahidul Alam, Abderrahim Fathan, and Jahangir Alam[✉]

Computer Research Institute of Montreal, Montreal, Quebec H3N 1M3, Canada
{abderrahim.fathan,jahangir.alam}@crim.ca

Abstract. The main objective of the audio deepfake detection system is to find out the artifacts within the input speech caused by the speech synthesis or voice conversion process. Recent trends in deepfake detection is to employ deep learning architectures in an end-to-end fashion to discriminate between bonafide and spoof speech signals. In deep learning, activation functions play an important role in deciding whether the neuron's input to the network is relevant or not in the process of prediction/classification. In this work, we propose to employ a Multiple Parametric Exponential Linear Unit (MPELU) activation function with the Residual Network (ResNet) architecture. The aim of the MPELU activation function is to generalize and unify the rectified and exponential linear units. Furthermore, we adopt an Attention Rectified Linear Unit (AReLU) which through the addition of element-wise sign-based attention mechanism with a ReLU module focuses on the enhancement of positive elements and a suppression of negative ones in a data-adaptive manner. The proposed frameworks was experimented on the logical access (LA) task of ASVSpoof2019 dataset, and outperformed the systems using the standard non-learnable and learnable activation functions.

Keywords: Audio deepfake detection · Activation function · MPELU · AReLU · ASVSpoof2019 · Logical access · ResNet

1 Introduction

In the past decade, attributed to the widespread deployment of smart devices, automatic speaker verification (ASV) has become an essential technology for user authentication. The ASV system takes the users speech as input and determines whether the user is enrolled to the system or not. In recent years, with the advent of deep learning, the capabilities of computing systems have been revolutionized, which led to a dramatic improvement in the speech synthesis and voice conversion technologies. As a result of which modern text-to-speech synthesis (TTS) and voice conversion (VC) techniques are capable of generating realistic

---

M. S. Alam, A. Fathan and J. Alam—These authors contributed equally to this work.

© The Author(s), under exclusive license to Springer Nature Switzerland AG 2023
A. Karpov et al. (Eds.): SPECOM 2023, LNAI 14339, pp. 307–321, 2023.
https://doi.org/10.1007/978-3-031-48312-7_25

fakes of human voices, also denoted as audio deepfakes or spoofs or spoofing attacks. Though there are many ethical applications of this technology there is a risk for its malicious use, e.g., cloning of a target speaker's voice for the purpose of (i) spreading misinformation (ii) creating false evidence (iii) gaining illegitimate access to/fooling an ASV system. Reliable detection of audio deepfakes or spoofing attacks can help mitigate such risks and is therefore an active area of research.

In order to countermeasure these audio deepfakes, various research were conducted to discriminate the synthetic speech samples from the genuine (bona fide) samples. The main objective for building a reliable voice spoofing countermeasure or audio deepfake detection system is to detect the artifacts from the synthetic speech spectrum. To achieve this, many attempts were made to exploit the techniques which have shown stable performance in the speaker recognition task. In the case of logical access (LA) spoofing detection task the most effective countermeasures are the frame-level acoustic features extracted at 10 ms intervals and designed to detect artifacts in the spoofed speech. Previously, the standard Gaussian Mixture Model (GMM) classifier in combination with frame-level acoustic [1,2,24,25,27,33,34] or deep features [3] was the most widely adopted spoofing detection approach [20,27,31,34]. But the recent trends in audio deepfake detection is to employ deep learning architectures in an end-to-end fashion on the top of raw signal/hand-crafted features to distinguish genuine speech from spoof speech signals [6,16,20–22,26,32,36,37]. Frequency masking-based on the fly data augmentation with the ResNet network using large margin cosine loss (LMCL) was introduced in [6]. In [37], one class softmax loss with ResNet18 architecture was proposed. Feature genuinization based light CNN system was presented in [36]. In order to improve generalization of anti-spoofing systems to unseen test data, several variants of softmax loss were also adopted [6,37]. Transfer learning approach with a ResNet has also been explored for spoofing detection task [26]. Recently, graph neural networks (GNNs) and RawNet have also been adopted as the backbone network in the deepfake detection task and achieved satisfactory performances [5,12,30,32]. Although these end-to-end systems outperformed the classical statistical-based spoofing systems (e.g., GMM, i-vector), their results suggest that there is still more room for improvement.

In neural network-based problem solving, the activation functions (AFs) play a very important role as it introduces non-linearity in the network and helps to learn abstract & discriminative features through nonlinear transformations [8]. As the selection of an activation function can affect the ability of the neural network to extract relevant information from the input data, diverse variants of the conventional rectified linear unit (ReLU) functions were proposed. For example, in [4], a trainable attention-based activation was introduced to efficiently focus on the relevant regions of the feature map. In [13], an investigative study on the effect of various AFs was presented and proposed to employ the activation ensemble to exploit the complementary information propagated through different activation functions.

In this work, with a view to boost end-to-end detection performance by effectively capturing the artifacts pertinent to the deepfakes within the given speech spectrogram, we propose to adopt a multiple parametric exponential linear unit (MPELU) activation function (AF), which aims to generalize and unify the rectified and exponential linear units AFs.

To evaluate the performance of the proposed scheme, we carry out a set of experiments using the ASVSpoof 2019 logical access dataset. The experimental results show that the MPELU-based end-to-end system outperforms the other variants of AF-based systems.

The contributions of this paper are as follows:

- We propose to employ MPELU for improving the performance of the end-to-end deepfake detection system.
- We also adopt an attentive activation function, more specifically attention rectified linear unit (AReLU), which by means of attention mechanism can help the countermeasure system to focus on the features related to the spoofing artifacts.
- We carry out an investigative study on the influence of different activation functions in the deepfake countermeasure task.
- We compare the performance of the proposed MPELU-based end-to-end system with other widely used AF-based end-to-end and conventional approaches.
- Although MPELU activation function was first proposed for computer vision application in [17], from the best of our knowledge, this is the first attempt on using the MPELU in speech processing applications, more specifically, for audio deepfake detection task.

2 Our Proposed System

2.1 End-to-End Deepfake Detection System

Most deep learning based spoofing detection systems employ deep neural architectures, such as Residual Network (ResNet), on top of hand-crafted/learned features for capturing more discriminative local descriptors which are then aggregated to generate final fixed dimensional utterance-level embeddings. The embeddings are then fed into a classifier which decides whether the input audio is a deepfake attack or genuine. Conventionally, a two-stage approach was popularly adopted, where the classifier (e.g., support vector machine (SVM)) and the embedding extraction network are trained separately. Recently, in order to mutually optimize the decision hyperplane and the embedding feature space, various end-to-end approaches [6,16,20–22,26,32,36,37] were proposed in the past few years, where the neural classifier is trained jointly with the embedding extraction network.

The proposed model also adopts the end-to-end framework for voice anti-spoofing as depicted in Fig. 1, which is composed of 2 networks: an embedding

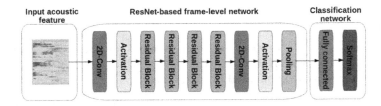

Fig. 1. The general architecture of the ResNet-based end-to-end deepfake detection system.

network and a classification network. For the embedding network, we experimented with one TDNN (Time Delay Neural Network)-based and two ResNet-based architectures, which have shown competitive performance in the speaker verification and image classification tasks:

– TDNN: also known as the x-vector architecture, which is composed of 5 TDNN layers. More information on the architecture can be found in [28].
– ResNet-18: It is an 18 layers deep convolutional network, which is composed of 4 residual blocks.
– SE-ResNet-18: a variant of the ResNet-18, where a squeeze-and-excitation (SE) block [11] is applied at the end of each non-identity branch of residual block to significantly decrease the computational cost of the system. More precisely, we utilize the SE-ResNet-18, which is an 18 layers deep convolutional network composed of 4 residual blocks. Table 1 presents a more detailed network architecture of SE-ResNet-18.

To aggregate the frame-level output of the ResNet, an attention statistics pooling layer is incorporated where the weighted first and second order (i.e., standard deviation) moments are pooled together across the temporal dimension [6,20–22,37] to obtain an utterance-level representation. The pooled statistics are then fed into a neural classifier, which consists of a fully-connected layer and a 2-dimensional softmax layer, where each softmax node represents the bona fide and deepfake classes, respectively.

The end-to-end system is trained via one-class softmax objective, which can be formulated as [37]:

$$L_{OCS} = -\frac{1}{N} \sum_{i=1}^{N} log(1 + e^{k(m_{y_i} - \hat{W}_0 \hat{\omega}_i)(-1)^{y_i}}) \tag{1}$$

where k is the scale factor, $\omega_i \in R^D$ and $y_i \in \{0,1\}$ are the D-dimensional embedding vector and label of the ith sample respectively. N is the mini-batch size and m_{y_i} defines the compactness margin for class label y_i. The larger is the margin, the more compact the embeddings will be. W_0 is the weight vector of our target class embeddings. Both $\hat{W}_0$ and $\hat{\omega}_i$ are normalizations of W_0 and ω_i respectively.

Table 1. The weight configuration of each layer in the SE-ResNet-18 end-to-end deep-fake detection system. In this table, ResBlock indicates the Residual Block component in Fig. 1 and L is the length of the 60-dimensional input feature (e.g., LFCC) sequence.

Layer	SE-ResNet-18		Output
Input	-		$1 \times 60 \times L$
2D-Conv	9×9, 16, stride (3, 1)		$16 \times 18 \times L$
ResBlock	$\begin{bmatrix} \text{2D-Conv } 3 \times 3, 64 \\ \text{2D-Conv } 3 \times 3, 64 \\ \text{FC } 64 \times 4 \\ \text{FC } 4 \times 64 \end{bmatrix}$	$\times 2$, stride 1	$64 \times 18 \times L$
ResBlock	$\begin{bmatrix} \text{2D-Conv } 3 \times 3, 128 \\ \text{2D-Conv } 3 \times 3, 128 \\ \text{FC } 128 \times 8 \\ \text{FC } 8 \times 128 \end{bmatrix}$	$\times 2$, stride 2	$128 \times 9 \times \frac{L}{2}$
ResBlock	$\begin{bmatrix} \text{2D-Conv } 3 \times 3, 256 \\ \text{2D-Conv } 3 \times 3, 256 \\ \text{FC } 256 \times 16 \\ \text{FC } 16 \times 256 \end{bmatrix}$	$\times 2$, stride 2	$256 \times 5 \times \frac{L}{4}$
ResBlock	$\begin{bmatrix} \text{2D-Conv } 3 \times 3, 512 \\ \text{2D-Conv } 3 \times 3, 512 \\ \text{FC } 512 \times 32 \\ \text{FC } 32 \times 512 \end{bmatrix}$	$\times 2$, stride 2	$512 \times 3 \times \frac{L}{8}$
2D-Conv	3×3, 256, stride 1		$256 \times 1 \times \frac{L}{8}$
Pooling	attentive statistics pooling		512
FC	512×256		256
Softmax	256×2		2

2.2 Multiple Parametric Exponential Linear Unit

One of the most popular activation functions is Rectified Linear Unit (ReLU) [23], which is a piecewise-linear function that outputs zero for all negative inputs. The standard ReLU activation function is formulated as:

$$f_{ReLU}(x_i) = \begin{cases} x_i & \text{if } x_i > 0 \\ 0 & \text{otherwise,} \end{cases} \tag{2}$$

where x_i is the input value. Since ReLU sets the same value (e.g., zero) to all negative inputs This prevents the network to learn from negative input representations and in a more extreme case, causes certain network parameters to be deactivated during training. To overcome this problem, various ReLU variants were proposed, where most of them attempt to relax the non-linear output of the ReLU function. The ELU (exponential linear unit) is one such variant that utilizes an exponential function for the negative value and, is formulated as:

$$f_{ELU}(x_i) = \begin{cases} x_i & \text{if } x_i > 0 \\ r(e^{x_i} - 1) & \text{otherwise,} \end{cases} \tag{3}$$

where r is a fixed parameter.

In this work, we propose to employ a new activation function, denoted as Multiple Parametric ELU (MPELU), for audio deepfake detection that covers the solution space of both the rectified and exponential linear units. MPELU is a generalization of ELU and is expressed mathematically as:

$$f_{MPELU}(x_i) = \begin{cases} x_i & \text{if } x_i > 0 \\ a(e^{bx_i} - 1)) & \text{otherwise,} \end{cases} \tag{4}$$

where a and b are learnable (channel shared) parameters, b is constrained to be greater than zero, and i is the index of input x. By tweaking the value of b MPELU can switch between the rectified and exponential linear units. More specifically, if b is set to a small number e.g., $b = 0.01$, the negative part of MPELU approximates to a linear function. Conversely, if b takes a large value e.g., $b = 1.0$, the negative part of MPELU is a non-linear function. As depicted in Fig. 2, the other activation functions can be special cases of MPELU, for example, with $a = 0$, MPELU is reduced to ReLU. If $a = 25.6302$ and $b = 0.01$, MPELU approximates to Parametric ReLU (PReLU); When $a = b = 1$, MPELU becomes ELU. We can see that the flexible form of MPELU makes it cover the solution space of its special cases, allowing it to obtain more powerful representation.

2.3   Attention Rectified Linear Unit (AReLU)

AReLU is a variant of the ReLU function, which employs the attention mechanism to boost the contribution of relevant input features while suppressing the irrelevant ones [4]. More specifically, the AReLU is a combination of the standard ReLU and the element-wise sign-based attention (ELSA). Given input x_i, which is the ith element of feature X, the AReLU is fomulated as follows:

$$f_{AReLU}(x_i) = f_{ReLU}(x_i) + g_{att}(x_i, \alpha, \beta) \tag{5}$$

$$= \begin{cases} C(\alpha)x_i & \text{if } x_i < 0 \\ (1 + \sigma(\beta))x_i & \text{otherwise,} \end{cases} \tag{6}$$

where α and β are learnable scaling parameters, C is the clamping operation which restricts the value to $[0.01, 0.99]$, and σ is the sigmoid function. While the β parameter amplifies the positive elements, the α parameter suppresses the negative elements. Unlike the standard ReLU which has a fixed scaling parameters, since the parameters of AReLU are learned in a data-adaptive fashion, it can effectively learn and emphasize the salient elements (e.g., artifacts caused by the spoofing) for deepfake countermeasure.

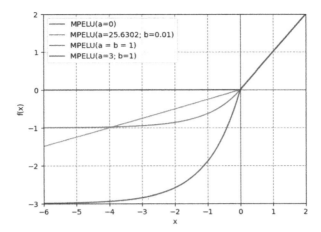

Fig. 2. Special cases of the MPELU activation function for different values of a & b. If we set $a = 0$, MPELU is reduced to ReLU, if $a = 25.6302$ and $b = 0.01$, MPELU approximates to Parametric ReLU (PReLU) and MPELU becomes ELU when $a = b = 1$.

In order to enable the end-to-end spoofing detection system to efficiently capture the artifacts within the input spectrogram, we used AReLU (or MPELU) as the very first activation of the frame-level network, which is placed right after the first 2D-Conv layer. Moreover, to ensure that the extracted embedding reflects the relevant elements of the frame-level representations, we also used AReLU (or MPELU) as the last activation of the frame-level network, which is prior to the pooling layer. In our experiments, we have used shared AReLU (or MPELU) parameters for the first and last layers.

3   Some Variants of ReLU Activation Function

In order to compare the performance of MPELU- amd AReLU-based end-to-end deepfake detection systems we consider ReLU, ELU, several variants of ReLU activation functions.

3.1   Leaky Rectified Linear Unit (LeakyReLU)

The LeakyReLU activation function modified the standard ReLU formulation by introducing a small slope to the negative input. The formulation for LeakyReLU is as follows [18]:

$$f_{LeakyReLU}(x_i) = \begin{cases} x_i & \text{if } x_i > 0 \\ \gamma x_i & \text{otherwise,} \end{cases} \qquad (7)$$

where γ is a fixed parameter. In this work, we set $\gamma = 0.2$.

3.2 Learnable Leaky Rectified Linear Unit (LLeakyReLU)

The LLeakyReLU activation function is a variant of the LeakyReLU, but with a learnable scaling parameter [19].

$$f_{LLeakyReLU}(x_i) = \begin{cases} hx_i & \text{if } x_i > 0 \\ 0.1\,hx_i & \text{otherwise,} \end{cases} \tag{8}$$

where h is a learnable parameter.

3.3 Randomized Leaky Rectified Linear Units (RReLU)

The RReLU is defined similarly to the LeakyReLU as follows:

$$f_{RReLU}(x_i) = \begin{cases} x_i & \text{if } x_i > 0 \\ a_i x_i & \text{otherwise,} \end{cases} \tag{9}$$

where a_i is randomly sampled from $unif(l, u)$ while training, and l and u is fixed parameters. When testing, the a_i is set to the mean of $unif(l, u)$, which is $\frac{l+u}{2}$. The initial value for l, and u were set to 0.125, 0.333, respectively in our experiments.

3.4 Parametric Rectified Linear Unit (PReLU)

The PReLU activation function is formulated similarly to the LeakyReLU, but uses a learnable parameter for the negative parameter. PReLU is expressed mathematically as [9]:

$$f_{PReLU}(x_i) = \begin{cases} x_i & \text{if } x_i > 0 \\ \xi_i x_i & \text{otherwise,} \end{cases} \tag{10}$$

where ξ_i is a learnable parameter. As an initial value, we set $\xi_i = 0.25$.

3.5 Parametric Exponential Linear Unit (PELU)

The PELU activation function is a variant of the ELU, but with learnable parameters [35].

$$f_{PELU}(x_i) = \begin{cases} \frac{k}{v}x_i & \text{if } x_i > 0 \\ k(e^{\frac{x_i}{v}} - 1) & \text{otherwise,} \end{cases} \tag{11}$$

where k and v are learnable parameters.

3.6 Scaled Exponential Linear Unit (SELU)

The SELU activation function is similar to ELU, that induce self-normalization with a scaling factor [15].

$$f_{SELU}(x_i) = c \cdot \begin{cases} x_i & \text{if } x_i > 0 \\ d(e^{x_i} - 1) & \text{otherwise,} \end{cases} \tag{12}$$

where c and d are fixed parameters.

3.7   Gaussian Error Linear Unit (GELU)

Unlike the activation functions mentioned above, the GELU is not based on the ReLU formulation where different functions are applied to the positive and degative input values. Instead, motivated by the success of stochastic regularizers (e.g., layer noise, dropout [29]), GELU adopts the cumulative distribution function for Gaussian distribution, which is a non-convex, non-monotonic function [10].

$$f_{GELU}(x_i) = x_i \Phi(x_i) = 0.5x_i(1 + tanh(\sqrt{\frac{2}{\pi}}(x_i + 0.44715x_i^3))) \qquad (13)$$

where $tanh$ is the hyperbolic tangent function . Unlike the ReLU-based functions, the GELU function has curvature at all points including the positive and negative domain. The GELU can be thought of as a smoother ReLU.

4   Experiments

4.1   Dataset

For training and evaluating the experimented systems, the ASVspoof 2019 challenge dataset was used, which provides a common framework with a standard corpus for conducting spoofing detection research on LA attacks. The LA dataset includes bonafide and spoof speech signals generated using various state-of-the-art voice conversion and speech synthesis algorithms. A summary of the LA corpora in terms of training (Train), development (Dev) and evaluation (Eval) partitions and number of recordings is presented in Table 2. The development and evaluation subsets constitute the seen and unseen test sets in terms of spoofing attacks. In our experiments, we have used the development subset as validation set for tuning the parameters of the systems and evaluation subset as our test set for reporting results. For more details about the corpora, the interested readers are referred to [7].

Table 2. Summary of ASVspoof2019 logical Access (LA) corpora in terms of training (Train), development (Dev) and evaluation (Eval) partitions and number of recordings.

Partition	#Speakers	#Recordings	
		Bona fide	Spoof
Training	20	2,580	22,800
Development	20	2,548	22,296
Evaluation	67	7,355	63,882

4.2   Experimental Setup

As local frame-level hand-crafted features we use 60-dimensional (including the delta and double delta coefficients) linear frequency cepstral coefficients (LFCC) extracted using 25ms analysis window over a frame shift of 10ms. No data augmentation was performed in our experiments.

For training all the experimented systems, balanced mini-batches of size 64 samples were used. The ADAM optimizer was used with initial learning rate of 0.0003 and exponential learning rate decay with rate of 0.5 was applied [21, 37].

For comparing the performance of different systems, the official evaluation metrics of ASVspoof2019 challenge, equal error rate (EER) and minimum tandem detection cost function (min-tDCF) [14], were used. The lower the values of EER and min-tDCF the better performance is attained. The ASV scores provided by the challenge organizer were used for computing min-tDCF.

4.3   Experimental Results

In the case of trainable activation functions, proper initialization of parameters ensure the convergence of the model as well as the performance improvement. In Table 3, we present the results of MPELU-based deepfake detection systems for different initial values of parameters a & b. It is observed from Table 3 that MPELU achieved optimal performance when the parameters were initialized with $a = 3$ & $b = 1$.

Performance with Different Frame-Level Networks. In this experiment, we compare the deepfake detection performance of the TDNN, ResNet-18 and SE-ResNet-18-based end-to-end systems with ReLU activation. As presented in Table 4, it could be seen that in all the experimented ReLU-based systems, the SE-ResNet-18 architecture outperformed the TDNN & ResNet-18 frame-level networks both in terms of EER & min-tDCF metrics. Again, from Table 4, it is evident that the MPELU & AReLU achieved better performances than the standard ReLU activation in terms of EER and min-tDCF. Especially in the SE-ResNet-18 architecture, the usage of AReLU achieved a relative improvement of

Table 3. The experimental results of the SE-ResNet-18-based end-to-end systems with MPELU activation function on the ASVSpoof2019 Logical Access evaluation set for different initial values of parameters a & b. All results are reported in respect of EER and min-tDCF evaluation metrics.

Initialization	EER [%]	min-tDCF
$a = 0.25, b = 1$	2.5154	0.0625
$a = 2.5, b = 1$	2.8114	0.0657
$a = 3, b = 1$	**2.0957**	**0.0506**
$a = 4, b = 1$	2.3394	0.0643

Table 4. The experimental results with ReLU activation function using TDNN, ResNet-18 and SE-ResNet-18 frame-level networks. Comparison of ReLU-, MPELU-, and AReLU activation functions-based deepfake detection performances employing SE-ResNet-18 frame-level network. All results are reported on the ASVSpoof2019 Logical Access (LA) evaluation set in terms of EER and min-tDCF.

Frame-level network	Activation	EER [%]	min-tDCF
TDNN	ReLU	5.6559	0.1315
ResNet-18	ReLU	3.1420	0.0735
SE-ResNet-18	ReLU	3.0589	0.0718
SE-ResNet-18	AReLU	2.3770	0.0586
SE-ResNet-18	MPELU	**2.0957**	**0.0506**

Table 5. The experimental results of the SE-ResNet-18-based end-to-end systems with different activation functions on the ASVSpoof2019 Logical Access evaluation set with regards to the EER and min-tDCF metrics.

Activation	EER [%]	min-tDCF
LFCC-GMM [7]	9.5700	0.2366
CQCC-GMM [7]	8.0900	0.2116
ReLU	2.9098	0.0763
LeakyReLU	2.7999	0.0696
RReLU	3.2104	0.0790
ELU	4.7026	0.0980
SELU	2.7045	0.0656
LLeakyReLU	2.4433	0.0536
PReLU	2.6515	0.0663
PELU	2.5407	0.0635
AReLU	2.3770	0.0586
MPELU	**2.0957**	**0.0506**
GELU	2.3525	0.0539

18.38% over the ReLU, in terms of min-tDCF. The MPELU activation demonstrated the best spoofing countermeasure performance with a relative improvement of 29.5% and 13.6% over the ReLU and AReLU activations, respectively in terms of min-tDCF metric.

Since the performance of an audio deepfake detection system is highly dependent on its ability to detect the artifacts within the speech spectrogram, we could safely assume that the MPELU & AReLU can enable the countermeasure system to focus more on the relevant features.

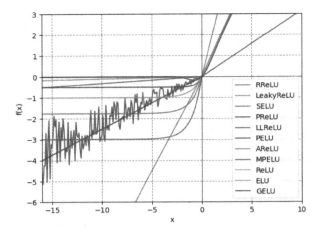

Fig. 3. Shapes of different activation functions considered in this work.

Comparison to Other Activation Functions. In Fig. 3 we present a comparison of the shapes of other the activation functions with the proposed the MPELU & AReLU for end-to-end deepfake detection task. As depicted in Fig. 3, ReLU suppresses the negative inputs which may lead to a significant portion of the neural network doing nothing. As a results, ReLU hinders the network to learn relevant features from negative input representations. The other activations of Fig. 3, on the other hand, focuses on learning discriminative features not only for positive but also negative input representations.

Table 5 shows the EER and min-tDCF results of the experimented systems with MPELU, AReLU, other ReLU variants and GELU activations as described in Sects. 2 and 3. As depicted in the results, it could be seen that 8 variants of the ReLU (i.e., LeakyReLU, LLeakyReLU, PReLU, AReLU, PELU, SELU, MPELU and GELU) were able to outperform the standard ReLU activation. This indicates that utilizing the potential useful information from the negative region of the inputs can help the network to focus more on the relevant features regarding the spoofing detection task from the input feature. However, as seen in the ELU and RReLU results, blindly exploiting the negative elements with no knowledge on the dataset does not always guarantee superior performance.

Another interesting point to notice from the results is that the learnable activation functions (i.e., LLeakyReLU, PReLU, AReLU, PELU, MPELU) were generally able to perform better than the fixed activations (i.e., ReLU, LeakyReLU, RReLU, ELU, SELU). This may be attributed to the fact that the learnable activation functions are more capable of suppressing the nuisance features as their scaling parameters are optimized in a data-adaptive fashion.

Among the learnable activations (i.e., LLeakyReLU, PReLU, AReLU, PELU, MPELU), the MPELU achieved the best performance, which outperformed the PReLU, PELU, AReLU and LLeakyReLU with a relative improvement of 23.7%, 20.3%, 13.7% and 5.6% respectively in terms of min-tDCF. Although the PReLU suppresses the negative elements similarly to the AReLU, it does not attempt to amplify the relevant features. Therefore, the AReLU may be more suited to focus on the artifacts caused by the spoofing process, as it can emphasize the positive elements via learnable scaling parameter β.

However, interestingly, the 2nd best performance was achieved by the GELU activation function, even outperforming all the considered learnable activation functions except the MPELU. The GELU achieved a relative improvement of 19.15% over the standard ReLU in terms of EER. This indicates that the curvature and non-monoticity of the GELU activation can allow the end-to-end system to capture the complicated deepfake artifacts within the input speech pattern.

5   Conclusion

The activation function plays a crucial role for learning representative features in deep learning-based problem solving. In this paper, we proposed the use of Multiple Parametric ELU (MPELU) & Attention ReLU (AReLU) activation functions for the end-to-end deepfake countermeasure system. The MPELU, with proper setting of the learnable parameters, can become the rectified or exponential linear units and can combine their benefits. The AReLU, on the other hand, with help of element-wise sign-based attention mechanism focuses on the detection of the artifacts created by the deepfakes generation process while suppressing the irrelevant features. In order to evaluate the proposed MPELU- and AReLU-based end-to-end frameworks, we conducted several experiments on the ASVSpoof2019 Challenge logical access dataset. Experimental results showed that the MPELU, AReLU and GELU can bring benefits to the deepfake detection performance and MPELU provided the best results over all considered activation functions.

Acknowledgments. The authors wish to acknowledge the funding from the Natural Sciences and Engineering Research Council of Canada (NSERC) through grant RGPIN-2019-05381.

References

1. Xiao, X., et al.: Spoofing speech detection using high dimensional magnitude and phase features: The NTU approach for asvspoof 2015 challenge. In: Proceedings of Interspeech (2015)
2. Alam, J., Kenny, P.: Spoofing detection employing infinite impulse response-constant q transform-based feature representations. In: Proceedings of EUSIPCO, pp. 101–105 (2017)
3. Alam, M.J., et al.: Spoofing detection on the asvspoof2015 challenge corpus employing deep neural networks. In: Proceedings of Odyssey, pp. 270–276 (2016)
4. Chen, D., Xu, K.: AReLU: attention-based rectified linear unit. arXiv preprint arXiv:2006.13858 (2020)

5. Chen, F., Deng, S., Zheng, T., He, Y., Han, J.: Graph-based spectro-temporal dependency modeling for anti-spoofing. In: IEEE ICASSP, pp. 1–5 (2023)
6. Chen, T., et al.: Generalization of Audio Deepfake Detection. In: Proceedings of Odyssey, pp. 132–137 (2020)
7. consortium, A.: ASVspoof 2019: automatic speaker verification spoofing and countermeasures challenge evaluation plan (2019). Accessed 13 May 2020. https://www.asvspoof.org/asvspoof2019/asvspoof2019_evaluation_plan.pdf
8. Dubey, S.R., Singh, S.K., Chaudhuri, B.B.: Activation functions in deep learning: a comprehensive survey and benchmark. Neurocomput. **503**, 92–108 (2022). https://www.sciencedirect.com/science/article/pii/S0925231222008426
9. He, K., et al.: Delving deep into rectifiers: Surpassing human-level performance on ImageNet classification. arXiv preprint arxiv:1502.01852 (2015)
10. Hendrycks, D., Gimpel, K.: Gaussian error linear units (GELUS) (2020)
11. Hu, J., Shen, L., Sun, G.: Squeeze-and-excitation networks. In: Proc. CVPR. pp. 7132–7141 (2018). https://doi.org/10.1109/Proc.CVPR.2018.00745
12. Weon Jung, J., et al.: Aasist: audio anti-spoofing using integrated spectro-temporal graph attention networks. In: IEEE ICASSP, pp. 6367–6371 (2021)
13. Kang, W.H., Alam, J., Fathan, A.: Investigation on activation functions for robust end-to-end spoofing attack detection system. In: Proceedings of 2021 Edition of the Automatic Speaker Verification and Spoofing Countermeasures Challenge, pp. 83–88 (2021)
14. Kinnunen, T., et al.: t-DCF: a detection cost function for the tandem assessment of spoofing countermeasures and automatic speaker verification. arXiv preprint arXiv:1804.09618 (2018)
15. Klambauer, G., Unterthiner, T., Mayr, A., Hochreiter, S.: Self-normalizing neural networks (2017)
16. Lavrentyeva, G., et al.: STC Antispoofing Systems for the ASVspoof2019 Challenge. In: Proceedings of Interspeech, pp. 1033–1037 (2019)
17. Li, Y., Fan, C., Li, Y., Wu, Q., Ming, Y.: Improving deep neural network with multiple parametric exponential linear units. Neurocomputing **301**, 11–24 (2018). https://www.sciencedirect.com/science/article/pii/S0925231218301255
18. Maas, A., et al.: Rectifier nonlinearities improve neural network acoustic models. In: Proceedings of ICML (2013)
19. Maniatopoulos, A., Mitianoudis, N.: Learnable leaky relu (LeLeLU): an alternative accuracy-optimized activation function. Information **12**(12), 513 (2021)
20. Monteiro, J., Alam, J.: Development of voice spoofing detection systems for 2019 edition of automatic speaker verification and countermeasures challenge. In: Proceedings of ASRU, pp. 1003–1010 (2019)
21. Monteiro, J., et al.: Generalized end-to-end detection of spoofing attacks to automatic speaker recognizers. Comput. Speech Lang. **63**, 101096 (2020)
22. Monteiro, J., et al.: A multi-condition training strategy for countermeasures against spoofing attacks to speaker recognizers. In: Proceedings of Odyssey, pp. 296–303 (2020)
23. Nair, V., Hinton, G.E.: Rectified linear units improve restricted boltzmann machines. In: Proceedings of the ICML, ICML 2010, pp. 807–814. Omnipress, Madison, WI, USA (2010)
24. Patel, T.B., Patil, H.A.: Combining evidences from MEL cepstral, cochlear filter cepstral and instantaneous frequency features for detection of natural vs. spoofed speech. In: Proceedings of Interspeech (2015)

25. Patel, T.B., Patil, H.A.: Effectiveness of fundamental frequency (f 0) and strength of excitation (SOE) for spoofed speech detection. In: Proceedings of ICASSP, pp. 5105–5109 (2016)
26. RahulT, P., et al.: Audio spoofing verification using deep convolutional neural networks by transfer learning. ArXiv abs/2008.03464 (2020)
27. Sahidullah, M., et al.: A comparison of features for synthetic speech detection. In: Proceedings of Interspeech, pp. 2087–2091 (2015)
28. Snyder, D., Garcia-Romero, D., Sell, G., Povey, D., Khudanpur, S.: X-vectors: robust DNN embeddings for speaker recognition. In: Proceedings of ICASSP, IEEE (2018)
29. Srivastava, N., Hinton, G., Krizhevsky, A., Sutskever, I., Salakhutdinov, R.: Dropout: a simple way to prevent neural networks from overfitting. J. Mach. Learn. Res. **15**(56), 1929–1958 (2014)
30. Tak, H., weon Jung, J., Patino, J., Todisco, M., Evans, N.W.D.: Graph attention networks for anti-spoofing. In: Interspeech (2021)
31. Tak, H., et al.: Spoofing attack detection using the non-linear fusion of sub-band classifiers. In: Proceedings of Interspeech, pp. 1106–1110 (2020)
32. Tak, H., et al.: End-to-end anti-spoofing with rawnet2. In: IEEE (ed.) Proceedings of ICASSP. Ontario (2021)
33. Tian, X., et al.: Spoofing detection from a feature representation perspective. In: Proceedings of ICASSP, pp. 2119–2123 (2016)
34. Todisco, M., et al.: Constant q cepstral coefficients: a spoofing countermeasure for automatic speaker verification. Comput. Speech Lang. **45**, 516–535 (2017)
35. Trottier, L., Giguère, P., Chaib-draa, B.: Parametric exponential linear unit for deep convolutional neural networks (2018)
36. Wu, Z., et al.: Light convolutional neural network with feature genuinization for detection of synthetic speech attacks. In: Proceedings of Interspeech, pp. 1101–1105 (2020)
37. Zhang, Y., et al.: One-class learning towards synthetic voice spoofing detection. IEEE Signal Process. Lett. **28**, 937–941 (2021)

A Comparison of Learned Representations with Jointly Optimized VAE and DNN for Syllable Stress Detection

Jhansi Mallela[✉], Prasanth Sai Boyina, and Chiranjeevi Yarra

Speech Processing Lab, Language Technologies Research Center (LTRC),
International Institute of Information and Technology, Hyderabad 500032, India
jhansi.mallela@research.iiit.ac.in, prasanth.sai@students.iiit.ac.in,
chiranjeevi.yarra@iiit.ac.in

Abstract. Automatic syllable stress detection is helpful in assessing L2 learners' pronunciation. In this work, for stress detection, we propose a representation learning framework by jointly optimizing VAE and DNN. The obtained representations from the proposed VAE plus DNN framework are compared with the implicit representations learned from DNN-based stress detection. Further, we compare the obtained representations from VAE plus DNN with those obtained from autoencoder (AE) plus DNN, and sparse-autoencoder (SAE) plus DNN considering with/without implicit representations from DNN. We perform the experiments on the ISLE corpus consisting of English utterances from German and Italian native speakers. We observe that the detection performance with the learned representations from VAE plus DNN is significantly better than that with the state-of-the-art method without any representation learning with the highest improvement of 2.2%, 5.1%, and 1.4% under matched, combined, and cross scenarios, respectively.

Keywords: Syllable stress detection · Joint representation learning · Computer-assisted language learning

1 Introduction

The technological advancements showed their impact on teaching with the development of different computer-assisted language learning (CALL) based modules [3,14]. In recent years, applications related to CALL have shown benefits for second language learning. The reasons for the benefits include, 1) flexibility in its availability, 2) low cost of usage, and 3) ability to provide personalized learning [24]. However, developing robust modules for CALL is a challenging task, mainly due to the variabilities in L2 learners' native languages and accents. One of the many different aspects that the CALL applications have been focusing on is the detection and diagnosis of prosodic errors such as stress/prominence and intonation [9,16,31] errors made by the L2 learners in their pronunciation. Syllable

A. Karpov et al. (Eds.): SPECOM 2023, LNAI 14339, pp. 322–334, 2023.
https://doi.org/10.1007/978-3-031-48312-7_26

stress plays a critical role in communication to convey the meaning and intent of the message. Also, correct syllable stress placements in a word convey correct pronunciation. In this work, we consider the problem of automatic syllable stress detection which could be useful for downstream tasks such as CALL systems.

Syllable stress is referred to as the emphasis on a particular syllable in a word. Stressed syllables appear more prominent than unstressed syllables. In [1,5,27], it is stated that stress is mirrored through the changes in intensity, pitch, and duration. In [7], it is defined that the stressed syllable can be longer in relative duration and with greater physical intensity than the unstressed syllables but pitch movement does not always contribute to stress. Also in the literature, there is no strong agreement on the definition of stress in terms of acoustics for non-native English learners. Aoyama et al. [1] hypothesized that Japanese speakers rely more on differences in F0 compare to intensity and duration to indicate stress in English. Because of the native language influence, the production and perception of L2 will differ which in turn affects the acoustic parameters responsible for stress perception [15]. It highlights the need for a clearer and more consistent representation of stress.

Typically, automatic syllable stress detection has a feature extraction step followed by a machine learning (ML) based classification step. In the literature, various methods were proposed for better performance at both steps. At the model level, different ML algorithms like support vector machines (SVM), deep neural networks (DNN), convolutional neural networks (CNN), and attention networks were used for stress detection. Johnson et al. [10] used five different machine learning classifiers namely, neural networks, SVM, decision tree, bagging, and boosting algorithms for automatic detection of Brazil's prominence syllables with seven sets of different acoustic features embedding with variations in intensity, pitch, and duration. Arnold et al. [2] used random forests for prominence detection in the German language. Tian et al. [30] used an attention-based neural network and bidirectional LSTMs for stress detection problem using Mel frequency cepstral coefficients (MFCCs), energy, and pitch features. Ruan et al. [22] performed stress detection using a transformer network. Further, there were attempts on non-native speech in French, Spanish, and Mandarin with SVM for stress detection using acoustic and context-based features [4,8]. The above works are based on different models and features. Also, there are works [27,31] that focused only on feature level to extract the best features that can capture the syllable prominence.

Neural networks are often seen as a black box and it is difficult to interpret the kind of representation that the network is learning. Neural network architectures like DNN, CNN, and LSTM involves complex, nonlinear, and structured dependencies and they have been gaining popularity in different speech applications with their better performance over traditional ML methods. In automatic classification tasks, these neural networks learn representations implicitly, referred to as implicit representations, of the given input and map it to a specific class by learning weights. Even though these networks are known for learning task-specific implicit representations, they are sensitive to factors like variation and entanglement [6] in the data which can't be eliminated in real data scenarios.

One of the ways to overcome these factors is by learning a good representation of the data explicitly, prior to the classification task. To resolve this, AEs [23] were proposed and used in several applications for learning representations explicitly [28], referred to as explicit representations. But, AEs are not consistent in generating disentangled representation and regularized latent space. By addressing these issues, variational autoencoders (VAE) [13] gained attention in the field of computer vision [17] and speech processing applications [18,25] to learn the disentangled explicit representation of the data.

Obtaining combined representations by incorporating both the explicit and implicit representations through a single framework would benefit the stress detection task. However, to the best of our knowledge, there is no work that learns the combined as well as the explicit representations from the acoustic features for the stress detection task. To obtain combined (explicit and implicit) representations, we propose to optimize VAE and DNN in a joint learning framework.

In this work, we analyze the representations in a task-specific manner using acoustic and context-based features by modelling in two ways. First, we consider a DNN which implicitly learns representation from state-of-the-art acoustic and context-based features and performs classification. Second, we use the proposed representation learning framework jointly with VAE and DNN to obtain effective explicit and implicit representations for the stress detection task. Further, we analyze the effectiveness of the jointly learned representations obtained with VAEs compare to those obtained with other autoencoders namely, simple autoencoder (AE), and sparse autoencoder (SAE). We perform experiments on the ISLE corpus which consists of polysyllabic English words uttered by nonnative speakers of German, and Italian. We conduct the experiments in three scenarios: 1) matched: train and test data are from the same language, 2) combined: train data is from both the speakers' but tested on each of them separately, and 3) cross: trained with German and tested on Italian, and vice-versa. The jointly learned representations from VAE outperform the state-of-the-art method (without any representation learning) and implicit representations from DNN for stress detection. We found an absolute improvement in the classification accuracies by 2.2% & 1.2%, 5.1% & 1.1%, and 1.4% & 1.1% on German & Italian under matched, combined, and cross scenarios, respectively.

Table 1. Details of train and test splits of GER and ITA showing the number of stressed and unstressed syllables.

	Train		Test	
	#Stressed	#Unstressed	#Stressed	#Unstressed
GER	3076	3905	2756	3492
ITA	4408	5854	2148	2754

2   Database

For the experiments in this work, we consider ISLE [20] corpus. From this corpus, we consider 7834 speech utterances from 46 non-native speakers learning English where each speaker uttered 160 sentences following the work [31]. Out of 46 speakers, 23 are German (GER), and 23 are Italian (ITA). The entire audio was phonetically annotated by a team of five linguists to reflect the speakers' pronunciation. Using the automatic force alignment process, each utterance is phonetically aligned. We use P2TK [26], syllabification software to obtain syllable transcriptions from the phone transcriptions. From the syllable transcriptions, we obtain the aligned syllable boundaries using aligned phone boundaries. Syllable stress markings were also manually labeled while ensuring only one stressed syllable for each word. Labelling resulted in a total of 48868 syllables as stressed and 16693 syllables as unstressed. For the experiments, we consider data containing all polysyllabic words which result 12388 stressed and 16005 unstressed syllables. Train and test splits of both GER and ITA are done by balancing the speakers' nativity, age, sex, and proficiency [20]. Table 1 shows the details of the train test splits considered in the experiments.

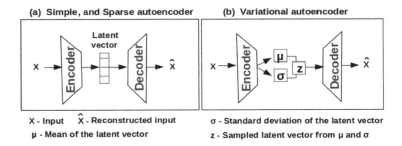

Fig. 1. Block diagrams of AE, SAE, and VAE.

3   Methodology

In this work, we consider VAE to learn the representations from the input features for the stress detection task. The VAEs are part of the autoencoder family, which includes AE, and SAE. In this section, we first briefly review AE, SAE, and VAE networks and then describe the framework of joint learning with VAE and DNN for syllable stress detection task.

3.1   Simple Autoencoder (AE):

Figure 1(a) illustrates the basic architecture of a simple autoencoder. It consists of an encoder and a decoder. The encoder encodes the d dimensional input feature vector X into a low dimensional latent vector and the decoder decodes the corresponding feature vector $\hat{X}$ from the latent vector. The entire encoder-decoder architecture is trained on the loss function which encourages the model to reconstruct the input from the latent vector at the output. Equation 1 shows the AE loss function, which is the mean square error between the encoder input and decoder output.

$$AE\ loss = (X - \hat{X})^2 \tag{1}$$

3.2   Sparse Autoencoder (SAE):

The autoencoders are usually prone to noise and learn more redundant information. In order to overcome this, sparse autoencoders were proposed. The sparse autoencoder architecture is the same as the autoencoder in Fig. 1(a) which has an encoder and decoder network. However, the loss function varies from AEs to SAEs. The SAE loss function includes a regularizer besides MSE loss in AE for penalizing the redundant information learning. The regularizer penalizes unnecessary nodes and activates selective nodes in the hidden layers of the encoder and decoder to avoid learning redundant information. Equation 2 shows the SAE loss function, in which the regularizer cost can be L_p norm (p=1 or 2) or Kullback-Leibler ($\mathbb{KL}$) - divergence on the parameters of encoder and decoder networks.

$$SAE\ loss = (X - \hat{X})^2 + regularizer \tag{2}$$

3.3   Variational Autoencoder (VAE):

Figure 1(b) illustrates the architecture of VAE. In VAE, for a given input vector X, unlike a fixed latent vector in AE and SAE encoder, $q_\theta(z|X)$ encodes the input feature vector to a latent vector space with a predefined random distribution $(p(z))$, typically a Gaussian density function with the mean μ and standard deviation σ. The decoder has two steps, the first step randomly samples the latent vectors $\mathbf{z}$ from the encoded latent space distribution using a reparametrization trick that uses unit normal Gaussian distribution, $z = \mu + \epsilon \cdot \sigma$, where $\epsilon \sim \mathcal{N}(0, \mathbf{I})$. The second step decodes the input feature vector $\hat{X}$ from the latent vector $\mathbf{z}$. Equation 3 shows the loss function for VAE, which is defined considering two objectives. 1) Reconstructing the input (MSE), 2) Constraining the latent space to Gaussian distribution with KL-divergence. With this formulation, VAEs have shown great success in the field of computer vision [11]. Further, these have gained attention in speech processing analysis requiring latent representation learning. Thus, we believe the learned representations from the VAE could be robust for the stress detection task.

$$VAE\ loss = (X - \hat{X})^2 + \mathbb{KL}(q_\theta(z|X)||p(z)) \tag{3}$$

3.4   Joint Learning with VAE and DNN

Figure 2 illustrates the block diagram of the joint learning with VAE and DNN for syllable stress detection[1]. It has two flows, the first one is training flow

---

[1] https://github.com/Prasanth-Sai-Boyina/Syllable_stress_detection.

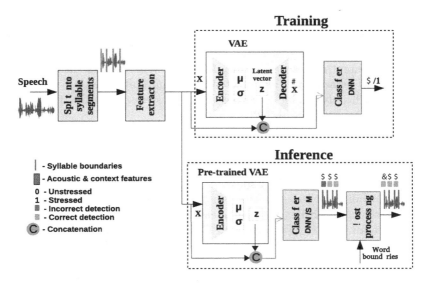

Fig. 2. Block diagram of joint learning approach.

and the second one is testing/inference flow. The two steps associated with the first two blocks are common for both training and testing flows. The first step obtains the syllable segments for a given speech utterance considering respective syllable transcriptions and their aligned boundaries. The second step computes input features for both training and testing. During training, we feed the input features to the VAE to learn the latent representations. The representations are learned by jointly training the VAE and the DNN classifier, which take latent representation and input features together (shown in the figure with blue lines) as input and stress markings (stressed and unstressed) as the output.

This joint training distinguishes our work from the typical training considered in the VAE. Equation 4 shows the loss function for the joint learning approach, which is defined considering two terms. 1) VAE loss consisting of MSE and KL-divergence, 2) Cross entropy (CE) loss between the predicted label ($\hat{Y}$) and ground truth (Y). λ_1 and λ_2 are the weight parameters. We hypothesize that by jointly optimizing the loss functions of VAE and DNN, we can learn the task-specific representations that would be robust for the detection task.

$$Joint\ loss = \lambda_1(VAE\ loss) + \lambda_2(CE(Y, \hat{Y})) \qquad (4)$$

These representations consist of 1) representations that are explicit to DNN i.e. the latent representations learned by VAE, and 2) representations that are implicitly learned by DNN. Thus, we consider the proposed approach uses both explicit and implicit representations for the detection task. On the other hand, the learned latent representations are considered as explicit to the DNN when VAE and DNN are jointly trained without the concatenation step shown in Fig. 2.

After training VAE and DNN jointly, we extract the latent representations for the test data from the trained encoder, as shown in the inference block of the figure. We then use latent representation along with the input features as input (or only latent representation) to detect the syllable stress using DNN and SVM classifiers separately. The detected stress markings are post-processed to ensure that each polysyllabic word has only one stressed syllable following the work proposed by Yarra et al. [32].

4   Experimental Setup

In this study, both GER and ITA speakers' data is split into two non-overlapping sets namely, train and test sets. For the train set, following the previous work [31], we consider 1st-12th & 1st-13th speakers data and 13th-23rd & 14th-23rd speakers data for test set respectively for GER, and ITA [9]. Table 1 presents the details of syllable count in train and test conditions for both GER and ITA. We consider the state-of-the-art 19-dim acoustic-based features along with 19-dim binary features representing context dependencies following the work by Yarra et al. [32]. We consider their method, which uses an SVM classifier in the detection task as the baseline. We perform experiments in a 5-fold cross-validation setup where the train set is equally split into five groups, and the number of stressed and unstressed syllables are similar across five groups. In each fold, we use four sets for training, and one set for validation following a round-robin fashion. We normalize the training and testing set with the mean and standard deviation of the vectors obtained from the training set.

Architecture Details: The approach that we consider for representation learning jointly with VAE and DNN and classification with DNN/SVM is referred to as VAE+classifer (x + y; x represents the autoencoder used for learning task-specific representations jointly with DNN, y represents the classifier in the test time, either DNN or SVM that is used for classification with the learned representations from x). In the proposed approach, along with the VAE, we analyse the latent representations learned with simple AE, and SAE jointly with DNN and the corresponding networks are referred to as AE+classifer, and SAE+classifer, respectively. The DNN model in each of these consists of 8 hidden layers. We consider *Relu* [21] as activation function for the hidden layers and *Adam* [12] as optimizer. Binary cross-entropy is the loss function in DNN. AE and SAE consists of 2 hidden layers in encoder and decoder with *Relu* activation function. In SAE, we use L1 regularizer in one of the hidden layers of encoder. VAE consists of 1 hidden layer each in encoder and decoder with *Relu* activation function. All the DNN, VAE, AE, and SAE parameters like number of layers, and number of nodes in each layer are optimal and we choose them by maximizing the performance on the validation set. The optimal values of the parameters λ_1 and λ_2 in joint loss are found to be 0.53 and 0.47, respectively. For the SVM, we consider radial basis kernel and the parameter C by optimizing on the validation set. We consider an average of classification accuracies on the test set obtained from five training folds as a performance metric. We perform experiments in three different scenarios. 1) **matched:** We train with GER & ITA train sets and test on the GER & ITA test sets, respectively, 2) **combined:** We train with pooled data of GER and ITA, and test on GER and ITA test sets separately, and 3) **cross:** We train with GER(ITA) train set and test on ITA(GER) test set.

5   Results and Discussion

We analyze the learned representations – 1) both explicit and implicit, 2) implicit, 3) explicit, with the accuracies shown in Table 2 and Fig. 4. Table 2 reports the average classification accuracies with (in brackets) and without post-processing obtained from baseline, DNN, VAE+DNN, and VAE+SVM on GER and ITA with acoustic (A) and acoustic plus context features (A+C) under all three scenarios. The results with VAE+DNN indicates the effectiveness of explicit and implicit representations combination. The results with DNN indicate the effectiveness of implicit representations. The explicit representations are analyzed with Fig. 4 by computing the accuracies without performing concatenation in Fig. 2 during testing/inference.

5.1   With Explicit and Implicit and Implicit Representations

Under Matched Scenario: From Table 2 under matched scenario, it is observed that in all the cases the accuracies obtained from VAE+DNN higher than those from baseline, DNN, and VAE+SVM with and without postprocessing. The highest improvements are found to be 2.2% & 1.2% and 1.9% & 1.4% on GER & ITA considering acoustic and acoustic plus context features, respectively. This indicates the benefit of both explicit and implicit representation compared to baseline (without any representations) and DNN (only with implicit representations). Further, the higher accuracies with DNN over baseline indicate the benefit of implicit representations. The higher accuracies with VAE+DNN compared to VAE+SVM indicate the effectiveness of implicit representations from DNN over SVM. The higher accuracies with the acoustic plus context features compared to acoustic features with the representation learning approach are consistent with the findings from the literature [27,29,32]. Altogether supports the benefit of the representation learning in stress detection task.

Under Combined Scenario: The comparisons made under matched scenario across baseline, DNN, VAE+DNN, and VAE+SVM are consistent under combined scenario also. From the table, the highest accuracies in GER and ITA are found in the combined scenario and those are 94.1% and 94.2%, respectively, obtained from VAE+DNN considering acoustic plus context features with postprocessing. Further, while comparing the accuracies between matched and combined scenarios, the accuracies are higher under combined than those under matched with VAE+DNN and DNN but not in all cases of baseline and VAE+SVM. Both these together suggest that the combined scenario has an advantage for the stress detection task compared to the matched scenario and

Table 2. Classification accuracies with (without) postprocessing considering acoustic (A) and acoustic plus context (A+C) features under three different scenarios.

Test data	Train scenario	SVM		DNN		VAE+DNN		VAE+SVM	
		A	A+C	A	A+C	A	A+C	A	A+C
GER	Matched	83.5 (80.3)	92.3 (88.7)	84.6 (81.1)	92.6 (88.3)	**85.7 (82.1)**	**93.5 (90.4)**	84.5 (81.3)	92.4 (89.1)
	Combined	83.2 (80.5)	89 (85.1)	84.1 (81.1)	92.7 (89.1)	**85.4 (82)**	**94.1 (90.9)**	84.6 (81.6)	92.3 (89.5)
	Cross	80.5 (77.7)	88.2 (84.5)	80.2 (77.4)	88.3 (84.5)	**80.9 (78.1)**	**89.6 (85.6)**	80.7 (78.5)	87.5 (83.6)
ITA	Matched	82.7 (80.5)	91.5 (88.2)	82.8 (81.1)	91.7 (87.7)	**84.6 (82.3)**	**92.9 (89.5)**	83.7 (81.4)	91.3 (88.4)
	Combined	83.4 (81)	93 (89.8)	83.8 (81.6)	93.3 (89.2)	**85.4 (82.6)**	**94.2 (90.6)**	84.5 (82.2)	92.6 (89.7)
	Cross	82.1 (79.3)	90.7 (86.6)	82.7 (79.4)	90.9 (86.2)	**83.6 (80)**	**91.8 (86.8)**	81.9 (79)	87.6 (84)

shows that VAE+DNN and DNN utilize the extra data in the stress detection task whereas baseline and VAE+SVM failed to do so.

Under Cross Scenario: From Table 2, it is observed that there is a drop in accuracies under cross scenario compared to those under matched scenario in baseline, DNN, VAE+DNN, and VAE+SVM. This could be due to the mismatch in the nativity. But the VAE+DNN is performing better over the baseline, and DNN in GER, and ITA in all the cases considering both with and without postprocessing. This indicates that the explicit and implicit representations learned with VAE+DNN could be independent of speakers' nativity and effective in learning the stress detection task-specific cues through the representations. From all the above comparisons, the significant improvements with the VAE+DNN over baseline, DNN, and VAE+SVM among all three scenarios indicate the robustness of the explicit and implicit representations for stress detection.

Fig. 3. t-SNE visualizations of learned representations under three approaches. ● Class 0, ● Class 1.

5.2   With Explicit Representations

Representations can be learned through different types of autoencoders. In this work, we consider VAE due to its effectiveness in learning representations. In order to analyze the same, we also compute the accuracies with the representations learned from other types – AE and SAE. We perform the analysis considering only explicit representations (without concatenation in Fig. 2) and comparing them with DNN and the baseline. The accuracies obtained from the autoencoders' (AE, SAE, and VAE) explicit representations and those from DNN and the baseline have similar trend across both GER and ITA, so for better readability, we present the accuracies averaged across GER and ITA.

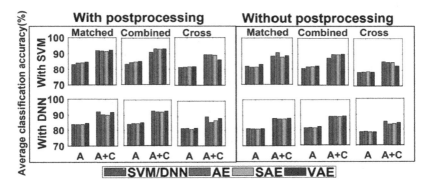

Fig. 4. Comparison of average classification accuracies obtained from explicit representations learned with AE, SAE, and VAE using classifier as SVM (first row) and DNN (second row) separately.

Figure 4 presents the average classification accuracies considering acoustic, and acoustic plus context features under all three scenarios with and without postprocessing. Each bar height represents average classification accuracy. The first and second rows correspond to the classification accuracies considering the test classifier as SVM, and DNN, respectively. From the figure, we observe that acoustic plus context features are significantly better than acoustic features with, and without postprocessing. From the first row, where the classifier is SVM, it is observed that classification with representation learning approaches (AE, SAE, and VAE) are higher than the baseline in majority of the cases. And there is an increasing trend in the performance among AE+SVM, SAE+SVM, and VAE+SVM in 3 out of 4 cases except in the cross scenarios. This indicates that the representations learned from VAE are comparable to and better than the other autoencoder types. On the other hand, a similar trend among the autoencoders is not consistent in the second row, where the classifier is DNN. Further, the accuracies with the DNN are higher than those with the AE+DNN, SAE+DNN, and VAE+DNN. This suggests that the explicit representations alone could be less effective compared to the implicit representations learned by

DNN. However, comparing Table 2 and Fig. 4, it is observed that the accuracies with the VAE+DNN considering explicit and implicit representation are higher than those with the DNN. Further, we observe that the accuracies with the VAE+DNN are higher than those with the AE+DNN and SAE+DNN considering explicit and implicit representations. These together indicate the benefit of the representations learned from VAE in the stress detection task considering the proposed explicit and implicit representation-based approaches compare to implicit, and explicit alone representations based approaches. The t-SNE [19] visualizations shown in Fig. 3 suggest that the explicit and implicit based representation learning approach is capable of discriminating the classes better.

6 Conclusion

In this work, we have considered a representation learning approach jointly with VAE and DNN for automatic syllable stress detection task using acoustic and context-based features. The learned representations include three sets of representations namely, 1) implicit, 2) explicit, and 3) explicit and implicit. The proposed joint learning approach learns both explicit and implicit representations. Experiments with ISLE corpus showed that stress detection performance with the proposed joint representation learning approach consistently performs better than the baseline, and DNN (implicit) in both GER and ITA under matched, combined, and cross-native scenarios. Further, representations learned from VAE were found to be better than those of AE, and SAE. In the future, we would like to investigate end-to-end based representation learning and self-supervised based representations for syllable stress detection to overcome the difficulty in manual labeling of stress markings.

References

1. Aoyama, K., Guion, S.G.: Prosody in second language acquisition. Language Experience in Second Language Speech Learning: in honor of James Emil Flege. Amsterdam (2007)
2. Arnold, D., Wagner, P., Baayen, R.H.: Using generalized additive models and random forests to model prosodic prominence in German. In: INTERSPEECH, Lyon, France, pp. 272–276. International Speech Communications Association (2017)
3. Bernhard, V., Schwab, S., Goldman, J.P.: Acoustic Stress Detection in Isolated English Words for Computer-Assisted Pronunciation Training. In: Proceedings of Interspeech 2022, pp. 3143–3147 (2022). https://doi.org/10.21437/Interspeech 2022-197
4. Christodoulides, G., Avanzi, M.: An evaluation of machine learning methods for prominence detection in French. In: INTERSPEECH, pp. 116–119 (2014)
5. Couper-Kuhlen, E.: An introduction to english prosody. (No Title) (1986)
6. Cunningham, P., Carney, J., Jacob, S.: Stability problems with artificial neural networks and the ensemble solution. Artif. Intell. Med. **20**(3), 217–225 (2000)
7. Cutler, A., Isard, S.D.: The production of prosody (1980)

8. Evin, D., Cossio Mercado, C., Torres, H.M., Gurlekian, J., Mixdorff, H.: Automatic prominence detection in Argentinian Spanish, Proceedings of Speech Prosody, Poznan, Poland, pp. 680–684 (2018)
9. Ferrer, L., Bratt, H., Richey, C., Franco, H., Abrash, V., Precoda, K.: Classification of lexical stress using spectral and prosodic features for computer-assisted language learning systems. Speech Commun. **69**, 31–45 (2015)
10. Johnson, D.O., Kang, O.: Automatic prominent syllable detection with machine learning classifiers. Int. J. Speech Technol. **18**(4), 583–592 (2015). https://doi.org/10.1007/s10772-015-9299-z
11. Kim, J.H., Zhang, Y., Han, K., Wen, Z., Choi, M., Liu, Z.: Representation learning of resting state fMRI with variational autoencoder. Neuroimage **241**, 118423 (2021)
12. Kingma, D.P., Ba, J.: Adam: a method for stochastic optimization. arXiv preprint arXiv:1412.6980 (2014)
13. Kingma, D.P., Welling, M.: Auto-encoding variational bayes. arXiv preprint arXiv:1312.6114 (2013)
14. Lewis, C.: The Role of Lexical Stress in English as a Lingua Franca in Southeast Asia. In: Pronunciation in Second Language Learning and Teaching Proceedings, vol. 12(1) (2022)
15. Li, A., Post, B.: L2 acquisition of prosodic properties of speech rhythm: evidence from l1 mandarin and German learners of English. Stud. Second. Lang. Acquis. **36**(2), 223–255 (2014)
16. Li, K., Mao, S., Li, X., Wu, Z., Meng, H.: Automatic lexical stress and pitch accent detection for L2 English speech using multi-distribution deep neural networks. Speech Commun. **96**, 28–36 (2018)
17. Lin, C.C., Hung, Y., Feris, R., He, L.: Video instance segmentation tracking with a modified vae architecture. In: Proceedings of the IEEE/CVF Conference on Computer Vision and Pattern Recognition, pp. 13147–13157 (2020)
18. Lin, S., Clark, R., Birke, R., Schönborn, S., Trigoni, N., Roberts, S.: Anomaly detection for time series using VAE-LSTM hybrid model. In: International Conference on Acoustics, Speech and Signal Processing (ICASSP), pp. 4322–4326. IEEE (2020)
19. Van der Maaten, L., Hinton, G.: Visualizing data using t-SNE. J. Mach. Learn. Res. **9**(11) (2008)
20. Menzel, W., et al.: The ISLE corpus of non-native spoken English. In: Proceedings of LREC: Language Resources and Evaluation Conference, vol. 2, pp. 957–964. European Language Resources Association (2000)
21. Nair, V., Hinton, G.E.: Rectified linear units improve restricted boltzmann machines. In: ICML (2010)
22. Ruan, Y., et al.: An end-to-end approach for lexical stress detection based on transformer. arXiv preprint arXiv:1911.04862 (2019)
23. Rumelhart, D.E., Hinton, G.E., Williams, R.J.: Learning representations by back-propagating errors. Nature **323**(6088), 533–536 (1986)
24. Su, P.H., Wu, C.H., Lee, L.S.: A recursive dialogue game for personalized computer-aided pronunciation training. IEEE/ACM Trans. Audio Speech Lang. Process. **23**(1), 127–141 (2014)
25. Sun, G., et al.: Generating diverse and natural text-to-speech samples using a quantized fine-grained VAE and autoregressive prosody prior. In: International Conference on Acoustics, Speech and Signal Processing (ICASSP), pp. 6699–6703. IEEE (2020)
26. Tauberer, J.: P2tk automated syllabifier (2008)

27. Tepperman, J., Narayanan, S.: Automatic syllable stress detection using prosodic features for pronunciation evaluation of language learners. In: Proceedings (ICASSP) IEEE International Conference on Acoustics, Speech, and Signal Processing, vol. 1, pp. I-937. IEEE (2005)
28. Tschannen, M., Bachem, O., Lucic, M.: Recent advances in autoencoder-based representation learning. arXiv preprint arXiv:1812.05069 (2018)
29. Umeda, N.: Vowel duration in American English. J. Acoustical Soc. Am. **58**(2), 434–445 (1975)
30. Xia, T., Rui, X., Huang, C.L., Chu, I.H., Wang, S., Han, M.: An Attention Based Deep Neural Network for Automatic Lexical Stress Detection. In: Global Conference on Signal and Information Processing (GlobalSIP), pp. 1–5. IEEE (2019)
31. Yarra, C., Deshmukh, O.D., Ghosh, P.K.: Automatic detection of syllable stress using sonority based prominence features for pronunciation evaluation. In: International Conference on Acoustics, Speech and Signal Processing (ICASSP), pp. 5845–5849. IEEE (2017)
32. Yarra, C., Ramanathi, M.K., Ghosh, P.K.: Comparison of automatic syllable stress detection quality with time-aligned boundaries and context dependencies. In: SLaTE, pp. 79–83 (2019)

On the Asymptotic Behaviour of the Speech Signal

Priyanka Gupta$^{(\boxtimes)}$, Rajul Acharya, Ankur T. Patil, and Hemant A. Patil

Speech Research Lab, DA-IICT Gandhinagar-382007, Gujarat, India
{priyanka_gupta,rajul_acharya,ankur_patil,hemant_patil}@daiict.ac.in

Abstract. In the time-frequency representation of a signal, the "richness" of information is given by the area of the Heisenberg's Box, whose value is determined by the *Time-Bandwidth Product* (TBP). The value of TBP determines the extent of asymptotic behaviour in a signal and also the characteristics of the stochastic (random) process that has produced the signal under consideration. A higher value of the TBP indicates better aysmptoticity of the signal. In this paper, the authors have analyzed the behaviour of the decay factor of the impulse response of the vocal tract system with the TBP. This is done by modelling voiced and unvoiced speech as the convolution of the impulse response of the vocal tract with a periodic impulse train and white Gaussian noise, respectively. Furthermore, variation of TBP is analyzed for five male speakers of the well-known TIMIT corpus. The outcome of effective bandwidth and effective duration on TBP is also analyzed. Finally, instantaneous frequency (IF) and group delay (GD) functions are estimated for asymptotic signals.

Keywords: Instantaneous Frequency · Group Delay Function · Asymptotic Signals · Heisenberg's Uncertainty Principle · Heisenberg's Box

1 Introduction

The asymptotic behaviour of a signal is useful to determine its instantaneous frequency from its group delay function and vice versa. Non-synthetic signals which exist in realistic scenarios are non-stationary signals. Speech signals and chirp signals have a time-varying frequency within a short interval of time. Therefore, the study of their asymptoticity is important to determine the instantaneous frequency and group delay functions for further analysis. One of the important conditions for asymptoticity is to have a high value of the TBP [13]. A high TBP indicates high uncertainty, as given by the Gabor-Heisenberg uncertainty analysis described in Sect. 2.

Signal representation in the time-frequency domain is a two-variable function of time and frequency [6]. Time-frequency representations, such as spectrograms and Time-Frequency Distributions (TFDs), such as Wigner-Ville distribution,

A. Karpov et al. (Eds.): SPECOM 2023, LNAI 14339, pp. 335–343, 2023.
https://doi.org/10.1007/978-3-031-48312-7_27

are well-known [7,14]. The TFDs (denoted by $\rho(t,\omega)$), are within the limits of the *Heisenberg's uncertainty principle* in signal processing framework [15]. To investigate the time-frequency content of a signal, energy density jointly in time and frequency is estimated using TFDs [20]. Therefore, we have a joint distribution function in terms of t and ω.

To the best of the authors' knowledge, speech signals, are highly non-stationary (i.e., the output of a random process representing speech production mechanism) and therefore, a high value of uncertainty is expected. This implies that speech signals have good asymptotic behaviour, which can further be used to determine the instantaneous frequency (IF) and group delay (GD) functions by their invertibility property in the case of asymptotic signals [].

2   The Time-Bandwidth Product (TBP)

The concept of *effective bandwidth* as defined by Gabor is important [11]. The duration of a signal $x(t)$ can be defined by its standard deviation, σ_t. If σ_t is small, we can say the duration of the signal is small. If σ_t is infinite, then the signal is of very long duration, however, its energy, $|x(t)|^2$, may be finite. Thus, in order to find the mean, we consider $|x(t)|^2$ as a probability density function (*pdf*). This explanation has the same analogy for the frequency domain. We can define effective bandwidth (σ_ω) as the second moment of $|X(\omega)|^2$ around $\omega = 0$, given that $x(t)$ is a zero-mean (i.e., $\langle \omega \rangle = 0$) finite-energy signal. Therefore, $\sigma_\omega{}^2 = \int_{\omega \in R} (\omega - \langle \omega \rangle)^2 \left| X(\omega) \right|^2 d\omega$. Since $\langle \omega \rangle = 0$,

$$\sigma_\omega{}^2 = \int_{-\infty}^{\infty} \omega^2 |X(\omega)|^2 d\omega. \tag{1}$$

The *effective duration* (σ_t) is given by:

$$\sigma_t{}^2 = \int_{t \in R} t^2 |x(t)|^2 dt. \tag{2}$$

Due to the time-scaling property of the Fourier transform, expansion in the time domain is equivalent to compression in the frequency domain [17]. Hence, $\sigma_t^2 \sigma_\omega^2 = constant$, where $\sigma_t^2 \sigma_\omega^2$ is the TBP. Furthermore, the value of the TBP is equal to the area of Heisenberg's box [15]. It has been found that for most of the practical signals, the value of TBP is constant with the definitions of σ_ω^2 and σ_t^2 in (1) and (2), respectively. The TBP gives the "richness" of the information content of such signals [3,13]. A subset of these types of signals are called as *asymptotic signals*. A large value of the TBP is an important characteristic of an asymptotic signal. For a signal to be asymptotic, the conditions are: σ_t and σ_ω should be finite, the value of TBP should be large, and the signal should have finite energy. Therefore, the condition relating to TBP has to be checked because the remaining conditions of asymptoticity are very well known to be satisfied by a speech signal [9].

Asymptotic signals hold an important property relating the IF and GD functions. For a monocomponent signal (a signal with a single frequency component) with a large value of TBP and having the IF function ($\omega_i(t)$) as a monotonic function in time, $\omega_i(t)$ approaches the GD function, $\tau_g(\omega)$ [5]. However, most of the practical signals (such as speech) are multicomponent in nature. They can be decomposed into a finite number of monocomponent signals by suitable subband filtering, and even if one of the subband signals shows asymptoticity, the multi-component signal as a whole can be said to have an asymptotic behaviour [3]. The definition of IF for an analytic signal $x_a(t) = a(t)e^{j\phi(t)}$ is given by:

$$\omega_i(t) = \frac{d\phi(t)}{dt}. \tag{3}$$

Clearly, the IF defined in (3) is a function of t only. However, the GD function is given by $\tau_g(\omega) = -\frac{d(\theta(\omega))}{d\omega}$. The GD depends on the unwrapped phase spectrum $\theta(\omega)$, and it further depends on both $a(t)$ and $\phi(t)$. This means that for IF and GD to be the *inverse* of each other, there has to be some condition. In particular, if TBP is large, the IF and GD functions are inverse of each other [4,9].

3   Asymptoticity via Heisenberg's Uncertainty Principle

A signal can be seen as a wave function whose location is analogous to *time* and its momentum is analogous to *frequency*. Thus, its TFD is within the limits given by *the uncertainty principle*. The uncertainty principle in a signal analysis states that if the effective bandwidth is σ_ω, then the effective duration has to be at least $1/\sigma_\omega$, which leads to $\sigma_t^2\sigma_\omega^2 \geq \frac{1}{4}$. The proof follows next.

The signal is assumed to be with zero-mean in time and zero-mean in frequency. To make the mean equal to zero, the signal is translated in time and frequency. Let the translated signal be denoted simply as $x(t)$. Because of being zero-mean, its effective bandwidth is $\int \omega^2 |X(\omega)|^2 d\omega = \int |x'(t)|^2 dt$, and the effective duration is $\int t^2 |x(t)|^2 dt$. And therefore, we have,

$$\sigma_t^2\sigma_\omega^2 = \int t^2 |x(t)|^2 dt \times \int |x'(t)|^2 dt. \tag{4}$$

Now, applying the Cauchy-Schwartz inequality given in (5) on (4), we get (6).

$$\int |f(t)|^2 dt \times \int |g(t)|^2 dt \geq \left| \int f^*(t)g(t)dt \right|^2. \tag{5}$$

$$\sigma_t^2\sigma_\omega^2 \geq \left| \int tx^*(t)x'(t)dt \right|^2. \tag{6}$$

Since $x(t)$ can be expressed as $A(t)e^{j\varphi(t)}$, the integrand in (6) can be solved as

$$tx^*(t)x'(t) = tA'(t)A(t) + jt\varphi'(t)A^2(t),$$
$$= \frac{1}{2}\frac{d}{dt}(tA^2(t)) - \frac{1}{2}A^2(t) + jt\varphi'(t)A^2(t). \tag{7}$$

Therefore, substituting the above integrand in (6) gives $\sigma_t{}^2\sigma_\omega{}^2 \geq \frac{1}{4} + Cov_{t\omega}{}^2$ where $\frac{1}{4} + Cov^2$, and since Cov^2 is always positive, it can be ignored. Hence, we get $\sigma_t^2\sigma_\omega^2 \geq \frac{1}{4}$. It should be noted that, the Cauchy-Schwartz inequality $|\langle a, b\rangle| \leq ||a||.||b||$ for two vectors a and b, becomes an equality when a and b are co-linear. This is the case for a Gaussian signal, where $\sigma_t^2\sigma_\omega^2$ becomes *exactly* equal to $\frac{1}{4}$ [15].

4   Experimental Analysis

In this section, we demonstrate the behaviour of TBP of synthetic speech signals to analyze their asymptotic nature. In addition, we have experimentally analyzed the individual effect of effective bandwidth and effective duration on the TBP.

4.1   Uncertainty *vs.* Decay Factor

Similar to the resonances of wind instruments, the human vocal tract system and the airflow from the glottis can be modelled as a linear filter with resonance. The resonant frequencies of the vocal tract system are called as *formants* [19] The formant frequencies can be determined from the locations of the peaks in the spectrum of a vocal tract system. It should be noted that not all peaks correspond to vocal tract resonances, and formant frequency is not equal to the resonance frequency of the vocal tract. The vocal tract system is modelled as a linear, time-invariant, all-pole system, to estimate the formants. Mathematically, the z-domain system function of the vocal tract system corresponding to the first four formants can be expressed as:

$$H(z) = \prod_{i=1}^{4} H_i(z) \quad \text{where,} \tag{8}$$

$$H_i(z) = \frac{b_0}{(1 - c_i z^{-1})(1 - c_i^* z^{-1})}, \tag{9}$$

where b_0 is the gain and c_is denote the poles of the transfer function, where $|c_i| < 1$. Therefore, the impulse response of the ith digital 2nd order resonator, corresponding to the ith formant, is given by $h_i[n] = \frac{b_{0i} r_i^n sin[\omega_i[n+1]]}{sin[\omega_i]} u[n]$, where r_i and w_i represent the pole radius and pole angle, respectively. Since the vocal tract system is considered to be linear and time-invariant, the speech signal is modelled as convolution of the glottal excitation source with the impulse response of the vocal tract system, as shown in Fig. 1. For voiced speech such as vowels, the glottal excitation source signal is represented as a periodic train of impulses, where the period of the train of impulses is called the (fundamental) pitch period (T_0) of the speaker [1,19].

From (8), the impulse response of the vocal tract system $h(n)$ can be modelled as a cascade system of four 2nd order resonators, such that the resonant frequency of each individual resonator is a formant frequency [18,19]. Therefore, the impulse response of the vocal tract system is expressed in terms of

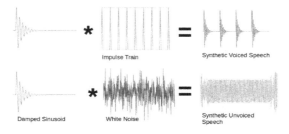

Fig. 1. Damped sinusoid convolved with (a) impulse-train and, (b) white Gaussian noise, to get synthetic voiced and unvoiced speech, respectively.

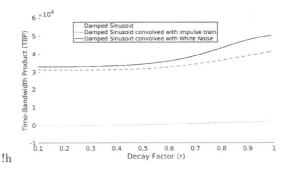

!h

Fig. 2. TBP trend for damped sinusoid convolved with impulse-train and white noise.

damped sinusoidal signal with a damping factor r, and for the stability in the z-domain, $|r| < 1$. Since the vocal tract system is a stable system, there are energy losses through the movement of articulators, such as the glottis, lips, and cheeks. Therefore, the damping in the sinusoid provides a mechanism to model various energy losses in the system (such as wall vibrations, viscosity, thermal, and lip radiation) [10]. In this paper, we have shown how uncertainty varies with the damping (decay) factor. Here, we have considered a decaying sinusoidal signal convoluted with a sequence of impulses and also a decaying sinusoid convolved with white noise, as shown in Fig. 1. It can be observed from Fig. 2 that as the decay factor r increases, the uncertainty (TBP) also increases. This is justified by the argument that a smaller decay factor of a sinusoid means that the signal attains its steady-state behaviour sooner and, hence, it is relatively *less uncertain*. However, if the decay factor is large, the signal is uncertain for a longer duration of time. Here, the signal being more uncertain means that its TBP is more.

We have visualized the TBP plot using Algorithm-7 for three cases- 1) decaying sinusoid, 2) when decaying sinusoid is convoluted with an impulse train (representing modelling of a synthetic voiced speech), and 3) when decaying sinusoid is convolved with white noise (i.e., modelling of synthetic unvoiced speech). We

---

Algorithm 1: TBP Computation

Input: Sampling frequency $F_s = 16000Hz$
Output: tbp_{gen}
/* Pass the speech signal x through the filterbank   */
1 window length $= 20ms$, window shift $= 10ms$
/* For each frame, do the following: */
2 **for** $j \leftarrow 1$ **to** *number of frames* **do**
3      $var_{gen} \leftarrow variance(Gen(j, :), mean_g en, t_{gen})$;
4      $mean_{freq} \leftarrow mean(fft(Gen(l, :)), freq)/(2 * pi)$;
5      $var_{freq} \leftarrow variance(A, mean_{freq}, freq)$;
6      $tbp_{gen} \leftarrow var_{gen} * var_{freq}$
7 **return** tbp_{gen}

---

observed a jump in the uncertainty *vs.* decay factor plot from case-1 to case-2. That is, we observed that the value of uncertainty for synthetically modelled unvoiced speech is more than that of the synthetically modelled voiced speech. This jump is primarily due to the change in the speech excitation source, i.e., more randomness is introduced when we convolve the damped sinusoid with white noise, as compared to when the damped sinusoid is convolved with an impulse-train signal.

Fig. 3. Waterfall plot of (a) time variance σ_t^2, (b) frequency variance σ_ω^2, and (c) TBP of the phoneme 'aa' from the TIMIT dataset for all the 630 male speakers.

4.2 TBP for Speech Signals

The authors have carried out experiments on the TIMIT dataset for five speakers, and the values of TBP for each vowel have been analyzed for each speaker as shown in Fig. 4. Notably, in a naturally occurring signal, such as speech, the uncertainty is very high as compared to the simulated signals, such as damped sinusoid as was shown in Fig. 3. The behaviour of TBP of each vowel for each speaker can be seen from the plot in Fig. 4. This behaviour can be used to determine if there is any speaker-specific characteristic, and it is an open research problem.

Figure 3 shows the waterfall plots for the vowel *'aa'* across the speakers from the TIMIT dataset for time variance, and frequency variance, respectively. A

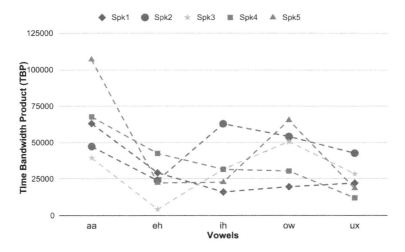

Fig. 4. Variation of TBP for vowels of five male speakers of the TIMIT dataset.

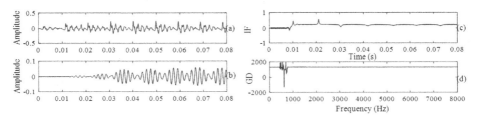

Fig. 5. (a) Speech signal corresponding to vowel 'aa' taken from the TIMIT corpus for one speaker as input, (b) output of 500 Hz resonator, (c) instantaneous frequency of the filtered signal, and (d) group delay function of the filtered signal.

Gabor filterbank was used to separate subband signals because of its optimal resolution both in time and frequency-domains [15]. Here, 15 linearly-spaced subband filters are used and for each of these subband signals thus obtained, variances in time and frequency-domains are estimated to get the TBP. It can be observed that the frequency variance is increasing very smoothly with an increase in the centre frequency of the bandpass filter. However, the time variance is not monotonically increasing with an increase in the center frequency of the bandpass filter. It can also be observed that the value of the time variance is significantly less than the value of the frequency variance. It shows that the contribution of the frequency variance is much larger than the time variance in TBP of a speech signal, thus, making speech *asymptotic*. We have then estimated the IF and GD for a synthetic speech excitation source and also for the vowel 'aa' taken from the TIMIT corpus for one male speaker [12]. For this, the signal is passed through a 500-Hz resonator (9), with poles at $0.922 - 0.382j$ and $0.922 + 0.382j$. The value of r is taken as 0.99. Figure 5 shows the IF and GD plots corresponding to vowel 'aa' from the TIMIT corpus. Notably, it remains an open research problem to express the *inverse* relationship between the GD and the IF functions of speech signals.

5   Future Work and Conclusion

In this study, the asymptotic behaviour of speech is investigated by invoking Heisenberg's uncertainty principle in a signal processing framework to estimate the area of Heisenberg's box (i.e., TBP). It was observed that the asymptoticity of a signal increases with an increase in TBP. The TBP of synthetic unvoiced speech is found to be greater than the TBP of synthetically modelled voiced speech. Further analysis has also been done by extracting vowels from the entire TIMIT corpus. The authors have analyzed the variation of the high TBP obtained for 5 male speakers. It was observed that the effective bandwidth contributes more to the high value of TBP. In the future, the distribution of TBP values can be used to have a discriminatory boundary between speaker-specific and speech-specific characteristics. Additional experiments on finding the IF and GD of a speech signal have been done. However, a distinct relation between the quantities is yet to be calculated and analyzed for a speech signal. This analysis may lead to numerous interesting feature extraction techniques for various Automatic Speech Recognition (ASR) system and Automatic Speaker Verification (ASV) systems [2,8,16].

References

1. Akande, O.O., Murphy, P.J.: Estimation of the vocal tract transfer function with application to glottal wave analysis. Speech Commun. **46**(1), 15–36 (2005)
2. Andersen, K.T., Moonen, M.: Adaptive time-frequency analysis for noise reduction in an audio filterbank with low delay. IEEE/ACM Trans. Audio Speech Lang. Process. **24**(4), 784–795 (2016)
3. Boashash, B.: Estimating and interpreting the instantaneous frequency of a signal. I. Fundam. Proc. IEEE **80**(4), 520–538 (1992)
4. Boashash, B.: Time-frequency signal analysis. In: Advances in Spectrum Estimation (1993)
5. Boashash, B., Jones, G., O'Shea, P.: Instantaneous frequency of signals: concepts, estimation techniques and applications. In: Advanced Algorithms and Architectures for Signal Processing IV, vol. 1152, pp. 382–400. International Society for Optics and Photonics (1989)
6. Boashash, B., Ouelha, S.: Designing high-resolution time-frequency and time-scale distributions for the analysis and classification of non-stationary signals: a tutorial review with a comparison of features performance. Digit. Sig. Process. **77**, 120–152 (2018)
7. Claasen, T., Mecklenbrauker, W.: The Wigner distribution - a tool for time-frequency signal analysis. Philips J. Res. **35**(3), 217–250 (1980)
8. Daneshvar, M., Salehi, P.: Optimization of multicomponent signals entered to the system using estimation of instantaneous frequency. J. Vib. Control **28**, 964–981 (2021)

9. Delprat, N., Escudié, B., Guillemain, P., Kronland-Martinet, R., Tchamitchian, P., Torresani, B.: Asymptotic wavelet and Gabor analysis: extraction of instantaneous frequencies. IEEE Trans. Inf. Theory **38**(2), 644–664 (1992)
10. Fant, G.: Acoustic Theory of Speech Production. Walter de Gruyter (1970)
11. Gabor, D.: Theory of Communication. Part 1: The analysis of information. J. Inst. Electr. Engi.-Part III: Radio Commun. Eng. **93**(26), 429–441 (1946)
12. Garofolo, J.S., et al.: TIMIT acoustic-phonetic continuous speech corpus LDC93s1. Linguistic Data Consortium (1993), Linguistic Data Consortium, Philadelphia, USA
13. L. Cohen: Time-Frequency Analysis, vol. 778. Prentice-Hall, Hoboken (1995)
14. Cohen, L.: Instantaneous frequency and group delay of a filtered signal. J. Franklin Inst. **337**(4), 329–346 (2000)
15. Mallat, S.: A wavelet tour of signal processing. The Sparse Way (1999)
16. Murthy, H.A., Yegnanarayana, B.: Group delay functions and its applications in speech technology. Sadhana **36**(5), 745–782 (2011)
17. Oppenheim, A., Schafer, R.: Signals and Systems, 2nd Ed., Prentice-Hall, New Jersey, USA
18. Portnoff, M.R.: A quasi-one-dimensional digital simulation for the time-varying vocal tract. Ph.D. thesis, Massachusetts Institute of Technology, USA (1973)
19. Quatieri, T.F.: Discrete-Time Speech Signal Processing: Principles and Practice. 2nd ed., Pearson Education India, India (2006)
20. Stankovic, L.: A method for time-frequency analysis. IEEE Trans. Signal Process. **42**(1), 225–229 (1994)

Improvement of Audio-Visual Keyword Spotting System Accuracy Using Excitation Source Feature

Salam Nandakishor[✉] and Debadatta Pati

Department of Electronics and Communication Engineering, National Institute of Technology Nagaland, Chumukedima, Dimapur 797103, Nagaland, India
salamnandu@gmail.com

Abstract. In this paper, we proposed a robust audio-visual keyword spotting (AVKS) system. This system is developed using DNN (Deep Neural Network) model with State Level Minimum Bayes Risk (sMBR) criteria. The symbols of International Phonetic Alphabet (IPA) are used for representing the speech sounds at phonetic level. Our proposed system can recognize 34 phonemes, silence region and can also detect the predefined keywords formed by these phonemes. Most of the audio-visual keyword spotting system used Mel-frequency cepstral coefficient (MFCC) as audio feature. This feature represents only the vocal-tract related information but does not contain excitation source information. Therefore, we explore the excitation source features as the supplementary information in this work. The excitation source features extracted from glottal flow derivative (GFD) and linear prediction (LP) residual through standard mel cepstral analysis are termed as Glottal Mel-Frequency Cepstral Coefficient (GMFCC) and Residual Mel-Frequency Cepstral Coefficient (RMFCC) respectively. The GFD signal is generated using Iterative Adaptive Inverse Filtering (IAIF) method whereas LP residual is estimated by inverse filtering process. In our experimental analysis, we observe that the performance of glottal based excitation feature is better than LP residual based excitation source feature in keyword spotting task. Hence, we consider the GMFCC features in development of our proposed system. The AVKS system using MFCC and DCT (Discrete Cosine Transform) based visual features extracted from mouth region provides an average accuracy of 93.87%, whereas the inclusion of GMFCC feature improves the performance to 94.93%. The experimental observations show the benefit of excitation source information for audio-visual keyword spotter under noisy condition.

Keywords: AVKS · Residual mel-frequency cepstral coefficient · Glottal mel-frequency cepstral coefficient · State level minimum bayes risk

1 Introduction

Keyword spotting system enables to detect the specific words from the continuous speech. This type of system can be used in many real time applications

© The Author(s), under exclusive license to Springer Nature Switzerland AG 2023
A. Karpov et al. (Eds.): SPECOM 2023, LNAI 14339, pp. 344–356, 2023.
https://doi.org/10.1007/978-3-031-48312-7_28

such as voice assistant, customer care service and smart speakers etc. However, such applications may not be working properly in noisy environment due to quality degradation of speech sound. This creates the difficulty in detection of keywords by the machine. To solve this problem, researchers use the visual features as complementary information along with audio feature for spotting the predefined keywords. This type of system is known as audio-visual keyword spotting (AVKS) system [1]. In this work, we developed a phoneme based audio-visual keyword spotting system. The MFCC audio feature is concatenated with DCT based visual feature by using feature level fusion approach which is known as early integration fusion [2]. As the rapid growth of machine learning techniques and availability of high computational machines, researchers used various neural networks approaches to improve the performance of keywords spotting systems [3–5]. Therefore, we employed DNN (Deep Neural Network) classifier for modeling the phonemes. We further improves the performance of the proposed system by using State Level Minimum Bayes Risk (sMBR) criteria. The main advantage of phoneme based audio-visual keyword spotter is that it can detect any keywords formed by combination of phonemes.

Speech production can considered as a process in which the time-varying vocal-tract system is excited by a time-varying excitation source [6]. Researchers used the audio feature MFCC for representing the vocal-tract characteristics in speech recognition tasks [7]. Some of speech sound units (phonemes) such as (/b/ and /p/, /t/ and /d/) have same place of articulation and same manner of articulation [8]. It means they are having similar vocal-tract characteristics. Moreover, these phonemes have similar lips shape or lips movements while producing the speech sounds [9]. Because of these similar vocal-tract characteristics and similar lips movements, it may create confusion in phoneme recognition and resulting inaccurate keyword detection from continuous speech. In this case, the supplementary feature; the excitation source information may be helpful to differentiate between similar sound units or phonemes by machine. The excitation source signal can be represented by linear prediction (LP) residual [10,11] or the glottal flow derivative (GFD) signal derived from speech signal. Several GFD extraction methods have been reported in [12–18]. In a recent work [19], the Iterative Adaptive Inverse Filtering (IAIF) approach is found effective for deriving the excitation source information from speech signal. In this work, GFD signal is computed by using IAIF algorithm and LP residual of speech signal is estimated by using inverse filtering approach.

The rest of the paper is organized as follows: Sect. 2 mentions some research works related to audio-visual keyword spotting task. Section 3 provides the details information about the database used in system development. Section 4 describes about the development of DNN-sMBR based audio-visual Keyword Spotting system. Experimental results analysis are discussed in Sect. 5. The conclusion of the paper is declared in Sect. 6.

2   Related Work

Very few research has been done to detect the keywords audio-visually [1]. In [20], authors developed an HMM based audio-visual keyword spotting system. The normalized histogram intensity of mouth region was used as visual feature. The MFCC audio feature was combined with visual feature using feature level fusion approach. The objective of proposed keyword spotter was to detect the 19 English keywords. The performance of this system was analyzed at various SNR levels. The noisy audio speech signals were generated by adding white noise. The audio-visual keyword spotter performed better than the audio based keyword spotter at all SNR levels.

In another work [21], authors used the conventional HMM garbage model in development of Mandarin based audio-visual keyword spotting system. They proposed a visual feature named as discriminative local spatial-temporal descriptor (disCLBP-TOP). The models built by acoustic feature MFCC and visual features were combined by adaptive integration approach with appropriate weights. A sigmoid function was used to generate these weights. The 30 Mandarin keywords belong to 12 male and 8 female speakers were used for system performance analysis. They also compared the performance between bimodal (audio-visual keyword spotter) and unimodal (audio or visual based keyword spotter) using white and babble noise added noisy speech signals.

In [1], authors presented a novel lip descriptor that comprise of both geometric features and appearance based features. The geometric features extracted from lips region were combined with appearance based spatiotemporal features. The audio features were extracted using mel cepstral analysis. Authors used two-step strategy HMM based keyword spotting system to make system more robust. At first stage, the acoustic and visual keyword with log-likelihoods were generated. The decision fusion was applied in the second stage to generate the final keyword. The OuluVS and PKU-AV database were used for experimental results analysis.

Table 1. The reported AVKS systems and their results.

Method	Accuracy (in %)
HMM based AVKS [20]	78
HMM-garbage based AVKS [21]	75.1
Two step strategy HMM based AVKS [1]	80.5

The results of the reported AVKS system are shown in Table 1. All of these reported works used the MFCC as audio feature in development of AVKS system. They were mainly focus on visual features to improve the system performance. It is interesting to explore the excitation source based audio feature as supplementary information for audio-visual keyword spotting task.

3   Database Description

Our proposed system is developed using train data set of track 1 of the 2nd 'CHiME' Challenge audio database [25]. The utterance structure of this database is shown below.

[command(4)] [color(4)] [preposition(4)] [letter(25)] [digit(10)] [adverb(4)]

The numerical value shown inside the bracket defines the number of different commands, colors, prepositions, letters, digits and adverbs present in the database. The commands are BIN, LAY, PLACE and SET. The different colors available in the utterances are BLUE, GREEN, RED and WHITE. Prepositions present in database are AT, BY, IN and WITH. The English alphabets from A-Z excluding W and digits from 0 to 9 are also available in the database. The words; AGAIN, NOW, PLEASE and SOON are the 4 adverbs utterances used in this database. The database belongs to 34 speakers (18 male, 16 female) [25].

Clean audio speech material was taken from the Grid corpus [26]. The clean audio speech were convolved with a set of binaural room impulse responses ((BRIRs) to simulate the speaker movements and reverberation. The background noise recorded from the living room were mixed with the audio speech signals to generate the noisy speech signals. These noisy speech signals were generated at six different SNRs (-6 dB, -3 dB, 0 dB, 3dB, 6 dB and 9 dB).

The track 1 of the 2nd 'CHiME' database comprises of 3 data sets. They are (1) training set (2) development set and (3) test set. Each speaker of training set has 500 utterances. The development data set consists of 600 speech utterances at each SNR level. Similarly test data set contain same number of utterances of development data set. The speech signals were recorded with 16 bits and sampled at 16 kHz. The video features are extracted from video data of Grid database.

4   Development of DNN-sMBR Based Audio-Visual Keyword Spotting System

The processing steps involved in development of our proposed DNN-sMBR based audio-visual keyword spotting system are (a) Data Preparation and Pronunciation dictionary (b) Feature Extraction (c) Modeling and (d) Keyword Decoder.

Data preparation is an important step required in development of this proposed system. This processing step provides information about; (a) mapping of each speaker ID to its corresponding utterances IDs (b) paths of audio speech wav files along with their corresponding utterance IDs (c) assignment of each utterance ID with corresponding speaker ID and (d) transcription of all the utterances. Pronunciation dictionary contains the information about phonemes present in the database used for system development, silence region information and lexicon. The silence region is denoted by word 'SIL'. In order to understand the speech sounds in phonetic level, we analyze the mentioned 2nd 'CHiME' database properly and represent the phonemes by using International Phonetic

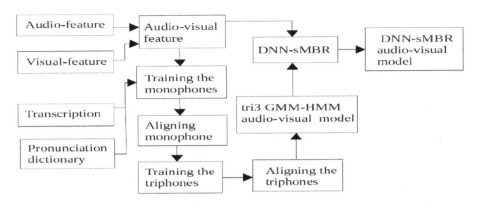

Fig. 1. Training phase of proposed audio-visual keyword spotting system.

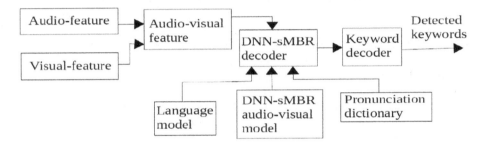

Fig. 2. Testing phase of proposed audio-visual keyword spotting system.

Alphabet (IPA) symbols. The IPA symbols and corresponding assigned ASCII of these phonemes are listed in Table 2.

The MFCC features are extracted from the input audio speech using standard mel cepstral analysis approach. The glottal excitation source based feature; GMFCC feature are derived from the GFD signal. These two features are concatenated to obtain a feature combination of vocal-tract and excitation source information. The dimension of the GMFCC is considered same as the 13 dimensional MFCC feature. Therefore, the total dimension of combined audio feature is 26. Image frames are extracted from the input video, then landmark points of mouth region are detected using Viola-Jones algorithm [27]. Discrete cosine transform (DCT) coefficients of landmark points of gray scale mouth region images are calculated to generate 63-dimensional visual features. In order to maintain same number of frames for both audio and visual features, the DCT coefficients are interpolated by using differential digital analyzer. Then the audio and visual features are concatenated in frame-wise manner to acquire 89 dimensional audio-visual features.

The block diagrams of training and testing phase of proposed audio-visual keyword spotting system are shown in Figs. 1 and 2. An audio-visual based

Table 2. List of phoneme used in development of audio-visual keyword spotting system.

Sl. No	Phoneme	Name in ASCII	Sl. No	Phoneme	Name in ASCII
1	b	B	18	w	W
2	ʃ	CH	19	y	Y
3	d	D	20	z	Z
4	ð	DH	21	aː	AA
5	f	F	22	æ	AE
6	g	G	23	ʌ	AH
7	ʤ	JH	24	ɔː	AO
8	k	K	25	ə	AX
9	l	L	26	ɛ	EX
10	m	M	27	i	IH
11	n	N	28	iː	IY
12	p	P	29	uː	UW
13	r	R	30	aʊ	AW
14	s	S	31	aɪ	AY
15	t	T	32	eɪ	EY
16	θ	TH	33	əʊ	OW
17	v	V	34	ɪə	IA

monophone GMM-HMM model is built using the audio-visual features, transcriptions and pronunciation dictionary. Contextual information of neighbouring phonemes that is front and back phoneme are not considered in monophone model. The audio-visual features are aligned with corresponding reference transcriptions using force alignment Viterbi algorithm. The monophone model is further extended to triphone GMM-HMM model. In this context-dependent triphone model, audio-visual features of neighbouring frames that is ± 3 frames are spliced to capture the dynamic information. Then, the dimension of this spliced audio-visual feature is reduced to 40 using Linear Discriminant Analysis (LDA) [28]. A popular speaker normalization technique, Maximum Likelihood Linear Transform is used to minimize the speakers variation. To make the proposed system more robust and speaker independent; speaker adaptation training (SAT) and feature-space Maximum Likelihood Linear Regression (fMLLR) [29] are used. This type of model is generally known as tri3 GMM-HMM audio-visual model. The pre-training of DNN is done by training the stack of Restricted Boltzmann machine (RBMs) through Contrastive Divergence (CD) approach. Updating of weights during the pre-training stage are used to initialize the DNN parameters, it allows the discriminative fine-tuning and reduce over fitting. During fine-tuning of DNN, the parameters are updated in a layer-wise manner by using back-propagation and Stochastic Gradient Descent (SGD) techniques. The sequence discriminative training method "state-level minimum Bayes risk (sMBR)" [30] is employed to emphasize the state sequence with better frame accuracy with respect to reference alignment. This model is represented as DNN-sMBR model. The model consists of 6 hidden layers with sigmoid activation function and used 18 beam for decoding. Each layer of DNN has 2048 neurons. At audio-visual keyword decoder stage, the system is ready to generate automatic transcriptions and detect the keywords of unknown test utterances. The system needs test input audio-visual feature, trained audio-visual model, language model and pronunciation dictionary to generate automatic transcription.

5   Experimental Results and Discussion

Visual keyword spotting systems are developed using different modeling approaches and compare their accuracies to select the best model for proposed AVKS system. We also compare the performance of LP based excitation source feature and glottal based excitation feature in context of keyword spotting task. Then, the outperforming model and excitation source feature are used in development of audio-visual keyword spotting system.

5.1   Visual Keywords Spotting System

Visual keyword spotting (VKS) is an automatic process of identifying the query keywords present in the video sequences using visual features. The 63-dimensional DCT coefficients visual features are extracted from mouth region images. These image frames are obtained from videos data of Grid database. The performance of the proposed visual keyword spotting system is evaluated using different models; GMM-HMM, DNN, DNN-sMBR-1 and DNN-sMBR-5 with visual features. The DNN-sMBR-1 and DNN-sMBR-5 represent the DNN model with state-level minimum Bayes risk (sMBR) criteria with 1 and 5 iterations respectively.

Table 3. Performance comparison of models for visual digits keyword spotting system.

Model	Accuracy (in %)
GMM-HMM	82.65
DNN	87.07
DNN-sMBR-1	88.27
DNN-sMBR-5	**89.29**

Digits are the most commonly used one time password (OTP) and input command words in real time applications like customer care service or automatic login system. Therefore, we consider the digits from zero to nine as the keywords for both visual keyword spotting system as well as audio-visual keyword spotting system. The development data set of Grid database is used for performance analysis of this visual keyword spotting system. From the experimental results provided in Table 3, we notice that DNN based system gives better accuracy than GMM-HMM based VKS system. The performance of DNN based system increases when the sMBR criteria is applied. We also analyze the performance of DNN-sMBR based system with different iterations, we observe the system performance improves when the number of iterations of sMBR training increase from 1 to 5. After 5th iteration, no further improvement in the system performance. Therefore, we adopt DNN-sMBR model with 5 iterations in development of proposed AVKS system.

5.2   Selection of Excitation Source Feature for Proposed AVKS System

The excitation source features have been explored for phoneme recognition task. The use of excitation source feature in speech recognition area is very limited as compare to other application like speaker recognition task. Some of the works related to excitation source features are reported in [7, 22–24]. They extracted the excitation source features from LP residual signal derived from speech signal. These excitation source features were used for improving the performance of phone recognizer. In this work, we explore the glottal based excitation source feature (GMFCC) and compared to the LP residual based excitation source feature (RMFCC).

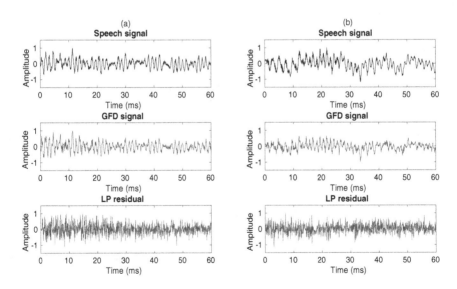

Fig. 3. Speech signal, GFD signal and LP residual of Alveolar Plosive sound units (a) t and (b) d.

Some of sound units such as (/p/ and /b/), (/t/ and /d/), (/k/ and /g/) are very confused among each other due to similar characteristics. We manually

extract the phoneme /t/ portion from speech sound of English letter 'T' occur
in utterance (srwt1n.wav) using linguistic tool 'Praat'. Similarly the phoneme
/d/ is extracted from sound 'D' present in utterance (lrwd1n.wav). The speech
signal, GFD signal and LP residual of these Alveolar plosive sound units are
shown in Fig. 3. The closeness between these Alveolar plosive sound units is
analyzed by plotting kernel density using GMFCC and RMFCC feature. Kernel
density estimation (KDE) method estimates the probability density function of
feature vectors using kernels as weights and smoothing the density function by
appropriate bandwidth. In this work, we used Gaussian kernel and bandwidth
equal to 1.8 for plotting the kernel density of Alveolar plosive sound units.

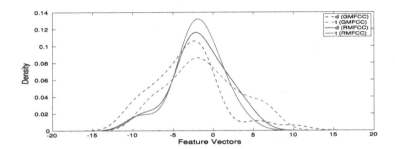

Fig. 4. The kernel density plot of Alveolar plosive sound units t and d using GMFCC
and RMFCC feature.

In Fig. 4, blue color lines represent kernel density plots for sound unit /d/ and
red color lines for phoneme /t/. The dotted lines belong to kernel density plots of
GMFCC features whereas the solid lines is for RMFCC features. The dotted lines
are less overlapping as compared to solid lines. This shows that GMFCC feature
has more discriminative ability than RMFCC feature to distinguish the similar
sound units like alveolar plosive. However, this type of analysis is a statistical
approach. We further evaluate the performance of GMFCC and RMFCC feature
in terms of keyword detection rate.

Table 4. Performance comparison of GMFCC and RMFCC at different SNR levels.

Feature	−6 dB	−3 dB	0 dB	3 dB	Average
GMFCC	68.73	76.12	88.66	92.27	**81.45**
RMFCC	61.34	63.75	77.84	83.16	71.45

The average accuracy of DNN-sMBR-5 based keyword spotter using GMFCC
feature is 81.45% whereas RMFCC feature gives 71.45%. At all SNR levels,
the glottal based excitation source feature performs better than LP residual

based excitation source feature for detecting keywords. The experimental results available in Table 4 reveal that the GMFCC feature are robust than RMFCC under noisy condition. Therefore, we consider this glottal based excitation source feature in development of proposed AVKS system.

5.3 Performance Analysis of Proposed DNN-sMBR-5 Based Keyword Spotting System

The accuracies of digits keyword spotting using vocal-tract feature (MFCC), glottal based excitation source feature (GMFCC), visual feature (V) and their combination are given in Table 5. At 3dB, the accuracy of keyword detection using MFCC feature is more than GMFCC feature as well as visual feature. However, the performance degraded from 0 dB to -6 dB due to background noise present in utterances of test data set. Similar problem also affects the performance of GMFCC feature as well.

Table 5. Accuracies of Digits keyword spotting system with different features and its feature combination.

Feature	−6 dB	−3 dB	0 dB	3 dB	Average
MFCC	76.80	84.71	92.96	95.25	87.43
GMFCC	68.73	76.12	88.66	92.27	81.45
V	89.29	89.29	89.29	89.29	89.29
MFCC + GMFCC	79.21	86.94	93.30	96.05	88.88
MFCC + V	92.00	93.81	94.19	95.50	93.87
GMFCC + V	91.07	92.44	92.44	93.64	92.40
MFCC + GMFCC + V	93.99	94.50	94.85	96.39	**94.93**

From experimental results analysis, we know that MFCC feature is better than GMFCC for keyword spotting task. However, the combination of these features perform better than individual feature; MFCC and GMFCC. At all SNR levels, the accuracies of keyword spotting using MFCC feature are improved by combining with GMFCC feature. This shows the glottal excitation source features can be used as supplementary feature along with MFCC feature for automatic transcription and keyword spotting under noisy environment. The performance improvement in keyword spotting when added excitation source information to vocal-tract information is because of confusion reduction between similar phonemes.

The audio features can be corrupted by acoustic background noise, therefore visual feature are combined together with them. The performance of audio-visual keyword spotting system is not that much fluctuate as compare to audio-based keyword spotting system. The audio-visual keyword spotting system performs well at all SNR levels. We compare the performance of audio-visual keyword spotting systems developed by using (MFCC with visual feature), (GMFCC with visual feature), and combination of MFCC with GMFCC and Visual feature. The average accuracy of keywords spotting of these three audio-visual systems are 93.87%, 92.40% and 94.93% respectively. The AVKS system develop using MFCC along with visual feature gives better accuracy than system develop using GMFCC and visual feature together. The best average accuracy of keyword spotting is observed when MFCC, GMFCC and visual feature are combined together. These experimental results reveal that glottal excitation source feature is useful to use as supplementary information for audio-visual keyword spotting system under noisy environment.

6 Conclusion

In this work, we explore a glottal based excitation source feature (GMFCC), particularly for detecting the audio-visual keywords under noisy background. This glottal based excitation source feature is found more suitable than RMFCC feature for keyword spotting task. The performance of DNN based visual keyword spotting system is improved by using 'sMBR' sequence discriminative training with 5 iterations. This DNN model also works very well for audio-visual keyword spotting system. The feature combination of MFCC and GMFCC gives better accuracy than individual features; MFCC and GMFCC in keywords detection task. The performance of these combined audio feature degraded under noisy condition. To solve this issue, a robust visual feature is combined to audio features. The AVKS system developed using MFCC and visual features is improved by adding the glottal excitation source feature. In future work, the performance of proposed system can be evaluated by using unseen speakers data.

References

1. Pingping, W., et al.: A novel lip descriptor for audio-visual keyword spotting based on adaptive decision fusion. IEEE Trans. Multimedia **18**(3), 326–338 (2016)
2. Nandakishor, S., Pati, D.: Analysis of lombard effect by using hybrid visual features for ASR. In: Pattern Recognition and Machine Intelligence (PReMI 2021) (2021)
3. Higuchi, T., Gupta, A., Dhir, C.: Multi-task learning with cross attention for keyword spotting. In: IEEE Automatic Speech Recognition and Understanding Workshop (2021)
4. Berg, A., Connor, M., Cruz, M.T.: Keyword transformer: a self-attention model for keyword spotting. In: Proceedings of INTERSPEECH (2021)
5. Li, Y., et al.: Audio-visual keyword transformer for unconstrained sentence-level keyword spotting. In: CAAI Transactions on Intelligence Technology (2023)
6. Rabiner, L.R., Juang, B.-H., Yegnanarayana, B.: Fundamentals of Speech Recognition. Pearson Education (2012)
7. Manjunath, K., Rao, K.S.: Source and system features for phone recognition. Int. J. Speech Technol. **18**(2), 257–270 (2015)
8. International Phonetic Association: Hand Book of the International Phonetic Association, Cambridge University Press (1999)

9. Bear, H.L., Harvey, R.: Phoneme-to-viseme mappings: the good, the bad, and the ugly. Speech Commun. **95**, 40–67 (2017)
10. Yengnanarayana, B., Murthy, P.S.: Enhancement of reverberant speech using LP residual signal. IEEE Trans. Speech Audio Process. **8**(3), 267–281 (2000)
11. Prasanna, S.R.M., Srinivasa, C., Yengnanarayana, B.: Extraction of speaker-specific excitation information from linear prediction residual of speech. Speech Commun. **48**(10), 1243–1261 (2006)
12. Drugman, T., et al.: Detection of glottal closure instants from speech signals: a quantitative review. IEEE Trans. Audio Speech Lang. Process. **20**(3), 994–1006 (2012)
13. Naylor, P.A., et al.: Estimation of glottal closure instants in voiced speech using the DYPSA algorithm. IEEE Trans. Audio Speech Lang. Process. **15**(1), 34–43 (2007)
14. Thomas, M.R., Gudnason, J., Naylor, P.A.: Estimation of glottal closing and opening instants in voiced speech using the YAGA algorithm. IEEE Trans. Audio Speech Lang. Process. **20**(1), 82–91 (2012)
15. Murthy, K.S.R., Yegnanarayana, B.: Epoch extraction from speech signals. IEEE Trans. Audio Speech Lang. Process. **16**(8), 1602–1613 (2008)
16. Prathosh, A., Ananthapadmanabha, T., Ramakrishnan, A.: Epoch extraction based on integrated linear prediction residual using plosion index. IEEE Trans. Audio Speech Lang. Process. **21**(12), 2471–2480 (2013)
17. Alku, P.: Glottal wave analysis with pitch synchronous iterative adaptive inverse filtering. Speech Commun. **11**(23), 109–118 (1992)
18. Alku, P., Vilkman, E.: A comparison of glottal voice source quantification parameters in breathy, normal and pressed phonation of female and male speakers. IEEE Trans. Audio Speech Lang. Process. **48**(5), 240–254 (1996)
19. Dutta, K., Singh, M., Pati, D.: Detection of replay signals using excitation source and shifted CQCC features. Int. J. Speech Technol. **24**(9), 497–507 (2009)
20. Liu, M., et al.: Audio visual word spotting. In: IEEE International Conference on Acoustics, Speech and Signal Processing (ICASSP), vol. 3, pp. 785–788 (2004)
21. Liu, H., et al.: Audio-visual keyword spotting for mandarin based on discriminative local spatial-temporal descriptors. In: International Conference on Pattern Recognition, pp. 785–790 (2014)
22. He, J., Liu, L., Palm, G.: On the use of residual cepstrum in speech recognition. In: IEEE International Conference on Acoustics, Speech and Signal Processing (ICASSP), vol. 1, pp. 5–8 (1996)
23. Chengalvarayan, R.: On the use of normalized LPC error towards better large vocabulary speech recognition systems. In: IEEE International Conference on Acoustics, Speech and Signal Processing (ICASSP) (1998)
24. Tripathi, K., Rao, K.S.: Improvement of phone recognition accuracy using speech mode classification. Int. J. Speech Technol. **21**(3), 489–500 (2018)
25. Vincent, E., et al.: The second "CHiME" speech separation and recognition challenge: datasets, tasks and baselines. In: International Conference on Acoustics, Speech, and Signal Processing (ICASSP), pp. 126–130 (2013)
26. Cooke, M., et al.: An audio-visual corpus for speech perception and automatic speech recognition. J. Acoust. Soc. Am. **120**(5), 2421–2424 (2006)
27. Ephraim, T., Himmelman, T., Siddiqi, K.: Real-time viola-jones face detection in a web browser. In: Canadian Conference on Computer and Robot Vision, pp. 321–328 (2009)
28. Rath, S.P., et al.: Improved feature processing for deep neural networks. In: Proceedings of the INTERSPEECH, pp. 109–113 (2013)

29. Povey, D., Saon, G.: Feature and model space speaker adaptation with full covariance Gaussians. In: Proceedings of the INTERSPEECH (2006)
30. Vesely, K., et al.: Sequence-discriminative training of deep neural networks. In: Proceedings of the INTERSPEECH (2013)

Developing a Question Answering System on the Material of Holocaust Survivors' Testimonies in Russian

Liudmila Bukreeva⬡, Daria Guseva⬡, Mikhail Dolgushin$^{(\boxtimes)}$⬡,
Vera Evdokimova⬡, and Vasilisa Obotnina⬡

Saint Petersburg State University, Universitetskaya emb., 7-9, St. Petersburg 199034, Russia
`v.evdokimova@spbu.ru`

Abstract. The paper makes use of the annotated task-oriented corpus of Holocaust testimonies in Russian (ruOHQA) to train a question-answer neural network model. We start from data preprocessing, present statistical analysis of the collected corpus for approximately 1500 pairs of questions and answers and describe its strengths and limitations. Also, we carry out experiments on automatic processing of the ruOHQA corpus using pre-trained transformer-based neural network models. Finally, we explore the capability of several models to generate simplified high-quality answers to questions and compare their results. The kind of research we present allows us to extract knowledge from oral history archives more productively.

Keywords: Question Answering · Corpora · Visual History Archives

1 Introduction

Question Answering Systems (QAS) have become an important field of research in natural language processing combining such tasks as information extraction and machine learning. QASs help to obtain answers to questions of interest asked in natural language which may be essential for various specific research issues [1]. In our paper we concentrate on extracting answers to questions from oral history archives. Oral history preserves historical records [2] in the form of an interview with people who witnessed historically significant events.

Oral history data encompasses multiple topics, one of which is Holocaust testimonies. The large amount of data includes The Visual History Archive of Holocaust testimonies compiled by the USC Shoah Foundation [3] with over 7,000 multimedia recordings and 25 freely available interviews with Holocaust survivors from the Yad Vashem Foundation in Russian [4]. Our aim is to summarize facts and stories from the interviews provided by the Yad Vashem Foundation. Our choice was made due to the fact that most of the video interviews contain manually typed subtitles. We enable the analysis and interpretation of these oral history archives by collecting tagged corpus for the presented records. It helps to satisfy the stable interest in materials of such kind [5–7] by turning this large amount

A. Karpov et al. (Eds.): SPECOM 2023, LNAI 14339, pp. 357–366, 2023.
https://doi.org/10.1007/978-3-031-48312-7_29

of data into a more attainable form as well as affects the accuracy of the forthcoming QAS.

QASs perform at their best when they deal with structured knowledge bases [1]. Therefore, we gather the Question-Answer corpus ruOHQA and further use this dataset to train neural network models for the question answering task. The corpus contains over 1,500 automatically gathered entries, further manually aligned and labeled by experts.

2 Related Work

There are several efforts to build QASs able to retrieve information from visual history data. The research [15] develops the dialogue system based on the international project MALACH (Multilingual Access to Large Spoken Archives). The QAS for English and Czech parts of the MALACH archive of Holocaust testimonies allows one to obtain answers using spoken natural language queries.

The paper [6] presents the QA model formulating queries in a natural language. Due to the colloquial form of speech in the researched mMQA corpus with 8914 entries of questions and answers, the final accuracy turns out to be very limited. The experimental results indicate that the further research on building QASs for oral history data remains relevant.

We were inspired by the paper [15], thus, our motivation was to retrieve information from oral history archives of Holocaust testimonies in Russian. To the best of our knowledge, there are no similar QA datasets and QAS for Russian oral history archives of such kind mentioned in the literature.

The main dataset used to solve the QA problem for Russian is SberQuAD [16] with approximately 50,000 question-answer pairs, which are splitted on 45,3 k train, 5,04 validation and 23.9k test rows. This reading comprehension dataset contains Wikipedia articles and questions to its segments posed by a group of crowdworkers. Each question presupposes an answer from the corresponding reading passage, however, might remain unanswered. The methodology used to create SberQuAD was similar to what was used for the development of the English SQuAD corpus [17], and SQuAD 2.0 [18]. The structure of these datasets has shown the significance of including unanswerable questions in the corpora.

We will follow the practice of earlier works published. Our tasks involve creating the QA dataset and applying it to train the QAS.

3 Corpus Creation

Research on building QAS has always been constrained by the limited availability of structured training data. Thus, collecting appropriate textual data and structuring it was the first step required in our work.

3.1 Text Collection

We started our corpus creation from collecting video recordings of interviews with Holocaust survivors from the Yad Vashem Foundation [4]. We decided to add into our corpus only recordings containing subtitles preprocessed by specialists of foundation. There were 4 recordings among 25 with automatic subtitles. We could not add them to the corpus since speech recognition technology is the error prone process, consequently, the quality of such subtitles might be low. As a result, we gathered 21 transcribed recordings with the total duration of approximately 26 h. We extracted all the subtitles from each recording. The total size of the unpreprocessed corpus reached 20200 unique pairs of questions and answers.

To identify video recordings and subtitle files, we assigned them an individual identification code. Keeping all the video materials in order was also necessary to further clarify the controversial points appearing during the corpus annotation. In particular, it ensured that potential context gaps, such as interruptions by the interviewer during the interviewee's response, were not overlooked.

3.2 The Annotation

The first step of dataset annotation involved dividing the interviewer's speech from one of the narrator's. The material in our unpreprocessed corpus already was in russian and contained punctuation, which allowed us to conduct preliminary annotation by rules. To extract the context of the expected replies, we followed the basic assumption that an interrogative sentence might be followed by an answer. Thus, we created a new corpus entry in case there was a question mark in a previous sentence. As a matter of course, questions following one another and building an interviewer's speech turned out to be divided, thereby we encountered false answer selection: e.g. *"Как ее звали? Вы помните?"*—*"What was her name? Do you remember?"*. It this example *"Do you remember?"* was automatically extracted as the answer, although we clearly understand that it is the question. Along with this, we mentioned that the false detection of questions occurred as well. It happened when there were rhetorical questions or questions within the context of a story in narrator's answer speech: e.g. *"и ему говорят: "Слушай, ты этого мальчика знаешь?" Он говорит…"*—*"and they say to him: "Listen, do you know this boy?" He says…"*.

With help of initial automatic preprocessing we extracted 4228 pairs of question-answer contexts with the preservation of the indexes from the subtitles. As might be expected, many errors occurred due to the specifics of automatic preprocessing, which does not take into account the peculiarities of the spoken form of the interviews and peculiar coloring of the speeches caused by the age of the narrators. These features made us decide to annotate the corpus manually using an expert assessment.

The next step of our work required dividing the corpus into parts equal in number of entries further given to 4 experts to annotate manually. The experts had access to all the materials and were required to act according to a unified set of instructions. The manual annotation included the following tasks: correction of errors caused by the automatic preprocessing and construction of the specialized format for our corpus useful for forthcoming QA training purposes. In case question entries were inaccurately assigned to the context of the answer or were not punctuated, we created new question entries for them. Punctuation was maintained if necessary. The context of the answer was cleared of possible interviewer's remarks along with grammatical and orthographic mistakes.

As a result, we managed to annotate 1555 entries that were composed into the Russian Oral History Question Answering dataset (ruOHQA). An example of the record with translation into English is presented in Table 1. The same structure is followed in every entry of the corpus.

Table 1. Corpus sample with translation.

id	question	answer	context
279_297	Это уже в какое время года было?	Это было, уже я пошла в школу, это к сентябрю.	Это я тебе сейчас скажу... Это было, уже я пошла в школу, это к сентябрю. Мы все лето, мы все время убегали от немцев. Нас даже там не высадили...
279_297	What time of year was this?	It was, I already went to school, this was by September.	I'll tell you now... It was, I already went to school, this was by September. We spent the whole summer, we ran away from the Germans all the time, they didn't even drop us off...

A corpus entry consists of four columns. The first column has unique indexes of the interrogative speech from the subtitles. The second column contains the interviewer's question to the narrator. The third column includes only direct answers to the interviewer's question. Finally, the fourth column contains the detailed context of the answer provided by the narrator within their story during the interview.

4 Data Analysis

In Table 2 we compare the ruOHQA dataset to the similar Russian QA corpus SberQuAD. A comprehensive description of all possible SberQuAD features is given in [16]. We compare such parameters as the average question, answer and context length in both QA corpora. As can be seen from Table 2, the average question length turns out to be similar in both datasets, while the average answer length shows noticeable differences. We explain the longer average length of answers in the ruOHQA corpus by the fact that the narrators make their speech more extended and often less concise by going into the details.

Table 2. Statistics of the ruOHQA and SberQuAD datasets.

Dataset	Total number of samples	Avg. question length (words)	Avg. answer length (words)	Avg. context length (words)
ruOHQA	1,555	7,076	5,444	22,858
SberQuAD	50,364	8,613	2,433	98,666

In order to analyze the content of the ruOHQA corpus, we counted 30 most common tokens in its question and answer parts. We lemmatized words with the Python library pymorphy2 [20] to conduct some preliminary processing. Further processing included removing of stop words, namely prepositions and conjunctions. In this way, we were able to extract only the tokens that were necessary to our query.

Finally, we obtained the token frequency graphs in Fig. 1 and Fig. 2 with nltk, the natural language processing library in Python [21].

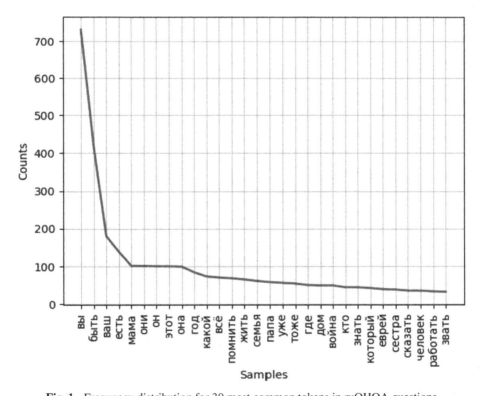

Fig. 1. Frequency distribution for 30 most common tokens in ruOHQA questions.

Figure 1 shows the most frequent lemmatized words counted in the question part of the ruOHQA corpus. We identify words connected with Holocaust, e.g. 'война' (war), 'помнить' (remember), 'еврей' (jew), with family or relatives, e.g. 'мама' (mom), 'сестра' (sister) etc. We intentionally did not remove pronouns and interrogative words in the questions' frequency list before counting, as they may also express an interviewer's appeal to narrators.

The solid curve in Fig. 2 represents the 30 most common lemmatized words found in answers of the ruOHQA corpus. We notice similar tokens including verbs related to memory, e.g. 'знать' (to know), 'помнить' (to remember), nouns naming family members, e.g. 'мама' (mom), 'папа' (dad), 'бабушка' (grandma) etc. An important frequently used word is 'еврей' (jew). It shows us the nationality of narrators and remains a core concept for specific topics discussed. Eventually, the frequency usage turns out to be quite representative for the content in our corpus based on the interviews with Jewish Holocaust survivors.

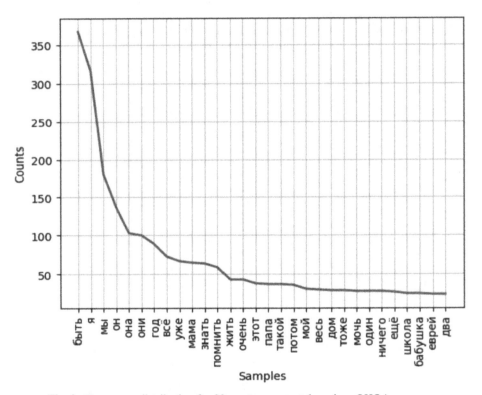

Fig. 2. Frequency distribution for 30 most common tokens in ruOHQA answers.

5 Experiments

Once we have the ruOHQA corpus ready for training our QAS, we start the experimental setup of the models. The initial step of experiments included fine-tuning using our corpus. We have selected the distilled versions of ruBERT models pretrained on informal texts from DeepPavlov [22] in the Huggingface framework [23]. Our choice has been made based on several reasons: 1) the informal texts used for pretraining the models correspond to the dialogue structure of our ruOHQA dataset; 2) the distilled versions of the models perform with relatively quick learning rate; 3) the performance of the distilled versions keeps up with the full models [24]; 4) finally, the ruBERT models show the high level of accuracy in automatic language processing tasks in Russian [25].

The ruOHQA dataset was divided into train and test subsets in the ratio of 0.7 to 0.3, for training and evaluation of the resulting model respectively. Thus, we received 929 entries of the corpus for training the model and 399 entries for testing. The size of the ruOHQA dataset is limited for the model to be trained only on it. Hence, we decided to evaluate the accuracy of our results on the corpus SberQuAD that was specifically collected to solve the QA problem for Russian. Finally, we trained our model on the combination of the SberQuAD and ruOHQA corpora to see whether the results improve.

To evaluate the performance of each model we have chosen two main metrics used for this task: F1 and Exact Match (EM) - and have implemented their realisation from [17]. We calculated F1 and EM on test sets from SberQuAD and ruOHQA using the *transformers.metrics* taken from the HuggingFace framework.

We used the same hyperparameter values as recommended in the HuggingFace documentation [26]:

- learning rate: $2 * 10{-5}$
- number of epochs: 3
- batch size: 16

Table 3. Evaluation of each pipeline's performance on SberQuAD and ruOHQA with 5.040 and 399 samples respectively. We report the exact match (EM) and F1 metrics.

DS for training	DS for test	distilrubert-tiny-cased-conversational		distilrubert-small-cased-conversational		Distilrubert-base-cased-conversational	
		F1	EM	F1	EM	F1	EM
SberQuAD	SberQuAD	52.206	33.459	52.231	33.141	78.114	58.161
	ruOHQA	54.581	26.202	30.843	56.925	63.234	38.795
SberQuAD+ruOHQA	SberQuAD	50.557	32.324	49.914	32.196	**78.160**	**58.503**
	ruOHQA	**80.558**	67.229	80.118	**67.470**	79.557	63.373

Table 3 compares the accuracy evaluation results for different combinations of train sets and three versions of the distilrubert model. The significant boost in performance appears after subjoining entries from the ruOHQA corpus to the SberQuAD dataset. The best accuracy value of F1 metric (80.558) tested on the ruOHQA dataset was achieved by the distilrubert-tiny-cased-conversational model trained on the combined SberQuAD and ruOHQA dataset. The best EM result (67.470) was achieved by the distilrubert-small-cased-conversational on the same dataset. However, we see significant differences if we compare the rates obtained for SberQuAD and ruOHQA to the lower accuracy results made only on the SberQuAD dataset. Such a high performance on the combined dataset represents an interesting finding. We might presume that the distilrubert-tiny-cased-conversational and distilrubert-small-cased-conversational show volatility when additional data is subjoined, consequently, models outperform the distilrubert-base-cased-conversational model in values.

In view of those considerations, we can conclude that the distilrubert-base-cased-conversational model fine-tuned on the combined SberQuAD and ruOHQA dataset can be considered as the most stable and simultaneously showing decent results on both datasets: 78.160 of F1 metric and 58.503 of EM.

Additionally, worth noticing is the fact that the models trained only on the SberQuAD dataset do not show high performance when tested on the ruOHQA set. We explain this by significant differences in the data structure of the sets, since entries in the SberQuAD corpus initially existed in written form while in the ruOHQA corpus they are compiled from oral history archives, i.e. have conversational spoken form.

6   Conclusion

This article presents the results of training the QAS models on ruOHQA and SberQuAD datasets. The content of our collected corpus initially has an oral form and is largely influenced by the emotional state and age of the respondents. Since training QAS requires structured training data, the ruOHQA corpus was annotated not only automatically, but also manually. In our paper, we described the method we followed to carry out the tagging. In addition, we presented some statistical characteristics of the resulting dataset.

As a result of our research, a demonstration dataset containing answers, questions and contexts based on interviews with Holocaust survivors was processed and published as a HuggingFace Dataset [27].

We used our corpus in combination with the SberQuAD dataset to conduct some experiments with three distilled ruBERT models. Incorporating of the ruOHQA dataset positively influences evaluation results. The best gotten F1 equals 80.558% reached by the distilrubert-tiny-cased-conversational model. However, our results showed that the distilrubert-base-cased-conversational model turns out to be more stable reaching appropriate F1 and EM scores at the same time. Moreover, it was found that results on RuOH-test in some situations are slightly better than those on SberQuAD-test before fine-tuning of tiny distied RuBERT, which will require deeper research. We are planning to try other training setups, for example, comparing the current setup with pretraining on SberQuAD and then fine tuning on ruOHQA, and also other state-of-the-art models, such as ELECTRA, T5 and LLMs.

In our future research, we plan to expand the ruOHQA corpus by processing other materials from oral history archives, e.g. the Shoah Foundation [3] containing about 7,000 video interviews with people who survived the Holocaust. These recordings in Russian have no annotated text presented. Our further work for this reason may include developing a speech recognition system.

References

1. Bouziane, A., Bouchiha, D., Doumi, N., Malki, M.: Question answering systems: survey and trends. Procedia Comput. Sci. **73**, 366–375 (2015). https://doi.org/10.1016/j.procs.2015.12.005

2. Abrams, L.: Oral History Theory. Routledge, London (2016). https://doi.org/10.4324/978131 564076
3. USC Shoah Foundation. https://sfi.usc.edu/. Accessed 22 Sept 2023
4. YouTube playlist of Holocaust survivors testimonies by Yad Vashem foundation. https://www. youtube.com/playlist?list=PLanQ0TFmIYBTV8sRAkSDWQLZNhbM-v1xp
5. Picheny, M., Tüske, Z., Kingsbury, B., Audhkhasi, K., Cui, X., Saon, G.: Challenging the boundaries of speech recognition: the MALACH corpus. In: Interspeech 2019, pp. 326–330 (2019). https://doi.org/10.21437/Interspeech.2019-1907
6. Psutka, J.V., Pražák, A., Vaněk, J.: Recognition of heavily accented and emotional speech of English and Czech Holocaust survivors using various DNN Architectures. In: Karpov, A., Potapova, R. (eds.) SPECOM 2021. LNCS, vol. 12997, pp. 553–564. Springer, Cham (2021). https://doi.org/10.1007/978-3-030-87802-3_50
7. Chýlek, A., Švec, J., Šmídl, L.: Initial experiments on question answering from the intrinsic structure of oral history archives. In: Karpov, A., Potapova, R. (eds.) SPECOM 2021. LNCS, vol. 12997, pp. 124–133. Springer, Cham (2021). https://doi.org/10.1007/978-3-030-87802-3_12
8. Project MALACH – Multilingual Access to Large Spoken Archives. https://malach.umiacs.umd.edu/
9. Byrne, W., et al.: Automatic recognition of spontaneous speech for access to multilingual oral history archives. IEEE Trans. Speech Audio Process. **12**(4), 420–435 (2004). https://doi.org/10.1109/TSA.2004.828702
10. Mihajlik, P., Fegyó, T., Németh, B., Tüske, Z., Trón, V.: Towards automatic transcription of large spoken archives in agglutinating languages – Hungarian ASR for the MALACH project. In: Matoušek, V., Mautner, P. (eds.) TSD 2007. LNCS, vol. 4629, pp. 342–349. Springer, Heidelberg (2007). https://doi.org/10.1007/978-3-540-74628-7_45
11. Psutka, J., Ircing, P., Psutka, J.V., Hajič, J., Byrne, W., Mírovský, J.: Automatic transcription of Czech, Russian and Slovak spontaneous speech in the MALACH project. In: Eurospeech 2005, pp. 1349–1352. ISCA (2005). https://doi.org/10.21437/Interspeech.2005-489
12. Ramabhadran, B., Huang, J., Picheny, M.: Towards automatic transcription of large spoken archives - English ASR for the MALACH project. In: ICASSP 2003, p. I (2003). https://doi.org/10.1109/ICASSP.2003.1198756
13. Ramabhadran, B., et al.: USC-SFI MALACH interviews and transcripts English. In: LDC2012S05. Web Download. Philadelphia: Linguistic Data Consortium (2012). https://doi.org/10.35111/7zfn-a492
14. Psutka, J., Radová, V., Ircing, P., Matoušek, J., Müller, L.: USC-SFI MALACH interviews and transcripts Czech. In: LDC2014S04. Web Download. Linguistic Data Consortium, Philadelphia (2014). https://doi.org/10.35111/v2nt-7j09
15. Chýlek, A., Šmídl, L., Švec, J.: Question-answering dialog system for large audiovisual archives. In: Ekštein, K. (ed.) TSD 2019. LNCS, vol. 11697, pp. 385–397. Springer, Cham (2019). https://doi.org/10.1007/978-3-030-27947-9_33
16. Efimov, P., Chertok, A., Boytsov, L., Braslavski, P.: SberQuAD – Russian reading comprehension dataset: description and analysis. In: Arampatzis, A., et al. (eds.) CLEF 2020. LNCS, vol. 12260, pp. 3–15. Springer, Cham (2020). https://doi.org/10.1007/978-3-030-58219-7_1
17. Rajpurkar, P., Zhang, J., Lopyrev, K., Liang, P.: SQuAD: 100,000+ questions for machine comprehension of text. In: Proceedings of the 2016 Conference on Empirical Methods in Natural Language Processing, Austin, Texas, November, pp. 2383–2392. Association for Computational Linguistics (2016). https://doi.org/10.48550/arXiv.1606.05250
18. Rajpurkar, P., Jia, R., Liang, P.: Know what you don't know: unanswerable questions for SQuAD. In: Proceedings of the 56th Annual Meeting of the Association for Computational Linguistics (Volume 2: Short Papers), Melbourne, Australia, pp. 784–789. Association for Computational Linguistics (2018). https://doi.org/10.18653/v1/P18-2124

19. Pisarevskaya, D., Shavrina, T.: WikiOmnia: filtration and evaluation of the generated QA corpus on the whole Russian Wikipedia. In: Proceedings of the 2nd Workshop on Natural Language Generation, Evaluation, and Metrics (GEM), Abu Dhabi, United Arab Emirates (Hybrid), pp. 125–135. Association for Computational Linguistics (2022). https://doi.org/10.18653/v1/2022.gem-1.10

20. Morphological analyzer pymorphy2. https://pymorphy2.readthedocs.io

21. NLTK documentation. https://www.nltk.org

22. Kolesnikova, A., Kuratov, Y., Konovalov, V., Burtsev, M.: Knowledge distillation of Russian language models with reduction of vocabulary. In: Proceedings of the International Conference «Dialogue 2022», Moscow, 15–18 June 2022. Computational Linguistics and Intellectual Technologies, vol. 21, pp. 295–310 (2022). https://www.dialog-21.ru/media/5770/kolesniko vaaplusetal036.pdf. ISBN 978-5-7281-3205-9

23. Wolf, T., Debut, L., Sanh, V., et al.: Transformers: state-of-the-art natural language processing. In: Proceedings of the 2020 Conference on Empirical Methods in Natural Language Processing: System Demonstrations, pp. 38–45. Association for Computational Linguistics (2020). https://doi.org/10.18653/v1/2020.emnlp-demos.6

24. Sanh, V., Debut, L., Chaumond, J., Wolf, T.: DistilBERT, a distilled version of BERT: smaller, faster, cheaper and lighter (2019). arXiv arXiv:1910.01108. https://arxiv.org/abs/1910.01108

25. Kuratov, Y., Arkhipov, M.: Adaptation of deep bidirectional multilingual transformers for Russian language, arXiv preprint (2019). arXiv:1905.07213. https://arxiv.org/abs/1905.07213

26. Question Answering, HuggingFace documentation. https://huggingface.co/docs/transform ers/tasks/question_answering

27. RuOHQA dataset on HuggingFace. https://huggingface.co/datasets/Mihaj/ruohqa_demo

Decoding Asian Elephant Vocalisations: Unravelling Call Types, Context-Specific Behaviors, and Individual Identities

Seema Lokhandwala[1]([envelope]) [iD], Rohit Sinha[1] [iD], Sreeram Ganji[2] [iD], and Balakrishna Pailla[2] [iD]

[1] Indian Institute of Technology Guwahati, Guwahati, India
{seema171655001,rsinha}@iitg.ac.in
[2] Reliance Jio AICoE, Hyderabad, India
{ganji.sreeram,balakrishna.pailla}@ril.com

Abstract. This paper investigates the automatic classification of four types of Asian elephant vocalizations (rumble, roar, trumpet, and chirp) recorded in Kaziranga National Park. Apart from the call type classification, the study explores individual identification and contextual analysis. Various classifiers using openSMILE features are developed to facilitate the classification process. The results demonstrate accurate classification of elephant call types and successful classification of context-specific behavior and individual identity based on trumpet and chirp calls, respectively. This study highlights the potential of acoustic analysis for understanding elephant communication and well-being, offering insights into their context-specific behavior and individual identities.

Keywords: Bioacoustics · Animal behavior · Animal communication · Elephant communication

1 Introduction

Asian elephants (*Elephas maximus*) are social and widely distributed mammals, relying on acoustic communication to navigate their complex social dynamics and geographically dispersed locations [3,28]. Acoustic communication plays a crucial role in various aspects of their lives, including, maintaining group cohesiveness, fostering cooperation, mating, and facilitating mother-infant interactions [11,17,22].

The repertoire of vocalizations produced by Asian elephants is remarkably diverse, encompassing a wide range of sounds that facilitate their communication. These vocalizations include low-frequency rumbles and growls, which can propagate over long distances, allowing elephants to communicate effectively over large areas [9,15]. Additionally, they are capable of producing high-frequency trumpets, chirps, roars, and barks, showcasing their remarkable vocal versatility in acoustic communication [14,22,25].

© The Author(s), under exclusive license to Springer Nature Switzerland AG 2023
A. Karpov et al. (Eds.): SPECOM 2023, LNAI 14339, pp. 367–379, 2023.
https://doi.org/10.1007/978-3-031-48312-7_30

However, despite the significance of elephant vocalizations, there is still limited research in the field of automatic classification of call types. Clemins *et al.* conducted a study utilizing a hidden Markov model (HMM) for classifying call types, which stands as one of the few studies in this domain. The authors utilized mel-frequency cepstral coefficients, log energy, and spectrally derived features to train HMM classifiers and reported an overall classification accuracy of 79.7% [4]. However, there is a need for further investigations to address the existing limitations and develop more refined and accurate call-type classifiers.

Recent research has found a connection between the acoustic structure of elephant vocalizations and their arousal or motivational states. Berg *et al.* classified elephant calls into ten types, with respect to their corresponding behaviors. High-frequency calls, like trumpets, were associated with emotionally charged situations, while low-frequency calls like rumbles were prevalent in relaxed social contexts [1]. The acoustic properties of elephant rumbles reflect individual emotional arousal [23]. For example, rumbles occurring during socializing and agitation exhibit increased fundamental frequencies and decreased duration [30]. Wesolek *et al.* found that post-nursing cessation rumbles had distinct acoustic characteristics [29].

In a recent study, Stoeger *et al.* investigated African elephants *(Loxodonta africana)* and their ability to produce various call types, including snorts, rumbles, and trumpets in response to verbal cues from trainers (mahouts). The study revealed that rumbles produced during social interactions with conspecifics had distinct acoustic characteristics compared to rumbles elicited by trainer cues [24]. Sharma *et al.* found that rumbles, but not trumpets, were modulated during disturbances among wild Asian elephants [21]. Fuchs *et al.* observed trumpet calls conveying individual identity information but no modulation between greeting and disturbance contexts [7].

For a complete understanding of a species' communication system, it is essential to comprehend the information conveyed by the various vocalizations in its vocal repertoire. The use of vocalizations by a number of non-human mammalian species to communicate sex, caller identity, emotional state, and context has been documented [13,19,20,26]. Caller identity is important in social species in particular, and this has been observed in the majority of mammal and bird species.

Individual anatomical and morphological variations in the sound-producing structures, as well as internal factors and the physiology of sound production, all affect vocal identity [26]. Soltis *et al.* [23] and Fuchs *et al.* [7] used discriminant functional analysis to study the individual identity of rumble and trumpet vocalizations respectively, revealing distinctive acoustic characteristics associated with each call type. In the assessment of individual identity for trumpet calls, the authors report a classification accuracy of 71.7% [7]. In the analysis carried out Soltis *et al.*, the accuracy of individual identity based on rumbles stood at 60.0% [23]. In speaker recognition experiments carried out on rumble calls, Clemins *et al.* report an individual identification accuracy of 82.5% [4]. Based on the findings from the aforementioned studies, we have been motivated to propose a framework and build models to classify call types followed by individual identity and context-specific behavior.

The remainder of the article is structured as follows. Information on the elephant vocalization data gathered for this study is described in Sect. 2. Section 3 describes the proposed framework for detecting call types, individual identities, and the broad nature of context-specific behaviors in the collected elephant vocalization database. Section 4 discusses the findings of the study. Section 5 summarizes the conclusions drawn.

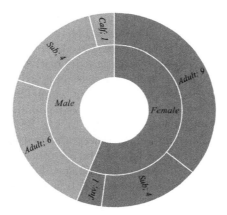

Fig. 1. Distribution of sexes and age groups among the studied subjects. (Sub refers to sub-adult and Juv refers to juvenile).

2 Database

2.1 Subjects and Study Site

The Kaziranga National Park and Tiger Reserve (hereinafter referred to as KNP), is a World Heritage Site in Assam (India), where the elephant vocalization data was collected. KNP houses around 60 semi-captive Asian elephants used for activities like patrolling, anti-poaching efforts, and tourism. Each elephant has a mahout to meet their daily needs. These elephants socialize, bathe together, play, freely browse in the forested area, and are accustomed to the presence of humans. For this study, based on their locations within KNP, a total of 25 elephants were selected with their ages spanning from less than 1 year to 60 years. They were categorized into four major age classes based on previous reports [27]: calf (below 1 year), juvenile (1–5 years), sub-adult (5–15 years), and adult (15 years and above). Figure 1 lists the sexes and age groups of the individuals under study.

2.2   Context-Specific Data Recording

The recording sessions were held throughout the field site, including the elephants' bathing areas, browsing areas, and places where they are tethered at night. No manipulative experiments to elicit responses from the elephants were carried out during these sessions. A round-robin approach was used during these sessions, with an average of 4 h spent monitoring each subject. A minimum of 15 min to an hour-long observation of their behavior per session was recorded at an interval of 30 s. We categorized elephant behavior into several broad categories, including locomotion, social interactions, handler interactions, self-directed actions, foraging, comfort, and other behaviors [12, 18].

In the study, close observation of elephant behavior allowed for interpretation in the context of their social interactions. Based on this interpretation, three specific context-specific behaviors were assigned: positive, negative, and neutral.

The positive context-specific behavior was assigned when elephants were observed interacting with other non-dominant elephants. These interactions involved socializing, playing, and engaging in behaviors such as physical contact and moving toward each other.

The negative context-specific behavior was assigned when elephants interacted with their mahouts (human caretakers) or other dominant individuals. During these interactions, elephants exhibited specific behaviors such as head bobbing and body swaying, which are commonly associated with stress or agitation. Head bobbing refers to repetitive and rhythmic movements of the head, while body swaying refers to rhythmic side-to-side movements of the body. These interactions often occurred when elephants displayed signs of fear or distress, such as retreating or showing avoidance behaviors.

Neutral context-specific behavior was assigned when individuals engaged in contact calls without clearly displaying positive or negative context-specific behavior. Contact calls are vocalizations made by elephants to communicate with each other over long distances.

2.3   Collection and Categorization of Acoustic Data

The elephant vocalization data was recorded during the daytime from February to April 2021. The data was recorded for a total of 47 d, yielding 103 h of acoustic data. Behavior, caller's identity, approximate recording distance, and context were noted for each recorded vocalization. The vocalizations were collected with a Sound Devices MixPre-3 II recorder connected to an Earthworks QTC-40 omni condenser microphone with a frequency response of 3 Hz to 40 kHz, sampling at a rate of 48 kHz, and a range of 5–100 meters. Nikon D5100 and a Cannon 1200-D digital single-lens reflex camera were used for video recordings.

Through field notes, auditory observation, and spectrogram analysis, all vocalizations were identified. Based on the results of earlier studies, the vocalizations were divided into four main call types and combination calls [1, 11, 22]. A total of 401 elephant calls, encompassing individuals of all age groups and sexes were captured during our fieldwork. Detailed information about the dataset can

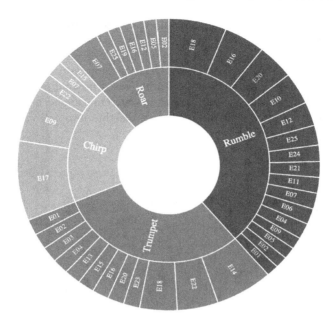

Fig. 2. Relative contribution of individual elephant in the data used for call type classification experiment.

be found in reference [10]. From this dataset, 226 calls, representing all call types, were selected for developing call type classifiers. The selection was based on the behavioral context and quality of the calls, as depicted in Fig. 2.

In order to conduct individual identification and context-specific behavior experiments, two types of calls: trumpet and chirp, were chosen. The rumble and roar call types were not selected due to the limited amount of data available per individual for rumble and roar calls. For the individual identification experiment, only the individuals who produced more than three calls were included. On average, we obtained 12.5 chirp calls from two individuals and 7.5 trumpet calls from eight individuals. Table 1 provides information regarding the number of calls used in chirp and trumpet call types for context-specific behavior experiments.

3   Proposed Framework

A comprehensive framework for analyzing elephant acoustic data is represented in Fig. 3. The process involves several key steps, starting with the segmentation of elephant calls. Once the calls are segmented, relevant features are extracted using advanced techniques. These features capture important acoustic characteristics of the elephant vocalizations. Next, the study utilizes five independent classifiers, each trained on the extracted features and associated with a specific label representing call type. Once the call type label is identified, we deployed five independent classifiers, each trained on the extracted features and associated with a specific label representing individual elephant and context-specific behavior for trumpet and chirp call types. Classification metrics are calculated to evaluate the performance of the classifiers and assess the quality of the classification results. Overall, this framework enables a systematic and effective analysis of elephant acoustics data, providing valuable insights into call type, individual identities, and behavioral patterns.

Table 1. Distribution of trumpet and chirp calls across three context-specific behaviors.

Context-specific behavior	Number of calls	
	Chirp	Trumpet
Positive	12	13
Neutral	5	22
Negative	8	25

3.1   Segmentation

The process of analyzing the acoustic recordings began with a visual examination using the PRAAT 6.2.03 software [2]. This involved opening the recordings and carefully observing the waveforms and spectrograms. We referred to our field notes and listened to the recordings to gather additional information about the calls. Once the calls were identified within the raw data, they were precisely located, marking the start and end times of each call. To extract relevant information, the calls were then trimmed, selecting the specific portions that contained the calls of interest.

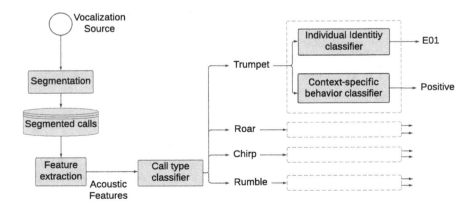

Fig. 3. A block diagram of the proposed framework. The modules within the dotted box are replicated for the rest of the call types, indicating their similar functionality.

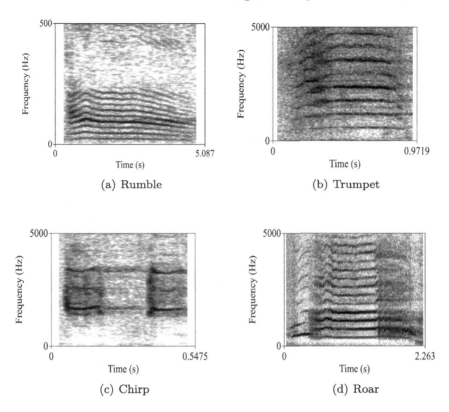

Fig. 4. Spectrograms depicting four types of elephant calls: (a) rumble, (b) trumpet, (c) chirp, and (d) roar. These visual representations highlight the unique characteristics of the rumble calls, allowing for a clear classification.

3.2   Feature Extraction and Acoustic Analysis

Features were extracted using the Python-based open-source feature extraction openSMILE toolkit [5]. The feature set is an acoustic parameter set for various areas of automatic voice analysis. The feature set was extracted from the openSMILE toolkit using an extended Geneva Minimalistic Acoustic Parameter Set (eGeMAPS) which resulted in 25 low-level descriptors (LLDs) and 88 functionals were extracted. The 25 LLDs are made up of voicing features, spectral features, cepstral features, and energy features. There are 88 functionals produced after statistics like the variances, arithmetic mean, standard deviations, and percentiles of the LLDs are calculated. These LLDs were obtained from 25 ms frames and extracted every 10 ms. Only the 88 functionals served as inputs for training individual classifiers associated with specific labels, representing particular individuals, context-specific behaviors, or call types. The spectrograms of rumbles, trumpet, and roar calls of elephants exhibited distinct features, reflecting the unique acoustic characteristics of each call type. Rumbles displayed strong energy in the lower frequency range, spanning from infrasound frequencies to several hundred Hertz, often with harmonic or quasi-harmonic patterns and various modulation patterns. Trumpet calls were characterized by a wide frequency range, showcasing broadband energy across the entire spectrum, an initial transient or burst of energy, and potential harmonic structures. Roar calls demonstrated a broadband distribution of energy with an emphasis on the mid-frequency range, irregular or modulated patterns, and the presence of harmonic structures or non-harmonic components. Chirp calls were characterized by their unique temporal structure. In comparison to the other calls, they were significantly shorter in duration, making them stand out noticeably. It's important to note that these spectrogram features can vary among individual elephants and may be influenced by factors such as age, sex, and social context. Further analysis utilizing advanced signal processing techniques can extract quantitative features from spectrograms to facilitate classification and in-depth analysis.

3.3   Classifiers

To classify the elephant calls based on context-specific behaviors, call types, and individual identification, three distinct models were developed, each utilizing different criteria or feature sets. The models employed five different classification algorithms: Support Vector Machine (SVM), K-Nearest Neighbors (KNN), Naive Bayes, Multi-layer Perceptron (MLP), and Random Forest. SVM determined an optimal hyperplane to separate data points of different classes, while KNN classified new data based on the majority class of its nearest neighbors. Naive Bayes calculated the probability of a data point belonging to a certain class based on the assumption of feature independence. MLP, a type of artificial neural network, learned complex relationships between inputs and outputs. Random Forest combined multiple decision trees to make predictions.

For the small size of the database, a k-fold validation methodology, with k set to 3, is employed to evaluate the classification performances of a model. The subsets were created so that the sets of utterances within each of the three subsets were mutually exclusive. Data from test utterances made up subsets 1, 2, and 3 respectively, with each subset accounting for 30% of the testing set. This approach allowed for comprehensive evaluation and validation of the performance of each of the models.

3.4   Evalution Metrics

In this study, Accuracy is used to determine how well the classification model performed. It can be defined as,

$$\text{Accuracy}(\%) = 100 \times \frac{TP + TN}{TP + FP + TN + FN} \tag{1}$$

where TP stands for "true positives", TN for "true negatives", FP for "false positives", and FN for "false negatives". The percentage accuracies for 3-fold of the data are calculated and reported in Tables 2 and 3.

4   Results and Discussion

4.1   Call Type Experiment

In the context of call type classification, the Random Forest model achieved the highest accuracy of 82.7%, followed by the Naive Bayes model. The confusion matrix for this experiment is presented in Fig. 5. Notably, rumbles were classified with the highest accuracy at 100% due to their low-frequency nature, whereas roars exhibited the lowest accuracy at 33%. One potential reason for this issue is the limited availability of training data for the "roar" call type. For the call type experiment, our findings are consistent with those reported by Clemins *et al.* [4].

Table 2. The following table showcases the average accuracy of the five models for call types.

Classification model	Average Accuracy (%)
Support Vector Machine	65.0
K-Nearest Neighbors	64.5
Naive Bayes	72.6
Multi-layer Perceptron	61.0
Random Forest	**82.7**

To determine which features play an important role in this classification, feature importance was analyzed. The top five features identified were alphaRatioV-sma3nz-stddevNorm, loudness-sma3-stddevNorm, loudnessPeaksPerSec, mfcc2-sma3-stddevNorm, and F1bandwidth-sma3nz-amean. The first feature, alpha-RatioV, represents the variation of the alpha ratio in an audio signal. This ratio provides insights into the spectral balance of the signal. The second feature, loudness-stddevNorm, reflects the normalized standard deviation of the signal's loudness. The third feature, loudnessPeaksPerSec, denotes the number of loudness peaks detected per second in the audio signal. These peaks represent instances of significantly high amplitude, such as trumpet, chirp, and roar which have higher frequency calls compared to rumble. Thus, loudness serves as a distinguishing factor in classifying these sounds, as evident from its inclusion in the top features for such classification. The fourth feature, mfcc2-stddevNorm, characterizes the second mel-frequency cepstral coefficient (MFCC), and is widely employed in audio signal analysis for tasks such as speech recognition and speaker identification. Finally, the fifth feature, F1bandwidth-sma3nz-amean refers to the width or range of frequencies around the first formant peak, which is an important component in speech analysis. The first formant represents the primary resonance frequency of the vocal tract during speech production.

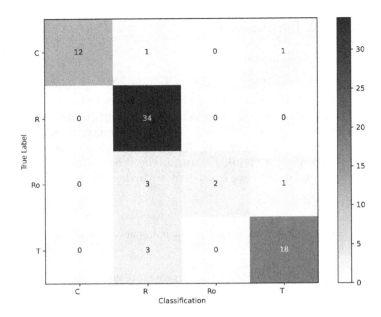

Fig. 5. Confusion matrix for call type experiment. (C-chirp, R-rumble, Ro-roar, T-trumpet).

4.2 Context-Specific Behavior and Individual Identification Experiment

For context-specific behavior and individual identification experiments, we utilized trumpet and chirp calls as the primary data. In the case of context-specific behavior classification, the Random Forest model achieved the highest accuracy of 75%, followed by the Naive Bayes model. Similarly, for chirp calls in the case of context-specific behavior classification, the Random Forest model achieved the highest accuracy of 72.6%, followed by the Naive Bayes model. Compared with earlier literature, Fuchs *et al.* observed trumpet calls in greeting and disturbance contexts, achieving a classification accuracy of 58.3%. In our own study, we observed trumpet calls in three different contexts and achieved a higher classification accuracy of 75%.

In terms of individual identification experiments, the Random Forest model is noted to outperform the others, achieving an accuracy of 91.6% for chirp calls compared to 71.6% for trumpet calls. Chirp calls had higher accuracy for individual identification because only data from two individuals were used, whereas eight individuals' data were used for trumpet calls. Compared with earlier literature, rumble, and trumpet calls were classified according to individual identity, indicating that acoustic characteristics varied based on the individual identity of the caller [7,23]. When specifically comparing trumpet calls, it is worth noting that Fuchs *et al.* [7] reported a classification accuracy of 71.7% for six individual

Table 3. The average accuracies of the five different models for context-specific behavior (Context) and individual identification (Identity) experiments for trumpet and chirp call types.

Classification model	Average Accuracy (%)			
	Trumpet		Chirp	
	Context	Identity	Context	Identity
Support Vector Machine	54.9	43.3	48.6	83.7
K-Nearest Neighbors	48.3	46.6	51.8	79.6
Naive Bayes	58.3	58.3	64.3	87.9
Multi-layer Perceptron	53.3	46.6	43.9	68.0
Random Forest	**75.0**	**71.6**	**72.6**	**91.6**

elephants, whereas our study achieves a closely similar classification accuracy of 71.6% for a slightly larger sample size of eight individual elephants.

Overall, these models employ different approaches and algorithms to classify elephant calls based on context-specific behaviors, call types, and individual identification. The Random Forest model demonstrated strong performance in classifying call types, context-specific behaviors, and individual identification. These results highlight the strengths and weaknesses of each model in capturing the underlying patterns in elephant calls for different classification tasks.

In the future, a detailed analysis needs to be conducted to determine which features play a significant role in the analysis. The Asian elephant is a social species which lives in matriarchal family groups [6,28]. They form social bonds (relationships) with unrelated individuals in captivity and even provide reassurance to distressed conspecifics [8,16]. Therefore, identifying the caller holds significant value as it fosters support and enhances social interactions among individuals. Playback experiments are recommended in the future to determine how well Asian elephants can identify and differentiate familiar conspecifics based on their vocalizations.

5 Conclusion

In conclusion, this study developed a framework to classify call types and then also demonstrated that the acoustic of elephant calls are context-specific, exhibiting distinct characteristics in relation to different context-specific behavioral states. Furthermore, the aim in the future is to develop an end-to-end architecture that can not only classifies context-specific behavior in all elephant calls but also recognize individual identity. This comprehensive understanding of elephant communication, encompassing both context-specific behavioral states and individual variations, contributes to a more nuanced comprehension of elephant behavior and communication. These findings have potential implications for conservation efforts, captive elephant welfare, and advancing our understanding of how elephants express themselves through vocalizations.

Acknowledgements. The first author extends sincere appreciation to the Assam Forest Department for graciously granting permission to gather the essential data required for this study. Their invaluable cooperation and consent have made it possible to conduct this research. Additionally, we would like to express heartfelt gratitude to the dedicated forest guards and diligent mahouts who wholeheartedly supported and actively participated in the fieldwork.

References

1. Berg, J.K.: Vocalizations and associated behaviors of the African elephant (Loxodonta africana) in captivity. Zeitschrift für Tierpsychologie **63**, 63–79 (1983). https://doi.org/10.1111/j.1439-0310.1983.tb00741.x
2. Boersma, P., Weenink, D.: Praat: doing phonetics by computer (version 5.1.13) (2009). http://www.praat.org
3. Calabrese, A., et al.: Conservation status of Asian elephants: the influence of habitat and governance. Biodivers. Conserv. **26**(9), 2067–2081 (2017). https://doi.org/10.1007/s10531-017-1345-5
4. Clemins, P.J., Johnson, M.T., Leong, K.M., Savage, A.: Automatic classification and speaker identification of African elephant (Loxodonta africana) vocalizations. J. Acoust. Soc. Am. **117**(2), 956–963 (2005)
5. Eyben, F., Wöllmer, M., Schuller, B.: openSMILE - the munich versatile and fast open-sourceaudio feature extractor. In: Proceedings of the 9th ACM International Conference on Multimedia, (MM), pp. 1459–1462 (2010)
6. Fernando, P., Lande, R.: Molecular genetic and behavioral analysis of social organization in the Asian elephant (Elephas maximus). Behav. Ecol. Sociobiol. **48**, 84–91 (2000)
7. Fuchs, E., Beeck, V.C., Baotic, A., Stoeger, A.S.: Acoustic structure and information content of trumpets in female Asian elephants (Elephas maximus). PLoS ONE **16**, 1–19 (2021). https://doi.org/10.1371/journal.pone.0260284
8. Gadgil, M., Nair, P.V.: Observations on the social behaviour of free ranging groups of tame Asiatic elephant (Elephas maximus Linn). Proc. Anim. Sci. **93**, 225–233 (1984)
9. Leighty, K.A., Soltis, J., Wesolek, C.M., Savage, A.: Rumble vocalizations mediate interpartner distance in African elephants Loxodonta africana. Anim. Behav. **76**(5), 1601–1608 (2008)
10. Lokhandwala, S., Sarmah, P., Sinha, R.: Classifying mahout and social interactions of Asian elephants based on trumpet calls. In: Prasanna, S.R.M., Karpov, A., Samudravijaya, K., Agrawal, S.S. (eds.) Speech and Computer. SPECOM 2022. Lecture Notes in Computer Science, vol. 13721, pp. 426–437. Springer, Cham (2022). https://doi.org/10.1007/978-3-031-20980-2_37
11. Nair, S., Balakrishnan, R., Seelamantula, C.S., Sukumar, R.: Vocalizations of wild Asian elephants (Elephas maximus): structural classification and social context. J. Acoust. Soc. Am. **126**, 2768–2778 (2009). https://doi.org/10.1121/1.3224717
12. Olson, D.: The Elephant Husbandry Resource Guide. American Zoo and Aquarium Association, Silver Spring, Maryland (2004)
13. Palacios, V., Font, E., Márquez, R., Carazo, P.: Recognition of familiarity on the basis of howls: a playback experiment in a captive group of wolves. Behaviour **152**(5), 593–614 (2015)

14. Pardo, M.A., et al.: Differences in combinatorial calls among the 3 elephant species cannot be explained by phylogeny. Behav. Ecol. **30**, 809–820 (2019). https://doi.org/10.1093/beheco/arz018
15. Payne, K.B., Langbauer, W.R., Thomas, E.M.: Infrasonic calls of the Asian elephant (Elephas maximus). Behav. Ecol. Sociobiol. **18**, 297–301 (1986)
16. Plotnik, J.M., De Waal, F.B.: Asian elephants (Elephas maximus) reassure others in distress. PeerJ **2**, e278 (2014)
17. Poole, J.H., Payne, K., Langbauer, W., Moss, C.: The social contexts of some very low-frequency calls of African elephants. Behav. Ecol. Sociobiol. **22**, 385–392 (1988). https://doi.org/10.1007/BF00294975
18. Rees, P.A.: Activity budgets and the relationship between feeding and stereotypic behaviors in Asian elephants (Elephas maximus) in a zoo. Zoo Biol. **28**, 79–97 (2009)
19. Rendall, D.: Acoustic correlates of caller identity and affect intensity in the vowel-like grunt vocalizations of baboons. J. Acoust. Soc. Am. **113**(6), 3390–3402 (2003)
20. Rendall, D., Rodman, P.S., Emond, R.E.: Vocal recognition of individuals and kin in free-ranging rhesus monkeys. Anim. Behav. **51**(5), 1007–1015 (1996)
21. Sharma, N., S, V.P., Kohshima, S., Sukumar, R.: Asian elephants modulate their vocalizations when disturbed. Anim. Behav. **160**, 99–111 (2020). https://doi.org/10.1016/j.anbehav.2019.12.004
22. Silva, S.D.: Acoustic communication in the Asian elephant Elephas maximus maximus. Behaviour **147**, 825–852 (2010). https://doi.org/10.1163/000579510X495762
23. Soltis, J., Leong, K., Savage, A.: African elephant vocal communication II: rumble variation reflects the individual identity and emotional state of callers. Anim. Behav. **70**, 589–599 (2005). https://doi.org/10.1016/j.anbehav.2004.11.016
24. Stoeger, A.S., Baotic, A.: Operant control and call usage learning in African elephants. Philos. Trans. R. Soc. B **376**(1836), 20200254 (2021)
25. Stoeger, A.S.: An Asian elephant imitates human speech. Curr. Biol. **22**, 2144–2148 (2012). https://doi.org/10.1016/j.cub.2012.09.022
26. Taylor, A.M., Reby, D.: The contribution of source-filter theory to mammal vocal communication research. J. Zool. **280**(3), 221–236 (2010)
27. Varma, S., Baskaran, N., Sukumar, R.: Field key for elephant population estimation and age and sex classification. Resource material for synchronized elephant population count using block count, line transect dung count method and waterhole count. Asian Nature Conservation Foundation, Innovation Centre, Indian Institute of Science, Bangalore - 560 012 (2012)
28. Vidya, T.N., Sukumar, R.: Social organization of the Asian elephant (Elephas maximus) in Southern India inferred from microsatellite DNA. J. Ethol. **23**, 205–210 (2005). https://doi.org/10.1007/s10164-005-0144-8
29. Wesolek, C.M., Soltis, J., Leighty, K.A., Savage, A.: Infant African elephant rumble vocalizations vary according to social interactions with adult females. Bioacoustics **18**, 227–239 (2009). https://doi.org/10.1080/09524622.2009.9753603
30. Wood, J.D., McCowan, B., Langbauer, W.R., Viljoen, J.J., Hart, L.A.: Classification of African elephant loxodonta Africana rumbles using acoustic parameters and cluster analysis. Bioacoustics **15**, 143–161 (2005). https://doi.org/10.1080/09524622.2005.9753544

Enhancing Children's Short Utterance Based ASV Using Data Augmentation Techniques and Feature Concatenation Approach

Shahid Aziz[(✉)] and Syed Shahnawazuddin

National Institute of Technology Patna, Bihar 800005, India
{shahida.phd20.ec,s.syed}@nitp.ac.in

Abstract. The task of developing an automatic speaker verification (ASV) system for children's speech is a challenging one due to a number of reasons. The dearth of domain-specific data is one among them. The challenge further intensifies with the introduction of short utterances of speech, a relatively unexplored domain in the case of children's ASV. To circumvent the issue arising due to data scarcity, the work in this paper extensively explores various in-domain and out-of-domain data augmentation techniques. A data augmentation approach is proposed that encompasses both in-domain and out-of-domain data augmentation techniques. The out-of-domain data used are from adult speakers which are known to have acoustic attributes in stark contrast to child speakers. Consequently, various techniques like prosody modification, formant modification and voice-conversion are employed in order to modify the adult acoustic features and render it acoustically similar to children's speech prior to augmentation. The in-domain data augmentation approach, on the other hand, involved speed perturbation of children's speech. The proposed data augmentation approach helps not only in increasing the amount of training data but also in effectively capturing the missing target attributes which helps in boosting the verification performance. A relative improvement of 43.91% in equal error rate (EER) with respect to the baseline system is a testimony of it. Furthermore, the commonly used Mel-frequency cepstral coefficients (MFCC) average out the higher-frequency components due to the larger bandwidth of the filter-bank. Therefore, effective preservation of higher-frequency contents in children's speech is another challenge which must be appropriately tackled for the development of a reliable and robust children'stion techniques and Feature Concatenation A ASV system. The feature concatenation of MFCC and IMFCC is carried out with the sole intention of effectively preserving the higher-frequency contents in the children's speech data. The feature concatenation approach, when combined with proposed data augmentation, helps in further improvement of the verification performance and results in an overall relative reduction of 48.51% for equal error rate.

© The Author(s), under exclusive license to Springer Nature Switzerland AG 2023
A. Karpov et al. (Eds.): SPECOM 2023, LNAI 14339, pp. 380–394, 2023.
https://doi.org/10.1007/978-3-031-48312-7_31

Keywords: Automatic speaker verification · In-domain data augmentation · Out-of-domain data augmentation · Mel-frequency cepstral coefficients · Inverse-Mel-frequency cepstral coefficients · Feature concatenation

1   Introduction

The web of cybernated applications in this digital age has fascinated people cutting across generations. In addition to the galore of positive aspects of cybernated applications is its dreary face. It is also fraught with the dangers of losing sensitive data and identity theft, if not accessed with caution. People accessing the online tools should be mindful of the cyber crimes and cyber frauds. To address such an intimidating issue, the field of biometrics have witnessed a meteoric rise in the recent past and is bound to remain at the center stage in the times to come. Voice/ Speech signal is one such biometric, which falls under the category of behavioral biometrics [6]. Even though the primary function of speech signal is human communication, it also captures information about the speaker's identity, age, emotions, gender, geographical origin and health. Voice biometrics or Automatic Speaker Verification (ASV) is a technology that uses algorithms and machine learning techniques to verify the identity of a speaker based on their speech characteristics. It is a biometric authentication method that relies on the unique patterns and traits in an individual's speech.

As compared to other competing biometrics, voice biometrics is increasingly becoming popular because of its low cost, ease of use, faster authentication process and higher level of security features [6]. But, the majority of the work reported in the literature deal with the design and development of ASV systems for adults. The fact that social networking websites and online learning tools are a rage among children and teenagers, with over half of youngsters in the age bracket of 6-15 obsessively indulging in internet and maintaining accounts on social media websites [1], cannot be denied. The children who are oblivious of the lurking perils in the usage of cyber related activities are the more vulnerable lot as opposed to the adults. This calls for the need of a robust ASV system for children. The literary works reported on building an ASV system for children are not vast as compared to adults [20,23,27]. Motivated by this, the authors' in this paper have focused their attention on developing robust ASV systems for child speakers.

State-of-the-art ASV systems employ deep learning architectures that necessitate estimation of a vast number of parameters. This, in turn, mandates a substantial quantity of domain-specific data. The road along the development of a reliable children's ASV system has many hindrances. The majority of children's speech corpora are not readily accessible. Moreover, these are limited in terms of data hours and the number of languages in which they are available. Developing an ASV system for languages without any children's speech corpus (zero-resource condition) is very demanding. Even if a small quantity of children's speech data is available (low-resource condition), designing an effective

ASV system for children using deep learning architectures is still a very challenging task. Some of the earlier works on children's ASV have investigated the effect of synthetically generating speech data and then pooling it for training in order to circumvent the problem posed by low- and zero-resource conditions. It has been reported that out-of-domain data augmentation and in-domain data augmentation is effective in this regard [23]. The performance of an ASV system for children is further dented when there is a reduction in the duration of the speech utterances during testing, commonly termed as short-utterance situation. Speech segments of duration 5-10 s are commonly termed as short-utterances in the literary domain. The unavailability of sufficiently longer duration of speech data can be tackled during training phase by some data augmentation techniques. However, it is not feasible to do the same during the testing phase [13]. The works reported on children's ASV hardly deal with such short utterances scenario.

Taking cognizance of the above literary gap, the authors' have explored the role of both the in-domain as well as out-of-domain data augmentation techniques in order to synthetically generate more speech data. The in-domain data augmentation technique used in this paper includes the default three-way speed perturbation of the original children's speech using Kaldi pipeline. To address the paucity of the domain-specific data, the impact of out-of-domain data augmentation techniques in the light of short-utterance based children's ASV system is also explored in this paper. This includes (i) voice conversion (VC) of adults' speech data through a cycle-consistent generative adversarial network (C-GAN) [7], (ii) prosody modification (PM) [21,22] of adults' speech i.e., optimally changing the pitch and duration of the speech data from adult speakers, and (iii) up-scaling the formant frequencies (FM) [8,11] of adults' speech data. All the explored techniques not only help in increasing the amount of training data but also in modifying the acoustic attributes of adult's speech so that the acoustic mismatch with child's speech is minimal. The proposed combination of in-domain and out-of-domain data augmentation technique is observed to be highly effective as is demonstrated and validated in the experimental evaluation section in this paper.

Besides data augmentation, this exploration also delves into the role of feature concatenation of two front end acoustic features namely the Mel-frequency cepstral coefficients (MFCC) and the inverse-Mel-frequency cepstral coefficients (IMFCC). In general, the Mel-frequency cepstral coefficients (MFCC) are the most commonly used front-end acoustic features and have been popular ever since its inception. They provide a compact and stable representation of the vocal-tract of a speaker, which can capture speaker-specific characteristics. When it comes to children's speech, a significant amount of relevant information is predominantly present in the high frequency region [2,19]. As resolution of Mel-filter-bank decreases with increase in frequency, the performance of children's ASV system based solely on MFCC features will be sub-optimal. In order to effectively preserve the higher-frequency contents in children's speech, the other front end acoustic feature explored in this paper is IMFCC. The IMFCC features are extracted using the inverse-Mel filter-banks. The inverse-Mel filter-banks is thus supposed to have better frequency resolution in higher-frequency range while the lower frequency components are down-sampled. As already highlighted, the use of Mel-filter-bank down-samples the spectral information in the higher-frequency range. The IMFCC due to its complementary nature of the filter-bank are supposed to better capture the acoustic information in the higher-frequency regions of children's speech, which are otherwise disregarded by the MFCC features. The feature fusion model of MFCC and IMFCC is thus expected to outperform the traditional MFCC, leading to an enhanced performance of children's ASV system.

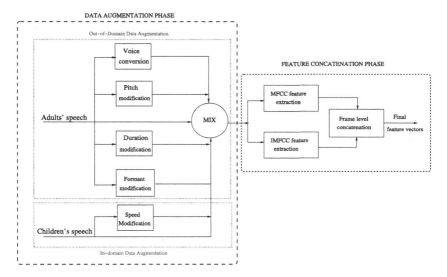

Fig. 1. Block diagram outlining the data augmentation and feature concatenation approaches proposed in this work in order to enhance the verification performance of a short-utterance-based children ASV system.

The aforementioned proposal of feature concatenation in addition to data augmentation is outlined in Fig. 1 and well validated in the experimental results section of the paper. The paper also illustrates the age-group wise as well as a gender-wise analysis of the children's ASV performance to unravel the effect of data augmentation and feature concatenation. The approach assists in considerably reducing the equal error rate (EER) as well as detection cost function (DCF) as compared to our baseline system trained exclusively on children's speech using MFCC features. The ASV system developed in this work for experimental evaluations employ x-vector-based speaker representation along with probabilistic linear discriminant analysis (PLDA) based scoring.

The rest of this paper is organized as follows: Sect. 2 deals with an exploration of in-domain data augmentation and various out-of-domain data augmentation techniques. Section 3, talks about the authors' motivation to delve into the scope of feature concatenation for children's ASV system. The experimental evaluations exhibiting the efficacy of our proposed techniques are presented in Sect. 4. Eventually, conclusion is drawn in Sect. 5.

2   Explored Data Augmentation Techniques

The state-of-the-art ASV system makes use of x-vectors-based speaker representation. For extracting x-vectors, a time-delay neural network (TDNN) [12,25,26] is trained. Deep learning models such as a TDNN have an inherent complexity owing to a number of hidden layers and hidden nodes per layer. They are resource intensive and require massive amount of data. As already mentioned, one of the hindrances in the development of a reliable ASV system for children is the paucity of domain-specific data. Hence, training an x-vector extractor on a limited amount of children's speech will result in sub-optimal performance. Data augmentation techniques offer a solution to these challenges. Data augmentation involves applying various transformations to the original training data to create new synthetic data samples. These synthetic samples are then used to augment the original data-set, thereby enhancing diversity of the captured acoustic attributes, increasing the amount of training data and improving the trained model's generalization capabilities. Taking cognizance of these facts, in-domain and out-of-domain data augmentation was performed to enhance the reliability and robustness of the developed children's ASV system.

2.1   Out-of-Domain Data Augmentation

Out-of-domain data augmentation refers to increasing the amount of training data by blending adults' data with children's speech. Since the acoustic attributes of adults' speech is in stark contrast to those of children, various modifications are applied to adults' speech so that the augmented data have attributes similar to those of children's speech.

The proposed out-of-domain data augmentation technique is pictorially outlined in Fig. 1. This augmentation technique involved using a limited quantity of original adults' speech. As noted earlier, we've used a variety of ways to adequately alter the acoustic characteristics of adults' speech. These are briefly addressed in the following:

In the first method, voice conversion (VC) was applied to the adults' speech using a cycle-consistent generative adversarial network (C-GAN) [7]. To train the C-GAN, about 10 minutes of speech samples from both adult and child speakers were employed. As seen throughout the hearing tests, VC makes adult speech utterances sound remarkably similar to kid speech. As a result, the problems with acoustic mismatch are much reduced when the voice-converted data is pooled.

The second method was prosody modification applied to adult speech prior to augmentation. It is commonly known that children's speech has a higher pitch and a slower speaking tempo [11,18]. As a result, the length of the speech data from the adult speakers was raised by 1.4 while the pitch was enhanced by a factor of 1.35. These scaling variables were chosen based on past studies that were published on children's speech recognition [21]. The method described in [16] was utilized to accomplish prosody modification (PM). Again, pooling data that has been prosody-modified helps keep the acoustic mismatch under control.

Compared to adult speakers, formant frequencies are greater in the case of children [11, 18]. As a result, the formant frequencies (FM) of adult speech samples were scaled-up by a factor of 0.08 in the third approach. The aforementioned scaling factor was taken from previous publication [10]. Similar to VC and PM, pooling the data of formant modified adults' speech increases the training data while substantially reducing acoustic mismatch.

All the modified versions of adults' data were then pooled into training along with the original adults' data. A more reliable estimate of the model parameters was achieved as a result of increasing the training data volume. Furthermore, altering the acoustic characteristics makes sure that the established ASV system does not become biased towards speakers who are adults.

2.2 In-Domain Data Augmentation

In-domain data augmentation refers to increasing the amount of children's speech available for training by synthetically generating more data from children's speech itself. In this regard speed perturbation technique was employed. The in-domain data augmentation technique is also pictorially represented in Fig. 1. **Speed perturbation** is one of the most well-known techniques for data augmentation reported in the scientific literature. In this technique the speaking-rate or speed is modified while preserving the linguistic content of the speech data. For this, the default three-way speed perturbation Kaldi pipeline is utilized. The speed of each of the utterances from children is modified simultaneously by a factor of 1.1 and 0.9, respectively. The speed perturbed data is then mixed with the unperturbed children's speech before learning the x-vector based speaker representation.

2.3 Proposed Data Augmentation

The authors' in this paper propose a combination of the out-of-domain data augmentation as well as in-domain data augmentation as discussed in the previous subsections individually. All the modified versions of adults' and children's data are pooled into training along with original children's and adults' speech. Consequently, the proposed data augmentation strategy addresses the challenges of acoustic variability posed by intra-speaker and inter-speaker variability, limited amount of training data, and potential adversarial attacks. The proposed data augmentation technique is pictorially summarized in Fig. 1. It is worth mentioning here, that even though the aforementioned techniques of synthetically generating speech data are well acclaimed in literary works, their combined effectiveness in the context of children's ASV systems for short utterances is relatively uncharted.

3 Motivation for Exploring Feature Concatenation

As mentioned earlier, the MFCC features are one of the most popular and commonly used front-end acoustic features in the context of an ASV system. MFCCs capture the spectral characteristics of speech signals and have proven to be effective in representing speaker-specific information. During the MFCC feature extraction process, the speech signal is first analyzed into overlapping frames of short duration followed by the computation of short-time Fourier transform (STFT). Next, spectral warping is done over a non-uniform frequency scale by using triangular Mel-filterbank. Resultant power spectrum undergoes logarithmic compression followed by discrete cosine transform (DCT). Applying DCT yields the real cepstrum (RC). The final feature vectors that are fed as input while training any classifier are obtained by low-time liftering of real cepstrum.

As mentioned in the previous section, in the case of children, there is a considerable amount of relevant spectral information in the higher-frequency region. Children's speech data are represented by a spectrogram in the bottom panel of the Fig. 2, which exhibits substantial power even between 4 and 8 kHz. Moreover, the spectrogram of children's speech fairly clearly illustrates the earlier literary works' assertion that the formant frequencies are higher in the case of child speakers [5,9]. For a comparative study, Fig. 2 also includes the spectrograms for the speech data from adult male (top panel) and adult female (middle panel).

Mel-scale warping is influenced by the findings of psycho-acoustics. It is based on the premise that human perception of pitch is linear up to 1000 Hz and then becomes non-linear for higher-frequencies [3]. The Mel-filter-bank provides better resolution to speech signals in the low-frequency range, while its frequency resolution deteriorates in the high-frequency range. The down-sampling of spectral information in the high-frequency band is a snag when dealing with children's speech [5,18]. The quest for the preservation of higher-frequency contents in children's speech led us towards the exploration of another front-end acoustic feature, namely the Inverse-Mel-Frequency Cepstral Coefficient. The IMFCC features are extracted by projecting the power spectra onto inverse-Mel-weighted filter-banks. The inverse-Mel-filter-bank is realized simply by flipping around the Mel-weighted filter-banks about the middle point of the frequency axis. The set up of this filter-bank is such that the high-frequency region's spectral information is better resolved and thus the IMFCC features are supposed to possess the acoustic attributes disregarded by the MFCC features. It is worth highlighting that due to the inherent nature of inverse-Mel-filter-bank, the spectral information in the lower frequency range of the children's speech will be down-sampled. Therefore, we have conceived the idea of concatenating the MFCC and IMFCC feature vectors in order to effectively preserve both the low as well as high-frequency components. The block diagram outlining the extraction process of the concatenated MFCC and IMFCC features is shown in Fig. 3.

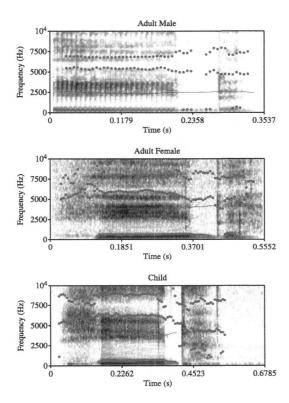

Fig. 2. Spectrograms corresponding to speech data from adult male (top panel), adult female (middle panel) and child (bottom panel) speaking the word *HEED*. The red speckles are the contours denoting the variation in formant frequencies, while the blue line denotes the pitch frequency variations.

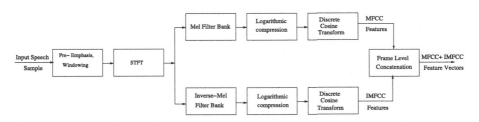

Fig. 3. Block diagram outlining the process of extracting concatenated MFCC and IMFCC features.

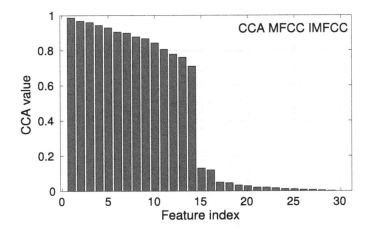

Fig. 4. Canonical correlation analysis of MFCC and IMFCC feature concatenation explored in the paper.

In order to substantiate the effect of feature concatenation, the canonical correlation analysis (CCA) was carried out. The CCA plot in Fig. 4 shows that the MFCC and IMFCC feature vectors are highly uncorrelated or less correlated for most of the coefficients except the starting few coefficients. Therefore the frame-level concatenation of MFCC and IMFCC features leads to capturing a wider range of acoustic attributes. The inherently complementary configuration of filter-banks employed in the extraction of MFCC and IMFCC features are the main force behind this development. Thus, the CCA plot of MFCC and IMFCC features upholds the complementary characteristic of IMFCC with respect to MFCC which assists their feature fusion model in representing a broader range of acoustic information in children's speech.

4   Experimental Evaluations

4.1   Speech Corpora and Experimental Set-Up

Three different speech corpora were employed for the development and evaluation of the speaker verification system in this paper. The CSLU kids corpus [24] consisted of spontaneous and prompted speech comprising of 100 h of data from 1, 100 children with a total of 73, 100 utterances. This speech corpus was used as the training set for the ASV system in this work. The CMU kids corpus [4] dataset comprised 9.1 h of data from 76 children having 5, 180 utterances. It served as our test data-set. A total of 423, 388 genuine trails and 26, 403, 832 impostor trails are present in this test set. The average duration of the data in this corpus is 6 seconds. Therefore, evaluation on this set represents the short-utterance case. Finally, the WSJCAM0 corpus [17] which is an adult speech data-set was used for the out-of-domain data augmentation. This speech corpus comprises 15.5 hours of data from 92 adult speakers having 7852 utterances.

After performing several data modification techniques like voice conversion (VC), prosody modification (PM) and formant modification (FM), a total of 63 hours of synthetic data is available for training purpose with acoustic attributes similar to those of children's speech.

The Kaldi toolkit was used to create the entire ASV system configuration and perform all the experiments [14]. As already stated earlier, two front-end acoustic features, namely the MFCC and IMFCC are used to represent the speech signal. Both these features were extracted using the Kaldi toolkit. Speech data were passed through a first-order high pass filter, having pre-emphasis factor of 0.97. To bring stationarity in the nature of speech signals, the speech signal is examined separately in short time frames of 25 ms with an overlapping of 10 ms. A 30-channel Mel-filter-bank was utilized for projecting the power spectrum into Mel-scale, followed by the computation of the 30-dimensional MFCC features. While, for the computation of the IMFCC features, a 30-channel inverse-Mel filter-bank was employed for warping the power spectra to inverse-Mel-scale, before computing the 30-dimensional IMFCC features.

For the extraction of highly discriminative speaker representations, a deep neural network was utilized. These fixed dimensional speaker-embeddings called as x-vectors are extracted from a time-delay neural network (TDNN) architecture [26], comprising of 7 hidden layers and trained for 6 epochs. Using the gradient descent algorithm, the network's parameters were trained [15,26]. Finally, each of the speech utterances is represented as a 512-dimensional x-vector.

4.2   Experimental Results

To keep a track on the performance of the aforementioned ASV system when subjected to short utterances of children's test data-set, an investigative study was undertaken. The first set of experiments were carried out to gauge the effectiveness of the explored/proposed data augmentation techniques on the performance of the ASV system. The corresponding experimental results in terms of EER and minDCF are displayed in Table 1. As evident from the table, the performance evaluation metrics undergo successive improvement with the application of subsequent explored data augmentation techniques. For instance, with the application of out-of-domain data augmentation techniques the system records a relative improvement of 33.57% in EER with respect to the system trained on the child dat-set alone. Next, when the in-domain data augmentation technique is put into action, the relative improvement in EER is 37.9%. Finally, as mentioned earlier, when the ASV system is trained using both the out-of-domain data augmentation technique and the in-domain data augmentation technique, which is the proposed data augmentation approach used in this paper, a staggering relative improvement of **43.91%** with respect to the baseline system trained solely on child data-set is achieved. Consequently, the EER for the employed children's ASV system comes down to a measly **12.31%**, which talks volumes about the effectiveness of the proposed data augmentation strategy.

The next round of experiments were carried out to assess the effectiveness of the proposed frame-level concatenation of the two front-end acoustic features

Table 1. EER and minDCF values for the short-utterances of children's speech test set demonstrating the effectiveness of out-of-domain, in-domain as well as the proposed data augmentation technique. The out-of-domain data augmentation scheme includes adult voice conversion (ADULT-VC), adult formant modification (ADULT-FM), adult prosody modification (ADULT-PM). The in-domain data augmentation scheme includes children's speech speed perturbation (CHILD-SP).

Type of Data Augmentation	Data used for training	Evaluation Metrics	
		EER(%)	minDCF
No Data Augmentation	CHILD	21.95	0.9975
Out-of-Domain Data Augmentation	CHILD + ADULT + ADULT-FM + ADULT-PM + ADULT-VC	14.58	0.9233
In-Domain Data Augmentation	CHILD + CHILD-SP	13.63	0.9031
In-Domain + Out-of-Domain Data Augmentation(**PROPOSED**)	CHILD+CHILD-SP+ADULT+ADULT-FM + ADULT-PM + ADULT-VC	**12.31**	**0.8464**

in the light of the employed short-utterance-based children's ASV system. The result of the evaluation metrics (EER and minDCF) obtained when MFCC features are concatenated with the IMFCC features for each frame of speech signal are shown in Table 2. It is to be kept in mind that the proposed data augmentation technique has been implemented prior to training the ASV system. The EER and minDCF values obtained when MFCC features alone are used to train the ASV system are also enlisted for comparison. Apparently, an absolute improvement of 1.01% is attained by the frame-level concatenation of MFCC and IMFCC features.

Table 2. EER and minDCF values for the short-utterance-based ASV system trained on the data-set obtained using the proposed data augmentation technique demonstrating the effectiveness of feature concatenation.

Acoustic features	Evaluation metric	
	EER (%)	minDCF
MFCC	12.31	0.8464
MFCC + IMFCC	**11.30**	**0.8351**

For an exhaustive analysis of the proposed strategy, the effect on the performance of the ASV system was monitored when subjected to an age-wise as well as gender-wise split-up of children's speech test set. For evaluating the effect of age variation, the evaluation metric results are noted for the complete test set, as well as with split-up of the test-set in two subgroups on the basis of age. The corresponding values for EER and minDCF for this study are exhibited in Table 3. Going by the results of the Table 3, it is quite evident that an ASV system shows a degraded results for children in the lower age bracket as compared

Table 3. Age group wise and gender-wise break up of EER and minimum DCF values highlighting the significance of feature concatenation approaches.

Features	Test-set	EER (%)	minDCF
MFCC	Full test set	12.31	0.8464
	6-7	14.63	0.9657
	8-9	12.12	0.8481
	Female	14.77	0.9113
	Male	9.229	0.7495
MFCC+IMFCC	Full test set	**11.30**	0.8351
	6-7	**13.61**	0.9221
	8-9	**10.98**	0.8273
	Female	**13.75**	0.8982
	Male	**8.625**	0.7311

to children in the higher age bracket or for the matter compared to children in the complete test-set. This can be attributed to the fact that younger children owing to their shorter vocal-track length have higher pitch frequency and formant frequencies. Also evident from the Table 3 is that the ASV system when trained exclusively on the MFCC features produce somewhat poorer results as those down-sample the higher-frequency contents of children's speech. On the contrary, the ASV system trained on the concatenated acoustic features yields superior results and this development can be attributed to the underlying fact that the feature fusion of MFCC and IMFCC takes into consideration the spectral information in the lower- as well as higher-frequency regions. Apart from the age-wise grouping of test set comprising children's short utterances, the effect of gender-wise grouping on the performance of the employed ASV system was also analyzed. The corresponding values for EER and minDCF for this study are also given in Table 3. As noticeable from the table that the ASV system performance drops when subjected to female speech test-set in contrast to the male children or as opposed to children in the complete test-set. This deterioration is due to the higher formant and pitch frequencies of female child in comparison to male child. The gender-wise results in Table 3 again reiterates the superior performance of the ASV system trained on the concatenated MFCC and IMFCC features as against the system trained solely on MFCC features. Moving on from the qualitative analysis towards the quantitative analysis of the effect of the proposed feature concatenation on the employed children's ASV system. The EER for the full test set registers a relative improvement of 8.20% when MFCC features are concatenated with the IMFCC features. When the speech test-set is split on the grounds of age variation, a relative reduction in EER for the age bracket of 6-7 years is calculated as 6.97% when the proposed feature concatenation is put into action. The corresponding relative improvement in EER for the age bracket of 8-9 years is 9.40%. When the speech test-set is split on the grounds of gender, a relative reduction in EER for the girl child is calculated as 6.90% upon frame-level concatenation of MFCC with the IMFCC features. Finally when the employed ASV system is subjected to short-utterances from the speech test set of the male child, it results in a relative reduction of 6.50% in EER.

5   Conclusion

Through the work in this paper, the authors' have examined the challenges surrounding the task of building a children's speaker verification system and their potential applications. Firstly, it was evident that the traditional speaker verification techniques designed for adult speakers are not directly applicable to children due to their physiological and psychological differences. The development of a robust and reliable children ASV system requires abundance of domain-specific data-set. Incorporating both in-domain and out-of-domain data augmentations in the proposed data augmentation approach, the amount of training data was increased, the diversity of the captured acoustic attributes was widened which also led to an improvement in the trained model's generalization capabilities, while keeping the acoustic mismatch in check. A relative improvement of 43.91% in equal error rate (EER) against the baseline system trained solely on the original child data-set authenticates the potency of the proposed data augmentation approach. Together with data augmentation, the effectiveness of frame-level concatenation of MFCC with the IMFCC features, is also analysed in this paper. The complementary nature of filter-banks employed in the extraction of IMFCC and MFCC features, helps in preserving spectral information in the higher-frequency range. The ASV system incorporating both the proposed data augmentation technique as well as feature concatenation culminates in an impressive overall relative improvement of 48.51% for equal error rate.

References

1. Badillo-Urquiola, K., Smriti, D., McNally, B., Golub, E., Bonsignore, E., Wisniewski, P.J.: Stranger danger! social media app features co-designed with children to keep them safe online. In: Proceedings of the 18th ACM International Conference on Interaction Design and Children, pp. 394–406 (2019)
2. D'Arcy, S., Russell, M.: A comparison of human and computer recognition accuracy for children's speech. In: Ninth European Conference on Speech Communication and Technology (2005)
3. Davis, S., Mermelstein, P.: Comparison of parametric representations for monosyllabic word recognition in continuously spoken sentences. IEEE Trans. Acoust. Speech Signal Process. **28**(4), 357–366 (1980). https://doi.org/10.1109/TASSP.1980.1163420
4. Eskenazi, M., Mostow, J., Graff, D.: The CMU Kids Corpus LDC97S63 (1997). https://catalog.ldc.upenn.edu/LDC97S63
5. Gerosa, M., Giuliani, D., Narayanan, S., Potamianos, A.: A review of ASR technologies for children's speech. In: Proceedings of the Workshop on Child, Computer and Interaction, pp. 7:1–7:8 (2009)

6. Hanifa, R.M., Isa, K., Mohamad, S.: A review on speaker recognition: technology and challenges. Comput. Electr. Eng. **90**, 107005 (2021)
7. Kaneko, T., Kameoka, H.: Parallel-data-free voice conversion using cycle-consistent adversarial networks. arXiv preprint arXiv:1711.11293 (2017)
8. Kathania, H.K., Kadiri, S.R., Alku, P., Kurimo, M.: Study of formant modification for children ASR. In: ICASSP 2020–2020 IEEE International Conference on Acoustics, Speech and Signal Processing (ICASSP), pp. 7429–7433. IEEE (2020)
9. Kathania, H.K., Shahnawazuddin, S., Ahmad, W., Adiga, N.: Role of linear, mel and inverse-mel filterbanks in automatic recognition of speech from high-pitched speakers. Circuits Syst. Sig. Process. **38**(10), 4667–4682 (2019)
10. Kumar, V., Kumar, A., Shahnawazuddin, S.: Creating robust children's ASR system in zero-resource condition through out-of-domain data augmentation. Circuits Syst. Signal Process. **41**(4), 2205–2220 (2022)
11. Lee, S., Potamianos, A., Narayanan, S.S.: Acoustics of children's speech: developmental changes of temporal and spectral parameters. J. Acoust. Soc. Am. **105**(3), 1455–1468 (1999)
12. Peddinti, V., Povey, D., Khudanpur, S.: A time delay neural network architecture for efficient modeling of long temporal contexts. In: Proceedings of the INTERSPEECH (2015)
13. Poddar, A., Sahidullah, M., Saha, G.: Speaker verification with short utterances: a review of challenges, trends and opportunities. IET Biometrics **7**(2), 91–101 (2018)
14. Povey, D., et al.: The kaldi speech recognition toolkit. In: Proceedings of the ASRU (2011)
15. Povey, D., Zhang, X., Khudanpur, S.: Parallel training of deep neural networks with natural gradient and parameter averaging. In: Proceedings of the ICLR (2015)
16. Prasanna, S.R.M., Govind, D., Rao, K.S., Yegnanarayana, B.: Fast prosody modification using instants of significant excitation. In: Proceedings of the International Conference on Speech Prosody (2010)
17. Robinson, T., Fransen, J., Pye, D., Foote, J., Renals, S.: WSJCAM0: a British English speech corpus for large vocabulary continuous speech recognition. In: Proceedings of the ICASSP, vol. 1, pp. 81–84 (1995)
18. Russell, M., D'Arcy, S.: Challenges for computer recognition of children's speech. In: Proceedings of the Speech and Language Technologies in Education (SLaTE) (2007)
19. Russell, M., D'Arcy, S., Qun, L.: The effects of bandwidth reduction on human and computer recognition of children's speech. IEEE Sig. Process. Lett. **14**(12), 1044–1046 (2007)
20. Safavi, S., Russell, M., Jancovic, P.: Automatic speaker, age-group and gender identification from children's speech. Comput. Speech Lang. **50**, 141–156 (2018)
21. Shahnawazuddin, S., Adiga, N., Kathania, H.K., Sai, B.T.: Creating speaker independent ASR system through prosody modification based data augmentation. Pattern Recogn. Lett. **131**, 213–218 (2020). https://doi.org/10.1016/j.patrec.2019.12.019
22. Shahnawazuddin, S., Adiga, N., Sai, B.T., Ahmad, W., Kathania, H.K.: Developing speaker independent ASR system using limited data through prosody modification based on fuzzy classification of spectral bins. Digit. Sig. Process. **93**, 34–42 (2019)
23. Shahnawazuddin, S., Ahmad, W., Adiga, N., Kumar, A.: In-domain and out-of-domain data augmentation to improve children's speaker verification system in limited data scenario. In: ICASSP 2020–2020 IEEE International Conference on Acoustics, Speech and Signal Processing (ICASSP), pp. 7554–7558 (2020)

24. Shobaki, K., Hosom, J.P., Cole, R.: CSLU: kids' speech version 1.1. Linguistic Data Consortium (2007)
25. Snyder, D., Garcia-Romero, D., Povey, D., Khudanpur, S.: Deep neural network embeddings for text-independent speaker verification. In: Proceedings of the INTERSPEECH, pp. 999–1003 (2017)
26. Snyder, D., Garcia-Romero, D., Sell, G., Povey, D., Khudanpur, S.: X-Vectors: Robust DNN embeddings for speaker recognition. In: Proceedings of the ICASSP, pp. 5329–5333 (2018)
27. Yeung, G., Alwan, A.: On the difficulties of automatic speech recognition for kindergarten-aged children. In: Interspeech 2018 (2018)

Studying the Effectiveness of Data Augmentation and Frequency-Domain Linear Prediction Coefficients in Children's Speaker Verification Under Low-Resource Conditions

Shahid Aziz[1]([✉])[iD], Shivesh Pushp[2], and Syed Shahnawazuddin[1][iD]

[1] National Institute of Technology Patna, Patna 800005, Bihar, India
{shahida.phd20.ec,s.syed}@nitp.ac.in
[2] Chandigarh University, Mohali, Punjab, India

Abstract. Developing an automatic speaker verification (ASV) system for children is extremely challenging due to the rarity of children's speech corpora. To deal with data scarcity, we have developed an out-of-domain data augmentation technique in this work. For that purpose, we have resorted to pitch scaling, formant modification, time-scale modification, and voice-conversion of adults' speech in order to render it acoustically similar to children's speech. The children's speech along with the modified and original adults' data are then pooled into training. Furthermore, two complementary front-end features namely, Mel-frequency cepstral coefficients (MFCC) and frequency-domain linear prediction (FDLP) coefficients have been concatenated so as to simultaneously capture the spectral as well as temporal envelopes. The feature concatenation approach when combined with data augmentation helps in achieving an overall relative reduction of 50.2% in equal error rate.

Keywords: Automatic speaker verification · Feature concatenation · Frequency-domain linear prediction coefficients · Out-of-domain data augmentation

1 Introduction

In the recent past, social networking websites and e-learning tools have become all rage among people of every generation. In addition to being an important source of information dissemination, these technological marvels are rife with the dangers of losing sensitive data and identity theft. Those keeping cheek-by-jowl with it, should be aware of these lurking perils. Even though such an intimidating issue can victimize anyone, but children who are oblivious of the repercussions following the loss of sensitive data and identity theft become more vulnerable targets. To address such jeopardising issues, a number of security measures are being deployed; an automatic speaker verification system is one such tool.

A. Karpov et al. (Eds.): SPECOM 2023, LNAI 14339, pp. 395–406, 2023.
https://doi.org/10.1007/978-3-031-48312-7_32

Automatic speaker verification (ASV) addresses the authentication issue of the claimed identity of a speaker. In this process, a speaker feeds in his/her data and claims the identity of a particular person. The deployed ASV system then digs into its stored templates/models and matches the stored template of the claimed identity with the input speech sample. The ASV system then states the claim to be genuine if the two samples match to a certain permissible degree; else the speaker is declared an impostor.

Although the primary function of speech signal is human communication, it also captures information about the speaker's identity, age, emotions, gender, geographical origin and health. An ASV system, exploits the speaker-specific information embedded in speech in order to determine the identity of the speaker. A lot of research and development has been done on automatic speaker recognition/verification in order to determine the speaker identity with a minimum error. Unfortunately, most of those works have focused on adult population. The scientific studies which discuss building children's ASV system are regrettably sparse [17–19, 21, 22].

Building a state-of-the-art children's ASV system is replete with several challenges. The lack of sizable domain-specific speech corpus which are freely available, act as a first hiccup. Further, children's speech databases are available in only a handful of languages spoken across the globe [22]. For the languages in which children's speech corpus is unavailable (zero-resource condition), developing an ASV system is quite a formidable task. Even if a limited amount of children's speech data is available (low-resource condition), developing a children's ASV system employing deep learning architectures is still very challenging. State-of-the-art ASV systems incorporate deep learning architectures that require estimating a huge number of parameters. This, in turn, requires a large amount of domain-specific data. To circumvent the low and zero-resource conditions, a few earlier works on children's ASV have studied the impact of synthetically generating speech data and then pooling it into training. Out-of-domain data augmentation has been reported to be effective in this regard [21]. Motivated by this fact, we have also studied the role of out-of-domain data augmentation in the context of children's ASV tasks. In this regard, we have studied the role of formant-modification-based data augmentation along with other existing augmentation methods. To the best of our knowledge, out-of-domain data augmentation based on formant scaling has not been studied in the context of low-resource children's ASV task.

In addition to data augmentation, we have also explored the effectiveness of concatenating two prominent front-end acoustic features, namely the Mel-frequency cepstral coefficients (MFCC) and the frequency-domain linear prediction (FDLP) coefficients. The MFCC are the most popular and the most widely used acoustic features which capture the spectral envelope. On the other hand, the FDLP features capture the temporal envelope of the speech signal. Earlier works have shown that modeling the temporal envelope aids in enhancing performance in several speech processing tasks, such as in the recognition of reverberant speech [26], replay spoofing attack detection [27] and spoken term detection [7]. While a log Mel-filterbank was engaged for warping the spectrum before extracting the MFCC features; FDLP feature extraction was carried out using three different filter-banks: Mel-, bark- and linear-filter-banks. To the best of the authors' awareness, the potency of FDLP features in the context of children's ASV tasks is an unexplored territory. Therefore, on top of data augmentation, we have also carried out frame-level concatenation of MFCC with FDLP features derived from three different filter-banks, in order to simultaneously model the spectral as well as temporal envelopes. The demonstrations in the later half of this paper reveal that the proposed frame-level concatenation of the two complementary front-end acoustic features increases the class separation among the speakers. This, in turn, assists in considerably reducing the equal error rate (EER) as well as the detection cost function (DCF) compared to our baseline system trained exclusively on children's speech using MFCC features.

The remainder of this paper is organized as follows: Sect. 2 describes the proposed out-of-domain data augmentation techniques to cope with paucity of domain specific data. In Sect. 3, we shed light on the role of feature concatenation and the different filter-banks employed for the extraction of FDLP features. The experimental evaluations illustrating the effectiveness of our proposed technique finds place in Sect. 4. Ultimately, the conclusion in Sect. 5 wraps up the paper.

2   Out-of-Domain Data Augmentation

A state-of-the-art ASV system makes use of an x-vectors-based speaker representation. For extracting x-vectors, a time-delay neural network (TDNN) [8,23,24] comprising a large number of hidden layers and hidden nodes per layer is trained. As already mentioned, one of the hurdles in the development of a reliable ASV system for children is the scarcity of domain-specific data. Hence, training an x-vector-based ASV systems on a meagre amount of children's speech, results in a sub-optimal performance. Out-of-domain data augmentation techniques can help mitigate this obstacle. Driven by this rationale, we have synthetically generated speech data, having acoustic attributes similar to those of children's speech using the available adults' speech corpus. The synthetically generated data was then pooled into training along with the children's speech for learning the model parameters. We have studied several ways by which data augmentation can be carried out and those are briefly discussed in the following:

– In the first approach, the adults' speech was subjected to voice conversion (VC) using a cycle-consistent generative adversarial network (CGAN) [4]. Nearly 10 min of speech data from each speaker group (adult and child speakers) was used to train the CGAN. As a result of VC, adults' speech utterances sound very similar to children's speech as noted during the listening tests. Therefore, on pooling the voice-converted data, the issues of acoustic mismatch reduce to a large extent.
– In the second approach, adults' speech was subjected to pitch scaling prior to augmentation. In this case, pitch of speech data from the adult speakers was increased by a factor of 1.35. These scaling factors were determined from

earlier reported works on children's speech recognition. The speech utterances from adult speakers were subjected to pitch modification so as to compensate for the difference in the pitch of adult and child speakers [6,15]. In order to perform pitch modification (PM), the technique reported in [12] was used.

- In case of child speakers, the formant frequencies are higher as well as average phoneme duration is longer compared to adult speakers [6,15]. As a consequence, the speaking-rate of children is slower as compared to adults'. These stark differences in the acoustic characteristics between the child and adult speakers paves way for our third and fourth approach of data augmentation. In the third approach the speaking-rate of adults' speech data was decreased by a factor of 1.4 through time-scale modification (TSM) [12]. While in the fourth approach, the formant frequencies (FM) of adults' speech data are upscaled by a factor of 0.08. All the modified versions of adults' speech data were then pooled together with the children's speech data and the unperturbed adult speech data. The mentioned scaling factors were adopted from our earlier studies [5,20].

- Finally, the pooled data was then passed through the default three-way speed perturbation Kaldi pipeline [10]. For each of the utterances, the speed is modified simultaneously by a factor of 1.1 and 0.9, respectively. The perturbed and unperturbed data were then mixed. Consequently, the amount of data used for training was further increased by a factor of three.

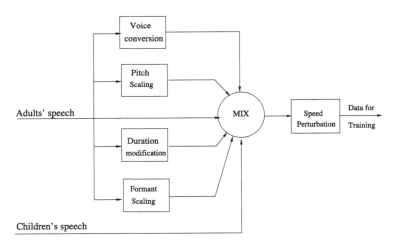

Fig. 1. Block diagram summarizing the out-of-domain data augmentation technique proposed in this paper.

These approaches account for the proposed data augmentation technique and has been pictorially summarized in Fig. 1. It is worth mentioning here, that even though the aforementioned techniques of synthetically generating speech data are acclaimed in the literary works, their combined efficaciousness in the context of a children's ASV systems are relatively uncharted. Among the approaches discussed, VC, PM and TSM have been explored in the context of children's ASV task to some extent. However, the effect of FM has not been studied yet. Moreover, the combined effectiveness of all the discussed approaches has also not been studied.

3   Acoustic Feature Concatenation

In the section, the idea behind concatenating complementary front-end acoustic features in order to enhance the performance of children's ASV system is discussed. As already mentioned, the considered acoustic features are MFCC and FDLP. Given the speech signal, first, we extract MFCC and FDLP features. Next, for each of the short-time frames, the corresponding MFCC and FDLP features are appended. The resulting feature vectors are then used as an input to the x-vector extractor instead of MFCC features alone.

The MFCC features model the spectral envelope corresponding to each of the short-time frames. However, the temporal structure is not effectively represented. In order to address this deficiency, the velocity and acceleration coefficients are generally appended to the base features. In recent times, time-splicing is employed in the place of appending velocity (delta) or acceleration (delta-delta) coefficients. FDLP features, on the other hand, capture the temporal envelope by applying linear predictive coding on the spectra. Prior reported works have shown that, effective modeling of the temporal peaks can aid in improving the efficacy of several speech processing tasks [7, 26, 27]. Having cognizance of the complementary nature of the two features, it is expected that frame-level concatenation of the two types of features will boost the performance of children's ASV task as well.

In order to examine the effect of feature concatenation, the following analysis was carried out. Three child speakers were randomly chosen from the available speech corpus. Next, we collected the MFCC features corresponding to all the speech utterances from those selected speakers. Finally, t-SNE plots were derived using the selected MFCC features, wherein each speaker was treated as one class. The t-SNE plot corresponding to this analysis is depicted in Fig. 2(a). This study was then repeated by replacing the MFCC features with FDLP features and again by frame-level concatenation of MFCC and FDLP features. The corresponding t-SNE plots are shown in Fig. 2(b) and Fig. 2(c), respectively. As evident from the t-SNE plots, the speaker clusters move further apart when FDLP features are employed in place of MFCC features. In addition to that, overlap among the speaker clusters significantly decreases when the two features are concatenated. Therefore, the proposed idea of frame-level concatenation is expected to enhance the discrimination among the speakers. The same has been experimentally substantiated in this paper.

In the following subsections the two types of front-end features are succinctly discussed for the sake of completeness. The discussion is in close adherence to the works reported in [1, 2], respectively.

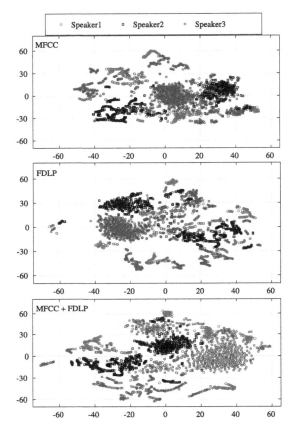

Fig. 2. t-SNE plots depicting the reduction of class overlap as a result of concatenating MFCC and FDLP features.

3.1   Mel-Frequency Cepstral Coefficients (MFCC)

For extracting MFCC features, the speech signal is first high-pass filtered through a pre-emphasis filter in order to emphasize the higher frequency components. Next, each of the speech utterances are analyzed into short-time frames using overlapping Hamming windows, followed by the computation of short-time Fourier-transform. Spectral warping is then carried out using a set of non-linearly spaced filters, called a Mel-filter-bank. Logarithmic compression of the filtered power spectrum is then performed. The de-correlated real cepstrum is then obtained by applying the discrete cosine transform. Finally, by low time liftering of the real cepstrum, MFCC features are extracted.

3.2   Frequency Domain Linear Prediction (FDLP) Coefficients

Formants are the frequency peaks in the power spectrum of the speech data. Each formant corresponds to a resonance in the vocal tract. These formants which are spectral structures convey vital linguistic details [1]. Still, this is only a partial depiction of speech signals. Temporal structures are also believed to encompass crucial information with regards to both the perception of natural sounds along with sensing stop bursts in a speech signal. These temporal envelopes can be obtained from frequency sub-bands of the signal using FDLP. Taking cue from the duality feature of time-domain and frequency-domain properties of signals, the temporal envelopes can be modeled through linear prediction analysis in frequency domain.

The residual signal from time-domain linear prediction applied to a speech signal contains the excitation source information of the signal. Thus, the spectral envelope and the residual signal are anticipated to carry complementary information. It is believed that the residual signal obtained from FDLP, carry complementary characteristics to the temporal envelope obtained using the FDLP process. As described in [27], this paper uses discrete cosine transform (DCT) to convert the time-domain signal into the frequency-domain. The DCT is applied to each long speech frame, and the DCT coefficients are grouped per sub-band, following which a linear prediction analysis is conducted in the frequency-domain on a per-subband basis. The all-pole magnitude response of the linear predictive filter thus obtained is taken as the temporal envelope.

The FDLP feature extraction employed in the paper was carried out using three different filter-banks: Mel-, bark- and linear-filter-banks. The brief detail of each of these non-linear scales are summarized in the following: Mel-scale filter-banks are a set of triangular filters with a peak response equal to unity at the center frequency. The central frequency of each Mel-scale filter bank is uniformly spaced till 1000 Hz and it follows a logarithmic scale thereafter. The mapping from linear frequency scale (f in Hz) to the Mel-frequency scale (m) is given by:

$$m = 2595 \log_{10} \left(1 + \frac{f}{700} \right) \tag{1}$$

The Bark scale provides an alternative perceptually motivated scale to the Mel-scale. The basilar membrane (BM) which is an important part of the inner ear performs the spectral analysis followed by speech intelligibility perception in humans. Each point on the BM can be considered as a band pass filter having a bandwidth equal to one critical bandwidth or one Bark. The bandwidth of several auditory filters were empirically observed and used to formulate the Bark scale. The transformation of linear frequency scale(f in Hz) into Bark-frequency scale (B) [13, 25] is given by:

$$B = 13 \arctan \left(\frac{0.76f}{1000} \right) + 3.5 \arctan \left(\frac{f}{7500} \right)^2 \tag{2}$$

The linear filter-bank's resolution is alike for all the frequency components of the spectral information. The linear-scale frequency of linear filter-bank may prove to be beneficial for children's ASV system as the filter-bank coefficients cover all speech frequency ranges equally and considers them equally important. Earlier works have shown that the higher-frequency components in children's speech are richer in speaker-specific information. Hence, effectively preserving those by the use of linear-filter-bank may improve the performance of an ASV system.

4   Experimental Evaluation

4.1   Speech Corpora and Experimental Set-Up

Three different speech corpora were employed for the development and evaluation of the speaker verification system in this paper. The **CMU kids corpus** [3] consisted of a 9.1 hours of data from 76 children. This speech corpus was used as the training set for the ASV system in this work. The **PF-STAR kid corpus** dataset [16] comprised of 8.3 hours of data from 121 children. It served as our test data-set. A total of 6,664 genuine trails and 995420 impostor trails are present in this test set. Finally, the **WSJCAM0 corpus** [14] which is an adult speech data-set was used for the out-of-domain data augmentation. This speech corpus comprises of 15.5 hours of data from 92 adult speakers.

The entire set-up for the ASV system was developed using kaldi toolkit [9]. As already mentioned, we have experimented with two front-end acoustic features. It must be pointed out that, the MFCC features were extracted using the Kaldi toolkit while FDLP-based front-end speech parametrization was performed using MATLAB. In the process to extract the MFCC features, speech data were first high-pass filtered having pre-emphasis factor of 0.97. Each of the speech utterances are divided into short-time frames using overlapping Hamming windows. The duration of the Hamming windows was chosen to be 25 ms with a frame shift of 10 ms. A 30-channel Mel-filter-bank was engaged for warping the linear spectra to Mel-scale, before computing the 30-dimensional MFCC features. On the other hand, FDLP feature extraction was accomplished using three different types of filter-banks, namely mel-scale, bark-scale and linear-scale filter-bank. The number of modulation components and cepstral components were 14 and 30, respectively. The frame length was chosen to be 25 ms with a frame shift of 10 ms, similar to that of MFCC specifications.

The x-vector extraction was performed using a time-delay neural network (TDNN) architecture [24] comprising of 7 hidden layers trained for 6 epochs. The parameters of the network was trained using gradient descent algorithm [11,24], followed by a 512-dimensional x-vector extraction as the final step. The metrics used for performance evaluation in this paper are equal error rate (EER) and minimum decision cost function (minDCF).

4.2   Experimental Results

The EER and minDCF values for the children's speech test-set with respect to an ASV system trained on either children's speech or a mix of children's and adults' speech along with the modified adults' speech are given in Table 1. As evident from the table, the EER and minDCF undergo appreciable improvement

Table 1. EER and minDCF values for the children's speech test set demonstrating the effectiveness of out-of-domain data augmentation techniques. The MODIFIED ADULT SPEECH in the out-of-domain data augmentation scheme includes adult voice conversion (ADULT-VC), adult time-scale modification (ADULT-TSM), adult formant modification (ADULT-FM) and adult pitch modification (ADULT-PM).

Data used for training	Evaluation Metric	
	EER(%)	minDCF
CHILD (Baseline)	4.235	0.6442
CHILD + ADULT	3.574	0.5432
CHILD + MODIFIED ADULT SPEECH	2.931	0.4565
CHILD + ADULT + MODIFIED ADULT SPEECH (**PROPOSED**)	**2.716**	**0.3655**

with the implementation of the proposed data augmentation technique. A relative improvement of 35.86% with respect to the baseline ASV system trained exclusively on child data-set is achieved when the proposed data augmentation techniques is employed. This shows that the missing targeted attributes have been well captured as the consequence of the proposed data augmentation. Consequently, the developed ASV system generalizes better for the children's speech. The separate impact of the augmented data for different setups are also enlisted in Table 1 for comparison with the data augmentation technique proposed in this paper.

Next, the effectiveness of the proposed feature concatenation approach was evaluated. The EER and minDCF values obtained when MFCC and FDLP features were concatenated are given in Table 2 for the entire test-set. The EER and minDCF values obtained when the ASV system is trained either using only MFCC features or using only FDLP features are also enlisted for comparison. Again, the proposed data augmentation technique has been employed prior to training the ASV system. As evident from the Table 2, relevant improvements are observed in the evaluation metrics when MFCC features are concatenated with the FDLP features. The frame-level concatenation of the MFCC features with the FDLP features extracted by the linear filter-bank out-classes all other feature concatenation pairs and culminates in a significant relative improvement of 22.34% in EER on the entire test-set.

Further, the effect on the performance of the ASV system was monitored when subjected to gender-wise split-up of children's speech test set. For evaluating the effect of gender variation, the evaluation metric results are noted for the complete test-set, as well as with split-up of the test-set in two subgroups on the basis of gender. The corresponding values for EER and minDCF for this study are exhibited in Table 3. Evident from the Table 3 is that the ASV system trained on the concatenated acoustic features yields superior results and this development can be attributed to the underlying fact that the feature fusion of MFCC and FDLP features represent the spectral as well as the temporal

Table 2. EER and minDCF values for the ASV system trained on the full data-set obtained using the proposed data augmentation technique, demonstrating the effectiveness of feature concatenation. This study was performed on x-vector-based children's ASV system.

Features	Test-set	EER (%)	minDCF
MFCC	Full	2.716	0.3655
FDLP_Linear	Full	2.412	0.3588
MFCC + FDLP_Bark	Full	2.395	0.3448
MFCC + FDLP_Mel	Full	2.287	0.3631
MFCC + FDLP_Linear	Full	**2.109**	**0.3313**

Table 3. EER and minimum DCF values highlighting the significance of feature concatenation approaches on the different test sets. This study was performed on x-vector-based children's ASV system.

Features	Test-set	EER (%)	minDCF
MFCC	Full test set	2.716	0.3655
	Female	2.407	0.2560
	Male	3.522	0.7470
MFCC + FDLP_Bark	Full test set	2.395	0.3448
	Female	2.148	0.2547
	Male	2.831	0.7070
MFCC + FDLP_Mel	Full test set	2.287	0.3631
	Female	2.519	0.2785
	Male	2.486	0.7100
MFCC + FDLP_Linear	Full test set	**2.109**	**0.3313**
	Female	**2.111**	**0.2813**
	Male	2.624	0.6840

structure effectively. This reiterates that an enhanced children ASV performance can be achieved by effectively modeling temporal envelope along with the spectral envelope.

5   Conclusion

The work in this paper presents our endeavour towards the development of a robust children's ASV system. To address the inevitable problem of speech data scarcity, we have proposed an out-of domain data augmentation technique wherein the available adults' speech was modified through techniques like voice conversion, pitch scaling, duration modification and formant modification. All the perturbed and unperturbed speech data were pooled together and the three-way speed modification was performed on them. Consequently, the amount of training data was increased three-folds while keeping acoustic mismatch in check to a large extent. Furthermore, we have also explored the effect of concatenating MFCC and FDLP coefficients in order to simultaneously model the spectral as well as temporal envelopes. The proposed data augmentation technique in combination with frame-level concatenation of MFCC with the FDLP features extracted through the linear filter-banks results in the most significant reduction in EER and minDCF compared to the baseline. As a future extension of this work, we would like to explore the performance of the children's ASV system with a larger amount of adults' speech data.

References

1. Athineos, M., Ellis, D.: Frequency-domain linear prediction for temporal features. In: 2003 IEEE Workshop on Automatic Speech Recognition and Understanding (IEEE Cat. No.03EX721), pp. 261–266 (2003)
2. Davis, S., Mermelstein, P.: Comparison of parametric representations for monosyllabic word recognition in continuously spoken sentences. IEEE Trans. Acoust. Speech Signal Process. **28**(4), 357–366 (1980). https://doi.org/10.1109/TASSP. 1980.1163420
3. Eskenazi, M., Mostow, J., Graff, D.: The CMU Kids Corpus LDC97S63. https:// catalog.ldc.upenn.edu/LDC97S63 (1997)
4. Kaneko, T., Kameoka, H.: Parallel-data-free voice conversion using cycle-consistent adversarial networks. arXiv preprint arXiv:1711.11293 (2017)
5. Kumar, V., Kumar, A., Shahnawazuddin, S.: Creating robust children's ASR system in zero-resource condition through out-of-domain data augmentation. Circuits Syst. Signal Process. **41**(4), 2205–2220 (2022)
6. Lee, S., Potamianos, A., Narayanan, S.S.: Acoustics of children's speech: developmental changes of temporal and spectral parameters. J. Acoust. Soc. Am. **105**(3), 1455–1468 (1999). https://doi.org/10.1121/1.426686
7. Mantena, G., Achanta, S., Prahallad, K.: Query-by-example spoken term detection using frequency domain linear prediction and non-segmental dynamic time warping. IEEE/ACM Trans. Audio Speech Lang. Process. **22**(5), 946–955 (2014)
8. Peddinti, V., Povey, D., Khudanpur, S.: A time delay neural network architecture for efficient modeling of long temporal contexts. In: Proceedings of the INTERSPEECH (2015)
9. Povey, D., et al.: The Kaldi Speech recognition toolkit. In: Proceedings of the ASRU (2011)
10. Povey, D., et al.: The kaldi speech recognition toolkit. In: IEEE 2011 Workshop on Automatic Speech Recognition and Understanding. No. CONF, IEEE Signal Processing Society (2011)
11. Povey, D., Zhang, X., Khudanpur, S.: Parallel training of DNNs with natural gradient and parameter averaging. arXiv preprint arXiv:1410.7455 (2014)
12. Prasanna, S.R.M., Govind, D., Rao, K.S., Yegnanarayana, B.: Fast prosody modification using instants of significant excitation. In: Proceedings of the International Conference on Speech Prosody (2010)
13. Quateier, T.F.: Discrete Time Processing of Speech Signals- Principles and Practice (1997)

14. Robinson, T., Fransen, J., Pye, D., Foote, J., Renals, S.: WSJCAMO: a British english speech corpus for large vocabulary continuous speech recognition. In: 1995 International Conference on Acoustics, Speech, and Signal Processing, vol. 1, pp. 81–84. IEEE (1995)

15. Russell, M., D'Arcy, S.: Challenges for computer recognition of children's speech. In: Proceedings of the Speech and Language Technologies in Education (SLaTE) (2007)

16. Russell, M., D'Arcy, S., Wong, M., Batliner, A., Blomberg, M., Gerosa, M.: The pf-star children's speech corpus. In: Interspeech 2005 (2005)

17. Safavi, S., Najafian, M., Hanani, A., Russell, M.J., Jancovic, P.: Comparison of speaker verification performance for adult and child speech. In: Proceedings of the WOCCI (2014)

18. Safavi, S., Najafian, M., Hanani, A., Russell, M.J., Jancovic, P., Carey, M.J.: Speaker recognition for children's speech. arXiv arXiv:1609.07498 (2012)

19. Safavi, S., Russell, M., Jancovic, P.: Automatic speaker, age-group and gender identification from children's speech. Comput. Speech Lang. **50**, 141–156 (2018)

20. Shahnawazuddin, S., Adiga, N., Kathania, H.K., Sai, B.T.: Creating speaker independent ASR system through prosody modification based data augmentation. Pattern Recogn. Lett. **131**, 213–218 (2020). https://doi.org/10.1016/j.patrec.2019.12.019

21. Shahnawazuddin, S., Ahmad, W., Adiga, N., Kumar, A.: In-domain and out-of-domain data augmentation to improve children's speaker verification system in limited data scenario. In: Proceedings of the ICASSP, pp. 7554–7558 (2020). https://doi.org/10.1109/ICASSP40776.2020.9053891

22. Shahnawazuddin, S., Ahmad, W., Adiga, N., Kumar, A.: Children's speaker verification in low and zero resource conditions. Digit. Signal Process. **116**, 103115 (2021)

23. Snyder, D., Garcia-Romero, D., Povey, D., Khudanpur, S.: Deep neural network embeddings for text-independent speaker verification. In: Proceedings of the INTERSPEECH, pp. 999–1003 (August 2017)

24. Snyder, D., Garcia-Romero, D., Sell, G., Povey, D., Khudanpur, S.: X-Vectors: Robust DNN embeddings for speaker recognition. In: 2018 IEEE International Conference on Acoustics, Speech and Signal Processing (ICASSP), pp. 5329–5333. IEEE (2018)

25. Stevens, S.S., Volkmann, J., Newman, E.B.: A scale for the measurement of the psychological magnitude pitch. J. Acoust. Soc. Am. **8**(3), 185–190 (1937)

26. Thomas, S., Ganapathy, S., Hermansky, H.: Recognition of reverberant speech using frequency domain linear prediction. IEEE Signal Process. Lett. **15**, 681–684 (2008)

27. Wickramasinghe, B., Irtza, S., Ambikairajah, E., Epps, J.: Frequency domain linear prediction features for replay spoofing attack detection. In: Interspeech, pp. 661–665 (2018)

Constant-Q Based Harmonic and Pitch Features for Normal *vs.* Pathological Infant Cry Classification

Aditya Pusuluri[✉], Aastha Kachhi, and Hemant A. Patil

Speech Research Lab, DA-IICT Gandhinagar Gujarat, Gandhinagar, India
{aditya_pss,aastha_k,hemant_patil}@daiict.ac.in

Abstract. Classification of normal *vs.* pathological infant cry is a socially relevant and challenging problem. Many feature sets, such as Mel Frequency Cepstral Coefficients (MFCC), Linear Frequency Cepstral Coefficients (LFCC), and Constant Q Cepstral Coefficients (CQCC) have been used for this task. However, an effective representation of the *spectral* and *pitch* components of a spectrum together is not achieved leaving scope for improvement. Also, the infant cry can be considered a melodic sound implying that the fundamental frequency and timbre-based features also carry vital information. This work proposes Constant Q Harmonic Coefficients (CQHC), and Constant Q Pitch Coefficients (CQPC) extracted by the decomposition of the Constant Q Transform (CQT) spectrum for the infant cry classification. This work uses Convolutional Neural Network (CNN) as the classifier along with traditional classifiers, such as Gaussian Mixture Models (GMM) and Support Vector Machines (SVM). The results using the CNN classifier are compared by considering the MFCC, LFCC, and CQCC feature sets as the baseline features. The feature-level fusion of MFCC with log-CQHC and MFCC with log-CQPC achieved a *5*-fold accuracy of *98.73%* and *98.96%* respectively, surpassing the baseline MFCC. Furthermore, the fusion of MFCC with log-CQHC and log-CQPC feature sets resulted in improved classification accuracy of *3%*, *4.7%*, and *5.85%* when compared with the baseline MFCC, LFCC, and CQCC feature sets, respectively. Further, our intensive experiments using three classifiers structures, namely, GMM, SVM, and CNN indicate superior results using the proposed feature extraction techniques.

Keywords: Infant cry classification · CQT · CQHC · CQPC · Feature-level fusion · Convolutional neural network · GMM · SVM

1 Introduction

Crying is the sole established means by which an infant communicates with parents or caregivers. Hence, the cry of an infant carries information, such as emotional needs, physical needs, or pathological needs. Even experienced mothers

A. Karpov et al. (Eds.): SPECOM 2023, LNAI 14339, pp. 407–420, 2023.
https://doi.org/10.1007/978-3-031-48312-7_33

and caregivers often find it challenging to pinpoint the precise cause of an infant's crying. Infant cry research involves diverse fields, such as prosody engineering, and neurology engineering. Normal *vs.* pathological infant cry classification is one of those [13]. World Health Organization (WHO) predicts that the infant mortality rate can be reduced by up to two-thirds if early diagnosis and treatments are given during the first week of life [10]. In this context, a cry-based recognition of infant was recently proposed by a collaborative research of Speech Brain and Ubenwa Health [5]. Study reported in [9], reports Infant Identification using Fingerprint I'D. To that effect, the classification of infant cries has been proven to be a vital study. Acoustic analysis of the infant cry is found to be useful for certain pathological conditions [12], where early detection of the pathological cry aids in diagnosing pathology in time.

Early 1960s mark the beginning of infant cry research and analysis [23]. The study reported in [26], identified ten distinct cry modes to describe the *manner* of variations of fundamental or pitch frequency (F_0) and its harmonics (kF_0, $k \in Z$). However, this study was limited to the analysis of normal infant cries and later extended to pathological infant cries, where dysphonation and hyperphonation cry modes were found to be correlated with the pathological cry [13]. These studies also used a narrowband spectrogram due to its capability of capturing the variation in kF_0, where formant structures are not clear due to quasi-periodic sampling of the vocal tract spectrum by the distantly-spared pitch source harmonics.

In the literature, studies using state-of-the-art feature sets, such as Mel Frequency Cepstral Coefficients (MFCC) are also explored for infant cry classification [1,15]. Nonetheless, the Short-Time Fourier Transform (STFT), employed in Mel Frequency Cepstral Coefficients (MFCC), exhibits a consistent time-frequency resolution across the entire time-frequency plane. Furthermore, it does not maintain the property of *form-invariance*, as the analysis window utilized in STFT is solely dependent on the time parameter. Constant-Q Transform (CQT) was found to preserve the form-invariance property as the window used in CQT is a function of both time and frequency. The MFCC captures the generalized timbre features and the multi-dimensional timbre feature cannot be captured using the Mel scale. Recently, there are many data-driven models used to obtain the timbre-based features, however, implicit learning is tied to specific training models and is not as explicit and interpretable as MFCCs, which are better at the characterization of sound signals.

Infants possess a remarkable innate inclination for music, where melody contour (i.e., F_0 and its harmonics) is most prominent for them [25]. Perception and memorization of melody and rhythm (i.e., prosody) start around the third trimester of pregnancy [2]. To that effect, motivated by Brown's original study on CQT for enhanced note resolution in western music [3], a CQT-based study was employed in [18] for infant cry classification. In this paper, we propose features based on the decomposition of the CQT spectrum giving, Constant Q Harmonic Coefficients (CQHC), and Constant Q Pitch Coefficients (CQPC) for the infant cry classification task.

The remainder of this paper is structured as follows: In Sect. 2, we introduce our proposed work on CQHC and CQPC features, along with the details of feature extraction. Section 3 provides insights into the database used and outlines the experimental setup. Section 4 presents the experimental results and provides an in-depth analysis of these findings. Lastly, Sect. 5 serves as the conclusion of the paper and offers a glimpse into potential directions for future research.

2   Proposed Work

In this Section, we describe details of CQT and its decomposition to obtain CQHC and CQPC feature sets. Figure 1 shows the functional block diagram of the proposed Constant-Q Based Harmonic and Pitch Features for Infant Cry Classification.

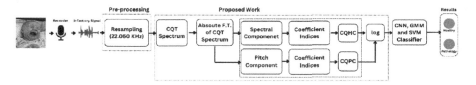

Fig. 1. Functional block diagram of the proposed Constant-Q Based Harmonic and Pitch Features for Infant Cry Classification.

2.1   Constant-Q Transform (CQT)

This frequency transform exhibits a logarithmic resolution that aligns with the tuning of Western music, where the octave is evenly divided into steps [3,4]. In contrast to the discrete Fourier transform (DFT), which maintains a constant window size for each frequency bin, the window size in the Constant-Q Transform (CQT) decreases as the frequency increases, thanks to the constant quality factor (Q), resulting in a logarithmic resolution [20].

Let x(n) be the discrete-time speech signal obtained with a sampling frequency of Fs. The STFT of x(n) is given by [3]:

$$X(\omega, \tau) = \sum_{n=-\infty}^{\infty} x(n) \cdot h(n, \tau) \cdot e^{-j\omega n}, \tag{1}$$

In this context, the symbol $h(n, \tau)$ signifies the analysis window, which is centred at a specific time point τ. It's important to note that this window function depends exclusively on the time parameter τ. Now, if we denote $z(n)$ as a frame of the speech signal, we can express the N-point Discrete Fourier Transform (DFT) for the kth spectral component of $z(n)$ which is given by $Z(k)$ as follows:

$$Z(k) = \sum_{n=0}^{N-1} z(n) \cdot e^{-j(\frac{2\pi}{N})kn}, \tag{2}$$

where k is the frequency bin index, and $\omega_{DFT} = (2\pi k)/N$. The CQT of a signal $z(n)$ is given as [20]:

$$Z^{CQT}(k) = \frac{1}{N(k)} \sum_{n=0}^{N(k)-1} z(n)h(n,k)e^{-j\left(\frac{2\pi}{N(k)}Qn\right)}, \tag{3}$$

and $\omega_{CQT} = (2\pi Qn)/N(k)$, and $h(n,k)$ represents the analysis window. It's important to note that this analysis window remains constant for each frequency bin f_k, but its length is determined by both n (time) and k (frequency), where $N(k) = Q(F_s/f_k)$.

The *quality factor* (Q) can be defined as the ratio of the center frequency to bandwidth, and it is calculated according to the formula provided in the reference [3]:

$$\therefore Q = \frac{f_k}{\Delta f_k} = \frac{f_k}{f_{k+1} - f_k} = \frac{1}{2^{1/B} - 1}, \tag{4}$$

where B represents the number of bins per octave, and f_k shows the frequency of kth spectral component, which is given by:

$$f_k = (2^{(k-1)/B})f_{min}, \tag{5}$$

where f_{min} is the minimum frequency of the signal.

2.2   Constant-Q Harmonic Coefficients (CQHC)

The logarithmic resolution of the CQT allows the harmonics to form a *constant pattern* in the frequency-domain, with their relative position remaining the same w.r.t F_0 [20]. As the harmonics are the spectral coefficients carrying the spectral information of the signal, they can be used in the *timbre* characterization of the signal, where timbre can be defined as the quality of the sound produced. Given the pitch can be normalized, the locations of harmonics can be inferred, and their energies be extracted leading to an efficient timbre feature set. The pitch normalization is achieved considering the assumption that the CQT spectrum can be represented as a convolution between a pitch-normalized spectral component, and energy-normalized pitch component as shown in Eq. (6) [20]. In particular, from Eq. (3), the CQT spectrum can be written as:

$$Z = S * P, \tag{6}$$

where Z represents the CQT spectrum, S represents the pitch-normalized spectral component, and P represents the energy-normalized pitch component. From the property that the magnitude of the Fourier transform is *shift-invariant*, the spectral component can be approximated by the magnitude Fourier transform of the CQT spectrum. The IFFT of the above approximation gives the estimate of the spectral component as stated in Eq. (7) [20]:

$$S = \mathcal{F}^{-1}(|\mathcal{F}(Z)|), \tag{7}$$

where $\mathcal{F}^{-1}(.)$ represents the inverse Fourier transform function. Given the octave resolution considered for the calculation of CQT, we can obtain the locations of harmonics in the spectral component, and then extract the harmonic coefficients. The coefficients from the spectral component are obtained by [20]:

$$i = round(O_r log_2(k)), \tag{8}$$

$$CQHC_k = S(i), \tag{9}$$

where k takes the value between 1 and N_c, O_r is the octave resolution, and N_c is the number of desired coefficients. The CQHC captures the harmonics information of the speech signal embedded in the CQT spectrum. In this work, along with CQHC, additionally, logarithmic CQHC is also considered.

Algorithm 1 Python pseudo code for CQHC and CQPC feature extraction

---

Input: Speech signal x(n) and sampling frequency Fs
Output: cqhc_feat, cqpc_feat

1: $cqt\_spec \leftarrow cqt(x(n), Fs)$ ▷ Constant Q transform
2: $power\_cqt \leftarrow power(cqt\_spec, 2)$ ▷ Power spectrum of the CQT
3: $ft\_cqt \leftarrow FT(power\_cqt)$ ▷ Fourier transform of the power spectrum
4: $absft\_cqt \leftarrow abs(ft\_cqt)$ ▷ Absolute value
5: $spect\_comp \leftarrow real(ifft((absft\_cqt)))$ ▷ Pitch normalized spectral
   component
6: $pitch\_comp \leftarrow real(ifft(ft\_cqt/absft\_cqt))$ ▷ Energy normalized pitch
   component
7: $indices \leftarrow round(octave\_resol * log(arrange(1, numcoeff + 1)))$ ▷ Indices
   values
8: $cqhc\_feat \leftarrow spect\_comp[indices, :]$
9: $cqpc\_feat \leftarrow pitch\_comp[indices, :]$

2.3   Constant-Q Pitch Coefficients (CQPC)

The decomposition of the CQT spectrum also results in an energy-normalized pitch component. This means that the information embedded in the fundamental frequency (F_0), and the first few formants are stored through the pitch component. The pitch component is calculated as [20]:

$$P = \mathcal{F}^{-1}(e^{jArg(\mathcal{F}(Z))}). \tag{10}$$

Furthermore, the coefficients for the pitch component are obtained in a similar manner shown in Eq. (8), and Eq. (10), where the spectral component is replaced by the pitch component. Algorithm 1 specifies the pseudocode for the feature extraction of CQHC and CQPC features. In addition, logarithm CQPC is also considered.

3   Experimental Setup

3.1   Datasets Used

This study utilizes the Baby Chillanto dataset, which was curated using recordings conducted by medical professionals and is a property of NIAOE-CONACYT in Mexico [21]. Each infant cry signal was divided into one-second segments, representing individual samples in our research. These cry segments were categorized into five groups, forming two sets for binary classification: healthy cry (comprising normal, hungry, and pain cries, totalling 1049 cry samples) and pathological cry (comprising asphyxia and deaf cries, totalling 1219 cry samples). All the samples are resampled to 22.05 kHz. An 80–20 split is followed for training and testing. A random seed value is fixed in order to remove the randomization across the train-test split. The cross-fold validation is included in order to show the robustness of the classifier and feature set. The statistical details of the dataset are shown in Table 1.

Table 1. Statistics of the Baby Chillanto dataset used. After [6,7,21].

Class	Category	# Utterances
Healthy	Normal	507
	Hungry	350
	Pain	192
Pathology	Asphyxia	340
	Deaf	879

3.2   Classifiers Used

Convolutional Neural Network (CNN) Classifier. This work uses CNN classifier, which is known to learn the spatial hierarchies from the data for classification. It is also known that infant cries contain major classification cues across the spatial axis in the spectrograms. [19] shows the important information embedded across the temporal axis of an infant cry. Table 2 shows a detailed description of CNN architecture. The model is trained using stratified 5-folds cross-validation strategy with a seed value and a train and validation split of *80%* and *20%* using *adam* optimizer [27], *binary cross-entropy* as a loss function, and *accuracy* as the evaluation metric. The stratified method ensures the distribution of data in each fold is similar to the distribution of the entire data. The algorithm was tuned using grid search to select the best learning rate, and batch size for 300 epochs. Two activation functions are used, namely, *ReLu* and *sigmoid*. A *ReLu* activation is used in order to improve the learning speed while reducing the computational cost [14], and the *sigmoid* activation is used at the final layer for binary classification. A normalization layer was added along with a dropout layer after each convolutional layer in order to avoid overfitting of

CNN model. The learning rate used is *0.001* and a batch size of *128*. The networks were implemented using the python library Keras v.2.24 [16] using the TensorFlow-GPU v.1.14.0 backend.

Table 2. CNN Architecture.

Output Size	Description
(20,130,1)	CQHC
(20,130,16)	convolution layer, 16 filters, BN, relu
(10,65,16)	max-pooling, (2,2), dropout (0.25)
(10,65,32)	convolution layer, 32 filters, BN, relu
(5,32,32)	max-pooling, (2,2), dropout (0.25)
(5,32,64)	convolution layer, 64 filters, BN, relu
(2,16,64)	max-pooling, (2,2), dropout (0.25)
(2,16,16)	convolution layer, 16 filters, BN, relu
(2,16,16)	dropout (0.25)
(2,16,16)	convolution layer, 16 filters, BN, relu
(2,16,16)	dropout (0.25), followed by flattening
128	dense layer, relu
64	dense layer, relu
64	dropout (0.25)
1	dense, sigmoid

Traditional Classifiers. Experiments were also performed on traditional classifiers such as Gaussian Mixture Model (GMM) and Support Vector Machine (SVM). 512 number of Gaussian mixtures were used to train the model on *5*-fold cross-validation. Similarly, the SVM was trained on a *5*-fold using a linear kernel. In this work, the focus will be on the results obtained using the CNN classifier and the traditional classifiers serve to support the discussions as the deep learning classifier have the ability to capture complex relations present across various features.

3.3 Baseline Features

In this work, three baseline features are considered, namely, Mel Frequency Cepstral Coefficients (MFCC), Linear Frequency Cepstral Coefficients (LFCC), and Constant Q Cepstral Coefficients (CQCC). All these features are evaluated by keeping a window size of 25 ms and a hop length of 10 ms, $F_{min} = 100$ Hz, and octave resolution of 14. All the features were extracted using librosa toolkit [17].

4   Results and Analysis

4.1   Spectrographic Analysis

Figure 2 represents the CQT-gram analysis of normal *vs.* asphyxia *vs.* deaf cries. From Panel III of Fig. 2, it can be observed that the pitch component of a normal cry is found to have a continuous contour plot (F_0 contour), however, it is seen to be discontinuous for the pathological cry. Furthermore, it is observed that the pitch component of pathology cries occurs at higher frequencies than the pitch component of the normal infant cry. These observations make the pitch component a vital differentiating factor for normal *vs.* pathology infant cry. However, the CQPC component does not contain the formant information. Panel II of Fig. 2 represents the spectral component of infant cries. For pathological cries, the harmonic structures are found to be smeared when compared with the normal infant cry. Due to the pitch normalization of the harmonics, the resolution of the harmonic component decreases. This makes the harmonic component a poor choice when considered alone.

4.2   Results Obtained for Baseline

The accuracy obtained using baseline features is reported in Table 3. It can be seen that the maximum 5-fold (test) accuracy of *96.95*% (97.88%) is achieved using the MFCC on the CNN classifier. Further, it can be seen that traditional classifiers, such as GMM, and SVM resulted in a test accuracy of 99.16% and 86.21%, respectively, for the MFCC. The MFCC results in the highest accuracy of all the baseline features across different classifiers because it contains generalized timbre information and pitch information [20]. It should also be noted that the introduction of the Mel scale features is primarily aimed at the musical signals [20], in particular, the Mel scale is derived from psychophysical measurement of just noticeable differences (JHD) pitch differences [22] and since the infant cry can be considered as a *melodic* signal, the Mel scaled features outperforms the linear scale-based features.

4.3   Results for CQT, CQHC, and CQPC

The CQT feature set using a CNN classifier resulted in an accuracy of 90.32% as shown in Table 4. The CQHC and CQPC feature sets, which are obtained by decomposing the CQT spectrum resulted in fold (test) accuracies of 80.85% (82%) and 83.47% (85.18%), respectively. A similar trend of results can be noticed using traditional classifiers, i.e., GMM and SVM. This result indicates the importance of the pitch component for the infant cry classification, which is captured by the CQPC feature set. This might be due to the fact that the pathology cry contains irregular breathing patterns which are caused due to affected vocal folds and it is known that the fundamental frequency (F_0) is tied to the rate of vocal fold vibration [11]. Hence, the F_0 or the pitch component contains distinguishing acoustic cues of the cry, which is vital for the classification task of normal *vs.* pathology cry. This result also indicates the fact that

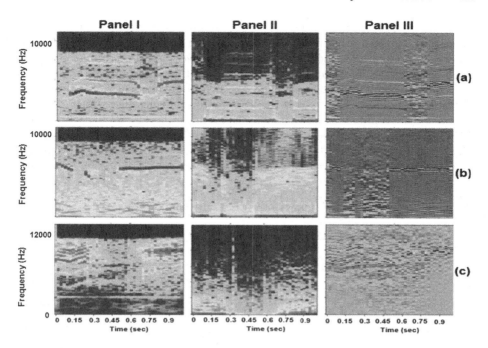

Fig. 2. Panel I, Panel II, and Panel III depicts CQT-gram, Spectral Component, and Pitch Component, respectively, for (a) normal cry, (b) asphyxia, and (c) deaf cries. Best viewed in colour.

Table 3. Results for Baseline Features.

Features	CNN Fold Acc.	CNN Test Acc.	GMM	SVM
MFCC	**96.95**	**97.88**	**99.16**	**86.21**
LFCC	94.42	96.47	**99.16**	84.76
CQCC	93.27	93	95.44	83.12

infant cries exhibit rich melodic features i.e., variation of fundamental frequency w.r.t time [24].

On the other hand, the CQHC feature set which is extracted by normalizing the spectrum w.r.t F_0 fails to perform when compared with the CQPC indicating the timbre information alone does not carry distinguishing factors for the normal and pathological infant cry. However, neither the harmonics component nor the pitch component alone is resulting in accuracy higher than the CQT feature set. These results can be supported by the spectrographic analysis performed in the previous section. Furthermore, the effect of the logarithm applied to the feature sets was investigated. The application of a log on any spectrum helps to increase the resolution of the spectrum.

It can be observed from Table 4 that the effect of the log is negligible in the case of CQPC as the increase of resolution of the energy normalized pitch component doesn't add much information *as compared to the spectral component which contains the information of the harmonics*, that is normalized to the lowest frequency. Similar conclusions can be drawn from the results obtained using traditional classifiers. The SVM is the least-performing classifier which might be because of its inability to deal with mapping features that are not linearly separable in lower-dimensional feature space into linearly separable higher-dimensional feature space, where they become linearly separable, which is nothing but the Cover's theorem on the separability of patterns [8].

Table 4. Accuracy of CQT, CQHC, and CQPC.

Feature	CNN 5-Fold Accuracy	CNN Test Accuracy	GMM	SVM
CQT	90.32	87.12	90.7	70.62
CQHC	80.85	82.00	85.77	64.49
CQPC	83.47	85.18	89.6	62.59
LOG CQHC	90.70	91.12	90.22	77.27
LOG CQPC	**91.24**	**92.12**	**93.61**	**80.31**

4.4 Effect of Feature-Level Fusion

This sub-Section discusses the results obtained from the feature-level fusion of MFCC, CQHC, CQT, and CQPC feature sets. This fusion is the concatenation of various feature sets extracted in different ways into a single feature set. The fusion of CQHC and CQPC outperforms the CQT feature set indicating that providing the pitch component separately results in a better performance. This result states that feeding the F_0 contour information separately along with harmonic information results in a better accuracy as can be seen from Fig. 2. The addition of log to the fusion of CQHC and CQPC performs comparable with MFCC features and outperforms LFCC and CQCC features. MFCC manages to capture generalized timbre information in it along with the pitch information [20]. The infant cry can be considered a melodic sound due to the continuous variations in the pitch of the cry. The timbre information provides the colour for the melodic sounds. Hence, both CQHC and MFCC capture the timbre information in a unique way.

The fusion of MFCC and log-CQHC features beat the baseline MFCC feature set by fold (test) accuracies of **1.78% (1.41%)**. This indicates that the harmonic features of the CQT spectrum carry additional information when compared with the generalized harmonic features captured by MFCC. Furthermore, the feature-level fusion of MFCC and log-CQPC feature set results in an improvement in the fold (test) accuracy of **2.01% (1.6%)** when compared with baseline MFCC features indicating that the additional pitch information is important for the infant cry classification task. The fusion of MFCC with log-CQPC and the fusion of MFCC with log-CQPC and log-CQHC managed to beat the baseline MFCC resulting in an improvement of **3% (1.6%)** in accuracy. This shows that the CQHC consists of unique information obtained from the CQT spectrum, which the MFCC fails to capture.

It also indicates the inability of the MFCC feature set to capture the pitch component when compared to the CQPC feature set. Hence, the fusion of the MFCC feature set with the CQT decomposed features (CQHC and CQPC) resulted in a noticeable amount of increase in accuracy, which can also be observed in traditional classifiers. The traditional classifiers, such as GMM and CNN also beat the baseline feature MFCC when compared with the fusion of MFCC with log-CQHC, log-CQPC by a margin of **0.65%** and **6.26%** (Table 5).

Table 5. Accuracy of Various Feature-Level Fusions.

Feature	CNN 5-Fold Accuracy	CNN Test Accurcy	GMM	SVM
CQHC+CQPC	91.92	94.17	93.26	70.66
LOG CQHC+ LOG CQPC	95.35	94.70	97.53	84.32
MFCC+LOG CQHC	98.73	99.29	99.34	89.91
MFCC+LOG CQPC	98.96	99.47	99.52	91.63
MFCC+LOG CQT	98.45	99.47	99.52	86.48
MFCC+LOG CQHC+LOG CQPC	**99.12**	**99.47**	**99.81**	**92.47**

4.5   Statistical Evaluation of Proposed Method

The statistical significance of results is shown using stratified k-fold cross-validation to ensure similar data distribution in each fold. 5-fold CV is performed 50 times to get violin plots as shown in Fig. 3 (all the results are obtained using GMM classifier), which shows relatively higher mean and median than the existing features for the proposed features. This states the statistical importance of the proposed CQHC and CQPC feature sets.

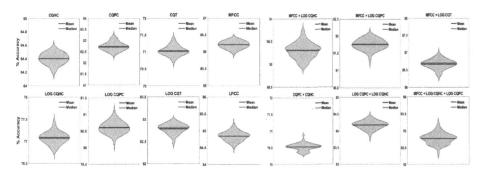

Fig. 3. Analysis of statistical significance via violin plots for various feature sets using GMM classifier.

5   Summary and Conclusion

This study proposed CQHC and CQPC feature sets for the infant cry classification task. The effect of the application of the log on the feature sets is studied. The fusion of MFCC with log CQHC and log CQPC outperforms the baseline MFCC by **3%** and LFCC by **4.7%** and CQCC by **5.85%**, respectively. Further, the study shows the importance of the fundamental frequency in normal *vs.* pathology infant cry classification tasks. Similar trends in the results are observed using traditional classifiers such as SVM and GMM. This work can be further extended by testing the feature sets on various time-based deep learning-based classifiers. Further in-depth analysis of CQHC and CQPC feature sets needs to be done. However, deep learning models require a large amount of training data, which is difficult to collect in the case of the infant cry dataset, more so, for pathological infant cry and it is computationally expensive. Hence, data augmentation of the infant cry can also be considered for future work. Further, this work can be extended to another database to investigate the generalizability of results and analyze the results for mismatched conditions of cross-database scenarios in training and testing. This will also motivate to development of a new In-House corpus for infant cry research. Furthermore, infant cries being private data (more so pathological cases), the development of application programming interfaces (APIs) along with real-time infant cry data acquisition remains another open research problem. Furthermore, for practical applications, it is crucial to ensure that the cry being analyzed is specifically recorded from the intended infant, rather than, for instance, potentially including cries from other infants in the same vicinity. To that effect, infant verification using a cry sample remains an open research problem statement.

Acknowledgements. The authors extend their heartfelt gratitude to the organizers of the National Institute of Astrophysics and Optical Electronics, CONACYT Mexico, for generously providing access to the Baby Chilanto database, which has proven to be statistically significant for their research. They would also like to express their appreciation to the Ministry of Electronics and Information Technology (MeitY) in New Delhi, Government of India, for their sponsorship of the consortium project titled 'Speech Technologies in Indian Languages' as part of the 'National Language Translation Mission (NLTM): BHASHINI.' This project, subtitled 'Building Assistive Speech Technologies for the Challenged,' carries the Grant ID: 11(1)2022-HCC (TDIL).

References

1. Alaie, H.F., Abou-Abbas, L., Tadj, C.: Cry-based infant pathology classification using GMMs. Speech Commun. **77**, 28–52 (2016)
2. Armbrüster, L., Mende, W., Gelbrich, G., Wermke, P., Götz, R., Wermke, K.: Musical intervals in infants' spontaneous crying over the first 4 months of life. Folia Phoniatr. Logop. **73**(5), 401–412 (2021)
3. Brown, J.C.: Calculation of a constant q spectral transform. J. Acoust. Soc. Am. **89**(1), 425–434 (1991)

4. Brown, J.C., Puckette, M.S.: An efficient algorithm for the calculation of a constant q transform. J. Acoust. Soc. Am. (JASA) **92**(5), 2698–2701 (1992)
5. Budaghyan, D., Gorin, A., Subakan, C., Onu, C.C.: Cryceleb: a speaker verification dataset based on infant cry sounds. arXiv preprint arXiv:2305.00969 (2023)
6. Buddha, N., Patil, H.A.: Corpora for analysis of infant cry. Oriental Cocosda, Vietnam (2007)
7. Chittora, A., Patil, H.A.: Data collection of infant cries for research and analysis. J. Voice **31**(2), 252-e15 (2017)
8. Cover, T.M.: Geometrical and statistical properties of systems of linear inequalities with applications in pattern recognition. IEEE Trans. Electron. Comput. **3**, 326–334 (1965)
9. Engelsma, J.J., Deb, D., Cao, K., Bhatnagar, A., Sudhish, P.S., Jain, A.K.: Infant-ID: fingerprints for global good. IEEE Trans. Pattern Anal. Mach. Intell. **44**, 3543–3559 (2021)
10. Ezbakhe, F., Pérez-Foguet, A.: Child mortality levels and trends. Demogr. Res. **43**, 1263–1296 (2020)
11. Feinberg, D.R., Jones, B.C., Little, A.C., Burt, D.M., Perrett, D.I.: Manipulations of fundamental and formant frequencies influence the attractiveness of human male voices. Anim. Behav. **69**(3), 561–568 (2005)
12. Hariharan, M., Yaacob, S., Awang, S.A.: Pathological infant cry analysis using wavelet packet transform and probabilistic neural network. Expert Syst. Appl. **38**(12), 15377–15382 (2011)
13. Hemant, A.: "Patil: Cry baby": using spectrographic analysis to assess neonatal health status from an infant's cry. In: Neustein, A. (ed.) Advances in Speech Recognition, pp. 323–348. Springer, Boston (2010). https://doi.org/10.1007/978-1-4419-5951-5_14
14. Ide, H., Kurita, T.: Improvement of learning for CNN with Relu activation by sparse regularization. In: 2017 International Joint Conference on Neural Networks (IJCNN), Anchorage, Alaska. pp. 2684–2691 (2017)
15. Ji, C., Mudiyanselage, T.B., Gao, Y., Pan, Y.: A review of infant cry analysis and classification. EURASIP J. Audio Speech Music Process. **2021**(1), 1–17 (2021)
16. Ketkar, N.: Introduction to Keras. In: Deep Learning with Python, pp. 95–109. Apress, Berkeley, CA (2017). https://doi.org/10.1007/978-1-4842-2766-4_7
17. McFee, B., et al.: Librosa: audio and music signal analysis in python. In: Proceedings of the 14th Python in Science Conference, vol. 8, pp. 18–25 (2015)
18. Patil, H.A., Patil, A.T., Kachhi, A.: Constant Q cepstral coefficients for classification of normal vs. pathological infant cry. In: IEEE International Conference on Acoustics, Speech and Signal Processing (ICASSP), Singapore, pp. 7392–7396 (2022)
19. Pusuluri, A., Kachhi, A., Patil, H.A.: Analysis of time-averaged feature extraction techniques on infant cry classification. In: Prasanna, S.R.M., Karpov, A., Samudravijaya, K., Agrawal, S.S. (eds.) SPECOM 2022. LNCS, vol. 13721, pp. 590–603. Springer, Cham (2022). https://doi.org/10.1007/978-3-031-20980-2_50
20. Rafii, Z.: The constant-Q harmonic coefficients: a timbre feature designed for music signals [Lecture Notes]. IEEE Signal Process. Mag. **39**(3), 90–96 (2022)
21. Rosales-Pérez, A., Reyes-García, C.A., Gonzalez, J.A., Reyes-Galaviz, O.F., Escalante, H.J., Orlandi, S.: Classifying infant cry patterns by the genetic selection of a fuzzy model. Biomed. Signal Process. Control **17**, 38–46 (2015)
22. Stevens, S.S., Volkmann, J., Newman, E.B.: A scale for the measurement of the psychological magnitude pitch. J. Acoust. Soc. Am. (JASA) **8**(3), 185–190 (1937)

23. Wasz-Höckert, O., Michelsson, K., Lind, J.: Twenty-five years of scandinavian cry research. In: Lester, B.M., Zachariah Boukydis, C.F. (eds.) Infant Crying, pp. 83–104. Springer, Boston (1985). https://doi.org/10.1007/978-1-4613-2381-5_4

24. Wermke, K., Mende, W.: Musical elements in human infants' cries: in the beginning is the melody. Musicae Scientiae **13**(2_suppl), 151–175 (2009)

25. Wermke, K., Robb, M.P., Schluter, P.J.: Melody complexity of infants' cry and non-cry vocalisations increases across the first six months. Sci. Rep. **11**(1), 1–11 (2021)

26. Xie, Q., Ward, R.K., Laszlo, C.A.: Automatic assessment of infants' levels-of-distress from the cry signals. IEEE Trans. Speech Audio Process. **4**(4), 253 (1996)

27. Zhang, Z.: Improved adam optimizer for deep neural networks. In: 2018 IEEE/ACM 26th International Symposium on Quality of Service (IWQoS), Banff, Canada, pp. 1–2 (2018)

Robustness of Whisper Features for Infant Cry Classification

Monil Charola$^{(\boxtimes)}$ ⓘ, Siddharth Rathod$^{(\boxtimes)}$ ⓘ, and Hemant A. Patil$^{(\boxtimes)}$ ⓘ

Dhirubhai Ambani Institute of Information and Communication Technology
(DA-IICT), Ganghinagar, India
{monil_charola,siddharth_rathod,hemant_patil}@daiict.ac.in

Abstract. Early intervention and correct identification of the pathology in infant cry is an important and socially relevant research problem, as it can save the lives of many infants, and also improve the quality of their life. This study proposes utilizing Web-scale Supervised Pre-training for Speech Recognition (WSPSR), also known as *Whisper*, pre-trained *Encoder Module* (WEM) for infant cry classification task. These features are contrasted with the state-of-the-art Mel Frequency Cepstral Coefficients (MFCC) feature set, for the purpose of classifying normal *vs.* pathological infant cries. Additionally, we introduce a multi-class classification approach for pathological infant cries using Convolutional Neural Network (CNN), and Bidirectional Long Short-Term Memory (Bi-LSTM) networks. Our study concludes that the combination of the WEM with Deep Neural Networks (DNN) classifiers, such as CNN and Bi-LSTM, outperforms the MFCC feature set by a significant margin. In addition, a series of comprehensive experiments were conducted to assess the noise robustness and the results indicate that WEM features are relatively more robust compared to MFCC. The experiments were performed utilizing a *10*-fold cross-validation on standard and statistically meaningful *Baby Chilanto* dataset, *In-House DA-IICT Corpus*, and a combined dataset derived from these two datasets.

Keywords: Infant cry classification · Whisper encoder features · Noise robustness of whisper encoder features · CNN · Bi-LSTM

1 Introduction

Infants primarily communicate their needs and overall emotional well-being through crying, making it a crucial aspect of their communication at an early age. Unfortunately, millions of infants die every year due to preventable illnesses, malnutrition, and diseases that could have been avoided with proper vaccination if being detected at an early stage. Some of the most common causes of infant mortality include conditions, such as asthma, asphyxia, and Sudden Infant Death Syndrome (SIDS) [13]. To clinically diagnose these illnesses, a variety of measures, including pictures from head ultrasound (HUS), computed tomography (CT), and magnetic resonance imaging (MRI) scans that indicate damaged

© The Author(s), under exclusive license to Springer Nature Switzerland AG 2023
A. Karpov et al. (Eds.): SPECOM 2023, LNAI 14339, pp. 421–433, 2023.
https://doi.org/10.1007/978-3-031-48312-7_34

regions of the brain, are employed. Unfortunately, pathology identification is time-consuming and expensive in many developing countries, which may have an impact on the infant's health because not all newborns have the luxury of quick access to healthcare and support from pediatricians.

As an example, asphyxia, which is one of the disorders that can lead to infant mortality, can be detected through visible signs, such as bluish and pale limbs. However, by the time these visual symptoms appear, the infant may have already sustained significant brain damage [12,13]. The degree of hearing loss, duration of treatment, and the age at which the condition is detected can all have an impact on the *acoustic* and *perceptual* characteristics of deaf infants' cries. As a result, there is a growing need to create diagnostic aids that use infant cries to help pediatricians identify the first symptoms of such illnesses [11]. Researchers can get insights about numerous aspects of infant health and development, such as discomfort, hunger, brain abnormalities, and emotional and social development by analyzing and studying the acoustic properties since this perception starts as early as the third trimester of pregnancy [4].

Although the use of signal processing techniques for infant cry analysis has shown a promise, there are several challenges that need to be addressed. These include a lack of sufficient pathological cry samples (i.e., data imbalance), difficulties in extracting excitation source and vocal tract-related features, and the issue of unbalanced data for classification. To overcome these challenges, recent studies have focused on utilizing advanced signal processing and machine learning algorithms for the analysis and classification of infant cries [22]. The use of Mel Frequency Cepstral Coefficients (MFCC), a state-of-the-art feature set, has been gaining traction for infant cry classification tasks. In these studies, Gaussian Mixture Models (GMM) have been commonly used as classifiers [2,9]. Furthermore, recent research on infant cry classification has focused on detecting various types of pain, such as belly pain, burping, discomfort, hunger, and tiredness, using traditional classifiers with MFCC features, however, there is less work focusing on various pathological infant cry [17].

In order to address the above-stated issues, transfer learning-based methods for infant cry classification tasks have been proposed in the literature [3,24]. This study proposes the use of the Whisper Encoder Module (WEM) features for infant cry classification task. Multiple whisper models, such as tiny and base, were compared using clean data. The performance of Whisper encoder-based features was compared to baseline MFCC using *CNN* and *Bi-LSTM* as *DNN* classifiers. Furthermore, since MFCC features are notoriously known to be affected by signal degradation conditions, analysis of noise robustness of proposed features was carried out by adding non-stationary noises at various Signal-to-Noise Ratio (*SNR*) levels. Experimental results indicate that WEM features outperform MFCC features for various noises at different SNR levels. Also, it was observed that with decreasing SNR levels, the performance degradation for WEM features was much less as compared to MFCC. Accurate diagnosis of the pathology is crucial in determining the early course of treatment, and it is necessary to be able to achieve this even for a shorter duration of speech.

Therefore, our study includes an analysis of latency periods and their comparison with MFCC features. To the best of the authors' knowledge and beliefs, this is the first work of its kind reported on the use of features generated from WEM for infant cry classification. The contributions of this study are summarized as follows:

- We propose an end-to-end pre-trained Whisper transformer encoder, using a transfer learning approach for the task of normal *vs.* pathological infant cry classification.
- Performance comparison between different whisper models with different numbers of layers and different numbers of trainable parameters.
- In practical applications, microphone conditions are often suboptimal, making it essential for a system to be resilient to noise. Hence, this study incorporates an assessment of the system's performance in the presence of degraded signals caused by noise.
- The precise identification of the pathology plays a critical role in determining the early course of treatment. It is crucial to achieve accurate diagnoses even when working with shorter speech durations. As a result, our study focuses on analyzing latency periods and comparing them to state-of-the-art feature sets to assess their effectiveness in this context.

The rest of the paper is organized as follows: Sect. 2 describes the differences between different whisper models along with the underlying motivation behind the training of a large weakly supervised corpus of audio data. Section 3 presents details of the proposed WEM feature extraction pipeline, whereas Sect. 4 gives details of the experimental setup. Section 5 presents experimental results, analysis, and discussion. Finally, Sect. 6 concludes the paper along with potential future research directions.

2   Proposed Work

Whisper is an open-source pre-trained sequence-to-sequence Transformer model on the lines of the model that is described in [23]. It was initially developed for multilingual and multitask automated speech recognition (ASR) and was made publicly available in September 2022 on GitHub at https://github.com/openai/whisper. The name Whisper is derived from the acronym **WSPSR**, which stands for **W**eb-scale **S**upervised **P**retraining for **S**peech **R**ecognition [15]. Whisper highlights the concept that training on a large and diverse supervised dataset, and focusing on zero-shot transfer greatly improves the system's robustness and performance.

The Whisper model is trained on a massive dataset consisting of weakly supervised audio paired with transcripts scraped from the Internet. This dataset comprises 680,000 h of audio data, including 117,000 h in other languages, and 125,000 h of translations from other languages to English [15]. This approach ensures that the model is trained on a highly diverse set of audio data, covering a broad range of sounds from various environments, recording setups, speakers, and languages. The large and varied dataset helps the Whisper models generate high-quality vector representations of audio signals, ensuring robustness and enhancing their ability to generalize to different domains.

There are five different whisper models, each characterized by an escalating number of encoder-decoder blocks and a varying count of trainable parameters. These models are designated as tiny, base, small, medium, and large and their detailed technical specifications can be referenced in [15]. The resulting output features generated by Whisper's Encoder-Decoder Models (WEM) have a fixed dimension depending on the size of the model. Specifically, in our study, we used Whisper's tiny and base models, with the output feature dimensions at the end of the encoder module fixed at $1 \times 1500 \times 384$ and $1 \times 1500 \times 512$, respectively. The size of the output vectors scales proportionally with the size of the Whisper model employed.

The authors hypothesize that the pre-trained Whisper model's sequence-to-sequence transformer encoder module effectively captures the sequential/melodic structure in cries, which can provide discriminatory information for various classes. We particularly chose this approach because Whisper's highly diversified training dataset takes advantage of the model's ability to generalize to previously unseen data and therby making the model more robust to signal degradation conditions. Moreover, fine-tuning the pre-trained model for our specific task also reduces training time while enhancing model performance.

3   Employed Pipeline and Its Workings

The pipeline used for this study is presented in Fig. 1. The first step involves the pre-processing of the speech signal to prepare it for feeding to the WEM. To achieve this, the input infant cry signal is first resampled to 16 kHz, and then padded to a time duration length of 30 s to maintain uniformity. An *80*-channel Log-Mel spectrogram is then computed using a window length of 25 ms and a stride of 10 ms, and the resulting coefficients are normalized to values between $[-1, 1]$. These values are then processed through two convolution layers of kernel size 3, using GELU as the activation function. Further, sinusoidal embeddings are utilized to aid the Whisper encoder in learning the relative positions within the input, as outlined in [15]. The processed signal is then passed through the Whisper encoder block, which produces a fixed-dimensional vector, which encompasses the learned representations of the signal as its final hidden state output. This output is then fed into a DNN classifier, which classifies the infant cry signal into its respective classes.

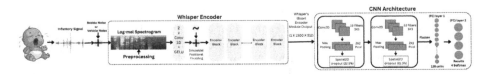

Fig. 1. Functional block diagram of proposed WEM features in tandem with CNN classifier.

During the training phase, the weights of the Whisper encoder are kept frozen, while only the DNN classifier's weights are modified through the back-propagation of errors. To ensure that WEM features are not biased w.r.t. DNN architecture, we conducted experiments using CNN and Bi-LSTM Network as classifiers [14, 20]. Furthermore, the number of classes can be modified by adjusting the number of units in the last dense layer, as shown in Fig. 1.

4   Experimental Setup

4.1   Datasets Used

- *Baby Chillanto Database (Dataset D1):* Baby Chillanto database used for this work was originally developed by the recordings conducted by NIAOE-CONACYT, Mexico [16, 18]. Baby Chillanto Data Base is a collection of Mexican cry samples from 98 babies. Six of them are from babies suffering from asphyxia, another six from deafness, and the rest are from normal healthy babies. The age of the babies were varying from 2 days upto 6 months. The cry samples were recorded in a controlled environment where a closed room was used and the only contamination in the sample was the noise from air conditioning, which was digitally removed once the samples were pre-processed. Each infant cry signal was resampled to achieve a common sampling frequency of 16 kHz. Within the dataset, the healthy cry signals were categorized into three distinct classes: normal, hungry, and pain, resulting in 1049 cry samples. Conversely, Pathology cry signals include two categories, namely, asphyxia and deaf resulting in 1219 cry samples. Consequently, our dataset encompassed a grand total of 2268 samples.
- *DA-IICT Infant Cry Database (Dataset D2):* This cry database was collected from the hospitals in India and is attributed to [6, 7]. Each cry signal of was uniformly resampled at 16 kHz. This dataset comprises a total of 793 samples of healthy cry samples and a total of 397 samples under *Pathology* class, which encompasses *Hypoxic Ischemic Encephalopathy (HIE)* and *Asthma* cries as subclass.
- *Multiclass Pathological Database (Dataset D3):* This database comprises all the cries under Pathology as parent class. It was meticulously curated, taking into account pathologies present in both the $D1$ and $D2$ datasets, resulting in a total of 4 distinct classes. The subclasses within this dataset include Asphyxia, Asthma, Deaf, and Hypoxic Ischemic Encephalopathy *(HIE)*. The number of cries in each subclass are 340, 182, 879, and 215, respectively, totaling to 1616 sample cries under this dataset.

Table 1 shows the statistics of all the three datasets employed for different experiments.

Table 1. # Cry Utterances in All Datasets Considered. After [6,7,16].

Class →	Healthy			Pathology			
Dataset ↓	Normal	Hungry	Pain	Asphyxia	Deaf	Asthma	HIE
D1	507	350	192	340	879	–	–
D2	793	–	–	–	–	215	182
D3	Not Applicable			340	879	215	182

4.2 Augmentation of Noisy Environment

The noisy data was augmented by superimposing various types of non-stationary noises onto the clean data. Non-stationary noise refers to those unpredictable and time-varying fluctuations in a signal that do not exhibit a consistent statistical pattern. Such noises can distort the signal and make it more challenging to identify and categorize. In our study, we specifically introduced two forms of non-stationary noises namely, babble noise and roadway noise or vehicle noise with different SNR levels of $-5\,$dB, $0\,$dB, and $5\,$dB, respectively. Our primary motivation for incorporating non-stationary noises was to ensure the reliability and effectiveness to classify infant cries accurately in real-world scenarios.

4.3 Specifications of the Classifiers and Feature Set Used

In this study, the classification performance of WEM features is contrasted with the state-of-the-art MFCC features [21]. The MFCCs were extracted from the audio files at a fixed sample rate of $16\,$kHz, using a window length of 512 samples, and a window shift of 256 samples. At the end, *13-D* MFCC features were extracted along with their delta and double-delta features, resulting in a total of *39-D* cepstral features.

Bi-LSTM: These networks are a type of Recurrent Neural Network (RNN) that can process input sequences in both forward and backward directions, allowing them to capture context from both the past and future. In this study, we employed a Bi-LSTM model consisting of two layers, with each layer containing 32 units, and a dropout probability of 0.1 at the end of each layer. Finally, we added a dense layer with 4 units and a softmax activation function as the output layer. The authors hypothesize that Bi-LSTM will be able to capture the discriminatory cues encompassed in the *melodic* structures in the cry samples [4], which are encompassed by WEM.

CNN: CNN works by imitating how a human brain perceives an image and hence, it was employed as one of the classifiers. The model consisted of two convolutional layers, each with a kernel size of 3×3 [5]. To reduce the spatial dimensionality, we incorporated a max-pooling layer of size 2×2 after each convolutional layer. We also included spatial 2D dropout layers along with a dropout probability of 0.225. The final layer of our model consisted of two Fully-Connected (FC) layers, with ReLU and softmax activation functions, respectively [1]. We employed the Adaptive Moment Estimation optimizer, commonly known as *Adam*, with a learning rate of 0.001, and used categorical cross-entropy as loss function [5, 25]. The classifier was trained for 10 epochs for each fold.

5   Experimental Results

All the experiments in this study were performed using *10*-fold cross-validation *(CV)*. The reported accuracy is averaged over all the folds.

5.1   Effect of the Size of Whisper Model

In this study, we tested two Whisper models, specifically the 'tiny' and 'base' variants, using both the CNN and Bi-LSTM classifiers on all the three datasets, namely, D1, D2, and D3. The results, as depicted in Fig. 2, clearly illustrate that as the number of trainable parameters in the Whisper model increases, the testing accuracy also rises. This consistent performance was observed across both classifiers. Given the higher accuracy achieved, we decided to utilize Whisper's Base model for all subsequent experiments discussed in this paper.

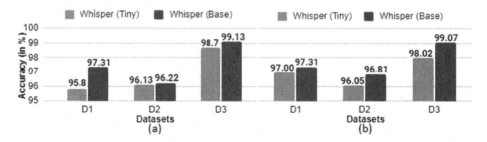

Fig. 2. Performance comparison between tiny *vs.* base whisper models: Results for (a) CNN, and (b) Bi-LSTM.

5.2   Results Under Clean Conditions

In this sub-Section, we present the results of our study on the binary classification of healthy *vs.* pathological cries using datasets *D*1 and *D*2, as well as the multiple pathological class detection on dataset *D*3. The datasets were clean and thus, free of any added noise. Table 2 presents the results obtained for proposed WEM features and MFCC features. Our findings show that WEM features outperform the baseline MFCC, and this can also be observed for both the classifiers, indicating no classifier bias for better performance given by proposed WEM features. This could be attributed to the fact that WEM is able to capture *sequential* information from signals and represent it in the form of a fixed-dimensional vector. A study reported in [4] showed that infants have melodic structures in their cries. Moreover, various pathologies have distinct cry patterns and melodic structures, each with unique characteristics. This supports our proposition that WEM features capture *sequential* information better than the MFCC. Further, the performance of the Bi-LSTM classifier is found to be comparable to that of the CNN classifier. Furthere, the performace comparion of MFCC feature set on Baby Chilanto dataset over existing studies is shown in Table 3. It is conspicuous that our proposed methodology yield high performance as compared to MFCC.

Table 2. Overall performance (in % Accuracy) of baselines and the proposed features on the three datasets (clean condition).

Classifier ↓	Dataset →	D1	D2	D3
CNN	**MFCC**	95.72	88.31	97.46
	Whisper	**97.31**	**96.22**	**99.13**
Bi-LSTM	**MFCC**	97.17	95.88	98.02
	Whisper	**97.31**	**96.81**	**99.07**

Table 3. Comparison of the proposed system over existing studies on the Baby Chilanto dataset.

Source	Features	Classifier	Accuracy (%)
[8]	Spectrogram + Prosodic + Wave	Hybrid-feature Multi-stage	95.10
[10]	MFCC + Prosodic	Neural Network	95.31
[13]	MFCC	SVM	85
[19]	MFCC	SVM	95.86
Proposed	**Whisper**	**CNN**	**97.31**

5.3   Effect of Signal Degradation Conditions

In this study, we introduced non-stationary noises at various Signal-to-Noise Ratio (SNR) levels. Here we are disclosing the findings of our binary classification experiments conducted on datasets $D1$ and $D2$, in addition to our multiclass pathological classification study performed on dataset $D3$. The results are shown in Fig. 3 shows that WEM features outperform MFCC for different SNR levels and more so for both the classifiers and once again reinforcing the fact that there is no classifier bias w.r.t. better performance of the proposed WEM features even under signal degradation conditions. Here, we also find that the Bi-LSTM classifier performs similarly to the CNN classifier. Additionally, for both classifiers, it's evident that MFCC's classification performance worsens more rapidly as the

Signal-to-Noise Ratio (*SNR*) decreases. This highlights the strength of Whisper encoder-based features when handling noisy conditions. The reason behind this could be attributed to Whisper's extensive pre-training on a vast dataset gathered from the internet, which encompasses a wide range of audio environments, microphone configurations, and various types and levels of background noise. This explains the superior performance of WEM features as compared to MFCC in noisy environments, which are closer to real-life scenarios.

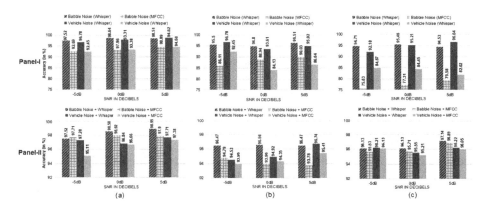

Fig. 3. Analysis of noise robustness of WEM features. Panel-I shows the results on CNN, whereas Panel-II shows the results on Bi-LSTM classifier. The dataset *D*1, *D*2, and *D*3 are represented as (a), (b) and (c), respectively.

5.4   Analysis of Latency Period

The latency period refers to the minimal amount of speech duration required for the classifier system to deliver acceptable % classification accuracy. The findings shown in Fig. 4 clearly show the superiority of Whisper-Encoder features over the state-of-the-art MFCC feature set. It is conspicuous that the whisper-based system consistently achieves comparable results, even when confronted with shorter speech instances, making it highly suitable for real-world applications characterized by shorter input speech durations. Moreover, its remarkable performance in processing smaller speech signal. This characteristic is particularly valuable in scenarios where computational resources are limited or constrained. By giving excellent in such conditions, it is clear that WEM features are an ideal choice for machines or systems with restricted computational capabilities.

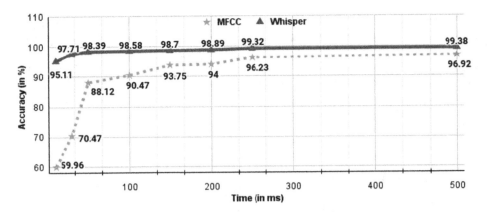

Fig. 4. Analysis of Latency Period for Multiclass Classification on Dataset D3.

5.5   Statistical Measures

Feature Space Visualization Using t-SNE Plots: The capability of multi-class pathology classification is also validated through the use of t-SNE plots, which were obtained by projecting WEM and MFCC features onto a 2-D space for various pathological classes. Figure 5(a) and Fig. 5(b) depict the scatter plots for WEM features and MFCC, respectively. The results displayed in Fig. 5 show that the inter-class distance between the clusters of different classes is greater for WEM features than the MFCC features. Further, the Whisper model can clearly distinguish between two closely correlated classes, namely, Asphyxia and HIE. On the other hand, MFCC fails to distinguish them indicating better class discrimination power of proposed WEM features than MFCC.

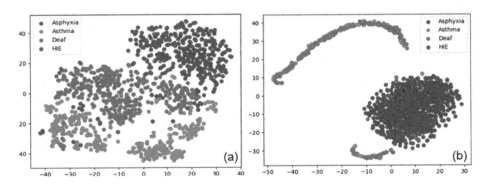

Fig. 5. Scatter Plots Obtained using t-SNE Plot for 4 Pathologies (a) WEM features, and (b) MFCC Features. Best viewed in colour.

6   Summary and Conclusion

This study investigated the significance and robustness of novel WEM features for infant cry classification in real-life scenarios. The proposed methodology outperforms baseline MFCC in various evaluation scenarios, including different datasets, noise types, and classifier structures. The authors hypothesize, this might be due to the sequential capturing characteristic of the whisper model, as infants are known to have melodic structures in cries. The proposed features demonstrate robustness to noise and suitability for practical system deployment, even for signal degradation conditions. Additionally, the proposed WEM features perform better even for a shorter duration of speech segments, as indicated in the latency period analysis, making them more suitable for practical purposes. Further discrimination capability of proposed features was analyzed using t-SNE plots. Our future work will be directed toward exploring different whisper models (such as, small, medium, and large) and data augmentation to enhance performance and relevance in analyzing and classifying various voiced pathologies and augmented cries.

To the best of the authors' knowledge and belief, the Baby Chilanto Dataset is the only corpus available for research and thus, to evaluate the performance in realistic hospital environments, it is important to develop a new *In-House* Corpus for infant cry research. Furthermore, infant cry signal being a private data (especially pathological cases), the development of an Application Programming Interface (API) along with real-time data acquisition for infant cry classification remains an open research question. In order to protect the privacy of such medical data, employing the recent approach of federated learning to transmit the parameters of the model (rather than the true data from edge devices, such as mobile, sensor, etc.) to the cloud servers remains another open research question. Additional research is required to assess the viability, effectiveness, and potential limitations of utilizing federated learning as a means to safeguard the privacy of medical data.

Acknowledgements. The authors are thankful to the Ministry of Electronics and Information Technology (MeitY), New Delhi, Government of India, for sponsoring the project, National Language Translation Mission (NLTM): BHASHINI with the objective of Building Assistive Speech Technologies for the Challenged (Grant ID: 11(1)2022-HCC (TDIL)). They also thank the organizers, namely, the National Institute of Astrophysics and Optical Electronics, CONACYT Mexico for the statistically meaningful Baby Chilanto Database.

References

1. Agarap, A.F.: Deep learning using rectified linear units (relu). CoRR abs/1803.08375 (2018). http://arxiv.org/abs/1803.08375. Accessed 6 Feb 2023
2. Alaie, H.F., Abou-Abbas, L., Tadj, C.: Cry-based infant pathology classification using GMMs. Speech Commun. **77**, 28–52 (2016)

3. Anjali, G., Sanjeev, S., Mounika, A., Suhas, G., Reddy, G.P., Kshiraja, Y.: Infant cry classification using transfer learning. In: TENCON 2022, Seoul, South Korea, pp. 1–7. IEEE (2022)
4. Armbrüster, L., Mende, W., Gelbrich, G., Wermke, P., Götz, R., Wermke, K.: Musical intervals in infants' spontaneous crying over the first 4 months of life. Folia Phoniatr. Logop. **73**(5), 401–412 (2021)
5. Bock, S., Weiß, M.: A proof of local convergence for the Adam optimizer. In: 2019 (IJCNN), pp. 1–8 (2019)
6. Buddha, N., Patil, H.A.: Corpora for analysis of infant cry. Oriental Cocosda, Vietnam (2007)
7. Chittora, A., Patil, H.A.: Data collection of infant cries for research and analysis. J. Voice **31**(2), 252-e15 (2017)
8. Ji, C., Basodi, S., Xiao, X., Pan, Y.: Infant sound classification on multi-stage CNNs with hybrid features and prior knowledge. In: Xu, R., De, W., Zhong, W., Tian, L., Bai, Y., Zhang, L.-J. (eds.) AIMS 2020. LNCS, vol. 12401, pp. 3–16. Springer, Cham (2020). https://doi.org/10.1007/978-3-030-59605-7_1
9. Ji, C., Mudiyanselage, T.B., Gao, Y., Pan, Y.: A review of infant cry analysis and classification. EURASIP J. Audio Speech Music Process. **2021**(1), 1–17 (2021)
10. Ji, C., Xiao, X., Basodi, S., Pan, Y.: Deep learning for asphyxiated infant cry classification based on acoustic features and weighted prosodic features. In: 2019 International Conference on Internet of Things (iThings) and IEEE Green Computing and Communications (GreenCom) and IEEE Cyber, Physical and Social Computing (CPSCom) and IEEE smart data (SmartData), pp. 1233–1240. IEEE (2019)
11. Manickam, K., Li, H.: Complexity analysis of normal and deaf infant cry acoustic waves. In: 4th International Workshop on Models and Analysis of Vocal Emissions for Biomedical Applications (2005)
12. Onu, C.C., Lebensold, J., Hamilton, W.L., Precup, D.: Neural transfer learning for cry-based diagnosis of perinatal asphyxia. In: International Conference on Learning Representations (ICLR) Workshop, Graz, Austria (2019)
13. Onu, C.C., et al.: Ubenwa: cry-based diagnosis of birth asphyxia. In: 31st Conference on Neural Information Processing Systems (NIPS), Long Beach, CA (2017)
14. O'Shea, K., Nash, R.: An introduction to convolutional neural networks. arXiv preprint arXiv:1511.08458 (2015). Accessed 25 Feb 2023
15. Radford, A., Kim, J.W., Xu, T., Brockman, G., McLeavey, C., Sutskever, I.: Robust speech recognition via large-scale weak supervision. arXiv preprint arXiv:2212.04356 (2022). Accessed 6 Mar 2023
16. Reyes-Galaviz, O.F., Cano-Ortiz, S.D., Reyes-García, C.A.: Validation of the cry unit as primary element for cry analysis using an evolutionary-neural approach. In: 2008 Mexican International Conference on Computer Science, pp. 261–267. IEEE (2008)
17. Rezaee, K., Ghayoumi Zadeh, H., Qi, L., Rabiee, H., Khosravi, M.R.: Can you understand why i am crying? a decision-making system for classifying infants' cry languages based on deepsvm model. ACM Transactions on Asian and Low-Resource Language Information Processing (2023)
18. Rosales-Pérez, A., Reyes-García, C.A., Gonzalez, J.A., Reyes-Galaviz, O.F., Escalante, H.J., Orlandi, S.: Classifying infant cry patterns by the genetic selection of a fuzzy model. Biomed. Signal Process. Control **17**, 38–46 (2015)

19. Sahak, R., Mansor, W., Lee, Y., Yassin, A., Zabidi, A.: Performance of combined support vector machine and principal component analysis in recognizing infant cry with asphyxia. In: 2010 Annual International Conference of the IEEE Engineering in Medicine and Biology, pp. 6292–6295. IEEE (2010)
20. Schuster, M., Paliwal, K.K.: Bidirectional recurrent neural networks. IEEE Trans. Signal Process. **45**(11), 2673–2681 (1997)
21. Strand, O.M., Egeberg, A.: Cepstral mean and variance normalization in the model domain. In: COST278 and ITRW on Robustness Issues in Conversational Interaction, Norwich, United Kingdom, 30–31 August 2004 (2004)
22. Ting, H.N., Choo, Y.M., Kamar, A.A.: Classification of asphyxia infant cry using hybrid speech features and deep learning models. Expert Syst. Appl. **208**, 118064 (2022)
23. Vaswani, A., et al.: Attention is all you need. In: Advances in NIPS, Long Beach California, United States of America 30 (2017)
24. Xu, H.t., Zhang, J., Dai, L.r.: Differential time-frequency log-mel spectrogram features for vision transformer based infant cry recognition. In: Proceedings of the INTERSPEECH, Incheon Songdo ConvensiA, Korea, pp. 1963–1967 (2022)
25. Zhang, Z., Sabuncu, M.: Generalized cross entropy loss for training deep neural networks with noisy labels. In: Advances in NIPS, vol. 31, 2018, Montreal Canada (2018)

Speaker and Language Identification, Verification, and Diarization

I-MSV 2022: Indic-Multilingual and Multi-sensor Speaker Verification Challenge

Jagabandhu Mishra$^{(\boxtimes)}$, Mrinmoy Bhattacharjee,
and S. R. Mahadeva Prasanna

Department of Electrical Engineering, Indian Institute of Technology (IIT) Dharwad,
Dharwad 580011, India
{jagabandhu.mishra.18,mrinmoy.b,prasanna}@iitdh.ac.in

Abstract. Speaker Verification (SV) is a task to verify the claimed identity of the claimant using his/her voice sample. Though there exists an ample amount of research in SV technologies, the development concerning a multilingual conversation is limited. In a country like India, almost all the speakers are polyglot in nature. Consequently, the development of a Multilingual SV (MSV) system on the data collected in the Indian scenario is more challenging. With this motivation, the Indic-Multilingual Speaker Verification (I-MSV) Challenge 2022 was designed to understand and compare the state-of-the-art SV techniques. An overview of the challenge and its outcomes is given here. For the challenge, approximately 100 h of data spoken by 100 speakers were collected using 5 different sensors in 13 Indian languages. The data is divided into development, training, and testing sets and has been made publicly available for further research. The goal of this challenge is to make the SV system robust to language and sensor variations between enrollment and testing. In the challenge, participants were asked to develop the SV system in two scenarios, viz. constrained and unconstrained. The best system in the constrained and unconstrained scenario achieved a performance of 2.12% and 0.26% in terms of Equal Error Rate (EER), respectively.

Keywords: Multilingual · Multi-Sensor · Speaker Verification Challenge

1 Introduction

Speaker Verification (SV) is the task of validating the identity of a speaker using the voice sample of the claimant. The tremendous development in SV technology in the last five decades has enabled the system to be deployed in various application areas, starting from voice-based attendance systems to authentication for bank transactions [1]. However, the performance of the systems suffers when multiple languages and sensors are involved during testing [9]. Hence, the scalability of SV systems is limited considering such scenarios. The citizens of

© The Author(s), under exclusive license to Springer Nature Switzerland AG 2023
A. Karpov et al. (Eds.): SPECOM 2023, LNAI 14339, pp. 437–445, 2023.
https://doi.org/10.1007/978-3-031-48312-7_35

India use approximately 122 major and 1599 other languages in their day-to-day conversation. Most importantly, they are polyglot in nature. Therefore, the flexibility in language and sensors during testing may restrict the reach of SV technologies. With this motivation, the Indian Institute of Technology Guwahati Multi Variability (IITG-MV) data was collected using five different sensors from the people coming from different geographical locations of India having variations in the native language, dialect, and accent [5].

In the literature, there exist few works on the development of SV in multilingual and domain mismatch scenarios [9]. The reported works contribute to the feature, model, and score level for minimizing the impact of language and domain mismatch [9]. Most of the reported work uses either an in-house dataset or publicly available data (mostly crawled from the public domain) for performing their studies. The in-house data are limited by the number of speakers, languages, and sensors. Though the publicly available data have a huge number of speakers, languages, and environmental variations, the unavailability of appropriate annotations (mostly done with automatic algorithms) poses a challenge for an in-depth analysis [9]. The current challenge was planned with the aim of resolving the above-mentioned issues by inviting the community to work on the development of the language and sensor invariant speaker representation.

This work considers the conversation recordings of the IITG-MV phase-I dataset. The dataset is divided into four parts, viz. (1) Development, (2) Enrollment, (3) Public test set, and (4) Private test set. The development set consists of speech utterances from 50 speakers recorded with all 5 sensors and in 13 languages. The enrollment set consists of utterances from the remaining 50 speakers, spoken in English language and through a headset microphone. The public test set consists of utterances from the 50 enrolled speaker in both matched and mismatched sensors and languages. The private test set only consists of cross-lingual and sensor utterances. Along with releasing the dataset, the challenge was offered in the form of two sub-tasks, (1) constrained and (2) unconstrained. The constrained sub-task restricts the participants to use only the provided data. On the other hand, no such restrictions are there in the unconstrained sub-task. The aim of the constrained sub-task here was to encourage the community to develop the SV with limited training data. Conversely, the aim of the unconstrained sub-task was to observe the performance of SV technologies developed with a sufficient amount of training data. The dataset is available at[1]. A baseline system implemented with the X-vector framework for both constrained and unconstrained sub-tasks was made available to the participants during the challenge (available at[2]). The performance of the baseline in public test data on both the sub-tasks were 9.32% and 8.15%, respectively.

The rest of the paper is organized as follows: the challenge rules are described in Sect. 2. The detailed description of the data preparation is described in Sect. 3. Section 4 reports the procedure of baseline system development and the performance measure used. A brief description of the top five systems along with their

---

[1] https://doi.org/10.5281/zenodo.7681049.
[2] https://github.com/jagabandhumishra/I-MSV-Baseline.

performance are described in Sect. 5. Finally, the summary and future directions are reported in Sect. 6.

2 Challenge Rules

As mentioned in the earlier section, the challenge consisted of two sub-tasks, viz. (1) constrained SV and (2) unconstrained SV.

- **Constrained SV**: Participants were not allowed to use speech data other than the speech data released as a part of the constrained SV challenge for the development of the SV system.
- **Unconstrained SV**: Participants were free to use any publicly available speech data in addition to the audio data released as a part of unconstrained SV.

The challenge was organized as a part of the 25th edition of the O-COCOSDA-2022 conference along with the Asian-Multilingual Speaker Verification (A-MSV) track. The participants were asked for registration. Upon agreeing to the data usage licenses agreement, the download link of the development, enrollment, and public test sets were provided. Through a license agreement, the participant teams agreed that they could use the data only for research purposes. Moreover, the top five systems in both the sub-tasks would have to submit the source code of their systems and a detailed report.

The public test set released during the time of registration had ground truth information. The purpose here was to tune the system parameter using the public test data. The participants were asked to upload their score files in a specific format on the challenge portal. The corresponding performance was evaluated by a back-end script and the results were uploaded to a online leader board. There was no constraint on uploading and evaluating the score files on the public test set. After around one month of the public test set release, the private test set was released without ground truth information. The participant teams were asked to submit their final results on the private test set within 24 h from the release of the private test set. A maximum of three successful attempts were allowed for each team for evaluating their system on the private test set.

3 Data Preparation

The IITG-MV speaker recognition dataset was recorded in four phases for dealing with various speaker recognition applications, viz. speaker identification, verification, and change detection, etc. [5]. Among the four phases, the phase-I dataset is considered for this study. The IITG-MV-Phase-I dataset consists of recordings from 100 speakers in reading and conversation mode. In both modes, each speaker has given their speech data in two sessions. The duration of each session is around 5–8 min. In addition, each speaker has given their data in two languages, viz. English and favorite language. Favorite language mostly meant their mother tongue/native language and varied from person to person. Furthermore, all the speech utterances were recorded through five different sensors, viz. H01, M01, M02, D01 and T01. The details of the dataset can be found at [5]. The utterances belonging to the conversation mode were only considered here. The total duration of the selected utterances is approximately 100 h. The selected utterances are named as the I-MSV dataset. Further, the I-MSV dataset is segregated into four parts, viz. development, enrollment, public test, and private test.

3.1   Development Set

This partition consists of recordings from 50 speakers. The utterances from each speaker are available in two languages, with two sessions, and with five sensors. The approximate duration of the development set is 50 h.

3.2   Enrollment Set

This partition consists of recordings from 50 speakers that are disjoint from the speakers used in the development set. The utterances belonging to both the sessions with the English language and the Headset (H01) sensor are used here. The first session utterances are completely used in this set. However, the utterances from the second session are segmented into two parts. Half of them are used in enrollment and the rest have been used in the public test set (to observe the performance in matched sensor and language conditions). The approximate duration of speech available for each speaker is 8–10 min.

3.3   Public Test Set

This set consists of the utterances from the second session recordings with three sensors and cross-languages along with the matched utterances. The second session utterances in the original IITG-MV-Phase-I dataset are segregated into two parts. Half of them are reserved for the preparation of the private test set. After that, each utterance is segmented into 10, 30, and 60 s utterances. The segments are split into silence regions using the knowledge of Voice Activity Detection. The segmented files were made available to the participants as the public test set. The total number of utterances available in this partition is 5907.

3.4   Private Test Set

This set consists of the utterances from the second session recordings with four sensors and cross-languages. This partition does not consist of matched sensors and language utterances. The selected utterances are segmented into 10 s, 30 s, and 60 s utterances and made available to the participants as the private test set. The total number of utterances available in this partition is 9521. The partition consists of cross-language utterances from 10 Indian languages.

Table 1. Baseline results on I-MSV dataset, UC: unconstrained condition.

Model	EER (%)	
	Overall	Matched Condition
I-vector	13.72	4.61
X-vector	9.32	2.40
X-vector (UC)	8.15	0.82

4   Performance Measures and Baselines

This challenge employs the Equal Error Rate (EER) measure to compare the performances of the different submissions with the baseline results. This section briefly describes the method of computing the EER measure and reports the baseline results on the I-MSV dataset. Let, N_P and N_N be the number of positive and negative test samples in the data, respectively. The number of samples out of a total of N_P positive samples predicted as positive are termed as True Positives (TP). On the other hand, the number of samples out of a total of N_N negative samples correctly predicted as negative are termed as True Negatives (TN). Incorrectly predicted positive and negative samples are termed as False Positives (FP) and False Negatives (FN), respectively. The prediction of a test sample as positive or negative is based on a pre-determined threshold τ which may be varied. The total number of TP, TN, FP, and FN for the whole test data can be used to compute two measures, viz., False Acceptance Rate (FAR) and False Rejection Rate (FRR). The FAR can be defined using Eq. 1.

$$\text{FAR} = \frac{FP}{FP + TN} \tag{1}$$

Similarly, the FRR can be defined as in Eq. 2.

$$\text{FRR} = \frac{FN}{TP + FN} \tag{2}$$

When τ is varied, different values of FAR and FRR can be obtained. Among all the different τ used, a specific threshold τ_{equal} can be identified which provides equal (or almost equal) values of FAR and FRR. The EER measure is computed as the mean of FAR and FRR at τ_{equal} (Eq. 3).

$$\text{EER} = \frac{1}{2} \left(FAR + FRR \right) \tag{3}$$

where, $\mid FAR - FRR \mid \rightarrow 0$.

The challenge organizers provided results on the I-MSV dataset using Kaldi-based I-vector and X-vector systems as a baseline for comparison. The baseline performances are reported in Table 1.

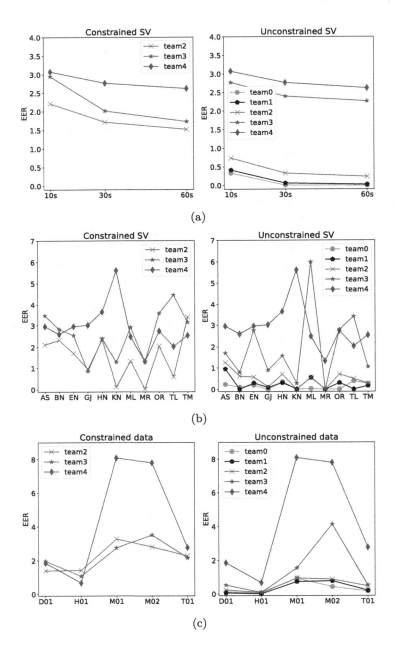

Fig. 1. Illustrating the effect of (a) different duration, (b) different languages, and (c) different sensors on the performance of submitted systems.

5   Systems and Results

A total of 25 teams registered for the I-MSV 2022 challenge. Among these, 10 teams submitted their results for the public test set evaluation. For the private test set evaluation, a total of 6 teams submitted their results and systems. The attributes of the best 5 participating systems are summarised in the next paragraph. Table 2 lists a brief summary of the top 5 systems.

Table 2. Summary of top 5 submissions to the challenge. FE:=*Frontend*, LF:=*Loss Function*, BE:=*Backend*, C-SV:=Constrained-SV, UC-SV:=Unconstrained-SV.

| Team | FE | LF | BE | EER (%) | |
				C-SV	UC-SV
T0	Rawnet3	Training: triplet margin loss; Fine-tuning: AAM Loss + K-Subcenter loss + Inter-topK loss	Cosine similarity	–	0.26
T1	ResNet with SE attention	Softmax + Angular Prototypical Loss	Model scoring (DNN, Random Forest and Gradient Boosting Trees)	–	0.36
T2	ECAPA-TDNN + SE-ResNet blocks	Weight Transfer loss + AAM-Softmax loss + L2 loss	Cosine similarity	2.12	0.63
T3	ECAPA-TDNN SE-ResNet blocks	AAM Loss	Cosine similarity	2.77	2.70
T4	ECAPA-TDNN + SE-ResNet blocks	Large Margin Cosine Loss	PLDA	2.97	2.97

The submission of *T0* obtained the best EER of 0.26 on the private test set using unconstrained training data. The best system of *T0* used the Rawnet3 architecture [8] as their front-end system. They initially trained the model with a Triplet Margin loss [11]. Subsequently, they fine-tuned their model with a combination of Adaptive Angular Margin (AAM) K-Subcenter loss [3] and Inter-TopK loss [13]. They performed the backend scoring using the cosine-similarity measure and used adaptive score normalization.

The second best EER of 0.36 using unconstrained data was obtained by *T1*. They used the ResNet-34 architecture proposed in [6] with Attentive Statistics Pooling [10] for their front-end. They trained the model using a combination of vanilla Softmax loss and Angular Prototypical loss [2]. They also proposed a two-layer model scoring system composed of Fully-Connected Feed-Forward layers, Random Forests and Gradient Boosting Trees.

The EER obtained by *T2* on the constrained data scenario was 2.12. They achieved an EER of 0.63 using unconstrained training data. They used combination of ECAPA-TDNN [4] and ResNet-34 [6] with Squeeze-and-Excitation (SE) attention as front-end models to obtain the best results in the constrained data scenario. However, only the ResNet-34-SE network provided the best performance in the unconstrained scenario. For the unconstrained scenario, they fine-tuned the backbone model using a combination of Weight-Transfer loss [12], AAM-Softmax loss and L_2 loss. The backend scoring was performed using cosine similarity measure.

The *T3* obtained an EER of 2.77 in the constrained scenario and EER of 2.70 in the unconstrained scenario. They used a similar front-end system as that of *T2* and trained it using the AAM loss. They also performed the backend scoring using cosine similarity.

The EER obtained by *T4* in the unconstrained scenario was 2.97. They also employed a similar front-end architecture as that of *T2* and used the Large Margin Cosine loss for training. They performed the backend scoring using Probabilistic Linear Discriminant Analysis (PLDA) [7].

6   Summary and Discussion

The results obtained by the submitted systems can be summarised along the following broad directions. First, the use of unconstrained training data is hugely beneficial in performing SV in low-resource scenarios like the current challenge. Second, automatic feature learning and end-to-end models can learn highly discriminating features. Third, the choice of loss function for the front-end system has a huge impact on the obtained performance of similar architectures. Fourth, simple backend scoring like cosine similarity might be enough if the learned speaker embedding is highly discriminating. Fifth, longer utterances (refer Fig. 1(a)) are more helpful in identifying the speakers. Sixth, a change in language (Fig. 1(b)) degrades the SV performance. However, it might also be noted that such an observation may also be the result of an imbalance in the number of utterances for the different languages in the I-MSV dataset. Seventh, the change in sensor (Fig. 1(a)) has a huge impact on the performance of SV systems. More specifically, SV systems fare poorly when presented with telephone channel recordings. In future, better SV systems may be developed by taking into consideration the observations made in this challenge.

Acknowledgments. The authors like to acknowledge the Ministry of Electronics and Information Technology (MeitY), Govt. of India, for supporting us through the "Bhashini: Speech technologies in Indian languages" project. We are also grateful to K. T. Deepak, Rajib Sharma and team (IIIT Dharwad, Karnataka), S. R. Nirmala, S. S. Chikkamath and team (KLETech, Hubballi, Karnataka), Debadatta Pati, and team (NIT Nagaland, Nagaland), Joyanta Basu, Soma Khan and team (CDAC Kolkata, WB), Akhilesh Kumar Dubey, Govind Menon and team (KLU Vijayawada, AP), Gayadhar Pradhan, Jyoti Prakash Singh and team (NIT Patna, Bihar), and S. R. M. Prasanna, Gayathri A. and team (IIT Dharwad, Karnataka) for their help and cooperation in successfully organizing this challenge.

References

1. Bai, Z., Zhang, X.L.: Speaker recognition based on deep learning: an overview. Neural Netw. **140**, 65–99 (2021)
2. Chung, J.S., et al.: In defence of metric learning for speaker recognition. In: Proceedings of the Interspeech 2020, pp. 2977–2981 (2020). https://doi.org/10.21437/Interspeech. 2020-1064

3. Deng, J., Guo, J., Xue, N., Zafeiriou, S.: Arcface: additive angular margin loss for deep face recognition. In: Proceedings of the IEEE/CVF Conference on Computer Vision and Pattern Recognition (CVPR), pp. 4690–4699 (2019)
4. Desplanques, B., Thienpondt, J., Demuynck, K.: ECAPA-TDNN: emphasized channel attention, propagation and aggregation in TDNN based speaker verification. In: Proceedings Interspeech 2020. pp. 3830–3834 (2020). https://doi.org/10.21437/Interspeech. 2020–2650
5. Haris, B.C., Pradhan, G., Misra, A., Prasanna, S., Das, R.K., Sinha, R.: Multivariability speaker recognition database in Indian scenario. Int. J. Speech Technol. **15**(4), 441–453 (2012)
6. Heo, H.S., Lee, B.J., Huh, J., Chung, J.S.: Clova baseline system for the voxceleb speaker recognition challenge 2020. arXiv preprint arXiv:2009.14153 (2020)
7. Jiang, Y., Lee, K.A., Tang, Z., Ma, B., Larcher, A., Li, H.: PLDA modeling in i-vector and supervector space for speaker verification. In: Proceeding of the Interspeech 2012, pp. 1680–1683 (2012). https://doi.org/10.21437/Interspeech. 2012–460
8. Jung, J.W., Kim, Y.J., Heo, H.S., Lee, B.J., Kwon, Y., Chung, J.S.: Raw waveform speaker verification for supervised and self-supervised learning. arXiv preprint arXiv:2203.08488 (2022)
9. Khosravani, A., Homayounpour, M.M.: A plda approach for language and text independent speaker recognition. Comput. Speech Lang. **45**, 457–474 (2017)
10. Okabe, K., Koshinaka, T., Shinoda, K.: Attentive statistics pooling for deep speaker embedding. In: Proceeding of the Interspeech 2018, pp. 2252–2256 (2018). https://doi.org/10.21437/Interspeech. 2018–993
11. Balntas, V., Riba, E., Ponsa, D.P., Mikolajczyk, K.: Learning local feature descriptors with triplets and shallow convolutional neural networks. In: Wilson, R.C., E.R.H., Smith, W.A.P. (eds.) Proc. British Machine Vision Conf. (BMVC), pp. 119.1-119.11. BMVA Press (2016). https://doi.org/10.5244/C.30.119
12. Zhang, L., Li, Y., Wang, N., Liu, J., Xie, L.: NPU-HC speaker verification system for far-field speaker verification challenge. In: Proceedings of the Interspeech 2022 (2022)
13. Zhao, M., Ma, Y., Ding, Y., Zheng, Y., Liu, M., Xu, M.: Multi-Query Multi-Head Attention Pooling and Inter-Topk Penalty for Speaker Verification. In: Proceedings of the IEEE International Conference on Acoustics, Speech and Signal Processing (ICASSP), pp. 6737–6741. IEEE (2022)

Multi-task Learning over Mixup Variants for the Speaker Verification Task

Abderrahim Fathan$^{(\boxtimes)}$, Jahangir Alam, and Xiaolin Zhu

Computer Research Institute of Montreal, Montreal, QC H3N 1M3, Canada
{abderrahim.fathan,jahangir.alam}@crim.ca

Abstract. Performance of the pseudo-label (PL)-based self-supervised training depends greatly on the quality of estimated PLs. Recent studies have shown that label noise can remarkably impact downstream performance. Recently, research has demonstrated that mixup regularization is effective against noise memorization. In this work, we extend this previous study by exploring several recent forms of mixup, namely 2-step interpolation double mixup to enhance model robustness, mixup over speech frames for better recognition at the frame-level, moment exchange mixup to encourage utilization of moment information of speaker speech as they can reveal speaker style, and virtual mixup training to regularize the areas in-between training points to be locally-Lipschitz and enforce consistent predictions. We analyze their effect on the generalization of some state-of-the-art speaker verification (SV) systems and explore their combination via different multi-task learning-based approaches. Our results show that the proposed mixup formulations are aligned with the SV task and that our proposed multi-task learning-based approach can be beneficial to improve the performance and robustness of SV systems.

Keywords: Speaker verification · Mixup · Multi-task learning

1 Introduction

Speaker verification (SV) is the task of confirming, based on a speaker's voice characteristics, that the identity of a speaker is who they purport to be. In recent years, it has become a key technology for personnel authentication in numerous applications [17]. Typically, utterance-level fixed-dimensional embedding vectors are extracted from the enrollment and test speech samples and then fed into a scoring algorithm (e.g., cosine distance) to measure their similarity/likelihood of being spoken by the same speaker. Classically, the i-vector framework has been one of the most dominant approaches for speech embedding [12,20] thanks to its ability to summarize the distributive patterns of the speech in an unsupervised manner and with a relatively small amount of training data. It generates fixed-sized compact vectors (i-vectors) that represent the speaker's identity in a speech utterance regardless of its length. In recent years, various other deep learning-based architectures have been proposed to extract embedding vectors [2]. They

A. Karpov et al. (Eds.): SPECOM 2023, LNAI 14339, pp. 446–460, 2023.
https://doi.org/10.1007/978-3-031-48312-7_36

have shown better performance than i-vectors when a large amount of training data is available, particularly with a sufficient number of speakers [31]. One widely employed architecture is ECAPA-TDNN [14], which has achieved state-of-the-art (SOTA) performance in text-independent speaker recognition. The ECAPA-TDNN uses squeeze-and-excitation (SE), employs channel- and context-dependent statistics pooling & multi-layer aggregation and applies self-attention pooling to obtain an utterance-level embedding vector.

Most of the deep embedding models are trained in a fully supervised manner and require large speaker-labeled datasets for training. However, well-annotated datasets can be time-consuming and expensive, which has lead to an increased interest in more affordable and larger but noisy/unlabeled datasets. One common way to solve this issue for SV systems is to use clustering to generate Pseudo-Labels (PLs) and train the speaker embedding network using these labels. More recently, better-performing frameworks have started to appear which are based on various SSL objectives [38] or two-stage progressive "clustering-classification" learning [8,33]. The first stage consists of Self-Supervised Learning (SSL) training (e.g., contrastive loss) to train an encoder to generate speaker embeddings, followed by a second stage of clustering those embeddings to produce PLs in order to jointly train the encoder with a classifier in a supervised manner. The two stages are repeated sequentially until no gains are obtained. Despite the impressive performance of PL-based Self-Supervised SV (SSSV) schemes, downstream performance relies greatly on accurate PLs. Indeed, due to the memorization effects [1], deep over-parameterized networks can easily overfit the noise and corruptions in the training PLs which leads to performance degradation. Indeed, PLs provided by the clustering algorithms are in general inaccurate and contain noise due to the discrepancy between the clustering objective(s) and the final SV task (speaker-identity ground truths). To mitigate these side effects, [15] has recently employed mixup [41] as an efficient strategy to augment data by interpolating different data samples alongside their labels, which leads to better generalization to out-of-set samples. Using mixup at both the instance input-level (i-mix) [21] and the latent space (l-mix) [19] of an autoencoder to create new synthetic samples of new target identities, they have demonstrated that mixup regularization is effective against noise memorization and leads to better performance, especially for PLs that form less compact or not well-distanced clusters.

In the same line of work, and following the same setup of [15,19], in this paper, we explore four other variants of mixup that we find, by definition, are naturally aligned with the SV task. Thus, can help to boost performance and further regularize our models to mitigate the memorization of wrongly identified speaker labels. Our investigation includes 2-step interpolation double mixup (DoubleMix) [7] to enhance model robustness, mixup over speech frames for better recognition/verification at the frame-level, moment exchange mixup (MoEx) to encourage utilization of moment information of speaker speech in order to reveal speaker style, and virtual mixup training (VMT) [24] to regularize the areas in-between training points to be locally-Lipschitz and enforce consistent predictions without the need for any ground truth labels, simply via online virtual soft-labels generated by the trained model itself.

To this end, we adapt these mixup formulations to both i-mix and l-mix SSSV embedding learning frameworks to produce robust embeddings which can perform well on verifying out-of-set speakers. Our approach is also an investigation attempt of which mixup formulations are helpful for the SV task, and takes advantage of multi-task learning (MTL) in order to combine the benefits of all our mixup strategies to enforce various inductive biases, improve sample efficiency (especially beneficial for small datasets), further prevent memorization of label noise, and enhance robustness at different levels by exploiting the complementary information available.

The contributions of this paper are as follows:

- We study different recent SV-related mixup strategies, some for the first time in the speech domain (e.g., DoubleMix and MoEx), and analyze their impact on the robustness and generalization of some recent SOTA SSSV systems. Our results show that the proposed mixup-based objectives are well aligned with the SV task, and that forms of mixup that do not employ PLs are better at mitigating label noise memorization.
- We provide a large study of different multi-task learning-based approaches to combine our various mixup strategies and show that our approach can often provide performance improvements and better generalization over the baselines.
- We provide a thorough discussion of our approach (benefits, challenges, and potential improvements) and several insights that could help future research in the field of noise-robust algorithms and MTL-based speaker verification.

2   Background and Related Work

2.1   Label Noise

Methods employed to learn from noisy labels can, in general, be categorized into two groups: approaches focusing on creating noise-robust algorithms to learn directly from noisy labels [4,18,29] and label-cleansing approaches that aim to remove or correct mislabeled data [5,32,35]. Our approach of employing several mixup strategies in a MTL fashion for SV is an attempt to propose a noise-robust self-supervised method that mitigates the effect of label noise, and generalizes well beyond discrepancies in the PLs. To this end, we attempt to enforce other inductive biases closely related to the SV task (our proposed mixup strategies) and make use of the variety of complementary information that can potentially be gained through the combination of the different tasks.

2.2   Instance-Mixup (i-Mix) for Speaker Verification

For an objective function $L_{pair}(x, y)$, where x is the input data and y is the corresponding PL, given two data instances (x_i, y_i) and (x_j, y_j), the i-mix loss [21] is defined as follows:

$$L_{pair}^{i-mix}((x_i, y_i), (x_j, y_j)) = L_{pair}(\lambda x_i + (1 - \lambda)x_j, \lambda y_i + (1 - \lambda)y_j),$$
$$= \lambda L_{pair}(\lambda x_i + (1 - \lambda)x_j, y_i) + (1 - \lambda)L_{pair}(\lambda x_i + (1 - \lambda)x_j, y_j). \tag{1}$$

where $\lambda \sim Beta(\alpha, \alpha)$ is a mixing coefficient from the Beta distribution. PLs are one-hot vectors. The i-mix augmentation strategy aims to generate synthetic training sample $\lambda x_i + (1 - \lambda)x_j$ with identity label $\lambda y_i + (1 - \lambda)y_j$ to improve generalization of the self-supervised speaker-embedding network. Leveraging the generated PLs, it can easily be applied to the SSSV system training process [19]. We also use additive angular margin softmax (AAMSoftmax) objective to train our self-supervised speaker embedding network, which is formulated as follows:

$$L_{AAMSoftmax} = -\frac{1}{N} \sum_{i=1}^{N} log(\frac{e^{s(cos(\theta_{y_i,i}+m))}}{K_1}), \tag{2}$$

where $K_1 = e^{s(cos(\theta_{y_i,i}+m))} + \sum_{j=1, j\neq i}^{C} e^{scos\theta_{j,i}}$, N is the batch size, C is the number of classes, y_i corresponds to PL index, $\theta_{j,i}$ represents the angle between the column vector of weight matrix W_j and the i-th embedding ω_i, where both W_j and ω_i are normalized. The scale factor $s = 30$ is the radius of the representation sphere, and $m = 0.35$ is a hyper-parameter for controlling the angular margin. Then we can incorporate the i-mix strategy into the self-supervised AAMSoftmax to boost generalization of our networks as follows:

$$L_{i-AAMSoftmax} = -\lambda \frac{1}{N} \sum_{i=1}^{N} log(\frac{exp(s(cos(\theta_{y_i,mix(i,r\neq i)} + m)))}{K_{mix,i}^{AAM}})$$
$$- (1 - \lambda)\frac{1}{N} \sum_{i=1}^{N} log(\frac{exp(s(cos(\theta_{y_{r\neq i},mix(i,r\neq i)} + m)))}{K_{mix,r\neq i}^{AAM}}), \tag{3}$$

$$K_{mix,i}^{AAM} = exp(s(cos(\theta_{y_i,mix(i,r\neq i)} + m))) + \sum_{j=1, j\neq i}^{c} exp(s(cos(\theta_{y_j,mix(i,r\neq i)}))) \tag{4}$$

where $\theta_{y_i,mix(i,r\neq i)}$ is the angle between the normalized W_j and $\omega_{mix(i,r\neq i)}$. $\omega_{mix(i,r\neq i)}$ is an embedding extracted from mixed utterance $\lambda x_i + (1 - \lambda)x_{r\neq i}$, where $x_{r\neq i}$ is a random utterance excluding x_i, and r is a random index.

2.3   Latent-Level Instance Mixup (l-Mix) for Speaker Verification

Although applying i-mix augmentation to the raw data has proven its strength in generalization in SV, due to the nature of linear interpolation, the standard i-mix strategy can only generate synthetic samples between the original samples. Since such limitation may restrict the overall diversity of the synthetic samples generated by the i-mix method, a latent-level i-mix (l-mix) was proposed [19].

In the l-mix framework, a variational autoencoder (VAE) is trained on Mel-frequency cepstral coefficients (MFCC) features prior to training the embedding network. Detailed information on the VAE used for l-mix can be found in [15,19]. Once the VAE has been trained, the VAE is used to perform mixup on the latent space, to generate new MFCC samples x_{l-mix}. Analogous to i-mix, l-mix can be applied to the self-supervised AAMSoftmax objective as follows:

$$L_{l-AAMSoftmax} = -\lambda \frac{1}{N} \sum_{i=1}^{N} log(\frac{exp(s(cos(\theta_{y_i,l-mix(i,r\neq i)} + m)))}{K_{l-mix,i}^{AAM}})$$
$$- (1-\lambda) \frac{1}{N} \sum_{i=1}^{N} log(\frac{exp(s(cos(\theta_{y_{r\neq i},l-mix(i,r\neq i)} + m)))}{K_{l-mix,r\neq i}^{AAM}}),$$

(5)

$$K_{l-mix,i}^{AAM} = exp(s(cos(\theta_{y_i,l-mix(i,r\neq i)} + m))) + \sum_{j=1,j\neq i}^{c} exp(s(cos(\theta_{y_j,l-mix(i,r\neq i)}))). \quad (6)$$

Attributed to the non-linear nature of the VAE, the resulting samples are expected to be more diverse than the standard i-mix strategy.

3   Our Proposed Mixup Strategies

Mixup is a highly effective approach for data augmentation. Indeed, [41] has shown that mixup not only reduces the memorization to adversarial samples, but also performs better than Empirical Risk Minimization [34].

DoubleMix - This simple interpolation-based data augmentation approach [7] has originally been proposed for text classification to enhance models' robustness by learning the "shifted" features in hidden space. It first leverages several augmentations to generate perturbed samples for each training data (a first-step mixup using coefficients from a Dirichlet distribution) and then uses the perturbed and original sample to carry out a second-step interpolation in the hidden space of neural models without the need for label mixing. Since we use suboptimal noisy PLs, we find DoubleMix to be a good candidate to help suppress the effect of wrong-labels memorization during training as it does not require PLs. As illustrated in Figs. 1a and 1b, we adapt it to both i-mix (input space) and l-mix (latent space) setups for SSSV to generate more diverse augmented samples which we believe would help to memorize less the specific augmentations used during training which induces better generalization and robustness. We add a Jensen-Shannon divergence (JSD) regularization term to our training objective to minimize the distance between the predicted distributions of the original data p_{org} and the perturbed variants p_{i-mix} and p_{l-mix} which stabilizes the training process. Additionally, we constrain the mixing weight of the original sample to be larger than the synthesized perturbed sample to balance the trade-off between proper perturbations and the potential injected noise.

Frames-based mixup - We explore this idea where instead of interpolating two entire MFCC inputs with a coefficient $\lambda \in [0,1]$, we select a percentage of random frames $(100 * \lambda)$ from one MFCC sample and replace them with frames from a second sample (selected randomly while respecting their order in the second sample). We interpolate labels similarly to classical mixup. We believe our frames-based mixup approach could help to further robustify our models and boost attention at the local frame level.

Moment Exchange Mixup (MoEx) - We also explore MoEx [22] to encourage utilization of moment information of speaker speech as they can reveal the

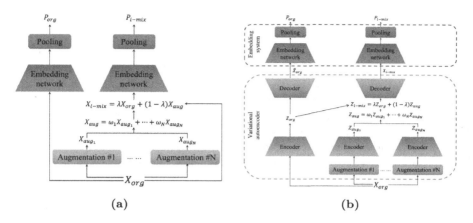

Fig. 1. The general frameworks for (a) our proposed double i-mix regularization strategy. (b) our proposed latent space double i-mix (double l-mix).

style of a speaker. In fact, studies have shown that the moments (mean and standard deviation) extracted from instance normalization and positional normalization can roughly capture style and shape information of an image. Instead of being discarded, in MoEx we replace the moments of the learned features of one training image by those of another and also interpolate the target labels, forcing the model to extract training recognition signals from the moments in addition to the normalized features. By analogy, we use MoEx over the speakers' speech frames to encourage the utilization of moment information during SV.

Virtual Mixup Training (VMT) - Inspired by VMT [24] which encourages the model to behave linearly in-between training points, we additionally adapt this regularization method to both i-mix and l-mix -based SV systems as an additional unsupervised task. Indeed, VMT, which was originally applied to unsupervised domain adaptation, helps to smooth the output distribution of neural networks by constructing surrounding points of the unlabeled training points and enforcing consistent predictions between the surrounding and training points [36]. We compute the VMT loss by minimizing the JSD or cosine distance between the generated speaker embeddings corresponding to every two mixed-up samples (two input MFCC features) and the interpolation of their separate embedding outputs respectively. As a result, VMT imposes local lipschitzness to the areas in-between training samples which is a critical factor in successful training of the cluster assumption [16]: if samples are in the same cluster, they come from the same class. In particular, we believe this VMT task could help to further mitigate the memorization of wrong PLs.

4   Multi-task Learning (MTL) over Mixup Variants

Leveraging several mixup strategies at the same time is not a trivial approach to follow, and choosing which tasks to be learned jointly is hard to know in advance. Indeed, learning different tasks does bring difficulties as these tasks may have conflicting needs [10]. To ensemble the aforementioned mixup strategies together, we follow a Multi-task learning (MTL) training paradigm in which each mixup objective is considered a different task. Thus, in addition to studying these strategies separately, we also train them simultaneously using shared representations with hard-parameters sharing to learn the common features and semantics between these tasks, and combine/transfer their different inductive biases to induce simpler and more generalizable hypotheses that can explain all the tasks. Since these strategies are all closely related to the SV task, we believe our approach could lead to better speaker embeddings and higher SV performance as this could implicitly serve as a self-correcting method for wrong PLs by guiding the model's attention to only focus on the most salient features. Besides, it has been found that hard parameter sharing between tasks greatly reduces the risk of overfitting [3]. In particular, this holds the potential to reduce the model's ability to accommodate random noise during training. Among the other advantages of our approach, we can cite the following: increased data efficiency for each sample (crucial for small datasets), potentially faster learning speed especially as our tasks are closely related, and reduced requirement for large-scale data in the domain of SV. However, MTL can also introduce several negative transfer challenges [30]: sometimes independent networks work better than multi-task approaches due to optimization issues such as cross-task interference, one or more tasks dominating the training process, tasks learning at different rates, or the limited representational capacity of a model. Indeed, [37] found that the output dimension of the shared module in MTL plays a fundamental role: if the shared module is large enough, interference between tasks can be avoided as each of them can be perfectly memorized in the shared module.

In this regard, our work provides an investigation of some MTL-based ideas and their effectiveness to overcome noisy labels in order to generalize well to out-of-set samples. Figure 2 depicts our proposed MTL framework. As presented in the figure, our approach follows a general architecture that consists of a global, shared feature extractor or embedding network (ECAPA-TDNN model) to generate utterance-level embeddings, followed by task-specific output branches (fully-connected layers) or modules to make predictions for each task [6]. The various task-specific loss objectives are combined into a single aggregated loss function $loss_{MTL}$ which the model is trained to minimize.

5   Results and Discussion

To evaluate our proposed approaches, we conduct a set of experiments based on the VoxCeleb2 dataset [9]. To train the embedding networks, we use the development subset of VoxCeleb2, consisting of 1,092,009 utterances collected from 5,994 speakers. The evaluation is performed according to the original VoxCeleb1 trials list [26], which consists of 4,874 utterances spoken by 40 speakers.

For our SV systems, the acoustic features used in the experiments were 40-dimensional MFCCs extracted at every 10 ms, using a 25 ms Hamming window

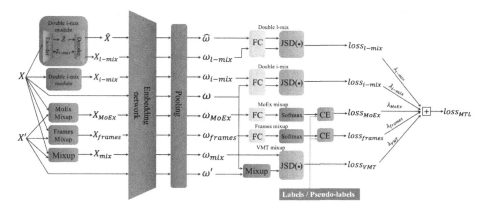

Fig. 2. General process for our proposed MTL-based framework using various mixup formulations. CE denotes the cross-entropy loss while JSD is the JS divergence. FC denotes a specific fully-connected layer for each task except for VMT mixup. X, X' are two original MFCC inputs and ω vectors are the various utterance-level embeddings manipulated throughout our training process.

via Kaldi toolkit [28]. We used waveform-level data augmentations including additive noise and room impulse response (RIR) simulation [31]. In addition, for the ECAPA-TDNN-based systems, we have also applied augmentation over the extracted MFCCs feature, analogous to the specaugment scheme [27]. We generate 512-dim speaker embeddings and use cosine similarity for final verification.

We have set 5000 as the optimal number of clusters, which [19] found to lead to the best results. Regarding our experiments, MTL is performed in 2 different ways: through multiple auxiliary tasks (addition of several auxiliary losses) all optimized via a single shared model (ECAPA-TDNN), and through a multi-head architecture (MHA) using multiple additional output headers (task-specific linear layers) each dedicated to a different task [6]. The aim is to learn speaker embeddings that encompass as many speaker characteristics as possible and that generalize well beyond the noisy PLs. Tables 1 and 2[1] provide the results of our large range of experiments with the 5 variants of mixup performed separately (added to the original i-mix or l-mix objective which employs normal mixup), or through MTL whether in a MHA form or simply via summing the auxiliary losses together. All experiments have been run for 7 days using a single RTX2080Ti GPU, with a batch size of 200 MFCC samples for all objectives.

We study various combinations with different weight coefficients for the added loss terms in order to control the strong regularization effect of the mixup-based MTL approaches, and different values of parameter α used to sample mixup-coefficient from a Beta distribution $\lambda \sim Beta(\alpha, \alpha)$, and $(\omega_1, ..., \omega_N) \sim Dirichlet(\alpha, ..., \alpha)$ in the case of double i-mix and double l-mix. Unless cosine distance is specified, double i-mix, double l-mix, and VMT objectives are opti-

---

[1] N.A. denotes the combinations that are not applicable.

Table 1. EER (%) performance comparison between the different studied systems based on the i-mix and l-mix training frameworks, tested with alpha values in {0.5, 1}. Systems are trained with pseudo-labels generated with AHC [11]. MHA denotes the use of a multi-head architecture for MTL with a different output linear layer for each task. Coef. refers to the weight coefficient of each loss function. The weights of i-mix and l-mix main loss terms are always 1.

Labels/Model		MHA	double i-mix	double l-mix	frames mixup	MoEx mixup	VMT mixup	i-mix (α=1)	i-mix (α=0.5)	l-mix (α=1)	l-mix (α=0.5)
AHC (mean-std scaling) [15]		✗	✗	✗	✗	✗	✗	3.478	3.51	3.377	3.409
AHC (l2-Norm)		✗	✗	✗	✗	✗	✗	3.42	3.399	3.314	3.372
AHC (l2-Norm)	Coef. 8	✗	✓	✗	✗	✗	✗	5.265	4.798	4.798	5.525
	Coef. 8	✓	✓	✗	✗	✗	✗	5.127	4.878	4.862	4.851
	Coef. 0.5	✗	✓	✗	✗	✗	✗	3.839	3.828	4.093	4.008
	Coef. 0.5 (Cos dist.)	✗	✓	✗	✗	✗	✗	4.051	3.993	3.855	3.897
	Coef. 0.5	✓	✓	✗	✗	✗	✗	4.093	4.003	4.024	3.95
	Coef. 0.5 (Cos dist.)	✓	✓	✗	✗	✗	✗	3.855	3.876	4.3	3.977
	Coef. 0.5 (Cos dist.)	✗	✓	✓	✗	✗	✗	N.A	N.A	10.811	3.886
	Coef. 0.5 (Cos dist.)	✓	✗	✓	✗	✗	✗	N.A	N.A	4.125	4.125
	Coef. 1	✗	✗	✓	✗	✗	✗	N.A	N.A	3.971	3.934
	Coef. 1	✓	✗	✓	✗	✗	✗	N.A	N.A	4.024	4.035
	Coef. 1	✗	✗	✗	✓	✗	✗	4.088	4.051	4.014	4.067
	Coef. 1	✓	✗	✗	✓	✗	✗	4.014	4.019	4.316	3.998
	Coef. 1	✗	✗	✗	✗	✓	✗	4.114	4.046	4.04	3.961
	Coef. 1	✓	✗	✗	✗	✓	✗	3.913	3.94	4.03	3.966
	Coef. 1	✗	✓	✗	✓	✗	✗	4.008	3.924	4.146	3.971
	Coef. 1	✓	✓	✗	✓	✓	✗	5.223	3.993	4.486	3.908
	Coef. 1	✗	✓	✓	✓	✓	✗	N.A	N.A	3.94	3.855
	Coef. 1	✓	✓	✓	✓	✓	✗	N.A	N.A	3.993	3.849
	Coef. 0.33	✗	✓	✓	✓	✓	✗	N.A	N.A	3.987	3.966
	Coef. 0.33	✓	✓	✓	✓	✓	✗	N.A	N.A	4.046	4.014
	Coef. 0.33	✗	✓	✗	✓	✓	✗	3.987	4.035	N.A	N.A
	Coef. 0.33	✓	✓	✗	✓	✓	✗	4.024	4.046	N.A	N.A
	Coef. 0.5	✗	✗	✗	✗	✗	✓	4.231	3.971	N.A	N.A
	Coef. 0.5 (Cos dist.)	✗	✗	✗	✗	✗	✓	4.21	3.971	4.114	3.961
	Coef. 0.5	✗	✗	✓	✗	✗	✓	N.A	N.A	3.966	4.024
	Coef. 0.5 (Cos dist.)	✗	✗	✓	✗	✗	✓	N.A	N.A	4.003	4.04
	Coef. 0.5	✗	✓	✗	✗	✗	✓	4.003	3.849	N.A	N.A
	Coef. 0.5 (Cos dist.)	✗	✓	✗	✗	✗	✓	3.77	3.807	N.A	N.A

mized using JSD. Code will be made available online upon acceptance of the paper. All systems in Table 1 are trained with PLs generated with Agglomerative Hierarchical Clustering (AHC) [11] (trained on top of compact i-vectors for efficiency reasons and to avoid high dimensionality of the MFCC acoustic features) which has outperformed all other algorithms used to generate speaker assignments in [15]. Unlike in the previous paper, and to avoid losing speaker information, we normalize 400-dim i-vectors (used during clustering) independently to unit l2-norm instead of mean and standard deviation scaling of i-vectors along the features axis, which helps to further improve performance across all systems in Table 1. Besides, in order to analyze the influence of sub-optimal PLs on our MTL-based setup and study the behavior of our models trained with the various proposed mixup-based objectives, in Table 2 we perform similar experiments using the original ground-truth labels to suppress the effect of label noise.

Results overall show that our adopted ECAPA-TDNN-based embedding systems trained with AAMSoftmax objective [13] are robust and able to generalize well, achieving comparable performance to the supervised baseline (see Table 2), despite the multitude of objectives been optimized or the massive noise in the PLs. Moreover, through our experiments, we could generally observe a more stable and steady improvement in validation performance when multiple objective functions are employed (see our visualization plots of the training accuracy and loss and the validation Equal Error Rate (EER) and Minimum Detection Cost

Table 2. EER (%) performance comparison between the different studied systems based on the i-mix and l-mix training frameworks, tested with alpha values in {0.5, 1}. Systems are trained with ground-truth labels. MHA denotes the use of a multi-head architecture for MTL with a different output linear layer for each task. Coef. refers to the weight coefficient of each loss function. The weights of i-mix and l-mix main loss terms are always 1.

Labels/Model		MHA	double i-mix	double l-mix	frames mixup	MoEx mixup	VMT mixup	i-mix (α=1)	i-mix (α=0.5)	l-mix (α=1)	l-mix (α=0.5)
True labels (Supervised baseline)		✗	✗	✗	✗	✗	✗	1.988	**1.341**	1.612	**1.458**
True labels	Coef. 0.5	✗	✓	✗	✗	✗	✗	1.925	1.538	1.787	**1.474**
	Coef. 0.5 (Cos dist.)	✗	✓	✗	✗	✗	✗	1.766	1.554	N.A	1.665
	Coef. 0.5	✓	✓	✗	✗	✗	✗	3.982	1.58	**1.723**	1.617
	Coef. 0.5	✗	✗	✓	✗	✗	✗	N.A	N.A	1.872	**1.575**
	Coef. 0.5	✓	✗	✓	✗	✗	✗	N.A	N.A	**1.718**	1.691
	Coef. 0.5	✗	✗	✗	✓	✗	✗	1.744	1.612	1.84	1.617
	Coef. 0.5	✓	✗	✗	✓	✗	✗	1.75	1.644	1.824	1.66
	Coef. 0.5	✗	✗	✗	✗	✓	✗	1.739	**1.511**	1.829	**1.543**
	Coef. 0.5	✓	✗	✗	✗	✓	✗	1.914	1.623	1.835	1.638
	Coef. 0.5 (Cos dist.)	✗	✗	✓	✗	✗	✗	N.A	N.A	**1.744**	1.723
	Coef. 0.5 (Cos dist.)	✓	✗	✓	✗	✗	✗	N.A	N.A	1.824	**1.543**
	Coef. 0.5 (Cos dist.)	✓	✓	✗	✗	✗	✗	3.977	1.697	N.A	N.A
	Coef. 0.5	✗	✗	✗	✗	✗	✓	1.988	1.633	N.A	N.A
	Coef. 0.5 (Cos dist.)	✓	✗	✗	✗	✗	✓	1.798	1.633	1.914	1.697
	Coef. 0.5	✗	✗	✓	✗	✗	✓	N.A	N.A	1.978	1.638
	Coef. 0.5 (Cos dist.)	✗	✗	✓	✗	✗	✓	N.A	N.A	1.962	N.A
	Coef. 0.5	✗	✓	✗	✗	✗	✓	1.856	1.569	N.A	N.A
	Coef. 0.5 (Cos dist.)	✗	✓	✗	✗	✗	✓	**1.681**	1.58	N.A	N.A
	Coef. 0.33	✗	✓	✗	✓	✓	✗	1.845	1.66	N.A	N.A
	Coef. 0.33	✓	✓	✗	✓	✓	✗	1.75	1.728	N.A	N.A
	Coef. 0.33	✗	✓	✓	✓	✓	✗	N.A	N.A	1.851	1.644
	Coef. 0.33	✓	✓	✓	✓	✓	✗	N.A	N.A	**1.707**	1.681

(MinDCF) of all studied systems at https://github.com/fathana/multi_task_learning_speaker_verification). In that case, MTL-based models start from a worse validation performance point, but then converge quickly to their best EER downstream performance (see Figs. 3a and 3b). Nevertheless, we can observe an overall degradation in downstream validation performance when multiple loss objectives were combined using AHC PLs, which shows that combining multiple related mixup-based objectives might not always be beneficial. Indeed, regularization induced by MTL to perform well on related tasks can be superior to regularization that penalizes model complexity, and slight data-manifold or task semantic shifts are sufficient to lead to adversarial competition of tasks [25]. We also notice that our proposed double i-mix and double l-mix strategies seem to slightly outperform all other forms of MTL-based mixup strategies, and that combining them with VMT mixup helps to further improve performance. This

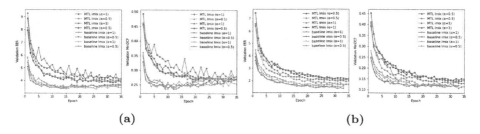

(a)   (b)

Fig. 3. Validation performance over time of the 4 types of our systems trained using (a) AHC pseudo-labels and (b) ground-truth labels (MTL vs. baselines).

Table 3. Results of some recent SOTA SSSV approaches in EER (%) compared to our best MTL-based system. All models are based on ECAPA-TDNN.

SSL Objective	EER (%)
MoBY [38]	8.2
InfoNCE [33]	7.36
MoCo [8]	7.3
ProtoNCE [38]	7.21
PCL [38]	7.11
MTL (Multi-objectives) (Ours)	3.77

can possibly be attributed to the fact that both double i-mix and double l-mix objectives and VMT mixup do not employ PLs, and are solely based on the JSD distance or cosine similarity between p_{org} and p_{i-mix} and p_{l-mix} respectively. On the contrary, MoEx and frames-mixup both rely on the noisy PLs which has the potential to exacerbate their negative impact on performance. Moreover, Cosine distance often leads to the best performance across the different systems which can be explained by its use in the final verification decision. Besides, employing a Multi-head architecture (MHA) does not seem to have a clear advantage in terms of performance over a single-head architecture, except for the case of l-mix with parameter $\alpha = 0.5$ and for the stability of validation performance (check our visualizations). On the other hand, in Table 2 we could observe that using true labels makes our MTL-based approach more advantageous by often providing validation performance gains or comparable results to the baselines that do not employ MTL. Figures 3a and 3b which compare the performance over time of our best setups versus the baselines further confirm this observation and show that validation performance is more stable and steady when using true labels despite simultaneously optimizing multiple objectives (e.g., 6 total objective functions combined in the case of our l-mix ($\alpha = 1$) MTL-based system). These observations highlight the fact that our MTL-based approach relies on good quality PLs to provide competitive performance, and demonstrate that our proposed mixup-based objectives are indeed aligned with the SV task, with very little or no negative interference. Additionally, we can often observe complementary information gained through the combination of the different tasks (e.g., see EER performance gains in the i-mix ($\alpha = 1$) system). We believe further fine-tuning of the hyperparameters could lead to further gains in the other systems as well. Interestingly, we can notice a clear degradation over time of MinDCF and EER validation performance of the PLs-based baselines (starting from the 12th epoch), a phenomenon that was mitigated by our MTL-based systems that better avoid overfitting. Figures also show that the MTL-based systems require more training epochs to converge to their best performance. Given this observation, we have extended the training of our MTL-based systems until no gain was observed.

Furthermore, since PLs provided by clustering are in general inaccurate and contain discrepancies between the clustering objective(s) and the final SV task, this causes that mixup may not perform well [44] and using MTL does lead to optimization conflicts between our regularizing mixup objectives and the main PL-based training objective or i-mix and l-mix. Some other plausible explanations for the slight performance degradation during MTL are the following: the destructive interference between the different concurrent tasks especially as optimization starts to happen sequentially across tasks (Hence the need for further finetuning), the strong regularizing effect of MTL-based approaches compared to other forms of regularization, or simply the need for more training of multi-objective functions. All these reasons are worth further future investigation.

Comparison to Other Baselines. Table 3 shows a comparison of our approach compared to recent SOTA SSSV approaches employing other SSL-based objectives with the same ECAPA-TDNN model encoder. The results show clearly that our approach outperforms all baselines and is on par with i-mix and l-mix.

Additional Advantages of Our Approach. Besides the aforementioned advantages, we can cite other potential benefits of our proposed method: (1) Our MTL-based framework could be particularly useful if learners operate in continuously changing environments (e.g., domain shift). (2) Since MTL strengthens adversarial robustness [23] , incorporating MoEx mixup that helps analyze the style of a speaker and frames-based mixup that boosts attention at the local frame-level, our approach can be particularly very promising against audio spoofing during automatic SV [39] as works such as [43] have done. (3) Instead of using large-scale datasets such is our Voxceleb use case, MTL can be useful when the data is limited (small datasets), as it allows the model to leverage the information shared across tasks to improve the generalization performance. (4) In cases where only much worse PLs are available (hard parameter sharing has an order N - where N is the number of tasks - smaller risk of overfitting the task-specific parameters [3]). Thus, less risk of memorizing highly random PLs.

Future Improvements. We would like to leave the reader with some potential future improvements to our framework: since multi-task networks often need to be larger than their single-task counterpart [37], scaling up our model width to better handle the different tasks is a promising avenue, use inter-tasks weights by forcing gradients to have similar magnitudes (to avoid negative competition) or by employing task uncertainty, encourage similar gradient directions between tasks [40] to avoid conflicting task gradients (using adversarial methods or by simply replacing gradient vectors), use MLP headers instead of single linear layers at the end of the model's output (this is to share fewer weights and provide more specific parameters for each task to prevent negative transfer), attention mechanisms can help to reduce negative transfer [42], use "soft parameter sharing" via $l1$-norm regularization between the specific weights of each task to constrain them to be closer as is common in several MTL-based works [10]. Since tasks compete with each other, a final fine-tuning with only i-mix or l-mix might provide better performance. Finally, our models could benefit from further fine-tuning of the different hyperparameters, and the investigation of additional combinations of our proposed loss objectives.

6   Conclusion

In this paper, we have proposed a noise-robust self-supervised (SS) method for speaker verification (SV) that can mitigate the effect of label noise and generalize well beyond discrepancies in pseudo-labels generated by clustering algorithms. Our approach leverages, for the first time in the speech domain, several recent mixup strategies used to train SS speaker embedding systems in a multi-task learning (MTL) fashion. These mixup forms are closely related to the SV task and we show indeed that they are aligned with the SV task and can potentially transfer well by providing performance gains. Our study analyzes their impact on the robustness and generalization of some recent SOTA SSSV systems, and provides an investigation of several MTL approaches to combine them. Finally, we provide a discussion of the different issues and shortcomings of our approach and insights to help guide future research in the field.

Acknowledgments. The authors wish to acknowledge the funding from the Government of Canada's New Frontiers in Research Fund (NFRF) through grant NFRFR-2021-00338 and Natural Sciences and Engineering Research Council of Canada (NSERC) through grant RGPIN-2019-05381.

References

1. Arpit, D., Jastrzębski, S., Ballas, N., Krueger, D., et al.: A closer look at memorization in deep networks. In: International Conference on Machine Learning (2017)
2. Bai, Z., Zhang, X.L.: Speaker recognition based on deep learning: an overview. Neural Netw. **140**, 65–99 (2021)
3. Baxter, J.: A bayesian/information theoretic model of learning to learn via multiple task sampling. Mach. Learn. **28**, 7–39 (1997)
4. Beigman, E., Klebanov, B.B.: Learning with annotation noise. In: Proceedings of ACL-IJCNLP (2009)
5. Brodley, C.E., Friedl, M.A.: Identifying mislabeled training data. J. Artif. Intell. Res. **11**, 131–167 (1999)
6. Caruana, R.: Multitask learning: A knowledge-based source of inductive bias. In: Proceedings of ICML, pp. 41–48. Citeseer (1993)
7. Chen, H., Han, W., Yang, D., Poria, S.: Doublemix: simple interpolation-based data augmentation for text classification. arXiv preprint arXiv:2209.05297 (2022)
8. Cho, J., et al.: The jhu submission to voxsrc-21: Track 3. arXiv preprint arXiv:2109.13425 (2021)
9. Chung, J.S., Nagrani, A., Zisserman, A.: Voxceleb2: deep speaker recognition. In: INTERSPEECH (2018)
10. Crawshaw, M.: Multi-task learning with deep neural networks: a survey. arXiv preprint arXiv:2009.09796 (2020)

11. Day, W.H.E., et al.: Efficient algorithms for agglomerative hierarchical clustering methods. J. Classif. **1**, 7–24 (1984)
12. Dehak, N., et al.: Front-end factor analysis for speaker verification. IEEE Trans. Audio Speech Lang. Process. **19**, 788–798 (2011)
13. Deng, J., et al.: Arcface: additive angular margin loss for deep face recognition. In: IEEE Transactions on Pattern Analysis and Machine Intelligence (2021)
14. Desplanques, B., et al.: ECAPA-TDNN: emphasized channel attention, propagation and aggregation in TDNN based speaker verification. In: Interspeech (2020)
15. Fathan, A., Alam, J., Kang, W.: On the impact of the quality of pseudo-labels on the self-supervised speaker verification task. In: NeurIPS ENLSP Workshop (2022). https://neurips2022-enlsp.github.io/papers/paper_51.pdf
16. Grandvalet, Y., Bengio, Y.: Semi-supervised learning by entropy minimization. In: Advances in Neural Information Processing Systems, vol. 17 (2004)
17. Hansen, J.H., Hasan, T.: Speaker recognition by machines and humans: a tutorial review. IEEE Signal Process. Mag. **32**, 74–99 (2015)
18. Joulin, A., van der Maaten, L., Jabri, A., Vasilache, N.: Learning visual features from large weakly supervised data. In: Leibe, B., Matas, J., Sebe, N., Welling, M. (eds.) ECCV 2016. LNCS, vol. 9911, pp. 67–84. Springer, Cham (2016). https://doi.org/10.1007/978-3-319-46478-7_5
19. Kang, W.H., Alam, J., Fathan, A.: l-mix: a latent-level instance mixup regularization for robust self-supervised speaker representation learning. JSTSP **16**, 1263–1272 (2022)
20. Kenny, P.: A Small Footprint I-vector Extractor. In: Odyssey, pp. 1–6 (2012)
21. Lee, K., et al.: I-mix: a domain-agnostic strategy for contrastive representation learning. In: ICLR (2021)
22. Li, B., Wu, F., et al.: On feature normalization and data augmentation. In: Proceedings of the IEEE-CVPR (2021)
23. Mao, C., et al.: Multitask learning strengthens adversarial robustness. In: Vedaldi, A., Bischof, H., Brox, T., Frahm, J.-M. (eds.) ECCV 2020. LNCS, vol. 12347, pp. 158–174. Springer, Cham (2020). https://doi.org/10.1007/978-3-030-58536-5_10
24. Mao, X., Ma, Y., Yang, Z., Chen, Y., Li, Q.: Virtual mixup training for unsupervised domain adaptation. arXiv preprint arXiv:1905.04215 (2019)
25. Mattick, A., Mayr, M., Maier, A., Christlein, V.: Is multitask learning always better? In: Uchida, S., Barney, E., Eglin, V. (eds.) DAS 2022. LNCS, vol. 13237, pp. 674–687. Springer, Cham (2022). https://doi.org/10.1007/978-3-031-06555-2_45
26. Nagrani, A., Chung, J.S., Zisserman, A.: Voxceleb: a large-scale speaker identification dataset. In: INTERSPEECH (2017)
27. Park, D.S., et al.: Specaugment: a simple data augmentation method for automatic speech recognition. In: Interspeech 2019, pp. 2613–2617 (2019)
28. Povey, D., et al.: The kaldi speech recognition toolkit. In: In IEEE workshop (2011)
29. Rolnick, D., et al.: Deep learning is robust to massive label noise. In: ICLR (2018)
30. Ruder, S.: An overview of multi-task learning in deep neural networks. arXiv preprint arXiv:1706.05098 (2017)
31. Snyder, D., et al.: X-vectors: robust DNN embeddings for speaker recognition. In: IEEE-CASSP (2018). https://doi.org/10.1109/ICASSP.2018.8461375
32. Sukhbaatar, S., et al.: Training convolutional networks with noisy labels. arXiv preprint arXiv:1406.2080 (2014)
33. Tao, R., et al.: Self-supervised speaker recognition with loss-gated learning. In: ICASSP. IEEE (2022)

34. Vapnik, V.N., Chervonenkis, A.Y.: On the uniform convergence of relative frequencies of events to their probabilities. In: Vovk, V., Papadopoulos, H., Gammerman, A. (eds.) Measures of Complexity, pp. 11–30. Springer, Cham (2015). https://doi.org/10.1007/978-3-319-21852-6_3

35. Veit, A., et al.: Learning from noisy large-scale datasets with minimal supervision. In: Proceedings of IEEE-CVPR (2017)

36. Verma, V., et al.: Interpolation consistency training for semi-supervised learning. Neural Netw. **145**, 90–106 (2022)

37. Wu, S., Zhang, H.R., Ré, C.: Understanding and improving information transfer in multi-task learning. arXiv preprint arXiv:2005.00944 (2020)

38. Xia, W., et al.: Self-supervised text-independent speaker verification using prototypical momentum contrastive learning. In: ICASSP. IEEE (2021)

39. Yamagishi, J., et al.: Asvspoof 2021: accelerating progress in spoofed and deepfake speech detection. arXiv preprint arXiv:2109.00537 (2021)

40. Yu, T., et al.: Gradient surgery for multi-task learning. Adv. Neural. Inf. Process. Syst. **33**, 5824–5836 (2020)

41. Zhang, H., Cisse, M., Dauphin, Y.N., Lopez-Paz, D.: mixup: beyond empirical risk minimization. arXiv preprint arXiv:1710.09412 (2017)

42. Zhao, J., et al.: Multiple relational attention network for multi-task learning. In: Proceedings of ACM SIGKDD, pp. 1123–1131 (2019)

43. Zhao, Y., Togneri, R., Sreeram, V.: Multi-task learning-based spoofing-robust automatic speaker verification system. Circ. Syst. Signal Process. **41**, 4068–6089 (2022)

44. Zhong, L., Fang, Z., Liu, F., et al.: How does the combined risk affect the performance of unsupervised domain adaptation approaches? In: Proceedings of AAAI-21 (2021)

Exploring the Impact of Different Approaches for Spoken Dialect Identification of Konkani Language

Sean Monteiro[1], Ananya Angra[2], Muralikrishna H.[3], Veena Thenkanidiyoor[1], and A. D. Dileep[2(✉)]

[1] Department of CSE, National Institute of Technology Goa, Ponda, Goa, India
veenat@nitgoa.ac.in
[2] MANAS Lab, SCEE, Indian Institute of Technology Mandi, Mandi, India
s22025@students.iitmandi.ac.in, addileep@iitmandi.ac.in
[3] Department of ECE, Manipal Institute of Technology,
Manipal Academy of Higher Education, Manipal, Karnataka, India
murali.h@manipal.edu

Abstract. This work aims to identify dialects for Konkani language. In this work, various state-of-the-art methods in language identification are explored for the identification of dialects of the Konkani language. The initial base model is constructed using fully connected neural network which is trained on frame-level Mel-frequency cepstral coefficient (MFCC) features. This base model trained on frame-level features is then used for comparison with state-of-the-art models from language identification task that are built for dialect identification (DID) that use utterance-level embeddings, namely x-vector and u-vector. The x-vector and u-vector based models are trained on segment-level features. This work explores segment-level features namely phone-state bottleneck features (BNFs) and wav2vec features extracted from pretrained feature extractors. The x-vector based model uses time delay neural network (TDNN) for the extraction of an utterance-level embedding from sequence of speech segments. A u-vector based model uses bidirectional LSTM (BLSTM) to extract utterance-level embeddings from sequence of speech segments. This work also proposes a novel transformer-based model to extract utterance-level embedding from sequence of speech segments. Results show the effectiveness of the proposed methods for DID of Konkani. It is observed that proposed transformer-based model outperform the other explored models. The results also show the superiority of wav2vec features over the phone-state BNFs for DID task.

Keywords: Konkani · Dialect Identification · X-vector · U-vector · Transformer · Bottleneck Feature · Wav2vec

---

S. Monteiro and A. Angra—Equal contribution.

A. Karpov et al. (Eds.): SPECOM 2023, LNAI 14339, pp. 461–474, 2023.
https://doi.org/10.1007/978-3-031-48312-7_37

1   Introduction

Dialect identification (DID) is an emerging research area which has gained a lot of importance in recent times and has attracted many speech recognition enthusiasts [2]. One of the main reasons for this development is that dialectal cues have been found responsible for considerably deteriorating the performance of automatic speech recognition systems [8]. Despite this not much work has been carried out for DID, especially for Indian languages [18]. A dialect is nothing but changes in speaking pattern and language vocabulary, grammar and pronunciation observed in speakers belonging to a particular geographic area. These changes are heavily dictated by factors like cultural backgrounds, social status, economic status, education and so on. Among the various factors, the most important factor is the geographic region [2]. If an effective dialect identification system is developed, it will give impetus to the improvement of speech recognition systems as well as speech based interactive systems. The experience of human-computer interaction will become more wholesome and rewarding [8] because of the realistic behaviour that will be introduced into such systems.

This work focuses on DID for Indian languages. There are a few attempts to dialect identification in Indian languages like Hindi and Kannada [3–6,9,13]. All these attempts focused on exploring the use of approaches to language identification for DID. These involve use of frame-level and prosodic features/representations [3,6,9,13], chroma features [5] as well as utterance-level representation such as i-vector [4]. Further these works also considered the use of different classification methods such as multiclass support vector machine (SVM) [4], ensemble of SVMs [5,6], extreme random forests [3] and artificial neural networks [9] for DID. A review on available literature on dialect identification for Indian languages shows that the said problem is less explored.

The focus of this work is on DID for Konkani, an Indian language which is the official and administrative language of the state of Goa [12]. As per our knowledge this is a first attempt for DID in Konkani language. Konkani is mostly spoken along the west coast of India involving the state of Goa, the Konkan region of the state of Maharashtra, Udupi, Dakshina Kannada, and Uttara Kannada districts of the state of Karnataka, along with several districts in the state of Kerala. The main objective of this work is to identify the dialect of Konkani from a given speech utterance.

In this work, we explore the effect of different state-of-the-art approaches to spoken language identification for DID of Konkani language. In this work we initially propose to work on frame-level features, followed by frame-level features over a longer context of several frames. Finally we explore segment-level features and utterance-level embeddings. Frame-level Mel-frequency cepstral coefficient(MFCC) features are used to train a fully connected neural network (FCNN) that serves as an initial base model. Next the frame-level MFCC features are used to create contextualized features that involves concatenation of MFCC features of 21 frames. These contextualized features are used to train an appropriate FCNN model. These base models which are trained on frame-level features are then used for comparison with DID models built using state-of-the-art language identification models, which use utterance-level embeddings such as x-vector [16] and u-vector [11]. These models are based on utterance-level embeddings and are trained using segment-level features. We propose to explore phone-state bottleneck features (BNFs) [7] and wav2vec features [1,14,15] extracted from pretrained feature extractors as segment-level features. These sequence of segment-level feature vectors are passed through time delay neural networks (TDNN) and bi-directional LSTM (BLSTM) respectively to obtain x-vector and u-vector.

In the recent past transformers [19] are widely used to capture the dependencies within the given input sequence and shown to work efficiently as compared to that of BLSTM. Hence, we propose a novel transformer-based model to extract u-vector from sequence of segment-level feature vectors. The proposed model replaces the BLSTM layers in u-vector based DID system by a transformer encoder. The proposed model is an end-to-end encoder-decoder model. The encoder uses multi-head attention to transform the sequence of segment-level feature vectors. These transformed feature vectors are then combined using attention based network to obtain u-vector. The decoder is a dense network that classifies an utterance. The main contributions of this work are : (i) exploring different state-of-the-art approaches of language identification for DID of Konkani language , and (ii) transformer-based model to extract utterance-level embedding and Konkani DID.

The rest of the paper is structured as follows: Sect. 2 of the paper discusses the different approaches considered to build DID system. This section also discusses the proposed transformer-based DID system. The experimental studies and results are presented in Sect. 3. Section 4 concludes the paper.

2   Dialect Identification System for Konkani

Typically a DID system contains feature extractor module in the front end, followed by a module that encodes the DID specific embedding and dialect classifier. We first discuss the features considered for building DID systems. Later, we discuss the proposed transformer-based dialect identification (DID) systems along with state-of-the-art language identification approaches explored for DID in Konkani language.

2.1   Features for DID

In this work, we explored both frame-level and segment-level features to build DID for Konkani language. Overall, a speech utterance is represented as sequence of feature vectors.

2.1.1   Frame-Level Features

We consider Mel-frequency cepstral coefficients (MFCC) as frame-level features for spoken dialect identification. A frame size of 25 ms and a shift of 10 ms are used for feature extraction from the speech signal of an utterance. Every frame is represented using a 39-dimensional feature vector. Here, the first 12 features are MFCC and 13th feature is log energy. The remaining 26 features are the delta and acceleration coefficients. Thus, a speech utterance is considered as a sequence of 39-dimensional feature vectors.

2.1.2 Segment-Level Features

In this work, we explore contextualised MFCC, phone-state bottleneck features (BNFs) and wav2vec features as different segment-level features.

Contextualised MFCC: These features are considered as segment-level features as they cover several frames. Contextualized vectors are obtained by concatenating several 39-dimensional vectors in a sequence. In this work, for each frame we have concatenated features of 10 previous frames and 10 future frames. Thus, each vector is of dimension 819 that captures a context of 21 frames i.e., 735 ms. Thus, a speech utterance is considered as a sequence of 819-dimensional feature vectors.

Phone-State Bottleneck Features (BNFs): These features are also segment-level features as they combine together the features of several frames and help to capture contextual information. We use 80-dimensional phone-state bottleneck features (BNFs) obtained using "BUT/Phonexia Bottleneck Feature Extractor" (BUT-BNF extractor) [7] as the segment-level features. This BNF extractor was originally trained with 3096 phone states from 17 languages as targets. Each of the extracted phone-state BNF vector covers a total context of 31 frames (i.e., 325 ms) of input speech. Successive phone-state BNFs are separated by 10 ms. Since wide variety of languages (including Indian languages) are used in the training, we assume that these extracted phone-state BNFs cover phonetics of the language used in this work. Thus, a speech utterance is considered as a sequence of 80-dimensional feature vectors.

Wav2vec Features: Wav2vec 2.0 is a framework that creates latent speech representation from raw audio data using self-supervised learning [1,15]. The extractor is pretrained for a different task and is then used to extract embeddings that are used as features for our DID task. The embeddings or latent speech representations are referred to as wav2vec features. The model used for extraction is pretrained on 53 different languages and gives feature vectors of dimension 512 [14]. These features are also segment-level features as they combine the features of several frames and help to capture contextual information. Each of the extracted wav2vec feature vector covers a total context of 210 ms of input speech. Thus, a speech utterance is considered as a sequence of 512-dimensional feature vectors.

2.2 State-of-the-Art Language Identification Approaches Explored for Konkani DID

In this work, we explore fully connected neural network (FCNN) based model as baseline DID system. This model is built on frame-level and segment-level features. We also explore x-vector based DID system for both frame-level and segment-level features. We explore u-vector based DID system using segment-level features. We also propose a transformer-based DID system that uses segment-level features.

2.2.1 Baseline DID System

We consider a FCNN with N_I number of hidden layers followed by a statistical pooling layer and then a classification layer as a baseline system. Let $\mathbf{H} = (\mathbf{h_1},\mathbf{h_2},...,\mathbf{h_t},...,\mathbf{h_T})$, be the sequence of feature vectors obtained from the last hidden layer by passing the input sequence of frame/segment-level feature vectors through the hidden layers of the baseline system. Here, T represents number of feature vectors in a sequence. The statistics pooling layer first computes the mean ($\mathbf{\mu}$) and standard deviation ($\mathbf{\sigma}$) of all last hidden layer outputs as follows.

$$\mathbf{\mu} = \tfrac{1}{T}\sum_{t=1}^{T} \mathbf{h}_t$$

$$\mathbf{\sigma} = \sqrt{\tfrac{1}{T}\sum_{t=1}^{T}(\mathbf{h}_t - \mathbf{\mu})^2}$$

The utterance-level embedding is then obtained by concatenating the mean vector with the standard deviation, $\mathbf{z} = [\mathbf{\mu}^\top, \mathbf{\sigma}^\top]^\top$. This z-vector (obtained using statistics pooling) is then fed to the classification layer for identifying the dialect.

2.2.2 X-Vector Based DID System

This system is an end-to-end system containing x-vector embedding extractor followed by a classification layer [16,17]. Figure 1 shows the block diagram of the x-vector based network. It contains a frame-level feature extractor at the front-end to convert the speech into a sequence of frame-level or segment-level feature vectors. The sequence of feature vectors is then analysed using a set of time delay neural network (TDNN) layers. The TDNN units are fully feed-forward in nature [16,17]. The TDNN layers in the x-vector network also consider a fixed context at each time index "t". Hence, the output of TDNN layers at a given time index can be visualized as a compact representation of DID-specific contents in a fixed-length chunk of size(N_B number of feature vectors). The output of TDNN layers (LID-senones) obtained over the entire speech sample are then processed by an utterance-level embedding extractor.

The standard x-vector architecture uses a statistics pooling layer, which computes mean and standard deviation of the output of TDNN layers, followed by a dense layer to obtain the utterance-level embedding called x-vector [16]. The x-vector is then fed to the output layer with softmax activation to predict the dialect label.We denote this end-to-end network as x-vec-Net.

2.2.3 U-Vector Based DID System

Block diagram of the LID-seq-senones based u-vector representation for DID is shown in Fig. 2. It is an end-to-end neural network, which contains a feature extractor block to extract an utterance-level embedding (represented as

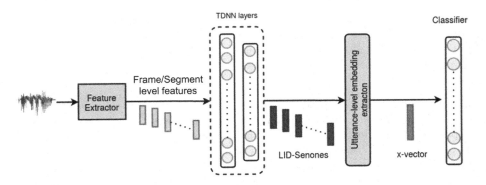

Fig. 1. Block diagram of x-vector based DID system (x-vec-Net).

u-vector in Fig. 2) and a dialect classifier block. The feature extractor block contains a segment-level feature extractor at the front-end to convert the speech into a sequence of segment-level feature vectors. A sequence of segment-level feature vectors is then fed to the BLSTM layers, which analyses it by dividing into fixed-size chunks (each containing N_B number of segment-level feature vectors). In other words, a sequence of N_B number of phone-state BNF vectors are grouped to form a fixed-size chunk, which acts as input to the BLSTM layers. The activations obtained at the output of last BLSTM layer is considered as a new intermediate representation. Since BLSTM network preserves the sequential information in the speech efficiently, these intermediate representations are termed as LID sequential senones (LID-seq-senones). Each LID-seq-senone is a compact representation of the given chunk (with N_B number of segment-level feature vectors) of speech sample. The sequence of LID-seq-senones obtained for a given speech sample is then processed by an utterance-level embedding extractor to produce the u-vector using attention-based strategy. The attention mechanism dynamically assigns the weights to LID-seq-senones depending on their relevance in determining the dialect label. The u-vector is obtained as weighted sum of LID-seq-senones [11]. This u-vector is then fed to the classifier network for identifying the dialect. We denote this end-to-end DID network as u-vec-Net.

In this work, we also propose to use an improved version of u-vector based system for DID. It uses a bi-resolution processing-based approach [11] where, a network processes the input at two different temporal resolutions using a set of two embedding extractors, which allows them to encode dissimilar contents in the speech. The outputs from these two-embedding extractors are then combined into the final utterance-level embedding (denoted as u-vector). Such arrangement allows the u-vector to gather the DID-specific contents in two different ways leading to better generalization [11]. The block diagram of the bi-resolution processing-based approach is given in Fig. 3. It is an end-to-end DID network which contains a feature extractor block to extract an utterance-level embedding (u-vector) of the input speech and a dialect classifier block. The feature extractor block contains a segment-level feature extractor at the front-end, followed by a

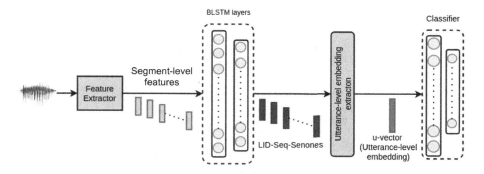

Fig. 2. Block diagram of u-vector based DID system (u-vec-Net).

set of two embedding extractors to provide two intermediate embeddings (represented as e_1 and e_2 in Fig. 3) of the speech, and an attention-based mechanism to combine these two embeddings into a single utterance-level embedding called u-vector. The architecture of both embedding extractors is identical, which is shown in Fig. 2. Despite having identical architectures, these two embedding extractors are designed to process the input sequence at two different temporal resolutions. Analysing the input at two different temporal resolutions allows the embedding extractors to encode the DID-specific contents in two different ways (due to its fast-changing nature) but encode similar information about the domain/background (which remain constant). As a result, when same input is fed to both embedding extractors, the embeddings e_1 and e_2 encode dissimilar DID-specific contents. The outputs from the two embedding extractors (e_1 and e_2) are then combined in the final utterance-level embedding called u-vector. This u-vector is then directly fed to the dialect classifier to form an end-to-end DID network as in Fig. 3. We denote this network as 2Arm-u-vec-Net.

Note that, unlike the u-vector in the simple u-vec-Net (given in Fig. 2) which uses only one embedding extractor to process the input, the u-vector in the 2Arm-u-vec-Net (Fig. 3) contains the DID-specific information gathered in two different ways. Since the two embedding extractors of the 2Arm-u-vec-Net are designed to encode dissimilar contents in the input, the corresponding u-vector should ideally carry more DID-specific information than its counterpart in the simple u-vec-Net.

In the recent days transformers are shown to capture the dependencies within the given input sequence better than BLSTM. Hence in the next section, we propose a transformer-based approach to extract u-vectors.

2.3   Proposed Transformer-Based DID System

The block diagram of the proposed transformer-based DID system is given in Fig. 4. It is an end-to-end DID network which contains a segment-level feature extractor at the front-end to convert the input speech utterance into a sequence of segment-level feature vectors. This is followed by a transformer network to

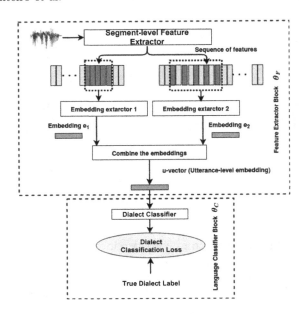

Fig. 3. Block diagram of the bi-resolution processing based approach. Orange coloured frames in sequence of segment-level features indicate the frames selected as input within an analysis window. This network is denoted as 2Arm-u-vec-Net. (Color figure online)

encode the sequence of segment-level features into an utterance-level embedding (u-vector) and classify to a dialect class. The proposed transformer network is an encoder-decoder network where the encoder unit includes LID-seq-senone generator followed by an utterance-level embedding extractor to transform the sequence of segment-level feature vectors into an u-vector and the decoder part is a dialect classifier, as shown in Fig. 4.

The LID-seq-senone generator is a multi-head attention network, which efficiently learns the dependencies within a given sequence of segment-level feature vectors in a chunk. It has N_e stacked encoder layers with N_h heads. As in [11], a sequence of segment-level feature vectors is fed to the LID-seq-senone generator, which analyses it by dividing into fixed-size chunks (each chunk containing N_B number of segment-level feature vectors). Each successive chunk is obtained with the shift of one segment-level feature vector. In other words, a sequence of N_B number of segment-level feature vectors are grouped to form a fixed size chunk, which acts as input to the stacked multi-head attention network and produces a sequence of transformed N_B number of segment-level feature vectors as output. These transformed segment-level feature vectors of a given chunk are then combined using attention mechanism to obtain a compact representation. Since the network preserves the sequential information in the speech efficiently, we continue to term these compact representation as LID-seq-senones. Each LID-seq-senone is a compact representation of the given chunk (with N_B number of segment-level feature vectors) of speech sample. We then perform weighted sum of the LID-seq-senones using attention mechanism to get the utterance-level embedding (u-vector), which is then processed by the classifier to predict the dialect. We denote this proposed end-to-end network as u-vec-transformer-Net.

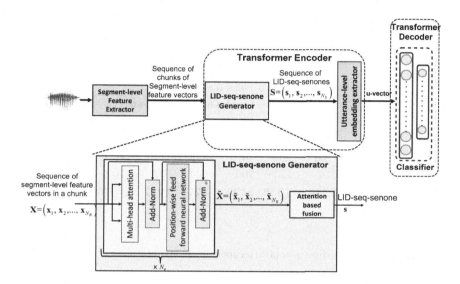

Fig. 4. Proposed transformer-based DID system (u-vec-transformer-Net). Here $\times N_e$ in LID-seq-senone generator indicate stacked N_e encoder layers, each with N_h heads.

In the next section we present the experimental study and performance of each of the approaches in identifying dialect of Konkani.

3   Experimental Studies and Results

In this section, we study the effectiveness of the proposed transformer based DID systems and compare it's performance with the other explored methods. Before that we present the details of the dataset considered for the studies.

3.1   Konkani Dataset

The dataset used for the experiment is a part of linguistic data consortium for Indian languages (LDC-IL) Konkani raw speech corpus [12]. This contains various content types like "Contemporary Text (News)", "Creative Text", "Sentences", "Command and Control Words", "Date", "Place Names", "Person Names", "Most Frequent Words", etc. Since our task is to identify dialects, which needs utterances with longer duration (at-least sentence level), we chose utterances from content type "Sentences". The dataset contains information for 4 dialects of Konkani collected from 4 regions namely, North Goa, South Goa, Sindhudurg and Karwar. The details of the data considered for our study is given in Table 1. The details of the duration of speech utterances in each dialect of Konkani are given in Table 2. In our study, 70% of the utterances from each class are considered for training and remaining 30% of utterances from each class are considered for testing. Both training and test set include good mix of male and female voices with balanced duration.

Table 1. Details of Konkani dialect dataset.

Age group	Number of speech utterances	Dialect (region) wise distribution							
		North Goa		South Goa		Karwari		Sindhudurg	
		Female	Male	Female	Male	Female	Male	Female	Male
16 to 20	1648	349	225	350	324	250	100	50	0
21 to 50	7294	1621	899	1075	1323	1150	1026	25	175
50+	3108	276	231	700	624	577	700	0	0
Total	**12050**	**2246**	**1355**	**2125**	**2272**	**1977**	**1826**	**75**	**175**

Table 2. Details of duration of utterances in Konkani dataset (in seconds).

Dialect	Min Duration	Max Duration	Avg Duration
Karwari	1.6	16.9	4.7
North Goa	1.2	11.5	4.4
South Goa	1.7	16.7	4.9
Sindhudurg	1.9	10.2	4.8

3.2   Experimental Studies on Konkani DID

All DID systems in this work are evaluated using two different metrics: Accuracy (%) and equal error rate (EER) (%). Accuracy is computed as the percentage of test utterances correctly classified to the respective dialect class. The EER (in %) is computed as EER = $\frac{FAR+FRR}{2} \times 100$ where, FAR is false acceptance rate and FRR is false rejection rate. Lower the values of EER, better is the performance.

3.2.1   Performance of Baseline DID System

We consider FCNN using MFCC and contextualised MFCC as baseline DID systems. We experimentally chose 3 hidden layer FCNN (here $N_I = 3$) with 40, 200 and 50 rectified linear neurons in each of the 3 hidden layers. The performance of the baseline DID systems is shown in the first two rows of the Table 3.

3.2.2   Performance of X-Vector Based DID System

The x-vector based DID system (x-vec-Net) uses time delay neural network (TDNN) architecture at the front-end, followed by a statistics pooling layer and a classification network. Final dense classification layer has 4 (which equals the number of dialects in the dataset) nodes. We experimentally consider N_B, the number of feature vectors in a chunk, as 30. We built x-vector based DID system using MFCC as frame-level feature and phone-state BNFs & wav2vec features as segment-level features. Their performance is given in the 3rd, 4th and 5th rows of Table 3. It is observed that x-vector based DID systems performed significantly better than the baseline DID systems. It is also seen that x-vec-Net using segment-level features (phone-state BNF and wav2vec) performed better than that of x-vec-Net built using frame-level features.

3.2.3   Performance of U-Vector Based DID System

We use two versions of u-vector based DID systems. The first version (u-vec-Net) uses BLSTM architecture followed by an attention network as embedding extractor to generate a u-vector. The second version (2Arm-u-vec-Net) uses a set of two embedding extractors followed by an attention network to combine the two embeddings and generate u-vector. The hyper-parameters of both the networks such as number of layers and number of nodes in each layer of BLSTM, the number of feature vectors in a chunk (N_B) and number of nodes in a single hidden layer based attention network are tuned experimentally. We experimentally consider two BLSTM layers with 256 and 64 nodes respectively in first and second layers, N_B as 30 and 128 nodes in the attention network. We built u-vec-Net and 2Arm-u-vec-Net using phone-state BNFs and wav2vec as segment-level features. Their performance is given in the 6th, 7th, 8th and 9th rows of Table 3. It is observed that u-vector based DID systems performed significantly better than the baseline DID systems and x-vector based DID systems. It is also observed that 2Arm-u-vec-Net performed better than that of u-vec-Net. This indicates that 2-Arm-u-vec-Net capture more DID-specific information than that of u-vec-Net.

3.2.4   Performance of Proposed Transformer Based DID System

We experimentally kept the number of encoder layers to 8 (here $N_e = 8$) and number of heads to 8 (here $N_h = 8$) as well. We built u-vec-transformer-Net using BNF and wav2vec as segment-level features. Their performance is given in the 10th and 11th rows of Table 3. It is observed that transformer based DID systems performed significantly better than all the models. This indicates that transformer capture better dependencies in the input sequence than BLSTM. Hence transformer-based u-vector representation capture better DID-specific information than u-vec-Net and 2Arm-u-vec-Net. It is seen in Table 3 that in all the models that build DID systems using segment-level features, models that use wav2vec features are performing significantly better than the models that use phone-state BNFs. In an attempt to reason the observed performance, we repeated the language identification experiments of [10] done using phone-state

BNFs with the wav2vec features. As an outcome of the experiment, we observed that for language identification task models using phone-state BNFs and wav2vec features both gave almost equal performance. This is possibly because phone-state BNFs capture the phone state information specific to each language (as some of the phone states are different for different languages). However, in the Konkani dialect identification task, phone states related to each of the dialects of Konkani are almost same. The wav2vec features are independent of phone states. Hence, the utterance-level embeddings learnt from x-vec-net, u-vec-net, 2Arm-u-vec-net and u-vec-transformer-Net using wav2vec features are more discriminative than that of utterance-level embeddings learnt using phone-state BNFs as observed in Table 3.

Table 3. Performance in accuracy and EER (both given in %) of different explored and proposed transformer-based DID for Konkani language.

Model	Features	Accuracy	EER
FCNN	MFCC	58.77%	34.21%
	Contextualised MFCC	56.95%	35.67%
x-vec-Net	MFCC	66.88%	31.23%
	Phone-state BNF	70.58%	26.43%
	wav2vec	72.19%	24.34%
u-vec-Net	Phone-state BNF	73.32%	23.56%
	wav2vec	76.42%	20.74%
2Arm-u-vec-Net	Phone-state BNF	74.85%	22.56%
	wav2vec	78.52%	19.69%
u-vec-transformer-Net	Phone-state BNF	74.42%	22.78%
	wav2vec	**80.59%**	**17.89%**

4   Conclusion

This work aimed at performing DID of Konkani language. Different state-of-the-art language identification approaches are explored to build DID system for Konkani language. A novel transformer-based DID system is also proposed in this work. MFCC as a frame-level feature and phone-state based BNF & wav2vec as segment-level feature are explored to build the DID systems. It is observed that the proposed transformer-based DID system outperformed other state-of-the art language identification systems explored for DID. It is also observed that the DID systems built using wav2vec performed significantly better than that of the DID systems built using phone-state based BNF.

Acknowledgement. This work resulted from research supported by Ministry of Electronics & Information Technology (MeitY), Government of India through project titled "National Language Translation Mission (NLTM) : BHASHINI".

References

1. Baevski, A., Zhou, Y., Mohamed, A., Auli, M.: wav2vec 2.0: a framework for self-supervised learning of speech representations. In: Advances in Neural Information Processing Systems 33, pp. 12449–12460 (2020)
2. Chambers, J.K., Trudgill, P.: Dialectology. Cambridge Textbooks in Linguistics, Cambridge University Press, 2 edn. (1998). https://doi.org/10.1017/CBO9780511805103
3. Chittaragi, N.B., Koolagudi, S.G.: Acoustic-phonetic feature based Kannada dialect identification from vowel sounds. Int. J. Speech Technol. **22**, 1099–1113 (2019)
4. Chittaragi, N.B., Koolagudi, S.G.: Automatic dialect identification system for Kannada language using single and ensemble SVM algorithms. Lang. Resour. Eval. **54**, 553–585 (2020)
5. Chittaragi, N.B., Koolagudi, S.G.: Dialect identification using chroma-spectral shape features with ensemble technique. Comput. Speech Lang. **70**, 101230 (2021)
6. Chittaragi, N.B., Prakash, A., Koolagudi, S.G.: Dialect identification using spectral and prosodic features on single and ensemble classifiers. Arab. J. Sci. Eng. **43**, 4289–4302 (2018)
7. Fer, R., Matějka, P., Grézl, F., Plchot, O., Veselý, K., Černockÿ, J.H.: Multilingually trained bottleneck features in spoken language recognition. Comput. Speech Lang. **46**, 252–267 (2017)
8. Ferragne, E., Pellegrino, F.: Automatic dialect identification: a study of British English, pp. 243–257 (2007). https://doi.org/10.1007/978-3-540-74122-0_19
9. Mothukuri, S.K.P., Hegde, P., Chittaragi, N.B., Koolagudi, S.G.: Kannada dialect classification using artificial neural networks. In: 2020 International Conference on Artificial Intelligence and Signal Processing (AISP), pp. 1–5. IEEE (2020)
10. Muralikrishna, H., Gupta, S., Dileep, A.D., Rajan, P.: Noise-robust spoken language identification using language relevance factor based embedding. In: 2021 IEEE Spoken Language Technology Workshop (SLT), pp. 644–651. IEEE (2021)
11. Muralikrishna, H., Kapoor, S., Dileep, A.D., Rajan, P.: Spoken language identification in unseen target domain using within-sample similarity loss. In: ICASSP 2021–2021 IEEE International Conference on Acoustics, Speech and Signal Processing (ICASSP), pp. 7223–7227. IEEE (2021)
12. Ramamoorthy, L., Choudhary, N., Varik, S., Tanawade, R.S.: Konkani Raw Speech Corpus. Central Institute of Indian Languages, Mysore (2019)
13. Rao, K.S., Koolagudi, S.G.: Identification of Hindi dialects and emotions using spectral and prosodic features of speech. IJSCI: Int. J. System. Cybern. Inf. **9**(4), 24–33 (2011)
14. Schneider, S., Baevski, A., Collobert, R., Auli, M.: wav2vec: unsupervised pre-training for speech recognition, pp. 3465–3469 (2019). https://doi.org/10.21437/Interspeech.2019-1873
15. Sharma, M.: Multi-lingual multi-task speech emotion recognition using wav2vec 2.0. In: ICASSP 2022–2022 IEEE International Conference on Acoustics, Speech and Signal Processing (ICASSP), pp. 6907–6911. IEEE (2022)
16. Snyder, D., Garcia-Romero, D., McCree, A., Sell, G., Povey, D., Khudanpur, S.: Spoken language recognition using x-vectors. In: Odyssey, vol. 2018, pp. 105–111 (2018)

17. Snyder, D., Garcia-Romero, D., Sell, G., Povey, D., Khudanpur, S.: x-vectors: Robust DNN embeddings for speaker recognition. In: 2018 IEEE International Conference on Acoustics, Speech and Signal Processing (ICASSP), pp. 5329–5333. IEEE (2018)

18. Soorajkumar, R., Girish, G.N., Ramteke, P.B., Joshi, S.S., Koolagudi, S.G.: Text-independent automatic accent identification system for Kannada language. In: Satapathy, S.C., Bhateja, V., Joshi, A. (eds.) Proceedings of the International Conference on Data Engineering and Communication Technology. AISC, vol. 469, pp. 411–418. Springer, Singapore (2017). https://doi.org/10.1007/978-981-10-1678-3_40

19. Vaswani, A., et al.: Attention is all you need. In: 31st Conference on Neural Information Processing Systems (NIPS 2017), Long Beach, CA, USA, pp. 2–7 (2017)

Adversarially Trained Hierarchical Attention Network for Domain-Invariant Spoken Language Identification

Urvashi Goswami[1], H. Muralikrishna[2], A. D. Dileep[1(✉)],
and Veena Thenkanidiyoor[3]

[1] MANAS Lab, SCEE, Indian Institute of Technology Mandi, Mandi, H.P., India
S22024@students.iitmandi.ac.in, addileep@iitmandi.ac.in
[2] Department of ECE, Manipal Institute of Technology, Manipal Academy of Higher
Education, Manipal, Karnataka, India
murali.h@manipal.edu
[3] Department of CSE, National Institute of Technology Goa, Ponda, Goa, India
veenat@nitgoa.ac.in

Abstract. State-of-the-art spoken language identification (LID) systems are sensitive to domain-mismatch between training and testing samples, due to which, they often perform unsatisfactorily in unseen target domain conditions. In order to improve the performance in domain-mismatched conditions, the LID system should be encouraged to learn domain-invariant representation of the speech. In this paper, we propose an adversarially trained hierarchical attention network for achieving this. Specifically, the proposed method first uses a transformer-encoder which uses attention mechanism at three different-levels to learn better representations at segment-level, suprasegmental-level and utterance-level. Such hierarchical attention mechanism allows the network to encode LID-specific contents of the speech in a better way. The network is then encouraged to learn domain-invariant representation of the speech using adversarial multi-task learning (AMTL). Results obtained on unseen target domain conditions demonstrate the superiority of proposed approach over state-of-the-art baselines.

Keywords: Spoken language identification (LID) ·
Domain-mismatch · Hierarchical attention · Adversarial multi-task
learning · Utterance-level embeddings · Indian languages

1 Introduction

An ideal spoken language identification (LID) system should accurately identify the language of the speech utterance irrespective of its duration and background conditions. Such accurate LID is useful in applications like multilingual automatic speech recognition (ASR), interactive voice response (IVR) systems, security and surveillance, archiving audio files, voice-based web search, etc. However, accurate identification of spoken language in real-world conditions is still a

A. Karpov et al. (Eds.): SPECOM 2023, LNAI 14339, pp. 475–489, 2023.
https://doi.org/10.1007/978-3-031-48312-7_38

challenging task for state-of-the-art systems [3,6]. One main reason is domain-mismatch which refers to the differences in background conditions, such as type of speech (e.g., spontaneous versus read speech), type of emotion in the speech (neutral versus emotional speech), type of pre-processing used (noise removal, encoding, compression), type of channels/devices used etc., between the samples used for training and samples used for testing [4,8,21]. Domain-mismatch is unavoidable in real-world scenarios, as the channel, speaker, background conditions, etc., present in a real-world test sample cannot be predicted ahead of time. In order to improve the performance of LID system in such unseen target domain conditions, we should improve its generalization. This can be achieved by learning LID-specific representation of the speech, which is invariant to domain-specific conditions.

In order to analyse the LID-specific contents in the speech, state-of-the-art LID systems use different type of frame-level features, such as Mel-frequency cepstral coefficients, Mel-filterbank coefficients, bottleneck features, etc. While all these features provide good representation at frame-level, they usually cover very short duration of speech and lack long-term contextual information. Furthermore, they provide a varying-length representation of the speech. Hence, it is very common practice to compute an utterance-level representation of the speech from these frame-level features before feeding to the classifier [14,19]. Such utterance-level embedding computation allows us to use simple classifiers in the back-end of the LID system.

In the literature, several approaches have been proposed for computing the utterance-level embedding from the frame-level features (sequence summarizing [16], time delay neural networks (TDNN) based x-vector [19], etc.). Note that, as these utterance-level embeddings are expected to compactly represent the LID-specific contents in the speech, the approach used to obtain the utterance-level embedding plays an important role in the performance of the system, especially in domain-mismatched conditions. In general, systems using attention modeling are showing very promising results [11,15]. For example, emphasized channel attention, propagation, and aggregation based time delay neural network (ECAPA-TDNN) [7], LID-seq-senone [14], etc., have shown superior performance.

Motivated by these, in this paper, we propose to use a hierarchical attention based network to learn LID-specific representation of the speech. Unlike the existing approaches (ECAPA-TDNN x-vector [7], bi-directional long short term memory (BiLSTM) u-vector [14], etc.), the proposed approach applies attention mechanism at three different levels which enable the system to efficiently encode LID-specific contents at segment-level, suprasegmental-level and utterance-level. For this purpose, we propose to use a transformer network which is an encoder-decoder network. We propose to learn LID-specific representation of the speech, using hierarchical attention, at the encoder part of the proposed transformer. Specifically, we first use a stacked multi-head attention for exploiting the sequential relationship in the input segment-level features. Followed by this, we propose to use a separate attention module, which applies attention on the output of stacked multi-head attention unit, to obtain suprasegmental-level embeddings (denoted as LID-seq-senones). A sequence of suprasegmental-level embeddings is then processed by another attention module, to obtain the final utterance-level embedding of the speech called u-vector. This u-vector is then given as input to the decoder (language classifier) of the transformer to predict the language label.

Apart from making utterance-level embeddings efficiently language dicriminative, we should also incorporate domain-invariance into it so that the robustness of the LID-network against domain-mismatch can be improved. For this, there must be sufficient training samples with different domain conditions, but collecting such kind of a training dataset is a difficult task. Hence, we need to utilize the available training dataset in a best possible way. Adversarial multi-task learning (AMTL) is one such way that has been used successfully to enforce domain invariance in many applications like speech recognition [17], speaker verification/recognition [10,20], speech emotion recognition [2], etc. AMTL forces the network to learn features invariant across domains by using training samples belonging to multiple domains that are available with their corresponding domain labels. Hence, we also propose to add adversarial learning on top of hierarchical attention mechanism in an end-to-end manner to obtain domain-invariant utterance-level embeddings. Thus the decoder part of the proposed transformer network include both language classifier and adversarial learning based domain classifier.

The major contributions of this work are summarized as follows:

– Hierarchical attention based network to extract LID-specific utterance-level embedding.
– Adversarially trained transformer network, a novel end-to-end structure to extract domain-invariant utterance-level embedding.
– Extensive experimentation of adversarially trained state-of-the-art utterance-level embeddings and comparison with proposed approach.

The later sections of this paper are organized as follows: In Sect. 2, we describe our proposed adversarial integrated transformer based approach for robust spoken language identification. A description of the databases used is given in Sect. 3. In Sect. 4, details of various experiments and corresponding results are given. It is further followed by conclusion in Sect. 5.

2   Proposed Approach for Domain Invariant LID-Specific Utterance-Level Embeddings

We propose to implement adversarially trained hierarchical attention network for designing domain-invariant utterance-level embeddings. The proposed end-to-end network is a transformer-based network which has following modules: (i) segment-level feature extractor, (ii) transformer encoder which acts as utterance-level feature extractor and (iii) transformer decoder which includes both language classifier and adversarial learning based domain classifier. Each module is explained in the following sub-sections.

2.1 Segment-Level Feature Extractor

In our work, we have used the phone-state bottleneck features (BNF) obtained using a pretrained BNF extractor [18] as segment-level feature vectors. Specifically, we use 80-dimensional BNF obtained using "BUT/Phonexia Bottleneck Feature Extractor" (BUT-BNF extractor) [18] as the segment-level features. This BNF extractor was originally trained with 3096 phone-states from 17 languages. BUT-BNF extractor processes the input speech using frames of 25 ms length, and having 10 ms shift. Each of the extracted phone-state BNF covers a total context of 31 frames (325 ms) of input speech and successive phone-state BNFs are separated by 10 ms. Thus, a speech utterance is represented as a sequence of phone-state BNF vectors.

2.2 Transformer-Encoder Based Utterance-Level Feature Extractor

The transformer encoder transforms the input sequence of segment-level feature vectors into an utterance-level embedding. We propose to implement a transformer-encoder as a hierarchical attention network which uses attention mechanism at three levels. The proposed network provides improved performance for domain-mismatch problem compared to the BiLSTM-based architecture, as it efficiently encodes the language dependencies within the given input speech sample. Also, the attention mechanism at three hierarchical levels, enables the model to focus on relevant language context at segment-level, suprasegmental-level and utterance-level. The block diagram of the proposed hierarchical attention based transformer encoder network is given in the Fig. 1.

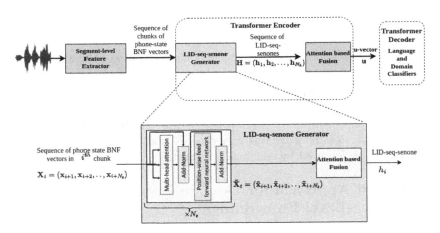

Fig. 1. Hierarchical attention network block for extracting utterance-level embedding. Here $\times N_e$ in LID-seq-senone generator indicate stacked N_e number of multi-head attention units, each with N_h heads.

The input sequence of phone-state BNF vectors are divided into fixed-size chunks, where each chunk includes sequence of N_b number of phone-state BNF vectors. Let $\mathbf{X}_i = (\mathbf{x}_{i+1}, \mathbf{x}_{i+2}, ..., \mathbf{x}_{i+N_b})$, where $\mathbf{X}_i \in \mathbb{R}^{N_b \times 80}$, be the ith chunk. Each successive chunk is shifted by one phone-state BNF vector. Let N_h be the number of such chunks. Every chunk $\mathbf{X}_i$ is passed onto the transformer encoder (see Fig. 1). The first block in the transformer encoder is the LID-seq-senone generator which include a stacked multi-head attention unit. There are N_e number of multi-head attention units are stacked. This stacked multi-head attention unit transform each of the chunks, so that it capture the dependencies in the sequence of phone-state BNFs in that chunk. Let $\tilde{\mathbf{X}}_i = (\tilde{\mathbf{x}}_{i+1}, \tilde{\mathbf{x}}_{i+2}, ..., \tilde{\mathbf{x}}_{i+N_b})$, where $\tilde{\mathbf{X}}_i \in \mathbb{R}^{N_b \times 80}$, be the transformed form of the chunk $\mathbf{X}_i$. We then propose to use an attention mechanism to dynamically assign the weights to each of the transformed phone-state BNF vectors in a chunk depending on their relevance in determining the language label. The weighted sum of these transformed phone-state BNF vectors in a chunk results into a suprasegmental feature vector. Since multi-head attention unit preserves the sequential information in the speech efficiently, we term this suprasegmental feature vector as LID sequential senone (LID-seq-senone) [14]. Each LID-seq-senone is a compact representation of the given chunk (with N_b number of phone-state BNF vectors) of speech sample. Thus, each of the chunks of phone-state BNF vectors are transformed into a LID-seq-senone.

Let $\mathbf{H} = (\mathbf{h}_1, \mathbf{h}_2, ..., \mathbf{h}_i, ..., \mathbf{h}_{N_h})$ be the sequence of LID-seq-senones obtained by passing the input chunks through LID-seq-senone generator unit of the transformer. Here, N_h represents number of chunks of speech which varies with the duration of the speech utterance, and $\mathbf{h}_i \in \mathbb{R}^{80}$ represents the ith LID-seq-senone. As shown in Fig. 1, we again apply attention-based fusion, which dynamically assigns the weights to each LID-seq-senones depending on their relevance in determining the language label to finally get a fixed-length utterance-level embedding called u-vector.

Note that the attention mechanisms used to obtain the suprasegmental representation (LID-seq-senone) [14] and utterance-level representation uses an attention network, which contains a dense (fully connected) layer with N_a number of nodes followed by a layer with single node. Both layers have $tanh$ activation function. Note that, this attention network can also be viewed as a fully connected neural network with 2 layers. More details on computation of u-vector from LID-seq-senones using attention mechanism can be seen in [12].

2.3 Transformer Decoder

The u-vector, obtained using hierarchical attention based network in transformer encoder, is then fed to the transformer decoder to predict the language label by minimising the impact of domain-mismatch. Further, in order to reduce the impact of domain-mismatch in attention based utterance level embedding, we propose to train the transformer network jointly with adversarial multi-task learning (AMTL) [17]. The utterance-level embedding (u-vector) extracted from transformer-encoder includes domain information along with LID-specific information which leads to domain-mismatch problem. In adversarial multi-task learning of multi-task networks in the transformer docoder, we use a multi-condition dataset where a class label associated with primary task (LID) and a class label associated with domain is given for each data point. This multi-task network simultaneously executes language classification and domain classification. It contains two output sub-networks, one for the primary task of language classification and the other for the secondary task of domain classification. Each output sub-network acts as a classifier to calculate posterior probabilities of classes given the u-vector representation.

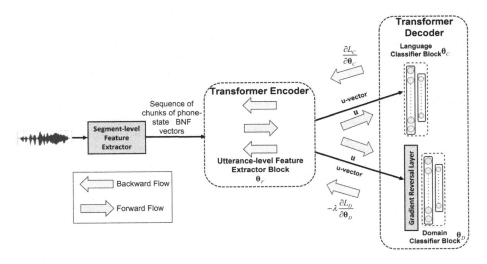

Fig. 2. Block diagram of the proposed transformer-network using AMTL for domain-invariant spoken language identification.

The block diagram of the proposed transformer-network using AMTL for domain-invariant spoken LID is given in Fig. 2. It is an end-to-end LID network which contains a transformer encoder acting as an utterance-level feature extractor block to extract an utterance-level embedding (represented as u-vector in Fig. 1) of the input speech with parameters $\boldsymbol{\theta}_F$ and a transformer decoder containing language classifier block with parameters $\boldsymbol{\theta}_C$ and domain classifier block with parameters $\boldsymbol{\theta}_D$. We denote this network as u-vec-HA-AMTL-Net. In AMTL, the u-vector is learned adversarially to the secondary task i.e., domain classification (and friendly to the primary task i.e., language classification), so that domain-dependent information is purged from the u-vector as it is irrelevant for the primary language classification task. During training, the parameters of the transformer-based LID network $\boldsymbol{\theta}_{net} = \{\boldsymbol{\theta}_F, \boldsymbol{\theta}_C, \boldsymbol{\theta}_D\}$ are tuned such that the network concentrates more on the LID-specific contents in the speech by ignoring domain-specific contents.

The cross-entropy loss functions for the primary task $L_C(\boldsymbol{\theta}_F, \boldsymbol{\theta}_C)$ and secondary task $L_D(\boldsymbol{\theta}_F, \boldsymbol{\theta}_D)$ are defined as

$$L_C(\boldsymbol{\theta}_F, \boldsymbol{\theta}_C) = -\sum_i \log P(l_i | \mathbf{u}_i; \boldsymbol{\theta}_F, \boldsymbol{\theta}_C)$$

$$L_D(\boldsymbol{\theta}_F, \boldsymbol{\theta}_D) = -\sum_i \log P(d_i | \mathbf{u}_i; \boldsymbol{\theta}_F, \boldsymbol{\theta}_D)$$

where, l_i and d_i respectively indicate the primary task label and secondary task label for i^{th} u-vector $\mathbf{u}_i$. Our aim is to minimize the primary task loss, so that the parameters of both utterance-level embedding extractor and language classifier are optimized. This ensures that u-vector learns LID-specific representation. This is done in conventional classification training process. To bring domain-invariance into the utterance-level embedding, adversarial learning is made by adjusting $\boldsymbol{\theta}_F$ to maximize the secondary task loss $L_D(\boldsymbol{\theta}_f, \boldsymbol{\theta}_D)$. This min-max optimization is achieved using gradient reversal layer (GRL), which is added in-front of secondary task classifier (as shown in Fig. 2). This transformer-based LID network (u-vec-HA-AMTL-Net) is trained in an end-to-end fashion using adversarial loss function as:

$$L_{net}(\boldsymbol{\theta}_{net}) = L_C(\boldsymbol{\theta}_F, \boldsymbol{\theta}_C) - \lambda L_D(\boldsymbol{\theta}_F, \boldsymbol{\theta}_D)$$

Due to this end-to-end adversarial training, the transformer encoder network learns u-vector (using hierarchical attention) to discriminate between languages, while ignoring domain-content in the input sample. These properties of the u-vector after adversarial learning in turn improves its robustness to the real-world domain-mismatch challenges.

3   Datasets Used in the Study

In this work, we consider three different Indian languages datasets, namely, Open-Speech-EkStep dataset (denoted as Ekstep-DS), IIT-Mandi Read Speech dataset (denoted as Readspeech-DS), and IIT-Mandi YouTube dataset (YouTube-DS). Among these, Ekstep-DS and Readspeech-DS are used for **training and validation** of the models, and YouTube-DS is used **only for testing**. All three datasets have 12 languages in common.

3.1   Open-Speech-EkStep Dataset (Ekstep-DS)

This is an open source dataset provided by Ekstep foundation, which was originally collected for building Vakyansh ASR toolkit [1]. It contains audio samples collected from different online resources [5]. In our experiments, we use two different subsets of this dataset. First subset contains audio samples collected from different domains such as TV programs and YouTube videos on sports, technology, religion, education, etc. We denote this subset as **Ekstep-Multi-Domain**. The second subset simulates extremely low-resource conditions, where, we assume that we do not have training data from multiple domains. Specifically, in all 12 languages we consider only audio samples from TV news broadcasts. We denote this subset as **Ekstep-TVnews**. In both Ekstep-Multi-Domain and Ekstep-TVnews, we collect approximately 5 h of speech in each language, which are divided into train (80%) and validation (remaining 20%). Details about these train and validation sets are given in Table 1.

Table 1. Details about the Open-Speech-EkStep dataset.

Language	Ekstep-Multi-Domain			Ekstep-TVnews		
	Train samples	Test samples	Total hours	Train samples	Test samples	Total hours
Assamese	1310	527	5.118	1218	305	5.018
Bengali	1360	485	5.236	1528	382	4.990
English	1015	364	4.852	1632	408	5.082
Gujarati	1536	456	5.197	1267	317	4.990
Hindi	1410	415	5.075	1090	272	5.049
Kannada	1390	389	4.799	1314	329	5.00
Malayalam	1378	368	4.503	1516	379	5.003
Marathi	1236	289	4.235	1332	333	5.100
Odia	1365	323	4.874	1459	365	5.001
Punjabi	1216	542	4.915	1132	283	5.003
Tamil	1364	336	4.816	960	240	5.007
Telugu	1489	403	5.184	1358	339	5.003

3.2 IIT-Mandi Read Speech Dataset (Readspeech-DS)

This dataset contains audio files obtained from news broadcasts in All India Radio (AIR) [13]. It contains samples recorded in studio environment, with good quality microphones. Each language in this dataset contains around 5 h of speech from at least 15 speakers. Like in the case of Ekstep-Multi-Domain and Ekstep-TVnews, we divide this dataset also into train (80%) and validation (remaining 20%) sets. Details about these train and test sets are given in Table 2.

Table 2. Details about the IIT-Mandi Read Speech dataset (Readspeech-DS).

Language	Train samples	Test samples	Total hours
Assamese	1270	617	4.288
Bengali	1540	360	5.381
English	955	239	5.012
Gujarati	1475	360	5.127
Hindi	1601	360	5.462
Kannada	1473	371	4.689
Malayalam	1423	357	4.583
Marathi	983	246	5.043
Odia	1418	354	4.474
Punjabi	966	242	5.012
Tamil	983	246	5.018
Telugu	1574	386	4.989

3.3   IIT-Mandi YouTube Dataset (YouTube-DS)

Third dataset used in this study is the IIT-Mandi YouTube dataset (YouTube-DS). This dataset contains audio samples from different YouTube videos from multiple domains (teaching, personal interviews, vlogs, etc.) [13]. In each language, it contains about 1 h of speech from at least 10 speakers. These samples are collected using different types of recording devices with different real-world background conditions. Hence, with respect to samples in Readspeech-DS and Ekstep-TVnews, samples from YouTube-DS has significant domain-mismatch. In this work, this dataset is used only for testing. Details about this dataset is given in Table 3.

Table 3. Details about the IIT-Mandi YouTube dataset (YouTube-DS).

Language	Num. of samples	Total hours
Assamese	366	1.017
Bengali	361	0.997
English	304	1.228
Gujarati	362	1.003
Hindi	367	1.014
Kannada	363	1.005
Malayalam	362	1.006
Marathi	395	1.573
Odia	363	1.003
Punjabi	439	1.797
Tamil	328	1.389
Telugu	366	1.029

4   Experiments and Results

In this section, we study the effectiveness of the proposed method. Performances are given in accuracy (%) and the equal error rate (EER) (%) metric. Lower values of EER indicates better performance.

We conduct the experiments in two different settings: i) training dataset with **extremely low domain-diversity** (which represents low-resource conditions), and ii) training dataset having **reasonable domain-diversity**.

4.1   Training Dataset with Extremely Low Domain-Diversity

In this case, we use the Ekstep-TVnews and Readspeech-DS as training datasets and use YouTube-DS as the test set. Note that, as both Ekstep-TVnews and Readspeech-DS contain samples from only news broadcasts (respectively from different TV channels and All India Radio), samples from the YouTube-DS have significant domain-mismatch with these two due to differences in channel, background conditions, type of speech, etc. Furthermore, as these domain conditions are unseen by the LID systems during the training, the YouTube-DS forms an **unseen test set** for the system trained on Ekstep-TVnews and Readspeech-DS. The combined validation set from Ekstep-TVnews and Readspeech-DS is considered as **seen test set**.

We first discuss the experiments conducted without AMTL, where, all systems are trained using only primary language classification loss. Later we discuss the effectiveness of AMTL, where, all systems are trained using primary language classification loss and secondary domain classification class.

4.1.1 Experiments on LID Systems Built Without AMTL. All systems are trained using a combined training dataset, obtained by combining Ekstep-TVnews and Readspeech-DS.

Experiments with Baseline LID Systems. We first give the performance of two baseline systems. First baseline is the state-of-the-art x-vector based LID system [9]. It contains a set of time-delay neural network (TDNN) layers in the front-end feature extractor block. These TDNN layers operate in a hierarchical manner such that the subsequent layers cover more temporal context than the preceding ones. The output of the last TDNN layer is then analyzed by a statistics pooling layer, which computes its mean and standard deviation. These concatenated mean and standard deviation form the utterance-level representation, which is then processed by a fully connected layer to get the utterance-level embedding x-vector. The x-vector is then processed by the classifier to predict the language label. We denote this LID system as x-vec-Net. The LID performance of the x-vec-Net for seen and unseen domain is given in the first row of Table 4.

Second baseline is u-vector based LID system [14], which has compact LID-seq-senones that are obtained using bidirectional long short-term memory (BiLSTM) units based networks. Since BiLSTM network models the sequential information in the input, the utterance-level embedding obtained from LID-seq-senones encode the temporal relations in a given speech better than x-vector. The LID-seq-senones are combined using attention-based mechanism to get the utterance-level embedding u-vector. The u-vector is then processed by the classifier to predict the language label. We denote this LID system as u-vec-Net. The LID performance of the u-vec-Net for seen and unseen domain is given in the second row of Table 4. It is seen that u-vec-Net performed significantly better than x-vec-Net, as expected.

Experiments with Proposed Transformer-Based Hierarchical Attention Network. Here, we demonstrate the effectiveness of the proposed transformer-based hierarchical attention network and compare it with two state-of-the-art baseline LID systems. We use the transformer encoder architecture whose structure is explained in Sect. 2.2 to extract the u-vector representation. However, we consider primary language classifier alone in the transformer decoder. We denote this proposed LID system as u-vec-HA-Net. Here, we only train primary language classifier of the system. We experimentally chose 8 stacked multi-head attention units ($N_e = 8$) with 8 heads ($N_h = 8$) in the transformer encoder module. The number of nodes (N_a) in the attention networks (used to obtain the suprasegmental representation LID-seq-senone and utterance-level representation u-vector) is chosen experimentally as 128. The LID performance of the u-vec-HA-Net for seen and unseen domain is given in the third row of Table 4.

From the results in Table 4, it is seen that, all LID systems performed satisfactorily on seen test set. As the seen test set contains similar domain conditions as in the training set, the LID system did not face any difficulty in identifying the language. However, all three systems performed poorly in unseen test set. This reduction in performance shows the impact of domain-mismatch in real-world conditions.

Among the three systems, the proposed u-vec-HA-Net performed significantly better than the baselines. Unlike the baselines, the proposed u-vec-HA-Net uses attention at three different levels, allowing the network to learn better representations at different levels. This leads to improved performance.

Table 4. Performance in accuracy and EER (both given in %) of proposed u-vec-HA-Net and baseline LID systems trained on low domain-diversity dataset.

LID System	Seen test set		Unseen test set	
	Accuracy	EER	Accuracy	EER
x-vec-Net	81.81	10.92	59.43	22.56
u-vec-Net	83.42	8.98	62.38	20.99
u-vec-HA-Net	85.99	7.55	67.69	18.09

4.1.2 Effect of AMTL on the Performance. Here, we study the effectiveness of AMTL on the proposed approach as well as on the baseline LID systems. All systems are trained using a combined training dataset, obtained by combining Ekstep-TVnews and Readspeech-DS. Hence the number of domains considered is 2. Note that, even though Ekstep-TVnews and Readspeech-DS contain samples from news broadcast, both have significant domain mismatch in terms of background noise and manner of speech.

Here, the baseline (x-vector and u-vector based) LID systems are also trained using AMTL where they include secondary domain classifier along with primary language classifier. We term the baseline AMTL-based LID systems as x-vec-AMTL-Net and u-vec-AMTL-Net. The LID performance of these baseline LID systems for seen and unseen domain is given in the first and second rows of Table 5.

The proposed transformer-based LID system is built by using the structure explained in Sect. 2. Here, the transformer decoder uses both primary language classifier and secondary domain classifier. All the hyperparameters are tuned experimentally as discussed in the Subsect. 4.1.1. Results obtained for the proposed u-vec-HA-AMTL-Net is given in the third row of Table 5.

It is seen that, inclusion of AMTL leads to slight improvement in all cases as compared to that of Table 4. Since the AMTL forces the system to learn a domain-invariant representation, systems trained with AMTL perform better compared to their counterparts trained without AMTL. It is interesting to observe that the performance of the proposed u-vec-HA-AMTL-Net is signifantly better compared to that of the baseline LID systems (with and without AMTL) even for unseen test set.

Table 5. Performance in accuracy and EER (both given in %) of proposed u-vec-HA-AMTL-Net and baseline AMTL-based LID systems trained on low domain-diversity dataset.

LID System	Seen test set		Unseen test set	
	Accuracy	EER	Accuracy	EER
x-vec-AMTL-Net	84.66	8.46	64.62	19.70
u-vec-AMTL-Net	86.56	7.23	66.11	18.88
u-vec-HA-AMTL-Net	**88.04**	**6.43**	**70.33**	**16.47**

4.2 Training Dataset with Reasonable Domain-Diversity

Note that, the Ekstep-DS actually contains speech samples collected from multiple domains. Hence, in this case, we replace the Ekstep-TVnews by Ekstep-Multi-Domain for training the systems. This allows us to evaluate the performance of LID system when a training dataset with better domain-diversity is available. Specifically, we use Ekstep-Multi-Domain and Readspeech-DS as training datasets, and use YouTube-DS as the **unseen test set**. All systems are trained using a combined training dataset, obtained by combining Ekstep-Multi-Domain and Readspeech-DS. The combined validation set from Ekstep-Multi-Domain and Readspeech-DS is considered as **seen test set**. Here also, for the AMTL-based LID systems the number of domains considered is 2.

Results obtained for proposed u-vec-HA-Net and baseline LID systems (trained without AMTL) are given in the first three rows of Table 6. Results obtained for proposed u-vec-HA-AMTL-Net and baseline AMTL-based LID systems are given in last three rows of Table 6. From the results, it is seen that, inclusion of AMTL is not much useful in this case. As the training dataset contains reasonable domain-diversity, all LID systems generalize very well and provide better performance compared to their counterparts trained with low domain-diversity (Table 4 and Table 5). However, among the three systems trained with AMTL, the proposed u-vec-HA-AMTL-Net has given the best performance. This again shows the superiority of the proposed approach.

Table 6. Performance in accuracy and EER (both given in %) of proposed transformer-based LID systems (with and without AMTL) and baseline LID systems (with and without AMTL) trained on reasonable domain-diversity dataset.

LID System	Seen test set		Unseen test set	
	Accuracy	EER	Accuracy	EER
x-vec-Net	83.63	8.86	60.27	22.15
u-vec-Net	85.23	8.24	63.59	20.23
u-vec-HA-Net	87.47	6.88	68.48	17.76
x-vec-AMTL-Net	85.34	8.09	65.49	19.03
u-vec-AMTL-Net	87.56	6.86	66.92	17.96
u-vec-HA-AMTL-Net	**89.57**	**6.12**	**71.68**	**15.52**

5   Conclusions

In this paper, we proposed a method to extract LID-specific utterance-level embeddings (u-vector) using hierarchical-attention based transformer-encoder network which is trained using adversarial learning. These embeddings are designed to capture the locally available language-specific information and ignoring the domain-specific information by learning representations at three different levels. Results obtained shows that these embeddings carry more language discriminative information and domain-invariance compared to state-of-the-art x-vector and u-vector embeddings.

Acknowledgement. This work resulted from research supported by Ministry of Electronics & Information Technology (MeitY), Government of India through project titled "National Language Translation Mission (NLTM) : BHASHINI".

References

1. Open-speech-ekstep dataset. https://github.com/Open-Speech-EkStep, (Accessed 23 Nov 2022)
2. Abdelwahab, M., Busso, C.: Domain adversarial for acoustic emotion recognition. IEEE/ACM Trans. Audio Speech Lang. Process. **26**(12), 2423–2435 (2018)
3. Abdullah, B.M., Avgustinova, T., Möbius, B., Klakow, D.: Cross-domain adaptation of spoken language identification for related languages: the curious case of Slavic languages. In: INTERSPEECH 2020, pp. 477–481 (2020)
4. Ambikairajah, E., Li, H., Wang, L., Yin, B., Sethu, V.: Language identification: a tutorial. IEEE Circuits Syst. Mag. **11**(2), 82–108 (2011)
5. Chadha, H.S., et al.: Vakyansh: ASR toolkit for low resource indic languages, pp. 1–5. arXiv preprint arXiv:2203.16512 (2022)
6. Dey, S., Saha, G., Sahidullah, M.: Cross-corpora language recognition: a preliminary investigation with indian languages. In: 2021 29th European Signal Processing Conference (EUSIPCO), pp. 546–550. IEEE (2021)
7. Dey, S., Sahidullah, M., Saha, G.: Cross-corpora spoken language identification with domain diversification and generalization. Comput. Speech Lang. **81**, 1–24 (2023)
8. Duroselle, R., Jouvet, D., Illina, I.: Metric learning loss functions to reduce domain mismatch in the x-vector space for language recognition. In: INTERSPEECH 2020, pp. 447–451 (2020)
9. Ganin, Y., Lempitsky, V.: Unsupervised domain adaptation by backpropagation. In: International Conference on Machine Learning, pp. 1180–1189. PMLR (2015)
10. Meng, Z., Zhao, Y., Li, J., Gong, Y.: Adversarial speaker verification. In: 2019 IEEE International Conference on Acoustics, Speech and Signal Processing (ICASSP 2019), pp. 6216–6220. IEEE (2019)
11. Mounika, K., Achanta, S., Lakshmi, H., Gangashetty, S.V., Vuppala, A.K.: An investigation of deep neural network architectures for language recognition in indian languages. In: INTERSPEECH, pp. 2930–2933 (2016)
12. Muralikrishna, H., Dileep, A.D.: Spoken language identification in unseen channel conditions using modified within-sample similarity loss. Pattern Recogn. Lett. **158**, 16–23 (2022)
13. Muralikrishna, H., Kapoor, S., Dileep, A.D., Rajan, P.: Spoken language identification in unseen target domain using within-sample similarity loss. In: 2021 IEEE International Conference on Acoustics, Speech and Signal Processing (ICASSP 2021), pp. 7223–7227. IEEE (2021)
14. Muralikrishna, H., Sapra, P., Jain, A., Dileep, A.D.: Spoken language identification using bidirectional LSTM based LID sequential senones. In: 2019 IEEE Automatic Speech Recognition and Understanding Workshop (ASRU), pp. 320–326. IEEE (2019)
15. Padi, B., Mohan, A., Ganapathy, S.: End-to-end language recognition using attention based hierarchical gated recurrent unit models. In: ICASSP 2019–2019 IEEE International Conference on Acoustics, Speech and Signal Processing (ICASSP), pp. 5966–5970. IEEE (2019)
16. Pešán, J., Burget, L., Černocký, J.: Sequence summarizing neural networks for spoken language recognition. In: Proceedings of interspeech 2016, pp. 3285–3288 (2016)
17. Shinohara, Y.: Adversarial multi-task learning of deep neural networks for robust speech recognition. In: Interspeech, pp. 2369–2372. San Francisco, CA, USA (2016)

18. Silnova, A., et al.: BUT/Phonexia bottleneck feature extractor. In: Odyssey, pp. 283–287 (2018)
19. Snyder, D., Garcia-Romero, D., McCree, A., Sell, G., Povey, D., Khudanpur, S.: Spoken language recognition using x-vectors. In: Odyssey, vol. 2018, pp. 105–111 (2018)
20. Suthokumar, G., Sethu, V., Sriskandaraja, K., Ambikairajah, E.: Adversarial multi-task learning for speaker normalization in replay detection. In: 2020 IEEE International Conference on Acoustics, Speech and Signal Processing (ICASSP 2020), pp. 6609–6613. IEEE (2020)
21. Zhou, K., Liu, Z., Qiao, Y., Xiang, T., Loy, C.C.: Domain generalization: a survey. IEEE Trans. Pattern Anal. Mach. Intell. **45**(4), 4396–4415 (2023)

Ensemble of Incremental System Enhancements for Robust Speaker Diarization in Code-Switched Real-Life Audios

Raj Gohil, Ramya Viswanathan, Saurabh Agrawal, C. M. Vikram,
Madhu R. Kamble[✉], Kamini Sabu, M. Ali Basha Shaik,
and Krishna K. S Rajesh

Samsung R & D Institute Bangalore, Bangalore, India
{raj.gohil,r.vishwanath,saurabh.a,vikram.cm,madhu.r,
kamini.sabu,m.shaik,ks.rajesh}@samsung.com

Abstract. Identifying individual speaker utterances in overlapped multi-speaker conversations pose a challenging problem in speaker diarization, specifically under multi-lingual scenarios. Standard speech diarization the system consists of a speech activity detector, a speaker-embedding extractor followed by clustering. We improve each of these components from the standard pipeline to enhance the speaker diarization in such complex cases. Our investigation focuses on addressing key sub-aspects of the task like the presence of noise variations, utterance duration variations, inclusion of enhanced ECAPA-TDNN embeddings for robustness etc. Finally, we use the DOVER-LAP approach to combine these system predictions so that complementary advantages of individual systems are efficiently incorporated. Our best-proposed systems outperform the baseline by achieving DER of 27.7% and 28.6% on Phase-1 and Phase-2 of Track-1 blind evaluation sets, respectively.

Keywords: Speaker diarization · ECAPA-TDNN · Spectral clustering

1 Introduction

In today's digital world, most of our communications and meetings tend to be online. In many applications like doctor visits, counsellor sessions, teacher-child interactions and customer support calls, it is necessary to know the time durations where each of the two parties are conversing. Precise time durations are one of the essential requirements in conversational scenarios to detect robust end-point detection [11], to generate high-quality transcription using automatic speech recognition [22] and to process using natural language understanding [24] and speech-to-speech translation [26]. In these cases, it is also important to label speech regions with the corresponding speakers to generate further enriched transcriptions. The segmentation of audio recordings by speaker labels, known as

ⓒ The Author(s), under exclusive license to Springer Nature Switzerland AG 2023
A. Karpov et al. (Eds.): SPECOM 2023, LNAI 14339, pp. 490–502, 2023.
https://doi.org/10.1007/978-3-031-48312-7_39

speaker diarization, is the process of recognizing *"who spoke when"* [21]. Diarization is considered as a major task in conversational AI systems and has applications in the processing of telephone conversations, broadcast news, meetings, clinical recordings, etc. [4,6,21].

An overview of speaker diarization system is shown in Fig. 1. It consists of speech activity detector (SAD), speaker embedding extractor and clustering technique.

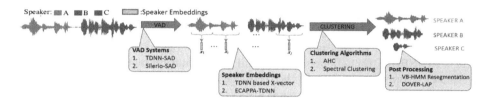

Fig. 1. Overview of Speaker Diarization System.

Recently, deep learning techniques are being widely used for speech diarization tasks. [30] proposed a deep neural network (DNN) with fully-connected hidden layers to classify all speakers in the training set, and then use bottleneck features as a speaker representation. Later, D-vectors were improved by a long short-term memory (LSTM) [10] network with a triplet loss function [13]. An improved version of D-Vectors with TDNN architecture and a statistical pooling layer was proposed in [6] and this work was further improved by generating robust speaker representations as X-Vectors in [28]. Emphasized Channel Attention, Propagation and Aggregation Time delay Neural networks (ECAPA-TDNN) were proposed [7], which is an enhanced structure based on X-Vectors' network. The basic TDNN layers are replaced with 1D-Convolutional Layers [9] and Res2Net-with-Squeeze-Excitation (SE-Res2Net) Blocks [9,12,14], while the basic statistical pooling layer is replaced with an Attentive Statistical Pooling. The ECAPA-TDNN system outperformed a strong X-Vectors baseline system as experimented in both speaker verification task and speaker diarization task [6,7]. Although all these approaches tried to address speaker diarization in clean conditions, however, challenges remain open under noisy and speech-overlapping conditions. Recently, deep learning-based end-to-end speaker diarization approaches are also proposed to solve the issue of overlapping speech [21].

Alternatively, most of the speaker diarization systems in the literature are developed by considering monolingual recordings. When a speaker speaks in multiple languages then the diarization becomes more challenging than the monolingual cases. In code-switched conversational speech, it is trivial that a single speaker could speak in multiple languages [19]. In this case, diarization becomes more complex as both the language and speaker compete during clustering [32]. The higher variance among the languages along with the speakers also poses challenge for the speaker diarization task [32].

In this paper, we propose a system for speaker diarization in multilingual code-switched scenarios for Track-1 of the DISPLACE 2023 Challenge. We start with the baseline architecture and improve each of its components as more robust substitutes. We use Silero VAD for improving performance in noisy and reverberant conditions. We validate the robustness of improved ECAPA-TDNN embeddings over X-vector variations for speaker diarization in the presence of multilingual code-switched data. We also observe that speaker clustering works much better than AHC for speaker diarization tasks. Observing that these incremental system enhancements improve the overall system performance for individual key aspects of the task, we combine these system outputs for final predictions on the evaluation set.

The remainder of this paper is organized as follows. Section 2 describes the Track-1 DISPLACE challenge dataset and the evaluation metric used during the system development. In Sect. 3, the technical details of our system are discussed. Experimental results and discussion are detailed in Sect. 4 along with case-by-case analysis. Finally, Sect. 5 provides the main conclusions of this work along with the future work directions.

2   DISPLACE Challenge Overview

In this section, we briefly describe the DIriazation of SPeaker and LAnguage in Conversational Environments (DISPLACE) Challenge [2] details. The challenge aims to detect and label all speaker or language segments automatically in each conversation. It features two tracks: Track-1 focuses on speaker diarization in multilingual scenarios, while Track-2 focuses on language diarization in multi-speaker settings.

Track-1 aims to perform speaker diarization *("who spoke when")* in multilingual conversational audio data, where the same speaker speaks in multiple code-mixed and/or code-switched languages. On the other hand, track-2 aims to perform language diarization *("which language was spoken when")* in multi-speaker conversational audio data, where the same speaker speaks in multiple languages within the same recording. We participated in the Track-1 speaker diarization challenge.

2.1   Challenge Dataset

The development set provided by the challenge was recorded in far-field conditions. The development and evaluation set consist of real-life multilingual, multi-speaker conversations. Each conversation is around 30 to 60 min long involving 3 to 5 participants. The participants show good proficiency in Indian languages along with English (though English is often observed to use the L1 accent). The development and evaluation set consists of approximately 15.5 h (27 recordings) and 16 h (29 recordings) of multilingual conversations, respectively. The evaluation was done in two phases, namely, Phase-1 and Phase-2. The Phase-1 evaluation set consists of a subset of the full evaluation set with 20 recordings spanning 11.5 h, and the Phase-2 evaluation set consisted of the full evaluation set.

The data was collected using a close-talking microphone worn by each speaker as well as a far-field microphone. The latter was provided to the participants for working on the challenge, while the organizers marked the ground truth using the close-talking microphone. The data contains natural code-mixing, code-switching, a variety of language dialects, reverberation, far-field effects, speaker overlaps, short turns, and short pauses.

The evaluation set features unseen languages as well. Participants were encouraged to use any publicly available datasets for training and developing the diarization systems.

2.2 Evaluation Metric

The performance metric is the diarization error rate (DER) calculated with overlap (the speech segments with multiple speakers speaking simultaneously are included during the evaluation) and without collar (tolerance around the actual speaker boundaries). Only the speech-based speaker activity regions are considered for evaluation. DER consists of three components: false alarm (FA), missed detection (Miss), and speaker confusion, among which FA and Miss are mostly caused by VAD errors. DER is defined as:

$$DER = \frac{D_{FA} + D_{miss} + D_{error}}{D_{total}} \tag{1}$$

where, D_{FA} is the total duration of wrongly detected non-speech, D_{miss} refers to the duration of wrongly detected speech, D_{error} refers to the duration of wrong speaker labeling, while D_{total} refers to the total speech duration in the given utterance.

3 Speaker Diarization System

This section explains the baseline system and the proposed system architectures in detail.

3.1 Core System

The core of the speaker diarization baseline is largely similar to the Third DIHARD Speech Diarization Challenge [23]. It uses basic components: speech activity detection, front-end feature extraction, X-vector extraction, and PLDA scoring followed by AHC. SAD is a TDNN model based on the Kaldi Aspire recipe ("egs/aspire/s5"). The speech intervals detected by the SAD are split into 1.5-sec windows with 0.25-sec shifts. For every window, 30-dimensional Mel Frequency Cepstral Coefficients (MFCCs) are computed with 25 ms window length and 10 ms hop. These are used to extract X-vectors at every 0.25 sec. The network used for X-vector extraction is the BigDNN architecture reported in [31] instead of the DNN network used in [23]. The X-vectors are centred and whitened every 3-sec using statistics estimated from the DISPLACE Dev set part 1. These vectors are then grouped into different speaker clusters using AHC (Agglomerative Hierarchical Clustering) and a similarity matrix produced by scoring with a Gaussian PLDA (Probabilistic Linear Discriminant Analysis) model. Finally, the speaker and non-speech labels are aligned temporally with the utterance waveform. The labels are further refined using Variational Bayes Hidden Markov Model (VB-HMM) and as Universal Background model-Gaussian Mixture Model (UBM-GMM). X-vector extractor as well as UBM-GMM and total variability matrix used for resegmentation are trained on VoxCeleb I and II [5,20] augmented with additive noise and reverberation.

3.2 Speech Activity Detection (SAD)

In our experiments, we investigate the use of TDNN-based SAD used in the baseline system [23], Silero VAD [29] and LSTM-based VAD [25]. The opensource Silero VAD [29] is trained on a large amount of data from over 100 languages and various background noises and reverberation conditions. It uses CNNs and transformers. It has been known to perform better than conventional VAD approaches in challenging noisy conditions both in terms of both precision and recall [29]. The model is trained using 30 ms frames and can also handle short frames without performance degradation.

Furthermore, we also evaluate our performance using the 2-layer LSTM VAD [25] system that predicts speech or non-speech decisions at frame-level. The system uses 20ms long frames to compute the input features: log energies of six frequency bands in the range 80 Hz to 4 kHz. The decisions may indicate some spurious unlikely short spurts of speech/silence. These are removed through post-processing where every speech region is expected to be at least 100 ms and every silence region is expected to be at least 200 ms.

3.3 Speaker Embeddings

Besides the X-vector used in the baseline, we try a different variation of the X-vector reported in [28] which is trained for the speaker verification task. In particular, we use the improved ECAPA-TDNN embeddings inspired by our previous work [6].

X-Vector. We used the X-vector described in the baseline system. This has been trained on the Voxceleb dataset augmented with additive noise and reverberation. The RIR dataset from [15] has been used to generate reverberation samples, while the additive noise sampled are taken from MUSAN [27], a corpus of music, speech and noise. The X-vectors are 512-dimensional vector embeddings computed every 1.5-s segments with a shift of 0.25 s.

VoxCeleb SID. We used Speaker Identification (SID) X-vector system in our experiments. It uses a smaller DNN network than a regular X-vector specifically trained for speaker recognition task [28]. The initial few layers use temporal context such that every frame sees a total context of 15 frames. The features are 24-dimensional filter banks with a frame length of 25 ms, mean-normalized over a sliding window of up to 3 s. The model is trained on VoxCeleb I and II [5,20] datasets augmented with additive noise and reverberation from Room Impulse Response and Noise Database [3] and MUSAN [27] datasets.

ECAPA-TDNN. We use the ECAPA-TDNN model inspired by our previous work [6] to extract enhanced speaker embeddings. It is an X-vector model improved to include Res2 blocks and channel- and context-dependent attention pooling. Multi-layer Feature Aggregation (MFA) is also used to merge complementary information before the statistics pooling. It has been trained on data with different augmentation strategies like waveform dropout, frequency dropout, speech perturbation, reverberation, addition noise, and noise with reverberation augmentation techniques. The data augmentation is applied on-the-fly to every speech utterance during training. This helps us more variety of data. The ECAPA-TDNN is trained using VoxCeleb I and VoxCeleb II [5,20] database with Room Impulse Response and Noise Database [3] and MUSAN [27] datasets used for the augmentation. 80-dimensional log Mel-filterbank energies mean-normalized across an input segment forms the input to the ECAPA-TDNN model. For every speech segment, 192-dimensional embeddings are extracted with a sliding window of size 1.5 s. In this work, we empirically try different hop sizes while computing the embeddings. Best performing hop sizes are 0.75 sec and 0.25 sec, and we refer to them as ECAPA-TDNN-1 and ECAPA-TDNN-2, respectively.

3.4   Clustering Algorithms

We tried different types of cluttering techniques in our experiments. In addition to using AHC from baseline setup, we also tried spectral clustering from [17] which has been shown to give high performance [6]. Spectral clustering is a graph-based clustering technique that uses an affinity matrix calculated using the cosine similarity metric. The affinity matrix is then enhanced and the Eigenvectors are computed. The Eigen-values are thresholded to get the number of speaker clusters k. The top Eigenvectors give the spectral embeddings which are more separable and give quite distinct speaker clusters through k-means clustering. We observed that AHC is better if there is hierarchy in the clusters while spectral clustering is useful if the data has connected clusters that do not form a globe.

4   Results and Discussion

The challenge provided baseline results on development dataset. Even though the challenge paper [1] reports DER to be 32.60%, we observe DER of 40.24%

in our implementation. We treat the latter as the baseline for all comparisons as indicated in Table 1. The baseline had UB-GMM and VB-HMM-based resegmentation modules as optional elements. We try modifying this module by using the default speaker shift probability as 0.45. The first two systems S1 and S2 in Table 1 show that adding resegmentation helps improve the DER of the baseline system. This holds not only for the baseline system but also for other systems as can be seen in Table 1.

Table 1. Diarization error rate on development set for different combinations of SAD, speaker embedding vectors and clustering methods.

System No	System Description	DER (%)
Baseline System		
S1	BL SAD+X-vector+PLDA+AHC [1]	40.24
S2	BL SAD+X-vector+PLDA+AHC+VB-HMM	38.74
VAD variation		
S3	Internal VAD+X-vector+PLDA+AHC	49.11
Replacing AHC with SC		
S4	BL SAD+X-vector+SC	51.49
S5	BL SAD+X-vector+PLDA+SC	37.67
S6	BL SAD+X-vector+PLDA+SC+VB-HMM	35.99
Finetuned Model		
S7	BL SAD+X-vector+PLDA+SC	**31.08**
Replacing X-vector with Voxceleb SID		
S8	BL SAD+VoxCeleb SID (0.25)	45.29
S9	BL SAD+VoxCeleb SID (0.25)+VB-HMM	38.23
Previous Work		
S10	Silero VAD+ECAPA-TDNN-1+SC [6]	39.29
S11	Silero VAD+ECAPA-TDNN-1+SC+VB-HMM	**39.02**
Towards Best System		
S12	BL SAD+ECAPA-TDNN-1+SC	36.93
S13	BL SAD+ECAPA-TDNN-1+SC+VB-HMM	**36.30**
S14	BL SAD+ECAPA-TDNN-2+SC+VB-HMM	**35.64**

4.1   Enhancements Using Clustering Techniques

We replaced the PLDA and AHC modules with spectral clustering. However, this gave poor performance compared to the baseline system. We observed that the input to the spectral clustering algorithm needs to consist of well-separated "connected components" [18] for robust clustering. As PLDA is expected to perform the required vector discrimination, we included the PLDA block before spectral clustering. The DER in Table 1 shows indeed a large improvement is observed when applied spectral clustering on X-vector with PLDA vectors (S5) than only X-vectors alone (S4).

4.2   Investigating the Separability of Speaker Embeddings

We observed that the spectral clustering works well if the speaker embedding vectors are well-separated, as shown in Sect. 4.1. We further explored different versions of speaker embeddings for their noticeable level of separability across speakers. As part of the analysis, we plot X-vector, X-vector with PLDA, Voxceleb SID and ECAPA-TDNN embeddings for audio in Fig. 2. The scatter plot in Fig. 2a shows that speaker discrimination is not sufficient enough with X-vectors. The PLDA scoring helps improve the speaker separation capability of the X-vectors resulting in better discrimination among the multi-lingual speakers as shown in Fig. 2c. The speaker distinction is the best using ECAPA-TDNN without the need for PLDA as seen from Fig. 2c.

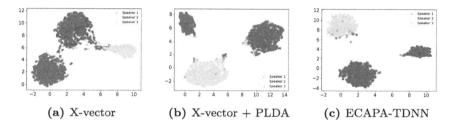

(a) X-vector   (b) X-vector + PLDA   (c) ECAPA-TDNN

Fig. 2. Scatter plots of (a) X-vector, (b) X-vector+PLDA, and (c) ECAPA-TDNN based enhanced embeddings after the U-map based dimensionality reduction. Red, blue and green color indicate three different speakers in an utterance. (Color figure online)

We were able to achieve 36.93% DER on Dev sets - a marginal improvement compared to Baseline numbers, using ECAPA-TDNN with a TDNN-based SAD system. We observe a further reduction in DER (S13 and S14) compared to baseline (S1) along with VB-HMM rescoring. As seen from Table 1, all the ECAPA-TDNN-based model performances are almost comparable with the X-vector+PLDA+SC approach. This is in line with the observations from Fig. 2. Furthermore, we observe from Table 1 that for the sliding window hop period, $p=0.25$ gives better results than when $p=0.75$. This is because the short speaker utterances like 'yes', 'no', 'oh', etc. can be easily accounted for with small hops.

4.3   Voice Activity Detection

As the DISPLACE challenge data was recorded in far-field conditions, we tried to remove noise or reverberation from the utterances using a DNN pre-processing model. This was followed by utterance segmentation into speech-only regions using LSTM VAD trained on noise-augmented Librispeech data discussed in Sect. 3.2.

In order to incorporate more data, we further tried replacing the TDNN based VAD with Silero VAD as discussed in Sect. 3.2. We see that the use of Silero VAD reduces the DER compared to when baseline TDNN SAD is used. However, a close analysis of failed cases indicates that the Silero VAD improves the performance for the utterances with high noise and reverberation, while TDNN SAD works best in the case of clean utterances. The development set did not contain many noisy utterances which led to aggregate performance deterioration for S13.

4.4 Results on Dev and Eval Datasets

Results on the development set using various experiments are shown in Table 1. Here, S7 is the finetuned version of the model S5. In general, overfitting happens when the model performs better with very low error rates on test data set [16]. On the contrary, the DERs are higher on the development data set due to the presence of largely divergent data conditions in this task. So, we finetuned the weights of model S5 using the development set and created model S7. In principle, it is not meaningful to measure the DER on the development set itself using system S7. However, as the DER is still on the higher scale even after the finetuning, we consider system S7 as one of the competing systems in our experiments.

Performance Evaluation on Phase-1. We selected four models based on development set results and observations, that is, S13, S14, S11 and S7. The corresponding evaluation set results are shown in Table 2. We observed that the Silero VAD proves to be more robust in the presence of noise variability and works well with short window and hop sizes. Corresponding system S11, therefore, outperforms very short and noisy utterances. That is, if a speaker speaks for a small time in a conversation, used ECAPA-TDNN embedding computed with a small window hop size provides an advantage in helping more accurate speaker change detection for system S14. We combine our four system's outputs for final submission, considering that each system has its characteristics which help in specific aspects of the task. We performed the fusion based on the maximum voting criteria. The speaker label which appears more times for a given frame is voted as the final speaker label. If none of the four systems claimed the same speaker label, we retained the labels from S7 - the system performing best on the development set. After fusion, the results improved further to achieve a lower DER of 27.70% as shown in Table 2.

Table 2. Results of different combination SAD, speaker vectors and clustering methods in DER (%) on eval phase 1 and phase 2 set.

System No	Systems	Dev	Phase-1	Phase-2
S1	BL X-vector + PLDA + AHC [1]	40.24	39.60	32.50
S13	BL SAD+ECAPA-TDNN (p 0.75)+SC+VB-HMM	36.30	28.11	29.45
S14	BL SAD+ECAPA-TDNN (p 0.25)+SC+VB-HMM	35.64	29.67	28.85
S11	Silero SAD +ECAPA-TDNN (p 0.75)+SC+VB-HMM	39.02	32.41	28.86
S7	BL SAD+X-vector+PLDA+SC	31.08	31.84	29.87
S15	Fusion of S13, S14, S11 and S7	NA	**27.67**	28.7
S16	Fusion of S14, S11 and S7	NA	27.89	**28.59**

Table 3. Individual DER results on the eval set for the individual audio files.

Audios → Sys ↓	B015	B016	B020	B023	B027	B029	B035	B039	B051	B053	B054	M007	M008	M010	M017	M044	M047	M048	M050	M053
S13	25.67	41.52	34.55	22.01	7.19	15.81	6.52	33.16	30.04	32.35	22.64	21.89	37.45	30.34	30.81	33.06	15.02	35.47	56.75	13.40
S14	25.60	41.94	34.75	23.94	7.32	15.76	6.45	33.25	29.96	32.33	23.20	30.30	37.37	30.18	30.69	34.70	30.55	35.44	62.32	16.54
S11	27.99	42.03	32.43	31.03	9.69	20.13	7.62	36.08	39.64	41.72	25.86	30.80	37.17	34.46	32.40	27.02	18.97	46.50	77.24	17.23
S7	41.75	48.65	38.53	22.01	7.19	27.48	19.82	33.33	34.08	34.21	22.64	23.57	38.97	50.44	32.61	33.06	15.02	37.90	56.75	13.40

Performance Evaluation on Phase-2. We decided to improve the fusion technique further based on the DOVER approach [8] for the Phase-2 part of the challenge. DOVER-LAP is a method to combine multiple diarization system hypotheses while handling the overlap between multiple speakers. The DOVER-LAP S15 and S16 systems were used to combine individual systems based on empirically selected custom weights. These weights were calculated based on the leave-one-out cross-validation performance on the development set.

4.5   Analysis After Phase-1 Evaluation

We performed a detailed analysis of the audio after the completion of the Phase-1 evaluation. The individual file-wise results for Phase 1 Eval-set are shown in Table 3. We observe that for a few files, the DER is relatively very less (e.g., file B027), while for some others the DER is very high (e.g., file M050).

We observe the scatter plots for the files M007 and M050 as shown in Fig. 3. For the M007 file the speakers are clearly distributed from each other which results in less DER (as reported in Table 3). In particular, with X-vector embeddings the DER obtained is relatively less compared to ECAPA-TDNN embeddings that are reflected from Fig. 3a and Fig. 3b. In addition, we also observe that the M050 recording is highly noisy. Figure 3c and 3d show the X-vector and ECAPA-TDNN embeddings respectively for this recording. In both cases, the speaker embeddings show a large overlap. Due to the noisy nature of speaker embeddings and distance metrics, the quality of the affinity matrix degrades affecting the spectral clustering, thereby leading to poor performance.

On the other hand, the audios B027 and B035, are near-field audios with relatively less noise and reverberation. Further, the gender-related speaker transitions in these audios are generally well-defined. That is, even within the same gender, different speakers have clearly distinct voices due to noticeable variations in pitch and timber. However, these audios do not have overlapping speakers. Each speaker speaks for a longer time as opposed to a short 2 to 3-sec duration. All these are helpful in getting better discrimination across embeddings of different speakers and hence better speaker diarization.

As shown in Table 2, stand-alone system S7 performed better on the dev set and did not perform well on the Eval set compared to other systems. Further investigation shows that most of the audios from the Dev set are clean, while the audios from the Eval set contain comparatively more noise under reverberation conditions. This indicates the importance of domain mismatch not only in terms of language and accent but also in terms of noise and reverberation as well.

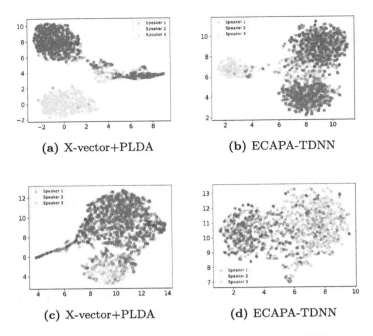

Fig. 3. Scatter plots of (a) X-vector+PLDA, and (b) ECAPA-TDNN embeddings for M007 recording. Scatter plots of (c) X-vector+PLDA, and (d) ECAPA-TDNN embeddings for M050 recording. The U-map based dimensionality reduction is performed before plotting scatter plots.

As shown in Table 3, we observe that all baseline VAD systems perform poorly for the M044 audio, while system S11 using Silero VAD performs much better. M044 audio is extremely noisy with very high pitch and loudness variations due to frequent switching between near-field and far-field conditions. This condition seems to have been captured well by Silero VAD compared to the baseline VAD.

5   Conclusion

In this paper, we built a system for Track-1 of the DISPLACE Challenge that aims at speaker diarization in multilingual scenarios. The system is implemented using different combinations of core sub-modules such as VAD, robust speaker embeddings, and clustering methods. The best system is the combination of different systems obtained using the DOVER-LAP fusion techniques. This represents a significant relative improvement over the baseline by 30.05% which led us to the **second** position for both phase-1 and phase-2 of the DISPLACE challenge. Although there is still room for improvement, we do believe that these are promising results. Our systems perform noticeably well with gender-specific transitions compared to same-gender conversations under multilingual and far-field conditions. The mismatch in the Dev and Eval sets due to huge reverberation and noisy data made the task more challenging. The use of models trained on large datasets helped with reducing the data mismatch under challenging acoustic conditions.

References

1. Displace challenge. https://codalab.lisn.upsaclay.fr/competitions/10588
2. Displace challenge evaluation plan. https://displace2023.github.io/docs/ DISPLACE_Evaluation_Plan_v1.pdf
3. openslr.org. https://www.openslr.org/28/
4. Anguera, X., Bozonnet, S., Evans, N., Fredouille, C., Friedland, G., Vinyals, O.: Speaker diarization: a review of recent research. IEEE Trans. Audio Speech Lang. Process. **20**(2), 356–370 (2012)
5. Chung, J.S., Nagrani, A., Zisserman, A.: VoxCeleb2: deep speaker recognition. In: Proceedings of the Interspeech 2018, pp. 1086–1090 (2018). https://doi.org/10. 21437/Interspeech.2018-1929
6. Dawalatabad, N., Ravanelli, M., Grondin, F., Thienpondt, J., Desplanques, B., Na, H.: ECAPA-TDNN embeddings for speaker diarization. In: Proceedings of the Interspeech 2021, pp. 3560–3564 (2021). https://doi.org/10.21437/Interspeech. 2021-941
7. Desplanques, B., Thienpondt, J., Demuynck, K.: ECAPA-TDNN: emphasized channel attention, propagation and aggregation in TDNN based speaker verification. In: Proceedings of the Interspeech 2020, pp. 3830–3834 (2020). https://doi. org/10.21437/Interspeech.2020-2650
8. Raj, D., et al.: DOVER-Lap: a method for combining overlap-aware diarization outputs. In: 2021 IEEE Spoken Language Technology Workshop (SLT) (2021)
9. Gao, S.H., Cheng, M.M., Zhao, K., Zhang, X.Y., Yang, M.H., Torr, P.: Res2net: a new multi-scale backbone architecture. IEEE Trans. Pattern Anal. Mach. Intell. **43**(2), 652–662 (2019)
10. Graves, A., Graves, A.: Long short-term memory. In: Supervised Sequence Labelling With Recurrent Neural Networks, pp. 37–45 (2012)
11. Gudepu, P., Koroth, M.J., Sabu, K., Shaik, M.A.B.: Dynamic encoder RNN for online voice activity detection in adverse noise conditions. In: Interspeech (Accepted for Publication). Dublin, Ireland (2023)
12. He, K., Zhang, X., Ren, S., Sun, J.: Deep residual learning for image recognition. In: Proceedings of the IEEE Conference on Computer Vision and Pattern Recognition, pp. 770–778 (2016)
13. Hermans, A., Beyer, L., Leibe, B.: In defense of the triplet loss for person re-identification. arXiv preprint arXiv:1703.07737 (2017)
14. Hu, J., Shen, L., Sun, G.: Squeeze-and-excitation networks. In: Proceedings of the IEEE Conference on Computer Vision and Pattern Recognition, pp. 7132–7141 (2018)
15. Ko, T., Peddinti, V., Povey, D., Seltzer, M.L., Khudanpur, S.: A study on data augmentation of reverberant speech for robust speech recognition. In: 2017 IEEE International Conference on Acoustics, Speech and Signal Processing (ICASSP), pp. 5220–5224. IEEE (2017)
16. Li, T.W., Lee, G.C.: Performance analysis of fine-tune transferred deep learning. In: IEEE 3rd Eurasia Conference on IOT, Communication and Engineering (ECICE), pp. 315–319 (2021)

17. Lin, Q., Yin, R., Li, M., Bredin, H., Barras, C.: LSTM based similarity measurement with spectral clustering for speaker diarization. In: Proceedings Interspeech 2019, pp. 366–370 (2019). https://doi.org/10.21437/Interspeech.2019-1388
18. von Luxburg, U.: A tutorial on spectral clustering. Stat. Comput. **17**, 395–416 (2007)
19. Lyu, D.C., Chng, E.S., Li, H.: Language diarization for code-switch conversational speech. In: 2013 IEEE International Conference on Acoustics, Speech and Signal Processing, pp. 7314–7318. IEEE (2013)
20. Nagrani, A., Chung, J.S., Zisserman, A.: VoxCeleb: a large-scale speaker identification dataset. In: Proceedings of the Interspeech 2017, pp. 2616–2620 (2017). https://doi.org/10.21437/Interspeech.2017-950
21. Park, T.J., Kanda, N., Dimitriadis, D., Han, K.J., Watanabe, S., Narayanan, S.: A review of speaker diarization: recent advances with deep learning. Comput. Speech Lang. **72**, 101317 (2022)
22. Prabhavalkar, R., Hori, T., Sainath, T.N., Schlüter, R., Watanabe, S.: End-to-end speech recognition: a survey. arXiv (2023). arXiv:2303.03329
23. Ryant, N., et al.: The third DIHARD diarization challenge. In: Proceedings of the Interspeech 2021, pp. 3570–3574 (2021). https://doi.org/10.21437/Interspeech.2021-1208
24. Sarikaya, R.: The technology behind personal digital assistants: an overview of the system architecture and key components. IEEE Signal Process. Mag. **34**(1), 67–81 (2017). https://doi.org/10.1109/MSP.2016.2617341
25. Sertsi, P., Boonkla, S., Chunwijitra, V., Kurpukdee, N., Wutiwiwatchai, C.: Robust voice activity detection based on LSTM recurrent neural networks and modulation spectrum. In: Proceedings of the APSIPA ASC, pp. 342–346 (2017). https://doi.org/10.21437/Interspeech.2021-941
26. Shankarappa, R., Tiwari, S.: A faster approach for direct speech to speech translation. In: IEEE WINTECHCON. Bangalore (2022)
27. Snyder, D., Chen, G., Povey, D.: MUSAN: a music, speech, and noise corpus. arXiv preprint arXiv:1510.08484 (2015)
28. Snyder, D., Garcia-Romero, D., Sell, G., Povey, D., Khudanpur, S.: X-vectors: robust DNN embeddings for speaker recognition. In: 2018 IEEE International Conference on Acoustics, Speech and Signal Processing (ICASSP), pp. 5329–5333. IEEE (2018)
29. Team, S.: Silero VAD: pre-trained enterprise-grade voice activity detector (VAD), number detector and language classifier. https://github.com/snakers4/silero-vad (2021)
30. Variani, E., Lei, X., McDermott, E., Moreno, I.L., Gonzalez-Dominguez, J.: Deep neural networks for small footprint text-dependent speaker verification. In: IEEE International Conference on Acoustics, Speech and Signal Processing (ICASSP), pp. 4052–4056 (2014)
31. Zeinali, H., Wang, S., Silnova, A., Matějka, P., Plchot, O.: BUT system description to VoxCeleb speaker recognition challenge 2019. arXiv preprint arXiv:1910.12592 (2019)
32. Zhou, Y., Tian, X., Li, H.: Language agnostic speaker embedding for cross-lingual personalized speech generation. IEEE/ACM Trans. Audio Speech Lang. Process. **29**, 3427–3439 (2021). https://doi.org/10.1109/TASLP.2021.3125142

Enhancing Language Identification in Indian Context Through Exploiting Learned Features with Wav2Vec2.0

Shivang Gupta[ID], Kowshik Siva Sai Motepalli[✉][ID], Ravi Kumar,
Vamsi Narasinga[ID], Sai Ganesh Mirishkar[ID], and Anil Kumar Vuppala[ID]

International Instituite of Information Technology Hyderabad, Hyderabad, India
{shivang.gupta,kowshik.siva}@students.iiit.ac.in,
anil.vuppala@iiit.ac.in

Abstract. This work proposes the utilization of a self-supervised pre-trained network for developing a Language Identification (LID) system catering to low-resource Indian languages. The framework employed is Wav2vec2.0-XLSR-53, pre-trained on 53k hours of unlabeled speech data. The unsupervised training of the model enables it to learn the acoustic patterns specific to a language. Given that languages share phonetic space, multi-lingual pre-training is instrumental in learning cross-lingual information and building systems that cater to low-resource languages. Further fine-tuning with a limited amount of labeled data significantly boosts the model's accuracy. The results showcase a relative improvement of 33.2% over the DNN-A (DNN with attention) model and 19.04% over Dense Resnets for the Language Identification task on the IIITH-ILSC database using the proposed features (Shivang Gupta and Kowshik Siva Sai Motepalli share first authorship).

Keywords: Language identification · Wav2vec2.0 · Self-attention mechanism · Equal error rate

1 Introduction

The objective of a Language Identification (LID) system is to categorize spoken language, upon being presented with a speech signal. Automated spoken language identification serves as a preliminary step for numerous speech-related applications, such as multi-lingual automatic speech recognition, speech-to-speech translation, customer routing in call centers, etc. [11]. In the case of code-switching, LID assumes an essential role as a fundamental component of any speech-based application system.

Several techniques have been devised for language identification, categorized broadly as explicit and implicit. Explicit LID systems typically involve the conversion of speech to an intermediate representation such as phones, followed by the extraction of features from this representation, which are then utilized for LID. Conversely, implicit methods involve the direct feeding of speech

© The Author(s), under exclusive license to Springer Nature Switzerland AG 2023
A. Karpov et al. (Eds.): SPECOM 2023, LNAI 14339, pp. 503–512, 2023.
https://doi.org/10.1007/978-3-031-48312-7_40

into the model to identify the language identity [21]. This paper focuses on an implicit Language Identification (LID) system utilizing wav2vec2.0-XLSR-53, which directly encodes raw speech into feature vectors that are subsequently used for LID.

DNN, DNN with attention, i-vector, LSTM, etc. have given good results for LID task [4,10,20]. But these models require a significant amount of language data for training. i-vector relies heavily on language data for training, and their effectiveness is influenced by the data parameters like speaker variability. Therefore, in low-resource language settings such as in India, where there are 22 official languages, regional dialects, and limited language data available, models that can learn cross-lingual information tend to perform better.

Features extracted from the Joint Acoustic Model(JAM) of a multi-lingual ASR trained using the LSTM-CTC framework along with a multi-head attention block have shown significant improvement for LID task [16]. It not only captures shared phonetic information across multiple languages but also learns long-range temporal information. However, ASR building requires a significant amount of labeled data, and getting labeled data is a bottleneck in low-resource languages. For some languages, we do have audio data available from various sources like films, videos, etc. but finding native speakers in the language for annotation is a challenge. Hence self-supervised models such as wav2vec2.0 are utilized to learn cross-lingual information from unlabeled data, which can then be fine-tuned with a minimal amount of labeled data. Features extracted from wav2vec2.0 are passed through the attention layer and then its performance is compared with different other approaches for LID task.

The paper is organized as follows. Section 2 contains the related work on LID. Section 3 describes the IIITH-ILSC database used. Sections 4 and 5 describes the wav2vec2.0 architecture and the experimental setup. Section 6 describes the experimental results of LID systems on the IIITH-ILSC database. Finally, the paper is concluded in Sect. 7.

2   Related Work

Gaussian mixture model (GMM), GMM-universal background model(UBM) [17], and i-vector model have been commonly used modeling techniques for developing LID systems. i-vector representation of speech summarizes information in an utterance [9]. Deep Neural Networks are also used for LID systems [11,15]. DNN systems have shown good performance since they capture temporal information quite efficiently. However, these models for LID are data-driven and require a larger amount of data as well as more number of speakers, both of which are insufficient in low-resource Indian languages. Earlier works used MFCC features that captured short-range acoustic properties and used quantization blocks to get discrete output which was then classified to represent the language identity of five Indian languages namely Hindi, Kannada, Malayalam, Telugu, and Tamil [2]. Later, auto-associative neural networks (AANN) were used for LID, which were trained on weighted LPCC (WLPCC) feature vectors to capture the distribution of spectral feature vectors and learn temporal dependencies in the language [13]. Further LID task was performed using Hilbert envelope and phase information of LP residual [14] on multilingual speech corpus, namely the Indian Institute of Technology Kharagpur-multilingual Indian language speech corpus (IITKGP-MLILSC) [12]. Various Deep Neural Networks like Deep Convolutional Recurrent Neural Networks [3], Resnets, etc. have also been used for LID task. Recently LID task for accented speech using various models like XLS-R-300M wav2vec2.0, Resnet, and ConvNet on ASR output have also been evaluated [7].

3 Database

The IIITH-ILSC [15] database was considered for model evaluation. It comprises 103.5 h of speech data collected from 1150 speakers across 23 languages, including 22 official Indian languages and Indian English. It has 4.5 h of data for each language. The corpus was pooled from various sources such as archives of Prasar Bharati, All Indian Radio, TED-talks, conversational speech from broadcasts, and speech recorded from students of IIITH, University of Hyderabad, Maulana Azad National Urdu University-Hyderabad, National Institute of Technology-Warangal, Goa University, Bodoland University, and the University of Jammu. Each language in the database contains utterances from 50 speakers (25 male and 25 female) with 5–10 min duration from each speaker. The database includes speech samples from both clean and noisy environments, and all speech files are in .wav format with a sampling rate of 16,000 samples/sec.

4 Methodology

4.1 Wav2Vec2.0

wav2vec2.0-XLSR-53 is a pre-trained model [1] trained on 53k hours of unlabeled speech and on 53 different languages. It takes raw speech waveform as input, segments into frames and each frame is passed through multiple stacked CNN layers, which give a latent representation $z_1....z_t$. Each z_i vector represents the vector for one time frame of the speech signal. These representations are masked and then passed to the context network to get representation $C = [c_1....c_t]$. Context network is a transformer encoder except that instead of using positional encoding, it uses grouped convolution layer to learn relative positions. Masked $z_1....z_t$ are also passed through quantization block to get $q_1....q_t$ vectors. Quantization block is introduced since speech is continuous and data is unlabeled, therefore there are no labeled speech units like phonemes, words, etc. Therefore it maps input to some different set of speech units. To generate $q_1....q_t$, there are code books(groups) from which codewords are taken and concatenated. 2 groups each having 320 entries(codewords) are used. Each group maps the input vector to a possible codeword by using a quantization matrix and then gumble softmax.

Then codewords from each group of the codebook are concatenated and multiplied by quantization projection matrix to get $q_1....q_t$. The concatenated word is a possible speech unit for each input vector we give to quantization module.

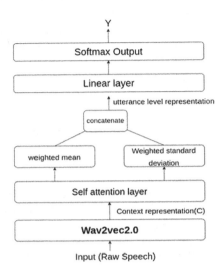

Fig. 1. Proposed architecture for Language identification.

Since there are 2 groups each containing 320 entries, thus it has 320*320 which is 102.4K possible speech units. Finally, the model is trained using contrastive learning. In contrastive learning for each masked position t, model tries to identify the true representation of c_t from a set say Q_t which contains q_t and K distractors. K = 100 distractors are uniformly sampled from masked positions other than at t^{th} position of that same utterance. Contrastive loss is calculated as

$$L_m = -log \frac{exp(sim(c_t, q_t)/\kappa)}{\Sigma_{\tilde{q} \sim Q_t} exp(sim(c_t, \tilde{q})/\kappa)}$$

where sim is cosine similarity , κ temperature in contrastive loss , Q_t is set which include q_t and K distractors.

Fine-tuning on the pre-trained model is done on labeled data and is optimized by minimizing the Connectionist Temporal Classification (CTC) loss.

Pre-trained wav2vec2.0-XLSR-53 model is taken, fine-tuned on the IIITH-ILSC database, and used for the LID task. Architecture is shown in Fig. 1. The context vectors $c_1....c_t$ obtained from 14th layer of XLSR-53 is taken and fed to the attention layer. In this layer following operations are done -

– Self-attention

$$a \; = \; softmax \; (w_2 GELU(W_1 c_T)) \; \in R_T$$

$$o_1 \; = \; \Sigma_{t=1}^{T} \, a_t \, c_t$$

$$o_2 \; = \; \sqrt{\Sigma_{t=1}^{T} \, a_t (c_t - \mu)^2 / T}$$

where $\mu = \Sigma_{t=1}^{T} \frac{c_t}{t}$, $W_1 \in R_U$, $w_2 \in R_U$ and o_1 is the weighted sum from context vector based on attention vector a and o_2 is weighted standard deviation.

o_1 and o_2 are concatenated and fed as a feature vector to the linear layer and then its output is normalized via softmax. Output(Y) is the probability vector where each Y_i indicates the probability of input speech belonging to the ith language.

5   Experimental Setup

5.1   Models

Resnet. A residual network is a feed-forward architecture in which for every layer along with the forward path from the previous layer, there is also a residual connection from the previous layer, and then the representation from forward and residual connections are added. These networks have shown better performances as they are more stable at larger depths [8,19]. DenseResNets are Resnets with a forward path and residual path not just from previous layer but from all the lower layers.

Stacked shifted delta cepstrum(SDC) features that capture longer temporal information are used for Resnet and DenseResnet [8]. A 56 dimensional SDC vector is obtained by appending 7-dimensional MFCC features with 49 dimensional SDC features [6]. For stacking, the temporal context of 2-1-2 is used which indicates the concatenation of SDC features from the previous 2 frames, the current frame and the next 2 frames. For a Resnet block, W1 weight matrix is taken that maps the input feature vector to 1024 dimensional output, then Relu activation is used, and then weight layer W2 that maps back the 1024 dimensional output of W1 to a same dimensional final output vector as that of the original input. 4 blocks are used for Resnet while for DenseResnet 7 dense blocks are used. For all blocks, a dropout factor of 0.1 is used.

Joint Acoustic Model. Joint acoustic model(JAM) of a multilingual ASR is taken and is trained using LSTM-CTC framework. It is built on 6 Indian languages namely Hindi, Marathi, Odia, Telugu, Tamil, and Gujarati. Data of Telugu, Tamil and Gujarati are taken from Microsoft Data which is released as a part of Low Resource Speech Recognition Challenge for Indian languages-Interspeech 2018, which has 50 h of data for each language. For Hindi, Marathi, Odia speech data is taken from [5] collected from the individual local speakers in a reading task. For Hindi, Marathi and Odia, 100 h of data is used for training. The model is then fine-tuned on 3.5 hrs of data for each of these six languages from the IIITH-ILSC database and then tested using 1 hr of data.

The combined data is converted to IT3 format using common phone set representation [18] which provides shared space representation and helps the model to learn cross-lingual information. For each acoustic vector(40-dimensional MFCC) extracted from speech, a posterior phone probability is calculated from JAM and then converted to scaled likelihood by dividing with phone prior probabilities to give CTC feature. The dimension of this multilingual CTC feature is 75 (number of unique phones in all six Indian languages using common phone set representation). These CTC features are then passed to attention layer and weighted mean and weighted standard deviation are concatenated, passed through linear layer and then softmax to predict the language identity.

Wav2Vec2.0. The wav2vec2.0-XLSR-53 pre-trained model is taken. The first block is feature encoder. Feature encoder is fed with 320 dimensional input which represents 20ms of audio sample which is sampled at 16 KHz frequency. Input sample is standardized to zero mean and unit variance. After that it is passed to convolution block which has 1d convolution layer, normalization layer and gelu activation function. 7 such blocks are used which constant channel size of 512, decreasing kernel width (10,3,3,3,3,2,2) and stride (5,2,2,2,2,2,2). Output is 512 dimensional vector which is fed to the transformer block. It has 24 encoder blocks with model dimension 1,024, inner dimension 4,096 and 16 attention heads. A projection layer is added above transformer block to map out the 1024 dimensional output from transformer block to 768 dimensional vector. Before feeding feature encoder output to context network(tranformer encoder) latent speech representation Z is masked by taking $p = 0.065$ random samples as starting indices and then masking the next $M = 5$ frames. For the quantization block, 512 dimensional input vector is fed to it which after quantization produces a 768 dimensional output vector. Overall, the model has 300 million parameters. The optimizer considered is adam optimizer with learning rate of 0.003.

Fine-Tuning with Labeled Data. wav2vec2.0 learns cross-lingual information and is able to learn speech representation units that can capture the common phonetic information across multiple languages. For fine-tuning, an 80-dimensional log Mel Spectrogram is considered. Window size of 30ms is chosen with an overlap of 15 ms, which is finally flattened to 1D vector and fed to the wav2ec2.0 model. Log mel Spectrogram is preferred over raw speech as different languages have different spectral features that are correctly captured by mel spectrogram. As shown in Fig. 1. The attention, linear, and softmax layers are stacked over the wav2vec encoder. Fine-tuning is done on the IIITH-ILSC database. To improve the learning of the model for low-resource languages, the database has been partitioned into three segments: 20 min, 2.5 h, and 12 h, with

Table 1. LID test Accuracy (%) and EER for 23 languages setup varying the dataset.

Duration	20 min	2.5 h	12 h
Accuracy	82.10	86.27	88.13
EER	13.18	11.56	10.14

each language having a nearly equal amount of labeled data with train, test split ratio as 80:20. The duration of labeled data for each language in these segments are approximately 1 min, 6 min, and 30 min, respectively. This approach aids in addressing the possibility of LID training for low-resource languages and also enhances the accuracy for high-resource languages.

Further audio samples are chopped to 6 s because attention cost is actually $O(n^2)$ in sequence_length, therefore using longer length explodes in complexity/memory. Classifier is fed with this 6 s speech input which gives out a 23-dimensional vector, where ith value represented the probability of the speech input belonging to ith language. The language with the highest probability in the vector is considered the final prediction. Table 1 depicts the EER of our model on different dataset sizes.

6   Experimental Results

The performance of the proposed LID system is compared with state-of-the-art LID systems on the IIITH-ILSC database. For comparison, an equal error rate is used. It is the point in the Receiver Operating Characteristic(ROC) curve where the false acceptance and false rejection rates are the same, hence lower EER depicts higher accuracy. Table 2. presents the results of various LID systems. EER mentioned is the average EER of all 23 languages. The results were compared with those obtained using i-vector, DNN, and DNN with attention. In these, for feature representation 39 dimensional (13 static + delta + delta-delta) Mel frequency cepstral features are used. Additionally, the performance of our model was compared with that of the Multi-head attention (MHA) model combined with DNN, ResNets, and DenseResNets with both MFCC and SDC features. SDC features performed better as they captured language-related information, hence it is observed that architectures that capture longer temporal dependencies perform better for LID.

For Joint Acoustic Model(JAM), The system was tested on six Indian languages, namely Hindi, Marathi, Odia, Telugu, Tamil, and Gujarati. When it is trained using combined data from all languages, it gives an average EER of 10.39. Although when JAM is trained monolingually it gives an EER of 24.21%, 17.43%, 25.81%, 17.90%, 17.33%, and 14.82% for Hindi, Marathi, Odia, Telugu, Tamil, and Gujarati respectively. So multilingual training helps in learning cross-lingual information and hence the combined accuracy of each language identification increases. Although multi-lingual training of JAM gives good results

Table 2. Performance comparison of the proposed Wav2vec model LID system to the other state-of-the-art works on the IIITH-ILSC database.

IIITH-ILSC		
Study	System	EER
Ravi et al. [15]	i-vector	17.77
	DNN	17.99
	DNN-A	15.18
Sequential model	LSTM	12.82
MHA	ResNets	12.34
	DenseResNets	12.06
XLSR-53 pre-trained (14th layer)	15.56	
Wav2vec2.0-XLSR-53 fine-tuned model	**10.14**	

but it has to be trained on large amount of labeled data which is a barrier for low-resource languages.

Residual and Dense Residual Networks were also explored using SDC features and Adam optimizer. Resnet is tested using 4 and 9 blocks and also using 0-1-0, 1-1-1, 2-1-2, and 3-1-3 stacked SDC features and the best result was obtained for 4 blocks and 2-1-2 features and learning rate of 0.001 for adam optimizer. For Dense Resnet 7 and 9 blocks are tested and 7 blocks performed better with 2-1-2 stacked SDC feature and learning rate of 0.0001.

The pre-trained Wav2vec2.0-XLSR-53 model was investigated without fine-tuning and coupled with multi-head attention system. Result shown in Table 2. are features from 14th encoder layer of transformer in wav2vec2.0 architecture. In terms of equal error rate, the trend shows a decrease in EER up to the 11th encoder layer, followed by a nearly constant EER until the 18th layer, and then a sharp increase. However, after fine-tuning, the features from the 24th layer outperform the rest, as the EER continuously decreased.

Fine-tuned wav2vec2.0-XLSR-53 was evaluated in comparison to these architectures, with the use of only 12 h of total labeled data (roughly 30 min for each language). The results of our model showed a substantial improvement in language identification performance.

7 Conclusion

This study explores features from wav2vec2.0-XLSR-53 for Language Identification task. By pre-training on multiple languages in a self-supervised manner, the acoustic modeling and cross-lingual information learning were significantly improved. This is particularly helpful for low-resource Indian languages that lack labeled data. For low-resource languages like Maithili, Sindhi where other LID systems like DNN-A gave an EER of around 28% EER, Resnets with MHA gave around 25% EER, our proposed features gave around 15% EER. The reason for this is that the model acquired knowledge of the phonetic space common to the languages, which aided in its ability to learn the acoustic properties of a new language with minimal fine-tuning. Additionally, the use of self-attention mechanism helps in learning long-range dependencies, further enhancing the performance. Therefore, the results show that the Wav2vec2.0 model is also scalable to other dialects and languages globally for the Language Identification task.

References

1. Baevski, A., Zhou, Y., Mohamed, A., Auli, M.: wav2vec 2.0: a framework for self-supervised learning of speech representations. Adv. Neural. Inf. Process. Syst. **33**, 12449–12460 (2020)
2. Balleda, J., Murthy, H.A., Nagarajan, T.: Language identification from short segments of speech. In: Sixth International Conference on Spoken Language Processing (2000)
3. Bartz, C., Herold, T., Yang, H., Meinel, C.: Language identification using deep convolutional recurrent neural networks. In: Liu, D., Xie, S., Li, Y., Zhao, D., El-Alfy, E.S.M. (eds.) Neural Information Processing, pp. 880–889. Springer International Publishing, Cham (2017). https://doi.org/10.1007/978-3-319-70136-3_93
4. Dehak, N., Torres-Carrasquillo, P.A., Reynolds, D., Dehak, R.: Language recognition via i-vectors and dimensionality reduction. In: Proceedings of INTERSPEECH (2011)
5. Diwan, A., et al.: MUCS 2021: multilingual and code-switching ASR challenges for low resource Indian languages. In: Interspeech 2021. ISCA (2021). https://doi.org/10.21437/interspeech.2021-1339
6. Jothilakshmi, S., Ramalingam, V., Palanivel, S.: A hierarchical language identification system for Indian languages. Digital Signal Process. **22**, 544–553 (2012). https://doi.org/10.1016/j.dsp.2011.11.008
7. Kukk, K., Alumäe, T.: Improving Language Identification of Accented Speech. In: Proceedings of Interspeech 2022, pp. 1288–1292 (2022). https://doi.org/10.21437/Interspeech.2022-10455
8. Kumar Vuddagiri, R., Vydana, H.K., Kumar Vuppala, A.: Improved language identification using stacked SDC features and residual neural network. In: Proceedings of the 6th International Workshop on Spoken Language Technologies for Under-Resourced Languages, pp. 210–214 (2018). https://doi.org/10.21437/SLTU.2018-44
9. Li, M., Narayanan, S.: Simplified supervised i-vector modeling with application to robust and efficient language identification and speaker verification. Comput. Speech Lang. **28**(4), 940–958 (2014)
10. Lopez-Moreno, I., Gonzalez-Dominguez, J., Plchot, O., Martinez, D., Gonzalez-Rodriguez, J., Moreno, P.: Automatic language identification using deep neural networks. In: Acoustics, Speech and Signal Processing (ICASSP), 2014 IEEE International Conference on, pp. 5337–5341. IEEE (2014)
11. Lopez-Moreno, I., Gonzalez-Dominguez, J., Plchot, O., Martinez, D., Gonzalez-Rodriguez, J., Moreno, P.: Automatic language identification using deep neural networks. In: 2014 IEEE International Conference on Acoustics, Speech and Signal Processing (ICASSP), pp. 5337–5341 (2014). https://doi.org/10.1109/ICASSP.2014.6854622

12. Maity, S., Vuppala, A.K., Rao, K.S., Nandi, D.: IITKGP-MLILSC speech database for language identification. In: Communications (NCC), 2012 National Conference on, pp. 1–5. IEEE (2012)

13. Mary, L., Yegnanarayana, B.: Autoassociative neural network models for language identification. In: International Conference on Intelligent Sensing and Information Processing, 2004. Proceedings of, pp. 317–320. IEEE (2004)

14. Nandi, D., Pati, D., Rao, K.S.: Language identification using Hilbert envelope and phase information of linear prediction residual. In: 2013 International Conference Oriental COCOSDA held jointly with 2013 Conference on Asian Spoken Language Research and Evaluation (O-COCOSDA/CASLRE), pp. 1–6. IEEE (2013)

15. Ravi Kumar, V., Gurugubelli, K., Jain, P., Vydana, H.K., Vuppala, A.K.: IIITH-ILSC speech database for Indian language identification. In: Proceedings in the 6th International Workshop on Spoken Language Technologies for Under-Resourced Languages (SLTU'18), pp. 56–60 (2018)

16. Tirusha, M., Kumar, V.R., Krishna, V.H., Kumar, V.A.: An investigation of LSTM-CTC based joint acoustic model for Indian language identification. In: 2019 IEEE Automatic Speech Recognition and Understanding Workshop (ASRU), pp. 389–396 (2019). https://doi.org/10.1109/ASRU46091.2019.9003784

17. Torres-Carrasquillo, P.A., Reynolds, D.A., Deller, J.R.: Language identification using Gaussian mixture model tokenization. In: Proceedings of the IEEE International Conference Acoustics, Speech and Signal Processing, vol. 1, pp. I-757–I-760. IEEE (2002)

18. Vydana, H.K., Gurugubelli, K., Raju, V.V.V., Vuppala, A.K.: An exploration towards joint acoustic modeling for Indian languages: IIIT-H submission for low resource speech recognition challenge for indian languages, INTERSPEECH 2018. In: Proceedings of Interspeech 2018, pp. 3192–3196 (2018). https://doi.org/10.21437/Interspeech.2018-1584

19. Zaeemzadeh, A., Rahnavard, N., Shah, M.: Norm-preservation: why residual networks can become extremely deep? CoRR abs/1805.07477 (2018). http://arxiv.org/abs/1805.07477

20. Zazo, R., Lozano-Diez, A., Gonzalez-Dominguez, J., Toledano, D., Gonzalez-Rodriguez, J.: Language identification in short utterances using long short-term memory (LSTM) recurrent neural networks. PloS one 11, e0146917 (2016). https://doi.org/10.1371/journal.pone.0146917

21. Zissman, M.A., Berkling, K.M.: Automatic language identification. Speech Commun. **35**(1–2), 115–124 (2001)

Design and Development of Voice OTP Authentication System

Pavanitha Manche[(✉)], Sahaja Nandyala, Jagabandhu Mishra,
Gayathri Ananthanarayanan, and S. R. Mahadeva Prasanna

Indian Institute of Technology Dharwad, Dharwad 580011, India
{200010027,200010032,jagabandhu.mishra.18,gayathri,prasanna}@iitdh.ac.in

Abstract. Voice OTP Authentication (VOA) provides authorization for a speaker by validating the spoken One-Time Password(OTP) and the speaker's identity. Even though Speaker Recognition and Digit Recognition techniques are fairly mature, the exploration in the direction of the development of VOA systems is limited. This work proposes a speaker and speech representation-based framework to develop the VOA system. Our design uses ECAPA-TDNN based speaker representation and wav2vec conformer-based digit representation to perform VOA. The achieved performance of the speaker identification, OTP identification, and the combined VOA system in the DigitUtter-IITDH dataset in terms of identification accuracy are 96.75%, 83.25% and 78.92%, respectively. Further, to deploy the VOA system on an edge device, we conduct a comprehensive performance analysis by deploying the proposed VOA system from a high-end server class machine to an embedded edge device. Our experimental results indicate that the average inference time for an OTP Authentication using an edge device is 3.14 seconds, while it takes 0.05 seconds on the server class system.

Keywords: Voice OTP · Speaker Identification · Digit Recognition

1 Introduction

The proliferation of businesses across the world with remote work and distributed teams necessitates the development and deployment of remote authentication systems [3,13]. Remote authentication systems allow users to access their accounts and resources from anywhere with an active internet connection. *Voice OTP Authentication* (VOA) is one such system that provides two-level authentication: (1) verifies the speaker's identity and (2) verifies the spoken OTP. Speaker Recognition (SR) and Digit Recognition (DR) are matured speech technologies and provide acceptable performance in practical deployments [3,17]. It also leverages the uniqueness of an individual's voice, making it difficult for unauthorized users to impersonate someone else. It is particularly beneficial for users with disabilities or those with difficulty typing or using traditional authentication methods. Hence, compared to other authentication alternatives, the VOA system is preferable as a low-cost, easy-to-use

A. Karpov et al. (Eds.): SPECOM 2023, LNAI 14339, pp. 513–528, 2023.
https://doi.org/10.1007/978-3-031-48312-7_41

solution. The VOA system can have a broad spectrum of applications and is not limited to online banking, remote logins to workstations, attendance systems, etc. However, the work related to VOA is still at a nascent stage in the literature.

In this work, we propose a VOA system framework, and Fig. 1 depicts a practical use case of the same. In the proposed framework, the user requests the authentication system to access his personal data. The authentication system in turn, sends a request to the OTP generator module to generate a N digit OTP, and the generated OTP is forwarded to the user. The user utters the received OTP, and using the user's utterance, the authentication system verifies the speaker's identity and deciphers the spoken OTP. Finally, if the identity and spoken OTP are correct, the authentication system provides access to the personal data and asks the user for another attempt if otherwise.

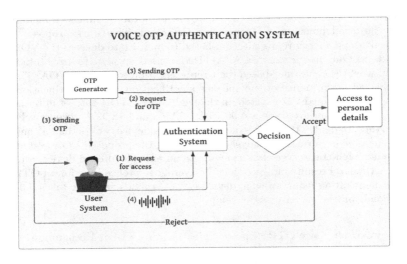

Fig. 1. Working of Voice OTP Authentication system.

In the early days, SR and DR were explored by proposing various feature extraction and modelling techniques [5,13]. The feature-based techniques have evolved over time by analyzing the production and perception mechanism of the speech signal [11,13–15,18]. The Mel frequency cepstral coefficient (MFCC), and perceptual linear prediction (PLP) have been proposed with respect to the perception mechanism of speech [12,13] while the linear prediction cepstral coefficient (LPCC), residual LPC, and residual phase-based features have been proposed for the production mechanism of speech [10,16,18]. Mostly, the formant (spectral resonances) locations and their dynamics play an important role in identifying both speaker and digit, hence parameterized in different ways [4,13]. Out of them, MFCC has shown to be successful over the rest for both digit and Speaker Recognition tasks [4,13]. Further, the features are modelled using `vector quantization (VQ)`, `Gaussian mixture model (GMM)`, and `i-vector` to perform the SI task while `GMM-hidden Markov model (GMM-HMM)` is largely used [5,8,13] for digit recognition. As acoustic features are sensitive to changes in acoustics in terms of device and environment variation, these systems are always built in a controlled scenario by constraining on the particular type of recording device and environment.

Deep Learning has become ubiquitous with applications across various fields. Recently, various Speaker Recognition techniques have been proposed using deep learning frameworks. Some of the existing works in the literature are Deep Neural Network–Hidden Markov Model (DNN-HMM) [17], Deepspeech2 [1], wav2vec-transformer [2], and wav2vec-conformer models [7] used to perform speech recognition task. Similarly, starting from the DNN-i-vector system, d-vector, x-vector, and emphasized channel attention, propagation, and aggregation (ECAPA-TDNN) based x-vector approaches have been proposed to perform the speaker identification task. The limitation of the traditional system design to a particular recording device and environment is relaxed by the use of pre-trained open-sourced task-specific deep learning models [2,3]. These models are trained with large amounts of speech data to perform a particular task. Further, these models achieve better performance for the SI task even when trained with a small utterance duration. However, the DI task in a given language is almost zero-shot. Motivated by these assumptions, the hypothesis is that *the use of speaker representation from the ECAPA-TDNN model* (trained in VoxCeleb [9]) and *digit representation from conformer-based wav2vec (W2V) model* (fine-tuned with Indian English [6]) can be helpful in developing the VOA system.

This work initially performs speaker identification (SI) with traditional approaches by considering MFCC-VQ and MFCC-GMM frameworks and compares the performance with the ECAPA TDNN-based speaker representation framework. Further, this work proposes a framework for training the speaker representation by generating utterances corresponding to the fixed OTP sequences. We then use the conformer-based W2V model to decode the uttered OTP sequence. We also augment this decoder with a rule-based wrapper algorithm to improve the accuracy of the decoded output. We use the combination of the output of the decoded OTP and the output of SI to evaluate the performance of the VOA system. Furthermore, for studying the feasibility of deploying the VOA system with different end devices, we consider the inference time as well as the run-time memory requirements.

The rest of the paper is organized as follows: Sect. 2 discusses the motivation for using the speaker and digit representation for designing the VOA system. Section 3 details the database used in this work. Section 4 provides the details of the proposed framework for the VOA system, while Sect. 5 discusses the experimental results. Finally, Sect. 6 presents the summary and future work directions.

2   Motivation for Using the Speaker and Digit Representations

We begin with the t-Distributed Stochastic Neighbor Embedding (t-SNE) distribution of the speaker and digit representations. The aim of this is to see whether the speaker representations of each speaker form a different cluster. Similarly, whether the digit representations of each digit form a different cluster. Figure 2 provides the t-SNE plots of speakers and digits representations.

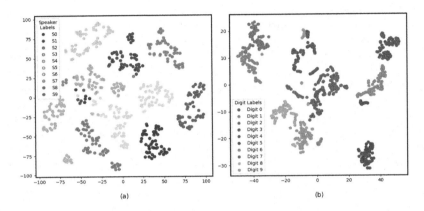

Fig. 2. t-SNE Visualization of (a) Speaker representations and (b) digits representations.

For this t-SNE study, we use utterances from 10 speakers and 100 utterances from each speaker. We consider any two random digits uttered by the speaker to observe the speaker's discrimination. Similarly, for each digit, we consider 10 utterances spoken by 10, different speakers to observe the digit discrimination. To obtain the speaker's representation for a given utterance, the filter bank features are extracted from the speech signal by considering 25 msec as the frame size and 10 msec as the frameshift. The filter bank features are then passed through the ECAPA-TDNN model (trained in the Voxceleb data and available at[1].) to obtain the 192 dimensional speaker representations. The obtained speaker representations for all the 10 speakers are projected in 2 dimension using t-SNE. The two-dimensional vectors are depicted in Fig. 2(a). From the figure, we can observe that the speaker representations are forming clusters with respect to the speakers, and overlapping between them is significantly less. This motivates us to use the ECAPA-TDNN-based speaker representations to perform the SI task. Similarly, as the W2V model works on signal level, the speech utterances are directly passed through the finetuned model (fine-tuned with 700 hours of Indian English data and available at[2]) to obtain the speech representations in every 20

---

[1] https://catalog.ngc.nvidia.com/orgs/nvidia/teams/nemo/models/ecapa_tdnn.

[2] https://github.com/Open-Speech-EkStep/vakyansh-models.

msec. For a given digit utterance, the speech representations are statistically pooled to obtain the digit representation. The digit representations for each digit are also projected using t-SNE to a two-dimensional plane, and the same is depicted in Fig. 2(b). From the figure, we can observe that similar to speakers', the digit representations also form distinct clusters, thus motivating us to use the digit representations to perform the OTP identification task.

3   Details of the Datasets

In this work, we use two databases: (1) In-house data and (2) Kaggle MNIST digit data to develop the VOA system. The dataset details are provided in the following subsections and summarized in Table 1.

3.1   In-House Dataset

The dataset was collected from students at IIT Dharwad, consisting of contributions from 50 speakers, with 47 being male and 3 being female speakers. The average age of the speakers is 20. Each speaker is asked to give 4 sessions, and in each session, speakers are asked to utter the digits $0-9$ with a pause after each digit. Further, after listening to the utterance, the speech belonging to each digit is manually segregated. The collected data is referred to as `DigitUtter-IITDH` dataset. The collected dataset is available at[3]DigitUtter-IITDH-dataset.

3.2   Kaggle MNIST Digit Dataset

The Kaggle MNIST Digit dataset is used as reference data to perform the initial experiments[4]. This dataset comprises voice recordings of 60 speakers, out of which 48 are male and 12 are female, all with an American accent. Each speaker contributed 50 sessions dedicated to pronouncing the digits 0 to 9. Throughout this work, we refer to this dataset as the `Kaggle Data`.

Table 1. Summary of Datasets.

Dataset	In-house Data	Kaggle Data
Speakers	50	60
Sessions	4	50
Digits	0–9	0–9

---

[3] https://github.com/mcqueen444/DigitUtter-IITDH-dataset.
[4] https://github.com/soerenab/AudioMNIST.

4   Proposed Framework for the Voice OTP Authentication System

The proposed VOA system consists of four modules (1) `OTP Generation`, (2) `Speaker Identification`, (3) `OTP Identification`, and (4) `Decision Logic`. Figure 3 presents the block diagram of the proposed VOA system. The details of each module are provided in the following subsections.

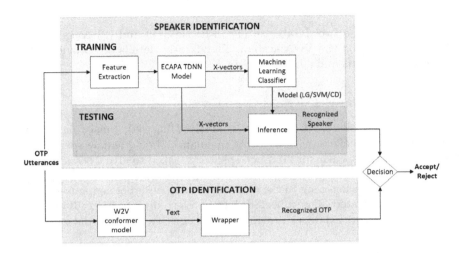

Fig. 3. Block diagram for Voice OTP Authentication system. LR, SVM, and CD denote Logistic Regression, Support Vector Machine, and Cosine Distance, respectively.

4.1   OTP Generation

In this work, OTPs with varying lengths of $1-4$ digits were generated using both DigitUtter-IITDH and Kaggle datasets. Using the DigitUtter-IITDH dataset, for a fixed OTP length of N digits, all possible combinations (i.e. 10^N) are generated as different OTPs. After that, the segregated digit-specific utterances are stitched together to form OTP utterances. Figure 4 depicts the OTP utterance generation process. The OTP utterances belonging to the first three sessions are used for training, and the fourth session is used for testing. The number of generated OTP utterances per speaker per session and the train test split is summarized in Table 2. Further, while generating OTP utterances from the Kaggle data, to make the number of training and testing utterances the same as the DigitUtter-IITDH data, the digits are sampled randomly from the sessions $1-40$ for training and $41-50$ for testing.

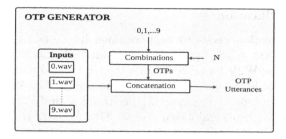

Fig. 4. Working principle of OTP Generator.

Table 2. Summary of OTP datasets that are generated, N refers to the Number of Digits in OTP.

Number of digits in the OTP (N)	1	2	3	4
Utterances per Speaker per Session	10	100	1000	10000
Total Training Utterances per Speaker	30	300	3000	30000
Total Testing Utterances per Speaker	10	100	1000	10000

4.2 Speaker Identification

After generating the OTP utterances, the speaker representations are extracted from the ECAPA-TDNN model. The ECAPA-TDNN model takes the filter bank features extracted from the speech signal (by considering 0.025 as the frame size and 0.01 secs as the frameshift) as input and is trained to classify the speakers. The model has several TDNN layers, a temporal pooling layer, and some fully connected layers. The architecture details can be found in [9]. The TDNN layers work on the frame level, the temporal pooling layer pools the frame-level information of a given utterance to a fixed-dimension vector, and then the fully connected layers work on the utterance level to classify the speaker. After training, the classifier layer is detached from the network and is used as a speaker representation extractor.

In this study, we use the ECAPA-TDNN model available in the NVIDIA NeMo toolkit [5]. The ECAPA-TDNN model is already pre-trained using the development set of the VoxCeleb-1 and two datasets having 7205 speakers with several thousands of hours of speech data. After obtaining the filter bank features from each utterance, the filter bank features are used to extract the speaker representations from the ECAPA-TDNN model. The extracted speaker representations from the ECAPA-TDNN model are well known as `x-vectors` [9]. We leverage the extracted x-vectors in two ways: (1) model-based and (2) model-free, to perform the SI task. The model-based approach includes the training of classifiers like Logistic Regression (LR) and Support Vector Machine (SVM), whereas the model-free approach uses a simple Cosine Distance (CD) based comparison.

---

[5] https://catalog.ngc.nvidia.com/orgs/nvidia/teams/nemo/models/ecapa_tdnn.

4.3 OTP Identification

The OTP Identification needs to be performed by decoding the OTP utterances through an Automatic Speech Recognition(ASR) model trained in Indian English. We use the W2V-based conformer model, trained and open-sourced by the Vakyansh team [6] to perform the OTP decoding. The W2V model training is generally done in two stages: (1) pre-training and (2) fine-tuning. The model is pre-trained using unlabeled speech data from 39 Indian languages of approximately 35000 hours. The pre-trained network is then finetuned with 700 hours of labelled Indian English speech data. The fine-tuned model is available at vakyansh-models.

This work uses the fine-tuned ASR model to decode the OTP utterances in the testing phase of the framework. The decoder generally outputs the orthographic form of the numbers. Hence, a wrapper algorithm is designed to convert them to numeric output. Further, in some cases, it is observed that instead of "two", "to" is decoded. The wrapper algorithm has also handled the same issue, i.e., if any of the letters are missing in the decoding, the same is substituted and converted to the corresponding numerical value. The wrapper algorithm is explained in Algorithm 1.

The decoded OTP from the W2V-based conformer model is directly given as input to the wrapper. Initially, the algorithm creates a dictionary D, storing all possible sub-words for each digit. Each sub-word is paired with its corresponding digit as the value. To construct D, the algorithm takes the alphabetical representation of the digits 0–9 in a list T. It then iterates over each element in T to generate all possible sub-words for each number, starting from a minimum length of 2 letters. Sub-words with only one letter are not considered as they cannot uniquely represent a digit. Once D is prepared, the decoded OTP words are processed individually. The algorithm checks each word against the keys in D to convert each digit to its original form. This process allows the algorithm to decode the OTP successfully.

4.4 Decision Logic

In this module, the final decision is made for the VOA system by combining the outputs given by the SI and the OTP Identification module. The identified speaker and decoded OTP are verified with the claimant's identity and generated OTP. The system will accept the trial only if both decisions are positive. If any one of the decisions is negative, the trial will be rejected.

5 Experimental Results and Discussions

In this section, we discuss the performance of the proposed system, along with the time to identify the speaker as well as the decoding of the OTP (inference time) and runtime memory consumption on various end devices.

We conducted several experiments to explore various aspects of the proposed VOA system.

Algorithm 1: Digit Recognition Wrapper

Input : transcription
Output: pred

```
1   T ← ["zero", "one", "two", "three", "four", "five", "six", "seven", "eight", "nine"];
2   D ← {} ;                                          // dictionary for Substrings and digits
3   for i ← 0 to len(T) do
4   │   S ← T[i] ;                                     // Current text
5   │   for L ← 2 to len(S) + 1 do
6   │   │   for start ← 0 to len(S) - L + 1 do
7   │   │   │   sub ← S[start : start + L] ;           // Substring
8   │   │   │   D[sub] ← i ;                           // Store
9   │   │   end
10  │   end
11  end
12  pred ← '' ;                                        // Prediction string
13  for w ∈ transcription.split() do
14  │   if w ∈ D then
15  │   │   d ← D[w] ;                                  // Retrieve digit
16  │   │   pred += str(d) ;                            // Append digit
17  │   end
18  end
```

---

1. We begin with experiments to quantify the gains of using x-vector representations over the traditional VQ and GMM-based framework to perform the SI task.
2. We then perform extensive studies using the model-based approach by varying the OTP length N and the number of training samples to understand its impact on the SI performance
3. We then evaluate the performance of the VOA system by implementing it in different end devices.

In this study, the following three different devices with varying performance capabilities were selected to understand the performance variation and assess the feasibility of practical deployment:

- **Server**: 24-Core Intel(R) Xeon(R) W-2265 CPU @ 3.50 GHz.
- **Desktop**: 8-Core Intel(R) Core(TM) i7-8550U CPU @ 1.80 GHz.
- **Edge Device**: 4-core ARM Cortex-A73 CPU @ 1.80 GHz and a 2-core ARM Cortex-A53 CPU @ 1.90 GHz.

5.1 SI with X-vector-based Speaker Representation

The aim of the experiment is to showcase the significance of the x-vector-based framework over the traditional VQ and GMM framework and quantify the achievable performance gains. We use the in-house `DigitUtter-IITDH` dataset to perform this set of experiments. From the dataset, we use the utterances from the first 3 sessions to train the VQ and GMM classifier by extracting the MFCC features from the speech signal (0.02 and 0.01 are the framesize and frameshift, respectively). We swift through a range of cluster sizes by varying the number of clusters from 32 to 256 and found that the cluster size of 64 performs the best. Thus, in our experiments, the VQ and GMM are trained with a cluster size of 64. Similarly, we extract the x-vectors from the training utterances and then model them using SVM and LR. We use the utterances belonging to the 4th session for the testing. The obtained result in terms of identification accuracy is tabulated in Table 3. From the table, it can be observed that the best performance obtained using the x-vector framework is 100%, in contrast to the best performance obtained in the traditional framework is 88%. This shows the significance of the x-vector-based framework over traditional frameworks to perform the SI task.

Table 3. Accuracy variation across various feature vectors.

Vectors	Model	Accuracy
MFCC	VQ	80%
	GMM	88%
x-vector	SVM	**100%**
	LR	98%

5.2   SI by Varying the OTP Length in both Training and Testing

This experiment aims to observe the variation in SI performance when varying OTP length during training and testing. For this, we use the OTP utterances generated from the first three sessions with a given OTP length N to extract the x-vectors and then train the LR and SVM classifier. The OTP length varies from one to four. We tabulate the obtained results with the LR classifier in Table 4 and with the SVM classifier in Table 5. From the tables, it can be observed that irrespective of the classifier, the performance improves with an increase in the OTP length. Further, it is also observed that the performance of the same OTP length training and testing is comparatively better than the cross-OTP length scenarios. We thus recommend using the same OTP length for both training and testing.

Table 4. Logistic Regression (%)

Train \ Test	1	2	3	4
1	**66.26**	53.06	42.26	23.33
2	55.28	**87.29**	87.29	81.30
3	39.72	78.05	**93.57**	92.96
4	29.54	66.13	86.58	**96.75**

Table 5. SVM (%)

Train \ Test	1	2	3	4
1	**29.34**	27.67	31.39	22.74
2	56.29	**86.09**	83.07	67.15
3	41.92	79.70	**93.99**	93.94
4	27.94	65.33	85.71	**96.40**

5.3 SI by Varying the Number of Training OTP Utterances

The aim of this experiment is to decide on the number of OTP utterances per speaker required to perform the SI task. The possible OTP utterances increase exponentially with an increase in the OTP length. Considering all the possible combinations will increase the enrollment time. Hence, we perform the SI experiment for $N = 4$ by randomly selecting 3000, 6000 OTP utterances per speaker from all possible OTP utterances and compared its performance with that of using all possible OTP utterances (i.e. 30000 per speaker). We provide the obtained performance in Table 6. Our results indicate that the performance achieved by randomly considering 6000 OTP utterance per speaker from all the possible 30000 OTP utterances is similar to the maximum achievable performance.

Table 6. Impact of Training Data Size on the SI performance.

# Utterances per Speaker in Train Data	LR Accuracy
3000	95.90%
6000	**96.75%**
30000	**96.75%**

5.4 SI with Model-Based and Model-Free Approach

We implement the SI task with model-based LR, SVM classifier, and model-free CD approach using both In-house and Kaggle data. In the CD-based approach, we extract the speaker-specific mean vectors and store them as a speaker representation. During testing, the test x-vector is compared with all the speaker representations using CD, and the speaker with the maximum cosine distance obtained is declared as the identified speaker.

We provide the obtained performance in Table 7. From the table, it can be observed that the LR with $N = 4$ performs better compared to the rest in both in-house and Kaggle datasets. The best performance in the in-house data is 96.75%, and with Kaggale data is 99.9%. The performance gap is due to the differences in the speaker's accent. Kaggle and Voxceleb have similar accents, whereas, in In-house data, all the speakers have Indian accents. Further, when using the model-free approach, the difference is even greater. The best performance achieved in In-house data is 74.45%, while in Kaggle data, it is 99.91%. Hence in the future, to further improve the performance of SI, the network should be fine-tuned with the in-house training data.

Table 7. Performance of SI

Model Name	N	In-house Data Accuracy	Kaggle Data Accuracy
SVM	1	2.00%	90.17%
	2	80.64%	99.55%
	3	94.01%	99.98%
	4	95.91%	**99.996%**
LR	1	66.27%	92.17%
	2	87.29%	99.68%
	3	94.23%	99.97%
	4	**96.75%**	**99.99%**
CD	1	53.87 %	91.83%
	2	64.68%	99.06%
	3	67.15%	99.72 %
	4	**74.45%**	**99.91%**

Table 8. Performance of OI

Number of Digits	Number of samples	Accuracy
1	500	50.70%
2	5000	74.58%
3	5000	78.89%
4	5000	**81.16%**

5.5 OTP Identification

We use the In-house data to evaluate the performance of the OTP Identification (OI) task. The total OTP utterances available with $N = 1,2, 3$ and 4 is 500, 5000, 50000 and 500000 (50×10^N), respectively. For evaluating the performance, instead of considering all the OTP utterances, for $N = 1$, all 500 and for $N = 2, 3$ and 4 randomly picked 5000 utterances are considered. We tabulate the resulting performance in Table 8. The OI task provides the best performance of 81.16% in terms of identification accuracy for $N = 4$. Like SI, it is observed that, with an increase in OTP length, the performance of the OI system also increases.

5.6 Performance Evaluation of VOA System

We evaluate the performance of SI and OI jointly with In-house `DigitUtter-IITDH` dataset, calculating combined accuracy by intersecting their probabilities. For SI, LR (model-based) and CD (model-free), we use the W2V conformer model and wrapper algorithm to perform the OI task. The results, as shown in

Table 9, reveal that the best accuracy achieved is 78.92% for model-based SI and 73.98% for model-free SI. The lower combined accuracy is due to the requirement for both SI and OI tasks to be simultaneously correct for authentication. Further, it can be observed from the table that the OI performance is inferior to the performance achieved in the SI task. In the future, the performance may be improved by finetuning the W2V conformer architecture with the training OTP utterances.

Table 9. The accuracy of the integrated processes involving Speaker identification (SI) and OTP Identification (OI). Note: OI is evaluated independently of LR and CD.

Model	Number of digits in test Data	SI Accuracy	OI Accuracy	Combined Accuracy
LR	1	66.26%	50.70%	32.87%
	2	87.29%	74.58%	66.14%
	3	93.58%	80.18%	75.89%
	4	96.75%	83.25%	**78.92%**
CD	1	53.09%	50.70%	33.27%
	2	64.69%	74.58%	61.10%
	3	67.15%	80.18%	65.99%
	4	74.45%	83.25%	**73.98%**

5.7   Memory Consumption Analysis

With the primary objective of implementing a VOA system on a device with limited resources, our focus was on reducing both computation time and memory usage. To address memory consumption concerns, we performed a detailed analysis of the runtime memory consumption of different steps in both tasks (SI and OI).

We conduct a comprehensive analysis of memory consumption throughout the VOA process. The modules that use larger amounts of memory are the module importation, ECAPA TDNN model loading, extraction of embeddings and vakyansh model loading (refer to Table 10). It is important to note that the memory consumption results mentioned above are specific to our model, which was trained and tested using data consisting of four-digit utterances. During the VOA process, the actual prediction stage requires less than 3 MiB of memory.

Table 10. Memory consumption at each step of the speaker verification process, CM, MI are Cumulative memory, Memory Increment at that step respectively.

Step	CM	MI
Importing modules	520 – 525 MiB	520 – 525 MiB
Loading ECAPA TDNN model	1930 – 1940 MiB	1407 – 1417 MiB
Extracting embeddings	3626 – 3628 MiB	1695 – 1698 MiB
Loading trained model and predicting	3626 – 3628 MiB	0.2 – 0.4 MiB
Loading vakyansh	4338 – 4340 MiB	711 – 713 MiB
Transcription	4340 – 4342 MiB	2.6 – 2.9 MiB

5.8   Feasibility Exploration on Different Platforms

The main objective is to study the feasibility of implementing a VOA system on low-resource devices. For this, a series of evaluations are performed to measure the proposed model's computational performance and memory usage on various devices mentioned in Sect. 5.

Table 11. Performance and Computational Time Comparison on Devices Server-CPU (SC), Laptop-CPU (LC), Odroid-N2 (OD) for Speaker Identification and OTP Identification with Logistic Regression (LR) and Cosine Distance (CD) methods.

# Digits	LR						CD					
	Accuracy(%)			Time(s)			Accuracy(%)			Time(s)		
	SC	LC	OD	SC	LC	OD	SC	LC	OD	SC	LC	OD
1	32.9	32.9	32.9	**0.0519**	0.5468	1.7357	33.3	33.3	33.3	0.0398	0.5284	1.5575
2	71.6	71.8	71.8	0.0555	0.7229	2.262	61.2	61.2	61.2	0.0424	0.9451	2.2203
3	85.4	85.4	85.4	0.0609	1.1859	2.759	63.4	63.4	63.4	0.4512	1.2341	2.9556
4	79	79	79	0.0593	1.3685	**3.1377**	70.6	70.6	70.6	0.0486	1.4675	3.0473

Table 11 presents the overall performance and computational time for both SI and OI tasks across various devices. The time values mentioned here are the average computational time taken by a particular model across the given OTPs for a specific digit. Also, the results shown here are from analyzing only a small number of OTP utterances. As seen, the accuracy scores for each device are consistent with one another. This suggests both the SI and OI modules deliver similar levels of accuracy across all the tested devices. Thus, this ensures the model can be deployed on any of the devices.

As seen from table, the time to process a 4-digit OTP on the edge device is ≈ 3 s while on the server, it is 0.05 seconds and 1.4 seconds on the desktop. Even though the edge device performs ≈ 50x slower than the server, with respect to the device footprint, power requirement, and cost, the edge devices are preferable for practical deployment. In the future, the aim is to optimize the model such that the computation time in the edge device can be improved.

6 Conclusion and Future Work

In summary, this work demonstrated the significance of speaker and digit representations obtained from the ECAPA-TDNN and W2V-conformer model to develop the VOA system. The SI component provides acceptable performance, while the OI component provides a little bit inferior performance. To address this limitation in the future, the models can be further fine-tuned with the In-house training data. Further, it is also observed that except for a lag in inference time, the performance of the VOA system is stable irrespective of the devices. In the future, the aim is to optimize the VOA system for resource-constrained environments and have a plan to integrate it into real-time applications like mobile banking.

Acknowledgements. The authors would like to acknowledge the Ministry of Electronics and Information Technology (MeitY), Govt. of India, for supporting us through different projects. Additionally, the authors also acknowledge the effort of the undergraduate students, who have contributed to the development of the DigitUtter-IITDh dataset.

References

1. Amodei, D., et al.: Deep speech 2: end-to-end speech recognition in English and mandarin. In: International Conference on Machine Learning, pp. 173–182. PMLR (2016)
2. Baevski, A., Zhou, Y., Mohamed, A., Auli, M.: wav2vec 2.0: a framework for self-supervised learning of speech representations. Adv. Neural. Inf. Process. Syst. **33**, 12449–12460 (2020)
3. Bai, Z., Zhang, X.L.: Speaker recognition based on deep learning: an overview. Neural Netw. **140**, 65–99 (2021)
4. Benesty, J., Sondhi, M.M., Huang, Y.A. (eds.): Springer Handbook of Speech Processing. SH, Springer, Heidelberg (2008). https://doi.org/10.1007/978-3-540-49127-9
5. Benzeghiba, M., De Mori, R., Deroo, O., Dupont, S., Erbes, T., Jouvet, D., Fissore, L., Laface, P., Mertins, A., Ris, C., et al.: Automatic speech recognition and speech variability: a review. Speech Commun. **49**(10–11), 763–786 (2007)
6. Chadha, H.S., et al.: Vakyansh: ASR toolkit for low resource Indic languages (2022)
7. Chung, Y.A., Zhang, Y., Han, W., Chiu, C.C., Qin, J., Pang, R., Wu, Y.: W2v-BERT: combining contrastive learning and masked language modeling for self-supervised speech pre-training. In: 2021 IEEE Automatic Speech Recognition and Understanding Workshop (ASRU), pp. 244–250. IEEE (2021)
8. Dehak, N., Kenny, P.J., Dehak, R., Dumouchel, P., Ouellet, P.: Front-end factor analysis for speaker verification. IEEE Trans. Audio Speech Lang. Process. **19**(4), 788–798 (2010)

9. Desplanques, B., Thienpondt, J., Demuynck, K.: ECAPA-TDNN: emphasized channel attention, propagation and aggregation in TDNN based speaker verification. In: Meng, H., Xu, B., Zheng, T.F. (eds.) Interspeech 2020, pp. 3830–3834. ISCA (2020)

10. Dutta, K., Mishra, J., Pati, D.: An effective combination scheme for improving speaker verification performance. In: TENCON 2017–2017 IEEE Region 10 Conference, pp. 1296–1299. IEEE (2017)

11. Dutta, K., Mishra, J., Pati, D.: Effective use of combined excitation source and vocal-tract information for speaker recognition tasks. Int. J. Speech Technol. **21**(4), 1057–1070 (2018)

12. Hermansky, H.: Perceptual linear predictive (PLP) analysis of speech. J. Acoust. Soc. Am. **87**(4), 1738–1752 (1990)

13. Kinnunen, T., Li, H.: An overview of text-independent speaker recognition: from features to supervectors. Speech Commun. **52**(1), 12–40 (2010)

14. Mishra, J., Singh, M., Pati, D.: LP residual features to counter replay attacks. In: 2018 International Conference on Signals and Systems (ICSigSys), pp. 261–266. IEEE (2018)

15. Mishra, J., Singh, M., Pati, D.: Processing linear prediction residual signal to counter replay attacks. In: 2018 International Conference on Signal Processing and Communications (SPCOM), pp. 95–99. IEEE (2018)

16. Murty, K.S.R., Yegnanarayana, B.: Combining evidence from residual phase and MFCC features for speaker recognition. IEEE Signal Process. Lett. **13**(1), 52–55 (2005)

17. Nassif, A.B., Shahin, I., Attili, I., Azzeh, M., Shaalan, K.: Speech recognition using deep neural networks: a systematic review. IEEE Access **7**, 19143–19165 (2019)

18. Prasanna, S.M., Gupta, C.S., Yegnanarayana, B.: Extraction of speaker-specific excitation information from linear prediction residual of speech. Speech Commun. **48**(10), 1243–1261 (2006)

End-to-End Native Language Identification Using a Modified Vision Transformer(ViT) from L2 English Speech

Kishan Pipariya[1]([✉]), Debolina Pramanik[2], Puja Bharati[2],
Sabyasachi Chandra[2], and Shyamal Kumar Das Mandal[2]

[1] Pandit Deendayal Energy University, Gandhinagar, Gujarat, India
Kishan.pce21@sot.pdpu.ac.in
[2] Indian Institute of Technology, Kharagpur, West Bengal, India
debolina96@kgpian.iitkgp.ac.in,
{pujabharati,sabyasachichandra}@iitkgp.ac.in, sdasmandal@cet.iitkgp.ac.in

Abstract. Native langauge identification involves identifying the mother tongue of a person from an audio recording of their speech in second language. Improving native language identification holds potential in advancing the development of more sophisticated human-computer interfaces that rely on audio inputs. Automatic speech recognition systems show a downgrade in performance when used on non-native speech, this can be mitigated by using L1 identification. Presently, the majority of research efforts in L1 identification have concentrated on employing Convolutional Neural Networks (CNNs) on audio spectrograms to predict the native language. With the emergence of Vision Transformers, which have demonstrated exceptional performance in object identification, we have adopted a modified version of the Vision Transformer model to analyze audio spectrograms for L1 identification. This approach has yielded promising outcomes on the NISP dataset which contains audio recordings of English speech of 5 regional lannguages(Hindi, Tamil, Telugu, Kannada, Malayalam) of 345 speakers. The proposed model was able to achieve an overall accuracy of 97.87% on the test dataset.

Keywords: Convolutional neural networks · End-to-end model · Mel spectrogram · L1 identification · Vision transformer

1 Introduction

The identification of an individual's native language (L1) can often be discerned through the distinct characteristics present in their speech when using a second language (L2). L1 identification, also known as native language identification, exploits this phenomenon to predict an individual's L1 based on the audio recordings of their L2 speech.

L1 identification shares similarities with accent and dialect identification, with similar models being employed for all three tasks. Enhancing the accuracy

© The Author(s), under exclusive license to Springer Nature Switzerland AG 2023
A. Karpov et al. (Eds.): SPECOM 2023, LNAI 14339, pp. 529–538, 2023.
https://doi.org/10.1007/978-3-031-48312-7_42

of these classification models can significantly contribute to the development of more precise audio-based human-computer interfaces.

This is due to the fact that a person's L1 introduces specific speech features into their L2 speech that are absent in native speakers of the L2 language. These differences negatively impact the performance of the interface.

To address the challenge of L1 identification, various models have been employed over the years to infer an individual's L1. Early models included Gaussian Mixture Models (GMMs), Hidden Markov Models (HMMs), and i-vector based models. These were subsequently succeeded by Convolutional Networks (CNNs) [12] and Recurrent Neural Networks (RNNs) [7]. These models have exhibited satisfactory performance in accurately predicting an individual's L1.

Recent advancements in L1 identification have closely followed the trends established by models used in object classification within the field of Computer Vision. Notably, Vision Transformers have recently achieved state-of-the-art performance in various computer vision tasks. [1]

Drawing inspiration from these advancements, a recent proposal introduced the Audio Spectrogram Transformer (AST) [2], which takes a spectrogram as input and employs a pre-trained Vision Transformer (ViT) model. Other transformer based models [8,13,14] are also being used more widely in various speech processing tasks and has yielded promising results.

In this paper a modified ViT architecture is proposed, which works on mel spectogram, to identify a person's L1 from l2 speech. Contribution of this paper are:

1. To the best of our knowledge ViT is nowhere used for L1 identification, this is the first time Vision Transformer is used to identify the native language of speakers.
2. This paper also checks whether macro level or micro level features of speech are important for identifying L1. Micro level features refer to features constrained to specific regions of the mel spectrogram, whereas macro level features deal with the entire mel spectrogram.

The subsequent sections of the paper proceed in the following order: we delve into the related work, followed by the end-to-end model description, experiments conducted, presentation of results, and finally, the conclusion. Section 2 describes the models proposed by other researchers for L1 identification. Section 3 provides details about the model proposed by the author. Section 4 describes the experimental setup of the author. Section 5 gives the results obtained by the author. Section 6 is the conclusion section and details the findings of the authors.

2   Related Work

There have been multiple approaches which have been used for the purpose of L1 identification over the years. One approach extracted MFCC features and used GMM, GMM-UBM and i-vector classifiers on the data. [5] This approach when tested on a custom dataset which consisted of 3 south Indian languages Kannada, Tamil, Telugu was able to achieve an overall accuracy of 93.3%.

Modified LeNet model, a type of convolutional neural network (CNN), has also been used to directly identify L1 from L2 recordings using spectrograms. [4] The experiments were conducted using the Cambridge English Corpus as dataset. The results showed an overall accuracy of 88.1% when only the raw audio file was utilized. Other CNN models such as ResNet with attentive pooling have also been used to predict L1. [12].

Hybrid model utilising both Deep Neural Networks(DNN) and Recurrent Neural Network have also seen uses for this task. [7] One such model was trained on the Native Language sub-challenge dataset from the ComParE Challenge [10]. This model first extracted short term and long term features from an audio clip. The DNN part of the model focused on the long term features whereas the RNN worked on short term features. This model was able to achieve an overall accuracy of 52.48%.

Mel frequency cepstral coefficients (MFCC) and Convolutional Restricted Boltzmann Machine (ConvRBM) can also be used for L1 prediction. One such model used the Native Language sub-challenge dataset from [10] for the purpose of training and evaluation and was able to achieve an accuracy of 40.2%. [9] Another model combined MFCCs with long term and short term CNNs for predictions. [6] This model was prepared use the NISP dataset which is the same dataset this paper is going to use in its experiment. This model achieved an overall acurracy of 79%.

Attention based models are also seeing a rise in usage with one such model taking inspiration from the Listen, Attend and Spell (LAS) model, [11]. This model took log mel filter bank features as inputs and provided probabilities for L1 identification. The Native Language sub-challenge dataset from [10] served as the corpus for experimentation. By combining multiple models, an overall accuracy of 83.32% was achieved.

Vision Transformer based models are seeing a rise in usage in a variety of speech processing tasks. But it has not yet been utilised for L1 identification. [2] [3]

3   End-to-End Model

ViT was the first image classification model which was completely based on attention mechanism and does not rely on using convolutions. ViT was able to achieve state of the art performance on the ImageNet dataset, which is the benchmark dataset for object classification. [1]

Figure 1 shows the proposed model which is a modified version of ViT. A mel spectogram of size of 384×384 pixels is fed to the model. This image is divided into multiple subimages/patches of sizes 32×32 pixels. These patches are subsequently flattened into 1-D vector representations and passed through the transformer module, resulting in a processing procedure similar to that of a standard transformer.

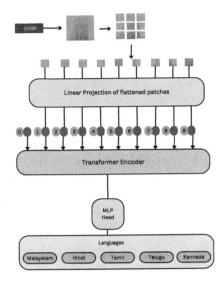

Fig. 1. Multi label L1 classification(Proposed architecture) from L2 English.

A multi-layer perceptron (MLP) head is used at the end to generate the probabilities for each language. The output of the transformer is fed to MLP as input which in turn outputs the probabilities for each label(Hindi, Kannada, Malayalam, Telugu, Tamil).

To prioritize simplicity, the relative positions of the patches were not passed to the proposed model. This decision was motivated by the relatively minor impact of spatial structure on the determination of L1 identification results. The model focuses on discerning distinctive features that distinctly characterize the L1, with the relative order of these features being inconsequential.

For the purpose of recording the baseline performance, a 4 layered CNN model, as shown in Fig. 2 anda pre-trained ResNet-18(an 18 layer CNN) is chosen. Similar models but with more layers have been used in other studies for purpose of L1 identification.

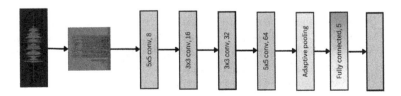

Fig. 2. Baseline CNN architecture.

4   Experiments

4.1   Corpora

The dataset utilized in this study is the NISP dataset, which was collaboratively prepared by NITK and IISc. This dataset comprises audio recordings of approximately 4-5 min from 345 speakers, encompassing both English and their respective native languages.

Within this dataset, there are five native languages represented: Hindi, Tamil, Telugu, Malayalam, and Kannada. Additionally, the dataset includes metadata such as age, nativity, language spoken with friends, medium of instruction, gender, and physical dimensions (height, weight, waist size, and shoulder size) for each speaker.

However, for the purpose of this paper, most of the metadata and the audio recordings of the speakers in their native languages have been disregarded. Instead, the focus of this experiment lies in utilizing the English recordings of the speakers and the information regarding their native language.

4.2   Experimental Setup

The experimental flow can be seen in Fig. 3.

Sampling. To ensure diversity in the dataset, a random selection process was employed, resulting in the sampling of 1500 audio clips for each language within the dataset. Subsequently, the chosen audio recordings were partitioned into three distinct sets: training, validation, and test. The training dataset consisted of 6000 clips, while the validation and testing sets comprised 750 clips each.

To leverage the parallel computing power of the GPU, each set was further divided into multiple batches, with each batch containing 64 samples. This division aimed to maximize the utilization of parallel processing capabilities.

Pre-processing. Each audio clip underwent padding or truncation to achieve a uniform length of 6 s. Additionally, random time shifting was applied to introduce variability to the clips. Finally, the clips were transformed into Mel spectrograms using a window length of 1024 ms and a hop length of 512 ms.

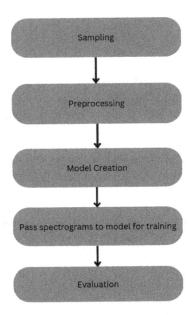

Fig. 3. The experimental flow.

In order to facilitate model compatibility, a label encoder was utilized to convert the language names into integers, as models cannot directly process strings.

Model Creation. A pre-trained Vision Transformer (ViT) model is used for L1 identification in this experiment along with a baseline 4 layer CNN model. Specifically, the "vit-patch32-384" variant, trained on the ImageNet-21k dataset and fine-tuned on the ImageNet dataset, was selected.

As the model expects images with a size of 384×384, the generated spectrograms had to be resized accordingly to ensure compatibility. To adapt the model for the task of L1 identification, the output categories were modified from the original 10,000 to 5.

For the purpose of training the model, a free instance of P100 GPU with 16 gb VRAM and system with 15 gb of RAM was used on Kaggle.

Training. The model was trained for 70 epochs using the Adam optimizer, with a scheduled learning rate (One Cycle LR) applied during training. The performance of the model on both the training and validation datasets was recorded during each epoch to facilitate the plotting of performance graphs, providing a visual representation of the model's training history.

Evaluation. The accuracy of the model was evaluated on the test dataset, followed by the creation of a confusion matrix to provide a more detailed assessment of the model's performance.

5 Result

Table 1 represents some other models, and datasets which have been used for L1 identification.

Table 1. Comparison with other models with respective datasets and accuracy.

Models	Dataset	Accuracy
Baseline	NISP	89.6%
GMM [5]	Custom	93.3%
LeNet [4]	Cambridge English Corpus	88.1%
CNN with attentive pooling [12]	ComParE challenge	86.05%
DNN +RNN [7]	ComParE challenge	52.48%
MFCC with ConvRBM [9]	ComParE challenge	40.2%
Modified LAS [11]	ComParE challenge	79%
Proposed model	NISP	**97.87%**

A simple CNN model was used as a baseline model. This CNN model showed an accuracy of 88.3%, 88.36% and 89.6% on training, validation and testing dataset respectively.

Th pre-trained ResNet-18 model show an accuracy of 99.8%, 96.7%, 96.8% on training, validation, and testing datasets respectively. The performance of Resnet-18 model can be seen in Fig. 4.

The overall accuracy of ViT model for training set was 99.8% and for validation set it was 98.9%. When the model's performance was benchmarked against test dataset its accuracy was found to be 97.87%. The comparison between the two models during training can be seen in Fig. 5 and their performance after training can be seen in Table 1.

The ViT based model showed a significant improvement over the baseline CNN model. For the chosen dataset this is the best performance recorded so far according to our knowledge.

The ViT model also does not show any major bias which can be observed from the confusion matrix in Fig. 6. Only notable observations are that Hindi was misclassified as Tamil 6 times and Kannada was misclassified as Hindi 4 times (Table 2).

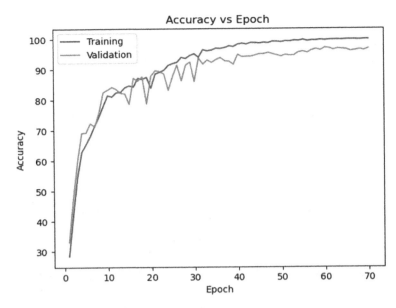

Fig. 4. ResNet-18 plot.

Table 2. Accuracies for the models on training, validation and test dataset.

	Baseline	Modified ViT(Proposed)
Training	88.3%	99.8%
Validation	88.36%	98.9%
Test	89.6%	97.87%

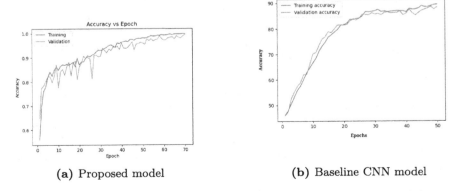

(a) Proposed model   **(b)** Baseline CNN model

Fig. 5. Training and Validation Accuracies vs Epochs for the models.

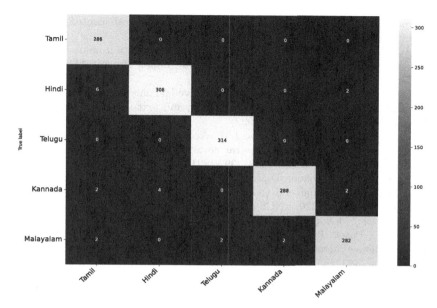

Fig. 6. Confusion Matrix for the ViT.

6   Conclusion

Proposed model showed great accuracy in predicting L1 from audio recordings in L2 compared to the baseline CNN model consisting of 4 layers. It showed an overall accuracy of 97.87% on test dataset compared to 89.6% showed by the CNN model. This shows that pure attention based models without convolutional layers are viable for L1 identification. Success of the ViT without passing additional information like the order of patches, also shows that micro features plays a major role for predicting L1. Models which focus on micro features are likely going to better perform for L1 identification.

We can also infer that other transformer based models for images which are currently existing such as beit or other transformer-based models which are created in future could also be used for this task.

References

1. Dosovitskiy, A., et al.: An image is worth 16x16 words: transformers for image recognition at scale. arXiv preprint arXiv:2010.11929 (2020)
2. Gong, Y., Chung, Y.A., Glass, J.: AST: audio spectrogram transformer. arXiv preprint arXiv:2104.01778 (2021)
3. Gong, Y., Lai, C.I., Chung, Y.A., Glass, J.: SSAST: self-supervised audio spectrogram transformer. In: Proceedings of the AAAI Conference on Artificial Intelligence, vol. 36, pp. 10699–10709 (2022)

4. Graham, C.: L1 identification from L2 speech using neural spectrogram analysis. In: Interspeech, vol. 2021, pp. 3959–3963 (2021)
5. Guntur, R.K., Ramakrishnan, K., Vinay Kumar, M.: An automated classification system based on regional accent. Circuits Syst. Signal Process **41**(6), 3487–3507 (2022)
6. Humayun, M.A., Yassin, H., Abas, P.E.: Native language identification for Indian-speakers by an ensemble of phoneme-specific, and text-independent convolutions. Speech Commun. **139**, 92–101 (2022)
7. Jiao, Y., Tu, M., Berisha, V., Liss, J.M.: Accent identification by combining deep neural networks and recurrent neural networks trained on long and short term features. In: Interspeech, pp. 2388–2392 (2016)
8. Kürzinger, L., Winkelbauer, D., Li, L., Watzel, T., Rigoll, G.: CTC-Segmentation of large corpora for German end-to-end speech recognition. In: Karpov, A., Potapova, R. (eds.) SPECOM 2020. LNCS (LNAI), vol. 12335, pp. 267–278. Springer, Cham (2020). https://doi.org/10.1007/978-3-030-60276-5_27
9. Rajpal, A., Patel, T.B., Sailor, H.B., Madhavi, M.C., Patil, H.A., Fujisaki, H.: Native language identification using spectral and source-based features. In: Interspeech, pp. 2383–2387 (2016)
10. Schuller, B., et al.: The interspeech 2016 computational paralinguistics challenge: Deception, sincerity & native language. In: 17TH Annual Conference of the International Speech Communication Association (Interspeech 2016), Vols. 1–5, vol. 8, pp. 2001–2005. ISCA (2016)
11. Ubale, R., Qian, Y., Evanini, K.: Exploring end-to-end attention-based neural networks for native language identification. In: 2018 IEEE Spoken Language Technology Workshop (SLT), pp. 84–91. IEEE (2018)
12. Ubale, R., Ramanarayanan, V., Qian, Y., Evanini, K., Leong, C.W., Lee, C.M.: Native language identification from raw waveforms using deep convolutional neural networks with attentive pooling. In: 2019 IEEE Automatic Speech Recognition and Understanding Workshop (ASRU), pp. 403–410. IEEE (2019)
13. Watzel, T., Kürzinger, L., Li, L., Rigoll, G.: Synchronized forward-backward transformer for end-to-end speech recognition. In: Karpov, A., Potapova, R. (eds.) SPECOM 2020. LNCS (LNAI), vol. 12335, pp. 646–656. Springer, Cham (2020). https://doi.org/10.1007/978-3-030-60276-5_62
14. Watzel, T., Kürzinger, L., Li, L., Rigoll, G.: Induced local attention for transformer models in speech recognition. In: Karpov, A., Potapova, R. (eds.) SPECOM 2021. LNCS (LNAI), vol. 12997, pp. 795–806. Springer, Cham (2021). https://doi.org/10.1007/978-3-030-87802-3_71

Dialect Identification in Ao Using Modulation-Based Representation

Moakala Tzudir[1], Rishith Sadashiv T.N.[1(✉)], Ayush Agarwal[2], and S.R. Mahadeva Prasanna[1]

[1] Department of Electrical Engineering, Indian Institute of Technology Dharwad, Dharwad 580011, India
{moakala.tzudir,221022005,prasanna}@iitdh.ac.in
[2] McAfee, Bengaluru, India
ayush_agarwal@mcafee.com

Abstract. This paper presents an automatic dialect identification in Ao using modulation-based approach. Ao is a low-resource, Tibeto-Burman tonal language spoken in Nagaland, a North-East state of India. This work aims to investigate dialect-specific characteristics to build a more robust DID system for classifying the three Ao dialects. In this direction, modulation-based representation is explored. Considering Ao is a tone language, the experiments were evaluated for 3 sec segment duration in order to capture the temporal information of the modulation spectrogram. In addition, the log Mel spectrogram is used as the feature for the baseline DID system. The proposed modulation spectrogram shows a significant performance of $\approx 8\%$ improvement in accuracy over the baseline Ao DID system. Hence, the result indicates the effectiveness of modulation-based representation in automatically identifying the three dialects of Ao.

Keywords: Ao · Tonal Language · Under-Resource · Dialect Identification · Modulation Spectrogram · CNN · Bi-GRU · Attention

1 Introduction

Adopting speech technologies is essential for a broad range of applications in today's technologically driven environment. Dialect Identification (DID) task is one of the major fields in the speech research community due to its significance in Automatic Speech Recognition (ASR) tasks [2]. The primary objective of a DID system is identifying differences amongst dialects within the same language family [2]. A dialect, in simple terms, is the speaker's pronunciation and vocabulary differences based on geographic location [4]. Variations in dialects may also come from syntactic and morphological differences. For instance, dialectal regions for the Arabic language are distributed over a large geographical area [23]. Contrary to this, in the case of Naga languages, dialectal variations can be observed within a small geographic area, sometimes even within the boundary

Table 1. Different tonal assignments in the word /mətsə/ [27].

Minimal set	Changki	Mongsen	Chungli	Meanings
	LH	HL	HL	'kick'
/mətsə/	LL	HH	HH	'salt'
	HL	MM	MM	'saliva'

of a village. A DID task is to identify one dialect from the other; however, capturing dialectal variations within a small region is extremely challenging [2]. The language of interest in this paper, Ao, is an under-resourced language spoken in the Northern part of Nagaland in the North-East region of India [9]. This work attempts to automatically classify the Ao dialects using the modulation-based approach.

Ao is a Tibeto-Burman language and is known to have three distinct dialects, namely, Chungli, Mongsen, and Changki, differing in terms of prosodic and phonemic properties [6,9]. It is a tone language with three distinct tones: High (H), Mid (M), and Low (L) [6,27]. Although all three Ao dialects consist of three tones, the tone assignment varies among the dialects, even with words of the same meaning. For instance, Table 1 shows the different tonal assignments across the three dialects of Ao. The word /mətsə/ is a minimal set across the dialects providing different meanings as the tone changes. However, the variation in tones is not systematic across the three Ao dialects [27]. The standard variety of the language is the Chungli dialect among the three dialects of Ao. As a result, all text materials are available only in the standard Chungli dialect. In addition, the Changki and Mongsen speakers can also read and write in the Chungli dialect. Consequently, as the textual resources are scarce in the language, speech analysis and modeling-related work in the Ao dialects becomes a formidable challenge.

1.1   Related Work

There are a number of works dedicated to DID systems built in major world languages, such as Arabic, Mandarin Chinese, English and Spanish. Several research studies have reported DID systems using hand-crafted features such as Mel Frequency Cepstral Coefficient (MFCC), Shifted Delta Cepstral (SDC), filter-banks, chroma-spectral shape, formants (F1-F3), and prosodic features like F_0, energy, intensity and duration using different Machine Learning (ML) and Deep Learning (DL) models [1,5,11,14,15,19,20]. The aforementioned studies were conducted in non-tonal languages such as Arabic, English, Spanish, Hindi, Kannada, and North Sámi. Time-frequency representation such as Mel-Single Frequency Filtering (SFF) spectrogram and Mel-Short Term Fourier Transform (STFT) spectrogram was implemented using an ML classifier in the English DID task [13]. At the same time, numerous works in dialect classification have been attempted for tonal languages such as Chinese, Vietnamese, Punjabi, and

Ao. Hand-crafted features like the tonal feature (F_0), MFCC, SDC, Linear Prediction Cepstral Coefficients (LPCC), Residual Mel Frequency Cepstral Coefficients (RMFCC), Mean Hilbert Envelope Coefficients (MHEC), filter-banks, and prosodic features were used with different ML and DL classifiers [10,16,18,23–28]. DID tasks with time-frequency representation have also been exploited in Ao, a tone language with features such as the Log Mel Spectrogram (LMS), Integrated Linear Prediction Residual Log Mel Spectrogram (ILPR-LMS), and Linear Prediction (LP)-gammatonegram using DL classifiers [21,22]. Most recently, self-supervised speech models were used in DID tasks to classify the North Sámi language [12].

1.2   Motivation

Based on the literature described in Subsect. 1.1, it is observed that there are numerous works in DID using hand-crafted features for both non-tonal and tonal languages. While there are a handful of works in DID with time-frequency representation, most of which are in the Ao language. However, to the best of our knowledge, frequency-frequency representation has not yet been explored in DID tasks. Hence, a modulation-based representation in DID is proposed in this work. As described in Magazine et al. [17], the long-term temporal characteristics of the speech signal are captured with the modulation spectrogram. As Ao is a tone language, there are variations in the tone assignment across the dialects, specifically for a longer speech duration. As a result, a speech segment of 2 sec from female speakers of each dialect was plotted in Fig. 1 with their corresponding modulation spectrogram. The speech segment exhibits a sentence with the same meaning but with lexical differences across the dialects. The modulation spectrogram in Fig. 1 (b), (d), and (f) shows different patterns across the three dialects, explicitly in the higher frequency regions. Motivated by the distinct differences across the dialects, the modulation spectrogram is explored in this work for dialect classification in Ao.

The contributions of this work are as follows:

1. DID task is attempted in an under-resourced language Ao, spoken in Nagaland, India.
2. Modulation spectrogram, a frequency-frequency representation, is used to classify the three Ao dialects.

The rest of the paper is arranged in the following: Sect. 2 gives a brief description of the speech corpus. The proposed Ao DID system is described in Sect. 3. Experiments and results are discussed in Sect. 4. The work is finally concluded in Sect. 5 with potential future directions.

2   Changki Mongsen Chungli-Ao Corpus

The current work is analyzed using the Changki Mongsen Chungli-Ao (CMC-Ao) Corpus. The CMC-Ao corpus comprises 96 read passages with $\approx$ 6 hours

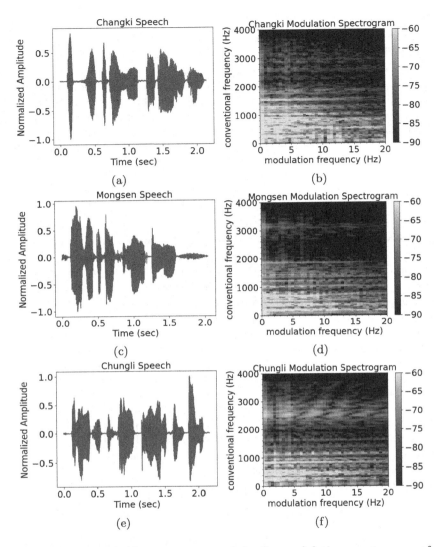

Fig. 1. The distinguishable patterns present in the modulation spectrogram of the three Ao dialects. Figure (a), (c), and (e) depicts the speech signal of the three dialects with their corresponding modulation spectrogram representation in (b), (d), and (f).

of recordings for the three Ao dialects. Each speaker was provided to read a brief narrative from the Bible, "The Parable of the prodigal son". As the Bible is available only in the standard dialect, the passage was translated for the speakers of the Changki and Mongsen dialects. The speech was recorded in a real-world environment using a TASCAM 2-channel digital recorder and a Shure head-mounted microphone. In order to add session variability, the speakers were

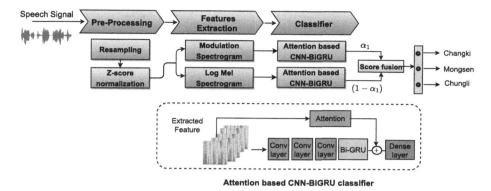

Fig. 2. Framework for Ao DID system.

asked to read the same passage in four sessions. The speech data was recorded from 24 native speakers in total, consisting of 4 males and 4 females from each dialect. All speakers spoke Ao as their first language, with English and Nagamese (a creolized variety of the Assamese language) as second or third languages.

3 Proposed Ao DID System

This section describes the proposed Ao DID system. The present work uses the optimized attention-based Convolutional Neural Network-Bidirectional Gated Recurrent Unit (CNN-BiGRU) classifier as the architecture proposed in our previous work [21]. Figure 2 shows the overall framework of the Ao DID system. Initially, the input speech signal is pre-processed by resampling and applying Z-score normalization. The pre-processed speech is then used to extract the modulation-based features. Next, the features are fed to the classifier for the three-class classification task.

3.1 Modulation Spectrogram

For the Ao DID system, the long-term temporal information captured by the modulation spectrogram is believed to carry distinguishing characteristics in classifying the three dialects. Figure 3 shows the generation procedure of the modulation spectrogram. The modulation spectrogram is a two-dimensional representation of a speech signal in terms of conventional frequency (f) and modulation frequency (f_{mod}). The modulation spectrogram $S(f, f_{mod})$ of the speech signal $s(t)$ is obtained by performing two transformations. As seen in the figure, frequency transformation is computed to the speech signal $s(t)$ to obtain its time-frequency representation $S(t, f)$. Following that, the time-frequency $S(t, f)$ to frequency-frequency $S(f, f_{mod})$ transformation is performed with the Fourier Transform (FT). The modulation spectrogram is obtained using Eq. 1 that consists of 161 feature dimensions.

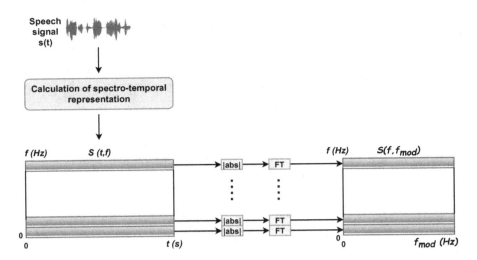

Fig. 3. Generation of modulation spectrogram where $|abs|$ represents the absolute value, and FT represents the use of the Fourier Transform [3].

$$S(f, f_{mod}) = FT|S(t, f)| \qquad (1)$$

For the detailed procedure of the modulation spectrogram extraction, the reader is encouraged to refer to the original paper [3]. The modulation spectrogram is represented as S_{mds} henceforth.

3.2   Attention-Based CNN-BiGRU Classifier

The optimized architecture presented in Fig. 4 is proposed in our previous study, where hyper-parameter tuning was conducted for the convolutional layers, Bi-GRU unit, and the dense node [21]. The architecture is incorporated with spatial and temporal information, complemented with frequency-based attention for the classification task. The convolutional layers are used to learn the spatial information of the modulation spectrogram. The temporal context across the dialects is captured using the Bi-GRU layer. Simultaneously, higher weights are assigned to frequency bins with more discriminative information to classify dialects through an attention mechanism along the conventional frequency direction. This work is computed on 3 sec segment duration (≈ 298 frames) as the decision units for classification.

The architecture comprises three 2D convolutional layers containing 32, 64, and 128 kernels. With a stride of $(2, 1)$, a kernel size of $(3, 3)$ is employed. Each convolutional layer's output is batch-normalized before being fed through a Max-pooling layer with a pool size of $(2, 1)$. The output of the last convolutional layer is then passed to the Bi-GRU layer with 128 units. In parallel, the input modulation spectrogram is fed to the attention mechanism and its output is concate-

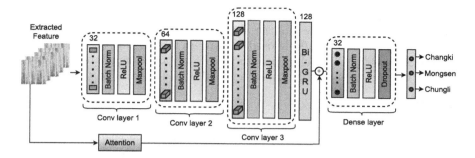

Fig. 4. Optimized architecture for Ao DID system [21].

nated with the output of the Bi-GRU layer. Next, the concatenated output is fed to the dense layer with 32 nodes. Lastly, in order to predict the class label, the output of the dense layer is fed into the output layer (size=3). The output layer employs *Softmax* activation, whereas the dense layer uses *ReLU* activation. In order to train the model, a mini-batch size of 33 is used for 50 epochs. A dropout of 0.4 is applied after the dense layer. Categorical cross-entropy loss is used to train the model, and the optimizer's initial learning rate is set to 0.0001.

4   Experiments and Results

This section discusses the experimental setup and results obtained in this work. The sub-section immediately following this briefly describes the baseline method. The subsequent sub-section describes the speech data augmentation carried out in this work. Finally, the setup for the speaker-independent strategy is discussed, followed by the classification results obtained.

4.1   Baseline Method

Log Mel Spectrogram (LMS) has been used previously in DID tasks [21,22]. The Mel spectrograms are generated using the Mel filter-bank, comprising 40 overlapping triangular filters. The Mel-spectrograms are subjected to a natural logarithmic operation, and the result time-frequency representation is referred to as Log Mel Spectrogram (S_{lms}). This work uses the S_{lms} as the baseline feature.

4.2   Speech Data Augmentation

A considerable amount of data are generally needed to compute the experiments based on DL classifiers. Therefore, original speech data is augmented to avoid overfitting the classification process and increase the CMC-Ao corpus. The following methods are used for speech data augmentation:

1. Telephonic Speech:
   A free software available on the International Telecommunication Union (ITU) website called G.191 is used to convert the original speech into telephonic speech [8]. A pipeline process is carried out to simulate the original speech into telephone quality speech signal with reference to the ITU users manual [7].
2. Reverberated Speech:
   The publicly available Roomsim toolbox is used to augment the original speech into two types of reverberated speech [29]. The generated reverberated speech differs in configuration settings, such as the source and room sensor.

After augmenting the original speech data, the CMC-Ao corpus yielded ≈ 24 hours of 384 passages across the three Ao dialects.

4.3   Classification Results

The usefulness of speech data augmentation is confirmed in our previous work [21]. Accordingly, the training is done using the original and augmented speech, while the original speech data is used for testing. The speech data is divided into four non-overlapping folds for the experimental setup. The folds are distributed in a manner that every fold contains the speech data of 1 male and 1 female speakers. For every iteration, training uses three folds of the speech data (including augmented data); the fourth remaining fold is used for testing. To obtain the training and validation sets, the training set is divided into a ratio of 70 : 30. Therefore, four distinct sets of train, validation, and test data are obtained from four-folds. As a result, the train set speakers differ from the test set speakers. Hence, the experiments are evaluated in a speaker-independent strategy. The model is trained for 3 sec segment duration to use the temporal context of the speech data.

Table 2 shows the classification performance for four-fold cross-validation computed with 3 sec segment duration. The results are reported in terms of mean (μ) and standard deviations (σ) for accuracy and F1-score. It is observed

Table 2. Classification performance of Ao dialects for 3 sec segment duration. Modulation spectrogram and log mel spectrogram are represented by S_{mds} and S_{lms}, respectively.

Features	Accuracy	F1-score			
		Changki	Mongsen	Chungli	Average
	($\mu \pm \sigma$)	($\mu \pm \sigma$)	($\mu \pm \sigma$)	($\mu \pm \sigma$)	($\mu \pm \sigma$)
S_{mds}	62.80±9.79	71.06±7.64	57.71±16.87	54.63±10.77	61.13±10.52
S_{lms} [21]	55.27±3.19	44.80±18.37	54.23±7.60	62.51±5.05	53.84±4.02
$S_{mds}+S_{lms}$	62.98±10.19	71.08±8.22	56.23±20.34	55.12±10.56	60.81±11.54

from the table that the proposed feature S_{mds} performs decently in classifying the three Ao dialects. The classification accuracy of S_{mds} is also significantly higher than the baseline feature S_{lms} that was reported in *Tzudir et al.* [21]. The decent performance of the individual features encouraged us to explore them further in combination. For the feature combination, the features are fused at score level and computed as shown in Eq. 2.

$$S_{comb} = \alpha S_{f_1} + (1 - \alpha)S_{f_2} \qquad (2)$$

S_{f_1} and S_{f_2} are the prediction scores from the two features, S_{mds} and S_{lms}. The value of α weight varies from $0 - 1$. Figure 5 shows the representation with different α values. It is noticed from the plot that the best accuracy is achieved for $\alpha = 0.9$, giving higher weight to the proposed feature S_{mds}. Hence, these results substantiate the efficacy of the modulation-based representation by capturing dialect-specific information in classifying the three Ao dialects.

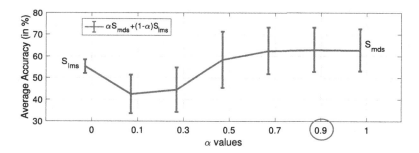

Fig. 5. Alpha variation for the combined features reported in Table 2.

5   Discussion and Conclusion

This paper presents an automatic DID system in Ao using modulation-based representation. Four cross-validations speaker-independent scheme was computed to get the performances of the system. The result shows that the proposed feature captures distinguishing characteristics to classify the three dialects of Ao. The proposed modulation spectrogram feature outperforms the baseline feature by about $\approx 8\%$. However, it is also seen that the performance of S_{mds} and $S_{mds} + S_{lms}$ are comparable with higher α weight assigned to the proposed feature. This shows that S_{lms} does not capture complementary information when fused with S_{mds}. Therefore, in the future, the feature combination of S_{mds} will be evaluated with the source features such as ILPR-LMS (S_{ilpr}) and LP-gammatonegram (S_{LP-gm}) that was proposed in our prior work [21, 22] for an improved DID system. Another point to be noted is the high standard deviation (σ) of S_{mds} compared to S_{lms}. As the experiment was computed in

4 iterations, there were differences in the performances for every fold in S_{mds}. Therefore, speaker-wise analysis can be conducted in the future, where every speaker will be subjected to a detailed analysis. Another possible extension is using self-supervised speech models in DID tasks to classify the Ao dialects.

References

1. Agrawal, S.S., Jain, A., Sinha, S.: Analysis and modeling of acoustic information for automatic dialect classification. Int. J. Speech Technol. **19**(3), 593–609 (2016). https://doi.org/10.1007/s10772-016-9351-7
2. Biadsy, F., Hirschberg, J., Habash, N.: Spoken Arabic dialect identification using phonotactic modeling. In: Proceedings of the EACL Workshop on Computational Approaches to Semitic Languages, pp. 53–61. Stroudsburg, PA, USA (2009)
3. Cassani, R., Albuquerque, I., Monteiro, J., Falk, T.H.: AMA: an open-source amplitude modulation analysis toolkit for signal processing applications. In: 2019 IEEE Global Conference on Signal and Information Processing (GlobalSIP), pp. 1–4. IEEE (2019)
4. Chambers, J.K., Trudgill, P.: Dialectology, vol. 2nd edition. Cambridge University Press (1998)
5. Chittaragi, N.B., Koolagudi, S.G.: Dialect identification using chroma-spectral shape features with ensemble technique. Comput. Speech Lang. **70**, 101230 (2021)
6. Coupe, A.R.: The acoustic and perceptual features of tone in the Tibeto-Burman language Ao naga. In: Proceedings of the 5th International Conference on Spoken Language Processing (1998)
7. G.191 ITU-T, R.: ITU-T software tool library. International Telecommunication Union, Geneva, Switzerland (2009)
8. G.191 ITU-T, R.: Software tools for speech and audio coding standardization. International Telecommunication Union, Geneva, Switzerland (2005). https://www.itu.int/rec/T-REC-G.191/en
9. Grierson, G.A.: Linguistic Survey of India, vol. 4. Office of the superintendent of government printing, India (1906)
10. Hung, P.N., Ha, N.T., Van Loan, T., Thang, V.X., Chien, N.D.: Vietnamese dialect identification on embedded system. UTEHY J. Sci. Technol. **24**, 82–87 (2019)
11. Kakouros, S., Hiovain, K., Vainio, M., Šimko, J.: Dialect identification of spoken north Sámi language varieties using prosodic features. arXiv preprint arXiv:2003.10183 (2020)
12. Kakouros, S., Hiovain-Asikainen, K.: North Sámi dialect identification with self-supervised speech models. arXiv preprint arXiv:2305.11864 (2023)
13. Kethireddy, R., Kadiri, S.R., Alku, P., Gangashetty, S.V.: Mel-weighted single frequency filtering spectrogram for dialect identification. IEEE Access **8**, 174871–174879 (2020)
14. Lei, Y., Hansen, J.H.L.: Dialect classification via text-independent training and testing for Arabic, Spanish, and Chinese. IEEE Trans. Audio Speech Lang. Process. **19**, 85–96 (2011)
15. Lin, W., Madhavi, M., Das, R.K., Li, H.: Transformer-based Arabic dialect identification. In: International Conference on Asian Language Processing (IALP), pp. 192–196. IEEE (2020)
16. Ma, B., Zhu, D., Tong, R.: Chinese dialect identification using tone features based on pitch flux. In: Proceedings of the IEEE International Conference on Acoustics Speech and Signal Processing, vol. 1 (2006)

17. Magazine, R., Agarwal, A., Hedge, A., Prasanna, S.M.: Fake speech detection using modulation spectrogram. In: International Conference on Speech and Computer, pp. 451–463. Springer (2022). https://doi.org/10.1007/978-3-031-20980-2_39

18. Mingliang, G., Yuguo, X., Yiming, Y.: Semi-supervised learning based Chinese dialect identification. In: Proceedings of the 9th International Conference on Signal Processing, pp. 1608–1611. IEEE (2008)

19. Rao, K.S., Koolagudi, S.G.: Identification of Hindi dialects and emotions using spectral and prosodic features of speech. IJSCI: Int. J. Syst. Cybern. Inf. **9**(4), 24–33 (2011)

20. Shon, S., Ali, A., Samih, Y., Mubarak, H., Glass, J.: ADI17: a fine-grained Arabic dialect identification dataset. In: Proceedings of the International Conference on Acoustics, Speech and Signal Processing (ICASSP), pp. 8244–8248. IEEE (2020)

21. Tzudir, M., Baghel, S., Sarmah, P., Prasanna, S.: Under-resourced dialect identification in Ao using source information. J. Acoust. Soc. Am. **152**(3), 1755–1766 (2022)

22. Tzudir, M., Baghel, S., Sarmah, P., Prasanna, S.M.: Excitation source feature based dialect identification in Ao-a low resource language. In: Proceedings of the INTERSPEECH, pp. 1524–1528 (2021)

23. Tzudir, M., Baghel, S., Sarmah, P., Prasanna, S.: Analyzing RMFCC feature for dialect identification in Ao, an under-resourced language. In: Proceedings of the National Conference on Communications (NCC), pp. 308–313. IEEE (2022)

24. Tzudir, M., Bhattacharjee, M., Sarmah, P., Prasanna, S.: Low-resource dialect identification in Ao using noise robust mean Hilbert envelope coefficients. In: Proc. of the National Conference on Communications (NCC), pp. 256–261. IEEE (2022)

25. Tzudir, M., Sarmah, P., Prasanna, S.R.M.: Dialect identification using tonal and spectral features in two dialects of Ao. In: Proceedings of the SLTU (2018)

26. Tzudir, M., Sarmah, P., Prasanna, S.M.: Tonal feature based dialect discrimination in two dialects in Ao. In: Proceedings of the Region 10 Conference, TENCON, pp. 1795–1799. IEEE (2017)

27. Tzudir, M., Sarmah, P., Prasanna, S.M.: Analysis and modeling of dialect information in Ao, a low resource language. J. Acoust. Soc. Am. **149**(5), 2976–2987 (2021)

28. Tzudir, M., Sarmah, P., Prasanna, S.M.: Prosodic information in dialect identification of a tonal language: the case of Ao. Proc. Interspeech **2022**, 2238–2242 (2022)

29. Vincent, E., Campbell, D.: Roomsimove. https://irisa.fr/metiss/members/evincent/Roomsimove.zip

Self-supervised Speaker Verification Employing Augmentation Mix and Self-augmented Training-Based Clustering

Abderrahim Fathan[(✉)] and Jahangir Alam

Computer Research Institute of Montreal, Montreal, QC H3N 1M3, Canada
{abderrahim.fathan,jahangir.alam}@crim.ca

Abstract. Using clustering algorithms to optimize speaker embedding networks via pseudo-labels is a widely used practice to train self-supervised speaker verification systems. Although pseudo-label-based self-supervised training scheme showed outstanding performance, this latter depends on high-quality pseudo-labels, and recent studies have shown that label noise can remarkably impact downstream performance. In this paper, we propose a general-purpose clustering algorithm called CAMSAT that outperforms all other baselines used to cluster speaker embeddings. Moreover, using the generated pseudo-labels to train our speaker embedding systems allows us to further improve speaker verification performance. CAMSAT is based on two principles: (1) Augmentation Mix (AM) by mixing predictions of augmented samples to provide a complementary supervisory signal for clustering and enforce symmetry within augmentations and (2) Self-Augmented Training (SAT) to enforce representation invariance and maximize the information-theoretic dependency between samples and their predicted pseudo-labels. We provide a thorough comparative analysis of the performance of our clustering method compared to all baselines using a variety of clustering metrics and perform an ablation study to analyze the contribution of each component of our system.

Keywords: Speaker verification · Speaker embeddings · Clustering algorithm · Pseudo-labels

1 Introduction

Speaker verification (SV) is the task of confirming, based on a speaker's known utterances, that the identity of a speaker is who they purport to be. In recent years, it has become a key technology for personnel authentication in numerous applications [27]. Typically, utterance-level fixed-dimensional embedding vectors are extracted from the enrollment and test speech samples and then fed into a scoring algorithm (e.g., cosine distance) to measure their similarity/likelihood of being spoken by the same speaker.

© The Author(s), under exclusive license to Springer Nature Switzerland AG 2023
A. Karpov et al. (Eds.): SPECOM 2023, LNAI 14339, pp. 550–563, 2023.
https://doi.org/10.1007/978-3-031-48312-7_44

Classically, the i-vector framework has been one of the most dominant approaches for speech embedding [12,35] thanks to its ability to summarize the distributive patterns of the speech in an unsupervised manner and with a relatively small amount of training data. It generates fixed-sized compact vectors (i-vectors) that represent the speaker's identity in a speech utterance regardless of its length. In the past years, various deep learning-based architectures and techniques have been proposed to extract embedding vectors [2,19,34]. They have shown great performance when a large amount of training data is available, particularly with a sufficient number of speakers [53]. One widely employed architecture for this purpose is ECAPA-TDNN [14], which has achieved state-of-the-art (SOTA) performance in text-independent speaker recognition. The ECAPA-TDNN uses squeeze-and-excitation (SE), employs channel- and context-dependent statistics pooling & multi-layer aggregation and applies self-attention pooling to obtain an utterance-level embedding vector.

Indeed, most of the deep embedding models are trained in a fully supervised manner and require large speaker-labeled datasets for training. However, well-annotated datasets can be expensive and time-consuming to prepare, which has lead the research community to explore more affordable self-supervised learning techniques using larger unlabeled datasets. One common way to solve this issue for SV systems is to use a one-stage "clustering-classification" scheme [19,33,34] by employing clustering algorithms (e.g., K-means, agglomerative hierarchical clustering, spectral clustering) or other SSL-based objectives (e.g., SimCLR, MoCo [62]) to generate Pseudo-Labels (PLs) and train the speaker embedding network using these labels in a discriminative fashion. More recently, better-performing ways have started to appear which are now widely adopted in the SV domain. These frameworks are based on two-stage progressive/iterative "clustering-classification" learning [47,55]. The first stage consists of SSL training (e.g., contrastive InfoNCE loss [55]) to train an encoder model to generate speaker embeddings, followed by a second stage of clustering those embeddings to produce pseudo-labels in order to jointly train the encoder with a classifier in a supervised manner. The two stages are repeated sequentially until no gains are obtained.

Despite the impressive performance of these PL-based Self-Supervised SV schemes, clustering performance remains a bottleneck in all above approaches [25,55] as downstream performance relies greatly on accurate PLs since these are in general inaccurate and contain noise due to the discrepancy between the clustering objective(s) and the final SV task (speaker-identity ground truths). Besides, even with iterative clustering-classification paradigms, the erroneous information from the wrong pseudo-labels keeps propagating iteratively, which drops the final performance [40,55]. On the other hand, due to the memorization effects [1], deep over-parameterized networks can easily overfit the noise and corruptions in the training PLs which leads to performance degradation and worse generalization. Thus, the need for better-performing clustering algorithms to generate less noisy and more accurate pseudo-labels.

In this paper, we propose a general-purpose clustering method called CAM-SAT (Clustering based on Augmentation Mix and Self-Augmented Training) which combines the benefits of the Information Maximizing Self-Augmented Training (IMSAT) clustering framework [31], and the simple data augmentation technique AUGMIX [29] used originally for image classifiers to improve their robustness and uncertainty estimates under data shift. Indeed, IMSAT is a general method for unsupervised discrete representation learning using deep models to maximize the information-theoretic dependency between data and their predicted discrete representations and which encourages the predictions to remain unchanged under data augmentation, while AUGMIX helps models generalize to unforeseen corruptions in the data inputs by utilizing stochasticity and a mix of diverse augmentations. For that it employs a Jensen-Shannon Divergence (JSD) consistency loss to achieve better robustness and stability against data perturbation. Instead of mixing augmented inputs for the sole goal of enforcing smoother model responses via the JSD consistency loss, our method leverages successfully this mix of augmentations at the predictions level as an additional supervisory signal to better guide the cluster assignment for more robust, stable, and better-performing data clustering.

The resulting algorithm is highly scalable, more robust to corruptions and shifts in the data during online clustering, enforces consistent embeddings across diverse perturbations through a JSD consistency loss, is simple to implement, and adds limited computational overhead to IMSAT. Besides, CAMSAT allows us to outperform all other clustering algorithms for speaker clustering, and to achieve better speaker verification performance than all other SOTA SV baselines.

We believe our proposed clustering method can be considerably beneficial to further optimize current self-supervised SV frameworks by replacing the simple clustering methods been employed (e.g. k-means, spectral clustering). It can also be used in speaker diarization frameworks to improve the clustering aspects of speaker diarization methods where clustering is one of the important modules. Finally, our proposed clustering approach is a general-purpose method and can be applied to other problems and domains other than speech.

The contributions of this paper are as follows:

- We propose a new general-purpose clustering algorithm called CAMSAT which combines the benefits of mutual information (MI) maximization of IMSAT clustering framework and the regularization benefit of AUGMIX (mix of augmentations at the predictions level) for better generalizability, robustness, and stability of clustering under data shift for large-scale datasets or/and a high number of clusters.
- Using a thorough comparative analysis via clustering metrics, we show that our proposed clustering method achieves a very high performance outperforming a large set of baselines. Besides, using the generated pseudo-labels to train our SV systems, we are able to outperform all other SV baselines.
- We perform an ablation study to analyze the contribution of the different components of our proposed framework.

2   Background and Related Work

Diverse methods for clustering have been proposed. For instance, classical models include K-means [28], Gaussian mixture model (GMM), variational GMM [3], BIRCH [65], CURE [24], Agglomerative Hierarchical Clustering (AHC) [11], Divisive Hierarchical Clustering (DHC) [45], and iterative quantization [23]. However, these methods are not suitable to model nonlinear structures of data and can only fit linear boundaries between data representations. Later on, other methods such as spectral clustering [44,61], kernel-based clustering [58,60], multi-exemplar clustering [57], or support vector clustering (SVC) [59] have been proposed to model the non-linearity of data. Nevertheless, their scalability to large datasets remains a difficult problem. Recently, the powerful representative ability of deep neural networks has been leveraged to model the non-linearity of complex data and to scale to large datasets. For instance, Deep Embedded Clustering (DEC) [63] proposed to use deep models to simultaneously learn feature representations and cluster assignments, while DeepCWRN [9] approach employs an autoencoder to simultaneously learn feature representations and embeddings suitable for clustering by encouraging the separation of natural clusters in the embedding space. Besides, methods such as [15,32] are proposed to model the data generation process by using deep generative models with Gaussian mixture models as prior distributions. More recently, a different approach called DeepDPM [50] proposed to use a split/merge framework, with a novel loss and a dynamic architecture that adapts to the changing number of clusters without the need for a predefined number of clusters.

While data augmentation remains a crucial component to regularize deep neural networks for clustering and unsupervised representation learning in order to model the invariance of learned representations [16], IMSAT imposes directly this invariance on the learned representations. We try to leverage AUGMIX augmentation technique at the output logits-level to enforce consistency prediction against the various augmentations and variants of cluster instances in order to further improve robustness and uncertainty estimates to previously unseen data/clusters during clustering, particularly when datasets are very large. Computing AUGMIX at the logits-level also allows us to leverage an additional complementary supervisory signal that is beneficial for clustering (see the case of AAMSoftmax). Closer to our idea of mixing predictions under different augmentations for clustering is [38] which shows that simply ensembling classifier predictions improves prediction calibration. Additionally, the pseudo-label method (or label guessing), used as an explicit regularization method to combat label noise, first computes the average of the model's predicted class distributions across all augmentations and then applies a temperature sharpening function to perform entropy minimization of the label distribution.

3   Our Proposed Clustering Approach

Given a clustering model f to train with a predefined number of clusters C, our CAMSAT approach imposes invariance to data augmentation on the output predictions of neural networks in an end-to-end fashion while maximizing the information-theoretic dependency between samples and their predicted discrete representations (cluster assignments). It minimizes the following L_{CAMSAT} objective:

$$
\begin{aligned}
L_{CAMSAT} &= L_{aug} + L_{IMSAT} + L_{symmetry}, \\
&= L_{aug} + R_{SAT}(\theta, T_{VAT}) + \lambda(H(Y|X) - \mu H(Y)) + L_{symmetry}.
\end{aligned}
\tag{1}
$$

where

$$
L_{aug} = \frac{1}{N} \sum_{i=1}^{N} KL(p_i^{aug_{r_i}} || p_i)
\tag{2}
$$

with $J = \{aug_1, ..., aug_{|J|}\}$ is the ensemble of available data augmentations and $r_i \in \{1, .., |J|\}$ refers to a random augmentation from J, and

$$
L_{symmetry} = \frac{1}{N} \sum_{i=1}^{N} \frac{1}{|J|} \sum_{j \in \{1, .., |J|\}} KL(p_i^{aug_j} || p_i^m)
\tag{3}
$$

$KL(.||.)$ refers to the Kullback-Leibler divergence. $p_i = f(x_i) \in \mathbb{R}^{1xC}$, $p_i^{aug_j} = f(x_i^{aug_j})$, and $p_i^m = \frac{1}{|J|+1}[\sum_{j \in \{1, .., |J|\}} \alpha_j p_i^{aug_j} + p_i]$ correspond to the predictions of data sample x_i, its augmented version $x_i^{aug_j}$, and a mixture of predictions for all available $x_i^{aug_j}$ respectively. N is the size of data (or mini-batches) and $\alpha_j \in [0, 1]$ is the weight (Dirichlet coefficient) corresponding to $x_i^{aug_j}$.

L_{aug} forces the predicted representations of augmented samples to be close to those of the original data points by minimizing the KL-divergence between both predictions. $H(.)$ and $H(.|.)$ are the marginal and conditional entropy, respectively, and their difference represents the MI between sample input X and label Y that we maximize. $H(Y) = h(p_\theta(y)) = h(\frac{1}{N} \sum_{i=1}^{N} p_\theta(y|x))$, and $H(Y|X) = \frac{1}{N} \sum_{i=1}^{N} h(p_\theta(y|x_i))$, where $p_\theta(y|x)$ is our probabilistic classifier modeled by parameters θ of a deep network, and $h(p(y)) = - \sum_{y'} p(y') \log p(y')$ is the entropy function.

Inspired from the Regularized Information Maximization method [37], and based on SAT regularization, $R_{SAT}(\theta; T) = \frac{1}{N} \sum_{n=1}^{N} R_{SAT}(\theta; x_n, T(x_n))$ is a loss term that allows the representations of the augmented samples to be further pushed close to those of the original samples while also regularizing the complexity of the network against local perturbations using Virtual Adversarial Training (VAT) [42]. $R_{SAT}(\theta; x, T(x)) = - \sum_{c=1}^{C} \sum_{y_c=0}^{1} p_{\hat{\theta}}(y_c|x) log p_\theta(y_c|T(x))$. Where $p_{\hat{\theta}}(y_c|x)$ is the prediction of original data point x, and $\hat{\theta}$ are the current parameters of the network. T_{VAT} is the augmentation function using local perturbations to enforce representation invariance with $T_{VAT}(x) = x + r$ and $r = \arg\max_{r'}\{R_{SAT}(\hat{\theta}; x, x + r'); ||r'||_2 \le \epsilon\}$ is an adversarial direction.

Hyper-parameters $\lambda, \mu \in \mathbb{R}$ control the trade-offs between the complexity regularization of the model (through R_{SAT}) and the MI maximization, and between the two entropy terms, respectively. Basically, increasing the entropy

$H(Y)$ amounts to encouraging the cluster sizes to be uniform and prevent collapsing into only a small number of clusters, while on the other hand, minimizing the conditional entropy $H(Y|X)$ enables less ambiguous cluster assignments and forces the classifier to be confident on the training samples [4]. For more details, please refer to [31,42].

Furthermore, we incorporate $L_{symmetry}$ objective function to harness the average/interpolation of different signals provided by the various augmented views as an additional supervisory signal during clustering to regularize our clustering model to produce consistent feature representations that will be labeled identically irrespective of any transformation/perturbation, generalize better, and generate more compact clusters. Besides, mixing augmentations allows us to generate further diverse transformations at the latent predictions level, which are important for inducing robustness and reducing the memorization of used augmentations for training [22,56], which helps to leave space to preserve more relevant discriminant information in the representations.

Indeed, inspired by the pseudo-label method [39], which was originally used for semi-supervised learning, $L_{symmetry}$ computes the KL-divergence between every data augmentation and the average mixture p_i^m which allows us to enforce representation smoothness and symmetry w.r.t data augmentations, and also to conduct entropy minimization implicitly. In our case, and following the work of [41], instead of directly averaging probabilities, the average is performed over logits, followed by softmax for better training and to prevent early information loss during the mix of probabilities of augmentations. Finally, and very importantly, our approach of bootstrapping/mixing predictions for clustering can be considered as a simple method to ensemble a majority vote among online pseudo-labels corresponding to diverse augmented versions of the same sample.

4   Clustering Algorithms and Metrics

To study the performance of our method against other benchmarks, we explored diverse clustering algorithms including widely used classical algorithms (GMM, variational GMM [3], K-means [28], BIRCH [65], CURE [24], Agglomerative Hierarchical Clustering (AHC) [11], Divisive Hierarchical Clustering (DHC) [45]), and 4 recent deep learning-based clustering models (IMSAT [31], DEC [63], DeepCWRN [9], SOM [36]), which allow us to generate diverse types of PLs depending on the optimization objective. To this aim, we employ 400-dim i-vectors as inputs to all of our clustering algorithms. The compact i-vectors, which are unsupervised speaker representations, allow us here to perform clustering in a more efficient way and to avoid high dimensionality of the MFCC acoustic features.

Besides, in order to thoroughly analyze the quality of PLs from various perspectives and the relationship with the downstream equal error rate (EER) performance, we use a list of 7 supervised metrics that are based on both the PLs and true labels (Unsupervised Clustering Accuracy (ACC), Normalized Mutual Information (NMI) [17], Adjusted MI (AMI) [64], Completeness score [51], Homogeneity score [51], Purity score, and Fowlkes-Mallows index (FMI) [21]). Among the criteria that these metrics assess, we can list the following: clustering accuracy and mutual information as measures of the consistency between the true labels and the generated PLs, homogeneity, completeness, and purity of clusters, and precision and recall. Additionally, we compute 3 unsupervised metrics (Silhouette score [52], Calinski-Harabasz score (CHS) [5], and Davies-Bouldin score (DBS) [10]) that are solely based on the generated PLs and the data samples, and which allow us to measure how compact or scattered are the clusters (e.g., intra-class dispersion, between-cluster distances, nearest-cluster distance). To compute these metrics, we use available implementations from the scikit-learn toolkit. More details and discussion about the clustering metrics are available at [19].

5   Results and Discussion

To evaluate the performance of our proposed clustering approach and the generated PLs for self-supervised speaker verification, we conducted a set of experiments based on the VoxCeleb2 dataset [7]. To train the embedding networks, we used the development subset of the VoxCeleb2 dataset, consisting of 1,092,009 utterances collected from 5,994 speakers. The evaluation was performed according to the original VoxCeleb1 trials list [43], which consists of 4,874 utterances spoken by 40 speakers. For our ECAPA-TDNN-based speaker verification system, the acoustic features used in the experiments were 40-dimensional Mel-frequency cepstral coefficients (MFCCs) extracted at every 10 ms, using a 25 ms Hamming window via Kaldi toolkit [49]. To improve generalization, we also use additive angular margin softmax (AAMSoftmax) objective to train our self-supervised speaker embedding network (with scale factor $s = 30$ and angular margin $m = 0.1$). Cosine similarity was used as a backend for verification scoring between enrollment and test embeddings.

Following IMSAT setup, we use the same MLP-based d-S-S-C architecture, where $d = 400$ and C are input and output dimensionality, respectively. S is the width of the network. We use RELU for all the hidden activations, apply batch normalization to hidden layers, and use softmax in the output layer. Regarding optimization, we used the Momentum algorithm with an initial learning rate of 0.01, a momentum of 0.9, and an exponential rate decay of 0.996. $\lambda = 0.5$, $\mu = 3.5$. Unless specified otherwise, we use by default a batch size of 10240 samples, $C = 5000$ as the number of clusters, $S = 5200$ neurons as the size of each fully connected layer, and ran experiments for 100 epochs. Additionally, our clustering benchmarks set 5000 as the default number of clusters, which [34] found to lead to the best results (except SOM where the number was set to be the size of the map 71*71 = 5041).

Moreover, we have used waveform-level data augmentations including additive noise and room impulse response (RIR) simulation [53]. In addition to the waveform-level augmentations, for the ECAPA-TDNN-based systems, we have also applied augmentation over the extracted MFCCs feature, analogous to the specaugment scheme [46]. For clustering, and to avoid altering speaker identity,

Table 1. A comparison study of our CAMSAT clustering compared to a large set of clustering benchmarks (classical and deep-learning based models). Results are reported in terms of Clustering performance (clustering metrics) and the corresponding EER (%) downstream SV evaluation performance when using the generated pseudo-labels to train our studied speaker verification system. S is the width of our MLP model and C the number of clusters. l2Norm refers to normalizing inputs independently to unit l2-norm instead of StandardScaler.

Model	Clustering Metrics											Speaker Verification
	ACC	AMI	NMI	No. of clusters	Completeness	Homogeneity	FMI	Purity	Silhouette	CHS	DBS	EER (%)
Supervised (True Labels)	1.0	1.0	1.0	5994	1.0	1.0	1.0	1.0	−0.006	31.708	4.692	**1.437**
GMM (Full cov.)	0.45	0.631	0.747	5000	0.767	0.728	0.312	0.566	−0.015	39.266	4.673	5.143
GMM (Full cov., l2Norm)	0.504	0.678	0.789	5000	0.792	0.785	0.415	0.633	−0.015	41.568	5.114	5.429
GMM (Spherical cov.)	0.427	0.587	0.711	5000	0.739	0.685	0.22	0.539	−0.037	38.665	4.864	5.265
GMM (Diagonal cov.)	0.425	0.6	0.721	5000	0.748	0.696	0.23	0.539	−0.033	38.455	4.874	5.451
GMM (Tied cov.)	0.457	0.66	0.767	5000	0.788	0.747	0.317	0.574	−0.016	38.922	4.726	5.164
Bayesian GMM (γ=1e-5, μ=1)	0.45	0.629	0.746	5000	0.766	0.727	0.312	0.566	−0.015	39.257	4.673	5.143
Bayesian GMM 1 (l2Norm, γ = 1e-5, μ = 1)	0.504	0.678	0.789	5000	0.792	0.785	0.415	0.633	−0.015	41.57	5.115	5.159
Bayesian GMM 2 (γ = 100, μ = 0.01)	0.449	0.63	0.746	5000	0.766	0.727	0.311	0.566	−0.015	39.258	4.675	4.958
Divisive HC	0.097	0.204	0.477	5000	0.479	0.474	0.035	0.132	−0.06	18.044	9.068	13.531
KMeans	0.302	0.468	0.591	5000	0.645	0.546	0.194	0.311	−0.114	24.936	**2.714**	6.978
CURE	0.151	0.218	0.393	5000	0.466	0.34	0.011	0.216	−0.052	17.77	5.372	6.994
BIRCH	0.299	0.374	0.54	5000	0.725	0.43	0.013	0.353	−0.027	24.348	4.901	5.642
DEC	0.029	0.122	0.365	4911	0.386	0.345	0.007	0.036	−0.084	8.734	7.266	11.957
SOM	0.025	0.088	0.402	5041	0.404	0.4	0.01	0.037	−0.041	10.148	18.402	15.806
DeepCWRN	0.003	0.006	0.15	1008	0.179	0.129	0.001	0.003	−0.217	3.841	41.521	38.171
IMSAT	0.393	0.491	0.649	4987	0.668	0.63	0.297	0.426	−0.044	22.887	6.668	5.912
AHC	0.587	0.74	0.825	5000	0.841	0.81	0.311	0.684	−0.01	39.561	4.991	3.685
AHC (l2Norm)	0.602	0.756	0.838	5000	0.849	0.827	0.375	0.693	−0.034	39.538	5.147	3.621
CAMSAT (S: 30k)	0.614	0.746	0.829	4993	0.843	0.816	0.557	0.636	−0.033	1.001	25.239	3.812
CAMSAT (l2Norm, S: 20k)	0.655	0.812	0.874	4596	0.888	0.86	0.641	0.675	−0.105	0.999	26.561	**3.065**
CAMSAT (l2Norm, S: 20k, C: 10k)	**0.709**	**0.83**	**0.889**	6364	**0.892**	**0.886**	**0.708**	**0.745**	−0.141	1.0	21.656	3.134

we additionally added light Gaussian noise to all augmented i-vectors (with a weighting factor of 0.2 to keep Gaussian noise low in inputs), used masking augmentation by randomly replacing 5–10% of input vectors with 0, and a mix of augmented inputs as an additional augmentation. Besides, inspired from techniques of noise-based exploration in the domain of reinforcement learning [20, 48] that add noise into observations, actions, or even parameter space. In our case, adding Gaussian noise to inputs helps the exploration of different clustering configurations, which we believe, in addition to the entropy loss terms that implicitly encourage exploration, helps to prevent early convergence to suboptimal cluster assignments, that we observed earlier in our experiments.

In Table 1, we provide the results for a large variety of clustering benchmarks compared to our CAMSAT method. According to the results, our approach outperforms by far all other baselines in terms of all supervised and unsupervised clustering metrics. For instance, we were able to boost unsupervised clustering accuracy from 60.2% and 39.3% corresponding to our strongest AHC baseline and IMSAT to 70.9% (17.8% and 80.4% improvements respectively). Using CAMSAT generated PLs to train our embedding system, also allowed us to boost downstream SV EER performance from 3.621% to 3.065% (18% improvement). Unlike in [18, 19], to avoid losing speaker information, we normalize i-vectors independently to unit l2-norm instead of mean and standard deviation scaling of i-vectors along the features axis, which helps to further improve performance across our systems and shows the importance of the type of data normalization.

Table 2. An ablation study of our proposed CAMSAT clustering model. Noise refers to adding light Gaussian noise to augmented inputs (with a weighting factor of 0.2 to keep Gaussian noise low in inputs). Masking augmentation replaces between 5 and 10% of input vectors with 0. Unless specified otherwise, we use by default a batch size of 10240 samples, $C = 5000$ as the number of clusters, $S = 5200$ neurons as the size of each fully connected layer in our MLP-based clustering models, and mean and standard deviation scaling (StandardScaler) of i-vectors along the features axis. l2Norm refers to normalizing i-vector inputs independently along the samples axis to unit l2-norm instead of StandardScaler.

Model					Clustering Metrics							Speaker Verification
	ACC	AMI	NMI	No. of clusters	Completeness	Homogeneity	FMI	Purity	Silhouette	CHS	DBS	EER (%)
IMSAT (no L_{aug}, no $L_{symmetry}$)	0.393	0.491	0.649	4987	0.668	0.63	0.297	0.426	-0.044	**22.887**	**6.668**	5.912
no $L_{symmetry}$	0.466	0.586	0.713	4967	0.736	0.693	0.316	0.529	-0.096	1.001	24.407	5.276
no $L_{symmetry}$, no R_{SAT}	0.401	0.585	0.733	5000	0.73	0.736	0.34	0.488	-0.016	1.0	26.5	6.188
no $L_{symmetry}$, no R_{SAT}, C: 10k	0.319	0.544	0.732	9998	0.705	0.761	0.275	0.519	-0.059	1.0	18.814	6.792
no $L_{symmetry}$, no R_{SAT}, C: 15k	0.266	0.497	0.715	14798	0.68	0.754	0.22	0.502	-0.13	1.0	15.194	7.015
no L_{aug}	0.498	0.646	0.765	4999	0.773	0.757	0.454	0.555	-0.051	1.001	25.671	5.329
no L_{aug}, no mix of inputs augmentation	0.492	0.644	0.763	5000	0.772	0.755	0.446	0.551	-0.083	0.999	25.866	5.027
no L_{aug}, dropout	0.473	0.664	0.783	5000	0.781	0.785	0.462	0.542	**-0.015**	1.0	25.558	5.488
no L_{aug}, no BatchNorm	0.491	0.674	0.787	5000	0.789	0.785	0.487	0.552	-0.018	1.001	25.856	5.313
no L_{aug}, only $KL(p_i\|p_i^m)$ term in $L_{symmetry}$	0.378	0.471	0.621	4957	0.654	0.591	0.197	0.417	-0.11	1.0	22.795	6.161
no L_{aug}, mixture in the input space alone	0.414	0.496	0.652	4989	0.671	0.633	0.301	0.451	-0.1	1.001	23.924	5.488
no L_{aug}, add another $L_{symmetry}$ version at the input level	0.428	0.624	0.757	5000	0.755	0.759	0.373	0.519	-0.017	0.999	25.697	5.541
CAMSAT	0.52	0.704	0.806	5000	0.809	0.803	0.48	0.602	-0.021	1.0	25.238	4.825
CAMSAT (S: 15k, C: 5994)	0.556	0.724	0.821	5994	0.821	0.822	0.524	0.644	-0.049	1.001	23.174	4.518
CAMSAT (S: 20k)	0.589	0.741	0.828	5000	0.836	0.821	0.559	0.639	-0.029	1.0	25.455	4.3
CAMSAT (l2Norm, Noise)	0.583	0.754	0.835	4923	0.848	0.823	0.552	0.636	-0.128	1.002	24.968	3.95
CAMSAT (l2Norm, S: 15k)	0.654	0.815	0.875	4664	**0.891**	0.86	0.643	0.673	-0.115	1.0	25.834	3.25
CAMSAT (l2Norm, S: 15k, C: 5994)	0.67	0.821	0.88	5238	**0.893**	0.867	0.662	0.692	-0.126	1.0	23.589	3.081
CAMSAT (Noise, Masking)	0.534	0.716	0.814	5000	0.817	0.81	0.493	0.614	-0.021	1.002	25.308	4.613
CAMSAT (Noise, Masking, S: 18k)	0.585	0.743	0.831	5000	0.835	0.826	0.559	0.642	-0.024	1.001	25.651	4.178
CAMSAT (Noise, Masking, S: 30k)	0.614	0.746	0.829	4993	0.843	0.816	0.557	0.636	-0.033	1.001	25.239	3.812
CAMSAT (l2Norm, Masking)	0.581	0.755	0.835	4907	0.849	0.822	0.544	0.632	-0.093	1.0	24.836	4.067
CAMSAT (l2Norm, Noise, Masking)	0.576	0.76	0.84	4993	0.85	0.83	0.544	0.633	-0.075	1.0	25.034	4.04
CAMSAT (l2Norm, Noise, Masking, S: 15k)	0.651	0.814	0.874	4665	0.89	0.859	0.639	0.67	-0.116	1.0	25.82	3.43
CAMSAT (l2Norm, Noise, Masking, S: 20k)	0.655	0.812	0.874	4596	0.888	0.86	0.641	0.675	-0.105	0.999	26.561	3.065
CAMSAT (l2Norm, Noise, Masking, S: 20k, C: 10k)	**0.709**	**0.83**	**0.889**	6364	0.892	0.886	**0.708**	**0.745**	-0.141	1.0	21.656	3.134
CAMSAT (l2Norm, Noise, Masking, S: 20k, C: 10k, 2xBatch size)	0.704	0.828	0.888	6424	0.891	0.884	0.703	0.74	-0.132	1.0	21.13	3.224
CAMSAT (l2Norm, Noise, Masking, S: 20k, C: 10k, Label smoothing)	0.707	**0.83**	**0.889**	6462	0.892	0.886	**0.708**	0.743	-0.141	0.999	21.24	3.203
CAMSAT (l2Norm, Noise, Masking, S: 20k, C: 5994)	0.669	0.816	0.878	5194	**0.888**	0.868	0.659	0.694	-0.122	1.0	24.627	3.309
CAMSAT (l2Norm, Noise, Masking, S: 30k)	0.656	0.801	0.867	4909	0.878	0.857	0.646	0.678	-0.1	0.999	25.923	3.33
CAMSAT (l2Norm, Noise, Masking, S: 45k)	0.638	0.776	0.851	4999	0.861	0.842	0.614	0.662	-0.09	0.999	26.241	3.462

Table 3. A study of our proposed CAMSAT clustering approach (no mixture weights, small size model) employing various distance metrics for optimization. Performance is reported in terms of clustering performance (clustering metrics) and the EER (%) downstream performance when using the generated pseudo-labels to train our speaker verification system.

Distance Metric					Clustering Metrics							Speaker Verification
	ACC	AMI	NMI	No. of clusters	Completeness	Homogeneity	FMI	Purity	Silhouette	CHS	DBS	EER (%)
KL divergence	**0.528**	**0.702**	**0.805**	5000	**0.809**	**0.801**	**0.485**	**0.608**	-0.026	1.001	25.465	**4.608**
JS divergence	0.376	0.541	0.706	4994	0.702	0.71	0.317	0.441	**-0.014**	1.001	25.1	6.267
Cosine distance	0.308	0.411	0.612	4897	0.616	0.609	0.259	0.335	-0.095	**1.002**	25.198	6.4
L2 loss	0.251	0.385	0.564	4895	0.59	0.541	0.134	0.275	-0.132	0.998	**23.428**	8.754
AAMSoftmax [13]	0.314	0.524	0.676	4729	0.691	0.661	0.251	0.361	-0.119	1.001	24.811	9.046
Squared Earth Mover's distance [30]	0.051	0.127	0.407	4996	0.416	0.399	0.014	0.063	-0.06	0.998	25.638	18.627
Sinkhorn distance [8]	0.018	0.052	0.331	4995	0.346	0.317	0.002	0.023	-0.083	1.001	23.661	12.275

Moreover, instead of using KL-divergence, in Table 3 we try to extend our approach to use other types of distance metrics such as the squared earth mover's distance (or the Wasserstein distance) [30], Sinkhorn distance [8], cosine distance, L2 loss, JS divergence. Results show that the KL divergence remains the best distance metric to use in our framework. Interestingly, we additionally incorporate the AAMSoftmax [13] loss at the output of our CAMSAT architecture and use the online generated pseudo-labels (stored at each epoch of the training to train our clustering model progressively in a supervised fashion during the following epoch). Following this approach, we were able to achieve pretty decent results without the need for any external labels and only by using the self-generated pseudo-labels of the clustering model itself. This successful training and the improvement of estimations over epochs also demonstrates that our mix of predictions provides effective information and an important signal for clustering that is able to progressively guide the clustering process to improve performance (compared to using predictions of clean samples alone where training was not stable and we couldn't even converge with the AAMSoftmax strong objective).

Additionally, we performed a large-scale ablation study in Table 2 to analyze the contribution of all components and the influence of a set of factors: batch size, model size, the predefined number of clusters, type of data normalization (l2-Norm vs StandardScaler), label smoothing, our proposed augmentations, dropout, etc. Results show that there is complementary information between all loss terms in our CAMSAT objective and that each help to boost the performance of the overall clustering framework. Performance degradation when performing mixture in the input space alone or only using $KL(p_i||p_i^m)$ term in $L_{symmetry}$ also demonstrates the importance of mixture in the logits space and the relevance of the notion of symmetry within augmentations. In addition, we can also observe that adversarial augmentations and our proposed augmentations are beneficial for clustering, dropout and label smoothing do not seem to be helpful, and a higher number of discovered clusters than ground truth tends to coincide with worse Silhouette, CHS, and DBS scores, which leads to slightly worse SV performance due to less compact and worse separated clusters. Results also show that scaling model size helps to boost performance up to 20000 neurons width, beyond which we didn't observe any improvement, which can be explained by the limited size of the VoxCeleb2 dataset. Besides, our experiments increasing the predefined number of clusters to 10000 and 15000 show that $L_{symmetry}$ is critical to recover/estimate the original 5994 ground truth number and that our CAMSAT method recovers it almost perfectly without the need for any memory queue of data samples or a prototypical memory bank [62]. On the contrary to other SV approaches [47] and other clustering algorithms, our clustering method shows constant stable performance, steady convergence, and is not sensitive to the predefined number of clusters. Last but not least, we observe that beyond some clustering performance, the marginal improvement in final downstream SV performance becomes minimal and requires much more accurate PLs.

Finally, Table 4 shows a comparison of our approach for Self-Supervised SV (SSSV) training using CAMSAT-based PLs compared to recent SOTA SSSV approaches employing a variety of SSL objectives with the same ECAPA-TDNN model encoder. The results show clearly that our approach outperforms all the baselines, and suggest that further gains can be made by improving the clustering modules of current self-supervised speaker recognition systems.

Table 4. Some recent SOTA self-supervised speaker verification approaches in EER (%) compared to our simple SV system trained with CAMSAT PLs. All models are based on ECAPA-TDNN.

SSL Objective	EER (%)
MoBY [62]	8.2
InfoNCE [55]	7.36
MoCo [6]	7.3
ProtoNCE [62]	7.21
PCL [62]	7.11
CA-DINO [26]	3.585
i-mix [18]	3.478
l-mix [18]	3.377
Iterative clustering [54]	3.09
CAMSAT (Ours)	**3.065**

Additional Advantages of Our CAMSAT Approach. Our approach is simple, sticks to an easy MLP architecture to avoid additional complex modules (e.g. autoencoders, overclustering, multiple outputs), and shows that improving clustering has a lot of advantages in improving speaker verification systems, without the need for complex and expensive multi-stage iterative clustering. Moreover, our method of maximizing MI while also imposing symmetry within augmentations is also rigorously grounded in information theory, effortlessly avoids degenerate solutions that other clustering methods are susceptible to, and has more capability to produce calibrated predictions. Interestingly, our clustering objective is also easily scalable since it does not depend on large batches of negative samples or large similarity matrices as is the case for instance with contrastive learning. Thus, it can use much larger batch sizes and is more suitable for large-scale datasets thanks to its robustness and stability against data shift.

Future Improvements. We would like to leave the reader with some potential improvements to our framework that could be the subject of future work: using compact i-vectors limits the upside performance of our clustering approach as these embeddings already lack important speaker information. Therefore, using higher-dimensional cepstral features such as MFCCs or even raw audio waveforms could present the model with richer information to mine (at the cost of more computations). In particular, this could help to better capture discriminative attributes from speech that are invariant to confounding low-level details (e.g., pitch contour, background noise). In addition, we didn't perform many hyper-parameters optimization , therefore further finetuning and exploration of other SOTA architectures could also be fruitful to improve performance.

6   Conclusion

In this paper, we propose a general-purpose clustering method called CAMSAT based on two principles: (1) mixing predictions of augmented samples to provide a complementary supervisory signal for clustering and enforce symmetry within augmentations and (2) Self-Augmented Training (SAT) to enforce representation invariance and maximize the information-theoretic dependency between samples and their predicted pseudo-labels. Our method is highly scalable and has better generalization capability, is robust under data shift, more stable during training, has the ability to produce more calibrated predictions, and is better suited for large-scale datasets or/and a high number of clusters. Our approach outperformed all other baselines used to cluster speaker embeddings. Moreover, using the generated pseudo-labels to train our speaker embedding systems allowed us to further improve speaker verification performance outperforming all other recent speaker verification benchmarks.

Acknowledgments. The authors wish to acknowledge the funding from the Government of Canada's New Frontiers in Research Fund (NFRF) through grant NFRFR-2021-00338.

References

1. Arpit, D., Jastrzębski, S., Ballas, N., Krueger, D., et al.: A closer look at memorization in deep networks. In: International Conference on Machine Learning (2017)
2. Bai, Z., Zhang, X.L.: Speaker recognition based on deep learning: an overview. Neural Netw. **140**, 65–99 (2021)
3. Blei, D.M., Jordan, M.I.: Variational inference for Dirichlet process mixtures. Bayesian analysis (2006)
4. Bridle, J., Heading, A., MacKay, D.: Unsupervised classifiers, mutual information and'phantom targets. In: Advances in Neural Information Processing Systems 4 (1991)
5. Caliński, T., Harabasz, J.: A dendrite method for cluster analysis. Commun. Stat.-Theory Methods **3**(1), 1–27 (1974)
6. Cho, J., et al.: The jhu submission to voxsrc-21: Track 3. arXiv preprint arXiv:2109.13425 (2021)
7. Chung, J.S., Nagrani, A., Zisserman, A.: Voxceleb2: deep speaker recognition. In: INTERSPEECH (2018)
8. Cuturi, M.: Sinkhorn distances: lightspeed computation of optimal transport. In: Advances in Neural Information Processing Systems 26 (2013)
9. Dahal, P.: Learning embedding space for clustering from deep representations. In: 2018 IEEE International Conference on Big Data (Big Data) (2018)
10. Davies, D.L., Bouldin, D.W.: A cluster separation measure. IEEE Trans. Pattern Anal. Mach. Intell. **2**, 224–227 (1979)
11. Day, W.H.E., et al.: Efficient algorithms for agglomerative hierarchical clustering methods. J. Classif. **1**, 7–24 (1984)
12. Dehak, N., et al.: Front-end factor analysis for speaker verification. IEEE Trans. Audio Speech Lang. Process. **19**, 788–798 (2011)
13. Deng, J., et al.: Arcface: additive angular margin loss for deep face recognition. IEEE Trans. Pattern Anal. Mach. Intell. (2021)
14. Desplanques, B., et al.: ECAPA-TDNN: emphasized channel attention, propagation and aggregation in TDNN based speaker verification. In: Interspeech (2020)

15. Dilokthanakul, N., et al.: Deep unsupervised clustering with gaussian mixture variational autoencoders. arXiv preprint arXiv:1611.02648 (2016)
16. Dosovitskiy, A., et al.: Discriminative unsupervised feature learning with convolutional neural networks. NeurIPS your (2014)
17. Estévez, P.A., et al.: Normalized mutual information feature selection. IEEE Trans. Neural Networks **20**(2), 189–201 (2009)
18. Fathan, A., Alam, J.: On the influence of the quality of pseudo-labels on the self-supervised speaker verification task: a thorough analysis. In: 2023 11th International Workshop on Biometrics and Forensics (IWBF), pp. 1–6. IEEE (2023)
19. Fathan, A., Alam, J., Kang, W.: On the impact of the quality of pseudo-labels on the self-supervised speaker verification task. In: NeurIPS ENLSP Workshop (2022)
20. Fortunato, M., et al.: Noisy networks for exploration. arXiv preprint arXiv:1706.10295 (2017)
21. Fowlkes, E.B., Mallows, C.L.: A method for comparing two hierarchical clusterings. J. Am. Stat. Assoc. **78**(383), 553–569 (1983)
22. Geirhos, R., et al.: Generalisation in humans and deep neural networks. In: Advances in Neural Information Processing Systems 31 (2018)
23. Gong, Y., et al.: Iterative quantization: a procrustean approach to learning binary codes for large-scale image retrieval. IEEE PAMI **35**(12), 2916–2929 (2012)
24. Guha, S., et al.: Cure: an efficient clustering algorithm for large databases. SIGMOD Rec. **27**(2), 73–84 (1998)
25. Han, B., Chen, Z., Qian, Y.: Self-supervised speaker verification using dynamic loss-gate and label correction. arXiv preprint arXiv:2208.01928 (2022)
26. Han, B., et al.: Self-supervised learning with cluster-aware-dino for high-performance robust speaker verification. arXiv preprint arXiv:2304.05754 (2023)
27. Hansen, J.H., Hasan, T.: Speaker recognition by machines and humans: a tutorial review. IEEE Signal Process. Mag. **32**, 74–99 (2015)
28. Hartigan, J.A., Wong, M.A.: A k-means clustering algorithm. JSTOR: Appl. Stat. **28**(1), 100–108 (1979)
29. Hendrycks, D., et al.: Augmix: a simple data processing method to improve robustness and uncertainty. arXiv preprint arXiv:1912.02781 (2019)
30. Hou, L., Yu, C.P., Samaras, D.: Squared earth mover's distance-based loss for training deep neural networks. arXiv preprint arXiv:1611.05916 (2016)
31. Hu, W., et al.: Learning discrete representations via information maximizing self-augmented training. PMLR (2017)
32. Jiang, Z., Zheng, Y., Tan, H., Tang, B., Zhou, H.: Variational deep embedding: a generative approach to clustering. CoRR, abs/1611.05148 1 (2016)
33. Kang, W.H., Alam, J., Fathan, A.: An analytic study on clustering-based pseudo-labels for self-supervised deep speaker verification. In: SPECOM. Springer, Cham (2022). https://doi.org/10.1007/978-3-031-20980-2_29
34. Kang, W.H., Alam, J., Fathan, A.: l-mix: a latent-level instance mixup regularization for robust self-supervised speaker representation learning. JSTSP (2022)
35. Kenny, P.: A small footprint I-vector extractor. In: Odyssey, pp. 1–6 (2012)
36. Kohonen, T.: Self-organizing maps. Springer Science & Business Media (2012)
37. Krause, A., et al.: Discriminative clustering by regularized information maximization. In: Advances in Neural Information Processing Systems 23 (2010)
38. Lakshminarayanan, B., Pritzel, A., Blundell, C.: Simple and scalable predictive uncertainty estimation using deep ensembles. NeurIPS 30 (2017)
39. Lee, D.H., et al.: Pseudo-label: The simple and efficient semi-supervised learning method for deep neural networks. In: Workshop on Challenges in Representation Learning, ICML, vol. 3, p. 896 (2013)

40. Li, Y., Hu, P., Liu, Z., Peng, D., Zhou, J.T., Peng, X.: Contrastive clustering. In: Proceedings of the AAAI Conference on Artificial Intelligence, vol. 35 (2021)
41. Mao, X., Ma, Y., Yang, Z., Chen, Y., Li, Q.: Virtual mixup training for unsupervised domain adaptation. arXiv preprint arXiv:1905.04215 (2019)
42. Miyato, T., Maeda, S.I., Koyama, M., Ishii, S.: Virtual adversarial training: a regularization method for supervised and semi-supervised learning. PAMI (2018)
43. Nagrani, A., Chung, J.S., Zisserman, A.: Voxceleb: a large-scale speaker identification dataset. In: INTERSPEECH (2017)
44. Ng, A., Jordan, M., Weiss, Y.: On spectral clustering: analysis and an algorithm. Advances in Neural Information Processing Systems 14 (2001)
45. Nielsen, F.: Hierarchical clustering. In: Introduction to HPC with MPI for Data Science. UTCS, pp. 195–211. Springer, Cham (2016). https://doi.org/10.1007/978-3-319-21903-5_8
46. Park, D.S., et al.: Specaugment: a simple data augmentation method for automatic speech recognition. In: Interspeech 2019, pp. 2613–2617 (2019)
47. Peng, J., et al.: Progressive contrastive learning for self-supervised text-independent speaker verification. In: Proceedings of Odyssey Workshop (2022)
48. Plappert, M., et al.: Parameter space noise for exploration. arXiv preprint arXiv:1706.01905 (2017)
49. Povey, D., et al.: The kaldi speech recognition toolkit. In: IEEE Workshop (2011)
50. Ronen, M., Finder, S.E., Freifeld, O.: Deepdpm: deep clustering with an unknown number of clusters. In: Proceedings of IEEE/CVF (2022)
51. Rosenberg, A., Hirschberg, J.: V-measure: a conditional entropy-based external cluster evaluation measure. In: Proceedings of EMNLP-CoNLL, pp. 410–420 (2007)
52. Rousseeuw, P.J.: Silhouettes: a graphical aid to the interpretation and validation of cluster analysis. J. Comput. Appl. Math. **20**, 53–65 (1987)
53. Snyder, D., et al.: X-vectors: Robust dnn embeddings for speaker recognition. In: IEEE-CASSP (2018)
54. Tao, R., Lee, K.A., Das, R.K., Hautamäki, V., Li, H.: Self-supervised speaker recognition with loss-gated learning (2021)
55. Tao, R., et al.: Self-supervised speaker recognition with loss-gated learning. In: ICASSP. IEEE (2022)
56. Vasiljevic, I., Chakrabarti, A., Shakhnarovich, G.: Examining the impact of blur on recognition by convolutional networks. arXiv preprint arXiv:1611.05760 (2016)
57. Wang, C.D., Lai, J.H., Suen, C.Y., Zhu, J.Y.: Multi-exemplar affinity propagation. IEEE Trans. Pattern Anal. Mach. Intell. **35**, 2223–2237 (2013)
58. Wang, C.D., Lai, J.H., Zhu, J.Y.: Conscience online learning: an efficient approach for robust kernel-based clustering. Knowl. Inf. Syst. **31**, 79–104 (2012)
59. Wang, C.D., Lai, J.: Position regularized support vector domain description. Pattern Recogn. **46**(3), 875–884 (2013)
60. Wang, C.D., et al.: A conscience on-line learning approach for kernel-based clustering. In: 2010 IEEE International Conference on Data Mining (2010)
61. Weiss, Y., Torralba, A., Fergus, R.: Spectral hashing. In: Advances in Neural Information Processing Systems 21 (2008)
62. Xia, W., et al.: Self-supervised text-independent speaker verification using prototypical momentum contrastive learning. In: ICASSP. IEEE (2021)
63. Xie, J., et al.: Unsupervised deep embedding for clustering analysis. In: International Conference on Machine Learning, pp. 478–487. PMLR (2016)
64. Xuan, N., et al.: Information theoretic measures for clusterings comparison: variants, properties, normalization and correction for chance (2010)
65. Zhang, T., et al.: BIRCH: a new data clustering algorithm and its applications. Data Mining and Knowledge Discovery (1997)

Author Index

© The Editor(s) (if applicable) and The Author(s), under exclusive license
to Springer Nature Switzerland AG 2023
A. Karpov et al. (Eds.): SPECOM 2023, LNAI 14339, pp. 565–568, 2023.
https://doi.org/10.1007/978-3-031-48312-7

Printed in the United States
by Baker & Taylor Publisher Services